75 Readings
Across the Curriculum

Chris Anson

McGraw Hill

Boston   Burr Ridge, IL   Dubuque, IA   Madison, WI   New York
San Francisco   St. Louis   Bangkok   Bogotá   Caracas   Kuala Lumpur
Lisbon   London   Madrid   Mexico City   Milan   Montreal   New Delhi
Santiago   Seoul   Singapore   Sydney   Taipei   Toronto

Higher Education

75 READINGS ACROSS THE CURRICULUM
Published by McGraw-Hill, a business unit of The McGraw-Hill Companies, Inc., 1221 Avenue of the Americas, New York, NY, 10020. Copyright © 2008 by The McGraw-Hill Companies, Inc. All rights reserved. No part of this publication may be reproduced or distributed in any form or by any means, or stored in a database or retrieval system, without the prior written consent of The McGraw-Hill Companies, Inc., including, but not limited to, in any network or other electronic storage or transmission, or broadcast for distance learning. Some ancillaries, including electronic and print components, may not be available to customers outside the United States.

This book is printed on acid-free paper.

1 2 3 4 5 6 7 8 9 0 DOC/DOC 0 9 8 7 6

ISBN-13: 978-0-07-340576-6
ISBN-10:   0-07-340576-0

Vice President and Editor-in-Chief:
Emily Barrosse
Publisher: *Lisa Moore*
Sponsoring Editor: *Victoria Fullard*
Editorial Assistant: *Jesse Hassenger*
Marketing Manager: *Lori DeShazo*
Managing Editor: *Jean Dal Porto*
Senior Project Manager:
Catherine R. Iammartino

Art Director: *Jeanne Schreiber*
Designer: *Marianna Kinigakis*
Senior Production Supervisor:
Carol A. Bielski
Composition: *10/12 Palatino,*
by Techbooks
Printing: *45# New Era Matte Plus,*
R. R. Donnelley & Sons

Credits: The credits section for this book begins on page 547 and is considered an extension of the copyright page.

Library of Congress Cataloging–in–Publication Data

Anson, Chris
    75 readings across the curriculum: an anthology / [edited by] Chris Anson.–1st ed.
    p. cm.
    Includes index.
    ISBN-13: 978-0-07-340576-6 (softcover : alk. paper)
    ISBN-10:   0-07-340576-0 (softcover : alk. paper)
    1. College readers. 2. English language—Rhetoric. I. Anson, Chris. II. Title.

PE1417.A129 2008
808.0427 22

The Internet addresses listed in the text were accurate at the time of publication. The inclusion of a Web site does not indicate an endorsement by the authors or McGraw-Hill, and McGraw-Hill does not guarantee the accuracy of the information presented at these sites.

www.mhhe.com

Contents

Chapter 3
RELIGION   87

Chapter 4
PHILOSOPHY AND ETHICS   121

Chapter 5
CULTURAL STUDIES   150

Chapter 9
MARRIAGE AND FAMILY   296

Chapter 10
POLITICAL SCIENCE   327

Chapter 11
ECONOMICS   384

Part 3
Sciences **435**

Chapter 12
BRAVE NEW WORLD 436

Chapter 13
ENVIRONMENT 473

Chapter 14
MEDICINE   517

RHETORICAL TABLE OF CONTENTS

Narration

Description

Comparison/Contrast

Definition

Classification

Process Analysis

Argumentation

Foreword

When most people think about academic writing and reading, their minds, like an electronic map program, zoom down from a broad view of the world of knowledge to one specific place: English departments, where serious material is read and where skills of written expression are practiced and honed. "Good writing" is to be found in novels, stories, poetry, and plays, preferably those of the greatest and most time-honored authors.

But consider this line describing the earth:

> Viewed from the distance of the moon, the astonishing thing about the Earth, catching the breath, is that it is alive. Photographs show the dry, pounded surface of the moon in the foreground, dead as an old bone. Aloft, floating free beneath the moist, gleaming membrane of bright blue sky, is the rising earth, the only exuberant thing in this part of the cosmos.

Elegant and engaging, this passage comes from the work not of a fiction writer or poet, but from biologist and cancer researcher Lewis Thomas. Effective writers like Thomas can be found in virtually every field of knowledge, every academic discipline, every nook and cranny of public life. They come from backgrounds in sociology, film studies, economics, philosophy, and genetics. They represent researchers, politicians, stay-at-home moms (and dads), chefs, newspaper columnists, educators, businesspeople, and even people who are homeless. In short, good writing isn't "located" anywhere; it comes from everywhere, wherever there are people with knowledge to share, opinions to argue, and experiences to recount.

In recent years, the Writing across the Curriculum movement has celebrated the diversity of writing in all fields, showing how communities of learners and thinkers work with their knowledge often in unique ways. True, much high-level writing in many disciplines is complicated and, for outsiders, baffling. But when the *ideas* of the work in these fields are made interesting for general readers like us, we're often fascinated. A technical report in textiles chemistry describing the processes of creating a new fabric that does not allow bacteria to grow may be stupefyingly dull to most of us outside the field. But explain to us that we might wear athletic socks for months at a stretch and still be able to share our space with polite company, and we get interested or amused—or we begin framing an argument for or against wash-free socks, extending the idea to other materials and situations.

Interesting writing that emerges from various disciplinary areas lets us into the conversations and innovations of people inhabiting these areas. Taken as a whole, the first, "general education" part of most students' college years is a journey through the worlds and ideas of psychology, history, biology, economics, literature, anthropology, art, or music. We may not become specialists in any more than the one field we choose for a major, but without broad exposure to many domains of intellect, we're not fully educated. And we miss out on a wealth of interesting ideas.

75 Readings Across the Curriculum is designed to give you, in one place, an impressive collection of material representing a world of information, opinions, and experience. In this collection, you'll find essays that explore a range of ideas. How are people best educated? What shapes our society's views about women and women's sexuality? What values should govern the way we live? What should we do about injustices—racial, economic, political, or gender-based? What sort of species are we, and where are we headed? What's it like to be homeless, or blind in one eye, or oppressed as a people? What is patriotism, and how is it defined? These and many other themes are interwoven with the observations and personal experiences of the several dozen authors whose works are collected here.

The readings also represent a range of genres, or types of writing, from highly personal essays to works of creative nonfiction to arguments for causes to engaging reflections on natural phenomena or social processes. Producing these genres is an impressive cast of authorial characters, from Plato (who comes to us from the fourth century BC) to Postman (who writes about the virtual and the digital). In these pages live some of the most readable, thoughtful, and important writers of our varied culture. They represent the voices of African Americans, Asians, Native Americans, Latinos and Latinas, immigrant Irish—old and young, ancient and modern, straight and gay, rich and impoverished, of many faiths and traditions. And like a complicated tapestry, their voices are interwoven through the themes and general disciplinary areas the collection brings together.

Throughout *75 Readings Across the Curriculum*, the essays find a common thread: they are engaging, capturing our imaginations, stirring our emotions, and stimulating our intellects. They urge us to act or give us a new perspective on an issue, making us see the world in new ways and understand how others see it. This process of "decentering,"—standing outside our own ideologies and opinions to consider other ways of knowing—is fundamental to becoming an educated citizen prepared to make informed judgments about the myriad issues that daily confront us. It also adds dimension to the specialized work we may end up doing, allowing us to bring to bear on that work many ideas, histories, and prior texts.

Deliberately absent from this collection is any apparatus for its use in the classroom. A website contains further information about the readings, including biographical information about the authors, bibliographical content regarding additional writings, and contextualizing cultural information. To access the Web site go to www.mhhe.com/75RAC and use the passcode G8JR-Y9P7-TTEH-9487-THW4. But *75 Readings Across the Curriculum* is intended to be integrated into courses with any number of structures, activities, writing assignments, and goals. Whole chapters can be worked through independently for immersion in their themes, disciplinary areas, and the crisscrossing ideas that their authors represent. Readings can also be grouped around certain rhetorical modes such as narration and argument, and writing assignments can be tailored to match the modes being studied.

Another aspect of this flexibility is the value price, which allows instructors to pair this reader with other teaching tools or textbooks of their choice without pushing students' budgets too far. With the ever-rising awareness of textbook prices, McGraw-Hill has recommitted to its value-priced "75" series. Also available in this series are *75 Readings*, *75 Readings Plus*, *75 Thematic Readings*, and (coming soon) *75 Arguments*. At less than half the price of most readers currently popular among college instructors, *75 Readings Across the Curriculum* offers excellent reading selections while addressing the very real concerns about textbook costs for students.

A world of possibilities for writing opens up from the essays in the collection: personal, journal-like responses to their ideas; electronic exchanges, blogs, or message boards used to bounce around reactions and explore the essays' nuances of meaning; formal papers analyzing topics or comparing a topic discussed in two or more readings; and research papers using one or more of the readings as a springboard for exploration. Readings can be assigned as stimuli for argumentative or persuasive pieces, or they can provide the specific focus for an essay. Students can be asked to read an essay through different lenses, such as economic, political, environmental, or religious, and then write analyses from those perspectives, comparing them with their peers'. In these and countless other creative uses of the book, the readings are intended not to dominate the course but to inspire the kind of thoughtfulness that gives life to good writing.

However you may be using *75 Readings Across the Curriculum*, there is no question that you'll find the material compelling to read and stimulating to write about.

Chris M. Anson
North Carolina State University

ACKNOWLEDGEMENTS

Special thanks are due to those instructors who reviewed and helped us shape this anthology with their suggestions, particularly

Phyllis Frus, *Hawaii Pacific University*

Phyllis Gobbell, *Nashville State Community College*

John Isaacs, *Waynesburg College*

Jacob Lewis, *University of Arkansas*

Anne Westrick, *Bowling Green State University*

Finally, we want to hear what you think about this text. Please e-mail English@mcgraw-hill.com to make suggestions or comments about *75 Readings Across the Curriculum* or to ask any questions about its use.

PART

1

Humanities

The Reflective Life

On Keeping a Notebook

Joan Didion

1   "'That woman Estelle,'" the note reads, "'is partly the reason why George Sharp and I are separated today.' *Dirty crepe-de-Chine wrapper, hotel bar, Wilmington RR, 9:45 a.m. August Monday morning.*"

2   Since the note is in my notebook, it presumably has some meaning to me. I study it for a long while. At first I have only the most general notion of what I was doing on an August Monday morning in the bar of the hotel across from the Pennsylvania Railroad station in Wilmington, Delaware (waiting for a train? missing one? 1960? 1961? why Wilmington?), but I do remember being there. The woman in the dirty crepe-de-Chine wrapper had come down from her room for a beer, and the bartender had heard before the reason why George Sharp and she were separated today. "Sure," he said, and went on mopping the floor. "You told me." At the other end of the bar is a girl. She is talking, pointedly, not to the man beside her but to a cat lying in the triangle of sunlight cast through the open door. She is wearing a plaid silk dress from Peck & Peck, and the hem is coming down.

3   Here is what it is: the girl has been on the Eastern Shore, and now she is going back to the city, leaving the man beside her, and all she can see ahead are the viscous summer sidewalks and the 3 a.m. long-distance calls that will make her lie awake and then sleep drugged through all the steaming mornings left in August (1960? 1961?). Because she must go directly from the train to lunch in New York, she wishes that she had a safety pin for the hem of the plaid silk dress, and she also wishes that she could forget about the hem and the lunch and stay in the cool bar that smells

2

of disinfectant and malt and make friends with the woman in the crepe-de-Chine wrapper. She is afflicted by a little self-pity, and she wants to compare Estelles. That is what that was all about.

Why did I write it down? In order to remember, of course, but ₄ exactly what was it I wanted to remember? How much of it actually happened? Did any of it? Why do I keep a notebook at all? It is easy to deceive oneself on all those scores. The impulse to write things down is a peculiarly compulsive one, inexplicable to those who do not share it, useful only accidentally, only secondarily, in the way that any compulsion tries to justify itself. I suppose that it begins or does not begin in the cradle. Although I have felt compelled to write things down since I was five years old, I doubt that my daughter ever will, for she is a singularly blessed and accepting child, delighted with life exactly as life presents itself to her, unafraid to go to sleep and unafraid to wake up. Keepers of private notebooks are a different breed altogether, lonely and resistant rearrangers of things, anxious malcontents, children afflicted apparently at birth with some presentiment of loss.

My first notebook was a Big Five tablet, given to me by my ₅ mother with the sensible suggestion that I stop whining and learn to amuse myself by writing down my thoughts. She returned the tablet to me a few years ago; the first entry is an account of a woman who believed herself to be freezing to death in the Arctic night, only to find, when day broke, that she had stumbled onto the Sahara Desert, where she would die of the heat before lunch. I have no idea what turn of a five-year-old's mind could have prompted so insistently "ironic" and exotic a story, but it does reveal a certain predilection for the extreme which has dogged me into adult life; perhaps if I were analytically inclined I would find it a truer story than any I might have told about Donald Johnson's birthday party or the day my cousin Brenda put Kitty Litter in the aquarium.

So the point of my keeping a notebook has never been, nor is ₆ it now, to have an accurate factual record of what I have been doing or thinking. That would be a different impulse entirely, an instinct for reality which I sometimes envy but do not possess. At no point have I ever been able successfully to keep a diary; my approach to daily life ranges from the grossly negligent to the merely absent, and on those few occasions when I have tried dutifully to record a day's events, boredom has so overcome me that the results are mysterious at best. What is this business about "shopping, typing piece, dinner with E, depressed"? Shopping for what? Typing what piece? Who is E? Was this "E" depressed, or was I depressed? Who cares?

7 In fact I have abandoned altogether that kind of pointless entry; instead I tell what some would call lies. "That's simply not true," the members of my family frequently tell me when they come up against my memory of a shared event. "The party was *not* for you, the spider was *not* a black widow, *it wasn't that way at all.*" Very likely they are right, for not only have I always had trouble distinguishing between what happened and what merely might have happened, but I remain unconvinced that the distinction, for my purposes, matters. The cracked crab that I recall having for lunch the day my father came home from Detroit in 1945 must certainly be embroidery, worked into the day's pattern to lend verisimilitude; I was ten years old and would not now remember the cracked crab. The day's events did not turn on cracked crab. And yet it is precisely that fictitious crab that makes me see the afternoon all over again, a home movie run all too often, the father bearing gifts, the child weeping, an exercise in family love and guilt. Or that is what it was to me. Similarly, perhaps it never did snow that August in Vermont; perhaps there never were flurries in the night wind, and maybe no one else felt the ground hardening and summer already dead even as we pretended to bask in it, but that was how it felt to me, and it might as well have snowed, could have snowed, did snow.

8 *How it felt to me:* that is getting closer to the truth about a notebook. I sometimes delude myself about why I keep a notebook, imagine that some thrifty virtue derives from preserving everything observed. See enough and write it down, I tell myself, and then some morning when the world seems drained of wonder, some day when I am only going through the motions of doing what I am supposed to do, which is write—on that bankrupt morning I will simply open my notebook and there it will all be, a forgotten account with accumulated interest, paid passage back to the world out there: dialogue overheard in hotels and elevators and at the hatcheck counter in Pavillon (one middle-aged man

shows his hatcheck to another and says, "That's my old football number"); impressions of Bettina Aptheker and Benjamin Sonnenberg and Teddy ("Mr. Acapulco") Stauffer; careful *apercus* about tennis bums and failed fashion models and Greek shipping heiresses, one of whom taught me a significant lesson (a lesson I could have learned from F. Scott Fitzgerald, but perhaps we all must meet the very rich for ourselves) by asking, when I arrived to interview her in her orchid-filled sitting room on the second day of a paralyzing New York blizzard, whether it was snowing outside.

I imagine, in other words, that the notebook is about other people. But of course it is not. I have no real business with what one stranger said to another at the hatcheck counter in Pavillon; in fact I suspect that the line "That's my old football number" touched not my own imagination at all, but merely some memory of something once read, probably "The Eighty-Yard Run." Nor is my concern with a woman in a dirty crepe-de-Chine wrapper in a Wilmington bar. My stake is always, of course, in the unmentioned girl in the plaid silk dress. *Remember what it was to be me:* that is always the point.

It is a difficult point to admit. We are brought up in the ethic that others, any others, all others, are by definition more interesting than ourselves; taught to be diffident, just this side of self-effacing. ("You're the least important person in the room and don't you forget it," Jessica Mitford's governess would hiss in her ear on the advent of any social occasion; I copied that into my notebook because it is only recently that I have been able to enter a room without hearing some such phrase in my inner ear.) Only the very young and the very old may recount their dreams at breakfast, dwell upon self, interrupt with memories of beach picnics and favorite Liberty lawn dresses and the rainbow trout in a creek near Colorado Springs. The rest of us are expected, rightly, to affect absorption in other people's favorite dresses, other people's trout.

And so we do. But our notebooks give us away, for however dutifully we record what we see around us, the common denominator of all we see is always, transparently, shamelessly, the implacable "I." We are not talking here about the kind of notebook that is patently for public consumption, a structural conceit for binding together a series of graceful *pensées;* we are talking about something private, about bits of the mind's string too short to use, an indiscriminate and erratic assemblage with meaning only for its maker.

12   And sometimes even the maker has difficulty with the meaning. There does not seem to be, for example, any point in my knowing for the rest of my life that, during 1964, 720 tons of soot fell on every square mile of New York City, yet there it is in my notebook, labeled "FACT." Nor do I really need to remember that Ambrose Bierce liked to spell Leland Stanford's name "£eland $tanford" or that "smart women almost always wear black in Cuba," a fashion hint without much potential for practical application. And does not the relevance of these notes seem marginal at best?

13   In the basement museum of the Inyo County Courthouse in Independence, California, sign pinned to a mandarin coat: This MANDARIN COAT was often worn by Mrs. Minnie S. Brooks when giving lectures on her TEAPOT COLLECTION." Redhead getting out of car in front of Beverly Wilshire Hotel, chinchilla stole, Vuitton bags with tags reading:

MRS. LOU FOX

HOTEL SAHARA

VEGAS

14   Well, perhaps not entirely marginal. As a matter of fact, Mrs. Minnie S. Brooks and her MANDARIN COAT pull me back into my own childhood, for although I never knew Mrs. Brooks and did not visit Inyo County until I was thirty, I grew up in just such a world, in houses cluttered with Indian relics and bits of gold ore and ambergris and the souvenirs my Aunt Mercy Farnsworth brought back from the Orient. It is a long way from that world to Mrs. Lou Fox's world, where we all live now, and is it not just as well to remember that? Might not Mrs. Minnie S. Brooks help me to remember what I am? Might not Mrs. Lou Fox help me to remember what I am not?

15   But sometimes the point is harder to discern. What exactly did I have in mind when I noted down that it cost the father of someone I know $650 a month to light the place on the Hudson in

which he lived before the Crash? What use was I planning to make of this line by Jimmy Hoffa: "I may have my faults, but being wrong ain't one of them"? And although I think it interesting to know where the girls who travel with the Syndicate have their hair done when they find themselves on the West Coast, will I ever make suitable use of it? Might I not be better off just passing it on to John O'Hara? What is a recipe for sauerkraut doing in my notebook? What kind of magpie keeps this notebook? *"He was born the night the Titanic went down."* That seems a nice enough line, and I even recall who said it, but is it not really a better line in life than it could ever be in fiction?

But of course that is exactly it: not that I should ever use the line, but that I should remember the woman who said it and the afternoon I heard it. We were on her terrace by the sea, and we were finishing the wine left from lunch, trying to get what sun there was, a California winter sun. The woman whose husband was born the night the *Titanic* went down wanted to rent her house, wanted to go back to her children in Paris. I remember wishing that I could afford the house, which cost $1,000 a month. "Someday you will," she said lazily. "Someday it all comes." There in the sun on her terrace it seemed easy to believe in someday, but later I had a low-grade afternoon hangover and ran over a black snake on the way to the supermarket and was flooded with inexplicable fear when I heard the checkout clerk explaining to the man ahead of me why she was finally divorcing her husband. "He left me no choice," she said over and over as she punched the register. "He has a little seven-month-old baby by her, he left me no choice." I would like to believe that my dread then was for the human condition, but of course it was for me, because I wanted a baby and did not then have one and because I wanted to own the house that cost $1,000 a month to rent and because I had a hangover.

It all comes back. Perhaps it is difficult to see the value in having one's self back in that kind of mood, but I do see it; I think we are well advised to keep on nodding terms with the people we used to be whether we find them attractive company or not. Otherwise they turn up unannounced and surprise us, come hammering on the mind's door at 4 a.m. of a bad night and demand to know who deserted them, who betrayed them, who is going to make amends. We forget all too soon the things we thought we could never forget. We forget the loves and the betrayals alike, forget what we whispered and what we screamed, forget who we were. I have already lost touch with a couple of people I used to be; one of them, a seventeen-year-old, presents little threat, although it would be of some interest to me to know again what it feels like to sit on a river levee drinking vodka-and-orange-juice and listening to Les Paul and Mary Ford and their echoes sing "How High the Moon" on the car radio. (You see I still have the scenes, but I no longer perceive myself among those present, no longer could even improvise the dialogue.) The other one, a twenty-three-year-old, bothers me more. She was always a good deal of trouble, and I suspect she will reappear when I least want to see her, skirts too long, shy to the point of aggravation, always the injured party, full of recriminations and little hurts and stories I do not want to hear again, at once saddening me and angering me with her vulnerability and ignorance, an apparition all the more insistent for being so long banished.

18   It is a good idea, then, to keep in touch, and I suppose that keeping in touch is what notebooks are all about. And we are all on our own when it comes to keeping those lines open to ourselves: your notebook will never help me, nor mine you. *"So what's new in the whiskey business?"* What could that possibly mean to you? To me it means a blonde in a Pucci bathing suit sitting with a couple of fat men by the pool at the Beverly Hills Hotel. Another man approaches, and they all regard one another in silence for a while. "So what's new in the whiskey business?" one of the fat men finally says by way of welcome, and the blonde stands up, arches one foot and dips it in the pool, looking all the while at the cabana where Baby Pignatari is talking on the telephone. That is all there is to that, except that several years later I saw the blonde coming out of Saks Fifth Avenue in New York with her California complexion and a voluminous mink coat. In the harsh wind that day she looked old and irrevocably tired to me, and even the skins in the mink coat were not worked the way they were doing them that year, not the way she would have wanted them done, and there is the point of the story. For a while after that I did not like to look in the mirror, and my eyes would skim the newspapers and pick out only the deaths, the cancer

victims, the premature coronaries, the suicides, and I stopped riding the Lexington Avenue IRT because I noticed for the first time
that all the strangers I had seen for years—the man with the seeing-
eye dog, the spinster who read the classified pages every day, the
fat girl who always got off with me at Grand Central—looked
older than they once had.

It all comes back. Even that recipe for sauerkraut: even that 19
brings it back. I was on Fire Island when I first made that sauerkraut, and it was raining, and we drank a lot of bourbon and ate
the sauerkraut and went to bed at ten, and I listened to the rain
and the Atlantic and felt safe. I made the sauerkraut again last
night and it did not make me feel any safer, but that is, as they
say, another story.

1966

Aria

Richard Rodriguez

Supporters of bilingual education today imply that students like 1
me miss a great deal by not being taught in their family's language. What they seem not to recognize is that, as a socially disadvantaged child, I considered Spanish to be a private language.
What I needed to learn in school was that I had the right—and
the obligation—to speak the public language of *los gringos*. The
odd truth is that my first-grade classmates could have become
bilingual, in the conventional sense of that word, more easily than
I. Had they been taught (as upper-middle-class children are often
taught early) a second language like Spanish or French, they could
have regarded it simply as that: another public language. In my
case such bilingualism could not have been so quickly achieved.
What I did not believe was that I could speak a single public
language.

Without question, it would have pleased me to hear my teach- 2
ers address me in Spanish when I entered the classroom. I would
have felt much less afraid. I would have trusted them and

responded with ease. But I would have delayed—for how long postponed?—having to learn the language of public society, I would have evaded—and for how long could I have afforded to delay?—learning the great lesson of school, that I had a public identity.

3   Fortunately, my teachers were unsentimental about their responsibility. What they understood was that I needed to speak a public language. So their voices would search me out, asking me questions. Each time I'd hear them, I'd look up in surprise to see a nun's face frowning at me. I'd mumble, not really meaning to answer. The nun would persist, "Richard, stand up. Don't look at the floor. Speak up. Speak to the entire class, not just to me!" But I couldn't believe that the English language was mine to use. (In part, I did not want to believe it.) I continued to mumble. I resisted the teacher's demands. (Did I somehow suspect that once I learned public language my pleasing family life would be changed?) Silent, waiting for the bell to sound, I remained dazed, diffident, afraid.

4   Because I wrongly imagined that English was intrinsically a public language and Spanish an intrinsically private one, I easily noted the difference between classroom language and the language of home. At school, words were directed to a general audience of listeners. ("Boys and girls.") Words were meaningfully ordered. And the point was not self-expression alone but to make oneself understood by many others. The teacher quizzed: "Boys and girls, why do we use that word in this sentence? Could we think of a better word to use there? Would the sentence change its meaning if the words were differently arranged? And wasn't there a better way of saying much the same thing?" (I couldn't say. I wouldn't try to say.)

5   Three months. Five. Half a year passed. Unsmiling, ever watchful, my teachers noted my silence. They began to connect my behavior with the difficult progress my older sister and brother were making. Until one Saturday morning three nuns arrived at the house to talk to our parents. Stiffly, they sat on the blue living room sofa. From the doorway of another room, spying the visitors, I noted the incongruity—the clash of two worlds, the faces and voices of school intruding upon the familiar setting of home. I overheard one voice gently wondering, "Do your children speak

only Spanish at home, Mrs. Rodriguez?" While another voice
added, "That Richard especially seems so timid and shy."

That Rich-heard!   6

With great tact the visitors continued, "Is it possible for you   7
and your husband to encourage your children to practice their
English when they are home?" Of course, my parents complied.
What would they not do for their children's well-being? And how
could they have questioned the Church's authority which those
women represented? In an instant, they agreed to give up the language (the sounds) that had revealed and accentuated our family's closeness. The moment after the visitors left, the change was
observed. "*Ahora,* speak to us *en inglés,* my father and mother
united to tell us.

At first, it seemed a kind of game. After dinner each night, the   8
family gathered to practice "our" English. (It was still then *inglès,*
a language foreign to us, so we felt drawn as strangers to it.) Laughing, we would try to define words we could not pronounce. We
played with strange English sounds, often overanglicizing our pro-
nunciations. And we filled the smiling gaps of our sentences with
familiar Spanish sounds. But that was cheating, somebody shouted.
Everyone laughed. In school, meanwhile, like my brother and sister, I was required to attend a daily tutoring session. I needed a full
year of special attention. I also needed my teachers to keep my
attention from straying in class by calling out, *Rich-heard*—their
English voices slowing prying loose my ties to my other name, its
three notes, *Ri-car-do.* Most of all I needed to hear my mother and
father speak to me in a moment of seriousness in broken—
suddenly heartbreaking—English. The scene was inevitable: One
Saturday morning I entered the kitchen where my parents were talking in Spanish. I did not realize that they were talking in Spanish
however until, at the moment they saw me, I heard their voices
change to speak English. Those *gringo* sounds they uttered startled
me. Pushed me away. In that moment of trivial misunderstanding
and profound insight, I felt my throat twisted by unsounded grief.
I turned quickly and left the room. But I had no place to escape to
with Spanish. (The spell was broken.) My brothers and sisters were
speaking English in another part of the house.

Again and again in the days following, increasingly angry, I   9
was obliged to hear my mother and father: "Speak to us *en inglés*"

(*Speak.*) Only then did I determine to learn classroom English. Weeks after, it happened: One day in school I raised my hand to volunteer an answer. I spoke out in a loud voice. And I did not think it remarkable when the entire class understood. That day, I moved very far from the disadvantaged child I had been only days earlier. The belief, that calming assurance that I belonged in public, had at last taken hold.

10   Shortly after, I stopped hearing the high and loud sounds of *los gringos*. A more and more confident speaker of English, I didn't trouble to listen to *how* strangers sounded, speaking to me. And there simply were too many English-speaking people in my day for me to hear American accents anymore. Conversations quickened. Listening to persons who sounded eccentrically pitched voices, I usually noted their sounds for an initial few seconds before I concentrated on *what* they were saying. Conversations became content-full. Transparent. Hearing someone's *tone* of voice—angry or questioning or sarcastic or happy or sad—I didn't distinguish it from the words it expressed. Sound and word were thus tightly wedded. At the end of a day, I was often bemused, always relieved, to realize how "silent," though crowded with words, my day in public had been. (This public silence measured and quickened the change in my life.)

11   At last, seven years old, I came to believe what had been technically true since my birth: I was an American citizen.

12   But the special feeling of closeness at home was diminished by then. Gone was the desperate, urgent, intense feeling of being at home, rare was the experience of feeling myself individualized by family intimates. We remained a loving family, but one greatly changed. No longer so close; no longer bound tight by the pleasing and troubling knowledge of our public separateness. Neither my older brother nor sister rushed home after school anymore. Nor did I. When I arrived home there would often be neighborhood kids in the house. Or the house would be empty of sounds.

13   Following the dramatic Americanization of their children, even my parents grew more publicly confident. Especially my mother. She learned the names of all the people on our block. And she decided we needed to have a telephone installed in the house. My father continued to use the word *gringo*. But it was no longer charged with the old bitterness or distrust. (Stripped of any

emotional content, the word simply became a name for those Americans not of Hispanic descent.) Hearing him, sometimes, I wasn't sure if he was pronouncing the Spanish word *gringo* or saying gringo in English.

Matching the silence I started hearing in public was a new 14 quiet at home. The family's quiet was partly due to the fact that, as we children learned more and more English, we shared fewer and fewer words with our parents. Sentences needed to be spoken slowly when a child addressed his mother or father. (Often the parent wouldn't understand.) The child would need to repeat himself. (Still the parent misunderstood.) The young voice, frustrated, would end up saying, "Never mind"—the subject was closed. Dinners would be noisy with the clinking of knives and forks against dishes. My mother would smile softly between her remarks; my father at the other end of the table would chew and chew at his food, while he stared over the heads of his children.

My *mother!* My *father!* After English became my primary lan- 15 guage, I no longer knew what words to use in addressing my parents. The old Spanish words (those tender accents of sound) I had used earlier—*mamá* and *papá*—I couldn't use anymore. They would have been too painful reminders of how much had changed in my life. On the other hand, the words I heard neighborhood kids call their parents seemed equally unsatisfactory. *Mother* and *Father; Ma, Papa, Pa, Dad, Pop* (how I hated the all American sound of that last word especially)—all these terms I felt were unsuitable, not really terms of address for my parents. As a result, I never used them at home. Whenever I'd speak to my parents, I would try to get their attention with eye contact alone. In public conversations, I'd refer to "my parents" or "my mother and father."

My mother and father, for their part, responded differently, as 16 their children spoke to them less. She grew restless, seemed troubled and anxious at the scarcity of words exchanged in the house. It was she who would question me about my day when I came home from school. She smiled at small talk. She pried at the edges of my sentences to get me to say something more. (What?) She'd join conversations she overheard, but her intrusions often stopped her children's talking. By contrast, my father seemed reconciled to the new quiet. Though his English improved somewhat, he retired into silence. At dinner he spoke very little. One night his children and even his wife helplessly giggled at his garbled English pronunciation of the Catholic Grace before Meals. Thereafter he made his wife recite the prayer at the start of each meal, even on formal occasions, when there were guests in the house. Hers became the public voice of the family. On official business, it was she, not my father, one would usually hear on the phone or in stores, talking to strangers. His children grew so accustomed to his silence that, years later, they would speak routinely of his shyness. (My mother would often try to explain: Both his parents died when he was eight. He was raised by an uncle who treated him like little more than a menial servant. He was never encouraged to speak. He grew up alone. A man of few words.) But my father was not shy, I realized, when I'd watch him speaking Spanish with relatives. Using Spanish, he was quickly effusive. Especially when talking with other men, his voice would spark, flicker, flare alive with sounds. In Spanish, he expressed ideas and feelings he rarely revealed in English. With firm Spanish sounds, he conveyed confidence and authority English would never allow him.

17   The silence at home, however, was finally more than a literal silence. Fewer words passed between parent and child, but more profound was the silence that resulted from my inattention to sounds. At about the time I no longer bothered to listen with care to the sounds of English in public, I grew careless about listening to the sounds family members made when they spoke. Most of the time I heard someone speaking at home and didn't distinguish his sounds from the words people uttered in public. I didn't even pay much attention to my parents' accented and ungrammatical speech. At least not at home. Only when I was with them in public would I grow alert to their accents. Though, even then, their sounds caused me less and less concern. For I was increasingly confident of my own public identity.

18   I would have been happier about my public success had I not sometimes recalled what it had been like earlier, when my family had conveyed its intimacy through a set of conveniently private sounds. Sometimes in public, hearing a stranger, I'd hark back to my past. A Mexican farmworker approached me downtown to ask directions to somewhere, "*¿Hijito . . .?*" he said. And his voice summoned deep longing. Another time, standing beside my mother

in the visiting room of a Carmelite convent, before the dense screen which rendered the nuns shadowy figures, I heard several Spanish-speaking nuns—their busy, singsong overlapping voices—assure us that yes, yes, we were remembered, all our family was remembered in their prayers. (Their voices echoed far-away family sounds.) Another day, a dark-faced old woman—her hand light on my shoulder—steadied herself against me as she boarded a bus. She murmured something I couldn't quite comprehend. Her Spanish voice came near, like the face of a never-before-seen relative in the instant before I was kissed. Her voice, like so many of the Spanish voices I'd hear in public, recalled the golden age of my youth. Hearing Spanish then, I continued to be a careful, if sad, listener to sounds. Hearing a Spanish-speaking family walking behind me, I turned to look. I smiled for an instance, before my glance found the Hispanic-looking faces of strangers in the crowd going by.

Today I hear bilingual educators say that children lose a degree of "individuality" by becoming assimilated into public society. Bilingual schooling was popularized in the seventies, that decade when middle-class ethics began to resist the process of assimilation—the American melting pot). But the bilingualists simplistically scorn the value and necessity of assimilation. They do not seem to realize that there are *two* ways a person is individualized. So they do not realize that while one suffers a diminished sense of *private* individuality by becoming assimilated into public society, such assimilation makes possible the achievement of *public* individuality. 19

The bilingualists insist that a student should be reminded of his difference from others in mass society, his heritage. But they equate mere separateness with individuality. The fact is that only in private—with intimates—is separateness from the crowd a prerequisite for individuality. (An intimate draws me apart, tells me that I am unique, unlike all others.) In public, by contrast, full individuality is achieved, paradoxically, by those who are able to consider themselves members of the crowd. Thus it happened for me: Only when I was able to think of myself as an American, no longer an alien in *gringo* society, could I seek the rights and opportunities necessary for full public individuality. The social 20 and political advantages I enjoy as a man result from the day that I came to believe that my name, indeed, is *Rich-heard Road-ree-guess.* It is true that my public society today is often impersonal. (My public society is usually mass society.) Yet despite the anonymity of the crowd and despite the fact that the individuality I achieve in public is often tenuous—because it depends on my being one in a crowd—I celebrate the day I acquired my new name. Those middle-class ethnics who scorn assimilation seem to me filled with decadent self-pity, obsessed by the burden of public life. Dangerously, they romanticize public separateness and they trivialize the dilemma of the socially disadvantaged.

21   My awkward childhood does not prove the necessity of bilingual education. My story discloses instead an essential myth of childhood—inevitable pain. If I rehearse here the changes in my private life after my Americanization, it is finally to emphasize the public gain. The loss implies the gain: The house I returned to each afternoon was quiet. Intimate sounds no longer rushed to the door to greet me. There were other noises inside. The telephone rang. Neighborhood kids ran past the door of the bedroom where I was reading my school-books—covered with shopping-bag paper. Once I learned public language, it would never again be easy for me to hear intimate family voices. More and more of my day was spent hearing words. But that may only be a way of saying that the day I raised my hand in class and spoke loudly to an entire roomful of faces, my childhood started to end.

1981

Coming to an Awareness of Language

Malcolm X

1 I've never been one for inaction. Everything I've ever felt strongly about, I've done something about. I guess that's why, unable to do anything else, I soon began writing to people I had known in

the hustling world, such as Sammy the Pimp, John Hughes, the gambling house owner, the thief Jumpsteady, and several dope peddlers. I wrote them all about Allah and Islam and Mr. Elijah Muhammad. I had no idea where most of them lived. I addressed their letters in care of the Harlem or Roxbury bars and clubs where I'd known them.

I never got a single reply. The average hustler and criminal 2 was too uneducated to write a letter. I have known many slick, sharp-looking hustlers, who would have you think they had an interest in Wall Street; privately, they would get someone else to read a letter if they received one. Besides, neither would I have replied to anyone writing me something as wild as "the white man is the devil."

What certainly went on the Harlem and Roxbury wires was 3 that Detroit Red was going crazy in stir, or else he was trying some hype to shake up the warden's office.

During the years that I stayed in the Norfolk Prison Colony, 4 never did any official directly say anything to me about those letters, although, of course, they all passed through the prison censorship. I'm sure, however, they monitored what I wrote to add to the files which every state and federal prison keeps on the conversion of Negro inmates by the teachings of Mr. Elijah Muhammad.

But at that time, I felt that the real reason was that the white 5 man knew that he was the devil.

Later on, I even wrote to the Mayor of Boston, to the Governor 6 of Massachusetts, and to Harry S. Truman. They never answered; they probably never even saw my letters. I handscratched to them how the white man's society was responsible for the black man's condition in this wilderness of North America.

It was because of my letters that I happened to stumble upon 7 starting to acquire some kind of a homemade education.

I became increasingly frustrated at not being able to express 8 what I wanted to convey in letters that I wrote, especially those to Mr. Elijah Muhammad. In the street, I had been the most articulate hustler out there—I had commanded attention when I said something. But now, trying to write simple English, I not only wasn't articulate, I wasn't even functional. How would I sound writing in slang, the way I would *say* it, something such as, "Look, daddy, let me pull your coat about a cat, Elijah Muhammad—"

9   Many who today hear me somewhere in person, or on television, or those who read something I've said, will think I went to school far beyond the eighth grade. This impression is due entirely to my prison studies.

10   It had really begun back in the Charlestown Prison, when Bimbi first made me feel envy of his stock of knowledge. Bimbi had always taken charge of any conversation he was in, and I had tried to emulate him. But every book I picked up had few sentences which didn't contain anywhere from one to nearly all of the words that might as well have been in Chinese. When I just skipped those words, of course, I really ended up with little idea of what the book said. So I had come to the Norfolk Prison Colony still going through only book-reading motions. Pretty soon, I would have quit even these motions, unless I had received the motivation that I did.

11   I saw that the best thing I could do was get hold of a dictionary—to study, to learn some words. I was lucky enough to reason also that I should try to improve my penmanship. It was sad. I couldn't even write in a straight line. It was both ideas together that moved me to request a dictionary along with some tablets and pencils from the Norfolk Prison Colony school.

12   I spent two days just riffling uncertainly through the dictionary's pages. I'd never realized so many words existed! I didn't know *which* words I needed to learn. Finally, just to start some kind of action, I began copying.

13   In my slow, painstaking, ragged handwriting, I copied into my tablet everything printed on that first page, down to the punctuation marks.

14   I believe it took me a day. Then, aloud, I read back, to myself, everything I'd written on the tablet. Over and over, aloud, to myself, I read my own handwriting.

15   I woke up the next morning, thinking about those words—immensely proud to realize that not only had I written so much at one time, but I'd written words that I never knew were in the world. Moreover, with a little effort, I also could remember what many of these words meant. I reviewed the words whose meanings I didn't remember. Funny thing, from the dictionary first page right now, that "aardvark" springs to my mind. The dictionary had a picture of it, a long-tailed, long-eared, burrowing

African mammal, which lives off termites caught by sticking out its tongue as an anteater does for ants.

I was so fascinated that I went on—I copied the dictionary's 16 next page. And the same experience came when I studied that. With every succeeding page, I also learned of people and places and events from history. Actually the dictionary is like a minia-ture encyclopedia. Finally the dictionary's A section had filled a whole tablet—and I went on into the B's. That was the way I started copying what eventually became the entire dictionary. It went a lot faster after so much practice helped me to pick up handwriting speed. Between what I wrote in my tablet, and writ-ing letters, during the rest of my time in prison I would guess I wrote a million words.

I suppose it was inevitable that as my word-base broadened, 17 I could for the first time pick up a book and read and now begin to understand what the book was saying. Anyone who has read a great deal can imagine the new world that opened. Let me tell you something: from then until I left that prison, in every free moment I had, if I was not reading in the library, I was reading on my bunk. You couldn't have gotten me out of books with a wedge. Between Mr. Muhammad's teachings, my correspondence, my visitors . . . and my reading of books, months passed without my even thinking about being imprisoned. In fact, up to then, I never had been so truly free in my life.

1965

The Death of the Moth

Virginia Woolf

Moths that fly by day are not properly to be called moths; they 1 do not excite that pleasant sense of dark autumn nights and ivy-blossom which the commonest yellow-underwing asleep in the shadow of the curtain never fails to rouse in us. They are hybrid creatures, neither gay like butterflies nor sombre like their own species. Nevertheless the present specimen, with his narrow hay-coloured wings, fringed with a tassel of the same colour, seemed to be content with life. It was a pleasant morning, mid-September, mild, benignant, yet with a keener breath than that of the summer months. The plough was already scoring the field opposite the window, and where the share had been, the earth was pressed flat and gleamed with moisture. Such vigour came rolling in from the fields and the down beyond that it was difficult to keep the eyes strictly turned upon the book. The rooks too were keeping one of their annual festivities; soaring round the tree tops until it looked as if a vast net with thousands of black knots in it had been cast up into the air; which, after a few moments sank slowly down upon the trees until every twig seemed to have a knot at the end of it. Then, suddenly, the net would be thrown into the air again in a wider circle this time, with the utmost clamour and vociferation, as though to be thrown into the air and settle slowly down upon the tree tops were a tremendously exciting experience.

2   The same energy which inspired the rooks, the ploughmen, the horses, and even, it seemed, the lean bare-backed downs, sent the moth fluttering from side to side of his square of the windowpane. One could not help watching him. One was, indeed, conscious of a queer feeling of pity for him. The possibilities of pleasure seemed that morning so enormous and so various that to have only a moth's part in life, and a day moth's at that, appeared a hard fate, and his zest in enjoying his meagre opportunities to the full, pathetic. He flew vigorously to one corner of his compartment, and, after waiting there a second, flew across to the other. What remained for him but to fly to a third corner and then to a fourth? That was all he could do, in spite of the size of the downs, the width of the sky, the far-off smoke of houses, and the romantic voice, now and then, of a steamer out at sea. What he could do he did. Watching him, it seemed as if a fibre, very thin but pure, of the enormous energy of the world had been thrust into his frail and diminutive body. As often as he crossed the pane, I could fancy that a thread of vital light became visible. He was little or nothing but life.

3   Yet, because he was so small, and so simple a form of the energy that was rolling in at the open window and driving its way

through so many narrow and intricate corridors in my own brain and in those of other human beings, there was something marvellous as well as pathetic about him. It was as if someone had taken a tiny bead of pure life and decking it as lightly as possible with down and feathers, had set it dancing and zigzagging to show us the true nature of life. Thus displayed one could not get over the strangeness of it. One is apt to forget all about life, seeing it humped and bossed and garnished and cumbered so that it has to move with the greatest circumspection and dignity. Again, the thought of all that life might have been had he been born in any other shape caused one to view his simple activities with a kind of pity.

After a time, tired by his dancing apparently, he settled on the 4 window ledge in the sun, and, the queer spectacle being at an end, I forgot about him. Then, looking up, my eye was caught by him. He was trying to resume his dancing, but seemed either so stiff or so awkward that he could only flutter to the bottom of the windowpane; and when he tried to fly across it he failed. Being intent on other matters I watched these futile attempts for a time without thinking, unconsciously waiting for him to resume his flight, as one waits for a machine, that has stopped momentarily, to start again without considering the reason of its failure. After perhaps a seventh attempt he slipped from the wooden ledge and fell, fluttering his wings, on to his back on the window sill. The helplessness of his attitude roused me. It flashed upon me that he was in difficulties; he could no longer raise himself; his legs struggled vainly. But, as I stretched out a pencil, meaning to help him to right himself, it came over me that the failure and awkwardness were the approach of death. I laid the pencil down again.

The legs agitated themselves once more. I looked as if for the 5 enemy against which he struggled. I looked out of doors. What had happened there? Presumably it was midday, and work in the fields had stopped. Stillness and quiet had replaced the previous animation. The birds had taken themselves off to feed in the brooks. The horses stood still. Yet the power was there all the same, massed outside, indifferent, impersonal, not attending to anything in particular. Somehow it was opposed to the little hay-coloured moth. It was useless to try to do anything. One could only watch the extraordinary efforts made by those tiny legs against an oncoming doom which could, had it chosen, have submerged an entire city, not merely a city, but masses of human beings; nothing, I knew, had any chance against death. Nevertheless after a pause of exhaustion the legs fluttered again. It was superb this last protest, and so frantic that he succeeded at last in righting himself. One's sympathies, of course, were all on the side of life. Also, when there was nobody to care or to know, this gigantic effort on the part of an insignificant little moth, against a power of such magnitude, to retain what no one else valued or desired to keep, moved one strangely. Again, somehow, one saw life, a pure bead. I lifted the pencil again, useless though I knew it to be. But even as I did so, the unmistakable tokens of death showed themselves. The body relaxed, and instantly grew stiff. The struggle was over. The insignificant little creature now knew death. As I looked at the dead moth, this minute wayside triumph of so great a force over so mean an antagonist filled me with wonder. Just as life had been strange a few minutes before, so death was now as strange. The moth having righted himself now lay most decently and uncomplainingly composed. O yes, he seemed to say, death is stronger than I am.

1942

Metaphors We Live By

George Lakoff and Mark Johnson

CONCEPTS WE LIVE BY

1 Metaphor is for most people device of the poetic imagination and the rhetorical flourish—a matter of extraordinary rather than ordinary language. Moreover, metaphor is typically viewed as characteristic of language alone, a matter of words rather than thought or action. For this reason, most people think they can get along perfectly well without metaphor. We have found, on the contrary, that metaphor is pervasive in everyday life, not just in language but in thought and action. Our ordinary conceptual system, in

terms of which we both think and act, is fundamentally metaphorical in nature.

The concepts that govern our thought are not just matters of 2 the intellect. They also govern our everyday functioning, down to the most mundane details. Our concepts structure what we perceive, how we get around in the world, and how we relate to other people. Our conceptual system thus plays a central role in defining our everyday realities. If we are right in suggesting that our conceptual system is largely metaphorical, then the way we think what we experience, and what we do every day is very much a matter of metaphor.

But our conceptual system is not something we are normally 3 aware of. In most of the little things we do every day, we simply think and act more or less automatically along certain lines. Just what these lines are is by no means obvious. One way to find out is by looking at language. Since communication is based on the same conceptual system that we use in thinking and acting, language is an important source of evidence for what that system is like.

Primarily on the basis of linguistic evidence, we have found 4 that most of our ordinary conceptual system is metaphorical in nature. And we have found a way to begin to identify in detail *just what the metaphors are that structure how we perceive,* how we think, and what we do.

To give some idea of what it could mean for a concept to be 5 metaphorical and for such a concept to structure an everyday activity, let us start with the concept ARGUMENT and the conceptual metaphor ARGUMENT IS WAR. This metaphor is reflected in our everyday language by a wide variety of expressions:

ARGUMENT IS WAR

Your claims are *indefensible.*

He *attacked* every weak point in my argument.

His criticisms were right on *target.*

I *demolished* his argument.

I've never *won* an argument with him.

You disagree? Okay, *shoot!*

If you use that *strategy,* he'll *wipe you out.*

He *shot down* all of my arguments.

6   It is important to see that we don't just talk about arguments
in terms of war. We can actually win or lose arguments. We see
the person we are arguing with as an opponent. We attack his
positions and we defend our own. We gain and lose ground. We
plan and use strategies. If we find a position indefensible, we can
abandon it and take a new line of attack. Many of the things we
do in arguing are partially structured by the concept of war.
Though there is no physical battle, there is a verbal battle, and the
structure of an argument—attack, defense, counter-attack, etc.—
reflects this. It is in this sense that the ARGUMENT IS WAR
metaphor is one that we live by in this culture; it structures the
actions we perform in arguing. Try to imagine a culture where
arguments are not viewed in terms of war, where no one wins or
loses, where there is no sense of attacking or defending, gaining
or losing ground. Imagine a culture where an argument is viewed
as a dance, the participants are seen as performers, and the goal
is to perform in a balanced and aesthetically pleasing way. In such
a culture, people would view arguments differently, experience
them differently, carry them out differently, and talk about them
differently. But we would probably not view them as arguing at
all: they would simply be doing something different. It would
seem strange even to call what they were doing "arguing." In perhaps the most neutral way of describing this difference between
their culture and ours would be to say that we have a discourse
form structured in terms of battle and they have one structured
in terms of dance. This is an example of what it means for a
metaphorical concept, namely, ARGUMENT IS WAR, to structure
(at least in part) what we do and how we understand what we
are doing when we argue. *The essence of metaphor is understanding
and experiencing one kind of thing in terms of another.* It is not that
arguments are a subspecies of war. Arguments and wars are
different kinds of things—verbal discourse and armed conflict—
and the actions performed are different kinds of actions. But
ARGUMENT is partially structured, understood, performed, and
talked about in terms of WAR. The concept is metaphorically
structured, the activity is metaphorically structured, and, consequently, the language is metaphorically structured.

7   Moreover, this is the ordinary way of having an argument and
talking about one. The normal way for us to talk about attacking

a position is to use the words "attack a position." Our conventional ways of talking about arguments presuppose a metaphor we are hardly ever conscious of. The metaphor is not merely in the words we use—it is in our very concept of an argument. The language of argument is not poetic, fanciful, or rhetorical; it is literal. We talk about arguments that way because we conceive of them that way—and we act according to the way we conceive of things.

The most important claim we have made so far is that metaphor is not just a matter of language, that is, of mere words. We shall argue that, on the contrary, human thought processes are largely metaphorical. This is what we mean when we say that the human conceptual system is metaphorically structured and defined. Metaphors as linguistic expressions are possible precisely because there are metaphors in a person's conceptual system. Therefore, whenever in this book we speak of metaphors, such as ARGUMENT IS WAR, it should be understood that metaphor means metaphorical concept.

THE SYSTEMATICITY OF METAPHORICAL CONCEPTS

Arguments usually follow patterns; that is, there are certain things we typically do and do not do in arguing. The fact that we in part conceptualize arguments in terms of battle systematically influences the shape arguments take and the way we talk about what we do in arguing. Because the metaphorical concept is systematic, the language we use to talk about that aspect of the concept is systematic.

We saw in the ARGUMENT IS WAR metaphor that expressions from the vocabulary of war, e.g., attack a position, indefensible, strategy, new line of attack, win, gain ground, etc., form a systematic way of talking about the battling aspects of arguing. It is no accident that these expressions mean what they mean when we use them to talk about arguments. A portion of the conceptual network of battle partially characterizes the concept of an argument, and the language follows suit. Since metaphorical expressions in our language are tied to metaphorical concepts in a systematic way, we can use metaphorical linguistic expressions to study the nature of metaphorical concepts and to gain an understanding of the metaphorical nature of our activities.

11   To get an idea of how metaphorical expressions in everyday language can give us insight into the metaphorical nature of the concept that structure our everyday activities, let us consider the metaphorical concept TIME IS MONEY as it is reflected in contemporary English.

TIME IS MONEY

You're *wasting* my time.

This gadget will save you hours. I don't have the time to give you.

How do you spend your time these days? That flat tire cost me an hour.

I've invested a lot of time in her.

I don't have enough time to spare for that. You're running out of time.

You need to budget your time.

Put aside some time for ping pong.

Is that *worth your while?*

Do you have much time *left?*

He's living on *borrowed* time.

You don't use your time *profitably.*

I *lost* a lot of time when I got sick.

Thank you for your time.

12   Time in our culture is a valuable commodity. It is a limited resource that we use to accomplish our goals. Because of the way that the concept of work has developed in modern Western culture, where work is typically associated with the time it takes and time is precisely quantified, it has become customary to pay people by the hour, week, or year. In our culture TIME IS MONEY in many ways: telephone message units, hourly wages, hotel room rates, yearly budgets, interest on loans, and paying your debt to society by "serving time." These practices are relatively new in the history of the human race, and by no means do they exist in all cultures. They have arisen in modern industrialized societies and structure our basic everyday activities in a very profound

way. Corresponding to the fact that we act as if time is a valuable commodity—a limited resource, even money—we conceive of time that way. Thus we understand and experience time as the kind of thing that can be spent, wasted, budgeted, invested wisely or poorly, saved, or squandered.

TIME IS MONEY, TIME IS A LIMITED RESOURCE, and 13 TIME IS A VALUABLE COMMODITY are all metaphorical concepts. They are metaphorical since we are using our everyday experiences with money, limited resources, and valuable commodities to conceptualize time. This isn't a necessary way for human beings to conceptualize time; it is tied to our culture. There are cultures where time is none of these things.

The metaphorical concepts TIME IS MONEY, TIME IS A 14 RESOURCE, and TIME IS A VALUABLE COMMODITY form a single system based on sub-categorization, since in our society money is a limited resource and limited resources are valuable commodities. These sub-categorization relationships characterize entailment relationships between the metaphors: TIME IS MONEY entails that TIME IS A LIMITED RESOURCE, which entails that TIME IS A VALUABLE COMMODITY. We are adopting the practice of using the most specific metaphorical concept, in this case TIME IS MONEY to characterize the entire system. Of the expressions listed under the TIME IS MONEY metaphor, some refer specifically to money (spend, invest, budget, probably cost), others to limited resources (use, use up, have enough of, run out of), and still others to valuable commodities (have, give, lose, thank you for). This is an example of the way in which metaphorical entailments can characterize a coherent system of metaphorical concepts and a corresponding coherent system of metaphorical expressions for those concepts.

The very systematicity that allows us to comprehend one 15 aspect of a concept in terms of another (e.g., comprehending an aspect of arguing in terms of battle) will necessarily hide other aspects of the concept. In allowing us to focus on one aspect of a concept (e.g., the battling aspects of arguing), metaphorical concept can keep us from focusing on other aspects of the concept that are inconsistent with that metaphor. For example, in the midst of a heated argument, when we are intent on attacking our opponent's position and defending our own, we may lose sight of the cooperative aspects of arguing. Someone who is arguing with you can be viewed as giving you his time, a valuable commodity, in an effort at mutual understanding. But when we are preoccupied with the battle aspects, we often lose sight of the cooperative aspects.

16   A far more subtle case of how a metaphorical concept can hide an aspect of our experience can be seen in what Michael Reddy has called the "conduit metaphor."' Reddy observes that our language about language is structured roughly by the following complex metaphor:

IDEAS (OF MEANINGS) ARE OBJECTS.
LINGUISTIC EXPRESSIONS ARE CONTAINERS.
COMMUNICATION IS SENDING.

17   The speaker puts ideas (objects) into words (containers) and sends them (along a conduit) to a bearer who takes the idea/objects out of the word/containers. Reddy documents this with more than a hundred types of expressions in English, which he estimates account for at least 70 percent of the expressions we use for talking about language. Here are some examples:

THE CONDUIT METAPHOR
It's hard to *get* that idea across to him.
I *gave* you that idea.
Your reasons *came through* to us.
It's difficult to *put* my ideas *into* words.
When you *have* a good idea, try to *capture* it immediately in words.
Try to *pack* more thought into fewer words.
You can't simply *stuff* ideas *into* a sentence any old way.
The meaning is right there *in* the words.
Don't *force* your meanings *into* the wrong words.
His words *carry* little meaning.
The introduction has a great deal of thought *content*.
Your words seem *hollow*.
The sentence is *without* meaning.
The idea is *buried in* terribly dense paragraphs.

In examples like these it is far more difficult to see that there
is anything hidden by the metaphor or even to see that there is a
metaphor here at all. This is so much the conventional way of
thinking about language that it is sometimes hard to imagine that
it might not fit reality. But if we look at what the conduit
metaphor entails, we can see some of the ways in which it masks
aspects of the communicative process.

First, the LINGUISTIC EXPRESSIONS ARE CONTAINERS
FOR MEANINGS aspect of the conduit metaphor entails that
words and sentences have meanings in themselves, independent
of any context or speaker. The MEANINGS ARE OBJECTS part of
the metaphor, for example, entails that meanings have an existence independent of people and contexts. The part of the
metaphor that says LINGUISTIC EXPRESSIONS ARE CON-
TAINERS FOR MEANING entails that words (and sentences)
have meanings, again independent of contexts and speakers.
These metaphors are appropriate in many situations—those
where context differences don't matter and where all the participants in the conversation understand the sentences in the same
way. These two entailments are exemplified by sentences like.

The meaning is right there in the words,

which, according to the CONDUIT metaphor, can correctly be said
of any sentence. But there are many cases where context does matter. Here is a celebrated one recorded in actual conversation by
Pamela Downing:

Please sit in the apple-juice seat.

In isolation this sentence has no meaning at all, since the
expression "apple-juice seat" is not a conventional way of referring to any kind of object. But the sentence makes perfect sense
in the context in which it was uttered. An overnight guest came
down to breakfast. There were four place settings, three with
orange juice and one with apple juice. It was clear what the apple-
juice seat was. And even the next morning, when there was no
apple juice, it was still clear which seat was the apple-juice seat.

In addition to sentences that have no meaning without context, there are cases where a single sentence will mean different
things to different people. Consider:

We need new alternative sources of energy.

22   This means something very different to the president of Mobil Oil from what it means to the president of Friends of the Earth. The meaning is not right there in the sentence—it matters a lot who is saying or listening to the sentence and what his social and political attitudes are. The CONDUIT metaphor does not fit cases where context is required to determine whether the sentence has any meaning at all and, if so, what meaning it has.

23   These examples show that the metaphorical concepts we have looked at provide us with a partial understanding of what communication, argument, and time are and that, in doing this, they hide other aspects of these concepts. It is important to see that the metaphorical structuring involved here is partial, not total. If it were total, one concept would actually be the other, not merely be understood in terms of it. For example, time isn't really money. If you spend your time trying to do something and it doesn't work, you can't get your time back. There are no time banks. I can give you a lot of time, but you can't give me back the same time, though you can give me back the same amount of time. And so on. Thus, part of a metaphorical concept does not and cannot fit.

24   On the other hand, metaphorical concepts can be extended beyond the range of ordinary literal ways of thinking and talking into the range of what is called figurative, poetic, colorful, or fanciful thought and language. Thus, if ideas are objects, we can dress them up in fancy clothes, juggle them, line them up nice and neat, etc. So when we say that a concept is structured by *a metaphor* we mean that it is partially structured and that it can be extended in some ways but not others.

ORIENTATIONAL METAPHORS

25 So far we have examined what we will call structural metaphors, cases where one concept is metaphorically structured in terms of another. But there is another kind of metaphorical concept, one that does not structure one concept in terms of another but instead organizes a whole system of concepts with respect to one another. We will call these *orientational metaphors*, since most of them have to do with spatial orientation: up-down, in-out, front-back, on-off, deep-shallow, central-peripheral. These spatial orientations arise

from the fact that we have bodies of the sort we have and that they function as they do in our physical environment. Orientational metaphors give a concept a spatial orientation; for example, happy is up. The fact that the concept HAPPY is oriented up leads to English expressions like "I'm feeling up today."

Such metaphorical orientations are not arbitrary. They have a 26 basis in our physical and cultural experience. Though the polar oppositions up-down, in-out, etc., are physical in nature, the orientational metaphors based on them vary from culture to culture. For example, in some cultures the future is in front of us, whereas in others it is in back. We will be looking at up-down spatialization metaphors, which have been studied intensively by William Nagy, as an illustration. In each case, we will give a brief hint about how such metaphorical concept might have arisen from our physical and cultural experience. These accounts are meant to be suggestive and plausible, not definitive.

HAPPY IS UP; SAD IS DOWN

I'm feeling up. That boosted my spirits. My spirits rose. You're in 27 high spirits. Thinking about her always gives me a lift. I'm feeling down. I'm depressed. He's really low these days. I fell into a depression. My spirits sank.

Physical basis: Drooping posture typically goes along with sadness 28 and depression, erect posture with a positive emotional state.

CONSCIOUS IS UP; UNCONSCIOUS IS DOWN

Wake up. Wake up. I'm up already. He rises early in the morning. 29 He fell asleep. He dropped off to sleep. He's under hypnosis. He sank into a coma.

Physical basis: Humans and most other mammals sleep lying 30 down and stand up when they awaken.

HEALTH AND LIFE ARE UP; SICKNESS AND DEATH ARE DOWN

He's at the peak of health. Lazarus rose from the dead. He's in 31 top shape. As to his health, he's way up there. He fell ill. He's sinking fast. He came down with the flu. His health is declining. He dropped dead.

32 Physical basis: Serious illness forces us to lie down physically. When you're dead, you are physically down.

HAVING CONTROL OR FORCE IS UP; BEING SUBJECT TO CONTROL OR FORCE IS DOWN

33 I have control over her. I am on top of the situation. He's in a superior position. He's at the height of his power. He's in the high command. He's in the upper echelon. His power rose. He ranks above me in strength. He is under my control. He fell from power. His power is on the decline. He is my social interior. He is low man on the totem pole.

34 Physical basis: Physical size typically correlates with physical strength, and the victor in a fight is typically on top.

MORE IS UP; LESS IS DOWN

35 The number of books printed each year keeps going up. His draft number is high. My income rose last year. The amount of artistic activity in this state has gone down in the past year. The number of errors he made is incredibly low. His income fell last year. He is underage. If you're 100 hot, turn the heat down.

36 Physical basis: If you add more of a substance of physical objects to a container or pile, the level goes up.

FORESEEABLE FUTURE EVENTS ARE UP (AND AHEAD)

37 All upcoming events are listed in the paper. What's coming up this week? I'm afraid of what's up ahead of us. What's up?

38 Physical basis: Normally our eyes look in the direction in which we typically move (ahead, forward). As an object approaches a person (or the person approaches the object), the object appears larger. Since the ground is perceived as being fixed, the top of the object appears to be moving upward in the person's field of vision.

HIGH STATUS IS UP; LOW STATUS IS DOWN

39 He has a lofty position. She'll rise to the top. He's at the peak of his career. He's climbing the ladder. He has little upward mobility. He's at the bottom of the social hierarchy. She fell in status.

Social and physical basis: Status is correlated with (social) power 40 and (physical) power is up.

GOOD IS UP; BAD IS DOWN

Things are looking up. We hit a peak last year, but it's been down- 41 hill ever since. Things are at an all-time low. He does high-quality work.

Physical basis for personal well-being: Happiness, health, life, and 42 control—the things that principally characterize what is good for a person—all are up.

VIRTUE IS UP; DEPRAVITY IS DOWN

He is high-minded. She has high standards. She is upright. She is 43 an up-standing citizen. That was a low trick. Don't be under-handed. I wouldn't stoop to that. That would be beneath me. He fell into the abyss of depravity. That was a low-down thing to do.

Physical and social basis: GOOD IS UP for a person (physical 44 basis), together with SOCIETY IS A PERSON (in the version where you are not identifying with your society). To be virtuous is to act in accordance with the standards set by the society/person to maintain its well-being. VIRTUE IS UP because virtuous actions correlate with social well-being from the society/person's point of view. Since socially based metaphors are part of the culture, it's the society/person's point of view that counts.

RATIONAL IS UP; EMOTIONAL IS DOWN

The discussion fell to the emotional level, but I raised it back up 45 to the rational plane. We put our feelings aside and had a high-level intellectual discussion of the matter. He couldn't rise above his emotions.

Physical and cultural basis: In our culture people view themselves 46 as being in control over animals, plants, and their physical envi-ronment, and it is their unique ability to reason that places human beings above other animals and gives them this control. CON-TROL IS UP thus provides a basis for MAN IS UP and therefore RATIONAL IS UP.

Languages and Literature

Whose Canon Is It, Anyway?

Henry Louis Gates, Jr.

1 William Bennett and Allan Bloom, the dynamic duo of the new cultural right, have become the easy targets of the cultural left, which I am defining here loosely and generously as that uneasy, shifting set of alliances formed by feminist critics, critics of so-called minority culture and Marxist and post-structuralist critics generally—in short, the rainbow coalition of contemporary critical theory. These two men (one a former United States Secretary of Education and now President Bush's "drug czar,"[1] the other a professor at the University of Chicago and author of "The Closing of the American Mind") symbolize the nostalgic return to what I think of as the "antebellum esthetic position," when men were men and men were white, when scholar-critics were white men and when women and people of color were voiceless, faceless servants and laborers, pouring tea and filling brandy snifters in the boardrooms of old boys' clubs. Inevitably, these two men have come to play the roles that George Wallace and Orville Faubus played for the civil rights movement, or that Richard Nixon and Henry Kissinger played during Vietnam—the "feel good" targets who, despite internal differences and contradictions, the cultural left loves to hate.

2   And how tempting it is to juxtapose their "civilizing mission" to the racial violence that has swept through our campuses since

---

[1]President George Bush (b. 1924), term 1989–1993, father of President George W. Bush

1986—at traditionally liberal Northern institutions such as the University of Massachusetts at Amherst, Mount Holyoke College, Smith College, the University of Chicago, Columbia, the University of Pennsylvania, and at Southern institutions such as the University of Alabama, the University of Texas and the Citadel. Add to this the fact that affirmative action programs on campus have become window dressing operations, necessary "evils" maintained to preserve the fiction of racial fairness and openness but deprived of the power to enforce their stated principles. When unemployment among black youth is 40 percent, when 44 percent of black Americans can't read the front page of a newspaper, when less than 2 percent of the faculty on campuses is black and when only 40 percent of black students in higher education are men, well, you look for targets close at hand.

And yet there's a real danger of localizing our grievances; of the 3
easy personification, assigning celebrated faces to the forces of reaction and so giving too much credit to a few men who are really symptomatic of a larger political current. (In a similar vein, our rhetoric sometimes depicts the high canonical as the reading matter of the power elite. You have to imagine James Baker curling up with the "Pisan Cantos," Dan Quayle leafing through "The Princess Casamassima.") Maybe our eagerness to do so reflects a certain vanity that academic cultural critics are prone to. We make dire predictions, and when they come true, we think we've changed the world.

It's a tendency that puts me in mind of my father's favorite 4
story about Father Divine, that historic con man of the cloth. In the 1930's, he was put on trial and convicted for using the mails to defraud. At sentencing, Father Divine stood up and told the judge: I'm warning you, you send me to jail, something terrible is going to happen to you. Father Divine, of course, was sent to prison, and a week later, by sheer coincidence, the judge had a heart attack and died. When the warden and the guards found out about it in the middle of the night, they raced to Father Divine's cell and woke him up. Father Divine, they said, your judge just dropped dead of a heart attack. Without missing a beat, Father Divine lifted his head and told them: "I hated to do it."

As writers, teachers or intellectuals, most of us would like to 5
claim greater efficacy for our labors than we're entitled to. These

days, literary criticism likes to think of itself as "war by other means." But it should start to wonder: have its victories come too easily? The recent turn toward politics and history in literary studies has turned the analysis of texts into a marionette theater of the political, to which we bring all the passions of our real-world commitments. And that's why it is sometimes necessary to remind ourselves of the distance from the classroom to the streets. Academic critics write essays, "readings" of literature, where the bad guys (you know, racism or patriarchy) lose, where the forces of oppression are subverted by the boundless powers of irony and allegory that no prison can contain, and we glow with hard-won triumph. We pay homage to the marginalized and demonized, and it feels almost as if we've righted an actual injustice. (Academic battles are so fierce—the received wisdom has it—because so little is truly at stake.) I always think of the folk tale about the fellow who killed seven with one blow: flies, not giants.

6   Ours was the generation that took over buildings in the late 1960's and demanded the creation of black and women's studies programs and now, like the return of the repressed, has come back to challenge the traditional curriculum. And some of us are even attempting to redefine the canon by editing anthologies. Yet it sometimes seems that blacks are doing better in the college curriculum than they are in the streets or even on the campuses.

7   This is not a defeatist moan, just an acknowledgment that the relation between our critical postures and the social struggles they reflect is far from transparent. That doesn't mean there's no relation, of course, only that it's a highly mediated one. In all events, I do think we should be clear about when we've swatted a fly and when we've toppled a giant. Still, you can't expect people who spend their lives teaching literature to be dispassionate about the texts they teach; no one went into literature out of an interest in literature-in-general.

8   I suppose the literary canon is, in no very grand sense, the commonplace book of our shared culture, the archive of those texts and titles we wish to remember. And how else did those of us who teach literature fall in love with our subject than through our very own commonplace books, in which we inscribed secretly, as we might in a private diary, those passages of books that named for us what we had deeply felt, but could not say?

I kept mine from the age of 12, turning to it to repeat those 9
marvelous words that named me in some private way. From
H. H. Munro to Dickens and Austen, to Hugo and de Maupas-
sant, each resonant sentence would find its way into my book.
(There's no point in avoiding the narcissism here: we are always
transfixed by those passages that seem to read *us*.) Finding James Baldwin and writing him down at an Episcopal
church camp in 1965—I was 15, and the Watts riots were
raging—probably determined the direction of my intellectual
life more than anything else I could name. I wrote and rewrote
verbatim his elegantly framed paragraphs, full of sentences that
were somehow both Henry Jamesian and King Jamesian, garbed
as they were in the figures and cadences of the spirituals. Of
course, we forget the private pleasures that brought us to the
subject in the first place once we adopt the alienating strategies
of formal analysis; our professional vanity is to insist that the
study of literature be both beauty and truth, style and politics
and everything in between.

In the swaddling clothes of our academic complacencies, then, 10
few of us are prepared when we bump against something hard, and
sooner or later, we do. One of the first talks I ever gave was to a
packed audience at a college honors seminar, and it was one of
those mistakes you don't make twice. Fresh out of graduate school,
immersed in the arcane technicalities of contemporary literary theory, I was going to deliver a crunchy structuralist analysis of a slave
narrative by Frederick Douglass, tracing the intricate play of its
"binary oppositions." Everything was neatly schematized, formal-
ized, analyzed; this was my Sunday-best structuralism: crisp white
shirt and shiny black shoes. And it wasn't playing. If you've seen
an audience glaze over, this was double glazing. Bravely, I finished
my talk and, of course, asked for questions. "Yeah, brother," said a
young man in the very back of the room, breaking the silence that
ensued, "all we want to know is, was Booker T. Washington an
Uncle Tom or not?"

The funny thing is, this happens to be an interesting question, a 11
lot more interesting than my talk was. It raised all the big issues
about the politics of style: about what it means to speak for another,
about how you were to distinguish between canny subversion and

simple co-optation—who was manipulating whom? And while I didn't exactly appreciate it at the time, the exchange did draw my attention, a little rudely perhaps, to the yawning chasm between our critical discourse and the traditions they discourse upon.

12   Obviously, some of what I'm saying is by way of *mea culpa*, because I'm speaking here as a participant in a moment of canon formation in a so-called marginal tradition. As it happens, W. W. Norton, the "canonical" anthology publisher, will be publishing "The Norton Anthology of Afro-American Literature." The editing of this anthology has been a great dream of mine for a long time, and it represents, in the most concrete way, the project of black canon formation. But my pursuit of this project has required me to negotiate a position between those on the cultural right who claim that black literature can have no canon, no masterpieces, and those on the cultural left who wonder why anyone wants to establish the existence of a canon, any canon, in the first place.

13   We face the outraged reactions of those custodians of Western culture who protest that the canon, that transparent decanter of Western values, may become—breathe the word—*politicized.* That people can maintain a straight face while they protest the irruption of politics into something that has always been political— well, it says something about how remarkably successful official literary histories have been in presenting themselves as natural objects, untainted by worldly interests.

14   I agree with those conservatives who have raised the alarm about our students' ignorance of history. But part of the history we need to teach has to be the history of the very idea of the "canon," which involves the history both of literary pedagogy and of the very institution of the school. One function of literary history is then to conceal all connections between institutionalized interests and the literature we remember. Pay no attention to the men behind the curtain, booms the Great Oz of literary history.

15   Cynthia Ozick once chastised feminists by warning that strategies become institutions. But isn't that really another way of warning that their strategies, Heaven forfend, may *succeed*?

16   Here we approach the scruples of those on the cultural left who worry about, well, the price of success. "Who's co-opting

whom?" might be their slogan. To them, the very idea of the canon is hierarchical, patriarchal and otherwise politically suspect. They'd like us to disavow it altogether.

But history and its institutions are not just something we 17 study, they're also something we live, and live through. And how effective and how durable our interventions in contemporary cultural politics will be depends upon the ability to mobilize the institutions that buttress and reproduce that culture. We could seclude ourselves from the real world and keep our hands clean, free from the taint of history. But that is to pay obeisance to the status quo, to the entrenched arsenal of sexual and racial authority, to say that things shouldn't change, become something other and, let's hope, better.

Indeed, this is one case where we've got to borrow a leaf from 18 the right, which is exemplarily aware of the role of education in the reproduction of values. We must engage in this sort of canon reformation precisely because Mr. Bennett is correct: the teaching of literature *is* the teaching of values, not inherently, no, but contingently, yes; it is—it has become—the teaching of an esthetic and political order, in which no person of color, no woman, was ever able to discover the reflection or representation of his or her cultural image or voice. The return of "the" canon, the high canon of Western masterpieces, represents the return of an order in which my people were the subjugated, the voiceless, the invisible, the unpresented and the unrepresentable.

Let me be specific. Those of us working in my own tradition 19 confront the hegemony of the Western tradition, generally, and of the larger American tradition, more locally, as we theorize about our tradition and engage in canon formation. Long after white American literature has been anthologized and canonized, and re-canonized, our efforts to define a black American canon are often decried as racist, separatist, nationalist, or "essentialist." Attempts to derive theories about our literary tradition from the black tradition—a tradition, I might add, that must include black vernacular forms as well as written literary forms—are often greeted by our colleagues in traditional literature departments as a misguided desire to secede from a union that only recently, and with considerable kicking and screaming, has been forged. What is *wrong* with you people? our friends ask

us in genuine passion and concern; after all, aren't we all just
citizens of literature here?

20   Well, yes and no. Every black American text must confess to
a complex ancestry, one high and low (that is, literary and vernacular) but also one white and black. There can be no doubt
that white texts inform and influence black texts (and vice
versa), so that a thoroughly integrated canon of American literature is not only politically sound, it is intellectually sound as
well. But the attempts of black scholars to define a black American canon, and to derive indigenous theories of interpretation
from within this canon, are not meant to refute the soundness of
these gestures of integration. Rather, it is a question of perspective, a question of emphasis. Just as we can and must cite a black
text within the larger American tradition, we can and must cite
it within its own tradition, a tradition not defined by a pseudo-
science of racial biology, or a mystically shared essence called
blackness, but by the repetition and revision of shared themes,
topoi and tropes, the call and response of voices, their music and
cacophony.

21   And this is our special legacy: what in 1849 Frederick Douglass
called the "live, calm, grave, clear, pointed, warm, sweet, melodi-
ous and powerful human voice." The presence of the past in the
African-American tradition comes to us most powerfully as *voice*,
a voice that is never quite our own—or *only* our own—however
much we want it to be. One of my earliest childhood memories tells
this story clearly.

22   I remember my first public performance, which I gave at the
age of 4 in the all-black Methodist church that my mother
attended, and that her mother had attended for 50 years. It was
a religious program, at which each of the children of the Sunday
school was to deliver a "piece"—as the people in our church
referred to a religious recitation. Mine was the couplet "Jesus was
a boy like me, / And like Him I want to be." Not much of a recitation, but then I *was* only 4. So, after weeks of practice in elocution, hair pressed and greased down, shirt starched and pants
pressed, I was ready to give my piece. I remember skipping along
to the church with all of the other kids, driving everyone crazy,
repeating that couplet over and over, "Jesus was a boy like me, /
And like Him I want to be."

Finally we made it to the church, and it was packed—bulging 23
and glistening with black people, eager to hear pieces, despite the
fact that they had heard all of the pieces already, year after year,
like bits and fragments of a repeated master text. Because I was
the youngest child on the program, I was the first to go. Miss
Sarah Russell (whom we called Sister Holy Ghost—behind her
back, of course) started the program with a prayer, then asked if
little Skippy Gates would step forward. I did so.

And then the worst happened: I completely forgot the words 24
of my piece. Standing there, pressed and starched, just as clean as
I could be, in front of just about everybody in our part of town,
I could not for the life of me remember one word of that piece.

After standing there I don't know how long, struck dumb and 25
captivated by all of those staring eyes, I heard a voice from near
the back of the church proclaim, "Jesus was a boy like me, / And
like Him I want to be."

And my mother, having arisen to find my voice, smoothed 26
her dress and sat down again. The congregation's applause lasted
as long as its laughter as I crawled back to my seat.

What this moment crystallizes for me is how much of my 27
scholarly and critical work has been an attempt to learn how to
speak in the strong, compelling cadences of my mother's voice.
As the black feminist scholar Hortense Spillers has recently
insisted, in moving words that first occasioned this very recollec-
tion, it is "the heritage of the *mother* that the African-American
male must regain as an aspect of his own personhood—the power
of 'yes' to the 'female' within."

To reform core curriculums, to account for the comparable elo- 28
quence of the African, the Asian and the Middle Eastern traditions,
is to begin to prepare our students for their roles as citizens of a
world culture, educated through a truly human notion of "the
humanities," rather than—as Mr. Bennett and Mr. Bloom would
have it—as guardians at the last frontier outpost of white male Western culture, the keepers of the master's pieces. And for us as scholar-
critics, learning to speak in the voice of the black mother is perhaps the ultimate challenge of producing a discourse of the Other.

1989

No Name Woman

Maxine Hong Kingston

1 "You must not tell anyone," my mother said, "what I am about to tell you. In China your father had a sister who killed herself. She jumped into the family well. We say that your father has all brothers because it is as if she had never been born.

2 "In 1924 just a few days after our village celebrated seventeen hurry-up weddings—to make sure that every young man who went 'out on the road' would responsibly come home—your father and his brothers and your grandfather and his brothers and your aunt's new husband sailed for America, the Gold Mountain. It was your grandfather's last trip. Those lucky enough to get contracts waved goodbye from the decks. They fed and guarded the stowaways and helped them off in Cuba, New York, Bali, Hawaii. 'We'll meet in California next year,' they said. All of them sent money home.

3 "I remember looking at your aunt one day when she and I were dressing; I had not noticed before that she had such a protruding melon of a stomach. But I did not think, 'She's pregnant,' until she began to look like other pregnant women, her shirt pulling and the white tops of her black pants showing. She could not have been pregnant, you see, because her husband had been gone for years. No one said anything. We did not discuss it. In early summer she was ready to have the child, long after the time when it could have been possible.

4 "The village had also been counting. On the night the baby was to be born the villagers raided our house. Some were crying. Like a great saw, teeth strung with lights, files of people walked zigzag across our land, tearing the rice. Their lanterns doubled in the disturbed black water, which drained away through the broken bunds. As the villagers closed in, we could see that some of them, probably men and women we knew well, wore white masks. The people with long hair hung it over their faces. Women with short hair made it stand up on end. Some had tied white bands around their foreheads, arms, and legs.

5 "At first they threw mud and rocks at the house. Then they threw eggs and began slaughtering our stock. We could hear the

animals scream their deaths—the roosters, the pigs, a last great roar from the ox. Familiar wild heads flared in our night windows; the villagers encircled us. Some of the faces stopped to peer at us, their eyes rushing like searchlights. The hands flattened against the panes, framed heads, and left red prints.

"The villagers broke in the front and the back doors at the 6 same time, even though we had not locked the doors against them. Their knives dripped with the blood of our animals. They smeared blood on the doors and walls. One woman swung a chicken, whose throat she had slit, splattering blood in red arcs about her. We stood together in the middle of our house, in the family hall with the pictures and tables of the ancestors around us, and looked straight ahead.

"At that time the house had only two wings. When the men 7 came back, we would build two more to enclose our courtyard and a third one to begin a second courtyard. The villagers pushed through both wings, even your grandparents' rooms, to find your aunt's, which was also mine until the men returned. From this room a new wing for one of the younger families would grow. They ripped up her clothes and shoes and broke her combs, grinding them underfoot. They tore her work from the loom. They scattered the cooking fire and rolled the new weaving in it. We could hear them in the kitchen breaking our bowls and banging the pots. They overturned the great waist-high earthenware jugs; duck eggs, pickled fruits, vegetables burst out and mixed in acrid torrents. The old woman from the next field swept a broom through the air and loosed the spirits-of-the-broom over our heads. 'Pig.' 'Ghost.' 'Pig,' they sobbed and scolded while they ruined our house.

"When they left, they took sugar and oranges to bless them- 8 selves. They cut pieces from the dead animals. Some of them took bowls that were not broken and clothes that were not torn. Afterward we swept up the rice and sewed it back up into sacks. But the smells from the spilled preserves lasted. Your aunt gave birth in the pigsty that night. The next morning when I went for the water, I found her and the baby plugging up the family well.

"Don't let your father know that I told you. He denies her. 9 Now that you have started to menstruate, what happened to her could happen to you. Don't humiliate us. You wouldn't like to be forgotten as if you had never been born. The villagers are watchful."

10 Whenever she had to warn us about life, my mother told stories that ran like this one, a story to grow up on. She tested our strength to establish realities. Those in the emigrant generations who could not reassert brute survival died young and far from home. Those of us in the first American generations have had to figure out how the invisible world the emigrants built around our childhoods fits in solid America.

11 The emigrants confused the gods by diverting their curses, misleading them with crooked streets and false names. They must try to confuse their offspring as well, who, I suppose, threaten them in similar ways—always trying to get things straight, always trying to name the unspeakable. The Chinese I know hide their names; sojourners take new names when their lives change and guard their real names with silence.

12 Chinese-Americans, when you try to understand what things in you are Chinese, how do you separate what is peculiar to childhood, to poverty, insanities, one family, your mother who marked your growing with stories, from what is Chinese? What is Chinese tradition and what is the movies?

13 If I want to learn what clothes my aunt wore, whether flashy or ordinary, I would have to begin, "Remember Father's drowned-in-the-well sister?" I cannot ask that. My mother has told me once and for all the useful parts. She will add nothing unless powered by Necessity, a riverbank that guides her life. She plants vegetable gardens rather than lawns; she carries the odd-shaped tomatoes home from the fields and eats food left for the gods.

14 Whenever we did frivolous things, we used up energy; we flew high kites. We children came up off the ground over the melting cones our parents brought home from work and the American movie on New Year's Day—*Oh, You Beautiful Doll* with Betty Grable one year, and *She Wore a Yellow Ribbon* with John Wayne another year. After the one carnival ride each, we paid in guilt; our tired father counted his change on the dark walk home.

15 Adultery is extravagance. Could people who hatch their own chicks and eat the embryos and the heads for delicacies and boil the feet in vinegar for party food, leaving only the gravel, eating even the gizzard lining—could such people engender a prodigal

aunt? To be a woman, to have a daughter in starvation time was a waste enough. My aunt could not have been the lone romantic who gave up everything for sex. Women in the old China did not choose. Some man had commanded her to lie with him and be his secret evil. I wonder whether he masked himself when he joined the raid on her family.

Perhaps she had encountered him in the fields or on the mountain where the daughters-in-law collected fuel. Or perhaps he first noticed her in the marketplace. He was not a stranger because the village housed no strangers. She had to have dealings with him other than sex. Perhaps he worked an adjoining field, or he sold her the cloth for the dress she sewed and wore. His demand must have surprised, then terrified her. She obeyed him; she always did as she was told. [16]

When the family found a young man in the next village to be her husband, she had stood tractably beside the best rooster, his proxy, and promised before they met that she would be his forever. She was lucky that he was her age and she would be the first wife, an advantage secure now. The night she first saw him, he had sex with her. Then he left for America. She had almost forgotten what he looked like. When she tried to envision him, she only saw the black and white face in the group photograph the men had had taken before leaving. [17]

The other man was not, after all, much different from her husband. They both gave orders: she followed. "If you tell your family, I'll beat you. I'll kill you. Be here again next week." No one talked sex, ever. And she might have separated the rapes from the rest of living if only she did not have to buy her oil from him or gather wood in the same forest. I want her fear to have lasted just as long as rape lasted so that the fear could have been contained. No drawn-out fear. But women at sex hazarded birth and hence lifetimes. The fear did not stop but permeated everywhere. She told the man, "I think I'm pregnant." He organized the raid against her. [18]

On nights when my mother and father talked about their life back home, sometimes they mentioned an "outcast table" whose business they still seemed to be settling, their voices tight. In a commensal tradition, where food is precious, the powerful older people made wrongdoers eat alone. Instead of letting them start [19] separate new lives like the Japanese, who could become samurais and geishas, the Chinese family, faces averted but eyes glowering sideways, hung on to the offenders and fed them leftovers. My aunt must have lived in the same house as my parents and eaten at an outcast table. My mother spoke about the raid as if she had seen it, when she and my aunt, a daughter-in-law to a different household, should not have been living together at all. Daughters-in-law lived with their husbands' parents, not their own; a synonym for marriage in Chinese is "taking a daughter-in-law." Her husband's parents could have sold her, mortgaged her, stoned her. But they had sent her back to her own mother and father, a mysterious act hinting at disgraces not told me. Perhaps they had thrown her out to deflect the avengers.

20   She was the only daughter; her four brothers went with her father, husband, and uncles "out on the road" and for some years became Western men. When the goods were divided among the family, three of the brothers took land, and the youngest, my father, chose an education. After my grandparents gave their daughter away to her husband's family, they had dispensed all the adventure and all the property. They expected her alone to keep the traditional ways, which her brothers, now among the barbarians, could fumble without detection. The heavy, deep-rooted women were to maintain the past against the flood, safe for returning. But the rare urge west had fixed upon our family, and so my aunt crossed boundaries not delineated in space.

21   The work of preservation demands that the feelings playing about in one's guts not be turned into action. Just watch their passing like cherry blossoms. But perhaps my aunt, my forerunner, caught in a slow life, let dreams grow and fade and after some months or years went toward what persisted. Fear at the enormities of the forbidden kept her desires delicate, wire and bone. She looked at a man because she liked the way the hair was tucked behind his ears, or she liked the question-mark line of a long torso curving at the shoulder and straight at the hip. For warm eyes or a soft voice or a slow walk—that's all—a few hairs, a line, a brightness, a sound, a pace, she gave up family. She offered us up for a charm that vanished with tiredness, a pigtail that didn't toss when the wind died. Why, the wrong lighting could erase the dearest thing about him.

It could very well have been, however, that my aunt did not 22
take subtle enjoyment of her friend, but, a wild woman, kept rol-
licking company. Imagining her free with sex doesn't fit, though.
I don't know any women like that, or men either. Unless I see her
life branching into mine, she gives me no ancestral help.

To sustain her being in love, she often worked at herself in 23
the mirror, guessing at the colors and shapes that would interest
him, changing them frequently in order to hit on the right combination. She wanted him to look back.

On a farm near the sea, a woman who tended her appearance 24
reaped a reputation for eccentricity. All the married women blunt-
cut their hair in flaps about their ears or pulled it back in tight
buns. No nonsense. Neither style blew easily into heart-catching
tangles. And at their weddings they displayed themselves in their
long hair for the last time. "It brushed the backs of my knees,"
my mother tells me. "It was braided, and even so, it brushed the
backs of my knees."

At the mirror my aunt combed individuality into her bob. A 25
bun could have been contrived to escape into black streamers
blowing in the wind or in quiet wisps about her face, but only the
older women in our picture album wear buns. She brushed her
hair back from her forehead, tucking the flaps behind her ears.
She looped a piece of thread, knotted into a circle between her
index fingers and thumbs, and ran the double strand across her
forehead. When she closed her fingers as if she were making a
pair of shadow geese bite, the string twisted together catching the
little hairs. Then she pulled the thread away from her skin, rip-
ping the hairs out neatly, her eyes watering from the needles of
pain. Opening her fingers, she cleaned the thread, then rolled it
along her hairline and the tops of her eyebrows. My mother did
the same to me and my sisters and herself. I used to believe that
the expression "caught by the short hairs" meant a captive held
with a depilatory string. It especially hurt at the temples, but my
mother said we were lucky we didn't have to have our feet bound
when we were seven. Sisters used to sit on their beds and cry
together, she said, as their mothers or their slaves removed the
bandages for a few minutes each night and let the blood gush
back into their veins. I hope that the man my aunt loved appreciated a smooth brow, that he wasn't just a tits-and-ass man.

26   Once my aunt found a freckle on her chin, at a spot that the almanac said predestined her for unhappiness. She dug it out with a hot needle and washed the wound with peroxide.

27   More attention to her looks than these pullings of hairs and pickings at spots would have caused gossip among the villagers. They owned work clothes and good clothes, and they wore good clothes for feasting the new seasons. But since a woman combing her hair hexes beginnings, my aunt rarely found an occasion to look her best. Women looked like great sea snails—the corded wood, babies, and laundry they carried were the whorls on their backs. The Chinese did not admire a bent back; goddesses and warriors stood straight. Still there must have been a marvelous freeing of beauty when a worker laid down her burden and stretched and arched.

28   Such commonplace loveliness, however, was not enough for my aunt. She dreamed of a lover for the fifteen days of New Year's, the time for families to exchange visits, money, and food. She plied her secret comb. And sure enough she cursed the year, the family, the village, and herself.

29   Even as her hair lured her imminent lover, many other men looked at her. Uncles, cousins, nephews, brothers would have looked, too, had they been home between journeys. Perhaps they had already been restraining their curiosity, and they left, fearful that their glances, like a field of nesting birds, might be startled and caught. Poverty hurt, and that was their first reason for leaving. But another, final reason for leaving the crowded house was the never-said.

30   She may have been unusually beloved, the precious only daughter, spoiled and mirror gazing because of the affection the family lavished on her. When her husband left, they welcomed the chance to take her back from the in-laws; she could live like the little daughter for just a while longer. There are stories that my grandfather was different from other people, "crazy ever since the little Jap bayoneted him in the head." He used to put his naked penis on the dinner table, laughing. And one day he brought home a baby girl, wrapped up inside his brown Western-style greatcoat. He had traded one of his sons, probably my father, the youngest, for her. My grandmother made him trade back. When he finally got a daughter of his own, he doted on her. They

must have all loved her, except perhaps my father, the only brother who never went back to China, having once been traded for a girl.

Brothers and sisters, newly men and women, had to efface 31 their sexual color and present plain miens. Disturbing hair and eyes, a smile like no other, threatened the ideal of five generations living under one roof. To focus blurs, people shouted face to face and yelled from room to room. The immigrants I know have loud voices, unmodulated to American tones even after years away from the village where they called their friendships out across the fields. I have not been able to stop my mother's screams in public libraries or over telephones. Walking erect (knees straight, toes pointed forward, not pigeon-toed, which is Chinese-feminine) and speaking in an inaudible voice, I have tried to turn myself American-feminine. Chinese communication was loud, public. Only sick people had to whisper. But at the dinner table, where the family members came nearest one another, no one could talk, not the outcasts nor any eaters. Every word that falls from the mouth is a coin lost. Silently they gave and accepted food with both hands. A preoccupied child who took his bowl with one hand got a sideways glare. A complete moment of total attention is due everyone alike. Children and lovers have no singularity here, but my aunt used a secret voice, a separate attentiveness.

She kept the man's name to herself throughout her labor and 32 dying; she did not accuse him that he be punished with her. To save her inseminator's name she gave silent birth.

He may have been somebody in her own household, but 33 intercourse with a man outside the family would have been no less abhorrent. All the village were kinsmen, and the titles shouted in loud country voices never let kinship be forgotten. Any man within visiting distance would have been neutralized as a lover—"brother," "younger brother," "older brother"—one hundred and fifteen relationship titles. Parents researched birth charts probably not so much to assure good fortune as to circumvent incest in a population that has but one hundred surnames. Everybody has eight million relatives. How useless then sexual mannerisms, how dangerous.

As if it came from an atavism deeper than fear, I used to add 34 "brother" silently to boys' names. It hexed the boys, who would or would not ask me to dance, and made them less scary and as familiar and deserving of benevolence as girls.

35   But, of course, I hexed myself also—no dates. I should have stood up, both arms waving, and shouted out across libraries, "Hey, you! Love me back." I had no idea, though, how to make attraction selective, how to control its direction and magnitude. If I made myself American-pretty so that the five or six Chinese boys in the class fell in love with me, everyone else—the Caucasian, Negro, and Japanese boys—would too. Sisterliness, dignified and honorable, made much more sense.

36   Attraction eludes control so stubbornly that whole societies designed to organize relationships among people cannot keep order, not even when they bind people to one another from child-hood and raise them together. Among the very poor and the wealthy, brothers married their adopted sisters, like doves. Our family allowed some romance, paying adult brides' prices and providing dowries so that their sons and daughters could marry strangers. Marriage promises to turn strangers into friendly relatives—a nation of siblings.

37   In the village structure, spirits shimmered among the live creatures, balanced and held in equilibrium by time and land. But one human being flaring up into violence could open up a black hole, a maelstrom that pulled in the sky. The frightened villagers, who depended on one another to maintain the real, went to my aunt to show her a personal, physical representation of the break she had made in the "roundness." Misallying couples snapped off the future, which was to be embodied in true offspring. The villagers punished her for acting as if she could have a private life, secret and apart from them.

38   If my aunt had betrayed the family at a time of large grain yields and peace, when many boys were born, and wings were being built on many houses, perhaps she might have escaped such severe punishment. But the men—hungry, greedy, tired of plant-ing in dry soil—had been forced to leave the village in order to send food-money home. There were ghost plagues, bandit plagues, wars with the Japanese, floods. My Chinese brother and sister had died of an unknown sickness. Adultery, perhaps only a mistake during good times, became a crime when the village needed food.

The round moon cakes and round doorways, the round tables 39
of graduated sizes that fit one roundness inside another, round
windows and rice bowls—these talismans had lost their power to
warn this family of the law: A family must be whole, faithfully
keeping the descent line by having sons to feed the old and the
dead, who in turn look after the family. The villagers came to
show my aunt and her lover-in-hiding a broken house. The villagers were speeding up the circling of events because she was
too shortsighted to see that her infidelity had already harmed the
village, that waves of consequences would return unpredictably,
sometimes in disguise, as now, to hurt her. This roundness had
to be made coin-sized so that she would see its circumference:
Punish her at the birth of her baby. Awaken her to the inexorable.
People who refused fatalism because they could invent small
resources insisted on culpability. Deny accidents and wrest fault
from the stars.

After the villagers left, their lanterns now scattering in vari- 40
ous directions toward home, the family broke their silence and
cursed her. "Aiaa, we're going to die. Death is coming. Death is
coming. Look what you've done. You've killed us. Ghost! Dead
ghost! Ghost! You've never been born." She ran out into the fields,
far enough from the house so that she could no longer hear their
voices, and pressed herself against the earth, her own land no
more. When she felt the birth coming, she thought that she had
been hurt. Her body seized together. "They've hurt me too much,"
she thought. "This is gall, and it will kill me." With forehead and
knees against the earth, her body convulsed and then relaxed. She
turned on her back, lay on the ground. The black well of sky and
stars went out and out and out forever; her body and her complexity seemed to disappear. She was one of the stars, a bright dot
in blackness, without home, without a companion, in eternal cold
and silence. An agoraphobia rose in her, speeding higher and
higher, bigger and bigger; she would not be able to contain it;
there would be no end to fear.

Flayed, unprotected against space, she felt pain return, focus- 41
ing her body. This pain chilled her—a cold, steady kind of surface
pain. Inside, spasmodically, the other pain, the pain of the child,
heated her. For hours she lay on the ground, alternately body and
space. Sometimes a vision of normal comfort obliterated reality:

She saw the family in the evening gambling at the dinner table, the young people massaging their elders' backs. She saw them congratulating one another, high joy on the mornings the rice shoots came up. When these pictures burst, the stars drew yet further apart. Black space opened.

42   She got to her feet to fight better and remembered that old fashioned women gave birth in their pigsties to fool the jealous, pain-dealing gods, who do not snatch piglets. Before the next spasms could stop her, she ran to the pigsty, each step a rushing out into emptiness. She climbed over the fence and knelt in the dirt. It was good to have a fence enclosing her, a tribal person alone.

43   Laboring, this woman who had carried her child as a foreign growth that sickened her every day, expelled it at last. She reached down to touch the hot, wet, moving mass, surely smaller than anything human, and could feel that it was human after all—fingers, toes, nails, nose. She pulled it up on to her belly, and it lay curled there, butt in the air, feet precisely tucked one under the other. She opened her loose shirt and buttoned the child inside. After resting, it squirmed and thrashed and she pushed it up to her breast. It turned its head this way and that until it found her nipple. There, it made little snuffling noises. She clenched her teeth at its preciousness, lovely as a young calf, a piglet, a little dog.

44   She may have gone to the pigsty as a last act of responsibility: She would protect this child as she had protected its father. It would look after her soul, leaving supplies on her grave. But how would this tiny child without family find her grave when there would be no marker for her anywhere, neither in the earth nor the family hall? No one would give her a family hall name. She had taken the child with her into the wastes. At its birth the two of them had felt the same raw pain of separation, a wound that only the family pressing tight could close. A child with no descent line would not soften her life but only trail after her, ghostlike, begging her to give it purpose. At dawn the villagers on their way to the fields would stand around the fence and look.

45   Full of milk, the little ghost slept. When it awoke, she hardened her breasts against the milk that crying loosens. Toward morning she picked up the baby and walked to the well.

46   Carrying the baby to the well shows loving. Otherwise abandon it. Turn its face into the mud. Mothers who love their children

take them along. It was probably a girl; there is some hope of forgiveness for boys.

"Don't tell anyone you had an aunt. Your father does not 47
want to hear her name. She has never been born." I have believed
that sex was unspeakable and words so strong and fathers so frail
that "aunt" would do my father mysterious harm. I have thought
that my family, having settled among immigrants who had also
been their neighbors in the ancestral land, needed to clean their
name, and a wrong word would incite the kins people even here.
But there is more to this silence: They want me to participate in
her punishment. And I have.

In the twenty years since I heard this story I have not asked for 48
details nor said my aunt's name; I do not know it. People who can
comfort the dead can also chase after them to hurt them further—a
reverse ancestor worship. The real punishment was not the raid
swiftly inflicted by the villagers, but the family's deliberately for-
getting her. Her betrayal so maddened them, they saw to it that she
would suffer forever, even after death. Always hungry, always need-
ing, she would have to beg food from other ghosts, snatch and steal
it from those whose living descendants give them gifts. She would
have to fight the ghosts massed at crossroads for the buns a few
thoughtful citizens leave to decoy her away from village and home
so that the ancestral spirits could feast unharassed. At peace, they
could act like gods, not ghosts, their descent lines providing them
with paper suits and dresses, spirit money, paper houses, paper
automobiles, chicken, meat, and rice into eternity—essences delivered up in smoke and flames, steam and incense rising from each
rice bowl. In an attempt to make the Chinese care for people outside the family, Chairman Mao encourages us now to give our paper
replicas to the spirits of outstanding soldiers and workers, no matter whose ancestors they may be. My aunt remains forever hungry.
Goods are not distributed evenly among the dead.

My aunt haunts me—her ghost drawn to me because now, 49
after fifty years of neglect, I alone devote pages of paper to her,
though not origamied into houses and clothes. I do not think she
always means me well. I am telling on her, and she was a spite
suicide, drowning herself in the drinking water. The Chinese are

always very frightened of the drowned one, whose weeping ghost, wet hair hanging and skin bloated, waits silently by the water to pull down a substitute.

1975

How to Tame a Wild Tongue

Gloria Anzaldúa

1 "We're going to have to control your tongue," the dentist says, pulling out all the metal from my mouth. Silver bits plop and tinkle into the basin. My mouth is a motherlode.

2   The dentist is cleaning out my roots. I get a whiff of the stench when I gasp. "I can't cap that tooth yet, you're still draining," he says.

3   "We're going to have to do something about your tongue," I hear the anger rising in his voice. My tongue keeps pushing out the wads of cotton, pushing back the drills, the long thin needles. "I've never seen anything as strong or as stubborn," he says. And I think, how do you tame a wild tongue, train it to be quiet, how do you bridle and saddle it? How do you make it lie down?

4   *"Who is to say that robbing a people of its*
    language is less violent than war?"
                —Ray Gwyn Smith[1]

5   I remember being caught speaking Spanish at recess—that was good for three licks on the knuckles with a sharp ruler. I remember being sent to the corner of the classroom for "talking back" to the Anglo teacher when all I was trying to do was tell her how to pronounce my name. "If you want to be American, speak 'American.' If you don't like it, go back to Mexico where you belong."

6   "I want you to speak English. *Pa' hallar buen trabajo tienes que saber hablar el inglés bien. Qué vale toda tu educación si todavía hablas inglé con un 'accent,'"* my mother would say, mortified that I spoke

---

[1]Ray Gwyn Smith, *Moorland Is Cold Country*, unpublished book.

English like a Mexican. At Pan American University, I and all Chicano students were required to take two speech classes. Their purpose: to get rid of our accents.

Attacks on one's form of expression with the intent to censor 7 are a violation of the First Amendment. *El Anglo con cara de inocente nos arrancó la lengua.* Wild tongues can't be tamed, they can only be cut out.

OVERCOMING THE TRADITION OF SILENCE

> *Abogadas, escupimos el oscuro.*   8
> *Peleando con nuestra propia sombra*
> *el silencio nos sepulta.*

En boca cerrada no entran moscas. "Flies don't enter a closed 9 mouth" is a saying I kept hearing when I was a child. *Ser habladora* was to be a gossip and a liar, to talk too much. *Muchachitas bien criadas,* well-bred girls don't answer back. *Es una falta de respeto* to talk back to one's mother or father. I remember one of the sins I'd recite to the priest in the confession box the few times I went to confession: talking back to my mother, *hablar pa' 'trás, repelar, Hocicona, repelona, chismosa,* having a big mouth, questioning, carrying tales are all signs of being *mal criada.* In my culture they are all words that are derogatory if applied to women—I've never heard them applied to men.

The first time I heard two women, a Puerto Rican and a 10 Cuban, say the word *"nosotras,"* I was shocked. I had not known the word existed. Chicanas use *nosotros* whether we're male or female. We are robbed of our female being by the masculine plural. Language is a male discourse.

> *And our tongues have become dry the*   11
> *wilderness has dried out our tongues*
> *and we have forgotten speech.*
> —Irena Klepfisz[2]

[2]Irena Klepfisz, *"Di rayze aheym/*The Journey Home," in *The Tribe of Dina: A Jewish Women's Anthology,* Melanie Kaye/Kontrowitz and Irena Klepfisz, eds. (Montpelier, VT: Sinister Wisdom Books, 1986), 49.

12   Even our own people, other Spanish speakers *nos quieren poner candados en la boca.* They would hold us back with their bag of *reglas de academia.*

OYÉ COMO LADRA: EL LENGUAJE DE LA FRONTERA

13   *Quien tiene boca se equivoca.*
                                   —Mexican saying

14   "*Pocho,* cultural traitor, you're speaking the oppressor's language by speaking English, you're ruining the Spanish language," I have been accused by various Latinos and Latinas. Chicano Spanish is considered by the purist and by most Latinos deficient, a mutilation of Spanish.

15   But Chicano Spanish is a border tongue which developed naturally. Change, *evolución, enriquecimiento de palabras nuevas por invención o adopción* have created variants of Chicano Spanish, *un nuevo lenguaje. Un lenguaje que corrésponde a un moda de vivir.* Chicano Spanish is not incorrect, it is a living language.

16   For a people who are neither Spanish nor live in a country in which Spanish is the first language; for a people who live in a country in which English is the reigning tongue but who are not Anglo; for a people who cannot entirely identify with either standard (formal, Castillian) Spanish or standard English, what recourse is left to them but to create their own language? A language which they can connect their identity to, one capable of communicating the realities and values true to themselves—a language with terms that are neither *español ni inglés,* but both. We speak a patois, a forked tongue, a variation of two languages.

17   Chicano Spanish sprang out of the Chicanos' need to identify ourselves as a distinct people. We needed a language with which we could communicate with ourselves, a secret language. For some of us, language is a homeland closer than the Southwest—for many Chicanos today live in the Midwest and the East. And because we are a complex, heterogeneous people, we speak many languages. Some of the languages we speak are:

   1. Standard English
   2. Working class and slang English

3. Standard Spanish
4. Standard Mexican Spanish
5. North Mexican Spanish dialect
6. Chicano Spanish (Texas, New Mexico, Arizona and California have regional variations)
7. Tex-Mex
8. *Pachuco* (called *caló*)

My "home" tongues are the languages I speak with my sister [18] and brothers, with my friends. They are the last five listed, with 6 and 7 being closest to my heart. From school, the media and job situations, I've picked up standard and working class English. From Mamagrande Locha and from reading Spanish and Mexican literature, I've picked up Standard Spanish and Standard Mexican Spanish. From *los recién llegados*, Mexican immigrants, and *braceros*, I learned the North Mexican dialect. With Mexicans I'll try to speak either Standard Mexican Spanish or the North Mexican dialect. From my parents and Chicanos living in the Valley, I picked up Chicano Texas Spanish, and I speak it with my mom, younger brother (who married a Mexican and who rarely mixes Spanish with English), aunts and older relatives.

With Chicanas from *Nuevo México* or *Arizona* I will speak [19] Chicano Spanish a little, but often they don't understand what I'm saying. With most California Chicanas I speak entirely in English (unless I forget). When I first moved to San Francisco, I'd rattle off something in Spanish, unintentionally embarrassing them. Often it is only with another Chicana *tejana* that I can talk freely.

Words distorted by English are known as anglicisms [20] or *pochismos*. The *pocho* is an anglicized Mexican or American of Mexican origin who speaks Spanish with an accent characteristic of North Americans and who distorts and reconstructs the language according to the influence of English.[3] Tex-Mex, or Spanglish, comes most naturally to me. I may switch back and forth

---

[3]R. C. Ortega *Dialectología Del Barrio,* trans. Hortencia S. Alwan (Los Angeles, CA: R. C. Ortega Publisher and Bookseller, 1977), 132.

from English to Spanish in the same sentence or in the same word. With my sister and my brother Nune and with Chicano *tejano* contemporaries I speak in Tex-Mex.

21   From kids and people my own age I picked up *Pachuco.* *Pachuco* (the language of the zoot suiters) is a language of rebellion, both against Standard Spanish and Standard English. It is a secret language. Adults of the culture and outsiders cannot understand it. It is made up of slang words from both English and Spanish. *Ruca* means girl or woman, *vato* means guy or dude, *chale* means no, *simón* means yes, *churo* is sure, talk is *periquiar, pigionear* means petting, *que gacho* means how nerdy, *ponte águila* means watch out, death is called *la pelona.* Through lack of practice and not having others who can speak it, I've lost most of the *Pachuco* tongue.

CHICANO SPANISH

22 Chicanos, after 250 years of Spanish/Anglo colonization, have developed significant differences in the Spanish we speak. We collapse two adjacent vowels into a single syllable and sometimes shift the stress in certain words such as *maíz/maiz, cohete/cuete.* We leave out certain consonants when they appear between vowels: *lado/lao, mojado/mojao.* Chicanos from South Texas pronounced *f* as *j* as in *jue* (*fue*). Chicanos use "archaisms," words that are no longer in the Spanish language, words that have been evolved out. We say *semos, truje, hiaga, ansina,* and *naiden.* We retain the "archaic" *j,* as in *jalar,* that derives from an earlier *h* (the French *halar* or the Germanic *halon* which was lost to standard Spanish in the 16th century), but which is still found in several regional dialects such as the one spoken in South Texas. (Due to geography, Chicanos from the Valley of South Texas were cut off linguistically from other Spanish speakers. We tend to use words that the Spaniards brought over from Medieval Spain. The majority of the Spanish colonizers in Mexico and the Southwest came from Extremadura—Hernán Cortés was one of them—and Andalucía. Andalucians pronounce *ll* like a *y,* and their *d*'s tend to be absorbed by adjacent

vowels: *tirado* becomes *tirao*. They brought *el lenguaje popular, dialectos y regionalismos.*[4])

Chicanos and other Spanish speakers also shift *ll* to *y* and *z* [23] to *s*.[5] We leave out initial syllables, saying *tar* for *estar, toy* for *estoy, hora* for *ahora* (*cubanos* and *puertorriqueños* also leave out initial letters of some words). We also leave out the final syllable such as *pa* for *para*. The intervocalic *y*, the *ll* as in *tortilla, ella, botella,* gets replaced by *tortia* or *tortiya, ea, botea*. We add an additional syllable at the beginning of certain words: *atocar* for *tocar, agastar* for *gastar*. Sometimes we'll say *lavaste las vacijas*, other time *lavates* (substituting the *ates* verb endings for the *aste*).

We use anglicisms, words borrowed from English: *bola* from [24] ball, *carpeta* from carpet, *máchina de lavar* (instead of *lavadora*) from washing machine. Tex-Mex argot, created by adding a Spanish sound at the beginning or end of an English word such as *cookiar* for cook, *watchar* for watch, *parkiar* for park, and *rapiar* for rape, is the result of the pressures on Spanish speakers to adapt to English.

We don't use the word *vosotros/as* or its accompanying verb [25] form. We don't say *claro* (to mean yes), *imagínate*, or *me emociona*, unless we picked up Spanish from Latinas, out of a book, or in a classroom. Other Spanish-speaking groups are going through the same, or similar, development in their Spanish.

LINGUISTIC TERRORISM

> *Deslenguadas. Somos los del español deficiente.* We are your lin- [26] guistic nightmare, your linguistic aberration, your linguistic *mestizaje*, the subject of your *burla*. Because we speak with tongues of fire we are culturally crucified. Racially, culturally and linguistically *somos huérfanos*—we speak an orphan tongue.

Chicanas who grew up speaking Chicano Spanish have internalized [27] the belief that we speak poor Spanish. It is illegitimate, a bastard language. And because we internalize how our language has been

---

[4]Eduardo Hernandéz-Chávez, Andrew D. Cohen, and Anthony F. Beltramo, *El Lenguaje de los Chicanos: Regional and Social Characteristics of Language Used by Mexican American* (Arlington, VA: Center for Applied Linguistics, 1975), 39.
[5]Hernandéz-Chávez, xvii.

used against us by the dominant culture, we use our language differences against each other.

28   Chicana feminists often skirt around each other with suspicion and hesitation. For the longest time I couldn't figure it out. Then it dawned on me. To be close to another Chicana is like looking into the mirror. We are afraid of what we'll see there. *Pena.* Shame. Low estimation of self. In childhood we are told that our language is wrong. Repeated attacks on our native tongue diminish our sense of self. The attacks continue throughout our lives.

29   Chicanas feel uncomfortable talking in Spanish to Latinas, afraid of their censure. Their language was not outlawed in their countries. They had a whole lifetime of being immersed in their native tongue; generations, centuries in which Spanish was a first language, taught in school, heard on radio and TV, and read in the newspaper.

30   If a person, Chicana or Latina, has a low estimation of my native tongue, she also has a low estimation of me. Often with *mexicanas y latinas* we'll speak English as a neutral language. Even among Chicanas we tend to speak English at parties or conferences. Yet, at the same time, we're afraid the other will think we're *agringadas* because we don't speak Chicano Spanish. We oppress each other trying to out-Chicano each other, vying to be the "real" Chicanas, to speak like Chicanos. There is no one Chicano language just as there is no one Chicano experience. A monolingual Chicana whose first language is English or Spanish is just as much a Chicana as one who speaks several variants of Spanish. A Chicana from Michigan or Chicago or Detroit is just as much as Chicana as one from the Southwest. Chicano Spanish is as diverse linguistically as it is regionally.

31   By the end of this century, Spanish speakers will comprise the biggest minority group in the U.S., a country where students in high schools and colleges are encouraged to take French classes because French is considered more "cultured." But for a language to remain alive it must be used.[6] By the end of this century English, and not Spanish, will be the mother tongue of most Chicanos and Latinos.

---

[6]Irena Klepfisz, "Secular Jewish Identity: Yidishkayt in America," in *The Tribe of Dina*, Kaye/Kantrowitz and Klepfisz, eds., 43

So, if you want to really hurt me, talk badly about my lan- ₃₂
guage. Ethnic identity is twin skin to linguistic identity—I am my
language. Until I can take pride in my language, I cannot take
pride in myself. Until I can accept as legitimate Chicano Texas
Spanish, Tex-Mex and all the other languages I speak, I cannot
accept the legitimacy of myself. Until I am free to write bilingually
and to switch codes without having always to translate, while I
still have to speak English or Spanish when I would rather speak
Spanglish, and as long as I have to accommodate the English
speakers rather than having them accommodate me, my tongue
will be illegitimate.

I will no longer be made to feel ashamed of existing. I will ₃₃
have my voice: Indian, Spanish, white. I will have my serpent's
tongue—my woman's voice, my sexual voice, my poet's voice. I
will overcome the tradition of silence.

> *My fingers*   ₃₄
> *move sly against your palm*
> *Like women everywhere, we speak in code. . . .*
> —Melanie Kaye/Kantrowitz[7]

1987

The Meanings of a Word

Gloria Naylor

Language is the subject. It is the written form with which I've ₁
managed to keep the wolf away from the door and, in diaries, to
keep my sanity. In spite of this, I consider the written word inferior to the spoken, and much of the frustration experienced by
novelists is the awareness that whatever we manage to capture in
even the most transcendent passages falls far short of the richness

---

[7]Melanie Kaye/Kantrowitz, "Sign," in *We speak in Code: Poems and Other Writings*
(Pittsburgh, PA: Motheroot Publications, Inc., 1980), 85.

of life. Dialogue achieves its power in the dynamics of a fleeting moment of sight, sound, smell, and touch.

2   I'm not going to enter the debate here about whether it is language that shapes reality or vice versa. That battle is doomed to be waged whenever we seek intermittent reprieve from the chicken and egg dispute. I will simply take the position that the spoken word, like the written word, amounts to a nonsensical arrangement of sounds or letters without a consensus that assigns "meaning." And building from the meanings of what we hear, we order reality. Words themselves are innocuous; it is the consensus that gives them true power.

3   I remember the first time I heard the word *nigger*. In my third-grade class, our math tests were being passed down the rows, and as I handed the papers to a little boy in back of me, I remarked that once again he had received a much lower mark than I did. He snatched his test from me and spit out that word. Had he called me a nymphomaniac or a necrophiliac, I couldn't have been more puzzled. I didn't know what a nigger was, but I knew that whatever it meant, it was something he shouldn't have called me. This was verified when I raised my hand, and in a loud voice repeated what he had said and watched the teacher scold him for using a "bad" word. I was later to go home and ask the inevitable question that every black parent must face—"Mommy, what does *nigger* mean?"

4   And what exactly did it mean? Thinking back, I realize that this could not have been the first time the word was used in my presence. I was part of a large extended family that had migrated from the rural South after World War II and formed a close-knit network that gravitated around my maternal grandparents. Their ground-floor apartment in one of the buildings they owned in Harlem was a weekend mecca for my immediate family, along with countless aunts, uncles, and cousins who brought along assorted friends. It was a bustling and open house with assorted neighbors and tenants popping in and out to exchange bits of gossip, pick up an old quarrel, or referee the ongoing checkers game in which my grandmother cheated shamelessly. They were all there to let down their hair and put up their feet after a week of labor in the factories, laundries, and shipyards of New York.

Amid the clamor, which could reach deafening proportions— 5
two or three conversations going on simultaneously, punctuated
by the sound of a baby's crying somewhere in the back rooms
or out on the street—there was still a rigid set of rules about
what was said and how. Older children were sent out of the living room when it was time to get into the juicy details about
"you-know-who" up on the third floor who had gone and gotten herself "p-r-e-g-n-a-n-t!" But my parents, knowing that
I could spell well beyond my years, always demanded that I follow the others out to play. Beyond sexual misconduct and
death, everything else was considered harmless for our young
ears. And so among the anecdotes of the triumphs and disappointments in the various workings of their lives, the word
nigger was used in my presence, but it was set within contexts
and inflections that caused it to register in my mind as something else.

In the singular, the word was always applied to a man who 6
had distinguished himself in some situation that brought their
approval for his strength, intelligence, or drive:

"Did Johnny *really* do that?"   7

"I'm telling you, that nigger pulled in $6,000 of overtime last 8
year. Said he got enough for a down payment on a house."

When used with a possessive adjective by a woman—"my 9
nigger"—it became a term of endearment for her husband or
boyfriend. But it could be more than just a term applied to a man.
In their mouths it became the pure essence of manhood—a disembodied force that channeled their past history of struggle and
present survival against the odds into a victorious statement of
being: "Yeah, that old foreman found out quick enough—you
don't mess with a nigger."

In the plural, it became a description of some group within 10
the community that had overstepped the bounds of decency
as my family defined it. Parents who neglected their children,
a drunken couple who fought in public, people who simply
refused to look for work, those with excessively dirty mouths or
unkempt households were all "trifling niggers." This particular circle could forgive hard times, unemployment, the occasional bout
of depression—they had gone through all of that themselves—but
the unforgivable sin was a lack of self-respect.

11   A woman could never be a "nigger" in the singular, with its connotation of confirming worth. The noun *girl* was its closest equivalent in that sense, but only when used in direct address and regardless of the gender doing the addressing. *Girl* was a token of respect for a woman. The one-syllable word was drawn out to sound like three in recognition of the extra ounce of wit, nerve, or daring that the woman had shown in the situation under discussion.

12   "G-i-r-l, stop. You mean you said that to his face?"

13   But if the word was used in a third-person reference or shortened so that it almost snapped out of the mouth, it always involved some element of communal disapproval. And age became an important factor in these exchanges. It was only between individuals of the same generation, or from any older person to a younger (but never the other way around), that *girl* would be considered a compliment.

14   I don't agree with the argument that use of the word *nigger* at this social stratum of the black community was an internalization of racism. The dynamics were the exact opposite: the people in my grandmother's living room took a word that whites used to signify worthlessness or degradation and rendered it impotent. Gathering there together, they transformed *nigger* to signify the varied and complex human beings they knew themselves to be. If the word was to disappear totally from the mouths of even the most liberal of white society, no one in that room was naive enough to believe it would disappear from white minds. Meeting the word head-on, they proved it had absolutely nothing to do with the way they were determined to live their lives.

15   So there must have been dozens of times that *nigger* was spoken in front of me before I reached the third grade. But I didn't "hear" it until it was said by a small pair of lips that had already learned it could be a way to humiliate me. That was the word I went home and asked my mother about. And since she knew that I had to grow up in America, she took me in her lap and explained.

1986

Language and Literature from a Pueblo Indian Perspective

Leslie Marmon Silko

Where I come from, the words that are most highly valued are 1
those which are spoken from the heart, unpremeditated and unrehearsed. Among the Pueblo people, a written speech or statement
is highly suspect because the true feelings of the speaker remain
hidden as he reads words that are detached from the occasion and
the audience. I have intentionally not written a formal paper to
read to this session because of this and because I want you to hear
and to experience English in a nontraditional structure, a structure that follows patterns from the oral tradition. For those of you
accustomed to a structure that moves from point A to point B to
point C, this presentation may be somewhat difficult to follow
because the structure of Pueblo expression resembles something
like a spider's web—with many little threads radiating from a center, criss-crossing each other. As with the web, the structure will
emerge as it is made and you must simply listen and trust, as the
Pueblo people do, that meaning will be made.

I suppose the task that I have today is a formidable one 2
because basically I come here to ask you, at least for a while, to
set aside a number of basic approaches that you have been using
and probably will continue to use in approaching the study of
English or the study of language; first of all, I come to ask you to
see language from the Pueblo perspective, which is a perspective
that is very much concerned with including the whole of creation
and the whole of history and time. And so we very seldom talk
about breaking language down into words. As I will continue to
relate to you, even the use of a specific language is less important
than the one thing—which is the "telling," or the storytelling. And
so, as Simon Ortiz has written, if you approach a Pueblo person

This essay is an edited transcript of an oral presentation. The author deliberately
did not read from a prepared paper so that the audience could experience first-
hand one dimension of the oral tradition—nonlinear structure.

and want to talk words or, worse than that, to break down an individual word into its components, ofttimes you will just get a blank stare, because we don't think of words as being isolated from the speaker, which, of course, is one element of the oral tradition. Moreover, we don't think of words as being alone: words are always with other words, and the other words are almost always in a story of some sort.

3   Today I have brought a number of examples of stories in English because I would like to get around to the question that has been raised, or the topic that has come along here, which is what changes we Pueblo writers might make with English as a language for literature. But at the same time I would like to explain the importance of storytelling and how it relates to a Pueblo theory of language.

4   So first I would like to go back to the Pueblo Creation story. The reason I go back to that story is because it is an all-inclusive story of creation and how life began. Tséitsínako, Thought Woman, by thinking of her sisters, and together with her sisters, thought of everything which is, and this world was created. And the belief was that everything in this world was a part of the original creation, and that the people at home realized that far away there were others—other human beings. There is even a section of the story which is a prophesy—which describes the origin of the European race, the African, and also remembers the Asian origins.

5   Starting out with this story, with this attitude which includes all things, I would like to point out that the reason the people are more concerned with story and communication and less with a particular language is in part an outgrowth of the area [pointing to a map] where we find ourselves. Among the twenty Pueblos there are at least six distinct languages, and possibly seven. Some of the linguists argue—and I don't set myself up to be a linguist at all—about the number of distinct languages. But certainly Zuni is all alone, and Hopi is all alone, and from mesa to mesa there are subtle differences in languages—very great differences. I think that this might be the reason that what particular language was being used wasn't as important as what a speaker was trying to say. And this, I think, is reflected and stems or grows out of a particular view of the story—that is, that language *is* story. At Laguna many words have stories which make them. So when one is

telling a story, and one is using words to tell the story, each word that one is speaking has a story of its own too. Often the speakers or tellers go into the stories of the words they are using to tell one story so that you get stories within stories, so to speak. This structure becomes very apparent in the storytelling, and what I would like to show you later on by reading some pieces that I brought is that this structure also informs the writing and the stories which are currently coming from Pueblo people. I think what is essential is this sense of story, and story within story, and the idea that one story is only the beginning of many stories, and the sense that stories never truly end. I would like to propose that these views of structure and the dynamics of storytelling are some of the contributions which Native American cultures bring to the English language or at least to literature in the English language.

First of all, a lot of people think of storytelling as something 6 that is done at bedtime—that is something that is done for small children. When I use the term storytelling, I include a far wider range of telling activity. I also do not limit storytelling to simply old stories, but to again go back to the original view of creation, which sees that it is all part of a whole; we do not differentiate or fragment stories and experiences. In the beginning, Tséitsínako, Thought Woman, thought of all these things, and all of these things are held together as one holds many things together in a single thought.

So in the telling (and today you will hear a few of the dimen- 7 sions of this telling) first of all, as was pointed out earlier, the storytelling always includes the audience and the listeners, and, in fact, a great deal of the story is believed to be inside the listener, and the storyteller's role is to draw the story out of the listeners. This kind of shared experience grows out of a strong community base. The storytelling goes on and continues from generation to generation.

The Origin story functions basically as a maker of our 8 identity—with the story we know who we are. We are the Lagunas. This is where we came from. We came this way. We came by this place. And so from the time you are very young, you hear these stories, so that when you go out into the wider world, when one asks who you are, or where are you from, you immediately know: we are the people who came down from the north. We are the people of these stories. It continues down into clans so that you are not just talking about Laguna Pueblo people, you are talking about your own clan. Within the clans there are stories which identify the clan.

9   In the Creation story, Antelope says that he will help knock a hole in the earth so that the people can come up, out into the next world. Antelope tries and tries, and he uses his hooves and is unable to break through; and it is then that Badger says, "Let me help you." And Badger very patiently uses his claws and digs a way through, bringing the people into the world. When the Badger clan people think of themselves, or when the Antelope people think of themselves, it is as people who are of *this* story, and this is *our* place, and we fit into the very beginning when the people first came, before we began our journey south.

10   So you can move, then, from the idea of one's identity as a tribal person into clan identity. Then we begin to get to the extended family, and this is where we begin to get a kind of story coming into play which some people might see as a different kind of story, though Pueblo people do not. Anthropologists and ethnologists have, for a long time, differentiated the types of oral language they find in the Pueblos. They tended to rule out all but the old and sacred and traditional stories and were not interested in family stories and the family's account of itself. But these family stories are just as important as the other stories—the older stories. These family stories are given equal recognition. There is no definite, pre-set pattern for the way one will hear the stories of one's own family, but it is a very critical part of one's childhood, and it continues on throughout one's life. You will hear stories of importance to the family—sometimes wonderful stories—stories about the time a maternal uncle got the biggest deer that was ever seen and brought back from the mountains. And so one's sense of who the family is, and who you are, will then extend from that—"I am from the family of my uncle who brought in this wonderful deer, and it was a wonderful hunt"—so you have this sort of building or sense of identity.

11   There are also other stories, stories about the time when another uncle, perhaps, did something that wasn't really acceptable. In other words, this process of keeping track, of telling, is an all-inclusive process which begins to create a total picture. So it is

very important that you know all of the stories— both positive and not so positive—about one's own family. The reason that it is very important to keep track of all the stories in one's own family is because you are liable to hear a story from somebody else who is perhaps an enemy of the family, and you are liable to hear a version which has been changed, a version which makes your family sound disreputable—something that will taint the honor of the family. But if you have already heard the story, you know your family's version of what *really* happened that night, so when somebody else is mentioning it, you will have a version of the story to counterbalance it. Even when there is no way around it— old Uncle Pete did a terrible thing—by knowing the stories that come out of other families, by keeping very close watch, listening constantly to·learn the stories about other families, one is in a sense able to deal with terrible sorts of things that might happen within one's own family. When a member of one's own family does something that cannot be excused, one always knows stories about similar things which happened in other families. And it is not done maliciously. I think it is very important to realize this. Keeping track of all the stories within the community gives a certain distance, a useful perspective which brings incidents down to a level we can deal with. If others have done it before, it cannot be so terrible. If others have endured, so can we.

The stories are always bringing us together, keeping this whole 12 together, keeping this family together, keeping this clan together. "Don't go away, don't isolate yourself, but come here, because we have all had these kinds of experiences"—this is what the people are saying to you when they tell you these other stories. And so there is this constant pulling together to resist what seems to me to be a basic part of human nature: when some violent emotional experience takes place, people get the urge to run off and hide or separate themselves from others. And of course, if we do that, we are not only talking about endangering the group, we are also talking about the individual or the individual family never being able to recover or to survive. Inherent in this belief is the feeling that one does not recover or get well by one's self, but it is together that we look after each other and take care of each other.

In the storytelling, then, we see this process of bringing people 13 together, and it works not only on the family level, but also on the level of the individual. Of course, the whole Pueblo concept of the individual is a little bit different from the usual Western concept of the individual. But one of the beauties of the storytelling is that when something happens to an individual, many people will come to you and take you aside, or maybe a couple of people will come and talk to you. These are occasions of storytelling. These occasions of storytelling are continuous; they are a way of life.

14   Storytelling lies at the heart of the Pueblo people, and so when someone comes in and says, "When did they tell the stories, or what time of day does the storytelling take place?" that is a ridiculous question. The storytelling goes on constantly—as some old grandmother puts on the shoes of a little child and tells the child the story of a little girl who didn't wear her shoes. At the same time somebody comes into the house for coffee to talk with an adolescent boy who has just been into a lot of trouble, to reassure him that *he* got into that kind of trouble, or somebody else's son got into that kind of trouble too. You have this constant ongoing process, working on many different levels.

15   One of the stories I like to bring up about helping the individual in crisis is a recent story, and I want to remind you that we make no distinctions between the stories—whether they are history, whether they are fact, whether they are gossip—these distinctions are not useful when we are talking about this particular experience with language. Anyway, there was a young man who, when he came back from the war in Vietnam, had saved up his Army pay and bought a beautiful red Volkswagen Beetle. He was very proud of it, and one night drove up to a place right across the reservation line. It is a very notorious place for many reasons, but one of the more notorious things about the place is a deep arroyo behind the place. This is the King's Bar. So he ran in to pick up a cold six-pack to take home, but he didn't put on his emergency brake. And his little red Volkswagen rolled back into the arroyo and was all smashed up. He felt very bad about it, but within a few days everybody had come to him and told him stories about other people who had lost cars to that arroyo. And probably the story that made him feel the best was about the time that George Day's station wagon, with his mother-in-law and kids in the back, rolled into that arroyo. So everybody was saying, "Well, at least your mother-in-law and kids weren't in the car

when it rolled in," and you can't argue with that kind of story. He felt better then because he wasn't alone anymore. He and his smashed-up Volkswagen were now joined with all the other stories of cars that fell into that arroyo. . . .

There are a great many parallels between Pueblo experiences 16 and the remarks that have been made about South Africa and the Caribbean countries—similarities in experiences so far as language is concerned. More specifically, with the experience of English being imposed upon the people. The Pueblo people, of course, have seen intruders come and intruders go. The first they watched come were the Spaniards; while the Spaniards were there, things had to be conducted in Spanish. But as the old stories say, if you wait long enough, they'll go. And sure enough, they went. Then another bunch came in. And old stories say, well, if you wait around long enough, not so much that they'll go, but at least their ways will go. One wonders now, when you see what's happening to technocratic-industrial culture, now that we've used up most of the sources of energy, you think perhaps the old people are right.

But anyhow, our experience with English has been different 17 because the Bureau of Indian Affairs schools were so terrible that we never heard of Shakespeare. There was Dick and Jane, and I can remember reading that the robins were heading south for winter, but I knew that all winter the robins were around Laguna. It took me a long time to figure out what was going on. I worried for quite a while about the robins because they didn't leave in the winter, not realizing that the textbooks were written in Boston. The big textbook companies are up here in Boston and *their* robins do go south in the winter. But this freed us and encouraged us to stay with our narratives. Whatever literature we received at school (which was damn little), at home the storytelling, the special regard for telling and bringing together through the telling, was going on constantly. It has continued, and so we have a great body of classical oral literature, both in the narratives and in the chants and songs.

As the old people say, "If you can remember the stories, you 18 will be all right. Just remember the stories." And, or course, usually when they say that to you, when you are young, you wonder what in the world they mean. But when I returned—I had been away from Laguna Pueblo for a couple of years, well more than a couple of years after college and so forth—I returned to Laguna and I went to Laguna-Acoma high school to visit an English class, and I was wondering how the telling was continuing, because Laguna Pueblo, as the anthropologists have said, is one of the more acculturated pueblos. So I walked into this high school English class and there they were sitting, these very beautiful Laguna and Acoma kids. But I knew that out in their lockers they had cassette tape recorders, and I knew that at home they had stereos, and they were listening to "Kiss" and Led Zeppelin and all those other things. I was almost afraid, but I had to ask—I had with me a book of short fiction (it's called *The Man to Send Rain Clouds* [New York: Viking Press, 1974]), and among the stories of other Native American writers, it has stories that I have written and Simon Ortiz has written. And there is one particular story in the book about the killing of a state policeman in New Mexico by three Acoma Pueblo men. It was an act that was committed in the early fifties. I was afraid to ask, but I had to. I looked at the class and I said, "How many of you heard this story before you read it in the book?" And I was prepared to hear this crushing truth that indeed the anthropologists were right about the old traditions dying out. But it was amazing, you know, almost all but one or two students raised their hands. They had heard that story, just as Simon and I heard it, when we were young. That was my first indication that storytelling continues on. About half of them had heard it in English, about half of them had heard it in Laguna. I think again, getting back to one of the original statements, that if you begin to look at the core of the importance of the language and how it fits in with the culture, it is the *story* and the feeling of the story which matters more than what language it's told in. . . .

1979

Politics and the English Language

George Orwell

1   Most people who bother with the matter at all would admit that the English language is in a bad way, but it is generally assumed

that we cannot by conscious action do anything about it. Our civilization is decadent and our language—so the argument runs—must inevitably share in the general collapse. It follows that any struggle against the abuse of language is a sentimental archaism, like preferring candles to electric light or hansom cabs to aeroplanes. Underneath this lies the half-conscious belief that language is a natural growth and not an instrument which we shape for our own purposes.

Now, it is clear that the decline of a language must ultimately 2 have political and economic causes: it is not due simply to the bad influence of this or that individual writer. But an effect can become a cause, reinforcing the original cause and producing the same effect in an intensified form, and so on indefinitely. A man may take to drink because he feels himself to be a failure, and then fail all the more completely because he drinks. It is rather the same thing that is happening to the English language. It becomes ugly and inaccurate because our thoughts are foolish, but the slovenliness of our language makes it easier for us to have foolish thoughts. The point is that the process is reversible. Modern English, especially written English, is full of bad habits which spread by imitation and which can be avoided if one is willing to take the necessary trouble. If one gets rid of these habits one can think more clearly, and to think clearly is a necessary first step towards political regeneration: so that the fight against bad English is not frivolous and is not the exclusive concern of professional writers. I will come back to this presently, and I hope by that time the meaning of what I have said here will have become clearer. Meanwhile, here are five specimens of the English language as it is now habitually written.

These five passages have not been picked out because they 3 are especially bad—I could have quoted far worse if I had chosen—but because they illustrate various of the mental vices from which we now suffer. They are a little below the average, but are fairly representative samples. I number them so that I can refer back to them when necessary:

> *"(1) I am not, indeed, sure whether it is not*
> *true to say that the Milton who once seemed*
> *not unlike a seventeenth-century Shelly had not*
> *become, out of an experience ever more bitter in*

each year, more alien [sic] *to the founder of that
Jesuit sect which nothing could induce him to
tolerate."*

Professor Harold Laski (Essay in
Freedom of Expression)

*"(2) Above all, we cannot play ducks and
drakes with a native battery of idioms which
prescribes such egregious collocations of voca-
bles as the Basic* put up with *for* tolerate *or*
put at a loss *for* bewilder.*"*

Professor Lancelot Hogben (*Interglossa*)

*"(3) On the one side we have the free personality:
by definition it is not neurotic, for it has neither
conflict nor dream. Its desires, such as they are,
are transparent, for they are just what institutional approval keeps in the forefront of consciousness; another institutional pattern would
alter their number and intensity; there is little in
them that is natural, irreducible, or culturally
dangerous. But* on the other *side, the social
bond itself is nothing but the mutual reflection of
these self-secure integrities. Recall the definition
of love. Is not this the very picture of a small
academic? Where is there a place in this hall of
mirrors for either personality or fraternity?"*

Essay on psychology in *Politics* (New York)

*"(4) All the 'best people' from the gentlemen's
clubs, and all the frantic fascist captains, united
in common hatred of Socialism and bestial horror of the rising tide of the mass revolutionary
movement, have turned to acts of provocation,
to foul incendiarism, to medieval legends of
poisoned wells, to legalize their own destruction
of proletarian organizations, and rouse the agitated petty-bourgeoisie to chauvinistic fervour
on behalf of the fight against the revolutionary
way out of the crisis."*

Communist pamphlet

*"(5) If a new spirit is to be infused into this
old country, there is one thorny and
contentious reform which must be tackled, and*

*that is the humanization and galvanization of
the B.B.C. Timidity here will bespeak cancer
and atrophy of the soul. The heart of Britain
may be sound and of strong beat, for instance,
but the British lion's roar at present is like that
of Bottom in Shakespeare's* Midsummer
Night's Dream—*as gentle as any sucking
dove. A virile new Britain cannot continue
indefinitely to be traduced in the eyes or rather
ears, of the world by the effete languors of
Langham Place, brazenly masquerading as
'standard English.' When the Voice of Britain is
heard at nine o'clock, better far and infinitely
less ludicrous to hear aitches honestly dropped
than the present priggish, inflated, inhibited,
school-ma'amish arch braying of blameless
bashful mewing maidens!"*

Letter in Tribune

Each of these passages has faults of its own, but, quite apart 4
from avoidable ugliness, two qualities are common to all of them.
The first is staleness of imagery: the other is lack of precision. The
writer either has a meaning and cannot express it, or he inadvertently says something else, or he is almost indifferent as to
whether his words mean anything or not. This mixture of vagueness and sheer incompetence is the most marked characteristic of
modern English prose, and especially of any kind of political
writing. As soon as certain topics are raised, the concrete melts
into the abstract and no one seems able to think of turns of
speech that are not hackneyed: prose consists less and less of
words chosen for the sake of their meaning, and more and more
of *phrases* tacked together like the sections of a prefabricated hen-
house. I list below, with notes and examples, various of the tricks
by means of which the work or prose-construction is habitually
dodged.

DYING METAPHORS

A newly invented metaphor assists thought by evoking a visual 5
image, while on the other hand a metaphor which is technically

"dead" (e.g. *iron resolution*) has in effect reverted to being an ordinary word and can generally be used without loss of vividness. But in between these two classes there is a huge dump of worn-out metaphors which have lost all evocative power and are merely used because they save people the trouble of inventing phrases for themselves. Examples are: *Ring the changes on, take up the cudgels for, toe the line, ride roughshod over, stand shoulder to shoulder with, play into the hands of, no axe to grind, grist to the mill, fishing in troubled waters, on the order of the day, Achilles' heel, swan song, hotbed.* Many of these are used without knowledge of their meaning (what is a "rift," for instance?), and incompatible metaphors are frequently mixed, a sure sign that the writer is not interested in what he is saying. Some metaphors now current have been twisted out of their original meaning without those who use them even being aware of the fact. For example, *toe the line* is sometimes written *tow the line.* Another example is *the hammer and the anvil,* now really used with the implication that the anvil gets the worst of it. In real life it is always the anvil that breaks the hammer, never the other way about: a writer who stopped to think what he was saying would be aware of this, and would avoid perverting the original phrase.

OPERATORS OR VERBAL FALSE LIMBS

6 These save the trouble of picking out appropriate verbs and nouns, and at the same time pad each sentence with extra syllables which give it an appearance of symmetry. Characteristic phrases are: *render inoperative, militate against, make contact with, be subjected to, give rise to, give grounds for, have the effect of, play a leading part (role) in, make itself felt, take effect, exhibit a tendency to, serve the purpose of, etc., etc.* The keynote is the elimination of simple verbs. Instead of being a single word, such as *break, stop, spoil, mend, kill,* a verb becomes a *phrase,* made up of a noun or adjective tacked on to some general-purposes verb such as *prove, serve, form, play, render.* In addition, the passive voice is wherever possible used in preference to the active, and noun constructions are used instead of gerunds (*by examination of* instead of *by examining*). The range of verbs is further cut down by means of the *-ize* and *de-* formation, and the banal statements are given an appearance of profundity by means of the *not un-* formation.

Simple conjunctions and prepositions are replaced by such phrases as *with respect to, having regard to, the fact that, by dint of, in view of, in the interests of, on the hypotheses that;* and the ends of sentences are saved from anticlimax by such resounding commonplaces as *greatly to be desired, cannot be left out of account, a development to be expected in the near future, deserving of serious consideration, brought to a satisfactory conclusion,* and so on and so forth.

PRETENTIOUS DICTION

Words like *phenomenon, element, individual* (as noun), *objective, categorical, effective, virtual, basic, primary, promote, constitute, exhibit, exploit, utilize, eliminate, liquidate,* are used to dress up simple statements and give an air of scientific impartiality to biased judgments. Adjectives like *epoch-making, epic, historic, unforgettable, triumphant, age-old, inevitable, inexorable, veritable,* are used to dignify the sordid processes of international politics, while writing that aims at glorifying war usually takes on an archaic color, its characteristic words being: *realm, throne, chariot, mailed fist, trident, sword, shield, buckler, banner, jackboot, clarion.* Foreign words and expressions such as *cul de sac, ancien régime, deus ex machina, mutatis mutandis, status quo, gleichschaltung, weltanschauung,* are used to give an air of culture and elegance. Except for the useful abbreviations *i.e., e.g.,* and *etc.,* there is no real need for any of the hundreds of foreign phrases now current in English. Bad writers, and especially scientific, political and sociological writers, are nearly always haunted by the notion that Latin or Greek words are grander than Saxon ones, and unnecessary words like *expedite, ameliorate, predict, extraneous, deracinated, clandestine, subaqueous,* and hundreds of others constantly gain ground from their Anglo-Saxon opposite numbers.[1] The

---

[1]An interesting illustration of this is the way in which the English flower names which were in use till very recently are being ousted by Greek ones, *snapdragon* becoming *antirrhinum, forget-me-not* becoming *myosotis, etc.* It is hard to see any practical reason for this change of fashion: it is probably due to an instinctive turning-away from the more homely word and vague feeling that the Greek word is scientific.

jargon peculiar to Marist writing (*hyena, hangman, cannibal, petty bourgeois, these gentry, lackey, flunky, mad dog, White Guard,* etc.) consists largely of words and phrases translated from Russian, German or French; but the normal way of coining a new word is to use a Latin or Greek root with the appropriate affix and, where necessary, the *-ize* formation. It is often easier to make up words of this kind (*deregionalize, impermissible, extramarital, nonfragmentatory,* and so forth) than to think up the English words that will cover one's meaning. The result, in general, is an increase in slovenliness and vagueness.

MEANINGLESS WORDS

8   In certain kinds of writing, particularly in art criticism and literary criticism, it is normal to come across long passages which are almost completely lacking in meaning.[2] Words like *romantic, plastic, values, human, dead, sentimental, natural, vitality,* as used in art criticism, are strictly meaningless in the sense that they not only do not point to any discoverable object, but are hardly ever expected to do so by the reader. When one critic writes, "The outstanding feature of Mr. X's work is its living quality," while another writes, "The immediately striking thing about Mr. X's work is its peculiar deadness," the reader accepts this as a simple difference of opinion. If words like *black* and *white* were involved, instead of the jargon words *dead* and *living,* he would see at once that language was being used in an improper way. Many political words are similarly abused. The word *Fascism* has now no meaning except in so far as it signifies "something not desirable." The words *democracy, socialism, freedom, patriotic, realistic, justice,* have each of them several different meanings which cannot be reconciled with one

---

[2]Example: "Comfort's catholicity of perception and image, strangely Whitmanesque in range, almost the exact opposite in aesthetic compulsion, continues to evoke that trembling atmospheric accumulative hinting at a cruel, an inexorably serene timelessness . . . Wrey Gardiner scores by aiming at simple bull's-eyes with precision. Only they are not so simple, and through this contented sadness runs more than the surface bittersweet of resignation" (*Poetry Quarterly*).

another. In the case of a word like *democracy,* not only is there no agreed definition, but the attempt to make one is resisted from all sides. It is almost universally felt that when we call a country democratic we are praising it: consequently the defenders of every kind of régime claim that it is a democracy, and fear that they might have to stop using the word if it were tied down to any one meaning. Words of this kind are often used in a consciously dishonest way. That is, the person who uses them has his own private definition, but allows his hearer to think he means something quite different. Statements like *Marshal Pétain was a true patriot, The Soviet Press is the freest in the world, The Catholic Church is opposed to persecution,* are almost always made with intent to deceive. Other words used in variable meanings, in most cases more or less dishonestly, are: *class, totalitarian, science, progressive, reactionary, bourgeois, equality.*

Now that I have made this catalog of swindles and perver- 9 sions, let me give another example of the kind of writing that they lead to. This time it must of its nature be an imaginary one. I am going to translate a passage of good English into modern English of the worst sort. Here is a well-known verse from *Ecclésiastes:*

> "I returned and saw under the sun, that the race is not to the swift, nor the battle to the strong, neither yet bread to the wise, nor yet riches to men of understanding, nor yet favor to men of skill; but time and chance happeneth to them all."

Here it is in modern English:

> "Objective consideration of contemporary phenomena compels the conclusion that success or failure in competitive activities exhibits no tendency to be commensurate with innate capacity, but that a considerable element of the unpredictable must invariably be taken into account."

This is a parody, but not a very gross one. Exhibit (3), above, 10 for instance, contains several patches of the same kind of English. It will be seen that I have not made a full translation. The beginning and ending of the sentence follow the original meaning fairly closely, but in the middle the concrete illustrations—race, battle, bread—dissolve into the vague phrase "success or failure in competitive activities." This had to be so, because no modern writer of the kind I am discussing—no one capable of using phrases like "objective consideration of contemporary phenomena"—would ever tabulate his thoughts in that precise and detailed way. The whole tendency of modern prose is away from concreteness. Now analyse these two sentences a little more closely. The first contains forty-nine words but only sixty syllables, and all its words are those of everyday life. The second contains thirty-eight words of ninety syllables: eighteen of its words are from Latin roots, and one from Greek. The first sentence contains six vivid images, and only one phrase ("time and chance") that could be called vague. The second contains not a single fresh, arresting phrase, and in spite of its ninety syllables it gives only a shortened version of the meaning contained in the first. Yet without a doubt it is the second kind of sentence that is gaining ground in modern English. I do not want to exaggerate. This kind of writing is not yet universal, and outcrops of simplicity will occur here and there in the worst-written page. Still, if you or I were told to write a few lines on the uncertainty of human fortunes, we should probably come much nearer to my imaginary sentence than to the one from *Ecclésiastes*.

11   As I have tried to show, modern writing at its worst does not consist in picking out words for the sake of their meaning and inventing images in order to make the meaning clearer. It consists in gumming together long strips of words which have already been set in order by someone else, and making the results presentable by sheer humbug. The attraction of this way of writing is that it is easier. It is easier—even quicker, once you have the habit—to say *In my opinion it is a not unjustifiable assumption that* than to say *I think*. If you use ready-made phrases, you not only don't have to hunt about for words; you also don't have to bother with the rhythms of your sentences, since these phrases are generally so arranged as to be more or less euphonious. When you are composing in a hurry—when you are dictating to a stenographer, for instance, or making a public speech—it is natural to fall into a pretentious, Latinized style. Tags like *a consideration which we should do well to bear in mind* or *a conclusion to which all of us would readily assent* will save many a sentence from coming down with a bump. By using stale metaphors, similes and idioms, you save much mental effort, at the cost of leaving your meaning vague, not only for your reader but for yourself. This is the

significance of mixed metaphors. The sole aim of a metaphor is to call up a visual image. When these images clash—as in *The Fascist octopus has sung its swan song, the jackboot is thrown into the melting pot*—it can be taken as certain that the writer is not seeing a mental image of the objects he is naming; in other words he is not really thinking. Look again at the examples I gave at the beginning of this essay. Professor Laski (1) uses five negatives in fifty-three words. One of these is superfluous, making nonsense of the whole passage, and in addition there is the slip *alien* for akin, making further nonsense, and several avoidable pieces of clumsiness which increase the general vagueness. Professor Hogben (2) plays ducks and drakes with a battery which is able to write prescriptions, and, while disapproving of the everyday phrase *put up with,* is willing to look *egregious* up in the dictionary and see what it means. (3), if one takes an uncharitable attitude towards it, is simply meaningless: probably one could work out its intended meaning by reading the whole of the article in which it occurs. In (4), the writer knows more or less what he wants to say, but an accumulation of stale phrases chokes him like tea leaves blocking a sink. In (5), words and meaning have almost parted company. People who write in this manner usually have a general emotional meaning—they dislike one thing and want to express solidarity with another—but they are not interested in the detail of what they are saying. A scrupulous writer, in every sentence that he writes, will ask himself at least four questions, thus: What am I trying to say? What words will express it? What image or idiom will make it clearer? Is this image fresh enough to have an effect? And he will probably ask himself two more: Could I put it more shortly? Have I said anything that is avoidably ugly? But you are not obliged to go to all this trouble. You can shirk it by simply throwing your mind open and letting the ready-made phrases come crowding in. They will construct your sentences for you—even think your thoughts for you, to a certain extent—and at need they will perform the important service of partially concealing your meaning even from yourself. It is at this point that the special connection between politics and the debasement of language becomes clear.

In our time it is broadly true that political writing is bad writing. Where it is not true, it will generally be found that the writer is some kind of rebel, expressing his private opinions and not a "party line." Orthodoxy, or whatever color, seems to demand a lifeless, imitative style. The political dialects to be found in pamphlets, leading articles, manifestos, White Papers and the speeches of under-secretaries do, our course, vary from party to party, but they are all alike in that one almost never finds in them a fresh, vivid, home-made turn of speech. When one watches some tired phrases—*bestial atrocities, iron heel, bloodstained tyranny, free peoples of the world, stand shoulder to shoulder*—one often has a curious feeling that one is not watching a live human being but some kind of dummy: a feeling which suddenly becomes stronger at moments when the light catches the speaker's spectacles and turns them into blank discs which seem to have no eyes behind them. And this is not altogether fanciful. A speaker who uses that kind of phraseology has gone some distance towards turning himself into a machine. The appropriate noises are coming out of his larynx, but his brain is not involved as it would be if he were choosing his words for himself. If the speech he is making is one that he is accustomed to make over and over again, he may be almost unconscious of what he is saying, as one is when one utters the responses in church. And this reduced state of consciousness, if not indispensable, is at any rate favorable to political conformity.

13   In our time, political speech and writing are largely the defense of the indefensible. Things like the continuance of British rule in India, the Russian purges and deportations, the dropping of the atom bombs on Japan, can indeed be defended, but only by arguments which are too brutal for most people to face, and which do not square with the professed aims of political parties. Thus political language has to consist largely of euphemism, question-begging and sheer cloudy vagueness. Defenseless villages are bombarded from the air, the inhabitants driven out into the countryside, the cattle machine-gunned, the huts set on fire with incendiary bullets: this is called *pacification*. Millions of peasants are robbed of their farms and sent trudging along the roads with no more than they can carry: this is called *transfer of population* or *rectification of frontiers*. People are imprisoned for years without trial, or shot in the back of the neck or sent to die of scurvy in Arctic lumber camps: this is called *elimination of unreliable elements*.

Such phraseology is needed if one wants to name things without calling up mental pictures of them. Consider for instance some comfortable English professor defending Russian totalitarianism. He cannot say outright, "I believe in killing off your opponents when you can get good results by doing so." Probably, therefore, he will say something like this:

"While freely conceding that the Soviet régime exhibits cer- 14 tain features which the humanitarian may be inclined to deplore, we must, I think, agree that a certain curtailment of the right to political opposition is an unavoidable concomitant of transitional periods, and that the rigors which the Russian people have been called upon to undergo have been amply justified in the sphere of concrete achievement."

The inflated style is itself a kind of euphemism. A mass of 15 Latin words falls upon the facts like soft snow, blurring the out-lines and covering up all the details. The great enemy of clear language is insincerity. When there is a gap between one's real and one's declared aims, one turns as it were instinctively to long words and exhausted idioms, like a cuttlefish squirting out ink. In our age there is no such thing as "keeping out of politics." All issues are political issues, and politics itself is a mass of lies, evasions, folly, hatred and schizophrenia. When the general atmosphere is bad, language must suffer. I should expect to find—this is a guess which I have not sufficient knowledge to verify—that the German, Russian and Italian languages have all deteriorated in the last ten or fifteen years, as a result of dictatorship.

But if thought corrupts language, language can also corrupt 16 thought. A bad usage can spread by tradition and imitation, even among people who should and do know better. The debased language that I have been discussing is in some ways very conven-ient. Phrases like *a not unjustifiable assumption, leaves much to be desired, would serve no good purpose, a consideration which we should do well to bear in mind,* are a continuous temptation, a packet of aspirins always at one's elbow. Look back through this essay, and for certain you will find that I have again and again committed the very faults I am protesting against. By this morning's post I have received a pamphlet dealing with conditions in Germany. The author tells me that he "felt impelled" to write it. I open it at random, and here is almost the first sentence that I see: "(The Allies) have an opportunity not only of achieving a radical transformation of Germany's social and political structure in such a way as to avoid a nationalistic reaction in Germany itself, but at the same time of laying the foundations of a cooperative and unified Europe." You see, he "feels impelled" to write—feels, presumable, that he has something new to say—and yet his words, like cavalry horses answering the bugle, group themselves automatically into the familiar dreary pattern. This invasion of one's mind by ready-made phrases (*lay the foundations, achieve a radical transformation*) can only be prevented if one is constantly on guard against them, and every such phrase anaesthetizes a portion of one's brain.

17   I said earlier that the decadence of our language is probably curable. Those who deny this would argue, if they produced an argument at all, that language merely reflects existing social conditions, and that we cannot influence its development by any direct tinkering with words and constructions. So far as the general tone or spirit of a language goes, this may be true, but it is not true in detail. Silly words and expressions have often disappeared, not through any evolutionary process but owing to the conscious action of a minority. Two recent examples were *explore every avenue* and *leave no stone unturned*, which were killed by the jeers of a few journalists. There is a long list of flyblown metaphors which could similarly be got rid of if enough people would interest themselves in the job; and it should also be possible to laugh the *not un-* formation out of existence,[3] to reduce the amount of Latin and Greek in the average sentence, to drive out foreign phrases and strayed scientific words, and, in general, to make pretentiousness unfashionable. But all these are minor points. The defense of the English language implies more than this, and perhaps it is best to start by saying what it does *not* imply.

18   To begin with it has nothing to do with archaism, with the salvaging of obsolete words and turns of speech, or with the setting up of a "standard English" which must never be departed from. On the contrary, it is especially concerned with the scrapping of every word or idiom which has outworn its usefulness. It

---

[3]One can cure oneself of the *not un-* formation by memorizing this sentence. *A not unblack dog was chasing a not unsmall rabbit across a not ungreen field.*

has nothing to do with correct grammar and syntax, which are of no importance so long as one makes one's meaning clear, or with the avoidance of Americanisms, or with having what is called a "good prose style." On the other hand it is not concerned with fake simplicity and the attempt to make written English colloquial. Nor does it even imply in every case preferring the Saxon word to the Latin one, though it does imply using the fewest and shortest words that will cover one's meaning. What is above all needed is to let the meaning choose the word, and not the other way about. In prose, the worst thing one can do with words is to surrender to them. When you think of a concrete object, you think wordlessly, and then, if you want to describe the thing you have been visualizing you probably hunt about till you find the exact words that seem to fit. When you think of something abstract you are more inclined to use words from the start, and unless you make a conscious effort to prevent it, the existing dialect will come rushing in and do the job for you, at the expense of blurring or even changing your meaning. Probably it is better to put off using words as long as possible and get one's meaning as clear as one can through pictures or sensations. Afterwards one can choose— not simply *accept*—the phrases that will best cover the meaning, and then switch round and decide what impression one's words are likely to make on another person. This last effort of the mind cuts out all stale or mixed images, all prefabricated phrases, needless repetitions, and humbug and vagueness generally. But one can often be in doubt about the effect of a word or a phrase, and one needs rules that one can rely on when instinct fails. I think the following rules will cover most cases:

(i)   Never use a metaphor, simile or other figure of speech which you are used to seeing in print.

(ii)   Never use a long word where a short one will do.

(iii)   If it is possible to cut a word out, always cut it out.

(iv)   Never use the passive where you can use the active.

(v)   Never use a foreign phrase, a scientific word or a jargon word if you can think of an everyday English equivalent.

(vi)   Break any of these rules sooner than say anything outright barbarous.

19 These rules sound elementary, and so they are, but they demand a
deep change of attitude in anyone who has grown used to writing
in the style now fashionable. One could keep all of them and still
write bad English, but one could not write the kind of stuff that I
quoted in those five specimens at the beginning of this article.

20   I have not here been considering the literary use of language,
but merely language as an instrument for expressing and not for
concealing or preventing thought. Stuart Chase and others have
come near to claiming that all abstract words are meaningless, and
have used this as a pretext for advocating a kind of political
quietism. Since you don't know what Fascism is, how can you
struggle against Fascism? One need not swallow such absurdities
as this, but one ought to recognize that the present political chaos
is connected with the decay of language, and that one can probably bring about some improvement by starting at the verbal end.
If you simplify your English, you are freed from the worst follies
of orthodoxy. You cannot speak any of the necessary dialects, and
when you make a stupid remark its stupidity will be obvious,
even to yourself. Political language—and with variations this is
true of all political parties, from Conservatives to Anarchists—is
designed to make lies sound truthful and murder respectable, and
to give an appearance of solidity to pure wind. One cannot change
this all in a moment, but one can at least change one's own habits,
and from time to time one can even, if one jeers loudly enough,
send some worn-out and useless phrase—some *jackboot, Achilles'
heel, hotbed, melting pot, acid test, veritable inferno* or other lump of
verbal refuse—into the dustbin where it belongs.

1946

Chapter 3

Religion

Salvation

Langston Hughes

I was saved from sin when I was going on thirteen. But not really 1
saved. It happened like this. There was a big revival at my Aun-
tie Reed's church. Every night for weeks there had been much
preaching, singing, praying, and shouting, and some very hardened sinners had been brought to Christ, and the membership of
the church had grown by leaps and bounds. Then just before the
revival ended, they held a special meeting for children, "to bring
the young lambs to the fold." My aunt spoke of it for days ahead.
That night I was escorted to the front row and placed on the
mourners' bench with all the other young sinners, who had not
yet been brought to Jesus.

My aunt told me that when you were saved you saw a light, 2
and something happened to you inside! And Jesus came into your
life! And God was with you from then on! She said you could see
and hear and feel Jesus in your soul. I believed her. I had heard
a great many old people say the same thing and it seemed to me
they ought to know. So I sat there calmly in the hot, crowded
church, waiting for Jesus to come to me.

The preacher preached a wonderful rhythmical sermon, all 3
moans and shouts and lonely cries and dire pictures of hell, and then
he sang a song about the ninety and nine safe in the fold, but one
little lamb was left out in the cold. Then he said: "Won't you come?
Won't you come to Jesus? Young lambs, won't you come?" And he
held out his arms to all us young sinners there on the mourners'
bench. And the little girls cried. And some of them jumped up and
went to Jesus right away. But most of us just sat there.

87

4   A great many older people came and knelt around us and prayed, old women with jet-black faces and braided hair, old men with work-gnarled hands. And the church sang a song about the lower lights are burning, some poor sinners to be saved. And the whole building rocked with prayer and song.

5   Still I kept waiting to *see* Jesus.

6   Finally all the young people had gone to the altar and were saved, but one boy and me. He was a rounder's son named Westley. Westley and I were surrounded by sisters and deacons praying. It was very hot in the church, and getting late now. Finally Westley said to me in a whisper: "God damn! I'm tired o' sitting here. Let's get up and be saved." So he got up and was saved.

7   Then I was left all alone on the mourners' bench. My aunt came and knelt at my knees and cried, while prayers and songs swirled all around me in the little church. The whole congregation prayed for me alone, in a mighty wail of moans and voices. And I kept waiting serenely for Jesus, waiting, waiting—but he didn't come. I wanted to see him, but nothing happened to me. Nothing! I wanted something to happen to me, but nothing happened.

8   I heard the songs and the minister saying: "Why don't you come? My dear child, why don't you come to Jesus? Jesus is waiting for you. He wants you. Why don't you come? Sister Reed, what is this child's name?"

9   "Langston," my aunt sobbed.

10   "Langston, why don't you come? Why don't you come and be saved? Oh, Lamb of God! Why don't you come?"

11   Now it was really getting late. I began to be ashamed of myself, holding everything up so long. I began to wonder what God thought about Westley, who certainly hadn't seen Jesus either, but who was now sitting proudly on the platform, swinging his knickerbockered legs and grinning down at me, surrounded by deacons and old women on their knees praying. God had not struck Westley dead for taking his name in vain or for lying in the temple. So I decided that maybe to save further trouble, I'd better lie, too, and say that Jesus had come, and get up and be saved.

12   So I got up.

Suddenly the whole room broke into a sea of shouting, as they 13
saw me rise. Waves of rejoicing swept the place. Women leaped
in the air. My aunt threw her arms around me. The minister took
me by the hand and let me to the platform.

When things quieted down, in a hushed silence, punctuated 14
by a few ecstatic "Amens," all the new young lambs were blessed
in the name of God. Then joyous singing filled the room.

That night, for the last time in my life but one—for I was a 15
big boy twelve years old—I cried. I cried, in bed alone, and
couldn't stop. I buried my head under the quilts, but my aunt
heard me. She woke up and told my uncle I was crying because
the Holy Ghost had come into my life, and because I had seen
Jesus. But I was really crying because I couldn't bear to tell her
that I had lied, that I had deceived everybody in the church, and
I hadn't seen Jesus, and that now I didn't believe there was a Jesus
any more, since he didn't come to help me.

1940

The Way to Rainy Mountain

N. Scott Momaday

A single knoll rises out of the plain in Oklahoma, north and west 1
of the Wichita range. For my people, the Kiowas, it is an old landmark, and they gave it the name Rainy Mountain. The hardest
weather in the world is there. Winter brings blizzards, hot tornadic
winds arise in the spring, and in summer the prairie is an anvil's
edge. The grass turns brittle and brown, and it cracks beneath your
feet. There are green belts along the rivers and creeks, linear groves
of hickory and pecan, willow and witch hazel. At a distance in July
or August the steaming foliage seems almost to writhe in fire. Great
green and yellow grasshoppers are everywhere in the tall grass,
popping up like corn to sting the flesh, and tortoises crawl about
on the red earth, going nowhere in the plenty of time. Loneliness
is an aspect of the land. All things in the plain are isolate; there is
no confusion of objects in the eye, but *one* hill *or one* tree or *one*

man. To look upon that landscape in the early morning, with the sun at your back, is to lose the sense of proportion. Your imagination comes to life, and this, you think, is where Creation was begun.

2   I returned to Rainy Mountain in July. My grandmother had died in the spring, and I wanted to be at her grave. She had lived to be very old and at last infirm. Her only living daughter was with her when she died, and I was told that in death her face was that of a child.

3   I like to think of her as a child. When she was born, the Kiowas were living the last great moment of their history. For more than a hundred years they had controlled the open range from the Smoky Hill River to the Red, from the headwaters of the Canadian to the fork of the Arkansas and Cimarron. In alliance with the Comanches, they had ruled the whole of the Southern Plains. War was their sacred business, and they were the finest horsemen the world has ever known. But warfare for the Kiowas was pre-eminently a matter of disposition rather than of survival, and they never understood the grim, unrelenting advance of the U.S. Cavalry. When at last, divided and ill provisioned, they were driven onto the Staked Plains in the cold of autumn, they fell into panic. In Palo Duro Canyon they abandoned their crucial stores to pillage and had nothing then but their lives. In order to save themselves, they surrendered to the soldiers at Fort Sill and were imprisoned in the old stone corral that now stands as a military museum. My grandmother was spared the humiliation of those high gray walls by eight or ten years, but she must have known from birth the affliction of defeat, the dark brooding of old warriors.

4   Her name was Aho, and she belonged to the last culture to evolve in North America. Her forebears came down from the high country in western Montana nearly three centuries ago. They were a mountain people, a mysterious tribe of hunters whose language has never been classified in any major group. In the late seventeenth century they began a long migration to the south and east. It was a journey toward the dawn, and it led to a golden age. Along the way the Kiowas were befriended by the Crows, who gave them the culture and religion of the Plains. They acquired horses, and their ancient nomadic spirit was suddenly free of the ground. They acquired Tai-me, the sacred sun-dance doll, from that moment the object and symbol of their worship, and so shared in the divinity

of the sun. Not least, they acquired the sense of destiny, therefore courage and pride. When they entered upon the Southern Plains they had been transformed. No longer were they slaves to the simple necessity of survival; they were a lordly and dangerous society of fighters and thieves, hunters and priests of the sun. According to their origin myth, they entered the world through a hollow log. From one point of view, their migration was the fruit of an old prophecy, for indeed they emerged from a sunless world.

Though my grandmother lived out her long life in the shadow 5 of Rainy Mountain, the immense landscape of the continental interior lay like memory in her blood. She could tell of the Crows, whom she had never seen, and of the Black Hills, where she had never been. I wanted to see in reality what she had seen more perfectly in the mind's eye, and drove fifteen hundred miles to begin my pilgrimage.

A dark mist lay over the Black Hills, and the land was like 6 iron. At the top of a ridge I caught sight of Devil's Tower upthrust against the gray sky as if in the birth of time the core of the earth had broken through its crust and the motion of the world was begun. There are things in nature that engender an awful quiet in the heart of man; Devil's Tower is one of them. Two centuries ago, because of their need to explain it, the Kiowas made a legend at the base of the rock. My grandmother said:

"Eight children were there at play, seven sisters and their 7 brother. Suddenly the boy was struck dumb; he trembled and began to run upon his hands and feet. His fingers became claws, and his body was covered with fur. There was a bear where the boy had been. The sisters were terrified; they ran, and the bear after them. They came to the stump of a great tree, and the tree spoke to them. It bade them climb upon it, and as they did so, it began to rise into the air. The bear came to kill them, but they were just beyond its reach. It reared against the tree and scored the bark all around with its claws. The seven sisters were borne into the sky, and they became the stars of the Big Dipper." From that moment, and so long as the legend lives, the Kiowas have kinsmen in the night sky. Whatever they were in the mountains, they could be no more. However tenuous their well-being, however much they had suffered and would suffer again, they had found a way out of the wilderness.

8   My grandmother had a reverence for the sun, a holy regard that now is all but gone out of mankind. There was a wariness in her, and an ancient awe. She was a Christian in her later years, but she had come a long way about, and she never forgot her birthright. As a child she had been to the sun dances; she had taken part in that annual rite, and by it she had learned the restoration of her people in the presence of Tai-me. She was about seven when the last Kiowa sun dance was held in 1887 on the Washita River above Rainy Mountain Creek. The buffalo were gone. In order to consummate the ancient sacrifice—to impale the head of a buffalo bull upon the Tai-me tree—a delegation of old men journeyed into Texas, there to beg and barter for an animal from the Goodnight herd. She was ten when the Kiowas came together for the last time as a living sun-dance culture. They could find no buffalo; they had to hang an old hide from the sacred tree. Before the dance could begin, a company of soldiers rode out from Fort Sill under orders to disperse the tribe. Forbidden without cause the essential act of their faith, having seen the wild herds slaughtered and left to rot upon the ground, the Kiowas backed away forever from the tree. That was July 20, 1890, at the great bend of the Washita. My grandmother was there. Without bitterness, and for as long as she lived, she bore a vision of deicide.

9   Now that I can have her only in memory, I see my grandmother in the several postures that were peculiar to her: standing at the wood stove on a winter morning and turning meat in a great iron skillet; sitting at the south window, bent above her beadwork, and afterwards, when her vision failed, looking down for a long time into the fold of her hands; going out upon a cane, very slowly as she did when the weight of age came upon her; praying. I remember her most often at prayer. She made long, rambling prayers out of suffering and hope, having seen many things. I was never sure that I had the right to hear, so exclusive were they of all mere custom and company. The last time I saw her she prayed standing by the side of the bed at night, naked to the waist, the light of a kerosene lamp moving upon her dark skin. Her long black hair, always drawn and braided in the day, lay upon her shoulders and against her breasts like a shawl. I do not speak Kiowa, and I never understood her prayers, but there was something inherently sad in

the sound, some merest hesitation upon the syllables of sorrow. She began in a high and descending pitch, exhausting her breath to silence; then again and again—and always the same intensity of effort, of something that is, and is not, like urgency in the human voice. Transported so in the dancing light among the shadows of her room, she seemed beyond the reach of time. But that was illusion; I think I knew then that I should not see her again.

Houses are like sentinels in the plain, old keepers of the 10 weather watch. There, in a very little while, wood takes on the appearance of great age. All colors wear soon away in the wind and rain, and then the wood is burned gray and the grain appears and the nails turn red with rust. The window panes are black and opaque; you imagine there is nothing within, and indeed there are many ghosts, bones given up to the land. They stand here and there against the sky, and you approach them for a longer time than you expect. They belong in the distance; it is their domain.

Once there was a lot of sound in my grandmother's house, a lot 11 of coming and going, feasting and talk. The summers there were full of excitement and reunion. The Kiowas are a summer people; they abide the cold and keep to themselves, but when the season turns and the land becomes warm and vital they cannot hold still; an old love of going returns upon them. The aged visitors who came to my grandmother's house when I was a child were made of lean and leather, and they bore themselves upright. They wore great black hats and bright ample shirts that shook in the wind. They rubbed fat upon their hair and wound their braids with strips of colored cloth. Some of them painted their faces and carried the scars of old and cherished enmities. They were an old council of warlords, come to remind and be reminded of who they were. Their wives and daughters served them well. The women might indulge themselves; gossip was at once the mark and compensation of their servitude. They made loud and elaborate talk among themselves, full of jest and gesture, fright and false alarm. They went abroad in fringed and flowered shawls, bright beadwork and German silver. They were at home in the kitchen, and they prepared meals that were banquets.

There were frequent prayer meetings, and nocturnal feasts. 12 When I was a child I played with my cousins outside, where the lamplight fell upon the ground and the singing of the old people rose up around us and carried away into the darkness. There were a lot of good things to eat, a lot of laughter and surprise. And afterwards, when the quiet returned, I lay down with my grandmother and could hear the frogs away by the river and feel the motion of the air.

13   Now there is a funereal silence in the rooms, the endless wake of some final word. The walls have closed in upon my grandmother's house. When I returned to it in mourning, I saw for the first time in my life how small it was. It was late at night, and there was a white moon, nearly full. I sat for a long time on the stone steps by the kitchen door. From there I could see out across the land; I could see the long row of trees by the creek, the low light upon the rolling plains, and the stars of the Big Dipper. Once I looked at the moon and caught sight of a strange thing. A cricket had perched upon the handrail, only a few inches away. My line of vision was such that the creature filled the moon like a fossil. It had gone there, I thought, to live and die, for there, of all places, was its small definition made whole and eternal. A warm wind rose up and purled like the longing within me.

14   The next morning, I awoke at dawn and went out on the dirt road to Rainy Mountain. It was already hot, and the grasshoppers began to fill the air. Still, it was early in the morning, and birds sang out of the shadows. The long yellow grass on the mountain shone in the bright light, and a scissortail hied above the land. There, where it ought to be, at the end of a long and legendary way, was my grandmother's grave. She had at last succeeded to that holy ground. Here and there on the dark stones were ancestral names. Looking back once, I saw the mountain and came away.

1967

Follow Your Bliss

Joseph Campbell

1 The man who never followed his bliss . . . may have a success in life, but then just think of it—what kind of life was it? What good was it—you've never done the thing you wanted to do in all your

life. I always tell my students, go where your body and soul want
to go. When you have the feeling, then stay with it, and don't let
anyone throw you off. . . .

    That is following your bliss. . . .   2

    When I taught at Sarah Lawrence, I would have an individ- 3
ual conference with every one of my students at least once a fort-
night, for a half hour or so. Now, if you're talking on about the
things that students ought to be reading, and suddenly you hit on
something that the student really responds to, you can see the
eyes open and the complexion change. The life possibility has
opened there. All you can say to yourself is, "I hope this child
hangs on to that." They may or may not, but when they do, they
have found life right there in the room with them. . . .

    It *is* miraculous. I even have a superstition that has grown on 4
me as the result of invisible hands coming all the time—namely,
that if you do follow your bliss you put yourself on a kind of track
that has been there all the while, waiting for you, and the life that
you ought to be living is the one you are living. When you can
see that, you begin to meet people who are in the field of your
bliss, and they open the doors to you. I say, follow your bliss and
don't be afraid, and doors will open where you didn't know they
were going to be.

1988

The Rival Conceptions of God

C. S. Lewis

I have been asked to tell you what Christians believe, and I am 1
going to begin by telling you one thing that Christians do not
need to believe. If you are a Christian you do not have to believe
that all the other religions are simply wrong all through. If you
are an atheist you do have to believe that the main point in all
the religions of the whole world is simply one huge mistake. If
you are a Christian, you are free to think that all these religions,
even the queerest ones, contain at least some hint of the truth.

When I was an atheist I had to try to persuade myself that most of the human race have always been wrong about the question that mattered to them most; when I became a Christian I was able to take a more liberal view. But, of course, being a Christian does mean thinking that where Christianity differs from other religions, Christianity is right and they are wrong. As in arithmetic—there is only one right answer to a sum, and all other answers are wrong: but some of the wrong answers are much nearer being right than others.

2   The first big division of humanity is into the majority, who believe in some kind of God or gods, and the minority who do not. On this point, Christianity lines up with the majority—lines up with ancient Greeks and Romans, modern savages, Stoics, Platonists, Hindus, Mohammedans, etc., against the modern Western European materialist.

3   Now I go on to the next big division. People who all believe in God can be divided according to the sort of God they believe in. There are two very different ideas on this subject. One of them is the idea that He is beyond good and evil. We humans call one thing good and another thing bad. But according to some people that is merely our human point of view. These people would say that the wiser you become the less you would want to call anything good or bad, and the more clearly you would see that everything is good in one way and bad in another, and that nothing could have been different. Consequently, these people think that long before you got anywhere near the divine point of view the distinction would have disappeared altogether. We call a cancer bad, they would say, because it kills a man; but you might just as well call a successful surgeon bad because he kills a cancer. It all depends on the point of view. The other and opposite idea is that God is quite definitely "good" or "righteous," a God who takes sides, who loves love and hates hatred, who wants us to behave in one way and not in another. The first of these views—the one that thinks God beyond good and evil—is called Pantheism. It was held by the great Prussian philosopher Hegel and, as far as I can understand them, by the Hindus. The other view is held by Jews, Mohammedans and Christians.

4   And with this big difference between Pantheism and the Christian idea of God, there usually goes another. Pantheists

usually believe that God, so to speak, animates the universe as you animate your body: that the universe almost *is* God, so that if it did not exist He would not exist either, and anything you find in the universe is a part of God. The Christian idea is quite different. They think God invented and made the universe—like a man making a picture or composing a tune. A painter is not a picture, and he does not die if his picture is destroyed. You may say, "He's put a lot of himself into it," but you only mean that all its beauty and interest has come out of his head. His skill is not in the picture in the same way that it is in his head, or even in his hands. I expect you see how this difference between Pantheists and Christians hangs together with the other one. If you do not take the distinction between good and bad very seriously, then it is easy to say that anything you find in this world is a part of God. But, of course, if you think some things really bad, and God really good, then you cannot talk like that. You must believe that God is separate from the world and that some of the things we see in it are contrary to His will. Confronted with a cancer or a slum the Pantheist can say, "If you could only see it from the divine point of view, you would realize that this also is God." The Christian replies, "Don't talk damned nonsense."[1] For Christianity is a fighting religion. It thinks God made the world—that space and time, heat and cold, and all the colors and tastes, and all the animals and vegetables, are things that God "made up out of His head" as a man makes up a story. But it also thinks that a great many things have gone wrong with the world that God made and that God insists, and insists very loudly, on our putting them right again.

And, of course, that raises a very big question. If a good God ₅ made the world why has it gone wrong? And for many years I simply refused to listen to the Christian answers to this question, because I kept on feeling "whatever you say, and however clever your arguments are, isn't it much simpler and easier to say that

---

[1] One listener complained of the word *damned* as frivolous swearing. But I mean exactly what I say—nonsense that is *damned* is under God's curse, and will (apart from God's grace) lead those who believe it to eternal death. [This note is the author's.]

the world was not made by any intelligent power? Aren't all your arguments simply a complicated attempt to avoid the obvious?" But then that threw me back into another difficulty.

6   My argument against God was that the universe seemed so cruel and unjust. But how had I got this idea of *just* and *unjust?* A man does not call a line crooked unless he has some idea of a straight line. What was I comparing this universe with when I called it unjust? If the whole show was bad and senseless from A to Z, so to speak, why did I, who was supposed to be part of the show, find myself in such violent reaction against it? A man feels wet when he falls into water, because man is not a water animal: a fish would not feel wet. Of course I could have given up my idea of justice by saying it was nothing but a private idea of my own. But if I did that, then my argument against God collapsed too—for the argument depended on saying that the world was really unjust, not simply that it did not happen to please my private fancies. Thus in the very act of trying to prove that God did not exist—in other words, that the whole of reality was senseless— I found I was forced to assume that one part of reality—namely my idea of justice—was full of sense. Consequently atheism turns out to be too simple. If the whole universe has no meaning, we should never have found out that it has no meaning: just as, if there were no light in the universe and therefore no creature with eyes, we should never know it was dark. *Dark* would be without meaning.

1952

The Mystery of Zen

Gilbert Highet

1 The mind need never stop growing. Indeed, one of the few expe- riences which never pall is the experience of watching one's own mind, and observing how it produces new interests, responds to new stimuli, and develops new thoughts, apparently without effort and almost independently of one's own conscious control.

I have seen this happen to myself a hundred times; and every time it happens again, I am equally fascinated and astonished.

Some years ago a publisher sent me a little book for review. 2 I read it, and decided it was too remote from my main interests and too highly specialized. It was a brief account of how a young German philosopher living in Japan had learned how to shoot with a bow and arrow, and how this training had made it possible for him to understand the esoteric doctrines of the Zen sect of Buddhism. Really, what could be more alien to my own life, and to that of everyone I knew, than Zen Buddhism and Japanese archery? So I thought, and put the book away.

Yet I did not forget it. It was well written, and translated into 3 good English. It was delightfully short, and implied much more than it said. Although its theme was extremely odd, it was at least highly individual; I had never read anything like it before or since. It remained in my mind. Its name was *Zen in the Art of Archery*, its author Eugen Herrigel, its publisher Pantheon of New York. One day I took it off the shelf and read it again; this time it seemed even stranger than before and even more unforgettable. Now it began to cohere with other interests of mine. Something I had read of the Japanese art of flower arrangement seemed to connect with it; and then, when I wrote an essay on the peculiar Japanese poems called *haiku*, other links began to grow. Finally I had to read the book once more with care, and to go through some other works which illuminated the same subject. I am still grappling with the theme; I have not got anywhere near understanding it fully; but I have learned a good deal, and I am grateful to the little book which refused to be forgotten.

The author, a German philosopher, got a job teaching philos- 4 ophy at the University of Tokyo (apparently between the wars), and he did what Germans in foreign countries do not usually do: he determined to adapt himself and to learn from his hosts. In particular, he had always been interested in mysticism—which, for every earnest philosopher, poses a problem that is all the more inescapable because it is virtually insoluble. Zen Buddhism is not the only mystical doctrine to be found in the East, but it is one of the most highly developed and certainly one of the most difficult to approach. Herrigel knew that there were scarcely any books which did more than skirt the edge of the subject, and that the best of all books on Zen (those by the philosopher D. T. Suzuki) constantly emphasize that Zen can never be learned from books, can never be studied as we can study other disciplines such as logic or mathematics. Therefore he began to look for a Japanese thinker who could teach him directly.

5   At once he met with embarrassed refusals. His Japanese friends explained that he would gain nothing from trying to discuss Zen as a philosopher, that its theories could not be spread out for analysis by a detached mind, and in fact that the normal relationship of teacher and pupil simply did not exist within the sect, because the Zen masters felt it useless to explain things stage by stage and to argue about the various possible interpretations of their doctrine. Herrigel had read enough to be prepared for this. He replied that he did not want to dissect the teachings of the school, because he knew that would be useless. He wanted to become a Zen mystic himself. (This was highly intelligent of him. No one could really penetrate into Christian mysticism without being a devout Christian; no one could appreciate Hindu mystical doctrine without accepting the Hindu view of the universe.) At this, Herrigel's Japanese friends were more forthcoming. They told him that the best way, indeed the only way, for a European to approach Zen mysticism was to learn one of the arts which exemplified it. He was a fairly good rifle shot, so he determined to learn archery; and his wife cooperated with him by taking lessons in painting and flower arrangement. How any philosopher could investigate a mystical doctrine by learning to shoot with a bow and arrow and watching his wife arrange flowers, Herrigel did not ask. He had good sense.

6   A Zen master who was a teacher of archery agreed to take him as a pupil. The lessons lasted six years, during which he practiced every single day. There are many difficult courses of instruction in the world: the Jesuits, violin virtuosi, Talmudic scholars, all have long and hard training, which in one sense never comes to an end; but Herrigel's training in archery equaled them all in intensity. If I were trying to learn archery, I should expect to begin by looking at a target and shooting arrows at it. He was not even allowed to aim at a target for the first four years. He had to begin by learning how to hold the bow and arrow, and then how to release the arrow; this took ages. The Japanese bow is not like our

sporting bow, and the stance of the archer in Japan is different from ours. We hold the bow at shoulder level, stretch our left arm out ahead, pull the string and the nocked arrow to a point either below the chin or sometimes past the right ear, and then shoot. The Japanese hold the bow above the head, and then pull the hands apart to left and right until the left hand comes down to eye level and the right hand comes to rest above the right shoulder; then there is a pause, during which the bow is held at full stretch, with the tip of the three-foot arrow projecting only a few inches beyond the bow; after that, the arrow is loosed. When Herrigel tried this, even without aiming, he found it was almost impossible. His hands trembled. His legs stiffened and grew cramped. His breathing became labored. And of course he could not possibly aim. Week after week he practiced this, with the Master watching him carefully and correcting his strained attitude; week after week he made no progress whatever. Finally he gave up and told his teacher that he could not learn: it was absolutely impossible for him to draw the bow and loose the arrow.

To his astonishment, the Master agreed. He said, "Certainly 7 you cannot. It is because you are not breathing correctly. You must learn to breathe in a steady rhythm, keeping your lungs full most of the time, and drawing in one rapid inspiration with each stage of the process, as you grasp the bow, fit the arrow, raise the bow, draw, pause, and loose the shot. If you do, you will both grow stronger and be able to relax." To prove this, he himself drew his massive bow and told his pupil to feel the muscles of his arms: they were perfectly relaxed, as though he were doing no work whatever.

Herrigel now started breathing exercises; after some time he 8 combined the new rhythm of breathing with the actions of drawing and shooting; and, much to his astonishment, he found that the whole thing, after this complicated process, had become much easier. Or rather, not easier, but different. At times it became quite unconscious. He says himself that he felt he was not breathing, but being breathed; and in time he felt that the occasional shot was not being dispatched by him, but shooting itself. The bow and arrow were in charge; he had become merely a part of them.

9   All this time, of course, Herrigel did not even attempt to discuss Zen doctrine with his Master. No doubt he knew that he was
approaching it, but he concentrated solely on learning how to
shoot. Every stage which he surmounted appeared to lead to
another stage even more difficult. It took him months to learn how
to loosen the bowstring. The problem was this. If he gripped the
string and arrowhead tightly, either he froze, so that his hands
were slowly pulled together and the shot was wasted, or else he
jerked, so that the arrow flew up into the air or down into the
ground; and if he was relaxed, then the bowstring and arrow simply *leaked* out of his grasp before he could reach full stretch, and
the arrow went nowhere. He explained this problem to the Master.
The Master understood perfectly well. He replied, "You must hold
the drawn bowstring like a child holding a grownup's finger. You
know how firmly a child grips; and yet when it lets go, there is
not the slightest jerk—because the child does not think of itself, it
is not self-conscious, it does not say, 'I will now let go and do
something else,' it merely acts instinctively. That is what you must
learn to do. Practice, practice, and practice, and then the string
will loose itself at the right moment. The shot will come as effortlessly as snow slipping from a leaf." Day after day, week after
week, month after month, Herrigel practiced this; and then, after
one shot, the Master suddenly bowed and broke off the lesson.
He said "Just then it shot. Not you, but *it*." And gradually thereafter more and more right shots achieved themselves; the young
philosopher forgot himself, forgot that he was learning archery for
some other purpose, forgot even that he was practicing archery,
and became part of that unconsciously active complex, the bow,
the string, the arrow, and the man.

10   Next came the target. After four years, Herrigel was allowed
to shoot at the target. But he was strictly forbidden to aim at it.
The Master explained that even he himself did not aim; and
indeed, when he shot, he was so absorbed in the act, so selfless
and unanxious, that his eyes were almost closed. It was difficult,
almost impossible, for Herrigel to believe that such shooting could
ever be effective; and he risked insulting the Master by suggesting that he ought to be able to hit the target blindfolded. But the
Master accepted the challenge, That night, after a cup of tea and
long meditation, he went into the archery hall, put on the lights

at one end and left the target perfectly dark, with only a thin taper
burning in front of it. Then, with habitual grace and precision, and
with that strange, almost sleepwalking, selfless confidence that is
the heart of Zen, he shot two arrows into the darkness. Herrigel
went out to collect them. He found that the first had gone to
the heart of the bull's eye, and that the second had actually hit
the first arrow and splintered it. The Master showed no pride. He
said, "Perhaps, with unconscious memory of the position of the
target, *I* shot the first arrow; but the second arrow? *It* shot the second arrow, and *it* brought it to the center of the target."

At last Herrigel began to understand. His progress became 11
faster and faster; easier, too. Perfect shots (perfect because perfectly unconscious) occurred at almost every lesson; and finally,
after six years of incessant training, in a public display he was
awarded the diploma. He needed no further instruction: he had
himself become a Master. His wife meanwhile had become expert
both in painting and in the arrangement of flowers—two of the
finest of Japanese arts. (I wish she could be persuaded to write a
companion volume, called *Zen in the Art of Flower Arrangement*—
it would have a wider general appeal than her husband's work.)
I gather also from a hint or two in his book that she had taken
part in the archery lessons. During one of the most difficult periods in Herrigel's training, when his Master had practically refused
to continue teaching him—because Herrigel had tried to cheat by
consciously opening his hand at the moment of loosing the
arrow—his wife had advised him against that solution, and sym-
pathized with him when it was rejected. She in her own way had
learned more quickly than he, and reached the final point together
with him. All their effort had not been in vain: Herrigel and his
wife had really acquired a new and valuable kind of wisdom.
Only at this point, when he was about to abandon his lessons forever, did his Master treat him almost as an equal and hint at the
innermost doctrines of Zen Buddhism. Only hints he gave; and
yet, for the young philosopher who had now become a mystic,
they were enough. Herrigel understood the doctrine, not with his
logical mind, but with his entire being. He at any rate had solved
the mystery of Zen.

Without going through a course of training as absorbing and 12
as complete as Herrigel's, we can probably never penetrate the

mystery. The doctrine of Zen cannot be analyzed from without: it must be lived.

13   But although it cannot be analyzed, it can be hinted at. All the hints that the adherents of this creed give us are interesting. Many are fantastic; some are practically incomprehensible, and yet unforgettable. Put together, they take us toward a way of life which is utterly impossible for westerners living in a western world, and nevertheless has a deep fascination and contains some values which we must respect.

14   The word Zen means "meditation." (It is the Japanese word, corresponding to the Chinese Ch'an and the Hindu Dhyana.) It is the central idea of a special sect of Buddhism which flourished in China during the Sung period (between A.D. 1000 and 1300) and entered Japan in the twelfth century. Without knowing much about it, we might be certain that the Zen sect was a worthy and noble one, because it produced a quantity of highly distinguished art, specifically painting. And if we knew anything about Buddhism itself, we might say that Zen goes closer than other sects to the heart of Buddha's teaching: because Buddha was trying to found, not a religion with temples and rituals, but a way of life based on meditation. However, there is something eccentric about the Zen life which is hard to trace in Buddha's teaching; there is an active energy which he did not admire, there is a rough grasp on reality which he himself eschewed, there is something like a sense of humor, which he rarely displayed. The gravity and serenity of the Indian preacher are transformed, in Zen, to the earthy liveliness of Chinese and Japanese sages. The lotus brooding calmly on the water has turned into a knotted tree covered with spring blossoms.

15   In this sense, "meditation" does not mean what we usually think of when we say a philosopher meditates: analysis of reality, a long-sustained effort to solve problems of religion and ethics, the logical dissection of the universe. It means something not divisive, but whole; not schematic, but organic; not long-drawn-out, but immediate. It means something more like our words "intuition" and "realization." It means a way of life in which there is no division between thought and action; none of the painful gulf, so well known to all of us, between the unconscious and the conscious mind; and no absolute distinction between the self and the external

world, even between the various parts of the external world and the whole.

When the German philosopher took six years of lessons in archery in order to approach the mystical significance of Zen, he was not given direct philosophical instruction. He was merely shown how to breathe, how to hold and loose the bowstring, and finally how to shoot in such a way that the bow and arrow used him as an instrument. There are many such stories about Zen teachers. The strangest I know is one about a fencing master who undertook to train a young man in the art of the sword. The relationship of teacher and pupil is very important, almost sacred, in the Far East; and the pupil hardly ever thinks of leaving a master or objecting to his methods, however extraordinary they may seem. Therefore this young fellow did not at first object when he was made to act as a servant, drawing water, sweeping floors, gathering wood for the fire, and cooking. But after some time he asked for more direct instruction. The master agreed to give it, but produced no swords. The routine went on just as before, except that every now and then the master would strike the young man with a stick. No matter what he was doing, sweeping the floor or weeding in the garden, a blow would descend on him apparently out of nowhere; he had always to be on the alert, and yet he was constantly receiving unexpected cracks on the head or shoulders. After some months of this, he saw his master stooping over a boiling pot full of vegetables; and he thought he would have his revenge. Silently he lifted a stick and brought it down; but without any effort, without even a glance in his direction, his master parried the blow with the lid of the cooking pot. At last, the pupil began to understand the instinctive alertness, the effortless perception and avoidance of danger, in which his master had been training him. As soon as he had achieved it, it was child's play for him to learn the management of the sword: he could parry every cut and turn every slash without anxiety, until his opponent, exhausted, left an opening for his counterattack. (The same principle was used by the elderly samurai for selecting his comrades in the Japanese motion picture *The Magnificent Seven*.)

These stories show that Zen meditation does not mean sitting and thinking. On the contrary, it means acting with as little thought as possible. The fencing master trained his pupil to guard against every attack with the same immediate, instinctive rapidity with which our eyelid closes over our eye when something threatens it. His work was aimed at breaking down the wall between thought and act, at completely fusing body and senses and mind so that they might all work together rapidly and effortlessly. When a Zen artist draws a picture, he does it in a rhythm almost the exact reverse of that which is followed by a Western artist. We begin by blocking out the design and then filling in the details, usually working more and more slowly as we approach the completion of the picture. The Zen artist sits down very calmly; examines his brush carefully; prepares his own ink; smoothes out the paper on which he will work; falls into a profound silent ecstasy of contemplation—during which he does not think anxiously of various details, composition, brushwork, shades of tone, but rather attempts to become the vehicle through which the subject can express itself in painting; and then, very quickly and almost unconsciously, with sure effortless strokes, draws a picture containing the fewest and most effective lines. Most of the paper is left blank; only the essential is depicted, and that not completely. One long curving line will be enough to show a mountainside; seven streaks will become a group of bamboos bending in the wind; and yet, though technically incomplete, such pictures are unforgettably clear. They show the heart of reality.

18   All this we can sympathize with, because we can see the results. The young swordsman learns how to fence. The intuitional painter produces a fine picture. But the hardest thing for us to appreciate is that the Zen masters refuse to teach philosophy or religion directly, and deny logic. In fact, they despise logic as an artificial distortion of reality. Many philosophical teachers are difficult to understand because they analyze profound problems with subtle intricacy: such is Aristotle in his *Metaphysics*. Many mystical writers are difficult to understand because, as they themselves admit, they are attempting to use words to describe experiences which are too abstruse for words, so that they have to fall back on imagery and analogy, which they themselves recognize to be poor media, far coarser than the realities with which they have been in contact. But the Zen teachers seem to deny the power of language and thought altogether. For example, if you ask a Zen master what is the ultimate reality, he will

answer, without the slightest hesitation, "The bamboo grove at the foot of the hill" or "A branch of plum blossom." Apparently he means that these things, which we can see instantly without effort, or imagine in the flash of a second, are real with the ultimate reality; that nothing is more real than these; and that we ought to grasp ultimates as we grasp simple immediates. A Chinese master was once asked the central question, "What is the Buddha?" He said nothing whatever, but held out his index finger. What did he mean? It is hard to explain; but apparently he meant "Here. Now. Look and realize with the effortlessness of seeing. Do not try to use words. Do not think. Make no efforts toward withdrawal from the world. Expect no sublime ecstasies. Live. All *that* is the ultimate reality, and it can be understood from the motion of a finger as well as from the execution of any complex ritual, from any subtle argument, or from the circling of the starry universe."

In making that gesture, the master was copying the Buddha   19 himself, who once delivered a sermon which is famous, but was hardly understood by his pupils at the time. Without saying a word, he held up a flower and showed it to the gathering. One man, one alone, knew what he meant. The gesture became renowned as the Flower Sermon.

In the annals of Zen there are many cryptic answers to the   20 final question, "What is the Buddha?"—which in our terms means "What is the meaning of life? What is truly real?" For example, one master, when asked "What is the Buddha?" replied, "Your name is Yecho." Another said, "Even the finest artist cannot paint him." Another said, "No nonsense here." And another answered, "The mouth is the gate of woe." My favorite story is about the monk who said to a Master, "Has a dog Buddha-nature too?" The Master replied, "Wu"—which is what the dog himself would have said.

Now, some critics might attack Zen by saying that this is the   21 creed of a savage or an animal. The adherents of Zen would deny that—or more probably they would ignore the criticism, or make some cryptic remark which meant that it was pointless. Their position—if they could ever be persuaded to put it into words— would be this. An animal is instinctively in touch with reality, and so far is living rightly, but it has never had a mind and so cannot perceive the Whole, only that part with which it is in touch. The philosopher sees both the Whole and the parts, and enjoys them all. As for the savage, he exists only through the group; he feels himself as part of a war party or a ceremonial dance team or a ploughing-and-sowing group or the Snake clan; he is not truly an individual at all, and therefore is less than fully human. Zen has at its heart an inner solitude; its aim is to teach us to live, as in the last resort we do all have to live, alone.

22   A more dangerous criticism of Zen would be that it is nihilism, that its purpose is to abolish thought altogether. (This criticism is handled, but not fully met, by the great Zen authority Suzuki in his *Introduction to Zen Buddhism.*) It can hardly be completely confuted, for after all the central doctrine of Buddhism is— Nothingness. And many of the sayings of Zen masters are truly nihilistic. The first patriarch of the sect in China was asked by the emperor what was the ultimate and holiest principle of Buddhism. He replied, "Vast emptiness, and nothing holy in it." Another who was asked the searching question "Where is the abiding place for the mind?" answered, "Not in this dualism of good and evil, being and nonbeing, thought and matter." In fact, thought is an activity which divides. It analyzes, it makes distinctions, it criticizes, it judges, it breaks reality into groups and classes and individuals. The aim of Zen is to abolish that kind of thinking, and to substitute—not unconsciousness, which would be death, but a consciousness that does not analyze but experiences life directly. Although it has no prescribed prayers, no sacred scriptures, no ceremonial rites, no personal god, and no interest in the soul's future destination, Zen is a religion rather than a philosophy. Jung points out that its aim is to produce a religious conversion, a "transformation": and he adds, "The transformation process is incommensurable with intellect." Thought is always interesting, but often painful; Zen is calm and painless. Thought is incomplete; Zen enlightenment brings a sense of completeness. Thought is a process; Zen illumination is a state. But it is a state which cannot be defined. In the Buddhist scriptures there is a dialogue between a master and a pupil in which the pupil tries to discover the exact meaning of such a state. The master says to him, "If a fire were blazing in front of you, would you know that it was blazing?"

"Yes, master."   23
"And would you know the reason for its blazing?"   24
"Yes, because it had a supply of grass and sticks."   25
"And would you know if it were to go out?"   26
"Yes, master."   27
"And on its going out, would you know where the fire had   28
gone? To the east, to the west, to the north, or to the south?"

"The question does not apply, master. For the fire blazed   29
because it had a supply of grass and sticks. When it had consumed this and had no other fuel, then it went out."

"In the same way," replies the master, "no question will apply   30
to the meaning of Nirvana, and no statement will explain it."

Such, then, neither happy nor unhappy but beyond all divi-   31
sive description, is the condition which students of Zen strive to
attain. Small wonder that they can scarcely explain it to us, the
unilluminated.

The Culture of Disbelief

Stephen L. Carter

Contemporary American politics faces few greater dilemmas than   1
deciding how to deal with the resurgence of religious belief. On
the one hand, American ideology cherishes religion, as it does all
matters of private conscience, which is why we justly celebrate a
strong tradition against state interference with private religious
choice. At the same time, many political leaders, commentators,
scholars, and voters are coming to view any religious element in
public moral discourse as a tool of the radical right for reshaping
American society. But the effort to banish religion for politics' sake
has led us astray: In our sensible zeal to keep religion from dom-
inating our politics, we have created a political and legal culture
that presses the religiously faithful to be other than themselves,
to act publicly, and sometimes privately as well, as though their
faith does not matter to them.

Recently, a national magazine devoted its cover story to an   2
investigation of prayer: how many people pray, how often, why,

how, and for what. A few weeks later came the inevitable letter from a disgruntled reader, wanting to know why so much space had been dedicated to such nonsense.[1]

3   Statistically, the letter writer was in the minority: by the magazine's figures, better than nine out of ten Americans believe in God and some four out of five pray regularly.[2] Politically and culturally, however, the writer was in the American mainstream, for those who do pray regularly—indeed, those who believe in God—are encouraged to keep it a secret, and often a shameful one at that. Aside from the ritual appeals to God that are expected of our politicians, for Americans to take their religions seriously, to treat them as ordained rather than chosen, is to risk assignment to the lunatic fringe.

4   Yet religion matters to people, and matters a lot. Surveys indicate that Americans are far more likely to believe in God and to attend worship services regularly than any other people in the Western world. True, nobody prays on prime-time television unless religion is a part of the plot, but strong majorities of citizens tell pollsters that their religious beliefs are of great importance to them in their daily lives. Even though some popular histories wrongly assert the contrary, the best evidence is that this deep religiosity has always been a facet of the American character and that it has grown consistently through the nation's history.[3] And today, to the frustration of many opinion leaders in both the legal and political cultures, religion, as a moral force and perhaps a political one too, is surging. Unfortunately, in our public life, we prefer to pretend that it is not.

5   Consider the following events:

- When Hillary Rodham Clinton was seen wearing a cross around her neck at some of the public events surrounding

---

[1]"Talking to God," *Newsweek,* Jan. 6, 1992, p. 38; Letter to the Editor, *Newsweek,* Jan. 1992, p. 10. The letter called the article a "theocratic text masquerading as a news article." [This and subsequent notes in the selection are the author's.]

[2]"Talking to God," p. 39. The most recent Gallup data indicate that 96 percent of Americans say they believe in God, including 82 percent who describe themselves as Christians (56 percent Protestant, 25 percent Roman Catholic) and 2 percent who describe themselves as Jewish. (No other faith accounted for as much as 1 percent.) See Ari L. Goldman, "Religion Notes," *New York Times,* Feb. 27, 1993, p. 9.

[3]See, for example, Jon Butler, *Awash in a Sea of Faith* (Cambridge: Harvard University Press, 1990).

her husband's inauguration as President of the United States, many observers were aghast, and one television commentator asked whether it was appropriate for the First Lady to display so openly a religious symbol. But if the First Lady can't do it, then certainly the President can't do it, which would bar from ever holding the office an Orthodox Jew under a religious compulsion to wear a yarmulke.

- Back in the mid-1980s, the magazine *Sojourners*—published by politically liberal Christian evangelicals—found itself in the unaccustomed position of defending the conservative evangelist Pat Robertson against secular liberals who, a writer in the magazine sighed, "see[m] to consider Robertson a dangerous neanderthal because he happens to believe that God can heal diseases."[4] The point is that the editors of *Sojourners*, who are no great admirers of Robertson, also believe that God can heal diseases. So do tens of millions of Americans. But they are not supposed to say so.

- In the early 1980s, the state of New York adopted legislation that, in effect, requires an Orthodox Jewish husband seeking a divorce to give his wife a *get*—a religious divorce— without which she cannot remarry under Jewish law. Civil libertarians attacked the statute as unconstitutional. Said one critic, the "barriers to remarriage erected by religious law . . . only exist in the minds of those who believe in the religion."[5] If the barriers are religious, it seems, then they are not real barriers, they are "only" in the woman's mind— perhaps even a figment of the imagination.

- When the Supreme Court of the United States, ostensibly the final refuge of religious freedom, struck down a Connecticut statute requiring employers to make efforts to allow their employees to observe the sabbath, one Justice observed that the sabbath should not be singled out because all employees would like to have "the right to select the day of the week

[4]Collum, "The Kingdom and the Power," *Sojourners*, Nov. 1986, p. 4. Some 82 percent of Americans believe that God performs miracles today. George Gallup, Jr., and Jim Castelli, *The People's Religion: American Faith in the '90s* (New York: Macmillan, 1989), p. 58.

[5]Madeline Kochen, "Constitutional Implications of New York's 'Get' Statute," *New York Law Journal*, Oct. 27, 1983, p. 32.

in which to refrain from labor."[6] Sounds good, except that, as one scholar has noted, "It would come as some surprise to a devout Jew to find that he has 'selected the day of the week in which to refrain from labor,' since the Jewish people have been under the impression for some 3,000 years that this choice was made by God."[7] If the sabbath is just another day off, then religious choice is essentially arbitrary and unimportant; so if one sabbath day is inconvenient, the religiously devout employee can just choose another.

- When President Ronald Reagan told religious broadcasters in 1983 that all laws passed since biblical times "have not improved on the Ten Commandments one bit," which might once have been considered a pardonable piece of rhetorical license, he was excoriated by political pundits, including one who charged angrily that Reagan was giving "short shrift to the secular laws and institutions that a president is charged with protecting."[8] And as for the millions of Americans who consider the Ten Commandments the fundaments on which they build their lives, well, they are no doubt subversive of these same institutions.

6   These examples share a common rhetoric that refuses to accept the notion that rational, public-spirited people can take religion seriously. It might be argued that such cases as these involve threats to the separation of church and state, the durable and vital doctrine that shields our public institutions from religious domination and our religious institutions from government domination. I am a great supporter of the separation of church and state . . . but that is not what these examples are about.

7   What matters about these examples is the *language* chosen to make the points. In each example, as in many more that I shall discuss, one sees a trend in our political and legal cultures toward treating religious beliefs as arbitrary and unimportant, a trend

---

[6]*Estate of Thornton v. Caldor, Inc.*, 472 U.S. 703, 711 (1985) (Justice Sandra Day O'Connor, concurring).

[7]Michael W. McConnell, "Religious Freedom at a Crossroads," *University of Chicago Law Review* 59 (1992):115.

[8]Robert G. Kaiser, "Hypocrisy: This Puffed-Up Piety Is Perfectly Preposterous," *Washington Post*, March 18, 1984, p. C1.

supported by a rhetoric that implies that there is something wrong with religious devotion. More and more, our culture seems to take the position that believing deeply in the tenets of one's faith represents a kind of mystical irrationality, something that thoughtful, public-spirited American citizens would do better to avoid. If you must worship your God, the lesson runs, at least have the courtesy to disbelieve in the power of prayer; if you must observe your sabbath, have the good sense to understand that it is just like any other day off from work.

The rhetoric matters. A few years ago, my wife and I were 8 startled by a teaser for a story on a network news program, which asked what was meant to be a provocative question: "When is a church more than just a place of worship?" For those to whom worship is significant, the subtle arrangement of words is arresting: *more than* suggests that what follows ("just a place of worship") is somewhere well down the scale of interesting or useful human activities, and certainly that whatever the story is about is *more than* worship; and *just*—suggests that what follows ("place of worship") is rather small potatoes.

A friend tells the story of how he showed his résumé to an 9 executive search consultant—in the jargon, a corporate head-hunter—who told him crisply that if he was serious about moving ahead in the business world, he should remove from the résumé any mention of his involvement with a social welfare organization that was connected with a church, but not one of the genteel mainstream denominations. Otherwise, she explained, a potential employer might think him a religious fanatic.

How did we reach this disturbing pass, when our culture 10 teaches that religion is not to be taken seriously, even by those who profess to believe in it? Some observers suggest that the key moment was the Enlightenment, when the Western tradition sought to sever the link between religion and authority. One of the playwright Tom Stoppard's characters observes that there came "a calendar date—*a moment*—when the onus of proof passed from the atheist to the believer, when, quite suddenly, the noes had it."[9] To

---

[9]Tom Stoppard, *Jumpers*, quoted in Jeffrey Stout, *The Flight from Authority: Religion, Morality and the Quest for Autonomy* (South Bend, Indiana: University of Notre Dame Press, 1981), p. 150.

which the philosopher Jeffrey Stout appends the following comment: "If so, it was not a matter of majority rule."[10] Maybe not—but a strong undercurrent of contemporary American politics holds that religion must be kept in its proper place and, still more, in proper perspective. There are, we are taught by our opinion leaders, religious matters and important matters, and disaster arises when we confuse the two. Rationality, it seems, consists in getting one's priorities straight. (Ignore your religious law and marry at leisure.) Small wonder, then, that we have recently been treated to a book, coauthored by two therapists, one of them an ordained minister, arguing that those who would put aside, say, the needs of their families in order to serve their religions are suffering from a malady the authors called "toxic faith"—for no normal person, evidently, would sacrifice the things that most of us hold dear just because of a belief that God so intended it.[11] (One wonders how the authors would have judged the toxicity of the faith of Jesus, Moses, or Mohammed.)

11   We are trying, here in America, to strike an awkward but necessary balance, one that seems more and more difficult with each passing year. On the one hand, a magnificent respect for freedom of conscience, including the freedom of religious belief, runs deep in our political ideology. On the other hand, our understandable fear of religious domination of politics presses us, in our public personas, to be wary of those who take their religion too seriously. This public balance reflects our private selves. We are one of the most religious nations on earth, in the sense that we have a deeply religious citizenry; but we are also perhaps the most zealous in guarding our public institutions against explicit religious influences. One result is that we often ask our citizens to split their public and private selves, telling them in effect that it is fine to be religious in private, but there is something askew when those private beliefs become the basis for public action.

12   We teach college freshmen that the Protestant Reformation began the process of freeing the church from the state, thus creating

[10]Ibid.
[11]Stephen Arterburn and Jack Felton, *Toxic Faith: Understanding and Overcoming Religious Addiction* (Nashville, Tenn.: Oliver-Nelson Books, 1991).

the possibility of a powerful independent moral force in society. As defenders of the separation of church and state have argued for centuries, autonomous religions play a vital role as free critics of the institutions of secular society. But our public culture more and more prefers religion as something without political significance, less an independent moral force than a quietly irrelevant moralizer, never heard, rarely seen. "[T]he public sphere," writes the theologian Martin Marty, "does not welcome explicit Reformed witness—or any other particularized Christian witness."[12] Or, for that matter, any religious witness at all.

Religions that most need protection seem to receive it least. [13] Contemporary America is not likely to enact legislation aimed at curbing the mainstream Protestant, Roman Catholic, or Jewish faiths. But Native Americans, having once been hounded from their lands, are now hounded from their religions, with the complicity of a Supreme Court untroubled when sacred lands are taken for road building or when Native Americans under a bona fide religious compulsion to use *peyote* in their rituals are punished under state antidrug regulations.[13] (Imagine the brouhaha if New York City were to try to take St. Patrick's Cathedral by eminent domain to build a new convention center, or if Kansas, a dry state, were to outlaw the religious use of wine.) And airports, backed by the Supreme Court, are happy to restrict solicitation by devotees of Krishna Consciousness, which travelers, including this one, find irritating.[14] (Picture the response should the airports try to regulate the wearing of crucifixes or yarmulkes on similar grounds of irritation.)

The problem goes well beyond our society's treatment of [14] those who simply want freedom to worship in ways that most Americans find troubling. An analogous difficulty is posed by those whose religious convictions move them to action in the public arena. Too often, our rhetoric treats the religious impulse to public action as presumptively wicked—indeed, as necessarily oppressive. But this is historically bizarre. Every time people

---

[12]Martin E. Marty, "Reformed America and America Reformed," *Reformed Journal* (March 1989): 8, 10.
[13]*Employment Division, Department of Human Resources v. Smith*, 494 U.S. 872 (1990).
[14]*International Society for Krishna Consciousness v. Lee*, 112 S. Ct. 2701 (1992).

whose vision of God's will moves them to oppose abortion rights are excoriated for purportedly trying to impose their religious views on others, equal calumny is implicitly heaped upon the mass protest wing of the civil rights movement, which was openly and unashamedly religious in its appeals as it worked to impose its moral vision on, for example, those who would rather segregate their restaurants.

15   One result of this rhetoric is that we often end up fighting the wrong battles. Consider what must in our present day serve as the ultimate example of religion in the service of politics: the 1989 death sentence pronounced by the late Ayatollah Ruhollah Khomeini upon the writer Salman Rushdie for his authorship of *The Satanic Verses*, which was said to blaspheme against Islam. The death sentence is both terrifying and outrageous, and the Ayatollah deserved all the fury lavished upon him for imposing it. Unfortunately, for some critics the facts that the Ayatollah was a religious leader and that the "crime" was a religious one lends the sentence a particular monstrousness; evidently they are under the impression that writers who are murdered for their ideas are choosy about the motivations of their murderers, and that those whose writings led to their executions under, say, Stalin, thanked their lucky stars at the last instant of their lives that Communism was at least godless.

16   To do battle against the death sentence for Salman Rushdie— to battle against the Ayatollah—one should properly fight against official censorship and intimidation, not against religion. We err when we presume that religious motives are likely to be illiberal, and we compound the error when we insist that the devout should keep their religious ideas—whether good or bad—to themselves. We do no credit to the ideal of religious freedom when we talk as though religious belief is something of which public-spirited adults should be ashamed.

17   The First Amendment to the Constitution, often cited as the place where this difficulty is resolved, merely restates it. The First Amendment guarantees the "free exercise" of religion but also prohibits its "establishment" by the government. There may have been times in our history when we as a nation have tilted too far in one direction, allowing too much religious sway over politics. But in late-twentieth-century America, despite some loud fears about the influence of the weak and divided Christian right, we

are upsetting the balance afresh by tilting too far in the other direction—and the courts are assisting in the effort. For example, when a group of Native Americans objected to the Forest Service's plans to allow logging and road building in a national forest area traditionally used by the tribes for sacred rituals, the Supreme Court offered the back of its hand. True, said the Justices, the logging "could have devastating effects on traditional Indian religious practices." But that was just too bad: "government simply could not operate if it were required to satisfy every citizen's religious needs and desires."[15]

A good point: but what, exactly, are the protesting Indians left 18 to do? Presumably, now that their government has decided to destroy the land they use for their sacred rituals, they are free to choose new rituals. Evidently, a small matter like the potential destruction of a religion is no reason to halt a logging project. Moreover, had the government decided instead to prohibit logging in order to preserve the threatened rituals, it is entirely possible that the decision would be challenged as a forbidden entanglement of church and state. Far better for everyone, it seems, for the Native Americans to simply allow their rituals to go quietly into oblivion. Otherwise, they run the risk that somebody will think they actually take their rituals seriously.

THE PRICE OF FAITH

When citizens do act in their public selves as though their faith 19 matters, they risk not only ridicule, but actual punishment. In Colorado, a public school teacher was ordered by his superiors, on pain of disciplinary action, to remove his personal Bible from his desk where students might see it. He was forbidden to read it silently when his students were involved in other activities. He was also told to take away books on Christianity he had added to the classroom library, although books on Native American religious traditions, as well as on the occult, were allowed to remain. A federal appeals court upheld the instruction, explaining that the teacher could not be allowed to create a religious atmosphere in

---

[15]*Lyng v. Northwest Indian Cemetery Protective Association*, 485 U.S. 439 (1988).

the classroom, which, it seems, might happen if the students knew he was a Christian.[16] One wonders what the school, and the courts, might do if, as many Christians do, the teacher came to school on Ash Wednesday with ashes in the shape of a cross imposed on his forehead—would he be required to wash them off? He just might. Early in 1993, a judge required a prosecutor arguing a case on Ash Wednesday to clean the ashes from his forehead, lest the jury be influenced by its knowledge of the prosecutor's religiosity.

20   Or suppose a Jewish teacher were to wear a yarmulke in the classroom. If the school district tried to stop him, it would apparently be acting within its authority. In 1986, after a Jewish Air Force officer was disciplined for wearing a yarmulke while on duty, in violation of a military rule against wearing head-gear indoors, the Supreme Court shrugged: "The desirability of dress regulations in the military is decided by the appropriate military officials," the justices explained, "and they are under no constitutional mandate to abandon their considered professional judgment."[17] The Congress quickly enacted legislation permitting the wearing of religious apparel while in uniform as long as "the wearing of the item would [not] interfere with the performance of the member's military duties," and—interesting caveat—as long as the item is "neat and conservative."[18] Those whose faiths require them to wear dreadlocks and turbans, one supposes, need not apply to serve their country, unless they are prepared to change religions.

21   Consider the matter of religious holidays. One Connecticut town recently warned Jewish students in its public schools that they would be charged with *six* absences if they missed two days instead of the officially allocated one for Yom Kippur, the holiest observance in the Jewish calendar. And Alan Dershowitz of Harvard Law School, in his controversial book *Chutzpah*, castigates Harry Edwards, a Berkeley sociologist, for scheduling an examination on Yom Kippur, when most Jewish students would be absent. According to Dershowitz's account, Edwards answered criticism by saying: "That's how I'm going to operate. If the students don't like it, they can drop the class." For Dershowitz, this was evidence that

---

[16]*Roberts v. Madigan*, 921 F. 2d 1047 (10th Cir. 1990).
[17]*Goldman v. Weinberger*, 475 U.S. 503 (1986).
[18]45 U.S.C. 774, as amended by Pub. L. No. 100-80, Dec. 4, 1987.

"Jewish students [are] second-class citizens in Professor Edwards's classes."[19] Edwards has heatedly denied Dershowitz's description of events, but even if it is accurate, it is possible that Dershowitz has identified the right crime and the wrong villain. The attitude that Dershowitz describes, if it exists, might reflect less a personal prejudice against Jewish students than the society's broader prejudice against religious devotion, a prejudice that masquerades as "neutrality." If Edwards really dared his students to choose between their religion and their grade, and if that meant that he was treating them as second-class citizens, he was still doing no more than the courts have allowed all levels of government to do to one religious group after another—Jews, Christians, Muslims, Sikhs, it matters not at all. The consistent message of modern American society is that whenever the demands of one's religion conflict with what one has to do to get ahead, one is expected to ignore the religious demands and act . . . well . . . rationally.

Consider Jehovah's Witnesses, who believe that a blood trans- 22 fusion from one human being to another violates the biblical prohibition on ingesting blood. To accept the transfusion, many Witnesses believe, is to lose, perhaps forever, the possibility of salvation. As the Witnesses understand God's law, moreover, the issue is not whether the blood transfusion is given against the recipient's will, but whether the recipient is, at the time of the transfusion, actively protesting. This is the reason that Jehovah's Witnesses sometimes try to impede the physical access of medical personnel to an unconscious Witness: lack of consciousness is no defense. This is also the reason that Witnesses try to make the decisions on behalf of their children: a child cannot be trusted to protest adequately.

The machinery of law has not been particularly impressed 23 with these arguments. There are many cases in which the courts have allowed or ordered transfusions to save the lives of unconscious Witnesses, even though the patient might have indicated a desire while conscious not to be transfused.[20] The machinery of

---

[19]Alan M. Dershowitz, *Chutzpah* (Boston: Little, Brown, 1991), pp. 329–30.

[20]In every decided case that I have discovered involving efforts by Jehovah's Witness parents to prevent their children from receiving blood transfusions, the court has allowed the transfusion to proceed in the face of parental objection. I say more about transfusions of children of Witnesses, and about the rights of parents over their children's religious lives, in chapter 11 [of my book].

modern medicine has not been impressed, either, except with the possibility that the Witnesses have gone off the deep end; at least one hospital's protocol apparently requires doctors to refer protesting Witnesses to psychiatrists.[21] Although the formal text of this requirement states as the reason the need to be sure that the Witness knows what he or she is doing, the subtext is a suspicion that the patient was not acting rationally in rejecting medical advice for religious reasons. After all, there is no protocol for packing *consenting* patients off to see the psychiatrist. But then, patients who consent to blood transfusions are presumably acting rationally. Perhaps, with a bit of gentle persuasion, the dissenting Witness can be made to act rationally too—even if it means giving up an important tenet of the religion.

24   And therein lies the trouble. In contemporary American culture, the religions are more and more treated as just passing beliefs—almost as fads, older, stuffier, less liberal versions of so-called New Age—rather than as the fundaments upon which the devout build their lives. (The noes have it!) And if religions *are* fundamental, well, too bad—at least if they're the wrong fundaments— if they're inconvenient, give them up! If you can't remarry because you have the *wrong* religious belief, well, hey, believe something else! If you can't take your exam because of a Holy Day, get a new Holy Day! If the government decides to destroy your sacred lands, just make some other lands sacred! If you must go to work on your sabbath, it's no big deal! It's just a day off! Pick a different one! If you can't have a blood transfusion because you think God forbids it, no problem! Get a new God! And through all of this trivializing rhetoric runs the subtle but unmistakable message: pray if you like, worship if you must, but whatever you do, do not on any account take your religion seriously.

1993

---

[21]See Ruth Macklin, "The Inner Workings of an Ethics Committee: Latest Battle over Jehovah's Witnesses," *Hastings Center Report* 18 (February/March 1988): 15.

Chapter 4

Philosophy and Ethics

The Value of Philosophy

Bertrand Russell

Having now come to the end of our brief and very incomplete 1
review of the problems of philosophy, it will be well to consider,
in conclusion, what is the value of philosophy and why it ought
to be studied. It is "the" more necessary to consider this question,
in view of the fact that many men, under the influence of science
or of practical affairs, are inclined to doubt whether philosophy
is anything better than innocent but useless trifling, hair-splitting
distinctions, and controversies on matters concerning which knowledge is impossible.

This view of philosophy appears to result, partly from a wrong 2
conception of the ends of life, partly from a wrong conception of
the kind of goods which philosophy strives to achieve. Physical science, through the medium of inventions, is useful to innumerable
people who are wholly ignorant of it; thus the study of physical
science is to be recommended, not only, or primarily, because of the
effect on the student, but rather because of the effect on mankind
in general. This utility does not belong to philosophy. If the study
of philosophy has any value at all for others than students of philosophy, it must be only indirectly, through its effects upon the lives
of those who study it. It is in these effects, therefore, if anywhere,
that the value of philosophy must be primarily sought.

But further, if we are not to fail in our endeavour to deter- 3
mine the value of philosophy, we must first free our minds from
the prejudices of what are wrongly called "practical" men. The

From: Bertrand Russell, *The Problems of Philosophy* (New York: Henry Holt and
Company, 1912) 237–250.

121

"practical" man, as this word is often used, is one who recognises only material needs, who realises that men must have food for the body, but is oblivious of the necessity of providing food for the mind. If all men were well off, if poverty and disease had been reduced to their lowest possible point, there would still remain much to be done to produce a valuable society; and even in the existing world the goods of the mind are at least as important as the goods of the body. It is exclusively among the goods of the mind that the value of philosophy is to be found; and only those who are not indifferent to these goods can be persuaded that the study of philosophy is not a waste of time.

4   Philosophy, like all other studies, aims primarily at knowledge. The knowledge it aims at is the kind of knowledge which gives unity and system to the body of the sciences, and the kind which results from a critical examination of the grounds of our convictions, prejudices, and beliefs. But it cannot be maintained that philosophy has had any very great measure of success in its attempts to provide definite answers to its questions. If you ask a mathematician, a mineralogist, a historian, or any other man of learning, what definite body of truths has been ascertained by his science, his answer will last as long as you are willing to listen. But if you put the same question to a philosopher, he will, if he is candid, have to confess that his study has not achieved positive results such as have been achieved by other sciences. It is true that this is partly accounted for by the fact that, as soon as definite knowledge concerning any subject becomes possible, this subject ceases to be called philosophy, and becomes a separate science. The whole study of the heavens, which now belongs to astronomy, was once included in philosophy; Newton's great work was called "the mathematical principles of natural philosophy." Similarly, the study of the human mind, which was, until very lately, a part of philosophy, has now been separated from philosophy and has become the science of psychology. Thus, to a great extent, the uncertainty of philosophy is more apparent than real: those questions which are already capable of definite answers are placed in the sciences, while those only to which, at present, no definite answer can be given, remain to form the residue which is called philosophy.

This is, however, only a part of the truth concerning the uncer- 5 tainty of philosophy. There are many questions—and among them those that are of the profoundest interest to our spiritual life— which, so far as we can see, must remain insoluble to the human intellect unless its powers become of quite a different order from what they are now. Has the universe any unity of plan or purpose, or is it a fortuitous concourse of atoms? Is consciousness a permanent part of the universe, giving hope of indefinite growth in wisdom, or is it a transitory accident on a small planet on which life must ultimately become impossible? Are good and evil of importance to the universe or only to man? Such questions are asked by philosophy, and variously answered by various philosophers. But it would seem that, whether answers be otherwise discoverable or not, the answers suggested by philosophy are none of them demonstrably true. Yet, however slight may be the hope of discovering an answer, it is part of the business of philosophy to continue the consideration of such questions, to make us aware of their importance, to examine all the approaches to them, and to keep alive that speculative interest in the universe which is apt to be killed by confining ourselves to definitely ascertainable knowledge.

Many philosophers, it is true, have held that philosophy could 6 establish the truth of certain answers to such fundamental questions. They have supposed that what is of most importance in religious beliefs could be proved by strict demonstration to be true. In order to judge of such attempts, it is necessary to take a survey of human knowledge, and to form an opinion as to its methods and its limitations. On such a subject it would be unwise to pronounce dogmatically; but if the investigations of our previous chapters have not led us astray, we shall be compelled to renounce the hope of finding philosophical proofs of religious beliefs. We cannot, therefore, include as part of the value of philosophy any definite set of answers to such questions. Hence, once more, the value of philosophy must not depend upon any supposed body of definitely ascertainable knowledge to be acquired by those who study it.

The value of philosophy is, in fact, to be sought largely in its 7 very uncertainty. The man who has no tincture of philosophy goes through life imprisoned in the prejudices derived from common sense, from the habitual beliefs of his age or his nation, and from convictions which have grown up in his mind without the co-operation or consent of his deliberate reason. To such a man the world tends to become definite, finite, obvious; common objects rouse no questions, and unfamiliar possibilities are contemptuously rejected. As soon as we begin to philosophise, on the contrary, we find, as we saw in our opening chapters, that even the most everyday things lead to problems to which only very incomplete answers can be given. Philosophy, though unable to tell us with certainty what is the true answer to the doubts which it raises, is able to suggest many possibilities which enlarge our thoughts and free them from the tyranny of custom. Thus, while diminishing our feeling of certainty as to what things are, it greatly increases our knowledge as to what they may be; it removes the somewhat arrogant dogmatism of those who have never travelled into the region of liberating doubt, and it keeps alive our sense of wonder by showing familiar things in an unfamiliar aspect.

8   Apart from its utility in showing unsuspected possibilities, philosophy has a value—perhaps its chief value—through the greatness of the objects which it contemplates, and the freedom from narrow and personal aims resulting from this contemplation. The life of the instinctive man is shut up within the circle of his private interests: family and friends may be included, but the outer world is not regarded except as it may help or hinder what comes within the circle of instinctive wishes. In such a life there is something feverish and confined, in comparison with which the philosophic life is calm and free. The private world of instinctive interests is a small one, set in the midst of a great and powerful world which must, sooner or later, lay our private world in ruins. Unless we can so enlarge our interests as to include the whole outer world, we remain like a garrison in a beleaguered fortress, knowing that the enemy prevents escape and that ultimate surrender is inevitable. In such a life there is no peace, but a constant strife between the insistence of desire and the powerlessness of will. In one way or another, if our life is to be great and free, we must escape this prison and this strife.

9   One way of escape is by philosophic contemplation. Philosophic contemplation does not, in its widest survey, divide the universe into two hostile camps—friends and foes, helpful and

hostile, good and bad—it views the whole impartially. Philosophic contemplation, when it is unalloyed, does not aim at proving that the rest of the universe is akin to man. All acquisition of knowledge is an enlargement of the Self, but this enlargement is best attained when it is not directly sought. It is obtained when the desire for knowledge is alone operative, by a study which does not wish in advance that its objects should have this or that character, but adapts the Self to the characters which it finds in its objects. This enlargement of Self is not obtained when, taking the Self as it is, we try to show that the world is so similar to this Self that knowledge of it is possible without any admission of what seems alien. The desire to prove this is a form of self-assertion and, like all self-assertion, it is an obstacle to the growth of Self which it desires, and of which the Self knows that it is capable. Self-assertion, in philosophic speculation as elsewhere, views the world as a means to its own ends; thus it makes the world of less account than Self, and the Self sets bounds to the greatness of its goods. In contemplation, on the contrary, we start from the not-Self, and through its greatness the boundaries of Self are enlarged; through the infinity of the universe the mind which contemplates it achieves some share in infinity.

For this reason greatness of soul is not fostered by those philosophies which assimilate the universe to Man. Knowledge is a form of union of Self and not-Self; like all union, it is impaired by dominion, and therefore by any attempt to force the universe into conformity with what we find in ourselves. There is a widespread philosophical tendency towards the view which tells us that Man is the measure of all things, that truth is man-made, that space and time and the world of universals are properties of the mind, and that, if there be anything not created by the mind, it is unknowable and of no account for us. This view, if our previous discussions were correct, is untrue; but in addition to being untrue, it has the effect of robbing philosophic contemplation of all that gives it value, since it fetters contemplation to Self. What it calls knowledge is not a union with the not-Self, but a set of prejudices, habits, and desires, making an impenetrable veil between us and the world beyond. The man who finds pleasure in such a theory of knowledge is like the man who never leaves the domestic circle for fear his word might not be law.

11   The true philosophic contemplation, on the contrary, finds its satisfaction in every enlargement of the not-Self, in everything that magnifies the objects contemplated, and thereby the subject contemplating. Everything, in contemplation, that is personal or private, everything that depends upon habit, self-interest, or desire, distorts the object, and hence impairs the union which the intellect seeks. By thus making a barrier between subject and object, such personal and private things become a prison to the intellect. The free intellect will see as God might see, without a *here* and *now*, without hopes and fears, without the trammels of customary beliefs and traditional prejudices, calmly, dispassionately, in the sole and exclusive desire of knowledge—knowledge as impersonal, as purely contemplative, as it is possible for man to attain. Hence also the free intellect will value more the abstract and universal knowledge into which the accidents of private history do not enter, than the knowledge brought by the senses, and dependent, as such knowledge must be, upon an exclusive and personal point of view and a body whose sense-organs distort as much as they reveal.

12   The mind which has become accustomed to the freedom and impartiality of philosophic contemplation will preserve something of the same freedom and impartiality in the world of action and emotion. It will view its purposes and desires as parts of the whole, with the absence of insistence that results from seeing them as infinitesimal fragments in a world of which all the rest is unaffected by any one man's deeds. The impartiality which, in contemplation, is the unalloyed desire for truth, is the very same quality of mind which, in action, is justice, and in emotion is that universal love which can be given to all, and not only to those who are judged useful or admirable. Thus contemplation enlarges not only the objects of our thoughts, but also the objects of our actions and our affections: it makes us citizens of the universe, not only of one walled city at war with all the rest. In this citizenship of the universe consists man's true freedom, and his liberation from the thraldom of narrow hopes and fears.

13   Thus, to sum up our discussion of the value of philosophy: Philosophy is to be studied, not for the sake of any definite answers to its questions, since no definite answers can, as a rule, be known to be true, but rather for the sake of the questions themselves; because these questions enlarge our conception of what is

possible, enrich our intellectual imagination, and diminish the dogmatic assurance which closes the mind against speculation; but above all because, through the greatness of the universe which philosophy contemplates, the mind also is rendered great, and becomes capable of that union with the universe which constitutes its highest good.

1912

Allegory of the Cave

Plato

And now, I said, let me show in a figure how far our nature is   1
enlightened or unenlightened: Behold! human beings living in an underground den, which has a mouth open towards the light and reaching all along the den; here, they have been from their childhood, and have their legs and necks chained so that they cannot move, and can only see before them, being prevented by the chains from turning round their heads. Above and behind them a fire is blazing at a distance, and between the fire and the prisoners there is a raised way; and you will see, if you look, a low wall built along the way, like the screen which marionette players have in front of them, over which they show the puppets.

I see.   2

And do you see, I said, men passing along the wall carrying   3
all sorts of vessels, and statues and figures of animals made of wood and stone and various materials, which appear over the wall? Some of them are talking, others silent.

You have shown me a strange image, and they are strange   4
prisoners.

Like ourselves, I replied; and they see only their own shad-   5
ows, or the shadows of one another, which the fire throws on the opposite wall of the cave?

True, he said; how could they see anything but the shadows   6
if they were never allowed to move their heads?

7 And of the objects which are being carried in like manner they would only see the shadows?

8 Yes, he said.

9 And if they were able to converse with one another, would they not suppose that they were naming what was actually before them?

10 Very true.

11 And suppose further that the prison had an echo which came from the other side, would they not be sure to fancy when one of the passers-by spoke that the voice which they heard came from the passing shadow?

12 No question, he replied.

13 To them, I said, the truth would be literally nothing but the shadows of the images.

14 That is certain.

15 And now look again, and see what will naturally follow if the prisoners are released and disabused of their error. At first, when any of them is liberated and compelled suddenly to stand up and turn his neck round and walk and look towards the light, he will suffer sharp pains; the glare will distress him and he will be unable to see the realities of which in his former state he had seen the shadows; and then conceive some one saying to him, that what he saw before was an illusion, but that now, when he is approaching nearer to being and his eye is turned towards more real existence, he has a clearer vision—what will be his reply? And you may further imagine that his instructor is pointing to the objects as they pass and requiring him to name them—will he not be perplexed? Will he not fancy that the shadows which he formerly saw are truer than the objects which are now shown to him?

16 Far truer.

17 And if he is compelled to look straight at the light, will he not have a pain in his eyes which will make him turn away to take refuge in the objects of vision which he can see, and which he will conceive to be in reality clearer than the things which are now being shown to him?

18 True, he said.

19 And suppose once more, that he is reluctantly dragged up a steep and rugged ascent, and held fast until he is forced into the

presence of the sun himself, is he not likely to be pained and irritated? When he approaches the light his eyes will be dazzled and he will not be able to see anything at all of what are now called realities.

Not all in a moment, he said. 20

He will require to grow accustomed to the sight of the upper 21 world. And first he will see the shadows best, next the reflections of men and other objects in the water, and then the objects themselves; then he will gaze upon the light of the moon and the stars and the spangled heaven; and he will see the sky and the stars by night better than the sun or the light of the sun by day?

Certainly. 22

Last of all he will be able to see the sun, and not mere reflec- 23 tions of him in the water, but he will see him in his own proper place, and not in another; and he will contemplate him as he is.

Certainly. 24

He will then proceed to argue that this is he who gives the 25 season and the years, and is the guardian of all that is in the visible world, and in a certain way the cause of all things which he and his fellows have been accustomed to behold?

Clearly, he said, he would first see the sun and then reason 26 about him.

And when he remembered his old habitation, and the wisdom 27 of the den and his fellow-prisoners, do you not suppose that he would felicitate himself on the change, and pity them?

Certainly, he would. 28

And if they were in the habit of conferring honors among 29 themselves on those who were quickest to observe the passing shadows and to remark which of them went before, and which followed after, and which were together; and who were therefore best able to draw conclusions as to the future, do you think that he would care for such honors and glories, or envy the possessors of them? Would he not say with Homer,

Better to be the poor servant of a poor master,

and to endure anything, rather than think as they do and live after their manner?

Yes, he said, I think that he would rather suffer anything than 30 entertain these false notions and live in this miserable manner.

31   Imagine once more, I said, such a one coming suddenly out of the sun to be replaced in his old situation; would he not be certain to have his eyes full of darkness?

32   To be sure, he said.

33   And if there were a contest, and he had to compete in measuring the shadows with the prisoners who had never moved out of the den, while his sight was still weak, and before his eyes had become steady (and the time which would be needed to acquire this new habit of sight might be very considerable) would he not be ridiculous? Men would say of him that up he went and down he came without his eyes; and that it was better not even to think of ascending; and if any one tried to loose another and lead him up to the light, let them only catch the offender, and they would put him to death.

34   No question, he said.

35   This entire allegory, I said, you may now append, dear Glaucon, to the previous argument; the prison-house is the world of sight, the light of fire is the sun, and you will not misapprehend me if you interpret the journey upwards to be the ascent of the soul into the intellectual world according to my poor belief, which, at your desire, I have expressed—whether rightly or wrongly God knows. But, whether true or false, my opinion is that in the world of knowledge the idea of good appears last of all, and is seen only with an effort; and, when seen, is also inferred to be the universal author of all things beautiful and right, parent of light and of the lord of light in this visible world, and the immediate source of reason and truth in the intellectual; and that this is the power upon which he who would act rationally either in public or private life must have his eye fixed.

36   I agree, he said, as far as I am able to understand you.

37   Moreover, I said, you must not wonder that those who attain to this beatific vision are unwilling to descend to human affairs; for their souls are ever hastening into the upper world where they desire to dwell; which desire of theirs is very natural, if our allegory may be trusted.

38   Yes, very natural.

39   And is there anything surprising in one who passes from divine contemplations to the evil state of man, misbehaving

himself in a ridiculous manner; if, while his eyes are blinking and before he has become accustomed to the surrounding darkness, he is compelled to fight in courts of law, or in other places, about the images or the shadows of images of justice, and is endeavoring to meet the conceptions of those who have never yet seen absolute justice?

Anything but surprising, he replied.   40

Any one who has common sense will remember that the 41
bewilderments of the eyes are of two kinds, and arise from two causes, either from coming out of the light or from going into the light, which is true of the mind's eye, quite as much as of the bodily eye; and he who remembers this when he sees any one whose vision is perplexed and weak, will not be too ready to laugh; he will first ask whether that soul of man has come out of the brighter light, and is unable to see because unaccustomed to the dark, or having turned from darkness to the day is dazzled by excess of light. And he will count the one happy in his condition and state of being, and he will pity the other; or, if he have a mind to laugh at the soul which comes from below into the light, there will be more reason in this than the laugh which greets him who returns from above out of the light into the den.

That, he said, is a very just distinction.   42

Fourth Century BCE

Death and Justice

Edward I. Koch

Last December a man named Robert Lee Willie, who had been 1
convicted of raping and murdering an 18-year-old woman, was executed in the Louisiana state prison. In a statement issued several minutes before his death, Mr. Willie said: "Killing people is wrong. . . . It makes no difference whether it's citizens, countries, or governments. Killing is wrong." Two weeks later in South Carolina, an admitted killer named Joseph Carl Shaw was put to death for murdering two teenagers. In an appeal to the governor

for clemency, Mr. Shaw wrote: "Killing is wrong when I did it. Killing is wrong when you do it. I hope you have the courage and moral strength to stop the killing."

2   It is a curiosity of modern life that we find ourselves being lectured on morality by cold-blooded killers. Mr. Willie previously had been convicted of aggravated rape, aggravated kidnapping, and the murders of a Louisiana deputy and a man from Missouri. Mr. Shaw committed another murder a week before the two for which he was executed, and admitted mutilating the body of the 14-year-old girl he killed. I can't help wondering what prompted these murderers to speak out against killing as they entered the death-house door. Did their newfound reverence for life stem from the realization that they were about to lose their own?

3   Life is indeed precious, and I believe the death penalty helps to affirm this fact. Had the death penalty been a real possibility in the minds of these murderers, they might well have stayed their hand. They might have shown moral awareness before their victims died, and not after. Consider the tragic death of Rosa Velez, who happened to be home when a man named Luis Vera burglarized her apartment in Brooklyn. "Yeah, I shot her," Vera admitted. "She knew me, and I knew I wouldn't go to the chair."

4   During my 22 years in public service, I have heard the pros and cons of capital punishment expressed with special intensity. As a district leader, councilman, congressman, and mayor, I have represented constituencies generally thought of as liberal. Because I support the death penalty for heinous crimes of murder, I have sometimes been the subject of emotional and outraged attacks by voters who find my position reprehensible or worse. I have listened to their ideas. I have weighed their objections carefully. I still support the death penalty. The reasons I maintain my position can be best understood by examining the arguments most frequently heard in opposition.

5   (1) *The death penalty is "barbaric."* Sometimes opponents of capital punishment horrify with tales of lingering death on the gallows, of faulty electric chairs, or of agony in the gas chamber. Partly in response to such protests, several states such as North Carolina and Texas switched to execution by lethal injection. The condemned person is put to death painlessly, without ropes, voltage, bullets, or gas. Did this answer the objections of death

penalty opponents? Of course not. On June 22, 1984, *The New York Times* published an editorial that sarcastically attacked the new "hygienic" method of death by injection, and stated that "execution can never be made humane through science." So it's not the method that really troubles opponents. It's the death itself they consider barbaric.

Admittedly, capital punishment is not a pleasant topic. How-   6
ever, one does not have to like the death penalty in order to support it any more than one must like radical surgery, radiation, or chemotherapy in order to find necessary these attempts at curing cancer. Ultimately we may learn how to cure cancer with a simple pill. Unfortunately, that day has not yet arrived. Today we are faced with the choice of letting the cancer spread or trying to cure it with the methods available, methods that one day will almost certainly be considered barbaric. But to give up and do nothing would be far more barbaric and would certainly delay the discovery of an eventual cure. The analogy between cancer and murder is imperfect, because murder is not the "disease" we are trying to cure. The disease is injustice. We may not like the death penalty, but it must be available to punish crimes of cold-blooded murder, cases in which any other form of punishment would be inadequate and, therefore, unjust. If we create a society in which injustice is not tolerated, incidents of murder—the most flagrant form of injustice—will diminish.

(2) *No other major democracy uses the death penalty.* No other   7
major democracy—in fact, few other countries of any description—are plagued by a murder rate such as that in the United States. Fewer and fewer Americans can remember the days when unlocked doors were the norm and murder was a rare and terrible offense. In America the murder rate climbed 122 percent between 1963 and 1980. During that same period, the murder rate in New York City increased by almost 400 percent, and the statistics are even worse in many other cities. A study at M.I.T. showed that based on 1970 homicide rates a person who lived in a large American city ran a greater risk of being murdered than an American soldier in World War II ran of being killed in combat. It is not surprising that the laws of each country differ according to differing conditions and traditions. If other countries had our murder

problem, the cry for capital punishment would be just as loud as it is here. And I daresay that any other major democracy where 75 percent of the people supported the death penalty would soon enact it into law.

8   (3) *An innocent person might be executed by mistake.* Consider the work of Adam Bedau, one of the most implacable foes of capital punishment in this country. According to Mr. Bedau, it is "false sentimentality to argue that the death penalty should be abolished because of the abstract possibility that an innocent person might be executed." He cites a study of the 7,000 executions in this country from 1893 to 1971, and concludes that the record fails to show that such cases occur. The main point, however, is this. If government functioned only when the possibility of error didn't exist, government wouldn't function at all. Human life deserves special protection, and one of the best ways to guarantee that protection is to assure that convicted murderers do not kill again. Only the death penalty can accomplish this end. In a recent case in New Jersey, a man named Richard Biegenwald was freed from prison after serving 18 years for murder; since his release he has been convicted of committing four murders. A prisoner named Lemuel Smith, who, while serving four life sentences for murder (plus two life sentences for kidnapping and robbery) in New York's Green Haven Prison, lured a woman corrections officer into the chaplain's office and strangled her. He then mutilated and dismembered her body. An additional life sentence for Smith is meaningless. Because New York has no death penalty statute, Smith has effectively been given a license to kill.

9   But the problem of multiple murder is not confined to the nation's penitentiaries. In 1981, 91 police officers were killed in the line of duty in this country. Seven percent of those arrested in the cases that have been solved had a previous arrest for murder. In New York City in 1976 and 1977, 85 persons arrested for homicide had a previous arrest for murder. Six of these individuals had two previous arrests for murder, and one had four previous murder arrests. During those two years the New York police were arresting for murder persons with a previous arrest for murder on the average of one every 8.5 days. This is not surprising when we learn that in 1975, for example, the median time served in

Massachusetts for homicide was less than two-and-a-half years. In 1976 a study sponsored by the Twentieth Century Fund found that the average time served in the United States for first-degree murder is ten years. The median time served may be considerably lower.

(4) *Capital punishment cheapens the value of human life.* On the contrary, it can be easily demonstrated that the death penalty strengthens the value of human life. If the penalty for rape were lowered, clearly it would signal a lessened regard for the victims' suffering, humiliation, and personal integrity. It would cheapen their horrible experience, and expose them to an increased danger of recurrence. When we lower the penalty for murder, it signals a lessened regard for the value of the victim's life. Some critics of capital punishment, such as columnist Jimmy Breslin, have suggested that a life sentence is actually a harsher penalty for murder than death. This is sophistic nonsense. A few killers may decide not to appeal a death sentence, but the overwhelming majority make every effort to stay alive. It is by exacting the highest penalty for the taking of human life that we affirm the highest value of human life.

(5) *The death penalty is applied in a discriminatory manner.* This factor no longer seems to be the problem it once was. The appeals process for a condemned prisoner is lengthy and painstaking. Every effort is made to see that the verdict and sentence were fairly arrived at. However, assertions of discrimination are not an argument for ending the death penalty but for extending it. It is not justice to exclude everyone from the penalty of the law if a few are found to be so favored. Justice requires that the law be applied equally to all.

(6) *Thou Shalt Not Kill.* The Bible is our greatest source of moral inspiration. Opponents of the death penalty frequently cite the sixth of the Ten Commandments in an attempt to prove that capital punishment is divinely proscribed. In the original Hebrew, however, the Sixth Commandment reads, "Thou Shalt Not Commit Murder," and the Torah specifies capital punishment for a variety of offenses. The biblical viewpoint has been upheld by philosophers throughout history. The greatest thinkers of the 19th century—Kant, Locke, Hobbes, Rousseau, Montesquieu, and Mill—agreed that natural law properly authorizes the sovereign

to take life in order to vindicate justice. Only Jeremy Bentham was ambivalent. Washington, Jefferson, and Franklin endorsed it. Abraham Lincoln authorized executions for deserters in wartime. Alexis de Tocqueville, who expressed profound respect for American institutions, believed that the death penalty was indispensable to the support of social order. The United States Constitution, widely admired as one of the seminal achievements in the history of humanity, condemns cruel and inhuman punishment, but does not condemn capital punishment.

13   (7) *The death penalty is state-sanctioned murder.* This is the defense with which Messrs. Willie and Shaw hoped to soften the resolve of those who sentenced them to death. By saying in effect, "You're no better than I am," the murderer seeks to bring his accusers down to his own level. It is also a popular argument among opponents of capital punishment, but a transparently false one. Simply put, the state has rights that the private individual does not. In a democracy, those rights are given to the state by the electorate. The execution of a lawfully condemned killer is no more an act of murder than is legal imprisonment an act of kidnapping. If an individual forces a neighbor to pay him money under threat of punishment, it's called extortion. If the state does it, it's called taxation. Rights and responsibilities surrendered by the individual are what give the state its power to govern. This contract is the foundation of civilization itself.

14   Everyone wants his or her rights, and will defend them jealously. Not everyone, however, wants responsibilities, especially the painful responsibilities that come with law enforcement. Twenty-one years ago a woman named Kitty Genovese was assaulted and murdered on a street in New York. Dozens of neighbors heard her cries for help but did nothing to assist her. They didn't even call the police. In such a climate the criminal understandably grows bolder. In the presence of moral cowardice, he lectures us on our supposed failings and tries to equate his crimes with our quest for justice.

15   The death of anyone—even a convicted killer—diminishes us all. But we are diminished even more by a justice system that fails to function. It is an illusion to let ourselves believe that doing away with capital punishment removes the murderer's deed from our conscience. The rights of society are paramount. When we

protect guilty lives, we give up innocent lives in exchange. When opponents of capital punishment say to the state: "I will not let you kill in my name," they are also saying to murderers: "You can kill in your *own* name as long as I have an excuse for not getting involved."

It is hard to imagine anything worse than being murdered 16 while neighbors do nothing. But something worse exists. When those same neighbors shrink back from justly punishing the murderer, the victim dies twice.

1985

What Really Ails America

William J. Bennett

A few months ago I lunched with a friend who now lives in Asia. 1 During our conversation the topic turned to America as seen through the eyes of foreigners. My friend had observed that while the world still regards the United States as the leading economic and military power on earth, this same world no longer beholds us with the moral respect it once did, as a "shining city on a hill." Instead, it sees a society in decline.

Recently, a Washington, D.C., cabdriver—a graduate student 2 from Africa—told me that when he receives his degree, he is returning to his homeland. His reason? He doesn't want his children to grow up in a country where his daughter will be an "easy target" for young men and where his son might also be a target for violence at the hands of other young males. "It is more civilized where I come from," he said.

Last year an article in the *Washington Post* described how 3 exchange students adopt the lifestyle of American teens. Paulina, a Polish high-school student studying in the United States, said that when she first came here she was amazed at the way teenagers spent their time. "In Warsaw, we would come home after school, eat with our parents and then do four or five hours of home-work. Now, I go to Pizza Hut and watch TV and do less work in school. I can tell it is not a good thing to get used to."

4   I have an instinctive aversion to foreigners harshly judging my nation; yet, I must concede that much of what they say is true. Something has gone wrong with us.

5   Yes, there are families, schools, churches and neighborhoods that work. But there is a lot less virtue than there ought to be.

6   Last year I compiled *The Index of Leading Cultural Indicators*, a statistical portrait of American behavioral trends of the past three decades. Among the findings: Since 1960, while the gross domestic product has nearly tripled, violent crime has increased at least 560 percent. Divorces have more than doubled. The percentage of children in single-parent homes has tripled. And by the end of the decade 40 percent of all American births and 80 percent of minority births will occur out of wedlock.

7   These are not good things to get used to.

8   The United States leads the industrialized world in murder, rape and violent crime. At the same time, our elementary-school students rank at or near the bottom in tests of math and science skills. Since 1960, average SAT scores in our high schools have dropped 75 points.

9   In 1940, teachers identified the top problems in America's schools as: talking out of turn, chewing gum, making noise and running in the hall. In 1990, teachers listed drugs, alcohol, pregnancy, suicide, rape and assault.

10   These are not good things to get used to, either.

11   There is a coarseness, a callousness and a cynicism to our era. The worst of it has to do with our children. Our culture seems almost dedicated to the corruption of the young.

12   Last year, Snoop Doggy Dogg, indicted for murder, saw his rap album "Doggystyle," which celebrates marijuana use and the degradation of women, debut at No. 1 on the pop chart. What will happen when young boys who grow up on mean streets, without fathers in their lives, are constantly exposed to such music?

13   On television, indecent exposure is celebrated by all ages as a virtue. There was a time when personal failures, subliminal desires and perverse tastes were accompanied by guilt, or at least silence. Today they are tickets to appear as guests on talk shows. In one recent two-week period, these shows featured cross-dressing

couples, a three-way love affair, a man who fools women into thinking he is using a condom during sex, and prostitutes who love their jobs. These shows present a two-edged problem: people want to expose themselves, and other people want to watch.

We have become inured to the cultural rot that is setting in. 14 People are losing their capacity for shock, disgust and outrage. During the 1992 Los Angeles riots, Damian Williams was filmed crushing an innocent man's skull with a brick, while Henry Watson held the victim down. When Williams was finished, he did a victory dance. Watson and William's lawyers then built a legal defense on the premise that people cannot be held accountable for getting caught up in mob violence. ("I guess maybe they were in the wrong place at the wrong time," one juror told *The New York Times*.) When these men were acquitted on most counts, the sound you heard throughout the land was not outrage, but relief.

This is not a good thing to get used to. 15

What's to blame for this change? The hard fact is that it was 16 not something done to us; it is something we have done to ourselves. Thoughtful people have pointed to materialism, an overly permissive society, or the legacy of the 1960s. There is truth in almost all these accounts. But in my view our real crisis is spiritual, a corruption of the heart.

The ancients called our problem acedia, an aversion to spiri- 17 tual things and an undue concern for the external and the worldly. Acedia also is the seventh capital sin—sloth—but it does not mean mere laziness. The slothful heart is steeped in the worldly and carnal, hates the spiritual and wants to be free of its demands.

When the novelist Walker Percy was asked what concerned 18 him most about America's future, he answered, "Probably the fear of seeing America, with all its great strength and beauty and freedom . . . gradually subside into decay through default and be defeated, not by the communist movement, but from within, from weariness, boredom, cynicism, greed and in the end helplessness before its great problems."

I realize this is a tough indictment. If my diagnosis is wrong, 19 then why, amid our economic prosperity and military security, do almost 70 percent of the public say we are off track? I submit that only when we turn to the right things—enduring, noble, spiritual things—will life get better.

20   During the last decade of the 20th century, there is a disturbing reluctance to talk seriously about matters spiritual and religious. We have become used to not talking about the things that matter most. One will often hear that religious faith is a private matter. But whatever your faith—or even if you have none at all—it is a fact that when millions of people stop believing in God, enormous public consequences follow. Dostoyevsky reminded us in *The Brothers Karamazov* that "if God does not exist, everything is permissible." We are now seeing "everything."

21   What can be done? For one, we must once again connect public policies to our deepest beliefs. Right now we say one thing and do another.

22   • We *say* we want law and order, but we allow violent criminals to return to the streets.

23   • We *say* we want to stop illegitimacy, but we subsidize behavior that leads to it.

24   • We *say* we want to discourage teenage sex, but educators across America treat teenagers as if they were young animals in heat, and are more eager to dispense condoms than moral guidance.

25   • We *say* we want more families to stay together, but we make divorce easier to attain.

26   • We *say* we want a colorblind society, but we continue to count people by race and skin pigment.

27   Furthermore, America desperately needs to recover the purpose of education, which is to provide for the intellectual *and* moral education of the young. Plato made the point that good education makes good men, and good men act nobly.

28   Until a quarter-century or so ago, this time-honored belief virtually went unchallenged. But having departed from it, we are now reaping the whirlwind. We say we desire more civility and responsibility from our children, but many schools refuse to teach right and wrong. And so we talk about "skills facilitation," "self-esteem" and being "comfortable with ourselves."

29   Most important, we must return religion to its proper place. Religion provides us with moral bearings, and the solution to our chief problem of spiritual impoverishment depends on spiritual renewal. The surrendering of strong beliefs, in our private and public lives, has demoralized society.

Today, much of society ridicules and mocks those who are ³⁰ serious about their faith. America's only respectable form of bigotry is bigotry against religious people. And the only reason for hatred of religion is that it forces us to confront matters many would prefer to ignore.

Nobel Prize-winning author William Faulkner once declared, ³¹ "I decline to accept the end of man." Man will prevail because, as Faulkner said, he alone among creatures "has a soul, a spirit capable of compassion and sacrifice and endurance."

In our time, we have seen America make enormous gains—a ³² standard of living unimagined 50 years ago, with extraordinary advances in medicine, science and technology. Life expectancy has increased by more than 20 years in the past seven decades. Opportunity has been extended to those who were once denied it. And, of course, America prevailed in our "long, twilight struggle" against communism.

Today we must carry on a new struggle for the country we ³³ love. We must push hard against an age that is pushing hard against us. If we have full employment and greater economic growth—if we have cities of gold and alabaster—but our children have not learned how to walk in goodness, justice and mercy, then the American experiment, no matter how gilded, will have failed.

Do not surrender. Get mad. Get in the fight. ³⁴

1993

If Hitler Asked You to Electrocute a Stranger, Would You? Probably

Philip Meyer

In the beginning, Stanley Milgram was worried about the Nazi ¹ problem. He doesn't worry much about the Nazis anymore. He worries about you and me, and, perhaps, himself a little bit too.

Stanley Milgram is a social psychologist, and when he began ² his career at Yale University in 1960 he had a plan to prove, scientifically, that Germans are different. The Germans-are-different hypothesis has been used by historians, such as William L. Shirer, to explain the systematic destruction of the Jews by the Third Reich.

3   The appealing thing about this theory is that it makes those of us who are not Germans feel better about the whole business. Obviously, you and I are not Hitler, and it seems equally obvious that we would never do Hitler's dirty work for him. But now, because of Stanley Milgram, we are compelled to wonder. Milgram developed a laboratory experiment which provided a systematic way to measure obedience. His plan was to try it out in New Haven on Americans and then go to Germany and try it out on Germans. He was strongly motivated by scientific curiosity, but there was also some moral content in his decision to pursue this line of research, which was, in turn, colored by his own Jewish background. If he could show that Germans are more obedient than Americans, he could then vary the conditions of the experiment and try to find out just what it is that makes some people more obedient than others. With this understanding, the world might, conceivably, be just a little bit better.

4   But he never took his experiment to Germany. He never took it any farther than Bridgeport. The first finding, also the most unexpected and disturbing finding, was that we Americans are an obedient people: Not blindly obedient, and not blissfully obedient, just obedient. "I found so much obedience," says Milgram softly, a little sadly, "I hardly saw the need for taking the experiment to Germany."

5   There is something of the theatre director in Milgram, and his technique, which he learned from one of the old masters in experimental psychology, Solomon Asch, is to stage a play with every line rehearsed, every prop carefully selected, and everybody an actor except one person. That one person is the subject of the experiment. The subject, of course, does not know he is in a play. He thinks he is in real life.

6   The experiment worked like this: If you were an innocent subjectin Milgram's melodrama, you read an ad in the newspaper or received one in the mail asking for volunteers for an educational experiment. The job would take about an hour and pay $4.50. So you make an appointment and go to an old Romanesque stone

structure on High Street with the imposing name of The Yale Interaction Laboratory. It looks something like a broadcasting studio. Inside, you meet a young, crew-cut man in a laboratory coat who says he is Jack Williams, the experimenter. There is another citizen, fiftyish, Irish face, an accountant, a little overweight, and very mild and harmless-looking. This other citizen seems nervous and plays with his hat while the two of you sit in chairs side by side and are told that the $4.50 checks are yours no matter what happens. Then you listen to Jack Williams explain the experiment.

It is about learning, says Jack Williams in a quiet, knowledge-   7 able way. Science does not know much about the conditions under which people learn and this experiment is to find out about negative reinforcement. Negative reinforcement is getting punished when you do something wrong, as opposed to positive reinforcement which is getting rewarded when you do something right. The negative reinforcement in this case is electric shock.

Then Jack Williams takes two pieces of paper, puts them in a   8 hat, and shakes them up. One piece of paper is supposed to say, "Teacher" and the other, "Learner." Draw one and you will see which you will be. The mild-looking accountant draws one, holds it close to his vest like a poker player, looks at it, and says, "Learner." You look at yours. It says; "Teacher." You do not know that the drawing is rigged, and both slips say "Teacher." The experimenter beckons to the mild-mannered "learner."

"Want to step right in here and have a seat, please?" he says.   9 "You can leave your coat on the back of that chair . . . roll up your right sleeve, please. Now what I want to do is strap down your arms to avoid excessive movement on your part during the experiment. This electrode is connected to the shock generator in the next room.

"And this electrode paste," he says, squeezing some stuff out   10 of a plastic bottle and putting it on the man's arm, "is to provide a good contact and to avoid a blister or burn. Are there any questions now before we go into the next room?"

You don't have any, but the strapped-in "learner" does.   11

"I do think I should say this," says the learner. "About two   12 years ago, I was at the veterans' hospital . . . they detected a heart condition. Nothing serious, but as long as I'm having these shocks, how strong are they—how dangerous are they?"

13   Williams, the experimenter, shakes his head casually. "Oh, no," he says. "Although they may be painful, they're not dangerous. Anything else?"

14   Nothing else. And so you play the game. The game is for you to read a series of word pairs: For example, blue-girl, nice-day, fat-neck. When you finish the list, you read just the first word in each pair and then a multiple-choice list of four other words, including the second word of the pair. The learner, from his remote, strapped-in position, pushes one of four switches to indicate which of the four answers he thinks is the right one. If he gets it right, nothing happens and you go on to the next one. If he gets it wrong, you push a switch that buzzes and gives him an electric shock. And then you go to the next word. You start with 15 volts and increase the number of volts by 15 for each wrong answer. The control board goes from 15 volts on one end to 450 volts on the other. So that you know what you are doing, you get a test shock yourself, at 45 volts. It hurts. To further keep you aware of what you are doing to that man in there, the board has verbal descriptions of the shock levels, ranging from "Slight Shock" at the left-hand side, through "Intense Shock" in the middle, to "Danger: Severe Shock" toward the far right. Finally, at the very end, under 435- and 450-volt switches, there are three ambiguous X's. If, at any point, you hesitate, Mr. Williams calmly tells you to go on. If you still hesitate, he tells you again.

15   Except for some terrifying details, which will be explained in a moment, this is the experiment. The object is to find the shock level at which you disobey the experimenter and refuse to pull the switch.

16   When Stanley Milgram first wrote this script, he took it to fourteen Yale psychology majors and asked them what they thought would happen. He put it this way: Out of one hundred persons in the teacher's predicament, how would their breakoff points be distributed along the 15-to-450-volt scale? They thought a few would break off very early, most would quit someplace in the middle and a few would go all the way to the end. The highest estimate of the number out of one hundred who would go all the way to the end was three. Milgram then informally polled some of his fellow scholars in the psychology department. They agreed that very few would go to the end. Milgram thought so too.

"I'll tell you quite frankly," he says, "before I began this exper- 17
iment, before any shock generator was built, I thought that most
people would break off at 'Strong Shock' or 'Very Strong Shock.'
You would get only a very, very small proportion of people going
out to the end of the shock generator, and they would constitute
a pathological fringe."

In his pilot experiments, Milgram used Yale students as sub- 18
jects. Each of them pushed the shock switches, one by one, all the
way to the end of the board.

So he rewrote the script to include some protests from the 19
learner. At first, they were mild, gentlemanly, Yalie protests, but,
"it didn't seem to have as much effect as I thought it would or
should," Milgram recalls. "So we had more violent protestation on
the part of the person getting the shock. All of the time, of course,
what we were trying to do was not to create a macabre situation,
but simply to generate disobedience. And that was one of the first
findings. This was not only a technical deficiency of the experiment, that we didn't get disobedience. It really was the first finding: That obedience would be much greater than we had assumed
it would be and disobedience would be much more difficult than
we had assumed."

As it turned out, the situation did become rather macabre. 20
The only meaningful way to generate disobedience was to have
the victim protest with great anguish, noise, and vehemence. The
protests were tape-recorded so that all the teachers ordinarily
would hear the same sounds and nuances, and they started with
a grunt at 75 volts, proceeded through a "Hey, that really hurts,"
at 125 volts, got desperate with, "I can't stand the pain, don't do
that," at 180 volts, reached complaints of heart trouble at 195,
an agonized scream at 285, a refusal to answer at 315, and only
heartrending, ominous silence after that.

Still, sixty-five percent of the subjects, twenty- to fifty-year-old 21
American males, everyday, ordinary people, like you and me, obe-
diently kept pushing those levers in the belief that they were
shocking the mild-mannered learner, whose name was Mr. Wallace,
and who was chosen for the role because of his innocent appearance, all the way up to 450 volts.

Milgram was now getting enough disobedience so that he 22
had something he could measure. The next step was to vary

the circumstances to see what would encourage or discourage obedience.

23   He put the learner in the same room with the teacher. He stopped strapping the learner's hand down. He rewrote the script so that at 150 volts the learner took his hand off the shock plate and declared that he wanted out of the experiment. He rewrote the script some more so that the experimenter then told the teacher to grasp the learner's hand and physically force it down on the plate to give Mr. Wallace his unwanted electric shock.

24   "I had the feeling that very few people would go on at that point, if any," Milgram says. "I thought that would be the limit of obedience that you would find in the laboratory."

25   It wasn't.

26   Although seven years have now gone by, Milgram still remembers the first person to walk into the laboratory in the newly rewritten script. He was a construction worker, a very short man. "He was so small," says Milgram, "that when he sat on the chair in front of the shock generator, his feet didn't reach the floor. When the experimenter told him to push the victim's hand down and give the shock, he turned to the experimenter, and he turned to the victim, his elbow went up, he fell down on the hand of the victim, his feet kind of tugged to one side, and he said, 'Like this, boss?' Zzumph!"

27   The experiment was played out to its bitter end. Milgram tried it with forty different subjects. And thirty percent of them obeyed the experimenter and kept on obeying.

28   "The protests of the victim were strong and vehement, he was screaming his guts out, he refused to participate, and you had to physically struggle with him in order to get his hand down on the shock generator," Milgram remembers. But twelve out of forty did it.

29   Milgram took his experiment out of New Haven. Not to Germany, just twenty miles down the road to Bridgeport. Maybe, he reasoned, the people obeyed because of the prestigious setting of Yale University.

30   The new setting was a suite of three rooms in a run-down office building in Bridgeport. The only identification was a sign with a fictitious name: "Research Associates of Bridgeport." Questions

about professional connections got only vague answers about "research for industry."

Obedience was less in Bridgeport. Forty-eight percent of the subjects stayed for the maximum shock, compared to sixty-five percent at Yale. But this was enough to prove that far more than Yale's prestige was behind the obedient behavior.

For more than seven years now, Stanley Milgram has been trying to figure out what makes ordinary American citizens so obedient. The most obvious answer—that people are mean, nasty, brutish and sadistic—won't do. The subjects who gave the shocks to Mr. Wallace to the end of the board did not enjoy it. They groaned, protested, fidgeted, argued, and in some cases, were seized by fits of nervous, agitated giggling.

"They even try to get out of it," says Milgram, "but they are somehow engaged in something from which they cannot liberate themselves. They are locked into a structure, and they do not have the skills or inner resources to disengage themselves."

Milgram's theory assumes that people behave in two different operating modes as different as ice and water. He does not rely on Freud or sex or toilet-training hang-ups for this theory. All he says is that ordinarily we operate in a state of autonomy, which means we pretty much have and assert control over what we do. But in certain circumstances, we operate under what Milgram calls a state of agency (after agent, *n* . . . one who acts for or in the place of another by authority from him; a substitute; a deputy— *Webster's Collegiate Dictionary*). A state of agency, to Milgram, is nothing more than a frame of mind.

"There's nothing bad about it, there's nothing good about it," he says. "It's a natural circumstance of living with other people. . . . I think of a state of agency as a real transformation of a person; if a person has different properties when he's in that state, just as water can turn to ice under certain conditions of temperature, a person can move to the state of mind that I call agency . . . the critical thing is that you see yourself as the instrument of the execution of another person's wishes. You do not see yourself as acting on your own. And there's a real transformation, a real change of properties of the person."

So, for most subjects in Milgram's laboratory experiments, the act of giving Mr. Wallace his painful shock was necessary, even though unpleasant, and besides they were doing it on behalf of somebody else and it was for science.

37   Stanley Milgram has his problems, too. He believes that in the laboratory situation, he would not have shocked Mr. Wallace. His professional critics reply that in his real-life situation he has done the equivalent. He has placed innocent and naïve subjects under great emotional strain and pressure in selfish obedience to his quest for knowledge. When you raise this issue with Milgram, he has an answer ready. There is, he explains patiently, a critical difference between his naïve subjects and the man in the electric chair. The man in the electric chair (in the mind of the naïve subject) is helpless, strapped in. But the naïve subject is free to go at any time.

38   Immediately after he offers this distinction, Milgram anticipates the objection.

39   "It's quite true," he says, "that this is almost a philosophic position, because we have learned that some people are psychologically incapable of disengaging themselves. But that doesn't relieve them of the moral responsibility."

40   The parallel is exquisite. "The tension problem was unexpected," says Milgram in his defense. But he went on anyway. The naïve subjects didn't expect the screaming protests from the strapped-in learner. But they went on.

41   "I had to make a judgment," says Milgram. "I had to ask myself, was this harming the person or not? My judgment is that it was not. Even in the extreme cases, I wouldn't say that permanent damage results."

42   Sound familiar? "The shocks may be painful," the experimenter kept saying, "but they're not dangerous."

43   After the series of experiments was completed, Milgram sent a report of the results to his subjects and a questionnaire, asking whether they were glad or sorry to have been in the experiment. Eighty-three and seven-tenths percent said they were glad and only 1.3 percent were sorry; 15 percent were neither sorry nor glad. However, Milgram could not be sure at the time of the experiment that only 1.3 percent would be sorry.

44   Kurt Vonnegut Jr. put one paragraph in the preface to *Mother Night*, in 1966, which pretty much says it for the people with their fingers on the shock-generator switches, for you and me, and

maybe even for Milgram. "If I'd been born in Germany," Vonnegut said, "I suppose I would have *been* a Nazi, bopping Jews and gypsies and Poles around, leaving boots sticking out of snowbanks, warming myself with my sweetly virtuous insides. So it goes."

Just so. One thing that happened to Milgram back in New 45 Haven during the days of the experiment was that he kept running into people he'd watched from behind the one-way glass. It gave him a funny feeling, seeing those people going about their everyday business in New Haven and knowing what they would do to Mr. Wallace if ordered to. Now that his research results are in and you've thought about it, you can get this funny feeling too. You don't need one-way glass. A glance in your own mirror may serve just as well.

1970

5

Cultural Studies

Why We Crave Horror Movies

Stephen King

1   I think that we're all mentally ill; those of us outside the asylums only hide it a little better—and maybe not all that much better, after all. We've all known people who talk to themselves, people who sometimes squinch their faces into horrible grimaces when they believe no one is watching, people who have some hysterical fear—of snakes, the dark, the tight place, the long drop . . . and, of course, those final worms and grubs that are waiting so patiently underground.

2   When we pay our four or five bucks and seat ourselves at tenth-row center in a theater showing a horror movie, we are daring the nightmare.

3   Why? Some of the reasons are simple and obvious. To show that we can, that we are not afraid, that we can ride this roller coaster. Which is not to say that a really good horror movie may not surprise a scream out of us at some point, the way we may scream when the roller coaster twists through a complete 360 or plows through a lake at the bottom of the drop. And horror movies, like roller coasters, have always been the special province of the young; by the time one turns 40 or 50, one's appetite for double twists or 360-degree loops may be considerably depleted.

4   We also go to re-establish our feelings of essential normality; the horror movie is innately conservative, even reactionary. Freda Jackson as the horrible melting woman in *Die, Monster, Die!* confirms for us that no matter how far we may be removed from the beauty of a Robert Redford or a Diana Ross, we are still light-years from true ugliness.

150

And we go to have fun.   5

Ah, but this is where the ground starts to slope away, isn't it? 6
Because this is a very peculiar sort of fun indeed. The fun comes
from seeing others menaced—sometimes killed. One critic has
suggested that if pro football has become the voyeur's version of
combat, then the horror film has become the modern version of
the public lynching.

It is true that the mythic, "fairytale" horror film intends to 7
take away the shades of gray. . . . It urges us to put away our
more civilized and adult penchant for analysis and to become children again, seeing things in pure blacks and whites. It may be that
horror movies provide psychic relief on this level because this
invitation to lapse into simplicity, irrationality and even outright
madness is extended so rarely. We are told we may allow our
emotions a free rein . . . or no rein at all.

If we are all insane, then sanity becomes a matter of degree. 8
If your insanity leads you to carve up women like Jack the Rip-
per or the Cleveland Torso Murderer, we clap you away in the
funny farm (but neither of those two amateur-night surgeons was
ever caught, heh-heh-heh); if, on the other hand your insanity
leads you only to talk to yourself when you're under stress or to
pick your nose on the morning bus, then you are left alone to go
about your business . . . though it is doubtful that you will ever
be invited to the best parties.

The potential lyncher is in almost all of us (excluding saints, 9
past and present; but then, most saints have been crazy in their
own ways), and every now and then, he has to be let loose to
scream and roll around in the grass. Our emotions and our fears
form their own body, and we recognize that it demands its
own exercise to maintain proper muscle tone. Certain of these
emotional muscles are accepted—even exalted—in civilized
society; they are, of course, the emotions that tend to maintain
the status quo of civilization itself. Love, friendship, loyalty,
kindness—these are all the emotions that we applaud, emotions
that have been immortalized in the couplets of Hallmark
cards and in the verses (I don't dare call it poetry) of Leonard
Nimoy.

When we exhibit these emotions, society showers us with 10
positive reinforcement; we learn this even before we get out of

diapers. When, as children, we hug our rotten little puke of a sister and give her a kiss, all the aunts and uncles smile and twit and cry, "Isn't he the sweetest little thing?" Such coveted treats as chocolate-covered graham crackers often follow. But if we deliberately slam the rotten little puke of a sister's fingers in the door, sanctions follow—angry remonstrance from parents, aunts and uncles; instead of a chocolate-covered graham cracker, a spanking.

11   But anticivilization emotions don't go away, and they demand periodic exercise. We have such "sick" jokes as, "What's the difference between a truckload of bowling balls and a truckload of dead babies?" (You can't unload a truckload of bowling balls with a pitchfork . . . a joke, by the way, that I heard originally from a ten-year-old.) Such a joke may surprise a laugh or a grin out of us even as we recoil, a possibility that confirms the thesis: If we share a brotherhood of man, then we also share an insanity of man. None of which is intended as a defense of either the sick joke or insanity but merely as an explanation of why the best horror films, like the best fairy tales, manage to be reactionary, anarchistic, and revolutionary all at the same time.

12   The mythic horror movie, like the sick joke, has a dirty job to do. It deliberately appeals to all that is worst in us. It is morbidity unchained, our most base instincts let free, our nastiest fantasies realized . . . and it all happens, fittingly enough, in the dark. For those reasons, good liberals often shy away from horror films. For myself, I like to see the most aggressive of them— *Dawn of the Dead,* for instance—as lifting a trap door in the civilized forebrain and throwing a basket of raw meat to the hungry alligators swimming around in that subterranean river beneath.

13   Why bother? Because it keeps them from getting out, man. It keeps them down there and me up here. It was Lennon and McCartney who said that all you need is love, and I would agree with that.

14   As long as you keep the gators fed.

1982

Talk TV: Tuning in to Trouble

Jeanne Albronda Heaton and Nona Leigh Wilson

"Panem et circenses!" Ancient Romans believed that people were 1
satisfied as long as they had bread and circuses. And their circuses
were both gruesome and popular. On the first day the Colosseum
opened in A.D. 80, nine thousand animals were slaughtered as
part of the show for a crowd of eighty thousand cheering spectators. Gladiators fought to the death with these beasts and with
one another. Christians, a disposable minority, were thrown to the
lions for entertainment. And the crowds came back for more.

Two thousand years later, the crowds yelled, "Why don't you 2
cut his balls off?" and "Kill, kill, kill!" These people weren't at the
Colosseum, however, they were in the audience of a TV talk show.
The transfixing power of sudden devastation runs deep throughout human history. Our desire for that particular blend of terror,
amazement, and awe that we can get only from the deep suffering of other people is just as strong now as it ever was, even if
our "circuses" are less fatal.

Tabloid character assassinations have replaced public execu- 3
tions (though Phil Donahue tried to offer the real thing, unsuc-
cessfully suing for the chance to broadcast a recent execution). The
Christians have been replaced by the emotionally wounded or the
socially outcast. "Psychic demons" stand in for the lions. And
while the show is less bloody, the crowd is bigger than ever and
roaring for more. The seating capacity appears to be unlimited.
All one needs to do, in any bus station, airport, bar room, dorm
room, or living room, is tune in Talk TV.

Shows that give viewers a chance to watch trouble and strife, 4
from murderous teenagers to sisters who sleep with each other's
husbands, are enormously popular. Talk TV also brings fair-
ground style freak shows into every home, and viewers lap them
up. It seems that viewers only want to see and hear about problems. Most of the shows that have attempted to focus on positive
topics have either dropped in the ratings or gone off the air completely. It is clear that viewers will tune in if there's trouble. What
is not clear is what happens to us individually and collectively as

a result of so many millions of people watching so many thousands of hours of troubled talk.

5   The early years of Talk TV accomplished some very important tasks. Information that was previously taboo or accessible only to those who had already sought professional help was suddenly made available to the general public. This made it possible for many people to finally understand that they were not alone, that help was available, and that differences could be respected by talking and listening.

6   Phil Donahue and Oprah Winfrey have performed an important public service by helping unveil many of America's best kept secrets. Naomi Wolf, the author of *The Beauty Myth,* and *Fire with Fire,* explains their contribution this way: "[Talk Shows did] something absolutely unique among our cultural institutions: that is, they treat[ed] the opinions of women of all classes, races, and educational levels as if they mattered . . . That daily act of listening, whatever its shortcomings, made for a revolution in what women were willing to ask for; the shows daily conditioned otherwise unheard women into the belief that they were entitled to a voice." Enormous credit for providing a platform for the voices of so many who needed to be heard belongs to these two hosts. We can all thank them for raising the American consciousness on many important topics, including domestic violence, child abuse, and other crucial problems.

7   But those pioneering days are over. As the number of shows has increased and the ratings wars have intensified, the manner in which issues are presented has changed. The shows now openly encourage conflict, name calling, and fights between the guests and the audience. Producers set up underhanded tricks and secret revelations. Hosts instruct guests to reveal their anger with "Let's fight it out!" The camera and our attention is turned to conflict, not resolution.

8   Consequently, it is our contention that in its current form Talk TV creates more problems than benefits for viewers. As we have seen, the more dramatic and bizarre the problems the better it is for the shows. The mental health experts are brought on to legitimize the discussion and offer "professional" advice about resolving the problem. But since all of this takes place in an entertainment driven, one-hour format, problems are exaggerated to heighten the drama and solutions are simplified to squeeze into the final moments of the shows. Consequently, mixed messages,

distorted representations, inaccurate information, and unrealistic solutions often result in problems for viewers.

Millions of people tune in every day, many of them perhaps 9 intending only to be entertained. However, all of them, no matter what their motivation for watching, absorb some part of the message. And even though the stated goal of Talk TV is informing the public, the amount of inaccurate information they give us about our own and others' problems is staggering.

BAD LESSONS IN MENTAL HEALTH

There is nothing inherently wrong with wanting to shock viewers, 10 or with providing disturbing information about problems we wish would go away. But when we are given information relating to mental health that is directly or indirectly supported by representatives of the mental health profession, the information should be valid. Viewers ought to be able to trust that they are not being deceived. Admittedly, one of the problems of trying to provide mental health information on television is the difficulty of keeping it manageable while still attempting to provide something of use. Unfortunately, the clichés, exaggerations, and inflated statistics that Talk TV provides do not achieve that balance and often seriously misinform viewers.

The primary focus of Talk TV has always been to entertain and 11 to do so by using sexual, familial, and personal problems. This leads to a predictable distortion of events, emotion, and truth. Producers claim viewers want shows that sizzle—so that's exactly what they produce. But all that sizzling means something's getting burned. And that something is mental health information.

DISTORTING NORMALLY

Although Talk TV shows are all about problems, they also indirectly 12 present viewers with a picture of normality. The shows set themselves up as reliable sources for information about what's really going on in America. And, in fact, they often cover what sound like common problems with work, love, and sex. But the information presented about these "normal" problems is skewed and confusing. Routine problems are exaggerated almost beyond recognition and extremely unusual problems are presented as though they are common.

Common problems such as depression and anxiety are rarely presented, yet these disorders affect millions. On the other hand, more exciting but less common problems involving sex-change operations and serial murders are presented so often they become clichés.

13   When ordinary problems *are* dealt with, they are transformed. Work problems, supposedly common to us all, become "fatal office feuds," "back-stabbing co-workers," and financial disasters." Problems concerning love, sex, or romance become "marriage with a fourteen-year-old," "women in love with the men who shoot them," or "man-stealing sisters." The hosts' constant reminders that the guests are "average" people with "common" problems certainly have the potential to create confusion for viewers. The lines between what is bizarre and alarming and what is typical and inconsequential are blurred.

14   Talk TV shows suggest that marrying a rapist, having a defiant teen, or discovering a cross-dressing neighbor are catastrophes about to happen to everyone. On an episode of *Salley Jessy Raphael* titled "Wives of Rapists," for example, Sally said to the woman on stage, "How would you ever know that this quiet man was a rapist? He could be anyone." As Sally described him, we were shown family pictures of him with his children. The wife cried as she described the quiet and angry withdrawal that preceded his rape of an eighty-year-old neighbor. Sally responded, "My husband withdraws when he is angry too."

15   This episode involves a number of potentially dangerous elements. First, the manner in which the topic is presented suggests that women are generally at considerable risk of marrying rapists. And while it is true that many rapists are married, it is not true that most married or marriageable men are rapists. Additionally, while it is true that wives might have a difficult time determining if they are married to a rapist, there was little discussion of what factors, other than being quiet and angry, might have been present to indicate that the man had a problem. Moreover, the implication that "quiet and angry" husbands might actually be rapists in disguise is of little use other than to inflame already strained relationships.

16   Day in and day out, the shows parade all the myriad traumas, betrayals, and afflictions that could possibly befall us. What can follow is the creeping sense that America is not the home of the brave, but of the depraved. And it is this sense that things are bad all over, not in terms of world politics but in terms of home and hearth, that

is one of the most damaging messages viewers get from Talk TV. Normality is lost in an artificially crafted sea of problems. Viewers can be left with the notion that everyone is really quite sick—another related problem we think Talk TV creates for viewers.

DENYING RESPONSIBILITY

With their incessant focus on individual problems, television talk shows are a major contributor to the recent trend of elevating personal concerns to the level of personal rights and then affording those "rights" infinitely more attention than their accompanying responsibilities. In other words, Talk TV helps maintain "A Nation of Whiners" (the title given to a *Crossfire* episode)—a nation in which everyone is entitled but no one is obligated.   17

Every day, we see guest after guest elaborate the ways in which their rights have been violated. Without a doubt, many of the guests have indeed been wronged, often seriously. But almost none of the guests ever talks about responsibility and rarely are the guests asked to do so. In order to give the appearance of being tough on responsibility, guests are brought on who have committed villainous acts (most often against other guests). Such guests serve as the token whipping boys and allow the host and audience to gratuitously "confront" the offenders about their wrongdoing and responsibilities. But these tirades never lead to an understanding of accountability; instead, they only serve to heighten outrage and defensiveness, which in turn leads to more excuses that offset any real culpability. Little to no time is devoted to discussing responsibilities or how to fulfill them.   18

Furthermore, the alleged offenders almost always refute their accountability with revelations that they too were previously wronged or "victimized," and therefore are not responsible. On *Sally Jessy Raphael*, a man appeared on stage with roses for the daughter he had sexually molested. To explain his wrongdoings, he revealed that he had been homosexually molested when he was five. He summed it up with, "I'am on this show too! I need help; I'll go through therapy." His revelation was met with a round of applause from the audience, which only moments before had been set up to despise him for his behavior.   19

His sudden turnaround was not unusual. In fact, viewers rarely see guests admit error early in the show, but a reversal often occurs   20 with just a few minutes remaining. This works well for the shows because they need the conflict to move steadily to a crescendo before the final "go to therapy" resolution. But before that, and for most of the show, viewers are treated to lots of conflict and a heavy dose of pseudopsychological explanations that are actually nothing more than excuses, and often lame ones as that.

21   This elevation of rights over responsibilities is problematic for viewers in a number of ways. It encourages viewers to focus on what others have or have not done as the source of their problems: *other* people are responsible. While this approach to resolving problems might initially seem appealing and comforting, it can actually increase feelings of despair and helplessness. When responsibility is completely lifted and shifted to others, the power to do anything other than complain goes with it. So while the shows might suggest that having the right to point the finger at others is the way to feel better, claiming one's share of responsibility may be more likely to produce useful change.

22   Although it would be hard to know it from what currently remains, Talk TV initially had great potential as a vehicle for disseminating accurate information and as a forum for public debate. But because the goal of Talk TV has become sensational entertainment that will increase ratings, that potential has been lost. We are left with cheap shots, cheap thrills, and sound-bite stereotypes. Taken on its own this combination is troubling enough, but when considered against the original opportunity for positive outcomes, what Talk TV delivers is truly disturbing.

Notes

P. 127, *On the first day the Colosseum opened:* Wiedemann, T. *Emperors and Gladiators.* London: Routledge & Kegan Paul, 1992, pp. 20, 60.

P. 128, *"something absolutely unique among our cultural institutions":* Wolf, N. *Fire with Fire: The New Female Power and How to Use It.* New York: Ballantine, 1993, p. 9.

P. 131, *damaging messages viewers get from Talk TV:* Howard Rosenberg, personal interview, Nov. 16, 1994.

P. 132, *forty to sixty million survivors of incest:* Goodman, W. "When Even Victimizers Say They Are Victims," *New York Times,* Mar. 28, 1994, p. C-14.

Money, Power, Elect: Where's the Hip-Hop Agenda?

Raquel Cepeda

Hip-hop culture has given my generation its tag line, if not its 1
very identity: For more than 20 years, rap—hip-hop's sometimes
furious, sometimes laid-back, rhythmic spoken-word expression—
has provided a mesmerizing sound track for the lives of many
young African-American and Latino people. Spawned from humble beginnings in New York City's South Bronx, hip-hop style
spread like wildfire, while rap rocked our neighborhood block
parties, turntables and boom boxes, and then White suburban
headphones all over the country. Eventually rap would generate
a $1.3 billion industry in the United States, exclusive of its still-
growing global influences.

But consider how rap music, back at the end of the cata- 2
strophic Reagan administration, was also identified as *the* platform to educate *and* entertain the nation on the realties of what
was going on socially and politically in Black and Latino America. Only a decade ago, rapper KRS-One and his crew BDP (Boo-
gie Down Productions) proclaimed in the title track to their 1990
album *Edutainment:* "Every time a Black man speaks up, KA-
POW!/See people concentrate on the leader. . . ." Other groups
such as Public Enemy, Brand Nubian, Poor Righteous Teachers
and even such West Coast pioneers as Compton, California's
gangsta-rappers N.W.A (Niggas With Attitude) penned tracks that
depicted and responded to the political agendas brewing in their
communities—namely, racial profiling, police brutality, the state
of public education and the prison system, Black-on-Black crime
and predatory drug peddling and abuse.

Compare that to the music that dominates the top of the 3
charts today: Rap is now a sample-heavy, benjamin-raking, crudely
individualistic pop-culture phenomenon that is very far from its
earlier countercultural and activist impulses. "There's no spiritual
content to the majority of records being made today," says cultural critic Nelson George, 42, author of *Hip-Hop America*. Icons like
Jay-Z, Puffy and Lil' Kim now compare themselves to high-profile

White celebrity entrepreneurs like Donald Trump, Donatella Versace and Martha Stewart. Ironically, traditional Black community leaders like the Reverend Jesse L. Jackson, Sr., NAACP president and CEO Kweisi Mfume, and even the Reverend Al Sharpton have been far less successful at appealing politically to these hip-hop megastars and the young people who follow them than folks like Trump and *Playboy* monarch Hugh Hefner have been in *partying* with them.

4   Meanwhile, today's post–civil-rights hip-hop civilian masses seem politically inert. Just as the rise of gangsta rap overwhelmed message rap, hip-hop's social energies have also been redirected by commercial success and corporate marketing. The popular mind, seduced by the ethic of getting paid, became preoccupied with rap's shiny, platinum-dipped dreams. Mogul Sean "Puffy" Combs almost single-handedly steered the sound of rap music into mainstream pop. Predictably, other popular hip-hop artists have followed suit.

5   Foxy Brown and Lil' Kim, in particular, enjoy new status as glam celebrity spokespeople-for-hire, successfully marketing luxury goods. But the media power this trend represents is rarely put to use for the benefit of our communities. "The so-called Black celebrities are created by companies to be advertisements for what companies promote," observes Public Enemy's Chuck D. "These celebrities lose focus and think it's all about them; that's individual instead of collective though."

6   But now, as we face the first national election season of the new century, will the hip-hop generation *stay* obsessed with living the ghetto-fabulons life? Will we remain unorganized and politically unresponsive to racism and police brutality, bad schools, economic gaps and other persistent problems in our communities? After all, this generation, however flaccid its political muscle may seem to be is heir to the Black Power era. We have witnessed two Republican administrations, the 1992 Los Angeles riots, the 1999 murder of our immigrant brother Amadou Diallo and most recently, California's passing of Proposition 21, which disproportionately criminalizes urban youth. So why haven't we been galvanized into an articulate and activist political movement by such events? Could the star power in merchandising and marketing, for example, ever be used successfully as a coalescing political force to get out our vote?

In fact, with the possible exceptions of Lauryn Hill and Queen 7 Latifah, few platinum-level artists have ever considered moving beyond conscious rhetoric and rhyme to organize our people. Many ask, why even expect a celebrity to take a particular political stand? The answer is simple: There's a long-standing tradition in our communities that unites the arts and activism (Paul Robeson is a historic example, as are Ossie Davis, Ruby Dee and Harry Belafonte). But cultural commentators agree that while our rap celebrities have an enormous influence on urban-youth culture, there's little interest in transferring it to politics. "What hip-hop has done is taken the strategies of grass-roots organizing and used it to sell records and images," explains Nelson George. "The same kind of kids who used to canvass a neighborhood door-to-door to get people registered to vote now give parties."

A similar observation comes from another older "hip-hop 8 head." Bill Stephney, 38, president of StepSun Music, board member of the National Urban League and founder of New York City's Families Organized for Liberty and Action (FOLA): "As Vernon Reid [musician and Black Rock Coalition founder] once said, the nineties were just the sixties turned upside down," recalls Stephney. "During the sixties, you had a generation of Black folks who were socially active and politically conscious. We wanted to change the world, but we really didn't have an idea, beyond the romance of revolution, how we were going to finance or set up any economic systems for Black and Latino people to survive. By the nineties, you have the kids of the sixties generation, who know how to make money, but who don't have the sociopolitical orientation their predecessors had. Imagine, if you will, having the social and political heart of Fannie Lou Hamer, Rosa Parks, Medgar Evers and Dr. King combined with the financial brains of Puffy."

Still, there *are* activist forces stirring within the twenty- 9 first–century hip-hop community. I'm not talking about well-publicized, star-sponsored operations like Puffy's Daddy's House (which finances camps and other activities for inner-city youth) and Lauryn Hill's Refugee Project (which also works with at-risk urban youth); even these operations have been criticized—perhaps unjustly—for being vanity charity activities, not really informed by an overall social or political strategy. No, I'm talking about a

largely unnoticed grass-roots hip-hop movement that is persistently making its way through urban neighborhoods all over the
country. Most of this so-called hip-hop activism began in New
York, just as rap did, but it has also cropped up among youths in
Los Angeles, San Francisco, Washington, D.C., Atlanta and cyberspace, according to Angela Ards, a senior associate editor at *Ms.*
magazine. Ards investigated hip-hop activism last year as a fellow
at the Nation Institute (the independent nonprofit organization
dedicated to protecting First Amendment freedoms and affiliated
with *The Nation* magazine).

10   These local groups identify with hip-hop expression but tap into
the energies of performers who are less well known than our stars.
One example: Last year Mos Def and Talib Kweli—Brooklyn-based
rappers–entrepreneurs who record individually and together as the
duo Black Star—rescued a local landmark Black bookstore from
going out of business by buying it. Black Star is also known for
spearheading anti–police brutality campaigns in the hip-hop industry, and other conscious artists like Common, OutKast and dead
prez have joined them in representing and working with the urban
neighborhoods they came from.

11   Such activity certainly deserves more recognition and support
from the hip-hop nation's everyday citizens. Although many of
our young adults seem to have little interest, or aspiration to participate, in politics or activism, a strident few, whom you will
meet below, show that the hip-hop generation has untapped
potential to become a serious political force. The question is, how
do we pump up the volume?

VOTER REGISTRATION AND PARTICIPATION

12 In this election year, young Black people are at best skeptical
about the political mainstream, and a few hardworking Black
political organizers are trying to change that. Donna Frisby-
Greenwood, former executive director of Rock the Vote (a non-
partisan, nonprofit organization dedicated to motivating young
people to participate in the political process) and a political orga-
nizer who has worked with urban youth for more than a decade,
points out that in the last Presidential election only about half the

8,928,000 eligible Black voters 18–34 registered to vote, and only 3.5 million of them—or about 72 percent—voted. (By comparison, about 68 percent of the 10,932,000 eligible Black voters 34–65 registered, and nearly 84 percent of them voted.) At Rock the Vote, Frisby-Greenwood organized the Hip-Hop Coalition for Political Power to reach out to the young Black voter. Artists like Public Enemy's Chuck D, Queen Latifah, LL Cool J and The Roots took an active role in the effort. Of the more than 500,000 voters Rock the Vote registered in 1996, at least 150,000 were registered through the efforts of the now-defunct Coalition.

Today, Frisby-Greenwood, 35, lives and works in Philadelphia 13 and cochairs the Black Youth Vote (BYV) Coalition—part of the National Coalition on Black Civic Participation, Inc., in Washington, D.C.—with BET talk-show host Tavis Smiley, 34, and Chuck D, 39. "We are now registering voters on-line, in the streets and on college campuses," says Frisby-Greenwood. "We've planned summer workshops to train young people to organize, educate and register voters in Pennsylvania, North Carolina, Alabama, Florida, D.C., Los Angeles, Ohio, Georgia, Texas and California."

The BYV works with an advisory committee of 21–to–40-year- 14 old leaders, including author and syndicated columnist Farai Chideya, 31; activists Conrad Muhammad, 35, and Ras Baraka, 31; and journalists Angela Ards, 31, and Kevin Powell, 34. "One of the things we emphasize in the BYV manifesto is awakening the sleeping giant of the hip-hop generation," says Chideya. "Black youths are such a force—I mean, we run American pop culture." Hoping to motivate at least 10 percent of young Black people between 18 and 29 to participate in the 2000 political process, BYV has been training local coordinators around the country. (For further information, see www.bigvote.com.)

These education and registration efforts are certainly needed, 15 according to my sample of attitudes. "*Politics* is a dangerous word," says Black Star's Kweli, 24, "because what it means to me is just a bunch of lies and rhetoric, not anything concrete." Still, Kweli, like many of his contemporaries, is motivated to do *something* about the issues that Black youths encounter every day in their own lives: police brutality and racial profiling, gun control, education and welfare reform, Black-on-Black crime and the racially slanted prison system, to name a few. But he feels neither elected politicians nor candidates speak to these issues directly in a language that makes sense to hip-hop youths. In fact, Black youths simply don't respond to politicians, including Black ones who, for the most part, have also made only token attempts to reach out to them.

16   One Black leader who insists that responsible Blacks in positions of authority can't give up on politically apathetic young people is Congresswoman Maxine Waters (D–CA). "I've tried to make the connection between rappers, young people and the Congressional Black Caucus," says Waters. "My main agenda is to connect to the hip-hop generation—more than to actual rappers—and close the communication gap between them and older adults." Freedom of speech and censorship issues have split the generations in Black communities. Some White politicians gleefully supported longtime Black political activist C. Delores Tucker in her 1996 campaign against gangsta rap, say Waters, "because they didn't like rap *or* young Black people." She also recalls the highly publicized congressional hearings, headed by then-Senator Carol Moseley Braun (D–IL): "I had to literally read lyrics from Snoop Dogg's records to show that all the words were not simply vulgar curse words. They were oftentimes deeply meaningful in describing young people's experiences, and they connected to many others who felt left outside of the system."

17   For the past few years at the annual Congressional Black Caucus Week in Washington, D.C., Waters has sponsored and moderated a workshop called Young, Gifted and Black, in which young people and rappers are given a platform before law-makers to define themselves and their issues. But a surprising number of Black politicians have essentially thrown up their hands. Congressman Jesse L. Jackson, Jr. (D–IL), himself a member of the hip-hop generation at age 35, points out that he didn't see any rappers in Decatur, Illinois, "when my father was fighting to get six young African-Americans back in school." (The young Black men, who got into a fistfight at a local high-school football game in September 1999, were expelled because of the school district's zero-tolerance policy on school violence, which the young men argue has been disproportionately applied to Decatur's Black students.) When Congressman Jackson was pressed to detail the extent of Rev. Jackson's previous outreach efforts to the hip-hop community, he

replied, "They probably wouldn't have shown up. I ain't blaming them. I'm just simply saying people are busy."

True. "Most rappers who say they're spokesmen for the gen- 18 eration generally are spokesmen only as it relates to social and cultural trends," says Conrad Muhammad, former minister of the Nation of Islam's Mosque No. 7 in Harlem and founder of A Movement for CHHANGE (Conscious Hip-Hop Activism Necessary for Global Empowerment), a national organization aimed at educating urban youth about the political process and registering young people to vote. CHHANGE aims to put 1 million Black young people on the rolls this November (call [718] 237-0064), and Muhammad has also targeted several popular rappers to groom as candidates for local political office. Although he reports "opening the minds" of rappers like Fat Joe, DJ Kool Here and Vinnie and Treach of Naughty by Nature, no actual campaigns have moved beyond the talking stage.

Similarly, in a 1998 *Essence* cover story, Sean "Puffy" Combs 19 himself expressed interest in political activism and maybe even running for office. So far he has committed, along with LL Cool J, Mary J. Blige and Rosie Perez, to appear in public-service announcements for Rap the Vote 2000. A joint project of rap mogul Russell Simmons's new Web site, 360HipHop.com, and Rock the Vote, Rap the Vote 2000 aims to get 850,000 new young voters to the polls this year under the slogan "Register. Vote. Represent."

POLICE BRUTALITY AND RACIAL PROFILING

The death of the 22-year-old West African immigrant Amadou 20 Diallo—an unarmed man shot 41 times by four New York Police Department officers who were later acquitted of all charges—forced the ever-present issue of police brutality and racial profiling to the top of urban America's political agenda. The Hip-Hop for Respect Foundation (HHFRF) project was one activist response from the community of hip-hop artists. "Most of the people that got killed by police this year and in the past have probably been some of your fans" wrote rapper Mos Def, 26, in an open letter to the rap-music industry. "We are the senators and the congressmen of our communities. We come from communities that don't have anybody to speak for them and that's why they love us." As fund-raisers for the foundation, which supports activist groups that effectively deal with police brutality issues, Mos Def and Talib Kweli went on to organize the recording session for the maxisingle "One for Love, Pt. 1," which also features Common, Rah Digga, Pharoahe Monch, Pos (from De La Soul) and others.

21   But the acquittal of the four officers charged with the Diallo shooting elicited strong statements from the hip-hop elite, like Russell Simmons (largely covered in the Black press and rap-music magazines), and, more important, thrust thousands of young protesters from a mix of races into the streets of Manhattan and the Bronx neighborhood where the killing took place. Some marchers replaced the slogans of yesteryear with a popular cho-rus from a Nas track: "I wanna talk to the mayor, to the governor and the muthaf—king President / I wanna talk to the FBI and the CIA and the muthaf—king congressmen." Here hip-hoppers took their music back to the streets to make a pointed political statement.

JUVENILE JUSTICE AND PROPOSITION 21

22 Another grassroots organization spawned by the hip-hop gener-ation is San Francisco's Third Eye Movement. This collective of 40 members became a major force in making the antigang–crime-prevention initiative Proposition 21 a centerpiece debate in California's elections last spring. A campaign spearheaded by for-mer Republican governor Pete Wilson put Prop 21 on the ballot. The measure gives police the right to make arrests under a num-ber of questionable charges that disproportionately target young people of color. It's possible for a young woman and two of her friends, dressed similarly, to be calssified as a gang and therefore arrested. "If I happen to be on the basketball court playing ball with somebody, and that person leaves and commits a crime, the doors are open for me to be put in jail under conspiracy charges because of my association," says Davey D. 35, a community-affairs director and on-air radio personality at 106 KMEL in Oakland. Prop 21 also allows courts to try juveniles as adults for felonies, as well as permit police surveillance and phone taps without a court order.

Jasmin de la Rosa, 24, coordinator and founder of Third Eye, 23 organized school walkouts, free concerts, rallies and sit-ins to protest the initiative. But Prop 21 was ultimately passed last March in the statewide count, although it was defeated in several districts, including San Francisco and Oakland, where young protesters were active. More than 170 hip-hop heads were arrested after more than 500 people staged a sit-in at the San Francisco Hilton because they believed a Hilton family member pumped money into the "Yes on Prop 21" campaign. Here hip-hop aficionados customized a chant from an old-school rap song: "Hotel, motel and the Hilton, say what / If you fund the war on youth, you ain't gonna win." Bay Area rappers, including Digital Underground, Boots, Money B. and Sugar T., joined the anti–Prop 21 rallies. But the biggest impact was at the grass-roots level, according to De la Rosa. "The cultural events and hip-hop parties—getting young people to organize those events was very effective in calling them to action," she says. "The people who organize the shows get skills in political organizing."

Davey D, who is also the Web master for the popular Internet 24 site Davey D's Hip-Hop Corner (www.daveyd.com), concludes: "The best way to bring people under one umbrella is for them to engage in politics on a local level first."

SCHOOLS, NOT JAILS

How can we cultivate strong leadership when the prison-industrial 25 complex has an obscene percentage of our generation on lockdown? If you are imprisoned for a felony, depending on the state, your voting rights may be revoked for life. Marc Maurer, expert analyst and author of *Race to Incarcerate* (New Press), points out that three out of every ten Black males and one in six Latinos born today can expect to do time in prison if current trends continue. African-Americans make up half the prison population, with an increasing number of drug arrests made among nonviolent offenders. Maurer also argues that the $40-billion prison-industrial complex has encroached on funds for higher education.

There is also the concern that the educational system teaches 26 young people a racially slanted, warped history of themselves and their place in society. "Next on Third Eye's agenda," says De la Rosa, "is exploring educational reform and reinforcing the allies we've made with teachers, principals and prison activists. We're studying how to frame these issues to have the most statewide appeal." (See its Web site, www.thirdeyemovement.org.)

27   Is the hip-hop generation going to do something effective to coalesce around these issues? The outlook is still uncertain. "Artists, whether we accept it or not, are more representative of their labels than they are of a community," says Angela Ards. But she adds, "The sixties generation saw power as a political thing, and our generation has come to understand that power is also economic. Mainstream artists could be using their capital to finance grass-roots movements."

28   But Bill Stephney puts it another way: "To think that the NAACP, the Urban League and other civil-rights organizations emerged in environments that, particularly for Black people, had nowhere near the level of capital finance and marketing the hip-hop generation has." In the final analysis, Stephney says, "It's never from the top down, anyway. It's always from the bottom up. That's the great thing about 'street' and 'neighborhood Black culture'—it grows like a beautiful flower, from the ground up." So it must be with the hip-hop agenda.

2000

Sex, Lies, and Advertising

Gloria Steinem

1   About three years ago, as *glasnost* was beginning and *Ms.* seemed to be ending, I was invited to a press lunch for a Soviet official. He entertained us with anecdotes about new problems of democracy in his country. Local Communist leaders were being criticized in their media for the first time, he explained, and they were angry.

2   "So I'll have to ask my American friends," he finished point-edly, "how more *subtly* to control the press." In the silence that followed, I said, "Advertising."

The reporters laughed, but later, one of them took me aside: 3
How *dare* I suggest that freedom of the press was limited? How
dare I imply that his newsweekly could be influenced by ads?

I explained that I was thinking of advertising's mediawide 4
influence on most of what we read. Even newsmagazines use "soft"
cover stories to sell ads, confuse readers with "advertorials," and
occasionally self-censor on subjects known to be a problem with big
advertisers.

But, I also explained, I was thinking especially of women's 5
magazines. There, it isn't just a little content that's devoted to
attracting ads, it's almost all of it. That's why advertisers—not
readers—have always been the problem for *Ms.* As the only
women's magazine that didn't supply what the ad world
euphemistically describes as "supportive editorial atmosphere"
or "complementary copy" (for instance, articles that praise
food/fashion/beauty subjects to "support" and "complement"
food/fashion/beauty ads), *Ms.* could never attract enough advertising to break even.

"Oh, *women's* magazines," the journalist said with contempt. 6
"Everybody knows they're catalogs—but who cares? They have
nothing to do with journalism."

I can't tell you how many times I've had this argument in 25 7
years of working for many kinds of publications. Except as mon-
eymaking machines—"cash cows" as they are so elegantly called
in the trade—women's magazines are rarely taken seriously.
Though changes being made by women have been called more far-
reaching than the industrial revolution—and though many editors
try hard to reflect some of them in the few pages left to them after
all the ad-related subjects have been covered—the magazines
serving the female half of this country are still far below the journalistic and ethical standards of news and general interest publications. Most depressing of all, this doesn't even rate an exposé.

If *Time* and *Newsweek* had to lavish praise on cars in general 8
and credit General Motors in particular to get GM ads, there
would be a scandal—maybe a criminal investigation. When
women's magazines from *Seventeen* to *Lear's* praise beauty products in general and credit Revlon in particular to get ads, it's just
business as usual.

I

9   When *Ms.* began, we didn't consider *not* taking ads. The most important reason was keeping the price of a feminist magazine low enough for most women to afford. But the second and almost equal reason was providing a forum where women and advertisers could talk to each other and improve advertising itself. After all, it was (and still is) as potent a source of information in this country as news or TV and movie dramas.

10   We decided to proceed in two stages. First, we would convince makers of "people products" used by both men and women but advertised mostly to men—cars, credit cards, insurance, sound equipment, financial services, and the like—that their ads should be placed in a women's magazine. Since they were accustomed to the division between editorial and advertising in news and general interest magazines, this would allow our editorial content to be free and diverse. Second, we would add the best ads for whatever traditional "women's products" (clothes, shampoo, fragrance, food, and so on) that surveys showed *Ms.* readers used. But we would ask them to come in *without* the usual quid pro quo of "complementary copy."

11   We knew the second step might be harder. Food advertisers have always demanded that women's magazines publish recipes and articles on entertaining (preferably ones that name their products) in return for their ads; clothing advertisers expect to be surrounded by fashion spreads (especially ones that credit their designers); and shampoo, fragrance, and beauty products in general usually insist on positive editorial coverage of beauty subjects, plus photo credits besides. That's why women's magazines look the way they do. But if we could break this link between ads and editorial content, then we wanted good ads for "women's products," too.

12   By playing their part in this unprecedented mix of *all* the things our readers need and use, advertisers also would be rewarded: ads for products like cars and mutual funds would find a new growth market; the best ads for women's products would no longer be lost in oceans of ads for the same category; and both would have access to a laboratory of smart and caring readers whose response would help create effective ads for other media as well.

I thought then that our main problem would be the imagery ₁₃
in ads themselves. Carmakers were still draping blondes in
evening gowns over the hoods like ornaments. Authority figures
were almost always male, even in ads for products that only
women used. Sadistic, he-man campaigns even won industry
praise. (For instance, *Advertising Age* had hailed the infamous
Silva Thin cigarette theme, "How to Get a Woman's Attention:
Ignore Her," as "brilliant.") Even in medical journals, tranquilizer
ads showed depressed housewives standing beside piles of dirty
dishes and promised to get them back to work.

Obviously, *Ms.* would have to avoid such ads and seek out ₁₄
the best ones—but this didn't seem impossible. *The New Yorker*
had been selecting ads for aesthetic reasons for years, a practice
that only seemed to make advertisers more eager to be in its
pages. *Ebony* and *Essence* were asking for ads with positive black
images, and though their struggle was hard, they weren't being
called unreasonable.

Clearly, what *Ms.* needed was a very special publisher and ad ₁₅
sales staff. I could think of only one woman with experience on
the business side of magazines—Patricia Carbine, who recently
had become a vice president of *McCall's* as well as its editor in
chief—and the reason I knew her name was a good omen. She
had been managing editor at *Look* (really *the* editor, but its owner
refused to put a female name at the top of his masthead) when I
was writing a column there. After I did an early interview with
Cesar Chavez, then just emerging as a leader of migrant labor, and
the publisher turned it down because he was worried about ads
from Sunkist, Pat was the one who intervened. As I learned later,
she had told the publisher she would resign if the interview
wasn't published. Mainly because *Look* couldn't afford to lose Pat,
it *was* published (and the ads from Sunkist never arrived).

Though I barely knew this woman, she had done two things ₁₆
I always remembered: put her job on the line in a way that editors often talk about but rarely do, and been so loyal to her colleagues that she never told me or anyone outside *Look* that she
had done so.

Fortunately, Pat did agree to leave *McCall's* and take a huge ₁₇
cut in salary to become publisher of *Ms.* She became responsible
for training and inspiring generations of young women who

joined the *Ms.* ad sales force, many of whom went on to become "firsts" at the top of publishing. When *Ms.* first started, however, there were so few women with experience selling space that Pat and I made the rounds of ad agencies ourselves. Later, the fact that *Ms.* was asking companies to do business in a different way meant our saleswomen had to make many times the usual number of calls—first to convince agencies and then client companies besides—and to present endless amounts of research. I was often asked to do a final ad presentation, or see some higher decision-maker, or speak to women employees so executives could see the interest of women they worked with. That's why I spent more time persuading advertisers than editing or writing for *Ms.* and why I ended up with an unsentimental education in the seamy underside of publishing that few writers see (and even fewer magazines can publish).

18   Let me take you with us through some experiences, just as they happened:

19 • Cheered on by early support from Volkswagen and one or two other car companies, we scrape together time and money to put on a major reception in Detroit. We know U.S. carmakers firmly believe that women choose the upholstery, not the car, but we are armed with statistics and reader mail to prove the contrary: a car is an important purchase for women, one that symbolizes mobility and freedom.

20   But almost nobody comes. We are left with many pounds of shrimp on the table, and quite a lot of egg on our face. We blame ourselves for not guessing that there would be a baseball pennant play-off on the same day, but executives go out of their way to explain they wouldn't have come anyway. Thus begins ten years of knocking on hostile doors, presenting endless documentation, and hiring a full-time saleswoman in Detroit—all necessary before *Ms.* gets any real results.

21   This long saga has a semihappy ending: foreign and, later, domestic carmakers eventually provided *Ms.* with enough advertising to make cars one of our top sources of ad revenue. Slowly, Detroit began to take the women's market seriously enough to put car ads in other women's magazines, too, thus freeing a few pages from the hothouse of fashion–beauty–food ads.

But long after figures showed a third, even a half, of many   22
car models being bought by women, U.S. makers continued to
be uncomfortable addressing women. Unlike foreign carmakers,
Detroit never quite learned the secret of creating intelligent ads
that exclude no one, and then placing them in women's magazines to overcome past exclusion. (*Ms.* readers were so grateful
for a routine Honda ad featuring rack and pinion steering, for
instance, that they sent fan mail.) Even now, Detroit continues
to ask, "Should we make special ads for women?" Perhaps
that's why some foreign cars still have a disproportionate share
of the U.S. women's market.

• In the *Ms.* Gazette, we do a brief report on a congressional   23
hearing into chemicals used in hair dyes that are absorbed
through the skin and may be carcinogenic. Newspapers report this
too, but Clairol, a Bristol-Myers subsidiary that makes dozens of
products—a few of which have just begun to advertise in *Ms.*—
is outraged. Not at newspapers or newsmagazines, just at us. It's
bad enough that *Ms.* is the only women's magazine refusing to
provide the usual "complementary" articles and beauty photos,
but to criticize one of their categories—*that* is going too far.

We offer to publish a letter from Clairol telling its side of
the story. In an excess of solicitousness, we even put this letter   24
in the Gazette, not in Letters to the Editors where it belongs.
Nonetheless—and in spite of surveys that show *Ms.* readers are
active women who use more of almost everything Clairol makes
than do the readers of any other women's magazine—*Ms.* gets
almost none of these ads for the rest of its natural life.

Meanwhile, Clairol changes its hair coloring formula, apparently in response to the hearings we reported.   25

• Our saleswomen set out early to attract ads for consumer   26
electronics: sound equipment, calculators, computers, VCRs,
and the like. We know that our readers are determined to be
included in the technological revolution. We know from reader
surveys that *Ms.* readers are buying this stuff in numbers as high
as those of magazines like *Playboy,* or "men 18 to 34," the prime
targets of the consumer electronics industry. Moreover, unlike
traditional women's products that our readers buy but don't

need to read articles about, these are subjects they want covered in our pages. There actually is a supportive editorial atmosphere.

27   "But women don't understand technology," say executives at the end of ad presentations. "Maybe not," we respond, "but neither do men—and we all buy it."

28   "If women *do* buy it," say the decision-makers, "they're asking their husbands and boyfriends what to buy first." We produce letters from *Ms.* readers saying how turned off they are when salesmen say things like "Let me know when your husband can come in."

29   After several years of this, we get a few ads for compact sound systems. Some of them come from JVC, whose vice president, Harry Elias, is trying to convince his Japanese bosses that there is something called a women's market. At his invitation, I find myself speaking at huge trade shows in Chicago and Las Vegas, trying to persuade JVC dealers that showrooms don't have to be locker rooms where women are made to feel unwelcome. But as it turns out, the shows themselves are part of the problem. In Las Vegas, the only women around the technology displays are seminude models serving champagne. In Chicago, the big attraction is Marilyn Chambers, who followed Linda Lovelace of *Deep Throat* fame as Chuck Traynor's captive and/or employee. VCRs are being demonstrated with her porn videos.

30   In the end, we get ads for a car stereo now and then, but no VCRs; some IBM personal computers, but no Apple or Japanese ones. We notice that office magazines like *Working Woman* and *Savvy* don't benefit as much as they should from office equipment ads either. In the electronics world, women and technology seem mutually exclusive. It remains a decade behind even Detroit.

31 •   Because we get letters from little girls who love toy trains, and who ask our help in changing ads and box-top photos that feature little boys only, we try to get toy-train ads from Lionel. It turns out that Lionel executives *have* been concerned about little girls. They made a pink train, and were surprised when it didn't sell.

32   Lionel bows to consumer pressure with a photograph of a boy *and* a girl—but only on some of their boxes. They fear that,

if trains are associated with girls, they will be devalued in the minds of boys. Needless to say, *Ms.* gets no train ads, and little girls remain a mostly unexplored market. By 1986, Lionel is put up for sale.

But for different reasons, we haven't had much luck with other kinds of toys either. In spite of many articles on child-rearing; an annual listing of nonsexist, multi-racial toys by Letty Cottin Pogrebin; Stories for Free Children, a regular feature also edited by Letty; and other prizewinning features for or about children, we get virtually no toy ads. Generations of *Ms.* sales-women explain to toy manufacturers that a larger proportion of *Ms.* readers have preschool children than do the readers of other women's magazines, but this industry can't believe feminists have or care about children.   33

• When *Ms.* begins, the staff decides not to accept ads for feminine hygiene sprays or cigarettes: they are damaging and carry no appropriate health warnings. Though we don't think we should tell our readers what to do, we do think we should provide facts so they can decide for themselves. Since the anti-smoking lobby has been pressing for health warnings on ciga-rette ads, we decided to take them only as they comply.   34

Philip Morris is among the first to do so. One of its brands, Virginia Slims, is also sponsoring women's tennis and the first national polls of women's opinions. On the other hand, the Virginia Slims theme, "You've come a long way, baby," has more than a "baby" problem. It makes smoking a symbol of progress for women.   35

We explain to Philip Morris that this slogan won't do well in our pages, but they are convinced its success with some women means it will work with *all* women. Finally, we agree to publish an ad for a Virginia Slims calendar as a test. The letters from readers are critical—and smart. For instance: Would you show a black man picking cotton, the same man in a Cardin suit, and symbolize the antislavery and civil rights movements by smoking? Of course not. But instead of honoring the test results, the Philip Morris people seem angry to be proven wrong. They take away ads for *all* their many brands.   36

37   This costs *Ms.* about $250,000 the first year. After five years, we can no longer keep track. Occasionally, a new set of executives listens to *Ms.* saleswomen, but because we won't take Virginia Slims, not one Philip Morris product returns to our pages for the next 16 years.

38   Gradually, we also realize our naiveté in thinking we *could* decide against taking cigarette ads. They became a disproportionate support of magazines the moment they were banned on television, and few magazines could compete and survive without them; certainly not *Ms.*, which lacks so many other categories. By the time statistics in the 1980s showed the women's rate of lung cancer was approaching men's, the necessity of taking cigarette ads has become a kind of prison.

39   • General Mills, Pillsbury, Carnation, DelMonte, Dole, Kraft, Stouffer, Hormel, Nabisco: you name the food giant, we try it. But no matter how desirable the *Ms.* readership, our lack of recipes is lethal.

40   We explain to them that placing food ads *only* next to recipes associates food with work. For many women, it is a negative that works *against* the ads. Why not place food ads in diverse media without recipes (thus reaching more men, who are now a third of the shoppers in supermarkets anyway), and leave the recipes to specialty magazines like *Gourmet* (a third of whose readers are also men)?

41   These arguments elicit interest, but except for an occasional ad for a convenience food, instant coffee, diet drinks, yogurt, or such extras as avocados and almonds, this mainstay of the publishing industry stays closed to us. Period.

42   • Traditionally, wines and liquors didn't advertise to women: men were thought to make the brand decisions, even if women did the buying. But after endless presentations, we begin to make a dent in this category. Thanks to the unconventional Michel Roux of Carillon Importers (distributors of Grand Marnier, Absolut Vodka, and others), who assumes that food and drink have no gender, some ads are leaving their men's club.

43   Beermakers are still selling masculinity. It takes *Ms.* fully eight years to get its first beer ad (Michelob). In general, however, liquor ads are less stereotyped in their imagery—and far

less controlling of the editorial content around them—than are women's products. But given the underrepresentation of other categories, these very facts tend to create a disproportionate number of alcohol ads in the pages of *Ms.* This in turn dismays readers worried about women and alcoholism.

• We hear in 1980 that women in the Soviet Union have been   44 producing feminist *samizdat* (underground, self-published books) and circulating them throughout the country. As punishment, four of the leaders have been exiled. Though we are operating on our usual shoestring, we solicit individual contributions to send Robin Morgan to interview these women in Vienna.

The result is an exclusive cover story that includes the first   45 news of a populist peace movement against the Afghanistan occupation, a prediction of *glasnost* to come, and a grass-roots, intimate view of Soviet women's lives. From the popular press to women's studies courses, the response is great. The story wins a Front Page award.

Nonetheless, this journalistic coup undoes years of efforts to   46 get an ad schedule from Revlon. Why? Because the Soviet women on our cover *are not wearing makeup.*

• Four years of research and presentations go into convincing   47 airlines that women now make travel choices and business trips. United, the first airline to advertise in *Ms.,* is so impressed with the response from our readers that one of its executives appears in a film for our ad presentations. As usual, good ads get great results.

But we have problems unrelated to such results. For   48 instance: because American Airlines flight attendants include among their labor demands the stipulation that they could choose to have their last names preceded by "Ms." on their name tags—in a long-delayed revolt against the standard, "I am your pilot, Captain Rothgart, and this is your flight attendant, Cindy Sue"—American officials seem to hold the magazine responsible. We get no ads.

There is still a different problem at Eastern. A vice president   49 cancels subscriptions for thousands of copies on Eastern flights. Why? Because he is offended by ads for lesbian poetry journals

in the *Ms.* Classified. A "family airline," as he explains to me
coldly on the phone, has to "draw the line somewhere."

50   It's obvious that *Ms.* can't exclude lesbians and serve
women. We've been trying to make that point ever since our
first issue included an article by and about lesbians, and both
Suzanne Levine, our managing editor, and I were lectured by
such heavy hitters as Ed Kosner, then editor of *Newsweek* (and
now of *New York Magazine*), who insisted that *Ms.* should
"position" itself *against* lesbians. But our advertisers have paid
to reach a guaranteed number of readers, and soliciting new
subscriptions to compensate for Eastern would cost $150,000
plus rebating money in the meantime.

51   Like almost everything ad-related, this presents an elaborate
organizing problem. After days of searching for sympathetic
members of the Eastern board, Frank Thomas, president of the
Ford Foundation, kindly offers to call Roswell Gilpatrick, a
director of Eastern. I talk with Mr. Gilpatrick, who calls Frank
Borman, then the president of Eastern. Frank Borman calls me
to say that his airline is not in the business of censoring magazines: *Ms.* will be returned to Eastern flights.

52 • Women's access to insurance and credit is vital, but with the
exception of Equitable and a few other ad pioneers, such financial
services address men. For almost a decade after the Equal Credit
Opportunity Act passes in 1974, we try to convince American
Express that women are a growth market—but nothing works.

53   Finally, a former professor of Russian named Jerry Welsh
becomes head of marketing. He assumes that women should be
cardholders, and persuades his colleagues to feature women in
a campaign. Thanks to this 1980s series, the growth rate for
female cardholders surpasses that for men.

54   For this article, I asked Jerry Welsh if he would explain why
American Express waited so long. "Sure," he said, "they were
afraid of having a 'pink' card."

55 • Women of color read *Ms.* in disproportionate numbers. This
is a source of pride to *Ms.* staffers, who are also more racially
representative than the editors of other women's magazines. But
this reality is obscured by ads filled with enough white women
to make a reader snowblind.

Pat Carbine remembers mostly "astonishment" when she   56
requested African American, Hispanic, Asian, and other diverse
images. Marcia Ann Gillespie, a *Ms.* editor who was previously
the editor in chief of *Essence,* witnesses ad bias a second time:
having tried for *Essence* to get white advertisers to use black
images (Revlon did so eventually, but L'Oréal, Lauder, Chanel,
and other companies never did), she sees similar problems getting integrated ads for an integrated magazine. Indeed, the ad
world often creates black and Hispanic ads only for black and
Hispanic media. In an exact parallel of the fear that marketing
a product to women will endanger its appeal to men, the
response is usually, "But your [white] readers won't identify."

In fact, those we are able to get—for instance, a Max Factor   57
ad made for *Essence* that Linda Wachner gives us after she
becomes president—are praised by white readers, too. But there
are pathetically few such images.

• By the end of 1986, production and mailing costs have risen   58
astronomically, ad income is flat, and competition for ads is
stiffer than ever. The 60/40 preponderance of edit over ads that
we promised to readers becomes 50/50; children's stories, most
poetry, and some fiction are casualties of less space; in order to
get variety into limited pages, the length (and sometimes the
depth) of articles suffers; and, though we do refuse most of the
ads that would look like a parody in our pages, we get so worn
down that some slip through. (See this issue's No Comment.)
Still, readers perform miracles. Though we haven't been able to
afford a subscription mailing in two years, they maintain our
guaranteed circulation of 450,000.

Nonetheless, media reports on *Ms.* often insist that our un-   59
profitability must be due to reader disinterest. The myth that
advertisers simply follow readers is very strong. Not one reporter
notes that other comparable magazines our size (say, *Vanity Fair*
or *The Atlantic*) have been losing more money in one year than
Ms. has lost in 16 years. No matter how much never-to-be-
recovered cash is poured into starting a magazine or keeping one
going, appearances seem to be all that matter. (Which is why we
haven't been able to explain our fragile state in public. Nothing
causes ad-flight like the smell of nonsuccess.)

60   My healthy response is anger. My not-so-healthy response is constant worry. Also an obsession with finding one more rescue. There is hardly a night when I don't wake up with sweaty palms and pounding heart, scared that we won't be able to pay the printer or the post office; scared most of all that closing our doors will hurt the women's movement.

61   Out of chutzpah and desperation, I arrange a lunch with Leonard Lauder, president of Estée Lauder. With the exception of Clinique (the brainchild of Carol Phillips), none of Lauder's hundreds of products has been advertised in *Ms.* A year's schedule of ads for just three or four of them could save us. Indeed, as the scion of a family-owned company whose ad practices are followed by the beauty industry, he is one of the few men who could liberate many pages in all women's magazines just by changing his mind about "complementary copy."

62   Over a lunch that costs more than we can pay for some articles, I explain the need for his leadership. I also lay out the record of *Ms.:* more literary and journalistic prizes won, more new issues introduced into the mainstream, new writers discovered, and impact on society than any other magazine; more articles that became books, stories that became movies, ideas that became television series, and newly advertised products that became profitable; and, most important for him, a place for his ads to reach women who aren't reachable through any other women's magazine. Indeed, if there is one constant characteristic of the ever-changing *Ms.* readership, it is their impact as leaders. Whether it's waiting until later to have first babies, or pioneering PABA as sun protection in cosmetics, *whatever* they are doing today, a third to a half of American women will be doing three to five years from now. It's never failed.

63   But, he says, *Ms.* readers are not *our* women. They're not interested in things like fragrance and blush-on. If they were, *Ms.* would write articles about them.

64   On the contrary, I explain, surveys show they are more likely to buy such things than the readers of, say, *Cosmopolitan* or *Vogue.* They're good customers because they're out in the world enough to need several sets of everything: home, work, purse, travel, gym, and so on. They just don't need to read articles about these things. Would he ask a men's magazine to publish monthly columns on how to shave before he advertised Aramis products (his line for men)?

He concedes that beauty features are often concocted more for 65
advertisers than readers. But *Ms.* isn't appropriate for his ads
anyway, he explains. Why? Because Estée Lauder is selling "a
kept-woman mentality."

I can't quite believe this. Sixty percent of the users of his prod- 66
ucts are salaried, and generally resemble *Ms.* readers. Besides, his
company has the appeal of having been started by a creative and
hardworking woman, his mother, Estée Lauder.

That doesn't matter, he says. He knows his customers, and 67
they would *like* to be kept women. That's why he will never
advertise in *Ms.*

In November 1987, by vote of the Ms. Foundation for Educa- 68
tion and Communication (*Ms.*'s owner and publisher, the media
subsidiary of the Ms. Foundation for Women), *Ms.* was sold to a
company whose officers, Australian feminists Sandra Yates and
Anne Summers, raised the investment money in their country that
Ms. couldn't find in its own. They also started *Sassy* for teenage
women.

In their two-year tenure, circulation was raised to 550,000 by 69
investment in circulation mailings, and, to the dismay of some
readers, editorial features on clothes and new products made a
more traditional bid for ads. Nonetheless, ad pages fell below previous levels. In addition, *Sassy*, whose fresh voice and sexual
frankness were an unprecedented success with young readers,
was targeted by two mothers from Indiana who began, as one of
them put it, "calling every Christian organization I could think
of." In response to this controversy, several crucial advertisers
pulled out.

Such links between ads and editorial content were a problem 70
in Australia, too, but to a lesser degree. "Our readers pay two
times more for their magazines," Anne explained, "so advertisers
have less power to threaten a magazine's viability."

"I was shocked," said Sandra Yates with characteristic direct- 71
ness. "In Australia, we think you have freedom of the press—but
you don't."

Since Anne and Sandra had not met their budget's projections 72
for ad revenue, their investors forced a sale. In October 1989, *Ms.*
and *Sassy* were bought by Dale Lang, owner of *Working Mother*,

Working Woman, and one of the few independent publishing companies left among the conglomerates. In response to a request from the original *Ms.* staff—as well as to reader letters urging that *Ms.* continue, plus his own belief that *Ms.* would benefit his other magazines by blazing a trail—he agreed to try the ad-free, reader-supported *Ms.* you hold now and to give us complete editorial control.

II

73 Do you think, as I once did, that advertisers make decisions based on solid research? Well, think again. "Broadly speaking," says Joseph Smith of Oxtoby-Smith, Inc., a consumer research firm, "there is no persuasive evidence that the editorial context of an ad matters."

74 Advertisers who demand such "complementary copy," even in the absence of respectable studies, clearly are operating under a double standard. The same food companies place ads in *People* with no recipes. Cosmetics companies support *The New Yorker* with no regular beauty columns. So where does this habit of controlling the content of women's magazines come from?

75 Tradition. Ever since *Ladies Magazine* debuted in Boston in 1828, editorial copy directed to women has been informed by something other than its readers' wishes. There were no ads then, but in an age when married women were legal minors with no right to their own money, there was another revenue source to be kept in mind: husbands. "Husbands may rest assured," wrote editor Sarah Joseph Hale, "that nothing found in these pages shall cause her [his wife] to be less assiduous in preparing for his reception or encourage her to 'usurp station' or encroach upon prerogatives of men."

76 Hale went on to become the editor of *Godey's Lady's Book,* a magazine featuring "fashion plates": engravings of dresses for readers to take to their seamstresses or copy themselves. Hale added "how to" articles, which set the tone for women's service magazines for years to come: how to write politely, avoid sunburn, and—in no fewer than 1,200 words—how to maintain a goose quill pen. She advocated education for women but avoided

controversy. Just as most women's magazines now avoid politics, poll their readers on issues like abortion but rarely take a stand, and praise socially approved lifestyles, Hale saw to it that *Godey's* avoided the hot topics of its day: slavery, abolition, and women's suffrage.

What definitively turned women's magazines into catalogs, 77 however, were two events: Ellen Butterick's invention of the clothing pattern in 1863 and the mass manufacture of patent medicines containing everything from colored water to cocaine. For the first time, readers could purchase what magazines encouraged them to want. As such magazines became more profitable, they also began to attract men as editors. (Most women's magazines continued to have men as top editors until the feminist 1970s.) Edward Bok, who became editor of *The Ladies' Home Journal* in 1889, discovered the power of advertisers when he rejected ads for patent medicines and found that other advertisers canceled in retribution. In the early 20th century, *Good Housekeeping* started its Institute to "test and approve" products. Its Seal of Approval became the grandfather of current "value added" programs that offer advertisers such bonuses as product sampling and department store promotions.

By the time suffragists finally won the vote in 1920, women's 78 magazines had become too entrenched as catalogs to help women learn how to use it. The main function was to create a desire for products, teach how to use products, and make products a crucial part of gaining social approval, pleasing a husband, and performing as a homemaker. Some unrelated articles and short stories were included to persuade women to pay for these catalogs. But articles were neither consumerist nor rebellious. Even fiction was usually subject to formula: if a woman had any sexual life outside marriage, she was supposed to come to a bad end.

In 1965, Helen Gurley Brown began to change part of that for- 79 mula by bringing "the sexual revolution" to women's magazines—but in an ad-oriented way. Attracting multiple men required even more consumerism, as the Cosmo Girl made clear, than finding one husband.

In response to the workplace revolution of the 1970s, traditional 80 women's magazines—that is, "trade books" for women working at home—were joined by *Savvy, Working Woman,* and other trade

books for women working in offices. But by keeping the fashion/
beauty/entertaining articles necessary to get traditional ads and
then adding career articles besides, they inadvertently produced the
antifeminist stereotype of Super Woman. The male-imitative, dress-
for-success woman carrying a briefcase became the media image of
a woman worker, even though a blue-collar woman's salary was
often higher than her glorified secretarial sister's, and though
women at a real briefcase level are statistically rare. Needless to say,
these dress-for-success women were also thin, white, and beautiful.

81   In recent years, advertisers' control over the editorial content
of women's magazines has become so institutionalized that it is
written into "insertion orders" or dictated to ad salespeople as
official policy. The following are recent typical orders to women's
magazines:

82 •   Dow's Cleaning Products stipulates that ads for its Vivid
and Spray 'n Wash products should be adjacent to "children or
fashion editorial"; ads for Bathroom Cleaner should be next to
"home furnishing/family" features; and so on for other brands.
"If a magazine fails for ½ the brands or more," the Dow order
warns, "it will be omitted from further consideration."

83 •   Bristol-Myers, the parent of Clairol, Windex, Drano, Bufferin,
and much more, stipulates that ads be placed next to "a full
page of compatible editorial."

84 •   S.C. Johnson & Son, makers of Johnson Wax, lawn and laundry products, insect sprays, hair sprays, and so on orders that
its ads *should not be opposite extremely controversial features or
material antithetical to the nature/copy of the advertised product."*
(Italics theirs.)

85 •   Maidenform, manufacturer of bras and other apparel, leaves
a blank for the particular product and states: "The creative concept of the _____ campaign, and the very nature of the product
itself appeal to the positive emotions of the reader/consumer.
Therefore, it is imperative that all editorial adjacencies reflect
that same positive tone. The editorial must not be negative in
content or lend itself contrary to the _____ product imagery/
message (e.g. *editorial relating to illness, disillusionment, large size
fashion, etc.*)." (Italics mine.)

- The De Beers diamond company, a big seller of engagement [86] rings, prohibits magazines from placing its ads with "adjacencies to hard news or anti/love-romance themed editorial."

- Procter & Gamble, one of this country's most powerful [87] and diversified advertisers, stands out in the memory of Anne Summers and Sandra Yates (no mean feat in this context): its products were not to be placed in *any* issue that included *any* material on gun control, abortion, the occult, cults, or the disparagement of religion. Caution was also demanded in any issue covering sex or drugs, even for educational proposes.

Those are the most obvious chains around women's maga- [88] zines. There are also rules so clear they needn't be written down: for instance, an overall "look" compatible with beauty and fashion ads. Even "real" nonmodel women photographed for a woman's magazine are usually made up, dressed in credited clothes, and retouched out of all reality. When editors do include articles on less-than-cheerful subjects (for instance, domestic violence), they tend to keep them short and unillustrated. The point is to be "upbeat." Just as women in the street are asked, "Why don't you smile, honey?" women's magazines acquire an institutional smile.

Within the text itself, praise for advertisers' products has [89] become so ritualized that fields like "beauty writing" have been invented. One of its frequent practitioners explained seriously that "It's a difficult art. How many new adjectives can you find? How much greater can you make a lipstick sound? The FDA restricts what companies can say on labels, but we create illusion. And ad agencies are on the phone all the time pushing you to get their product in. A lot of them keep the business based on how many editorial clippings they produce every month. The worst are products," like Lauder's as the writer confirmed, "with their own name involved. It's all ego."

Often, editorial becomes one giant ad. Last November, for [90] instance, *Lear's* featured an elegant woman executive on the cover. On the contents page, we learned she was wearing Guerlian makeup and Samsara, a new fragrance by Guerlain. Inside were full-page ads for Samsara and Guerlain antiwrinkle cream. In the cover profile, we learned that this executive was responsible for launching Samsara and is Guerlain's director of public relations.

When the *Columbia Journalism Review* did one of the few articles to include women's magazines in coverage of the influence of ads, editor Frances Lear was quoted as defending her magazine because "this kind of thing is done all the time."

91   Often, advertisers also plunge odd-shaped ads into the text, no matter what the cost to the readers. At *Woman's Day*, a magazine originally founded by a supermarket chain, editor in chief Ellen Levine said, "The day the copy had to rag around a chicken leg was not a happy one."

92   Advertisers are also adamant about where in a magazine their ads appear. When Revlon was not placed as the first beauty ad in one Hearst magazine, for instance, Revlon pulled its ads from *all* Hearst magazines. Ruth Whitney, editor in chief of *Glamour*, attributes some of these demands to "ad agencies wanting to prove to a client that they've squeezed the last drop of blood out of a magazine." She also is, she says, "sick and tired of hearing that women's magazines are controlled by cigarette ads." Relatively speaking, she's right. To be as censoring as are many advertisers for women's products, tobacco companies would have to demand articles in praise of smoking and expect glamorous photos of beautiful women smoking their brands.

93   I don't mean to imply that the editors I quote here share my objections to ads: most assume that women's magazines have to be the way they are. But it's also true that only former editors can be completely honest. "Most of the pressure came in the form of direct project mentions," explains Sey Chassler, who was editor in chief of *Redbook* from the sixties to the eighties. "We got threats from the big guys, the Revlons, blackmail threats. They wouldn't run ads unless we credited them.

94   "But it's not fair to single out the beauty advertisers because these pressures came from everybody. Advertisers want to know two things: What are you going to charge me? What *else* are you going to do for me? It's a holdup. For instance, management felt that fiction took up too much space. They couldn't put any advertising in that. For the last ten years, the number of fiction entries into the National Magazine Awards has declined.

95   "And pressures are getting worse. More magazines are more bottom-line oriented because they have been taken over by companies with no interest in publishing.

"I also think advertisers do this to women's magazines espe- 96
cially," he concluded, "because of the general disrespect they have
for women."

Even media experts who don't give a damn about women's 97
magazines are alarmed by the spread of this ad–edit linkage. In a
climate *The Wall Street Journal* describes as an unacknowledged
Depression for media, women's products are increasingly able to
take their low standards wherever they go. For instance:
newsweeklies publish uncritical stories on fashion and fitness. *The
New York Times Magazine* recently ran an article on "firming
creams," complete with mentions of advertisers. *Vanity Fair* published a profile of one major advertiser, Ralph Lauren, illustrated
by the same photographer who does his ads, and turned the
lifestyle of another, Calvin Klein, into a cover story. Even the outrageous *Spy* has toned down since it began to go after fashion ads.

And just to make us really worry, films and books, the last 98
media that go directly to the public without having to attract ads
first, are in danger, too. Producers are beginning to depend on
payments for displaying products in movies, and books are now
being commissioned by companies like Federal Express.

But the truth is that women's products—like women's maga- 99
zines—have never been the subjects of much serious reporting
anyway. News and general interest publications, including the
"style" or "living" sections of newspapers, write about food and
clothing as cooking and fashion, and almost never evaluate such
products by brand name. Though chemical additives, pesticides,
and animal fats are major health risks in the United States, and
clothes, shoddy or not, absorb more consumer dollars than cars, this
lack of information is serious. So is ignoring the contents of beauty
products that are absorbed into our bodies through our skins, and
that have profit margins so big they would make a loan shark blush.

III

What could women's magazines be like if they were as free as 100
books? as realistic as newspapers? as creative as films? as diverse
as women's lives? We don't know.

101   But we'll only find out if we take women's magazines seriously. If readers were to act in a concerted way to change traditional practices of *all* women's magazines and the marketing of *all* women's products, we could do it. After all, they are operating on our consumer dollars, money that we now control. You and I could:

- write to editors and publishers (with copies to advertisers) that we're willing to pay *more* for magazines with editorial independence, but will *not* continue to pay for those that are just editorial extensions of ads;
- write to advertisers (with copies to editors and publishers) that we want fiction, political reporting, consumer reporting—whatever is, or is not, supported by their ads;
- put as much energy into breaking advertising's control over content as into changing the images in ads, or protesting ads for harmful products like cigarettes;
- support only those women's magazines and products that take *us* seriously as readers and consumers.

102   Those of us in the magazine world can also use the carrot-and-stick technique. For instance: pointing out that, if magazines were a regulated medium like television, the demands of advertisers would be against FCC rules. Payola and extortion could be punished. As it is, there are probably illegalities. A magazine's postal rates are determined by the ratio of ad to edit pages, and the former costs more than the latter. So much for the stick.

103   The carrot means appealing to enlightened self-interest. For instance: there are many studies showing that the greatest factor in determining an ad's effectiveness is the credibility of its surroundings. The "higher the rating of editorial believability," concluded a 1987 survey by the *Journal of Advertising Research*, "the higher the rating of the advertising." Thus, an impenetrable wall between edit and ads would also be in the best interest of advertisers.

104   Unfortunately, few agencies or clients hear such arguments. Editors often maintain the false purity of refusing to talk to them at all. Instead, they see ad salespeople who know little about editorial, are trained in business as usual, and are usually paid by commission. Editors might also band together to take on controversy. That happened once when all the major women's magazines

did articles in the same month on the Equal Rights Amendment.
It could happen again.

It's almost three years away from life between the grindstones   105
of advertising pressures and readers' needs. I'm just beginning to
realize how edges got smoothed down—in spite of all our resistance.

I remember feeling put upon when I changed "Porsche" to   106
"car" in a piece about Nazi imagery in German pornography by
Andrea Dworkin—feeling sure Andrea would understand that
Volkswagen, the distributor of Porsche and one of our few supportive advertisers, asked only to be far away from Nazi subjects.
It's taken me all this time to realize that Andrea was the one with
a right to feel put upon.

Even as I write this, I get a call from a writer for *Elle*, who is   107
doing a whole article on where women part their hair. Why, she
wants to know, do I part mine in the middle?

It's all so familiar. A writer trying to make something of a   108
nothing assignment; an editor laboring to think of new ways to
attract ads; readers assuming that other women must want this
ridiculous stuff; more women suffering for lack of information,
insight, creativity, and laughter that could be on these same pages.

I ask you: Can't we do better than this?   109

1990

Red, White, and Beer

Dave Barry

Lately I've been feeling very patriotic, especially during commer-   1
cials. Like, when I see those strongly pro-American Chrysler commercials, the ones where the winner of the Bruce Springsteen
Sound-Alike Contest sings about how The Pride Is Back, the ones
where Lee Iacocca himself comes striding out and practically challenges the president of Toyota to a knife fight, I get this warm,
proud feeling inside, the same kind of feeling I get whenever we
hold routine naval maneuvers off the coast of Libya.

2   But if you want to talk about *real* patriotism, of course, you
have to talk about beer commercials. I would have to say that
Miller is the most patriotic brand of beer. I grant you it tastes like
rat saliva, but we are not talking about taste here. What we are
talking about, according to the commercials, is that Miller is by
God an *American* beer, "born and brewed in the U.S.A.," and the
men who drink it are American men, the kind of men who aren't
afraid to perspire freely and shake a man's hand. That's mainly
what happens in Miller commercials: Burly American men go
around, drenched in perspiration, shaking each other's hands in
a violent and patriotic fashion.

3   You never find out exactly why these men spend so much time
shaking hands. Maybe shaking hands is just their simple straightforward burly masculine American patriotic way of saying to each
other: "Floyd, I am truly sorry I drank all that Miller beer last night
and went to the bathroom in your glove compartment." Another
possible explanation is that, since there are never any women in
the part of America where beer commercials are made, the burly
men have become lonesome and desperate for any form of physical contact. I have noticed that sometimes, in addition to shaking
hands, they hug each other. Maybe very late at night, after the
David Letterman show, there are Miller commercials in which the
burly men engage in slow dancing. I don't know.

4   I do know that in one beer commercial, I think this is for
Miller—although it could be for Budweiser, which is also a very
patriotic beer—the-burly men build a house. You see them all getting together and pushing up a brand-new wall. Me, I worry some
about a house built by men drinking beer. In my experience, you
run into trouble when you ask a group of beer-drinking men to
perform any task more complex than remembering not to light
the filter ends of cigarettes.

5   For example, in my younger days, whenever anybody in my
circle of friends wanted to move, he'd get the rest of us to help,
and, as an inducement, he'd buy a couple of cases of beer. This
almost always produced unfortunate results, such as the time we
were trying to move Dick "The Wretch" Curry from a horrible
fourth-floor walk-up apartment in Manhattan's Lower East Side to
another horrible fourth-floor walk-up apartment in Manhattan's
Lower East Side, and we hit upon the labor-saving concept of,

instead of carrying The Wretch's possessions manually down the stairs, simply dropping them out the window, down onto the street, where The Wretch was racing around, gathering up the broken pieces of his life and shrieking at us to stop helping him move, his emotions reaching a fever pitch when his bed, which had been swinging wildly from a rope, entered the apartment two floors below his through what had until seconds earlier been a window.

This is the kind of thinking you get, with beer. So I figure 6 what happens, in the beer commercial where the burly men are building the house, is they push the wall up so it's vertical, and then, after the camera stops filming them, they just keep pushing, and the wall crashes down on the other side, possibly onto somebody's pickup truck. And then they all shake hands.

But other than that, I'm in favor of the upsurge in retail patri- 7 otism, which is lucky for me because the airwaves are saturated with pro-American commercials. Especially popular are commercials in which the newly restored Statue of Liberty—and by the way, I say Lee Iacocca should get some kind of medal for that, or at least be elected president—appears to be endorsing various products, as if she were Mary Lou Retton or somebody. I saw one commercial strongly suggesting that the Statue of Liberty uses Sure brand underarm deodorant.

I have yet to see a patriotic laxative commercial, but I imag- 8 ine it's only a matter of time. They'll show some actors dressed up as hard-working country folk, maybe at a church picnic, smiling at each other and eating pieces of pie. At least one of them will be a black person. The Statue of Liberty will appear in the background. Then you'll hear a country-style singer singing:

> Folks' round here they love this land;
> They stand by their beliefs;
> An' when they git themselves stopped up;
> They want some quick relief.

Well, what do you think? Pretty good commercial concept, huh? 9

Nah, you're right. They'd never try to pull something like 10 that. They'd put the statue in the *foreground*.

1997

6

Education

Learning to Read and Write

Frederick Douglass

1 I lived in Master Hugh's family about seven years. During this time, I succeeded in learning to read and write. In accomplishing this, I was compelled to resort to various stratagems. I had no regular teacher. My mistress, who had kindly commenced to instruct me, had, in compliance with the advice and direction of her husband, not only ceased to instruct, but had set her face against my being instructed by any one else. It is due, however, to my mistress to say of her, that she did not adopt this course of treatment immediately. She at first lacked the depravity indispensable to shutting me up in mental darkness. It was at least necessary for her to have some training in the exercise of irresponsible power, to make her equal to the task of treating me as though I were a brute.

2 My mistress was, as I have said, a kind and tender-hearted woman; and in the simplicity of her soul she commenced, when I first went to live with her, to treat me as she supposed one human being ought to treat another. In entering upon the duties of a slaveholder, she did not seem to perceive that I sustained to her the relation of a mere chattel, and that for her to treat me as a human being was not only wrong, but dangerously so. Slavery proved as injurious to her as it did to me. When I went there, she was a pious, warm, and tender-hearted woman. There was no sorrow or suffering for which she had not a tear. She had bread for the hungry, clothes for the naked, and comfort for every mourner that came within her reach. Slavery soon proved its ability to divest her of these heavenly qualities. Under its influence, the tender heart became stone, and the lamb-like disposition gave way to one of

tiger-like fierceness. The first step in her downward course was in her ceasing to instruct me. She now commenced to practise her husband's precepts. She finally became even more violent in her opposition than her husband himself. She was not satisfied with simply doing as well as he had commanded; she seemed anxious to do better. Nothing seemed to make her more angry than to see me with a newspaper. She seemed to think that here lay the danger. I have had her rush at me with a face made all up of fury, and snatch from me a newspaper, in a manner that fully revealed her apprehension. She was an apt woman; and a little experience soon demonstrated, to her satisfaction, that education and slavery were incompatible with each other.

From this time I was most narrowly watched. If I was in a separate room any considerable length of time, I was sure to be suspected of having a book, and was at once called to give an account of myself. All this, however, was too late. The first step had been taken. Mistress, in teaching me the alphabet, had given me the *inch*, and no precaution could prevent me from taking the *ell*. 3

The plan which I adopted, and the one by which I was most successful, was that of making friends of all the little white boys whom I met in the street. As many of these as I could, I converted into teachers. With their kindly aid, obtained at different times and in different places, I finally succeeded in learning to read. When I was sent on errands, I always took my book with me, and by doing one part of my errand quickly, I found time to get a lesson before my return. I used also to carry bread with me, enough of which was always in the house, and to which I was always welcome; for I was much better off in this regard than many of the poor white children in our neighborhood. This bread I used to bestow upon the hungry little urchins, who, in return, would give me that more valuable bread of knowledge. I am strongly tempted to give the names of two or three of those little boys, as a testimonial of the gratitude and affection I bear them; but prudence forbids:—not that it would injure me, but it might embarrass them; for it is almost an unpardonable offence to teach slaves to read in this Christian country. It is enough to say of the dear little fellows, that they lived on Philpot Street, very near Durgin and Bailey's shipyard. I used to talk this matter of slavery over with them. I would sometimes say to them, I wished I could be 4 as free as they would be when they got to be men. "You will be free as soon as you are twenty-one, *but I am a slave for life!* Have not I as good a right to be free as you have?" These words used to trouble them; they would express for me the liveliest sympathy, and console me with the hope that something would occur by which I might be free.

5   I was now about twelve years old, and the thought of being *a slave for life* began to bear heavily upon my heart. Just about this time, I got hold of a book entitled "The Columbian Orator." Every opportunity I got, I used to read this book. Among much of other interesting matter, I found in it a dialogue between a master and his slave. The slave was represented as having run away from his master three times. The dialogue represented the conversation which took place between them, when the slave was retaken the third time. In this dialogue, the whole argument in behalf of slavery was brought forward by the master, all of which was disposed of by the slave. The slave was made to say some very smart as well as impressive things in reply to his master—things which had the desired though unexpected effect; for the conversation resulted in the voluntary emancipation of the slave on the part of the master.

6   In the same book, I met with one of Sheridan's mighty speeches on and in behalf of Catholic emancipation. These were choice documents to me. I read them over and over again with unabated interest. They gave tongue to interesting thoughts of my own soul, which had frequently flashed through my mind, and died away for want of utterance. The moral which I gained from the dialogue was the power of truth over the conscience of even a slaveholder. What I got from Sheridan was a bold denunciation of slavery, and a powerful vindication of human rights. The reading of these documents enabled me to utter my thoughts, and to meet the arguments brought forward to sustain slavery; but while they relieved me of one difficulty, they brought on another even more painful than the one of which I was relieved. The more I read, the more I was led to abhor and detest my enslavers. I could regard them in no other light than a band of successful robbers, who had left their homes, and gone to Africa, and stolen us from our homes, and in a strange land reduced us to slavery. I loathed them as being the meanest as well as the most wicked of men. As

I read and contemplated the subject, behold! that very discontentment which Master Hugh had predicted would follow my learning to read had already come, to torment and sting my soul to unutterable anguish. As I writhed under it, I would at times feel that learning to read had been a curse rather than a blessing. It had given me a view of my wretched condition, without the remedy. It opened my eyes to the horrible pit, but to no ladder upon which to get out. In moments of agony, I envied my fellow-slaves for their stupidity. I have often wished myself a beast. I preferred the condition of the meanest reptile to my own. Any thing, no matter what, to get rid of thinking! It was this everlasting thinking of my condition that tormented me. There was no getting rid of it. It was pressed upon me by every object within sight or hearing, animate or inanimate. The silver trump of freedom had roused my soul to eternal wakefulness. Freedom now appeared, to disappear no more forever. It was heard in every sound, and seen in every thing. It was ever present to torment me with a sense of my wretched condition. I saw nothing without seeing it, I heard nothing without hearing it, and felt nothing without feeling it. It looked from every star, it smiled in every calm, breathed in every wind, and moved in every storm.

I often found myself regretting my own existence, and wishing myself dead; and but for the hope of being free, I have no doubt but that I should have killed myself, or done something for which I should have been killed. While in this state of mind, I was eager to hear anyone speak of slavery. I was a ready listener. Every little while, I could hear something about the abolitionists. It was some time before I found what the word meant. It was always used in such connections as to make it an interesting word to me. If a slave ran away and succeeded in getting clear, or if a slave killed his master, set fire to a barn, or did any thing very wrong in the mind of a slaveholder, it was spoken of as the fruit of *abolition*. Hearing the word in this connection very often, I set about learning what it meant. The dictionary afforded me little or no help. I found it was "the act of abolishing;" but then I did not know what was to be abolished. Here I was perplexed. I did not dare to ask any one about its meaning, for I was satisfied that it was something they wanted me to know very little about. After a patient waiting, I got one of our city papers, containing an account of the number of petitions from the north, praying for the abolition of slavery in the District of Columbia, and of the slave trade between the States. From this time I understood the words *abolition* and *abolitionist,* and always drew near when that word was spoken, expecting to hear something of importance to myself and fellow-slaves. The light broke in upon me by degrees. I went one day down on the wharf of Mr. Waters; and seeing two Irishmen unloading a scow of stone, I went, unasked, and helped them. When we had finished, one of them came to me and asked me if I were a slave. I told him I was. He asked, "Are ye a slave for life?" I told him that I was. The good Irishman seemed to be deeply affected by the statement. He said to the other that it was a pity so fine a little fellow as myself should be a slave for life. He said it was a shame to hold me. They both advised me to run away to the north; that I should find friends there, and that I should be free. I pretended not to be interested in what they said, and treated them as if I did not understand them; for I feared they might be treacherous. White men have been known to encourage slaves to escape, and then, to get the reward, catch them and return them to their masters. I was afraid that these seemingly good men might use me so; but I nevertheless remembered their advice, and from that time I resolved to run away. I looked forward to a time at which it would be safe for me to escape. I was too young to think of doing so immediately; besides, I wished to learn how to write, as I might have occasion to write my own pass. I consoled myself with the hope that I should one day find a good chance. Meanwhile, I would learn to write.

8   The idea as to how I might learn to write was suggested to me by being in Durgin and Bailey's ship-yard, and frequently seeing the ship carpenters, after hewing, and getting a piece of timber ready for use, write on the timber the name of that part of the ship for which it was intended. When a piece of timber was intended for the larboard side, it would be marked thus—"L." When a piece was for the starboard side, it would be marked thus—"S." A piece for the larboard side forward, would be marked thus—"L. F." When a piece was for starboard side forward, it would be marked thus—"S. F." For larboard aft, it would be marked thus—"L. A." For starboard aft, it would be marked thus—"S. A." I soon learned the names of these letters, and for what they were intended when

placed upon a piece of timber in the ship-yard. I immediately commenced copying them, and in a short time was able to make the four letters named. After that, when I met with any boy who I knew could write, I would tell him I could write as well as he. The next word would be, "I don't believe you. Let me see you try it." I would then make the letters which I had been so fortunate as to learn, and ask him to beat that. In this way I got a good many lessons in writing, which it is quite possible I should never have gotten in any other way. During this time, my copy-book was the board fence, brick wall, and pavement; my pen and ink was a lump of chalk. With these, I learned mainly how to write. I then commenced and continued copying the Italics in Webster's Spelling Book, until I could make them all without looking on the book. By this time, my little Master Thomas had gone to school, and learned how to write, and had written over a number of copy-books. These had been brought home, and shown to some of our near neighbors, and then laid aside. My mistress used to go to class meeting at the Wilk Street meetinghouse every Monday afternoon, and leave me to take care of the house. When left thus, I used to spend the time in writing in the spaces left in Master Thomas's copy-book, copying what he had written. I continued to do this until I could write a hand very similar to that of Master Thomas. Thus, after a long, tedious effort for years, I finally succeeded in learning how to write.

1845

Graduation

Maya Angelou

The children in Stamps[1] trembled visibly with anticipation. Some 1
adults were excited too, but to be certain the whole young population had come down with graduation epidemic. Large classes were graduating from both the grammar school and the high

---

[1] A rural, segregated town in Arkansas.

school. Even those who were years removed from their own day
of glorious release were anxious to help with preparations as a
kind of dry run. The junior students who were moving into the
vacating classes' chairs were tradition-bound to show their talents
for leadership and management. They strutted through the school
and around the campus exerting pressure on the lower grades.
Their authority was so new that occasionally if they pressed a little too hard it had to be overlooked. After all, next term was coming, and it never hurt a sixth grader to have a play sister in the
eighth grade, or a tenth-year student to be able to call a twelfth
grader Bubba. So all was endured in a spirit of shared understanding. But the graduating classes themselves were the nobility.
Like travelers with exotic destinations on their minds, the graduates were remarkably forgetful. They came to school without their
books, or tablets or even pencils. Volunteers fell over themselves
to secure replacements for the missing equipment. When
accepted, the willing workers might or might not be thanked, and
it was of no importance to the pregraduation rites. Even teachers
were respectful of the now quiet and aging seniors, and tended
to speak to them, if not as equals, as being only slightly lower
than themselves. After tests were returned and grades given, the
student body, which acted like an extended family, knew who did
well, who excelled, and what piteous ones had failed.

2   Unlike the white high school, Lafayette County Training
School distinguished itself by having neither lawn, nor hedges,
nor tennis court, nor climbing ivy. Its two buildings (main classrooms, the grade school and home economics) were set on a dirt
hill with no fence to limit either its boundaries or those of bordering farms. There was a large expanse to the left of the school
which was used alternately as a baseball diamond or basketball
court. Rusty hoops on swaying poles represented the permanent
recreational equipment, although bats and balls could be borrowed from the P.E. teacher if the borrower was qualified and if
the diamond wasn't occupied.

3   Over this rocky area relieved by a few shady tall persimmon
trees the graduating class walked. The girls often held hands and
no longer bothered to speak to the lower students. There was a
sadness about them, as if this old world was not their home and
they were bound for higher ground. The boys, on the other hand,

had become more friendly, more outgoing. A decided change from the closed attitude they projected while studying for finals. Now they seemed not ready to give up the old school, the familiar paths and classrooms. Only a small percentage would be continuing on to college—one of the South's A & M (agricultural and mechanical) schools, which trained Negro youths to be carpenters, farmers, handymen, masons, maids, cooks and baby nurses. Their future rode heavily on their shoulders, and blinded them to the collective joy that had pervaded the lives of the boys and girls in the grammar school graduating class.

Parents who could afford it had ordered new shoes and 4 ready-made clothes for themselves from Sears and Roebuck or Montgomery Ward. They also engaged the best seamstresses to make the floating graduating dresses and to cut down second-hand pants which would be pressed to a military slickness for the important event.

Oh, it was important, all right. Whitefolks would attend the 5 ceremony, and two or three would speak of God and home, and the Southern way of life, and Mrs. Parsons, the principal's wife, would play the graduation march while the lower-grade graduates paraded down the aisles and took their seats below the platform. The high school seniors would wait in empty classrooms to make their dramatic entrance.

In the Store I was the person of the moment. The birthday 6 girl. The center. Bailey had graduated the year before, although to do so he had had to forfeit all pleasures to make up for his time lost in Baton Rouge.

My class was wearing butter-yellow piqué dresses, and 7 Momma launched out on mine. She smocked the yoke into tiny crisscrossing puckers, then shirred the rest of the bodice. Her dark fingers ducked in and out of the lemony cloth as she embroidered raised daisies around the hem. Before she considered herself finished she had added a crocheted cuff on the puff sleeves, and a point crocheted collar.

I was going to be lovely. A walking model of all the various 8 styles of fine hand sewing and it didn't worry me that I was only twelve years old and merely graduating from the eighth grade. Besides, many teachers in Arkansas Negro schools had only that diploma and were licensed to impart wisdom.

9   The days had become longer and more noticeable. The faded beige of former times had been replaced with strong and sure colors. I began to see my classmates' clothes, their skin tones, and the dust that waved off pussy willows. Clouds that lazed across the sky were objects of great concern to me. Their shiftier shapes might have held a message that in my new happiness and with a little bit of time I'd soon decipher. During that period I looked at the arch of heaven so religiously my neck kept a steady ache. I had taken to smiling more often, and my jaws hurt from the unaccustomed activity. Between the two physical sore spots, I suppose I could have been uncomfortable, but that was not the case. As a member of the winning team (the graduating class of 1940) I had outdistanced unpleasant sensations by miles. I was headed for the freedom of open fields.

10   Youth and social approval allied themselves with me and we trammeled memories of slights and insults. The wind of our swift passage remodeled my features. Lost tears were pounded to mud and then to dust. Years of withdrawal were brushed aside and left behind, as hanging ropes of parasitic moss.

11   My work alone had awarded me a top place and I was going to be one of the first called in the graduating ceremonies. On the classroom blackboard, as well as on the bulletin board in the auditorium, there were blue stars and white stars and red stars. No absences, no tardinesses, and my academic work was among the best of the year. I could say the preamble to the Constitution even faster than Bailey. We timed ourselves often: "WethepeopleoftheUnitedStatesinordertoformamoreperfectunion. . . ." I had memorized the Presidents of the United States from Washington to Roosevelt in chronological as well as alphabetical order.

12   My hair pleased me too. Gradually the black mass had lengthened and thickened, so that it kept at last to its braided pattern, and I didn't have to yank my scalp off when I tried to comb it.

13   Louise and I had rehearsed the exercises until we tired out ourselves. Henry Reed was class valedictorian. He was a small, very black boy with hooded eyes, a long, broad nose and an oddly shaped head. I had admired him for years because each term he and I vied for the best grades in our class. Most often he bested me, but instead of being disappointed I was pleased that we shared top places between us. Like many Southern Black children,

he lived with his grandmother, who was as strict as Momma and as kind as she knew how to be. He was courteous, respectful and soft-spoken to elders, but on the playground he chose to play the roughest games. I admired him. Anyone, I reckoned, sufficiently afraid or sufficiently dull could be polite. But to be able to operate at a top level with both adults and children was admirable.

His valedictory speech was entitled "To Be or Not to Be." The 14 rigid tenth-grade teacher had helped him write it. He'd been working on the dramatic stresses for months.

The weeks until graduation were filled with heady activities. 15 A group of small children were to be presented in a play about buttercups and daisies and bunny rabbits. They could be heard throughout the building practicing their hops and their little songs that sounded like silver bells. The older girls (non-graduates, of course) were assigned the task of making refreshments for the night's festivities. A tangy scent of ginger, cinnamon, nutmeg and chocolate wafted around the home economics building as the budding cooks made samples for themselves and their teachers.

In every corner of the workshop, axes and saws split fresh 16 timber as the woodshop boys made sets and stage scenery. Only the graduates were left out of the general bustle. We were free to sit in the library at the back of the building or look in quite detachedly, naturally, on the measures being taken for our event.

Even the minister preached on graduation the Sunday before. 17 His subject was, "Let your light so shine that men will see your good works and praise your Father, Who is in Heaven." Although the sermon was purported to be addressed to us, he used the occasion to speak to backsliders, gamblers and general ne'er-do-wells. But since he had called our names at the beginning of the service we were mollified.

Among Negroes the tradition was to give presents to children 18 going only from one grade to another. How much more important this was when the person was graduating at the top of the class. Uncle Willie and Momma had sent away for a Mickey Mouse watch like Bailey's. Louise gave me four embroidered handkerchiefs. (I gave her crocheted doilies.) Mrs. Sneed, the minister's wife, made me an undershirt to wear for graduation, and nearly every customer gave me a nickel or maybe even a dime with the instruction, "Keep on moving to higher ground," or some such encouragement.

19   Amazingly the great day finally dawned and I was out of bed before I knew it. I threw open the back door to see it more clearly, but Momma said, "Sister, come away from that door and put your robe on."

20   I hoped the memory of that morning would never leave me. Sunlight was itself young, and the day had none of the insistence maturity would bring it in a few hours. In my robe and barefoot in the backyard, under cover of going to see about my new beans, I gave myself up to the gentle warmth and thanked God that no matter what evil I had done in my life He had allowed me to live to see this day. Somewhere in my fatalism I had expected to die, accidentally, and never have the chance to walk up the stairs in the auditorium and gracefully receive my hard-earned diploma. Out of God's merciful bosom I had won reprieve.

21   Bailey came out in his robe and gave me a box wrapped in Christmas paper. He said he had saved his money for months to pay for it. It felt like a box of chocolates, but I knew Bailey wouldn't save money to buy candy when we had all we could want under our noses.

22   He was as proud of the gift as I. It was a soft-leather-bound copy of a collection of poems by Edgar Allan Poe, or, as Bailey and I called him, "Eap." I turned to "Annabel Lee" and we walked up and down the garden rows, the cool dirt between our toes, reciting the beautifully sad lines.

23   Momma made a Sunday breakfast although it was only Friday. After we finished the blessing, I opened my eyes to find the watch on my plate. It was a dream of a day. Everything went smoothly and to my credit. I didn't have to be reminded or scolded for anything. Near evening I was too jittery to attend to chores, so Bailey volunteered to do all before his bath.

24   Days before, we had made a sign for the Store, and as we turned out the lights Momma hung the cardboard over the door-knob. It read clearly: CLOSED. GRADUATION.

25   My dress fitted perfectly and everyone said that I looked like a sunbeam in it. On the hill, going toward the school, Bailey walked behind with Uncle Willie, who muttered, "Go on, Ju." He wanted him to walk ahead with us because it embarrassed him to have to walk so slowly. Bailey said he'd let the ladies walk together, and the men would bring up the rear. We all laughed, nicely.

Little children dashed by out of the dark like fireflies. Their 26
crepe-paper dresses and butterfly wings were not made for running and we heard more than one rip, dryly, and the regretful "uh
uh" that followed.

The school blazed without gaiety. The windows seemed cold 27
and unfriendly from the lower hill. A sense of ill-fated timing
crept over me, and if Momma hadn't reached for my hand I
would have drifted back to Bailey and Uncle Willie, and possibly
beyond. She made a few slow jokes about my feet getting cold,
and tugged me along to the now-strange building.

Around the front steps, assurance came back. There were my 28
fellow "greats," the graduating class. Hair brushed back, legs
oiled, new dresses and pressed pleats, fresh pocket handkerchiefs
and little handbags, all homesewn. Oh, we were up to snuff, all
right. I joined my comrades and didn't even see my family go in
to find seats in the crowded auditorium

The school band struck up a march and all classes filed in as 29
had been rehearsed. We stood in front of our seats, as assigned, and
on a signal from the choir director, we sat. No sooner had this been
accomplished than the band started to play the national anthem.
We rose again and sang the song, after which we recited the pledge
of allegiance. We remained standing for a brief minute before the
choir director and the principal signaled to us, rather desperately I
thought, to take our seats. The command was so unusual that our
carefully rehearsed and smooth-running machine was thrown off.
For a full minute we fumbled for our chairs and bumped into each
other awkwardly. Habits change or solidify under pressure, so in
our state of nervous tension we had been ready to follow our usual
assembly pattern: the American national anthem, then the pledge
of allegiance, then the song every Black person I knew called the
Negro National Anthem. All done in the same key, with the same
passion and most often standing on the same foot.

Finding my seat at last, I was overcome with a presentiment 30
of worse things to come. Something unrehearsed, unplanned, was
going to happen, and we were going to be made to look bad. I
distinctly remember being explicit in the choice of pronoun. It was
"we," the graduating class, the unit, that concerned me then.

The principal welcomed "parents and friends" and asked the 31
Baptist minister to lead us in prayer. His invocation was brief and

punchy, and for a second I thought we were getting on the high road to right action. When the principal came back to the dais, however, his voice had changed. Sounds always affected me profoundly and the principal's voice was one of my favorites. During assembly it melted and lowed weakly into the audience. It had not been in my plan to listen to him, but my curiosity was piqued and I straightened up to give him my attention.

32   He was talking about Booker T. Washington, our "late great leader," who said we can be as close as the fingers on the hand, etc. . . . Then he said a few vague things about friendship and the friendship of kindly people to those less fortunate than themselves. With that his voice nearly faded, thin, away. Like a river diminishing to a stream and then to a trickle. But he cleared his throat and said, "Our speaker tonight, who is also our friend, came from Texarkana to deliver the commencement address, but due to the irregularity of the train schedule, he's going to, as they say, 'speak and run.'" He said that we understood and wanted the man to know that we were most grateful for the time he was able to give us and then something about how we were willing always to adjust to another's program, and without more ado—"I give you Mr. Edward Donleavy."

33   Not one but two white men came through the door off-stage. The shorter one walked to the speaker's platform, and the tall one moved to the center seat and sat down. But that was our principal's seat, and already occupied. The dislodged gentleman bounced around for a long breath or two before the Baptist minister gave him his chair, then with more dignity than the situation deserved, the minister walked off the stage.

34   Donleavy looked at the audience once (on reflection, I'm sure that he wanted only to reassure himself that we were really there), adjusted his glasses and began to read from a sheaf of papers.

35   He was glad "to be here and to see the work going on just as it was in the other schools."

36   At the first "Amen" from the audience I willed the offender to immediate death by choking on the word. But Amens and Yes, sir's began to fall around the room like rain through a ragged umbrella.

37   He told us of the wonderful changes we children in Stamps had in store. The Central School (naturally, the white school was

Central) had already been granted improvements that would be in use in the fall. A well-known artist was coming from Little Rock to teach art to them. They were going to have the newest microscopes and chemistry equipment for the laboratory. Mr. Donleavy didn't leave us long in the dark over who made these improvements available to Central High. Nor were we to be ignored in the general betterment scheme he had in mind.

He said that he had pointed out to people at a very high level 38 that one of the first-line football tacklers at Arkansas Agricultural and Mechanical College had graduated from good old Lafayette County Training School. Here fewer Amen's were heard. Those few that did break through lay dully in the air with the heaviness of habit.

He went on to praise us. He went on to say how he had 39 bragged that "one of the best basketball players at Fisk sank his first ball right here at Lafayette County Training School."

The white kids were going to have a chance to become 40 Galileos and Madame Curies and Edisons and Gauguins, and our boys (the girls weren't even in on it) would try to be Jesse Owenses and Joe Louises.

Owens and the Brown Bomber were great heroes in our 41 world, but what school official in the white-goddom of Little Rock had the right to decide that those two men must be our only heroes? Who decided that for Henry Reed to become a scientist he had to work like George Washington Carver, as a bootblack, to buy a lousy microscope? Bailey was obviously always going to be too small to be an athlete, so which concrete angel glued to what county seat had decided that if my brother wanted to become a lawyer he had to first pay penance for his skin by picking cotton and hoeing corn and studying correspondence books at night for twenty years?

The man's dead words fell like bricks around the auditorium 42 and too many settled in my belly. Constrained by hard-learned manners I couldn't look behind me, but to my left and right the proud graduating class of 1940 had dropped their heads. Every girl in my row had found something new to do with her handkerchief. Some folded the tiny squares into love knots, some into triangles, but most were wadding them, then pressing them flat on their yellow laps.

43   On the dais, the ancient tragedy was being replayed. Professor Parsons sat, a sculptor's reject, rigid. His large, heavy body seemed devoid of will or willingness, and his eyes said he was no longer with us. The other teachers examined the flag (which was draped stage right) or their notes, or the windows which opened on our now-famous playing diamond.

44   Graduation, the hush-hush magic time of frills and gifts and congratulations and diplomas, was finished for me before my name was called. The accomplishment was nothing. The meticulous maps, drawn in three colors of ink, learning and spelling decasyllabic words, memorizing the whole of *The Rape of Lucrece*—it was for nothing. Donleavy had exposed us.

45   We were maids and farmers, handymen and washerwomen, and anything higher that we aspired to was farcical and presumptuous.

46   Then I wished that Gabriel Prosser and Nat Turner had killed all whitefolks in their beds and that Abraham Lincoln had been assassinated before the signing of the Emancipation Proclamation, and that Harriet Tubman had been killed by that blow on her head and Christopher Columbus had drowned in the *Santa Maria*.

47   It was awful to be a Negro and have no control over my life. It was brutal to be young and already trained to sit quietly and listen to charges brought against my color with no chance of defense. We should all be dead. I thought I should like to see us all dead, one on top of the other. A pyramid of flesh with the white-folks on the bottom, as the broad base, then the Indians with their silly tomahawks and teepees and wigwams and treaties, the Negroes with their mops and recipes and cotton sacks and spirituals sticking out of their mouths. The Dutch children should all stumble in their wooden shoes and break their necks. The French should choke to death on the Louisiana Purchase (1803) while silkworms ate all the Chinese with their stupid pigtails. As a species, we were an abomination. All of us.

48   Donleavy was running for election, and assured our parents that if he won we could count on having the only colored paved playing field in that part of Arkansas. Also—he never looked up to acknowledge the grunts of acceptance—also, we were bound to get some new equipment for the home economics building and the workshop.

He finished, and since there was no need to give any more 49
than the most perfunctory thank-you's, he nodded to the men on
the stage, and the tall white man who was never introduced joined
him at the door. They left with the attitude that now they were off
to something really important. (The graduation ceremonies at
Lafayette County Training School had been a mere preliminary.)

The ugliness they left was palpable. An uninvited guest who 50
wouldn't leave. The choir was summoned and sang a modern
arrangement of "Onward, Christian Soldiers," with new words
pertaining to graduates seeking their place in the world. But it
didn't work. Elouise, the daughter of the Baptist minister, recited
"Invictus," and I could have cried at the impertinence of "I am
the master of my fate, I am the captain of my soul."

My name had lost its ring of familiarity and I had to be 51
nudged to go and receive my diploma. All my preparations had
fled. I neither marched up to the stage like a conquering Amazon,
nor did I look in the audience for Bailey's nod of approval. Marguerite Johnson,[2] I heard the name again, my honors were read,
there were noises in the audience of appreciation, and I took my
place on the stage as rehearsed.

I thought about colors I hated: ecru, puce, lavender, beige and 52
black.

There was shuffling and rustling around me, then Henry Reed 53
was giving his valedictory address, "To Be or Not to Be." Hadn't
he heard the whitefolks? We couldn't *be,* so the question was a
waste of time. Henry's voice came out clear and strong. I feared
to look at him. Hadn't he got the message? There was no "nobler
in the mind" for Negroes because the world didn't think we had
minds, and they let us know it. "Outrageous fortune"? Now, that
was a joke. When the ceremony was over I had to tell Henry Reed
some things. That is, if I still cared. Not "rub," Henry, "erase."
"Ah, there's the erase." Us.

Henry had been a good student in elocution. His voice rose 54
on tides of promise and fell on waves of warnings. The English
teacher had helped him to create a sermon winging through

[2]Maya Angelou was born Marguerite Johnson in 1928; married Tosh Angelou
(divorced 1952); took the name of Maya Angelou in her early twenties.

Hamlet's soliloquy. To be a man, a doer, a builder, a leader, or to
be a tool, an unfunny joke, a crusher of funky toadstools. I mar-
veled that Henry could go through with the speech as if we had
a choice.

55   I had been listening and silently rebutting each sentence with
my eyes closed; then there was a hush, which in an audience
warns that something unplanned is happening. I looked up and
saw Henry Reed, the conservative, the proper, the A student, turn
his back to the audience and turn to us (the proud graduating
class of 1940) and sing, nearly speaking,

> "Lift ev'ry voice and sing
> Till earth and heaven ring
> Ring with the harmonies of Liberty . . ."

It was the poem written by James Weldon Johnson. It was the
music composed by J. Rosamond Johnson. It was the Negro
National Anthem. Out of habit we were singing it.

56   Our mothers and fathers stood in the dark hall and joined the
hymn of encouragement. A kindergarten teacher led the small
children onto the stage and the buttercups and daisies and bunny
rabbits marked time and tried to follow:

> "Stony the road we trod
> Bitter the chastening rod
> Felt in the days when hope, unborn, had died.
> Yet with a steady beat
> Have not our weary feet
> Come to the place for which our fathers sighed?"

57   Each child I knew had learned that song with his ABC's and
along with "Jesus Loves Me This I Know." But I personally had
never heard it before. Never heard the words, despite the thousands of times I had sung them. Never thought they had anything
to do with me.

58   On the other hand, the words of Patrick Henry had made such
an impression on me that I had been able to stretch myself tall
and trembling and say, "I know not what course others may take,
but as for me, give me liberty or give me death."

And now I heard, really for the first time: 59

> "We have come over a way that with tears
> has been watered,
> We have come, treading our path through
> the blood of the slaughtered."

While echoes of the song shivered in the air, Henry Reed   60
bowed his head, said "Thank you," and returned to his place in
the line. The tears that slipped down many faces were not wiped
away in shame.

We were on top again. As always, again. We survived. The   61
depths had been icy and dark, but now a bright sun spoke to our
souls. I was no longer simply a member of the proud graduating
class of 1940; I was a proud member of the wonderful, beautiful
Negro race.

Oh, Black known and unknown poets, how often have your   62
auctioned pains sustained us? Who will compute the only nights
made less lonely by your songs, or the empty pots made less
tragic by your tales?

If we were a people much given to revealing secrets, we might   63
raise monuments and sacrifice to the memories of our poets, but
slavery cured us of that weakness. It may be enough, however, to
have it said that we survive in exact relationship to the dedica-
tion of our poets (include preachers, musicians and blues singers).

1970

"I Just Wanna Be Average"

Mike Rose

Some people who manage to write their way out of the working   1
class describe the classroom as an oasis of possibility. It became
their intellectual playground, their competitive arena. Given the
richness of my memories of this time, it's funny how scant are my

recollections of school. I remember the red brick building of St. Regina's itself, and the topography of the playground: the swings and basketball courts and peeling benches. There are images of a few students: Erwin Petschaur, a muscular German boy with a strong accent; Dave Sanchez, who was good in math; and Sheila Wilkes, everyone's curly-haired heartthrob. And there are two nuns: Sister Monica, the third-grade teacher with beautiful hands for whom I carried a candle and who, to my dismay, had wedded herself to Christ; and Sister Beatrice, a woman truly crazed, who would sweep into class, eyes wide, to tell us about the Apocalypse.

2   All the hours in class tend to blend into one long, vague stretch of time. What I remember best, strangely enough, are the two things I couldn't understand and over the years grew to hate: grammar lessons and mathematics. I would sit there watching a teacher draw her long horizontal line and her short, oblique lines and break up sentences and put adjectives here and adverbs there and just not get it, couldn't see the reason for it, turned off to it. I would hide by slumping down in my seat and page through my reader, carried along by the flow of sentences in a story. She would test us, and I would dread that, for I always got Cs and Ds. Mathematics was a bit different. For whatever reasons, I didn't learn early math very well, so when it came time for more complicated operations, I couldn't keep up and started day-dreaming to avoid my inadequacy. This was a strategy I would rely on as I grew older. I fell further and further behind. A memory: The teacher is faceless and seems very far away. The voice is faint and is discussing an equation written on the board. It is raining, and I am watching the streams of water form patterns on the windows.

3   I realize now how consistently I defended myself against the lessons I couldn't understand and the people and events of South L.A. that were too strange to view head-on. I got very good at watching a blackboard with minimum awareness. And I drifted more and more into a variety of protective fantasies. I was lucky in that although my parents didn't read or write very much and had no more than a few books around the house, they never debunked my pursuits. And when they could, they bought me what I needed to spin my web.

One early Christmas they got me a small chemistry set. My 4
father brought home an old card table from the secondhand store,
and on that table I spread out my test tubes, my beaker, my Erlen-
meyer flask, and my gas-generating apparatus. The set came
equipped with chemicals, minerals, and various treated papers—all
in little square bottles. You could send away to someplace in Mary-
land for more, and I did, saving pennies and nickels to get the
substances that were too exotic for my set, the Junior Chem-craft:
Congo red paper, azurite, glycerine, chrome alum, cochineal—this
from female insects!—tartaric acid, chameleon paper, logwood. I
would sit before my laboratory and play for hours. My father
rested on the purple couch in front of me watching wrestling or
Gunsmoke while I measured powders or heated crystals or blew
into solutions that my breath would turn red or pink. I was taken
by the blends of names and by the colors that swirled through the
beaker. My equations were visual and phonetic. I would hold a
flask up to the hall light, imagining the veils of a million atoms
dancing. Sulfur and alcohol hung in the air. I wanted to shake
down the house.

One day my mother came home from Coffee Dan's with an 5
awful story. The teenage brother of one of her waitress friends was
in the hospital. He had been fooling around with explosives in his
garage "where his mother couldn't see him," and something happened, and "he blew away part of his throat. For God's sake, be
careful," my mother said. "Remember poor Ada's brother." Wow!
I thought. How neat! Why couldn't my experiments be that dangerous? I really lost heart when I realized that you could probably eat the chemicals spread across my table.

I knew what I had to do. I saved my money for a week and 6
then walked with firm resolve past Walt's Malts, past the brake
shop, across Ninetieth Street, and into Palazzolla's market. I bought
a little bottle of Alka-Seltzer and ran home. I chopped up the
wafers and mixed them into a jar of white crystals. When my
mother came home, dog tired, and sat down on the edge of my
couch to tell me and Dad about her day, I gravely poured my con-
coction into a beaker of water, cried something about the unexpected, and ran out from behind my table. The beaker foamed
ominously. My father swore in Italian. The second time I tried it,
I got something milder—in English. And by my third near-miss

with death, my parents were calling my behavior cute. Cute! Who wanted cute? I wanted to toy with the disaster that befell Ada Pendleton's brother. I wanted all those wonderful colors to collide in ways that could blow your voice box right off.

7 But I was limited by the real. The best I could do was create a toxic antacid. I loved my chemistry set—its glassware and its intriguing labels—but it wouldn't allow me to do the things I wanted to do. St. Regina's had an all-purpose room, one wall of which was lined with old books—and one of those shelves held a row of plastic-covered space novels. The sheen of their covers was gone, and their futuristic portraits were dotted with erasures and grease spots like a meteor shower of the everyday. I remember the rockets best. Long cylinders outfitted at the base with three slick fins, tapering at the other end to a perfect conical point, ready to pierce out of the stratosphere and into my imagination: X-fifteens and Mach 1, the dark side of the moon, the Red Planet, Jupiter's Great Red Spot, Saturn's rings—and beyond the solar system to swirling wisps of galaxies, to stardust.

8 I would check out my books two at a time and take them home to curl up with a blanket on my chaise lounge, reading, sometimes, through the weekend, my back aching, my thoughts lost between galaxies. I became the hero of a thousand adventures, all with intricate plots and the triumph of good over evil, all many dimensions removed from the dim walls of the living room. We were given time to draw in school, so, before long, all this worked itself onto paper. The stories I was reading were reshaping themselves into pictures. My father got me some butcher paper from Palazolla's, and I continued to draw at home. My collected works rendered the Horsehead Nebula, goofy space cruisers, robots, and Saturn. Each had its crayon, a particular waxy pencil with mood and meaning: rust and burnt sienna for Mars, yellow for the Sun, lime and rose for Saturn's rings, and bright red for the Jovian spot. I had a little sharpener to keep the points just right. I didn't write any stories; I just read and drew. I wouldn't care much about writing until late in high school.

9 The summer before the sixth grade, I got a couple of jobs. The first was at a pet store a block or so away from my house. Since I was still small, I could maneuver around in breeder cages, scraping the heaps of parakeet crap from the tin floor, cleaning the

water troughs and seed trays. It was pretty awful. I would go home after work and fill the tub and soak until all the fleas and bird mites came floating to the surface, little Xs in their multiple eyes. When I heard about a job selling strawberries door-to-door, I jumped at it. I went to work for a white-haired Chicano named Frank. He would carry four or five kids and dozens of crates of strawberries in his ramshackle truck up and down the avenues of the better neighborhoods: houses with mowed lawns and petunia beds. We'd work all day for seventy-five cents, Frank dropping pairs of us off with two crates each, then picking us up at preassigned corners. We spent lots of time together, bouncing around on the truck bed redolent with strawberries or sitting on a corner, cold, listening for the sputter of Frank's muffler. I started telling the other kids about my books, and soon it was my job to fill up that time with stories.

Reading opened up the world. There I was, a skinny bookworm   10 drawing the attention of street kids who, in any other circumstances, would have had me for breakfast. Like an epic tale-teller, I developed the stories as I went along, relying on a flexible plot line and a repository of heroic events. I had a great time. I sketched out trajectories with my finger on Frank's dusty truck bed. And I stretched out each story's climax, creating cliffhangers like the ones I saw in the Saturday serials. These stories created for me a temporary community.

It was around this time that fiction started leading me   11 circuitously to a child's version of science. In addition to the space novels, St. Regina's library also had half a dozen books on astronomy—*The Golden Book of Planets* and stuff like that—so I checked out a few of them. I liked what I read and wheedled enough change out of my father to enable me to take the bus to the public library. I discovered star maps, maps of lunar seas, charts upon charts of the solar system and the planetary moons: Rhea, Europa, Callisto, Miranda, Io. I didn't know that most of these moons were named for women—I didn't know classical mythology—but I would say their names to myself as though they had a woman's power to protect: Europa, Miranda, Io. . . . The distances between stars fascinated me, as did the sizes of the big telescopes. I sent away for catalogs. Then prices fascinated me too. I wanted to drape my arm over a thousand-dollar scope and hear its motor drive whirr. I conjured a twelve-year-old's life of the astronomer: sitting up all night with potato chips and the stars, tracking the sky for supernovas, humming "Earth Angel" with the Penguins. What was my mother to do but save her tips and buy me a telescope?!

12   It was a little reflecting job, and I solemnly used to carry it out to the front of the house on warm summer nights, to find Venus or Alpha Centauri or trace the stars in Orion or lock onto the moon. I would lay out my star maps on the concrete, more for their magic than anything else, for I had trouble figuring them out. I was no geometer of the constellations; I was their balladeer. Those nights were very peaceful. I was far enough away from the front door and up enough from the sidewalk to make it seem as if I rested on a mound of dark silence, a mountain in Arizona, perhaps, watching the sky alive with points of light. Poor Freddie, toothless Lester whispering promises about making me feel good, the flat days, the gang fights—all this receded, for it was now me, the star child, lost in an eyepiece focused on a reflecting mirror that cradled, in its center, a shimmering moon.

———————

13   The loneliness in Los Angeles fosters strange arrangements. Lou Minton was a wiry man with gaunt, chiseled features and prematurely gray hair, combed straight back. He had gone to college in the South for a year of two and kicked around the country for many more before settling in L.A. He lived in a small downtown apartment with a single window and met my mother at the counter of Coffee Dan's. He had been alone too long and eventually came to our house and became part of the family. Lou repaired washing machines, and he had a car, and he would take me to the vast, echoing library just west of Pershing Square and to the Museum of Science and Industry in Exposition Park. He bought me astronomy books, taught me how to use tools, and helped me build model airplanes from balsa wood and rice paper. As my father's health got worse, Lou took care of him.

14   My rhapsodic and prescientific astronomy carried me into my teens, consumed me right up till high school, losing out finally, and only, to the siren call of pubescence—that endocrine hoodoo that transmogrifies nice boys into gawky flesh fiends. My mother used

to bring home *Confidential* magazine, a peep-show rag specializing in the sins of the stars, and it beckoned me mercilessly: Jayne Mansfield's cleavage, Gina Lollobrigida's eyes, innuendos about deviant sexuality, ads for Frederick's of Hollywood—spiked heels, lacy brassieres, the epiphany of silk panties on a mannequin's hips. Along with Phil Everly, I was through with counting the stars above.

Budding manhood. Only adults talk about adolescence budding. Kids have no choice but to talk in extremes; they're being wrenched and buffeted, rabbit-punched from inside by systemic thugs. Nothing sweet and pastoral here. Kids become ridiculous and touching at one and the same time: passionate about the trivial, fixed before the mirror, yet traversing one of the most important rites of passage in their lives—liminal people, silly and profoundly human. Given my own expertise, I fantasized about concocting the fail-safe aphrodisiac that would bring Marianne Bilpusch, the cloakroom monitor, rushing into my arms or about commanding a squadron of bosomy, linguistically mysterious astronauts like Zsa Zsa Gabor. My parents used to say that their son would have the best education they could afford. Maybe I would be a doctor. There was a public school in our neighborhood and several Catholic schools to the west. They had heard that quality schooling meant private, Catholic schooling, so they somehow got the money together to send me to Our Lady of Mercy, fifteen or so miles southwest of Ninety-first and Vermont. So much for my fantasies. Most Catholic secondary schools then were separated by gender.

It took two buses to get to Our Lady of Mercy. The first started deep in South Los Angeles and caught me at midpoint. The second drifted through neighborhoods with trees, parks, big lawns, and lots of flowers. The rides were long but were livened up by a group of South L.A. veterans whose parents also thought that Hope had set up shop in the west end of the county. There was Christy Biggars, who, at sixteen, was dealing and was, according to rumor, a pimp as well. There were Bill Cobb and Johnny Gonzales, grease-pencil artists extraordinaire, who left Nembutal-enhanced swirls of "Cobb" and "Johnny" on the corrugated walls of the bus. And then there was Tyrrell Wilson. Tyrrell was the coolest kid I knew. He ran the dozens like a metric halfback, laid down a rap that outrhymed and outpointed Cobb, whose rap was good but not great—the curse of a moderately soulful kid trapped in white skin. But it was Cobb who would sneak a radio onto the bus, and thus underwrote his patter with Little Richard, Fats Domino, Chuck Berry, the Coasters, and Ernie K. Doe's mother-in-law, an awful woman who was "sent from down below." And so it was that Christy and Cobb and Johnny G. and Tyrrell and I and assorted others picked up along the way passed our days in the back of the bus, a funny mix brought together by geography and parental desire.

17   Entrance to school brings with it forms and releases and assessments. Mercy relied on a series of tests, mostly the Stanford-Binet, for placement, and somehow the results of my tests got confused with those of another student named Rose. The other Rose apparently didn't do very well, for I was placed in the vocational track, a euphemism for the bottom level. Neither I nor my parents realized what this meant. We had no sense that Business Math, Typing, and English–Level D were dead ends. The current spate of reports on the schools criticizes parents for not involving themselves in the education of their children. But how would someone like Tommy Rose, with his two years of Italian schooling, know what to ask? And what sort of pressure could an exhausted waitress apply? The error went undetected, and I remained in the vocational track for two years. What a place.

18   My homeroom was supervised by Brother Dill, a troubled and unstable man who also taught freshman English. When his class drifted away from him, which was often, his voice would rise in paranoid accusations, and occasionally he would lose control and shake or smack us. I hadn't been there two months when one of his brisk, face-turning slaps had my glasses sliding down the aisle. Physical education was also pretty harsh. Our teacher was a stubby ex-lineman who had played old-time pro ball in the Midwest. He routinely had us grabbing our ankles to receive his stinging paddle across our butts. He did that, he said, to make men of us. "Rose," he bellowed on our first encounter; me standing geeky in line in my baggy shorts. "'Rose'? What the hell kind of name is that?"

19   "Italian, sir," I squeaked.

20   "Italian! Ho. Rose, do you know the sound a bag of shit makes when it hits the wall?"

"No, sir." 21

"Wop!" 22

Sophomore English was taught by Mr. Mitropetros. He was a 23
large, bejeweled man who managed the parking lot at the Shrine
Auditorium. He would crow and preen and list for us the stars
he'd brushed against. We'd ask questions and glance knowingly
and snicker, and all that fueled the poor guy to brag some more.
Parking cars was his night job. He had little training in English,
so his lesson plan for his day work had us reading the district's
required text, *Julius Caesar,* aloud for the semester. We'd finish the
play way before the twenty weeks was up, so he'd have us switch
parts again and again and start again: Dave Snyder, the fastest
guy at Mercy, muscling through Caesar to the breathless squeals
of Calpurnia, as interpreted by Steve Fusco, a surfer who owned
the school's most envied paneled wagon. Week ten and Dave and
Steve would take on new roles, as would we all, and render a
waterlogged Cassius and a Brutus that are beyond my powers of
description.

Spanish I—taken in the second year—fell into the hands of a 24
new recruit. Mr. Montez was a tiny man, slight, five foot six at the
most, soft-spoken and delicate. Spanish was a particularly rowdy
class, and Mr. Montez was as prepared for it as a doily maker at
a hammer throw. He would tap his pencil to a room in which
Steve Fusco was propelling spitballs from his heavy lips, in which
Mike Dweetz was taunting Billy Hawk, a half-Indian, half-Spanish,
reed-thin, quietly explosive boy. The vocational track at Our Lady
of Mercy mixed kids traveling in from South L.A. with South Bay
surfers and a few Slavs and Chicanos from the harbors of San
Pedro. This was a dangerous miscellany: surfers and hodads and
South-Central blacks all ablaze to the metronomic tapping of
Hector Montez's pencil.

One day Billy lost it. Out of the corner of my eye I saw him 25
strike out with his right arm and catch Dweetz across the neck.
Quick as a spasm, Dweetz was out of his seat, scattering desks,
cracking Billy on the side of the head, right behind the eye. Snyder and Fusco and others broke it up, but the room felt hot and
close and naked. Mr. Montez's tenuous authority was finally
ripped to shreds, and I think everyone felt a little strange about
that. That charade was over, and when it came down to it, I don't

think any of the kids really wanted it to end this way. They had pushed and pushed and bullied their way into a freedom that both scared and embarrassed them.

---

26   Students will float to the mark you set. I and the others in the vocational classes were bobbing in pretty shallow water. Vocational education has aimed at increasing the economic opportunities of students who do not do well in our schools. Some serious programs succeed in doing that, and through exceptional teachers—like Mr. Gross in *Horace's Compromise*—students learn to develop hypotheses and troubleshoot, reason through a problem, and communicate effectively—the true job skills. The vocational track, however, is most often a place for those who are just not making it, a dumping group for the disaffected. There were a few teachers who worked hard at education; young Brother Slattery, for example, combined a stern voice with weekly quizzes to try to pass along to us a skeletal outline of world history. But mostly the teachers had no idea of how to engage the imaginations of us kids who were scuttling along at the bottom of the pond.

27   And the teachers would have needed some inventiveness, for none of us was groomed for the classroom. It wasn't just that I didn't know things—didn't know how to simplify algebraic fractions, couldn't identify different kinds of clauses, bungled Spanish translations—but that I had developed various faulty and inadequate ways of doing algebra and making sense of Spanish. Worse yet, the years of defensive tuning out in elementary school had given me a way to escape quickly while seeming at least half alert. During my time in Voc. Ed., I developed further into a mediocre student and a somnambulant problem solver, and that affected the subjects I did have the wherewithal to handle: I detested Shakespeare; I got bored with history. My attention flitted here and there. I fooled around in class and read my books indifferently—the intellectual equivalent of playing with your food. I did what I had to do to get by, and I did it with half a mind.

28   But I did learn things about people and eventually came into my own socially. I liked the guys in Voc. Ed. Growing up where I did, I understood and admired physical prowess, and there was an abundance of muscle here. There was Dave Snyder, a sprinter

and halfback of true quality. Dave's ability and his quick wit gave him a natural appeal, and he was welcome in any clique, though he always kept a little independent. He enjoyed acting the fool and could care less about studies, but he possessed a certain maturity and never caused the faculty much trouble. It was a testament to his independence that he included me among his friends—I eventually went out for track, but I was no jock. Owing to the Latin alphabet and a dearth of *R*s and *S*s, Snyder sat behind Rose and we started exchanging one-liners and became friends.

There was Ted Richard, a much-touted Little League pitcher.   29 He was chunky and had a baby face and came to our Lady of Mercy as a seasoned street fighter. Ted was quick to laugh and he had a loud, jolly laugh, but when he got angry he'd smile a little smile, the kind that simply raises the corner of the mouth a quarter of an inch. For those who knew, it was an eerie signal. Those who didn't found themselves in big trouble, for Ted was very quick. He loved to carry on what we would come to call philosophical discussions: What is courage? Does God exist? He also loved words, enjoyed picking up big ones like *salubrious* and *equivocal* and using them in our conversations—laughing at himself as the word hit a chuckhole rolling off his tongue. Ted didn't do all that well in school—baseball and parties and testing the courage he'd speculated about took up his time. His textbooks were *Argosy* and *Field and Stream*, whatever newspapers he'd find on the bus stop—from the *Daily Worker* to pornography—conversations with uncles or hobos or businessmen he'd meet in a coffee shop, *The Old Man and the Sea*. With hindsight, I can see that Ted was developing into one of those rough-hewn intellectuals whose sources are a mix of the learned and the apocryphal, whose discussions are both assured and sad.

And then there was Ken Harvey. Ken was good-looking in a   30 puffy way and had a full and oily ducktail and was a car enthusiast . . . a hodad. One day in religion class, he said the sentence that turned out to be one of the most memorable of the hundreds of thousands I heard in those Voc. Ed. years. We were talking about the parable of the talents, about achievement, working hard, doing the best you can do, blah-blah-blah, when the teacher called on the restive Ken Harvey for an opinion. Ken thought about it, but just for a second, and said (with studied, minimal affect), "I just wanna be average." That woke me up. Average?! Who wants to be average? Then the athletes chimed in with the clichés that make you want to laryngectomize them, and the exchange became a platitudinous melee. At the time, I thought Ken's assertion was stupid, and I wrote him off. But his sentence has stayed with me all these years, and I think I am finally coming to understand it.

31   Ken Harvey was gasping for air. School can be a tremendously disorienting place. No matter how bad the school, you're going to encounter notions that don't fit with the assumptions and beliefs that you grew up with—maybe you'll hear these dissonant notions from teachers, maybe from the other students, and maybe you'll read them. You'll also be thrown in with all kinds of kids from all kinds of backgrounds, and that can be unsettling—this is especially true in places of rich ethnic and linguistic mix, like the L.A. basin. You'll see a handful of students far excel you in courses that sound exotic and that are only in the curriculum of the elite: French, physics, trigonometry. And all this is happening while you're trying to shape an identity; your body is changing, and your emotions are running wild. If you're a working-class kid in the vocational track, the options you'll have to deal with this will be constrained in certain ways: You're defined by your school as "slow"; you're placed in a curriculum that isn't designed to liberate you but to occupy you, or, if you're lucky, train you, though the training is for work the society does not esteem; other students are picking up the cues from your school and your curriculum and interacting with you in particular ways. If you're a kid like Ted Richard, you turn your back on all this and let your mind roam where it may. But youngsters like Ted are rare. What Ken and so many others do is protect themselves from such suffocating madness by taking on with a vengeance the identity implied in the vocational track. Reject the confusion and frustration by openly defining yourself as the Common Joe. Champion the average. Rely on your own good sense. F—— this bull——. Bull——, of course, is everything you—and the others—fear is beyond you: books, essays, tests, academic scrambling, complexity, scientific reasoning, philosophical inquiry.

32   The tragedy is that you have to twist the knife in your own gray matter to make this defense work. You'll have to shut down, have to reject intellectual stimuli or diffuse them with sarcasm,

have to cultivate stupidity, have to convert boredom from a malady into a way of confronting the world. Keep your vocabulary simple, act stoned when you're not or act more stoned than you are, flaunt ignorance, materialize your dreams. It is a powerful and effective defense—it neutralizes the insult and the frustration of being a vocational kid and, when perfected, it drives teachers up the wall, a delightful secondary effect. But like all strong magic, it exacts a price.

My own deliverance from the Voc. Ed. world began with 33 sophomore biology. Every student, college prep to vocational, had to take biology, and unlike the other courses, the same person taught all sections. When teaching the vocational group, Brother Clint probably slowed down a bit or omitted a little of the fundamental biochemistry, but he used the same book and more or less the same syllabus across the board. If one class got tough, he could get tougher. He was young and powerful and very handsome, and looks and physical strength were high currency. No one gave him any trouble.

I was pretty bad at the dissecting table, but the lectures and 34 the textbook were interesting: plastic overlays that, with each turned page, peeled away skin, then veins and muscle, then organs, down to the very bones that Brother Clint, pointer in hand, would tap out on our hanging skeleton. Dave Snyder was in big trouble, for the study of life—versus the living of it—was sticking in his craw. We worked out a code for our multiple-choice exams. He'd poke me in the back: once for the answer under *A*, twice for *B*, and so on: and when he'd hit the right one, I'd look up to the ceiling as though I were lost in thought. Poke: cytoplasm. Poke, poke: methane. Poke, poke, poke: William Harvey. Poke, poke, poke, poke: islets of Langerhans. This didn't work out perfectly, but Dave passed the course, and I mastered the dreamy look of a guy on a record jacket. And something else happened. Brother Clint puzzled over this Voc. Ed. kid who was racking up 98s and 99s on his tests. He checked the school's records and discovered the error. He recommended that I begin my junior year in the College Prep program. According to all I've read since, such a shift, as one report put it, is virtually impossible. Kids at that level rarely cross tracks. The telling thing is how chancy both my placement into and exit from Voc. Ed. was; neither I nor my parents had anything to do with it. I lived in one world during spring semester, and when I came back to school in the fall, I was living in another.

1989

keeping close to home: class and education

bell hooks

1 We are both awake in the almost dark of 5 a.m. Everyone else is sound asleep. Mama asks the usual questions. Telling me to look around, make sure I have everything, scolding me because I am uncertain about the actual time the bus arrives. By 5:30 we are waiting outside the closed station. Alone together, we have a chance to really talk. Mama begins. Angry with her children, especially the ones who whisper behind her back, she says bitterly, "Your childhood could not have been that bad. You were fed and clothed. You did not have to do without—that's more than a lot of folks have and I just can't stand the way y'all go on." The hurt in her voice saddens me. I have always wanted to protect mama from hurt, to ease her burdens. Now I am part of what troubles. Confronting me, she says accusingly, "It's not just the other children. You talk too much about the past. You don't just listen." And I do talk. Worse, I write about it.

2 Mama has always come to each of her children seeking different responses. With me she expresses the disappointment, hurt, and anger of betrayal: anger that her children are so critical, that we can't even have the sense to like the presents she sends. She says, "From now on there will be no presents. I'll just stick some money in a little envelope the way the rest of you do. Nobody wants criticism. Everybody can criticize me but I am supposed to say nothing." When I try to talk, my voice sounds like a twelve year old. When I try to talk, she speaks louder,

interrupting me, even though she has said repeatedly, "Explain it to me, this talk about the past." I struggle to return to my thirty-five year old self so that she will know by the sound of my voice that we are two women talking together. It is only when I state firmly in my very adult voice, "Mama, you are not listening," that she becomes quiet. She waits. Now that I have her attention, I fear that my explanations will be lame, inadequate. "Mama," I begin, "people usually go to therapy because they feel hurt inside, because they have pain that will not stop, like a wound that continually breaks open, that does not heal. And often these hurts, that pain has to do with things that have happened in the past, sometimes in childhood, often in childhood, or things that we believe happened." She wants to know, "What hurts, what hurts are you talking about?" "Mom, I can't answer that. I can't speak for all of us, the hurts are different for everybody. But the point is you try to make the hurt better, to heal it, by understanding how it came to be. And I know you feel mad when we say something happened or hurt that you don't remember being that way, but the past isn't like that, we don't have the same memory of it. We remember things differently. You know that. And sometimes folk feel hurt about stuff and you just don't know or didn't realize it, and they need to talk about it. Surely you understand the need to talk about it."

Our conversation is interrupted by the sight of my uncle walking across the park toward us. We stop to watch him. He is on his way to work dressed in a familiar blue suit. They look alike, these two who rarely discuss the past. This interruption makes me think about life in a small town. You always see someone you know. Interruptions, intrusions are part of daily life. Privacy is difficult to maintain. We leave our private space in the car to greet him. After the hug and kiss he has given me every year since I was born, they talk about the day's funerals. In the distance the bus approaches. He walks away knowing that they will see each other later. Just before I board the bus I turn, staring into my mother's face. I am momentarily back in time, seeing myself eighteen years ago, at this same bus stop, staring into my mother's face, continually turning back, waving farewell as I returned to college—that experience which first took me away from our town, from family. Departing was as painful then as it is now. Each movement away makes return harder. Each separation intensifies distance, both physical and emotional.

4   To a southern black girl from a working-class background who had never been on a city bus, who had never stepped on an escalator, who had never travelled by plane, leaving the comfortable confines of a small town Kentucky life to attend Stanford University was not just frightening; it was utterly painful. My parents had not been delighted that I had been accepted and adamantly opposed my going so far from home. At the time, I did not see their opposition as an expression of their fear that they would lose me forever. Like many working-class folks, they feared what college education might do to their children's minds even as they unenthusiastically acknowledged its importance. They did not understand why I could not attend a college nearby, an all-black college. To them, any college would do. I would graduate, become a school teacher, make a decent living and a good marriage. And even though they reluctantly and skeptically supported my educational endeavors, they also subjected them to constant harsh and bitter critique. It is difficult for me to talk about my parents and their impact on me because they have always felt wary, ambivalent, mistrusting of my intellectual aspirations even as they have been caring and supportive. I want to speak about these contradictions because sorting through them, seeking resolution and reconciliation has been important to me both as it affects my development as a writer, my effort to be fully self-realized, and my longing to remain close to the family and community that provided the groundwork for much of my thinking, writing, and being.

5   Studying at Stanford, I began to think seriously about class differences. To be materially underprivileged at a university where most folks (with the exception of workers) are materially privileged provokes such thought. Class differences were boundaries no one wanted to face or talk about. It was easier to downplay them, to act as though we were all from privileged backgrounds, to work around them, to confront them privately in the solitude of one's room, or to pretend that just being chosen to study at such an institution meant that those of us who did not come from privilege were already in transition toward privilege. To not long for such transition marked one as rebellious, as

unlikely to succeed. It was a kind of treason not to believe that it was better to be identified with the world of material privilege than with the world of the working class, the poor. No wonder our working-class parents from poor backgrounds feared our entry into such a world, intuiting perhaps that we might learn to be ashamed of where we had come from, that we might never return home, or come back only to lord it over them.

Though I hung with students who were supposedly radical and chic, we did not discuss class. I talked to no one about the sources of my shame, how it hurt me to witness the contempt shown the brown-skinned Filipina maids who cleaned our rooms, or later my concern about the $100 a month I paid for a room off-campus which was more than half of what my parents paid for rent. I talked to no one about my efforts to save money, to send a little something home. Yet these class realities separated me from fellow students. We were moving in different directions. I did not intend to forget my class background or alter my class allegiance. And even though I received an education designed to provide me with a bourgeois sensibility, passive acquiescence was not my only option. I knew that I could resist. I could rebel. I could shape the direction and focus of the various forms of knowledge available to me. Even though I sometimes envied and longed for greater material advantages (particularly at vacation times when I would be one of few if any students remaining in the dormitory because there was no money for travel), I did not share the sensibility and values of my peers. That was important—class was not just about money; it was about values which showed and determined behavior. While I often needed more money, I never needed a new set of beliefs and values. For example, I was profoundly shocked and disturbed when peers would talk about their parents without respect, or would even say that they hated their parents. This was especially troubling to me when it seemed that these parents were caring and concerned. It was often explained to me that such hatred was "healthy and normal." To my white, middle-class California roommate, I explained the way we were taught to value our parents and their care, to understand that they were not obligated to give us care. She would always shake her head, laughing all the while, and say, "Missy, you will learn that it's different here, that we think differently." She was right. Soon, I lived alone, like the one Mormon student who kept to himself as he made a concentrated effort to remain true to his religious beliefs and values. Later in graduate school I found that classmates believed "lower class" people had no beliefs and values. I was silent in such discussions, disgusted by their ignorance.

7   Carol Stack's anthropological study, *All Our Kin,* was one of the first books I read which confirmed my experiential understanding that within black culture (especially among the working class and poor, particularly in southern states), a value system emerged that was counter-hegemonic, that challenged notions of individualism and private property so important to the maintenance of white-supremacist, capitalist patriarchy. Black folk created in marginal spaces a world of community and collectivity where resources were shared. In the preface to *Feminist Theory: from margin to center,* I talked about how the point of difference, this marginality can be the space for the formation of an oppositional world view. That world view must be articulated, named if it is to provide a sustained blueprint for change. Unfortunately, there has existed no consistent framework for such naming. Consequently both the experience of this difference and documentation of it (when it occurs) gradually loses presence and meaning.

8   Much of what Stack documented about the "culture of poverty," for example, would not describe interactions among most black poor today irrespective of geographical setting. Since the black people she described did not acknowledge (if they recognized it in theoretical terms) the oppositional value of their world view, apparently seeing it more as a survival strategy determined less by conscious efforts to oppose oppressive race and class biases than by circumstance, they did not attempt to establish a framework to transmit their beliefs and values from generation to generation. When circumstances changed, values altered. Efforts to assimilate the values and beliefs of privileged white people, presented through media like television, undermine and destroy potential structures of opposition.

9   Increasingly, young black people are encouraged by the dominant culture (and by those black people who internalize the values of this hegemony) to believe that assimilation is the only possible way to survive, to succeed. Without the framework of an organized civil rights or black resistance struggle, individual and

collective efforts at black liberation that focus on the primacy of self-definition and self-determination often go unrecognized. It is crucial that those among us who resist and rebel, who survive and succeed, speak openly and honestly about our lives and the nature of our personal struggles, the means by which we resolve and reconcile contradictions. This is no easy task. Within the educational institutions where we learn to develop and strengthen our writing and analytical skills, we also learn to think, write, and talk in a manner that shifts attention away from personal experience. Yet if we are to reach our people and all people, if we are to remain connected (especially those of us whose familial backgrounds are poor and working-class), we must understand that the telling of one's personal story provides a meaningful example, a way for folks to identify and connect.

Combining personal with critical analysis and theoretical per- 10 spectives can engage listeners who might otherwise feel estranged, alienated. To speak simply with language that is accessible to as many folks as possible is also important. Speaking about one's personal experience or speaking with simple language is often considered by academics and/or intellectuals (irrespective of their political inclinations) to be a sign of intellectual weakness or even anti-intellectualism. Lately, when I speak, I do not stand in place—reading my paper, making little or no eye contact with audiences—but instead make eye contact, talk extemporaneously, digress, and address the audience directly. I have been told that people assume I am not prepared, that I am anti-intellectual, unprofessional (a concept that has everything to do with class as it determines actions and behavior), or that I am reinforcing the stereotype of black people as non-theoretical and gutsy.

Such criticism was raised recently by fellow feminist scholars 11 after a talk I gave at Northwestern University at a conference on "Gender, Culture, Politics" to an audience that was mainly students and academics. I deliberately chose to speak in a very basic way, thinking especially about the few community folks who had come to hear me. Weeks later, Kum-Kum Sangari, a fellow participant who shared with me what was said when I was no longer present, and I engaged in quite rigorous critical dialogue about the way my presentation had been perceived primarily by privileged white female academics. She was concerned that I not mask my knowledge of theory, that I not appear anti-intellectual. Her critique compelled me to articulate concerns that I am often silent about with colleagues. I spoke about class allegiance and revolutionary commitments, explaining that it was disturbing to me that intellectual radicals who speak about transforming society, ending the domination of race, sex, class, cannot break with behavior patterns that reinforce and perpetuate domination, or continue to use as their sole reference point how we might be or are perceived by those who dominate, whether or not we gain their acceptance and approval.

12   This is a primary contradiction which raises the issue of whether or not the academic setting is a place where one can be truly radical or subversive. Concurrently, the use of a language and style of presentation that alienate most folks who are not also academically trained reinforces the notion that the academic world is separate from real life, that everyday world where we constantly adjust our language and behavior to meet diverse needs. The academic setting is separate only when we work to make it so. It is a false dichotomy which suggests that academics and/or intellectuals can only speak to one another, that we cannot hope to speak with the masses. What is true is that we make choices, that we choose our audiences, that we choose voices to hear and voices to silence. If I do not speak in a language that can be understood, then there is little chance for dialogue. This issue of language and behavior is a central contradiction all radical intellectuals, particularly those who are members of oppressed groups, must continually confront and work to resolve. One of the clear and present dangers that exists when we move outside our class of origin, our collective ethnic experience, and enter hierarchical institutions which daily reinforce domination by race, sex, and class, is that we gradually assume a mindset similar to those who dominate and oppress, that we lose critical consciousness because it is not reinforced or affirmed by the environment. We must be ever vigilant. It is important that we know who we are speaking to, who we most want to hear us, who we most long to move, motivate, and touch with our words.

13   When I first came to New Haven to teach at Yale, I was truly surprised by the marked class divisions between black folks—students and professors—who identify with Yale and those

black folks who work at Yale or in surrounding communities. Style of dress and self-presentation are most often the central markers of one's position. I soon learned that the black folks who spoke on the street were likely to be part of the black community and those who carefully shifted their glance were likely to be associated with Yale. Walking with a black female colleague one day, I spoke to practically every black person in sight (a gesture which reflects my upbringing), an action which disturbed my companion. Since I addressed black folk who were clearly not associated with Yale, she wanted to know whether or not I knew them. That was funny to me. "Of course not," I answered. Yet when I thought about it seriously, I realized that in a deep way, I knew them for they, and not my companion or most of my colleagues at Yale, resemble my family. Later that year, in a black women's support group I started for undergraduates, students from poor backgrounds spoke about the shame they sometimes feel when faced with the reality of their connection to working-class and poor black people. One student confessed that her father is a street person, addicted to drugs, someone who begs from passersby. She, like other Yale students, turns away from street people often, sometimes showing anger or contempt; she hasn't wanted anyone to know that she was related to this kind of person. She struggles with this, wanting to find a way to acknowledge and affirm this reality, to claim this connection. The group asked me and one another what we do to remain connected, to honor the bonds we have with working-class and poor people even as our class experience alters.

Maintaining connections with family and community across 14 class boundaries demands more than just summary recall of where one's roots are, where one comes from. It requires knowing, naming, and being ever-mindful of those aspects of one's past that have enabled and do enable one's self-development in the present, that sustain and support, that enrich. One must also honestly confront barriers that do exist, aspects of that past that do diminish. My parent's ambivalence about my love for reading led to intense conflict. They (especially my mother) would work to ensure that I had access to books, but would threaten to burn the books or throw them away if I did not conform to other expectations. Or they would insist that reading too much would drive me insane. Their ambivalence nurtured in me a like uncertainty about the value and significance of intellectual endeavor which took years for me to unlearn. While this aspect of our class reality was one that wounded and diminished, their vigilant insistence that being smart did not make me a "better" or "superior" person (which often got on my nerves because I think I wanted to have that sense that it did indeed set me apart, make me better) made a profound impression. From them I learned to value and respect various skills and talents folk might have, not just to value people who read books and talk about ideas. They and my grandparents might say about somebody, "Now he don't read nor write a lick, but he can tell a story," or as my grandmother would say, "call out the hell in words."

15   Empty romanticization of poor or working-class backgrounds undermines the possibility of true connection. Such connection is based on understanding difference in experience and perspective and working to mediate and negotiate these terrains. Language is a crucial issue for folk whose movement outside the boundaries of poor and working-class backgrounds changes the nature and direction of their speech. Coming to Stanford with my own version of a Kentucky accent, which I think of always as a strong sound quite different from Tennessee or Georgia speech, I learned to speak differently while maintaining the speech of my region, the sound of my family and community. This was of course much easier to keep up when I returned home to stay often. In recent years, I have endeavored to use various speaking styles in the classroom as a teacher and find it disconcerts those who feel that the use of a particular patois excludes them as listeners, even if there is translation into the usual, acceptable mode of speech. Learning to listen to different voices, hearing different speech challenges the notion that we must all assimilate—share a single, similar talk—in educational institutions. Language reflects the culture from which we emerge. To deny ourselves daily use of speech patterns that are common and familiar, that embody the unique and distinctive aspect of our self is one of the ways we become estranged and alienated from our past. It is important for us to have as many languages on hand as we can know or learn. It is important for those of us who are black, who speak in particular patois as well as standard English to express ourselves in both ways.

Often I tell students from poor and working-class back- 16
grounds that if you believe what you have learned and are learning in schools and universities separates you from your past, this
is precisely what will happen. It is important to stand firm in the
conviction that nothing can truly separate us from our pasts when
we nurture and cherish that connection. An important strategy for
maintaining contact is ongoing acknowledgement of the primacy
of one's past, of one's background, affirming the reality that such
bonds are not severed automatically solely because one enters a
new environment or moves toward a different class experience.

Again, I do not wish to romanticize this effort, to dismiss the 17
reality of conflict and contradiction. During my time at Stanford,
I did go through a period of more than a year when I did not
return home. That period was one where I felt that it was simply
too difficult to mesh my profoundly disparate realities. Critical
reflection about the choice I was making, particularly about why
I felt a choice had to be made, pulled me through this difficult
time. Luckily I recognized that the insistence on choosing between
the world of family and community and the new world of privileged white people and privileged ways of knowing was imposed
upon me by the outside. It is as though a mythical contract had
been signed somewhere which demanded of us black folks that
once we entered these spheres we would immediately give up all
vestiges of our underprivileged past. It was my responsibility to
formulate a way of being that would allow me to participate fully
in my new environment while integrating and maintaining
aspects of the old.

One of the most tragic manifestations of the pressure black 18
people feel to assimilate is expressed in the internalization of
racist perspectives. I was shocked and saddened when I first
heard black professors at Stanford downgrade and express contempt for black students, expecting us to do poorly, refusing to
establish nurturing bonds. At every university I have attended as
a student or worked at as a teacher, I have heard similar attitudes
expressed with little or no understanding of factors that might
prevent brilliant black students from performing to their full
capability. Within universities, there are few educational and
social spaces where students who wish to affirm positive ties to
ethnicity—to blackness, to working-class backgrounds—can

receive affirmation and support. Ideologically, the message is clear—assimilation is the way to gain acceptance and approval from those in power.

19   Many white people enthusiastically supported Richard Rodriguez's vehement contention in his autobiography, *Hunger of Memory,* that attempts to maintain ties with his Chicano background impeded his progress, that he had to sever ties with community and kin to succeed at Stanford and in the larger world, that family language, in his case Spanish, had to be made secondary or discarded. If the terms of success as defined by the standards of ruling groups within white-supremacist, capitalist patriarchy are the only standards that exist, then assimilation is indeed necessary. But they are not. Even in the face of powerful structures of domination, it remains possible for each of us, especially those of us who are members of oppressed and/or exploited groups as well as those radical visionaries who may have race, class, and sex privilege, to define and determine alternative standards, to decide on the nature and extent of compromise. Standards by which one's success is measured, whether student or professor, are quite different for those of us who wish to resist reinforcing the domination of race, sex, and class, who work to maintain and strengthen our ties with the oppressed, with those who lack material privilege, with our families who are poor and working-class.

20   When I wrote my first book, *Ain't I A Woman: black women and feminism,* the issue of class and its relationship to who one's reading audience might be came up for me around my decision not to use footnotes, for which I have been sharply criticized. I told people that my concern was that footnotes set class boundaries for readers, determining who a book is for. I was shocked that many academic folks scoffed at this idea. I shared that I went into working-class black communities as well as talked with family and friends to survey whether or not they ever read books with footnotes and found that they did not. A few did not know what they were, but most folks saw them as indicating that a book was for college-educated people. These responses influenced my decision. When some of my more radical, college-educated friends freaked out about the absence of footnotes, I seriously questioned how we could ever imagine revolutionary transformation of society if such a small shift in direction could be viewed as threatening. Of course,

many folks warned that the absence of footnotes would make the work less credible in academic circles. This information also highlighted the way in which class informs our choices. Certainly I did feel that choosing to use simple language, absence of footnotes, etc. would mean I was jeopardizing the possibility of being taken seriously in academic circles but then this was a political matter and a political decision. It utterly delights me that this has proven not to be the case and that the book is read by many academics as well as by people who are not college-educated.

Always our first response when we are motivated to conform 21 or compromise within structures that reinforce domination must be to engage in critical reflection. Only by challenging ourselves to push against oppressive boundaries do we make the radical alternative possible, expanding the realm and scope of critical inquiry. Unless we share radical strategies, ways of rethinking and revisioning with students, with kin and community, with a larger audience, we risk perpetuating the stereotype that we succeed because we are the exception, different from the rest of our people. Since I left home and entered college, I am often asked, usually by white people, if my sisters and brothers are also high achievers. At the root of this question is the longing for reinforcement of the belief in "the exception" which enables race, sex, and class biases to remain intact. I am careful to separate what it means to be exceptional from a notion of "the exception."

Frequently I hear smart black folks, from poor and working- 22 class backgrounds, stressing their frustration that at times family and community do not recognize that they are exceptional. Absence of positive affirmation clearly diminishes the longing to excel in academic endeavors. Yet it is important to distinguish between the absence of basic positive affirmation and the longing for continued reinforcement that we are special. Usually liberal white folks will willingly offer continual reinforcement of us as exceptions—as special. This can be both patronizing and very seductive. Since we often work in situations where we are isolated from other black folks, we can easily begin to feel that encouragement from white people is the primary or only source of support and recognition. Given the internalization of racism, it is easy to view this support as more validating and legitimizing than similar support from black people. Still, nothing takes the place of being valued and appreciated by one's own, by one's family and community. We share a mutual and reciprocal responsibility for affirming one another's successes. Sometimes we have to talk to our folks about the fact that we need their ongoing support and affirmation, that it is unique and special to us. In some cases we may never receive desired recognition and acknowledgement of specific achievements from kin. Rather than seeing this as a basis for estrangement, for severing connection, it is useful to explore other sources of nourishment and support.

23   I do not know that my mother's mother ever acknowledged my college education except to ask me once, "How can you live so far away from your people?" Yet she gave me sources of affirmation and nourishment, sharing the legacy of her quilt-making, of family history, of her incredible way with words. Recently, when our father retired after more than thirty years of work as a janitor, I wanted to pay tribute to this experience, to identify links between his work and my own as writer and teacher. Reflecting on our family past, I recalled ways he had been an impressive example of diligence and hard work, approaching tasks with a seriousness of concentration I work to mirror and develop, with a discipline I struggle to maintain. Sharing these thoughts with him keeps us connected, nurtures our respect for each other, maintaining a space, however large or small, where we can talk.

24   Open, honest communication is the most important way we maintain relationships with kin and community as our class experience and backgrounds change. It is as vital as the sharing of resources. Often financial assistance is given in circumstances where there is no meaningful contact. However helpful, this can also be an expression of estrangement and alienation. Communication between black folks from various experiences of material privilege was much easier when we were all in segregated communities sharing common experiences in relation to social institutions. Without this grounding, we must work to maintain ties, connection. We must assume greater responsibility for making and maintaining contact, connections that can shape our intellectual visions and inform our radical commitments.

25   The most powerful resource any of us can have as we study and teach in university settings is full understanding and appreciation of the richness, beauty, and primacy of our familial and

community backgrounds. Maintaining awareness of class differences, nurturing ties with the poor and working-class people who are our most intimate kin, our comrades in struggle, transforms and enriches our intellectual experience. Education as the practice of freedom becomes not a force which fragments or separates, but one that brings us closer, expanding our definitions of home and community.

1988

The Recoloring of Campus Life

Shelby Steele

In the past few years, we have witnessed what the National Institute Against Prejudice and Violence calls a "proliferation" of racial incidents on college campuses around the country. Incidents of on-campus "intergroup conflict" have occurred at more than 160 colleges in the last two years, according to the institute. The nature of these incidents has ranged from open racial violence—most notoriously, the October 1986 beating of a black student at the University of Massachusetts at Amherst after an argument about the World Series turned into a racial bashing, with a crowd of up to three thousand whites chasing twenty blacks—to the harassment of minority students and acts of racial or ethnic insensitivity, with by far the greatest number of episodes falling in the last two categories. At Yale last year, a swastika and the words "white power" were painted on the university's Afro-American cultural center. Racist jokes were aired not long ago on a campus radio station at the University of Michigan. And at the University of Wisconsin at Madison, members of the Zeta Beta Tau fraternity held a mock slave auction in which pledges painted their faces black and wore Afro wigs. Two weeks after the president of Stanford University informed the incoming freshmen class last fall that "bigotry is out, and I mean it," two freshmen defaced a poster of Beethoven—gave the image thick lips—and hung it on a black student's door.

2   In response, black students around the country have rediscovered the militant protest strategies of the sixties. At the University of Massachusetts at Amherst, Williams College, Penn State
University, University of California–Berkeley, UCLA, Stanford
University, and countless other campuses, black students have sat
in, marched, and rallied. But much of what they were marching
and rallying about seemed less a response to specific racial incidents than a call for broader action on the part of the colleges and
universities they were attending. Black students have demanded
everything from more black faculty members and new courses on
racism to the addition of "ethnic" foods in the cafeteria. There is
the sense in these demands that racism runs deep. Is the campus
becoming the battleground for a renewed war between the races?
I don't think so, not really. But if it is not a war, the problem of
campus racism does represent a new and surprising hardening
of racial lines within the most traditionally liberal and tolerant of
America's institutions—its universities.

3   As a black who has spent his entire adult life on predomi-
nantly white campuses, I found it hard to believe that the problem of campus racism was as dramatic as some of the incidents
seemed to make it. The incidents I read or heard about often
seemed prankish and adolescent, though not necessarily harmless. There is a meanness in them but not much menace; no
one is proposing to reinstitute Jim Crow on campus. On the
California campus where I now teach, there have been few
signs of racial tension.

4   And, of course, universities are not where racial problems
tend to arise. When I went to college in the mid-sixties, colleges
were oases of calm and understanding in a racially tense society;
campus life—with its traditions of tolerance and fairness, its
very distance from the "real" world—imposed a degree of broad-
mindedness on even the most provincial students. If I met whites
who were not anxious to be friends with blacks, most were at least
vaguely friendly to the cause of our freedom. In any case, there
was no guerrilla activity against our presence, no "mine field of
racism" (as one black student at Berkeley recently put it to me) to
negotiate. I wouldn't say that the phrase "campus racism" is a
contradiction in terms, but until recently it certainly seemed an
incongruence.

But a greater incongruence is the generational timing of this 5
new problem on the campuses. Today's undergraduates were born
after the passage of the 1964 Civil Rights Act. They grew up in an
age when racial equality was for the first time enforceable by law.
This too was a time when blacks suddenly appeared on television,
as mayors of big cities, as icons of popular culture, as teachers, and
in some cases even as neighbors. Today's black and white college
students, veterans of "Sesame Street" and often of integrated
grammar and high schools, have had more opportunities to know
each other than any previous generation in American history. Not
enough opportunities, perhaps, but enough to make the notion of
racial tension on campus something of a mystery, at least to me.

To look at this mystery, I left my own campus with its bur- 6
den of familiarity and talked with black and white students at
California schools where racial incidents had occurred: Stanford,
UCLA, and Berkeley. I spoke with black and white students—not
with Asians and Hispanics—because, as always, blacks and
whites represent the deepest lines of division, and because I hesitate to wander onto the complex territory of other minority
groups. A phrase by William H. Gass—"the hidden internality of
things"—describes, with maybe a little too much grandeur, what
I hoped to find. But it is what I wanted to find, for this is the kind
of problem that makes a black person nervous, which is not to say
that it doesn't unnerve whites as well. Once every six months or
so someone yells "nigger" at me from a passing car. I don't like
to think that these solo artists might soon make up a chorus, or
worse, that this chorus might one day soon sing to me from the
paths of my own campus.

I have long believed that the trouble between the races is sel- 7
dom what it appears to be. It was not hard to see after my first
talks with students that racial tension on campus is a problem that
misrepresents itself. It has the same look, the archetypal pattern,
of America's timeless racial conflict—white racism and black
protest. And I think part of our concern over it comes from the
fact that it has the feel of a relapse, illness gone and come again.
But if we are seeing the same symptoms, I don't believe we are
dealing with the same illness. For one thing, I think racial tension
on campus is more the result of racial equality than inequality.

8   How to live with racial difference has been America's profound social problem. For the first hundred years or so following
emancipation it was controlled by a legally sanctioned inequality
that kept the races from each other. No longer is this the case. On
campuses today, as throughout society, blacks enjoy equality
under the law—a profound social advancement. No student may
be kept out of a class or a dormitory or an extracurricular activity because of his or her race. But there is a paradox here: on a
campus where members of all races are gathered, mixed together
in the classroom as well as socially, differences are more exposed
than ever. And this is where the trouble starts. For members of
each race—young adults coming into their own, often away from
home for the first time—bring to this site of freedom, exploration,
and (now, today) equality, very deep fears, anxieties, inchoate feelings of racial shame, anger, and guilt. These feelings could lie dor-
mant in the home, in familiar neighborhoods, in simpler days of
childhood. But the college campus, with its structures of interaction and adult-level competition—the big exam, the dorm, the
mixer—is another matter. I think campus racism is born of the rub
between racial difference and a setting, the campus itself, devoted
to interaction and equality. On our campuses, such concentrated
micro-societies, all that remains unresolved between blacks and
whites, all the old wounds and shames that have never been
addressed, present themselves for attention—and present our
youth with pressures they cannot always handle.

9   I have mentioned one paradox: racial fears and anxieties
among blacks and whites, bubbling up in an era of racial equality under the law, in settings that are among the freest and fairest
in society. But there is another, related paradox, stemming from
the notion of—and practice of—affirmative action. Under the provisions of the Equal Employment Opportunity Act of 1972, all
state governments and institutions (including universities) were
forced to initiate plans to increase the proportion of minority and
women employees and, in the case of universities, of students too.
Affirmative action plans that establish racial quotas were ruled
unconstitutional more than ten years ago in *University of California*
v. *Bakke,* but such plans are still thought by some to secretly exist,
and lawsuits having to do with alleged quotas are still very much
with us. But quotas are only the most controversial aspect of

affirmative action; the principal of affirmative action is reflected in various university programs aimed at redressing and overcoming past patterns of discrimination. Of course, to be conscious of past patterns of discriminations—the fact, say, that public schools in the black inner cities are more crowded and employ fewer top-notch teachers than a white suburban public school, and that this is a factor in student performance—is only reasonable. But in doing this we also call attention quite obviously to difference: in the case of blacks and whites, racial difference. What has emerged on campus in recent years—as a result of the new equality and of affirmative action and, in a sense, as a result of progress—is a *politics of difference*, a troubling, volatile politics in which each group justifies itself, its sense of worth and its pursuit of power, through difference alone.

In this context, racial, ethnic, and gender differences become 10 forms of sovereignty, campuses become balkanized, and each group fights with whatever means are available. No doubt there are many factors that have contributed to the rise of racial tension on campus: What has been the role of fraternities, which have returned to campus with their inclusions and exclusions? What role has the heightened notion of college as some first step to personal, financial success played in increasing competition, and thus tension? But mostly, what I sense is that in interactive settings, fighting the fights of "difference," old ghosts are stirred and haunt again. Black and white Americans simply have the power to make each other feel shame and guilt. In most situations, we may be able to deny these feelings, keep them at bay. But these feelings are likely to surface on college campuses, where young people are groping for identity and power, and where difference is made to matter so greatly. In a way, racial tension on campus in the eighties might have been inevitable.

I would like, first, to discuss black students, their anxieties 11 and vulnerabilities. The accusation black Americans have always lived with is that they are inferior—inferior simply because they are black. And this accusation has been too uniform, too ingrained in cultural imagery, too enforced by law, custom, and every form of power not to have left a mark. Black inferiority was a precept accepted by the founders of this nation; it was a principle of social organization that relegated blacks to the sidelines of American life. So when young black students find themselves on white campuses surrounded by those who have historically claimed superiority, they are also surrounded by the myth of their inferiority.

12   Of course, it is true that many young people come to college with some anxiety about not being good enough. But only blacks come wearing a color that is still, in the minds of some, a sign of inferiority. Poles, Jews, Hispanics, and other groups also endure degrading stereotypes. But two things make the myth of black inferiority a far heavier burden—the broadness of its scope and its incarnation in color. There are not only more stereotypes of blacks than of other groups, but these stereotypes are also more dehumanizing, more focused on the most despised human traits: stupidity, laziness, sexual immorality, dirtiness, and so on. In America's racial and ethnic hierarchy, blacks have clearly been relegated to the lowest level—have been burdened with an ambiguous, animalistic humanity. Moreover, this is made unavoidable for blacks by sheer visibility of black skin, a skin that evokes the myth of inferiority on sight. Today this myth is sadly reinforced for many black students by affirmative action programs, under which blacks may often enter college with lower test scores and high school grade point averages than whites. "They see me as an affirmative action case," one black student told me at UCLA. This reinforces the myth of inferiority by implying that blacks are not good enough to make it into college on their own.

13   So when a black student enters college, the myth of inferiority compounds the normal anxiousness over whether he or she will be good enough. This anxiety is not only personal but also racial. The families of these students will have pounded into them the fact that blacks are not inferior. And probably more than anything it is this pounding that finally leaves the mark. If I am not inferior, why the need to say so?

14   This myth of inferiority constitutes a very sharp and ongoing anxiety for young blacks, the nature of which is very precise: it is the terror that somehow, through one's actions or by virtue of some "proof" (a poor grade, a flubbed response in class), one's fear of inferiority—inculcated in ways large and small by society—will be confirmed as real. On a university campus where intelligence itself is the ultimate measure, this anxiety is bound to be triggered.

A black student I met at UCLA was disturbed a little when 15 I asked him if he ever felt vulnerable—anxious about "black inferiority"—as a black student. But after a long pause, he finally said, "I think I do." The example he gave was of a large lecture class he'd taken with over three hundred students. Fifty or so black students sat in the back of the lecture hall and "acted out every stereotype in the book." They were loud, ate food, came in late—and generally got lower grades than whites in the class. "I knew I would be seen like them, and I didn't like it. I never sat by them." Seen like what, I asked, though we both knew the answer. "As lazy, ignorant, and stupid," he said sadly.

Had the group at the back been white fraternity brothers, they 16 would not have been seen as dumb whites, of course. And a frat brother who worried about his grades would not worry *that he had been seen* "like them." The terror in this situation for the black student I spoke with was that his own deeply buried anxiety would be given credence, that the myth would be verified, and that he would feel shame and humiliation not because of who he was but simply because he was black. In this lecture hall his race, quite apart from his performance, might subject him to four unendurable feelings—diminishment, accountability to the preconceptions of whites, a powerlessness to change those preconceptions, and finally, shame. These are the feelings that make up his racial anxiety, and that of all blacks on any campus. On a white campus a black is never far from these feelings, and even his unconscious knowledge that he is subject to them can undermine his self-esteem. There are blacks on any campus who are not up to doing good college-level work. Certain black students may not be happy or motivated or in the appropriate field of study—*just like whites.* (Let us not forget that many white students get poor grades, fail, drop out.) Moreover, many more blacks than whites are not quite prepared for college, may have to catch up, owing to factors beyond their control: poor previous schooling, for example. But the white who has to catch up will not be anxious that his being behind is a matter of his whiteness, of his being racially inferior. The black student may well have such a fear.

This, I believe, is one reason why black colleges in America 17 turn out 37 percent of all black college graduates though they enroll only 16 percent of black college students. Without whites around on campus, the myth of inferiority is in abeyance and, along with it, a great reservoir of culturally imposed self-doubt. On black campuses, feelings of inferiority are personal; on campuses with a white majority, a black's problems have a way of becoming a "black" problem.

18   But this feeling of vulnerability a black may feel, in itself, is not as serious a problem as what he or she does with it. To admit that one is made anxious in integrated situations about the myth of racial inferiority is difficult for young blacks. It seems like admitting that one is racially inferior. And so, most often, the student will deny harboring the feelings. This is where some of the pangs of racial tension begin, because denial always involves distortion.

19   In order to deny a problem we must tell ourselves that the problem is something different from what it really is. A black student at Berkeley told me that he felt defensive every time he walked into a classroom of white faces. When I asked why, he said, "Because I know they're all racists. They think blacks are stupid." Of course, it may be true that some whites feel this way, but the singular focus on white racism allows this student to obscure his own underlying racial anxiety. He can now say that his problem—facing a classroom of white faces, *fearing* that they think he is dumb—is entirely the result of certifiable white racism and has nothing to do with his own anxieties, or even that this particular academic subject may not be his best. Now all the terror of his anxiety, its powerful energy, is devoted to simply *seeing* racism. Whatever evidence of racism he finds—and looking this hard, he will no doubt find some—can be brought in to buttress his distorted view of the problem while his actual deep-seated anxiety goes unseen.

20   Denial, and the distortion that results, places the problem *outside* the self and in the world. It is not that I have any inferiority anxiety because of my race; it is that I am going to school with people who don't like blacks. This is the shift in thinking that allows black students to reenact the protest pattern of the sixties. *Denied racial anxiety–distortion–reenactment* is the process by which feelings of inferiority are transformed into an exaggerated white menace—which is then protested against with the techniques of the past. Under the sway of this process, black students believe that history is repeating itself, that it's just like the sixties, or fifties.

In fact, it is not-yet-healed wounds from the past, rather than the inequality that created the wounds, that is the real problem.

This process generates an unconscious need to exaggerate the 21 level of racism on campus—to make it a matter of the system, not just a handful of students. Racism is the avenue away from the true inner anxiety. How many students demonstrating for black theme dorms—demonstrating in the style of the sixties, when the battle was to win for blacks a place on campus—might be better off spending their time reading and studying? Black students have the highest dropout rate and the lowest grade point average of any group in American universities. This need not be so. And it is not the result of not having black theme dorms.

It was my very good fortune to go to college in 1964, when 22 the question of black "inferiority" was openly talked about among blacks. The summer before I left for college, I heard Martin Luther King speak in Chicago, and he laid it on the line for black students everywhere: "When you are behind in a footrace, the only way to get ahead is to run faster than the man in front of you. So when your white roommate says he's tired and goes to sleep, you stay up and burn the midnight oil." His statement that we were "behind in a footrace" acknowledged that, because of history, of few opportunities, of racism, we were, in a sense, "inferior." But this had to do with what had been done to our parents and their parents, not with inherent inferiority. And because it was acknowledged, it was presented to us as a challenge rather than a mark of shame.

Of the eighteen black students (in a student body of one thou- 23 sand) who were on campus in my freshman year, all graduated, though a number of us were not from the middle class. At the university where I currently teach, the dropout rate for black students is 72 percent, despite the presence of several academic support programs, a counseling center with black counselors, an Afro-American studies department, black faculty, administrators, and staff, a general education curriculum that emphasizes "cultural pluralism," an Educational Opportunities Program, a mentor program, a black faculty and staff association, and an administration and faculty that often announce the need to do more for black students.

24   It may be unfair to compare my generation with the current one. Parents do this compulsively and to little end but self-congratulation. But I don't congratulate my generation. I think we were advantaged. We came along at a time when racial integration was held in high esteem. And integration was a very challenging social concept for both blacks and whites. We were remaking ourselves—that's what one did at college—and making history. We had something to prove. This was a profound advantage; it gave us clarity and a challenge. Achievement in the American mainstream was the goal of integration, and the best thing about this challenge was its secondary message—that we *could* achieve.

25   There is much irony in the fact that black power would come along in the late sixties and change all this. Black power was a movement of uplift and pride, and yet it also delivered the weight of pride—a weight that would burden black students from then on. Black power "nationalized" the black identity, made blackness itself an object of celebration, an allegiance. But if it transformed a mark of shame into a mark of pride, it also, in the name of pride, required the denial of racial anxiety. Without a frank account of one's anxieties, there is no clear direction, no concrete challenge. Black students today do not get as clear a message from their racial identity as my generation got. They are not filled with the same urgency to prove themselves because black pride has said, *You're already proven, already equal, as good as anybody.*

26   The "black identity" shaped by black power most forcefully contributes to racial tensions on campuses by basing entitlement more on race than on constitutional rights and standards of merit. With integration, black entitlement derived from constitutional principles of fairness. Black power changed this by skewing the formula from rights to color—if you were black, you were entitled. Thus the United Coalition Against Racism (UCAR) at the University of Michigan could "demand" two years ago that all black professors be given immediate tenure, that there is a special pay incentive for black professors, and that money be provided for an all-black student union. In this formula, black becomes the very color of entitlement, an extra right in itself, and a very dangerous grandiosity is promoted in which blackness amounts to specialness.

Race is, by any standard, an unprincipled source of power. 27 And on campuses the use of racial power by one group makes racial, ethnic, or gender difference a currency of power for all groups. When I make my *difference* into power, other groups must seize upon their difference to contain my power and maintain their position relative to me. Very quickly a kind of politics of difference emerges in which racial, ethnic, and gender groups are forced to assert their entitlement and vie for power based on the single quality that makes them different from one another.

On many campuses today academic departments and pro- 28 grams are established on the basis of difference—black studies, women's studies, Asian studies, and so on—despite the fact that there is nothing in these "difference" departments that cannot be studied within traditional academic disciplines. If their rationale is truly past exclusion from the mainstream curriculum, shouldn't the goal now be complete inclusion rather than separateness? I think this logic is overlooked because those groups are too interested in the power their difference can bring, and they insist on separate departments and programs as tribute to that power.

This politics of difference makes everyone on campus a mem- 29 ber of a minority group. It also makes racial tension inevitable. To highlight one's difference as a source of advantage is also, indirectly, to inspire the enemies of that difference. When blackness (and femaleness) become power, then white maleness is also sanctioned as power. A white male student I spoke with at Stanford said, "One of my friends said the other day that we should get together and start up a white student union and come up with a list of demands."

It is certainly true that white maleness has long been an unfair 30 source of power. But the sin of white male power is precisely its use of race and gender as a source of entitlement. When minorities and women use their race, ethnicity, and gender in the same way, they not only commit the same sin but also, indirectly, sanction the very form of power that oppressed them in the first place. The politics of difference is based on a tit-for-tat sort of logic in which every victory only calls one's enemies to arms.

This elevation of difference undermines the communal impulse 31 by making each group foreign and inaccessible to others. When difference is celebrated rather than remarked, people must think in terms of difference, they must find meaning in difference, and this meaning comes from an endless process of contrasting one's group with other groups. Blacks use whites to define themselves as different, women use men, Hispanics use whites and blacks, and on it goes. And in the process each group mythologizes and mystifies its difference, puts it beyond the full comprehension of outsiders. Difference becomes inaccessible preciousness toward which outsiders are expected to be simply and uncomprehendingly reverential. But beware: in this world, even the insulated world of the college campus, preciousness is a balloon asking for a needle. At Smith College graffiti appears: "Niggers, spics, and chinks. Quit complaining or get out."

32   I think that those who run our colleges and universities are every bit as responsible for the politics of difference as are minority students. To correct the exclusions once caused by race and gender, universities—under the banner of affirmative action—have relied too heavily on race and gender as criteria. So rather than break the link between difference and power, they have reinforced it. On most campuses today, a well-to-do black student with two professional parents is qualified by his race for scholarship monies that are not available to a lower-middle-class white student. A white female with a private school education and every form of cultural advantage comes under the affirmative action umbrella. This kind of inequity is an invitation to backlash.

33   What universities are quite rightly trying to do is compensate people for past discrimination and the deprivations that followed from it. But race and gender alone offer only the grossest measure of this. And the failure of universities has been their backing away from the challenge of identifying principles of fairness and merit that make finer and more equitable distinctions. The real challenge is not simply to include a certain number of blacks, but to end discrimination against all blacks and to offer special help to those with talent who have also been economically deprived.

34   With regard to black students, affirmative action has led universities to correlate color with poverty and disadvantage in so absolute a way as to encourage the politics of difference. But why have they gone along with this? My belief is that it is due to the specific form of racial anxiety to which whites are most subject.

35   Most of the white students I talked with spoke as if from under a faint cloud of accusation. There was always a ring of

defensiveness in their complaints about blacks. A white student I spoke to at UCLA told me: "Most white students on this campus think the black student leadership here is made up of oversensitive crybabies who spend all their time looking for things to kick up a ruckus about." A white student at Stanford said, "Blacks do nothing but complain and ask for sympathy when everyone really knows that they don't do well because they don't try. If they worked harder, they could do as well as everyone else."

That these students felt accused was most obvious in their 36 compulsion to assure me that they were not racist. Oblique versions of some-of-my-best-friends-are stories came ritualistically before or after critiques of black students. Some said flatly, "I am not a racist, but . . ." Of course, we all deny being racist, but we only do this compulsively, I think, when we are working against an accusation of bias. I think it was the color of my skin itself that accused them.

This was the meta-message that surrounded these conversa- 37 tions like an aura, and it is, I believe, the core of white American racial anxiety. My skin not only accused them; it judged them. And this judgment was a sad gift of history that brought them to account whether they deserved such accountability or not. It said that wherever and whenever blacks were concerned, they had reason to feel guilt. And whether it was earned or unearned, I think it was guilt that set off the compulsion in these students to disclaim. I believe it is true that, in America, black people make white people feel guilty.

Guilt is the essence of white anxiety just as inferiority is the 38 essence of black anxiety. And the terror that it carries for whites is the terror of discovering that one has reason to feel guilt where blacks are concerned—not so much because of what blacks might think but because of what guilt can say about oneself. If the darkest fear of blacks is inferiority, the darkest fear of whites is that their better lot in life is at least partially the result of their capacity for evil—their capacity to dehumanize an entire people for their own benefit and then to be indifferent to the devastation their dehumanization has wrought on successive generations of their victims. This is the terror that whites are vulnerable to regarding blacks. And the mere fact of being white is sufficient to feel it, since even whites with hearts clean of racism benefit from being white—benefit at the expense of blacks. This is a conditional guilt having nothing to do with individual intentions or actions. And it makes for a very powerful anxiety because it threatens whites with a view of themselves as inhuman, just as inferiority threatens blacks with a similar view of themselves. At the dark core of both anxieties is a suspicion of incomplete humanity.

39   So, the white students I met were not just meeting me; they were also meeting the possibility of their own inhumanity. And this, I think, is what explains how some young white college students in the late eighties could so frankly take part in racially insensitive and outright racist acts. They were expected to be cleaner of racism than any previous generation—they were born into the Great Society. But this expectation overlooks the fact that, for them, color is still an accusation and judgment. In black faces there is a discomforting reflection of white collective shame. Blacks remind them that their racial innocence is questionable, that they are the beneficiaries of past and present racism, and the sins of the father may well have been visited on the children.

40   And yet young whites tell themselves that they had nothing to do with the oppression of black people. They have a stronger belief in their racial innocence than any previous generation of whites and a natural hostility toward anyone who would challenge that innocence. So (with a great deal of individual variation) they can end up in the paradoxical position of being hostile to blacks as a way of defending their own racial innocence.

41   I think this is what the young white editors of the *Dartmouth Review* were doing when they harassed black music professor William Cole. Weren't they saying, in effect, I am so free of racial guilt that I can afford to attack blacks ruthlessly and still be racially innocent? The ruthlessness of these attacks was a form of denial, a badge of innocence. The more they were charged with racism, the more ugly and confrontational their harassment became (an escalation unexplained even by the serious charges against Professor Cole). Racism became a means of rejecting racial guilt, a way of showing that they were not, ultimately, racists.

42   The politics of difference sets up a struggle for innocence among all groups. When difference is the currency of power, each group must fight for the innocence that entitles it to power. To gain this innocence, blacks sting whites with guilt, remind them

of their racial past, accuse them of new and more subtle forms of racism. One way whites retrieve their innocence is to discredit blacks and deny their difficulties, for in this denial is the denial of their own guilt. To blacks this denial looks like racism, a racism that feeds black innocence and encourages them to throw more guilt at whites. And so the cycle continues. The politics of difference leads each group to pick at the vulnerabilities of the other.

Men and women who run universities—whites, mostly— 43 participate in the politics of difference because they handle their guilt differently than do many of their students. They don't deny it, but still they don't want to *feel* it. And to avoid this feeling of guilt they have tended to go along with whatever blacks put on the table rather than work with them to assess their real needs. University administrators have too often been afraid of guilt and have relied on negotiation and capitulation more to appease their own guilt than to help blacks and other minorities. Administrators would never give white students a racial theme dorm where they could be "more comfortable with people of their own kind," yet more and more universities are doing this for black students, thus fostering a kind of voluntary segregation. To avoid the anxieties of integrated situations blacks ask for theme dorms; to avoid guilt, white administrators give theme dorms.

When everyone is on the run from their anxieties about race, 44 race relations on campus can be reduced to the negotiation of avoidances. A pattern of demand and concession develops in which both sides use the other to escape themselves. Black studies departments, black deans of student affairs, black counseling programs, Afro houses, black theme dorms, black homecoming dances and graduation ceremonies—black students and white administrators have slowly engineered a machinery of separatism that, in the name of sacred difference, redraws the ugly lines of segregation.

Black students have not sufficiently helped themselves, and 45 universities, despite all their concessions, have not really done much for blacks. If both faced their anxieties, I think they would see the same thing: academic parity with all other groups should be the overriding mission of black students, and it should also be the first goal that universities have for their black students. Blacks can only *know* they are as good as others when they are, in fact, as good—when their grades are higher and their dropout rate lower. Nothing under the sun will substitute for this, and no amount of concessions will bring it about.

46 Universities can never be free of guilt until they truly help black students, which means leading and challenging them rather than negotiating and capitulating. It means inspiring them to achieve academic parity, nothing less, and helping them to see their own weaknesses as their greatest challenge. It also means dismantling the machinery of separatism, breaking the link between difference and power, and skewing the formula for entitlement away from race and gender and back to constitutional rights.

47 As for the young white students who have rediscovered swastikas and the word "nigger," I think that they suffer from an exaggerated sense of their own innocence, as if they were incapable of evil and beyond the reach of guilt. But it is also true that the politics of difference creates an environment that threatens their innocence and makes them defensive. White students are not invited to the negotiating table from which they see blacks and others walk away with concessions. The presumption is that they do not deserve to be there because they are white. So they can only be defensive, and the less mature among them will be aggressive. Guerrilla activity will ensue. Of course this is wrong, but it is also a reflection of an environment where difference carries power and where whites have the wrong "difference."

48 I think universities should emphasize commonality as a higher value than "diversity" and "pluralism"—buzzwords for the politics of difference. Difference that does not rest on a clearly delineated foundation of commonality is not only inaccessible to those who are not part of the ethnic or racial group, but also antagonistic to them. Difference can enrich only the common ground.

49 Integration has become an abstract term today, having to do with little more than numbers and racial balances. But it once stood for a high and admirable set of values. It made difference second to commonality, and it asked members of all races to face whatever fears they inspired in each other. I doubt the world will have a new vogue, but the values, under whatever name, are worth working for.

1989

Race

The Harmful Myth of Asian Superiority

Ronald Takaki

Asian Americans have increasingly come to be viewed as a "model 1 minority." But are they as successful as claimed? And for whom are they supposed to be a model?

Asian Americans have been described in the media as 2 "excessively, even provocatively" successful in gaining admission to universities. Asian American shopkeepers have been congratu-lated, as well as criticized, for their ubiquity and entrepreneurial effectiveness.

If Asian Americans can make it, many politicians and pundits 3 ask, why can't African Americans? Such comparisons pit minori-ties against each other and generate African American resentment toward Asian Americans. The victims are blamed for their plight, rather than racism and an economy that has made many young African American workers superfluous.

The celebration of Asian Americans has obscured reality. For 4 example, figures on the high earnings of Asian Americans relative to Caucasians are misleading. Most Asian Americans live in Cal-ifornia, Hawaii, and New York—states with higher incomes and higher costs of living than the national average.

Even Japanese Americans, often touted for their upward mo- 5 bility, have not reached equality. While Japanese American men in California earned an average income comparable to Caucasian men in 1980, they did so only by acquiring more education and working more hours.

253

6   Comparing family incomes is even more deceptive. Some Asian American groups do have higher family incomes than Caucasians. But they have more workers per family.

7   The "model minority" image homogenizes Asian Americans and hides their differences. For example, while thousands of Vietnamese American young people attend universities, others are on the streets. They live in motels and hang out in pool halls in places like East Los Angeles; some join gangs.

8   Twenty-five percent of the people in New York City's Chinatown lived below the poverty level in 1980, compared with 17 percent of the city's population. Some 60 percent of the workers in the Chinatowns of Los Angeles and San Francisco are crowded into low-paying jobs in garment factories and restaurants.

9   "Most immigrants coming into Chinatown with a language barrier cannot go outside this confined area into the mainstream of American industry," a Chinese immigrant said. "Before, I was a painter in Hong Kong, but I can't do it here. I got no license, no education. I want a living; so it's dishwasher, janitor, or cook."

10   Hmong and Mien refugees from Laos have unemployment rates that reach as high as 80 percent. A 1987 California study showed that three out of ten Southeast Asian refugee families had been on welfare for four to ten years.

11   Although college-educated Asian Americans are entering the professions and earning good salaries, many hit the "glass ceiling"—the barrier through which high management positions can be seen but not reached. In 1988, only 8 percent of Asian Americans were "officials" and "managers," compared with 12 percent for all groups.

12   Finally, the triumph of Korean immigrants has been exaggerated. In 1988, Koreans in the New York metropolitan area earned only 68 percent of the median income of non-Asians. More than three-quarters of Korean greengrocers, those so-called paragons of bootstrap entrepreneurialism, came to America with a college education. Engineers, teachers, or administrators while in Korea, they became shopkeepers after their arrival. For many of them, the greengrocery represents dashed dreams, a step downward in status.

13   For all their hard work and long hours, most Korean shopkeepers do not actually earn very much: $17,000 to $35,000 a year, usually representing the income from the labor of an entire family.

But most Korean immigrants do not become shopkeepers. 14
Instead, many find themselves trapped as clerks in grocery stores,
service workers in restaurants, seamstresses in garment factories,
and janitors in hotels.

Most Asian Americans know their "success" is largely a myth. 15
They also see how the celebration of Asian Americans as a "model
minority" perpetuates their inequality and exacerbates relations
between them and African Americans.

1990

How It Feels to Be Colored Me

Zora Neale Hurston

I am colored but I offer nothing in the way of extenuating circum- 1
stances except the fact that I am the only Negro in the United States
whose grandfather on the mother's side was *not* an Indian chief.

I remember the very day that I became colored. Up to my thir- 2
teenth year I lived in the little Negro town of Eatonville, Florida.
It is exclusively a colored town. The only white people I knew
passed through the town going to or coming from Orlando. The
native whites rode dusty horses, the Northern tourists chugged
down the sandy village road in automobiles. The town knew the
Southerners and never stopped cane chewing when they passed.
But the Northerners were something else again. They were peered
at cautiously from behind curtains by the timid. The more ven-
turesome would come out on the porch to watch them go past
and got just as much pleasure out of the tourists as the tourists
got out of the village.

The front porch might seem a daring place for the rest of the 3
town, but it was a gallery seat for me. My favorite place was atop
the gate-post. Proscenium box for a born first-nighter. Not only
did I enjoy the show, but I didn't mind the actors knowing that I
liked it. I usually spoke to them in passing. I'd wave at them and
when they returned my salute, I would say something like this:

"Howdy-do-well-I-thank-you-where-you-goin'?" Usually automobile or the horse paused at this, and after a queer exchange of compliments, I would probably "go a piece of the way" with them, as we say in farthest Florida. If one of my family happened to come to the front in time to see me, of course negotiations would be rudely broken off. But even so, it is clear that I was the first "welcome-to-our-state" Floridian, and I hope the Miami Chamber of Commerce will please take notice.

4   During this period, white people differed from colored to me only in that they rode through town and never lived there. They liked to hear me "speak pieces" and sing and wanted to see me dance the parse-me-la, and gave me generously of their small silver for doing these things, which seemed strange to me for I wanted to do them so much that I needed bribing to stop. Only they didn't know it. The colored people gave no dimes. They deplored any joyful tendencies in me, but I was their Zora nevertheless. I belonged to them, to the nearby hotels, to the county—everybody's Zora.

5   But changes came in the family when I was thirteen, and I was sent to school in Jacksonville. I left Eatonville, the town of the oleanders, as Zora. When I disembarked from the river-boat at Jacksonville, she was no more. It seemed that I had suffered a sea change. I was not Zora of Orange County any more, I was now a little colored girl. I found it out in certain ways. In my heart as well as in the mirror, I became a fast brown—warranted not to rub nor run.

6   But I am not tragically colored. There is no great sorrow dammed up in my soul, nor lurking behind my eyes. I do not mind at all. I do not belong to the sobbing school of Negrohood who hold that nature somehow has given them a low-down dirty deal and whose feelings are all hurt about it. Even in the helter-skelter skirmish that is my life, I have seen that the world is to the strong regardless of a little pigmentation more or less. No, I do not weep at the world—I am too busy sharpening my oyster knife.

7   Someone is always at my elbow reminding me that I am the granddaughter of slaves. It fails to register depression with me. Slavery is sixty years in the past. The operation was successful and the patient is doing well, thank you. The terrible struggle that made me an American out of a potential slave said "On the line!"

The Reconstruction said "Get set!"; and the generation before said "Go!" I am off to a flying start and I must not halt in the stretch to look behind and weep. Slavery is the price I paid for civilization, and the choice was not with me. It is a bully adventure and worth all that I have paid through my ancestors for it. No one on earth ever had a greater chance for glory. The world to be won and nothing to be lost. It is thrilling to think—to know that for any act of mine, I shall get twice as much praise or twice as much blame. It is quite exciting to hold the center of the national stage, with the spectators not knowing whether to laugh or to weep.

The position of my white neighbor is much more difficult. No 8 brown specter pulls up a chair beside me when I sit down to eat. No dark ghost thrusts its leg against mine in bed. The game of keeping what one has is never so exciting as the game of getting.

I do not always feel colored. Even now I often achieve the un- 9 conscious Zora of Eatonville before the Hegira. I feel most colored when I am thrown against a sharp white background.

For instance at Barnard. "Beside the waters of the Hudson" I 10 feel my race. Among the thousand white persons, I am a dark rock surged upon, and overswept, but through it all, I remain myself. When covered by the waters, I am; and the ebb but reveals me again.

Sometimes it is the other way around. A white person is set 11 down in our midst, but the contrast is just as sharp for me. For instance, when I sit in the drafty basement that is The New World Cabaret with a white person, my color comes. We enter chatting about any little nothing that we have in common and are seated by the jazz waiters. In the abrupt way that jazz orchestras have, this one plunges into a number. It loses no time in circumlocutions, but gets right down to business. It constricts the thorax and splits the heart with its tempo and narcotic harmonies. This orchestra grows rambunctious, rears on its hind legs and attacks the tonal veil with primitive fury, rending it, clawing it until it breaks through to the jungle beyond. I follow those heathen—follow them exultingly. I dance wildly inside myself; I yell within, I whoop; I shake my assegai above my head, I hurl it true to the mark *yeeeeoowww!* I am in the jungle and living in the jungle way. My face is painted red and yellow and my body is painted blue. My pulse is throbbing like a war drum. I want to slaughter something—give pain, give death to what, I do not know. But the piece ends. The men of the orchestra wipe their lips and rest their fingers. I creep back slowly to the veneer we call civilization with the last tone and find the white friend sitting motionless in his seat, smoking calmly.

12   "Good music they have here," he remarks, drumming the table with his fingertips.

13   Music. The great blobs of purple and red emotion have not touched him. He has only heard what I felt. He is far away and I see him but dimly across the ocean and the continent that have fallen between us. He is so pale with his whiteness then and I am *so* colored.

14   At certain times I have no race. I am *me*. When I set my hat at a certain angle and saunter down Seventh Avenue, Harlem City, feeling as snooty as the lions in front of the Forty-Second Street Library, for instance. So far as my feelings are concerned, Peggy Hopkins Joyce on the Boule Mich with her gorgeous rainment, stately carriage, knees knocking together in a most aristocratic manner, has nothing on me. The cosmic Zora emerges. I belong to no race nor time. I am the eternal feminine with its string of beads.

15   I have no separate feeling about being an American citizen and colored. I am merely a fragment of the Great Soul that surges within the boundaries. My country, right or wrong.

16   Sometimes, I feel discriminated against, but it does not make me angry. It merely astonishes me. How *can* any deny themselves the pleasure of my company? It's beyond me.

17   But in the main, I feel like a brown bag of miscellany propped against a wall. Against a wall in company with other bags, white, red and yellow. Pour out the contents, and there is discovered a jumble of small things priceless and worthless. A first-water diamond, an empty spool, bits of broken glass, lengths of string, a key to a door long since crumbled away, a rusty knife-blade, old shoes saved for a road that never was and never will be, a nail bent under the weight of things too heavy for any nail, a dried flower or two still a little fragrant. In your hand is the brown bag. On the ground before you is the jumble it held—so much like the jumble in the bags, could they be emptied, that all might be dumped in a single heap and the bags refilled without altering the content of any greatly. A bit of colored glass more or less would not

matter. Perhaps that is how the Great Stuffer of Bags filled them in the first place—who knows?

1928

Black Men and Public Spaces

Brent Staples

My first victim was a woman—white, well dressed, probably in her 1
early twenties. I came upon her late one evening on a deserted street in Hyde Park, a relatively affluent neighborhood in an otherwise mean, impoverished section of Chicago. As I swung onto the avenue behind her, there seemed to be a discreet, uninflammatory distance between us. Not so. She cast back a worried glance. To her, the youngish black man—a broad six feet two inches with a beard and billowing hair, both hands shoved into the pockets of a bulky military jacket—seemed menacingly close. After a few more quick glimpses, she picked up her pace and was soon running in earnest. Within seconds she disappeared into a cross street.

That was more than a decade ago. I was twenty-two years old, 2
a graduate student newly arrived at the University of Chicago. It was in the echo of that terrified woman's footfalls that I first began to know the unwieldy inheritance I'd come into—the ability to alter public space in ugly ways. It was clear that she thought herself the quarry of a mugger, a rapist, or worse. Suffering a bout of insomnia, however, I was stalking sleep, not defenseless wayfarers. As a softy who is scarcely able to take a knife to a raw chicken—let alone hold it to a person's throat—I was surprised, embarrassed, and dismayed all at once. Her flight made me feel like an accomplice in tyranny. It also made it clear that I was indistinguishable from the muggers who occasionally seeped into the area from the surrounding ghetto. That first encounter, and those that followed, signified that a vast, unnerving gulf lay between nighttime pedestrians—particularly women—and me. And I soon gathered that being perceived as dangerous is a hazard in itself.

I only needed to turn a corner into a dicey situation, or crowd some frightened, armed person in a foyer somewhere, or make an errant move after being pulled over by a policeman. Where fear and weapons meet—and they often do in urban America—there is always the possibility of death.

3   In that first year, my first away from my hometown, I was to become thoroughly familiar with the language of fear. At dark, shadowy intersections in Chicago, I could cross in front of a car stopped at a traffic light and elicit the *thunk, thunk, thunk* of the driver—black, white, male, or female—hammering down the door locks. On less traveled streets after dark, I grew accustomed to but never comfortable with people who crossed to the other side of the street rather than pass me. Then there were the standard unpleasantries with police, doormen, bouncers, cabdrivers, and others whose business is to screen out troublesome individuals *before* there is any nastiness.

4   I moved to New York nearly two years ago and I have remained an avid night walker. In central Manhattan, the near-constant crowd cover minimizes tense one-on-one street encounters. Elsewhere—visiting friends in SoHo, where sidewalks are narrow and tightly spaced buildings shut out the sky—things can get very taut indeed.

5   Black men have a firm place in New York mugging literature. Norman Podhoretz in his famed (or infamous) 1963 essay, "My Negro Problem—And Ours," recalls growing up in terror of black males; they "were tougher than we were, more ruthless," he writes—and as an adult on the Upper West Side of Manhattan, he continues, he cannot constrain his nervousness when he meets black men on certain streets. Similarly, a decade later, the essayist and novelist Edward Hoagland extols a New York where once "Negro bitterness bore down mainly on other Negroes." Where some see mere panhandlers, Hoagland sees "a mugger who is clearly screwing up his nerve to do more than just *ask* for money." But Hoagland has "the New Yorker's quick-hunch posture for broken-field maneuvering," and the bad guy swerves away.

6   I often witness that "hunch posture," from women after dark on the warrenlike streets of Brooklyn where I live. They seem to set their faces on neutral and, with their purse straps strung across their chests bandolier style, they forge ahead as though bracing

themselves against being tackled. I understand, of course, that the danger they perceive is not a hallucination. Women are particularly vulnerable to street violence, and young black males are drastically overrepresented among the perpetrators of that violence. Yet these truths are no solace against the kind of alienation that comes of being ever the suspect, against being set apart, a fearsome entity with whom pedestrians avoid making eye contact.

It is not altogether clear to me how I reached the ripe old age 7 of twenty-two without being conscious of the lethality nighttime pedestrians attributed to me. Perhaps it was because in Chester, Pennsylvania, the small, angry industrial town where I came of age in the 1960s, I was scarcely noticeable against a backdrop of gang warfare, street knifings, and murders. I grew up one of the good boys, had perhaps a half-dozen fistfights. In retrospect, my shyness of combat has clear sources.

Many things go into the making of a young thug. One of those 8 things is the consummation of the male romance with the power to intimidate. An infant discovers that random flailings send the baby bottle flying out of the crib and crashing to the floor. Delighted, the joyful babe repeats those motions again and again, seeking to duplicate the feat. Just so, I recall the points at which some of my boyhood friends were finally seduced by the perception of themselves as tough guys. When a mark cowered and surrendered his money without resistance, myth and reality merged—and paid off. It is, after all, only manly to embrace the power to frighten and intimidate. We, as men, are not supposed to give an inch of our lane on the highway; we are to seize the fighter's edge in work and in play and even in love; we are to be valiant in the face of hostile forces.

Unfortunately, poor and powerless young men seem to take all 9 this nonsense literally. As a boy, I saw countless tough guys locked away; I have since buried several, too. They were babies, really—a teenage cousin, a brother of twenty-two, a childhood friend in his midtwenties—all gone down in episodes of bravado played out in the streets. I came to doubt the virtues of intimidation early on. I chose, perhaps even unconsciously, to remain a shadow—timid, but a survivor.

The fearsomeness mistakenly attributed to me in public places 10 often has a perilous flavor. The most frightening of these confusions occurred in the late 1970s and early 1980s when I worked as a journalist in Chicago. One day, rushing into the office of a magazine I was writing for with a deadline story in hand, I was mistaken for a burglar. The office manager called security and, with an ad hoc posse, pursued me through the labyrinthine halls, nearly to my editor's door. I had no way of proving who I was. I could only move briskly toward the company of someone who knew me.

11   Another time I was on assignment for a local paper and killing time before an interview. I entered a jewelry store on the city's affluent Near North Side. The proprietor excused herself and returned with an enormous red Doberman pinscher straining at the end of a leash. She stood, the dog extended toward me, silent to my questions, her eyes bulging nearly out of her head. I took a cursory look around, nodded, and bade her good night. Relatively speaking, however, I never fared as badly as another black male journalist. He went to nearby Waukegan, Illinois, a couple of summers ago to work on a story about a murderer who was born there. Mistaking the reporter for the killer, police hauled him from his car at gunpoint and but for his press credentials would probably have tried to book him. Such episodes are not uncommon. Black men trade tales like this all the time.

12   In "My Negro Problem—And Ours," Podhoretz writes that the hatred he feels for blacks makes itself known to him through a variety of avenues—one being his discomfort with that "special brand of paranoid touchiness" to which he says blacks are prone. No doubt he is speaking here of black men. In time, I learned to smother the rage I felt at so often being taken for a criminal. Not to do so would surely have led to madness—via that special "paranoid touchiness" that so annoyed Podhoretz at the time he wrote the essay.

13   I began to take precautions to make myself less threatening. I move about with care, particularly late in the evening. I give a wide berth to nervous people on subway platforms during the wee hours, particularly when I have exchanged business clothes for jeans. If I happen to be entering a building behind some people who appear skittish, I may walk by, letting them clear the lobby before I return, so as not to seem to be following them. I have been calm and extremely congenial on those rare occasions when I've been pulled over by the police.

And on late-evening constitutionals along streets less traveled 14
by, I employ what has proved to be an excellent tension-reducing
measure: I whistle melodies from Beethoven and Vivaldi and the
more popular classical composers. Even steely New Yorkers hunch-
ing toward nighttime destinations seem to relax, and occasionally
they even join in the tune. Virtually everybody seems to sense that
a mugger wouldn't be warbling bright, sunny selections from
Vivaldi's *Four Seasons*. It is my equivalent of the cowbell that
hikers wear when they know they are in bear country.

1986

The Myth of the Latin Woman: I Just Met a Girl Named Maria

Judith Ortiz Cofer

On a bus trip to London from Oxford University where I was earn- 1
ing some graduate credits one summer, a young man, obviously
fresh from a pub, spotted me and as if struck by inspiration went
down on his knees in the aisle. With both hands over his heart he
broke into an Irish tenor's rendition of "Maria" from *West Side Story*.
My politely amused fellow passengers gave his lovely voice the
round of gentle applause it deserved. Though I was not quite as
amused, I managed my version of an English smile: no show of
teeth, no extreme contortions of the facial muscles—I was at this
time of my life practicing reserve and cool. Oh, that British control,
how I coveted it. But "Maria" had followed me to London, reminding me of a prime fact of my life: you can leave the island, master
the English language, and travel as far as you can, but if you are a
Latina, especially one like me who so obviously belongs to Rita
Moreno's gene pool, the island travels with you.

This is sometimes a very good thing. It may win you that extra 2
minute of someone's attention. But with some people, the same
things can make *you* an island—not a tropical paradise but an
Alcatraz, a place nobody wants to visit. As a Puerto Rican girl

living in the United States and wanting like most children to "belong," I resented the stereotype that my Hispanic appearance called forth from many people I met.

3   Growing up in a large urban center in New Jersey during the 1960s, I suffered from what I think of as "cultural schizophrenia." Our life was designed by my parents as a microcosm of their *casas* on the island. We spoke in Spanish, ate Puerto Rican food bought at the *bodega,* and practiced strict Catholicism at a church that allotted us a one-hour slot each week for mass, performed in Spanish by a Chinese priest trained as a missionary for Latin America.

4   As a girl I was kept under strict surveillance by my parents, since my virtue and modesty were, by their cultural equation, the same as their honor. As a teenager I was lectured constantly on how to behave as a proper *senorita*. But it was a conflicting message I received, since the Puerto Rican mothers also encouraged their daughters to look and act like women and to dress in clothes our Anglo friends and their mothers found too "mature" and flashy. The difference was, and is, cultural; yet I often felt humiliated when I appeared at an American friend's party wearing a dress more suitable to a semiformal than to a playroom birthday celebration. At Puerto Rican festivities, neither the music nor the colors we wore could be too loud.

5   I remember Career Day in our high school, when teachers told us to come dressed as if for a job interview. It quickly became obvious that to the Puerto Rican girls "dressing up" meant wearing their mother's ornate jewelry and clothing, more appropriate (by mainstream standards) for the company Christmas party than as daily office attire. That morning I had agonized in front of my closet, trying to figure out what a "career girl" would wear. I knew how to dress for school (at the Catholic school I attended, we all wore uniforms), I knew how to dress for Sunday mass, and I knew what dresses to wear for parties at my relatives' homes. Though I do not recall the precise details of my Career Day outfit, it must have been a composite of these choices. But I remember a comment my friend (an Italian American) made in later years that coalesced my impressions of that day. She said that at the business school she was attending, the Puerto Rican girls always stood out for wearing "everything at once." She meant, of course, too much jewelry, too many accessories. On that day at

school we were simply made the negative models by the nuns, who were themselves not credible fashion experts to any of us. But it was painfully obvious to me that to the others, in their tailored skirts and silk blouses, we must have seemed "hopeless" and "vulgar." Though I now know that most adolescents feel out of step much of the time, I also know that for the Puerto Rican girls of my generation that sense was intensified. The way our teachers and classmates looked at us that day in school was just a taste of the cultural clash that awaited us in the real world, where prospective employers and men on the street would often misinterpret our tight skirts and jingling bracelets as a "come-on."

Mixed cultural signals have perpetuated certain stereotypes— 6 for example, that of the Hispanic woman as the "hot tamale" or sexual firebrand. It is a one-dimensional view that the media have found easy to promote. In their special vocabulary, advertisers have designated "sizzling" and "smoldering" as the adjectives of choice for describing not only the foods but also the women of Latin America. From conversations in my house I recall hearing about the harassment that Puerto Rican women endured in factories where the "boss-men" talked to them as if sexual innuendo was all they understood, and worse, often gave them the choice of submitting to their advances or being fired.

It is custom, however, not chromosomes, that leads us to 7 choose scarlet over pale pink. As young girls it was our mothers who influenced our decisions about clothes and colors— mothers who had grown up on a tropical island where the natural environment was a riot of primary colors, where showing your skin was one way to keep cool as well as to look sexy. Most important of all, on the island, women perhaps felt freer to dress and move more provocatively since, in most cases, they were protected by the traditions, mores, and laws of a Spanish/Catholic system of morality and machismo whose main rule was: *You may look at my sister, but if you touch her I will kill you.* The extended family and church structure could provide a young woman with a circle of safety in her small pueblo on the island; if a man "wronged" a girl, everyone would close in to save her family honor.

My mother has told me about dressing in her best party 8 clothes on Saturday nights and going to the town's plaza to promenade with her girlfriends in front of the boys they liked. The males were thus given an opportunity to admire the women and to express their admiration in the form of *piropos:* erotically charged street poems they composed on the spot. (I have myself been subjected to a few *piropos* while visiting the island, and they can be outrageous, although custom dictates that they must never cross into obscenity.) This ritual, as I understand it, also entails a show of studied indifference on the woman's part; if she is "decent," she must not acknowledge the man's impassioned words. So I do understand how things can be lost in translation. When a Puerto Rican girl dressed in her idea of what is attractive meets a man from the mainstream culture who has been trained to react to certain types of clothing as a sexual signal, a clash is likely to take place. I remember the boy who took me to my first formal dance leaning over to plant a sloppy, overeager kiss painfully on my mouth; when I didn't respond with sufficient passion, he remarked resentfully: "I thought you Latin girls were supposed to mature early," as if I were expected to *ripen* like a fruit or vegetable, not just grow into womanhood like other girls.

9   It is surprising to my professional friends that even today some people, including those who should know better, still put others "in their place." It happened to me most recently during a stay at a classy metropolitan hotel favored by young professional couples for weddings. Late one evening after the theater, as I walked toward my room with a colleague (a woman with whom I was coordinating an arts program), a middle-aged man in a tuxedo, with a young girl in satin and lace on his arm, stepped directly into our path. With his champagne glass extended toward me, he exclaimed "Evita!"

10   Our way blocked, my companion and I listened as the man half-recited, half-bellowed "Don't Cry for Me, Argentina." When he finished, the young girl said: "How about a round of applause for my daddy?" We complied, hoping this would bring the silly spectacle to a close. I was becoming aware that our little group was attracting the attention of the other guests. "Daddy" must have perceived this too, and he once more barred the way as we tried to walk past him. He began to shout-sing a ditty to the tune of "La Bamba"—except the lyrics were about a girl named Maria

whose exploits rhymed with her name and gonorrhea. The girl kept saying "Oh, Daddy" and looking at me with pleading eyes. She wanted me to laugh along with the others. My companion and I stood silently waiting for the man to end his offensive song. When he finished, I looked not at him but at his daughter. I advised her calmly never to ask her father what he had done in the army. Then I walked between them and to my room. My friend complimented me on my cool handling of the situation, but I confessed that I had really wanted to push the jerk into the swimming pool. This same man—probably a corporate executive, well-educated, even worldly by most standards—would not have been likely to regale an Anglo woman with a dirty song in public. He might have checked his impulse by assuming that she could be somebody's wife or mother, or at least *somebody* who might take offense. But, to him, I was just an Evita or a Maria: merely a character in his cartoon-populated universe.

Another facet of the myth of the Latin woman in the United   11 States is the menial, the domestic—Maria the housemaid or countergirl. It's true that work as domestics, as waitresses, and in factories is all that's available to women with little English and few skills. But the myth of the Hispanic menial—the funny maid, mispronouncing words and cooking up a spicy storm in a shiny California kitchen—has been perpetuated by the media in the same way that "Mammy" from *Gone with the Wind* became America's idea of the black woman for generations. Since I do not wear my diplomas around my neck for all to see, I have on occasion been sent to that "kitchen" where some think I obviously belong.

One incident has stayed with me, though I recognize it as a   12 minor offense. My first public poetry reading took place in Miami, at a restaurant where a luncheon was being held before the event. I was nervous and excited as I walked in with notebook in hand. An older woman motioned me to her table, and thinking (foolish me) that she wanted me to autograph a copy of my newly published slender volume of verse, I went over. She ordered a cup of coffee from me, assuming that I was the waitress. (Easy enough to mistake my poems for menus, I suppose.) I know it wasn't an intentional act of cruelty. Yet of all the good things that happened later, I remember that scene most clearly, because it reminded me of what I had to overcome before anyone would take me seriously. In retrospect I understand that my anger gave my reading fire. In fact, I have almost always taken any doubt in my abilities as a challenge, the result most often being the satisfaction of winning a convert, of seeing the cold, appraising eyes warm to my words, the body language change, the smile that indicates I have opened some avenue for communication. So that day as I read, I looked directly at that woman. Her lowered eyes told me she was embarrassed at her faux pas, and when I willed her to look up at me, she graciously allowed me to punish her with my full attention. We shook hands at the end of the reading and I never saw her again. She has probably forgotten the entire incident, but maybe not.

13   Yet I am one of the lucky ones. There are thousands of Latinas without the privilege of an education or the entrees into society that I have. For them life is a constant struggle against the misconceptions perpetuated by the myth of the Latina. My goal is to try to replace the old stereotypes with a much more interesting set of realities. Every time I give a reading, I hope the stories I tell, the dreams and fears I examine in my work, can achieve some universal truth that will get my audience past the particulars of my skin color, my accent, or my clothes.

14   I once wrote a poem in which I called all Latinas "God's brown daughters." This poem is really a prayer of sorts, offered upward, but also, through the human-to-human channel of art, outward. It is a prayer for communication and for respect. In it, Latin women pray "in Spanish to an Anglo God/with a Jewish heritage," and they are "fervently hoping/that if not omnipotent,/at least He be bilingual."

I Have a Dream

Martin Luther King, Jr.

1   Five score years ago, a great American, in whose symbolic shadow we stand, signed the Emancipation Proclamation. This momentous decree came as a great beacon light of hope to millions of Negro slaves who had been seared in the flames of withering injustice. It came as a joyous daybreak to end the long night of captivity.

But one hundred years later, we must face the tragic fact that 2 the Negro is still not free. One hundred years later, the life of the Negro is still sadly crippled by the manacles of segregation and the chains of discrimination. One hundred years later, the Negro lives on a lonely island of poverty in the midst of a vast ocean of material prosperity. One hundred years later, the Negro is still languishing in the corners of American society and finds himself an exile in his own land. So we have come here today to dramatize an appalling condition.

In a sense we have come to our nation's capital to cash a 3 check. When the architects of our republic wrote the magnificent words of the Constitution and the Declaration of Independence, they were signing a promissory note to which every American was to fall heir. This note was a promise that all men would be guaranteed the unalienable rights of life, liberty, and the pursuit of happiness.

It is obvious today that America has defaulted on this prom- 4 issory note insofar as her citizens of color are concerned. Instead of honoring this sacred obligation, America has given the Negro people a bad check; a check which has come back marked "insufficient funds." But we refuse to believe that the bank of justice is bankrupt. We refuse to believe that there are insufficient funds in the great vaults of opportunity of this nation. So we have come to cash this check—a check that will give us upon demand the riches of freedom and the security of justice. We have also come to this hallowed spot to remind America of the fierce urgency of *now*. This is no time to engage in the luxury of cooling off or to take the tranquilizing drugs of gradualism. *Now* is the time to make real the promises of Democracy. *Now* is the time to rise from the dark and desolate valley of segregation to the sunlit path of racial justice. *Now* is the time to open the doors of opportunity to all of God's children. *Now* is the time to lift our nation from the quick-sands of racial injustice to the solid rock of brotherhood.

It would be fatal for the nation to overlook the urgency of the 5 moment and to underestimate the determination of the Negro. This sweltering summer of the Negro's legitimate discontent will not pass until there is an invigorating autumn of freedom and equality. 1963 is not an end, but a beginning. Those who hope that the Negro needed to blow off steam and will now be content will have a rude awakening if the nation returns to business as usual. There will be neither rest nor tranquility in America until the Negro is granted his citizenship rights. The whirlwinds of revolt will continue to shake the foundations of our nation until the bright day of justice emerges.

6   But there is something that I must say to my people who stand on the warm threshold which leads into the palace of justice. In the process of gaining our rightful place we must not be guilty of wrongful deeds. Let us not seek to satisfy our thirst for freedom by drinking from the cup of bitterness and hatred. We must forever conduct our struggle on the high plane of dignity and discipline. We must not allow our creative protest to degenerate into physical violence. Again and again we must rise to the majestic heights of meeting physical force with soul force. The marvelous new militancy which has engulfed the Negro community must not lead us to a distrust of all white people, for many of our white brothers, as evidenced by their presence here today, have come to realize that their destiny is tied up with our destiny and their freedom is inextricably bound to our freedom. We cannot walk alone.

7   And as we walk, we must make the pledge that we shall march ahead. We cannot turn back. There are those who are asking the devotees of civil rights, "When will you be satisfied?" We can never be satisfied as long as the Negro is the victim of the unspeakable horrors of police brutality. We can never be satisfied as long as our bodies, heavy with the fatigue of travel, cannot gain lodging in the motels of the highways and the hotels of the cities. We cannot be satisfied as long as the Negro's basic mobility is from a smaller ghetto to a larger one. We can never be satisfied as long as a Negro in Mississippi cannot vote and a Negro in New York believes he has nothing for which to vote. No, no, we are not satisfied, and will not be satisfied until justice rolls down like waters and righteousness like a mighty stream.

8   I am not unmindful that some of you have come here out of great trials and tribulations. Some of you have come fresh from narrow jail cells. Some of you have come from areas where your quest for freedom left you battered by the storms of persecution and staggered by the winds of police brutality. You have been the veterans of creative suffering. Continue to work with the faith that unearned suffering is redemptive.

Go back to Mississippi, go back to Alabama, go back to South 9
Carolina, go back to Georgia, go back to Louisiana, go back to the
slums and ghettos of our northern cities, knowing that somehow
this situation can and will be changed. Let us not wallow in the valley of despair.

I say to you today, my friends, that in spite of the difficulties 10
and frustrations of the moment I still have a dream. It is a dream
deeply rooted in the American dream.

I have a dream that one day this nation will rise up and live 11
out the true meaning of its creed: "We hold these truths to be self-
evident; that all men are created equal."

I have a dream that one day on the red hills of Georgia the sons 12
of former slaves and the sons of former slaveowners will be able to
sit down together at the table of brotherhood.

I have a dream that one day even the state of Mississippi, a 13
desert state sweltering with the heat of injustice and oppression,
will be transformed into an oasis of freedom and justice.

I have a dream that my four little children will one day live in 14
a nation where they will not be judged by the color of their skin but
by the content of their character.

I have a dream today. 15

I have a dream that one day the state of Alabama, whose gov- 16
ernor's lips are presently dripping with the words of interposition
and nullification, will be transformed into a situation where little
black boys and black girls will be able to join hands with little white
boys and white girls and walk together as sisters and brothers.

I have a dream today. 17

I have a dream that one day every valley shall be exalted, 18
every hill and mountain shall be made low, the rough places will
be made plain, and the crooked places will be made straight, and
the glory of the Lord shall be revealed, and all flesh shall see it
together.

This is our hope. This is the faith with which I return to the 19
South. With this faith we will be able to hew out of the mountain
of despair a stone of hope. With this faith we will be able to transform the jangling discords of our nation into a beautiful symphony
of brotherhood. With this faith we will be able to work together,
to pray together, to struggle together, to go to jail together, to stand
up for freedom together, knowing that we will be free one day.

20   This will be the day when all of God's children will be able to sing with new meaning

> My country, 'tis of thee,
> Sweet land of liberty,
>   Of thee I sing:
> Land where my fathers died,
> Land of the pilgrims' pride,
> From every mountain-side
>   Let freedom ring.

21   And if America is to be a great nation this must become true. So let freedom ring from the prodigious hilltops of New Hampshire. Let freedom ring from the mighty mountains of New York. Let freedom ring from the heightening Alleghenies of Pennsylvania!

22   Let freedom ring from the snowcapped Rockies of Colorado!

23   Let freedom ring from the curvaceous peaks of California!

24   But not only that; let freedom ring from Stone Mountain of Georgia!

25   Let freedom ring from Lookout Mountain of Tennessee!

26   Let freedom ring from every hill and molehill of Mississippi. From every mountainside, let freedom ring.

27   When we let freedom ring, when we let it ring from every village and every hamlet, from every state and every city, we will be able to speed up that day when all of God's children, black men and white men, Jews and Gentiles, Protestants and Catholics, will be able to join hands and sing in the words of the old Negro spiritual, "Free at last! free at last! thank God almighty, we are free at last!"

1963

8

Gender Studies

Ain't I a Woman?

Sojourner Truth

Well, children, where there is so much racket there must be some- 1
thing out of kilter. I think that 'twixt the negroes of the South and
the women of the North, all talking about rights, the white men
will be in a fix pretty soon. But what's all this here talking about?

That man over there says that women need to be helped into 2
carriages, and lifted over ditches, and to have the best place everywhere. Nobody ever helps me into carriages, or over mud-puddles,
or gives me any best place! And ain't I a woman? Look at me! Look
at my arm! I have ploughed and planted, and gathered into barns,
and no man could head me! And ain't I a woman? I could work as
much and eat as much as a man—when I could get it—and bear
the lash as well! And ain't I a woman? I have borne thirteen children, and seen them most all sold off to slavery, and when I cried
out with my mother's grief, none but Jesus heard me! And ain't I
a woman?

Then they talk about this thing in the head; what's this they 3
call it? [Intellect, someone whispers.] That's it, honey. What's that
got to do with women's rights or negro's rights? If my cup won't
hold but a pint, and yours holds a quart, wouldn't you be mean
not to let me have my little half-measure full?

Then that little man in black there, he says women can't have 4
as much rights as men, 'cause Christ wasn't a woman! Where did
your Christ come from? From God and a woman! Man had nothing to do with Him.

If the first woman God ever made was strong enough to turn 5
the world upside down all alone, these women together ought to

273

be able to turn it back, and get it right side up again! And now they is asking to do it, the men better let them.

6   Obliged to you for hearing me, and now old Sojourner ain't got nothing more to say.

1851

"I'm Sorry, I'm Not Apologizing": Conversational Rituals

Deborah Tannen

1 Conversation is a ritual. We say things that seem the thing to say, without thinking of the literal meaning of our words any more than we expect the question "How are you?" to call forth a detailed account of aches and pains. On the job, the meat of the work that has to be done is held together, made pleasant and possible, by the ketchup, relish, and bun of conversational rituals. But people have different habits for using these rituals, and when a ritual is not recognized, the words spoken are taken literally. I have heard visitors to the United States complain that Americans are hypocritical because they ask how you are but aren't interested in the answer. And Americans in Burma are puzzled when Burmese ask, "Have you eaten yet?"—and show no sign of inviting them to lunch.[1] In the Philippines, people ask each other, "Where are you going?"—which may seem rather intrusive to Americans, who don't realize that the only reply expected is, "Over there."[2]

2   It is easy, and entertaining, to notice different rituals in foreign countries, as did the Briton who spent a year working in France and was amused that everyone ceremoniously shook hands and said *"Bonjour"* to everyone else when they arrived at work in the morning—and again when they left for lunch, returned from lunch,

---

[1] *"And Americans in Burma are puzzled when Burmese ask, 'Have you eaten yet?'—and show no sign of inviting them to lunch."* My source for the Burmese greeting ritual is personal conversation with A. L. Becker.

[2] *". . . Americans, who don't realize that the only reply expected is, 'Over there.'"* Mary Catherine Bateson mentions this Philippine greeting ritual in *Peripheral Visions*.

and left at the end of the day. He even observed elementary-school children shaking each other's hands in greeting when they met on their way to school. We expect rituals at points of transition like greetings, and we expect them to be different—and those differences to cause confusion—when we go to foreign countries. But we don't expect differences, and are far less likely to recognize the ritual nature of our conversations, among other Americans at work. Our differing rituals are even more problematic when we think we're all speaking the same language.

SAYING "I'M SORRY" WHEN YOU'RE NOT

One conversational ritual that can differ from one person to the next and cause trouble at work is apologizing. ₃

I had been interviewed by a well-known columnist who ₄ ended our friendly conversation by giving me the number of her direct telephone line in case I ever wanted to call her. Some time later, I did want to call her but had misplaced her direct number and had to go through the newspaper receptionist to get through to her. When our conversation was ending, and we had both uttered ending-type remarks, I remembered that I wanted to get her direct number for the future and said, "Oh, I almost forgot—last time you gave me your direct number, but I lost it: I wondered if I could get it again." "Oh, I'm sorry," she came back instantly. "It's . . ." And she gave me the number. I laughed because she had just done something I had mentioned in our interview: said "I'm sorry" when an apology was not called for. She had done nothing wrong; I was the one who lost the number. But in fact she was not apologizing; she was just uttering an automatic conversational smoother to assure me she had no intention of rushing me off the phone or denying me her number. . . .

Sometimes a tone of self-deprecation is heard as an apology ₅ even without the word "sorry" being spoken. In another tape of a conversation recorded for me, a manager named Kristin was explaining to a computer-support manager named Herb why she invited him to a meeting, even though she wasn't sure he was the right person:

KRISTIN: Just 'cause, you know, I'd worked with him and then you came and I   I didn't know . . . what his schedule was.

And I wasn't sure who [laughing] the head of that group was!
[Herb also laughs.] To tell you the truth! So . . .
HERB: No, don't—don't apologize.

Many women are frequently told, "Don't apologize" or "You're
always apologizing." The reason "apologizing" is seen as something they should stop doing is that it seems synonymous with
putting oneself down. But for many women, and a fair number
of men, saying "I'm sorry" isn't literally an apology; it is a ritual
way of restoring balance to a conversation. "I'm sorry," spoken in
this spirit, if it has any literal meaning at all, does not mean "I
apologize," which would be tantamount to accepting blame, but
rather "I'm sorry that happened." To understand the ritual nature
of apologies, think of a funeral at which you might say, "I'm so
sorry about Reginald's death." When you say that, you are not
pleading guilty to a murder charge. You're expressing regret that
something happened without taking or assigning blame. In other
words, "I'm sorry" can be an expression of understanding—and
caring—about the other person's feelings rather than an apology.[3]

6   That an apology can be a routinized way of taking the other
person's feelings into account becomes clear in the following
example. When professional pool player Ewa Mataya, who is
regarded as one of the top female pool players in the world, was
being bested in a tournament by amateur Julie Nogiac, Mataya
said of Nogiac, "She's very sweet. She kept apologizing." I doubt
Nogiac actually regretted that she was beating the champion; she
was simply expressing her awareness that her doing so must have
been making Mataya feel bad.[4]

7   This is not to say that "I'm sorry" is never an apology. But when
it is, in the sense of accepting responsibility for something that went

---

[3]*"'I'm sorry' can be an expression of understanding—and caring—about the other person's
feelings rather than an apology."* Linguist Amy Sheldon uses the term "double-voice
discourse" to describe how the little girls in a day care center talked in ways that
took account of both their own and others' interests and goals. She contrasts this
with the "single-voice discourse" that typified the boys' talk: Each pursued his own
goal, leaving it to others to pursue theirs. (Sheldon, "Preschool Girls' Discourse
Competence")

[4]My information about and quotation from pool champion Ewa Mataya are taken
from "Pool's Reigning Hot Shot," by Marcia Froelke Coburn, *Know-How* magazine,
Fall 1993, pp. 58–60. The quotation is from p. 60.

wrong, it is often assumed to be the first step in a two-step ritual: I say "I'm sorry" and take half the blame; then you take the other half. A secretary told me she liked working for her boss because, if he said, "When you typed this letter, you missed this phrase that I inserted," and she said, "Oh, I'm sorry. I'll fix it," he would usually follow up, "Well, I wrote it so small it was easy to miss."

Admitting fault can be experienced as taking a one-down 8 position. When both parties share the blame, they end up on an equal footing. That is the logic behind the ritual sharing of blame in response to an apology. It's a mutual face-saving device. Someone who feels that an apology requires a ritualized sharing of blame might even make up a fault to admit, in order to seal off the interchange in an appropriate way. And those who share an understanding of the ritual will not take that admission of fault literally, but will simply appreciate it as an attempt to save face for them. Put another way, it is a courteous way of not leaving the apologizer in the one-down position.

Someone, on the other hand, who does not use apologies rit- 9 ually may well take them all literally. And this can lead to resentment on the part of the ritual apologizer. If I say "I'm sorry" and you say "I accept your apology," then my attempt to achieve balance has misfired, and I think you have put me in a one-down position, though you probably think I put myself there. (Sensing this, people sometimes make a joke of preserving the imbalance following an apology: "Okay, just make sure it doesn't happen again." It's funny because it is obvious that is not the way the exchange is supposed to go.)

Ritual apologies—like other conversational rituals—work fine 10 when both parties share assumptions about their use. But people who utter frequent ritual apologies when others don't may end up seeming to be taking blame for mishaps that are not their fault. When they are partly at fault, they come out looking entirely so. There are cultural as well as gender influences on how likely people are to use apologies in this way, but research on Americans by Nessa Wolfson and on New Zealanders by Janet Holmes shows that women are more likely to do it than men. Holmes found that women uttered the most apologies to other women and far fewer to men, while men uttered very few to other men and slightly more to women. . . .

GIVING PRAISE

11   Giving praise is also a conversational ritual, and here too there are cultural as well as gender patterns, as the next two examples show.

12   Lester had been on his new job only six months when he heard that some of the women reporting to him were deeply dissatisfied. When he talked to them, they erupted; two were on the verge of quitting, they said, because they weren't happy working for someone who didn't appreciate their work. They were convinced that Lester didn't think they were doing a good job, and they preferred to quit rather than wait to be fired. Lester was dumbfounded. He believed they were doing a fine job and had never thought otherwise. Surely, he had said nothing to give them the impression he didn't like their work. And indeed he hadn't. That was the problem. He had said nothing. The women expected him to praise their work if he liked it, and to show interest in what they were doing by asking about it from time to time. When he said nothing about the job they were doing, they assumed he was following the adage, "If you can't say something nice, don't say anything." He thought he was showing confidence in them by leaving them alone. To him, everything was fine unless he corrected them. To them, unless he told them everything was fine, there must be a problem.

13   Vince had a similar experience by which he learned there is no right amount of praise and attention to give. He supervised a group of eight people who reported directly to him. He believed in keeping in touch with his group, so he made a point of checking in with each one, even if briefly, at least once a day. Certain he was being a responsible and caring boss, he was shocked when a new system of soliciting evaluations from subordinates was instituted. Though there were some who were pleased with his style of management, the complaints of others ranged from, "He's always looking over my shoulder; he doesn't seem to trust me to do the work" to "He rarely shows any interest in what I'm doing; he doesn't seem to care about it, so why should I care?" It turned out that checking once a day was too much attention for some in his group and too little for others. Those who saw his visits as too brief were interpreting them in terms of power: He's my superior, he's checking on me. Those who saw them as too brief were interpreting them in terms of rapport: He's not interested enough to spend more time.

In Vince's case, it turned out that those who took the first tack were men, and those who took the second were women.

Praise is a very special form of feedback. Although I heard 14 many men and women mention that they got more thanks and praise from women than from men, I never heard anyone say they resented receiving praise.[5] I frequently heard from men that they did not mind not getting feedback; if they didn't hear anything, they felt they were doing okay. But when they had a boss who praised them often, they always said they liked it. "It's a problem," one man joked, "because it's habit-forming. The more praise you get, the more you want!"

"I don't know where I stand with you," a woman complained 15 to her boss. "You're not giving me any signals." This is a complaint I heard frequently from women who worked for men. But I also heard it from many men who work for women. I suspect it is not a matter of women or men not sending out signals, but of their sending different signals, which are more likely to be missed by those of the other gender. Another possibility is that many men feel women don't tell them directly enough if they are doing something wrong, and many women feel that men don't tell them directly enough if they are doing well. . . .

"WHICH WAY IS RIGHT?"

Someone who is told, "Stop apologizing" rarely thinks of reply- 16 ing, "It's just a ritual; you should say, 'I'm sorry' more. It would make you more likable." She is more likely to say, or think, "What's wrong with me? Why do I apologize all the time?" Our understanding of language inclines us to look for literal rather than ritual meanings in words. And many of us are also inclined to look for individual psychological problems to explain the way we talk. It is easy to make someone who has spoken indirectly feel guilty: "Why do I do that? What's wrong with me?" But few people wonder why they speak as they do when they are talking

---

[5]*"I never heard anyone say they resented receiving praise."* Actually, there was one exception: One woman said she cried when, on her first job, all she got from her boss was praise. Since she couldn't believe she was doing everything right, she took the unalloyed praise as lack of caring.

to others who share their conversational rituals. It's only when our rituals fail that we question them.

17   I have described in this chapter a number of conversational rituals (by no means all) that can differ from one person to the next. Many readers will wonder, "Which way is best?" There is no one best way. Any style of speaking will work just fine in some situations with those who share the style. The most common culprit is style differences. (This is not to imply that misunderstandings or other tensions will never arise when styles are shared. Discord can result from ill intentions or conflicts of interest, and all styles have built-in liabilities that can cause problems in some situations.) But all styles will at times fail with others who don't share or understand them, just as your language won't do you much good if you try to speak it to someone who doesn't know that language. It's not that you are no longer speaking a good language; it will still work fine to express your ideas. But if what you're after is not just self-expression but communication—getting others to understand what you say—then it's not enough for language to be right; it has to be shared—or at least understood.

1990

Beauty: When the Other Dancer Is the Self

Alice Walker

1 It is a bright summer day in 1947. My father, a fat, funny man with beautiful eyes and a subversive wit, is trying to decide which of his eight children he will take with him to the county fair. My mother, of course, will not go. She is knocked out from getting most of us ready: I hold my neck stiff against the pressure of her knuckles as she hastily completes the braiding and the beribboning of my hair.

2   My father is the driver for the rich old white lady up the road. Her name is Miss Mey. She owns all the land for miles around, as well as the house in which we live. All I remember

about her is that she once offered to pay my mother thirty-five cents for cleaning her house, raking up piles of her magnolia leaves, and washing her family's clothes, and that my mother—she of no money, eight children, and a chronic earache—refused it. But I do not think of this in 1947. I am two-and-a-half years old. I want to go everywhere my daddy goes. I am excited at the prospect of riding in a car. Someone has told me fairs are fun. That there is room in the car for only three of us doesn't faze me at all. Whirling happily in my starchy frock, showing off my biscuit-polished patent-leather shoes and lavender socks, tossing my head in a way that makes my ribbons bounce, I stand, hands on hips, before my father. "Take me, Daddy," I say with assurance; "I'm the prettiest!"

Later, it does not surprise me to find myself in Miss Mey's shiny 3 black car, sharing the back seat with the other lucky ones. Does not surprise me that I thoroughly enjoy the fair. At home that night I tell the unlucky ones all I can remember about the merry-go-round, the man who eats live chickens, and the teddy bears, until they say: that's enough, baby Alice. Shut up now, and go to sleep.

It is Easter Sunday, 1950. I am dressed in a green, flocked, 4 scalloped-hem dress (handmade by my adoring sister, Ruth) that has its own smooth satin petticoat and tiny hot-pink roses tucked into each scallop. My shoes, new T-strap patent leather, again highly biscuit-polished. I am six years old and have learned one of the longest Easter speeches to be heard that day, totally unlike the speech I said when I was two: "Easter lilies/pure and white/blossom in/the morning light." When I rise to give my speech I do so on a great wave of love and pride and expectation. People in the church stop rustling their new crinolines. They seem to hold their breath. I can tell they admire my dress, but it is my spirit, bordering on sassiness (womanishness), they secretly applaud.

"That girl's a little *mess*," they whisper to each other, pleased. 5

Naturally I say my speech without stammer or pause, unlike 6 those who stutter, stammer, or, worst of all, forget. This is before the word "beautiful" exists in people's vocabulary, but "Oh, isn't she the *cutest* thing!" frequently floats my way. "And got so much sense!" they gratefully add . . . for which thoughtful addition I thank them to this day.

7   *It was great fun being cute. But then, one day, it ended.*

8   I am eight years old and a tomboy. I have a cowboy hat, cowboy boots, checkered shirt and pants, all red. My playmates are my brothers, two and four years older than I. Their colors are black and green, the only difference in the way we are dressed. On Saturday nights we all go to the picture show, even my mother; Westerns are her favorite kind of movie. Back home, "on the ranch," we pretend we are Tom Mix, Hopalong Cassidy, Lash LaRue (we've even named one of our dogs Lash LaRue); we chase each other for hours rustling cattle, being outlaws, delivering damsels from distress. Then my parents decide to buy my brothers guns. These are not "real" guns. They shoot BBs, copper pellets my brothers say will kill birds. Because I am a girl, I do not get a gun. Instantly I am relegated to the position of Indian. Now there appears a great distance between us. They shoot and shoot at everything with their new guns. I try to keep up with my bow and arrows.

9   One day while I am standing on top of our makeshift "garage"—pieces of tin nailed across some poles—holding my bow and arrow and looking out toward the fields, I feel an incredible blow in my right eye. I look down just in time to see my brother lower his gun.

10   Both brothers rush to my side. My eye stings, and I cover it with my hand. "If you tell," they say, "we will get a whipping. You don't want that to happen, do you?" I do not. "Here is a piece of wire," says the older brother, picking it up from the roof; "say you stepped on one end of it and the other flew up and hit you." The pain is beginning to start. "Yes," I say. "Yes, I will say that is what happened." If I do not say this is what happened, I know my brothers will find ways to make me wish I had. But now I will say anything that gets me to my mother.

11   Confronted by our parents we stick to the lie agreed upon. They place me on a bench on the porch and I close my left eye while they examine the right. There is a tree growing from underneath the porch that climbs past the railing to the roof. It is the last thing my right eye sees. I watch as its trunk, its branches, and then its leaves are blotted out by the rising blood.

12   I am in shock. First there is intense fever, which my father tries to break using lily leaves bound around my head. Then there

are chills: my mother tries to get me to eat soup. Eventually, I do not know how, my parents learn what has happened. A week after the "accident" they take me to see a doctor. "Why did you wait so long to come?" he asks, looking into my eye and shaking his head. "Eyes are sympathetic," he says. "If one is blind, the other will likely become blind too."

This comment of the doctor's terrifies me. But it is really how   13 I look that bothers me most. Where the BB pellet struck there is a glob of whitish scar tissue, a hideous cataract, on my eye. Now when I stare at people—a favorite pastime, up to now—they will stare back. Not at the "cute" little girl, but at her scar. For six years I do not stare at anyone, because I do not raise my head.

Years later, in the throes of a mid-life crisis, I ask my mother   14 and sister whether I changed after the "accident." "No," they say, puzzled. "What do you mean?"

What do I mean?   15

I am eight, and, for the first time, doing poorly in school, where   16 I have been something of a whiz since I was four. We have just moved to the place where the "accident" occurred. We do not know any of the people around us because this is a different county. The only time I see the friends I knew is when we go back to our old church. The new school is the former state penitentiary. It is a large stone building, cold and drafty, crammed to overflowing with boisterous, ill-disciplined children. On the third floor there is a huge circular imprint of some partition that has been torn out.

"What used to be here?" I ask a sullen girl next to me on our   17 way past it to lunch.

"The electric chair," says she.   18

At night I have nightmares about the electric chair, and about   19 all the people reputedly "fried" in it. I am afraid of the school, where all the students seem to be budding criminals.

"What's the matter with your eye?" they ask, critically.   20

When I don't answer (I cannot decide whether it was an   21 "accident" or not), they shove me, insist on a fight.

My brother, the one who created the story about the wire,   22 comes to my rescue. But then brags so much about "protecting" me, I become sick.

After months of torture at the school, my parents decide to   23 send me back to our old community, to my old school. I live with my grandparents and the teacher they board. But there is no room for Phoebe, my cat. By the time my grandparents decide there is room, and I ask for my cat, she cannot be found. Miss Yarborough, the boarding teacher, takes me under her wing, and begins to teach me to play the piano. But soon she marries an African—a "prince," she says—and is whisked away to his continent.

24   At my old school there is at least one teacher who loves me. She is the teacher who "knew me before I was born" and bought my first baby clothes. It is she who makes life bearable. It is her presence that finally helps me turn on the one child at the school who continually calls me "one-eyed bitch." One day I simply grab him by his coat and beat him until I am satisfied. It is my teacher who tells me my mother is ill.

25   My mother is lying in bed in the middle of the day, something I have never seen. She is in too much pain to speak. She has an abscess in her ear. I stand looking down on her, knowing that if she dies, I cannot live. She is being treated with warm oils and hot bricks held against her cheek. Finally a doctor comes. But I must go back to my grandparents' house. The weeks pass but I am hardly aware of it. All I know is that my mother might die, my father is not so jolly, my brothers still have their guns, and I am the one sent away from home.

26   "You did not change," they say.

27   *Did I imagine the anguish of never looking up?*

28   I am twelve. When relatives come to visit I hide in my room. My cousin Brenda, just my age, whose father works in the post office and whose mother is a nurse, comes to find me. "Hello," she says. And then she asks, looking at my recent school picture, which I did not want taken, and on which the "glob," as I think of it, is clearly visible, "You still can't see out of that eye?"

29   "No," I say, and flop back on the bed over my book.

30   That night, as I do almost every night, I abuse my eye. I rant and rave at it, in front of the mirror. I plead with it to clear up before morning. I tell it I hate and despise it. I do not pray for sight. I pray for beauty.

31   "You did not change," they say.

I am fourteen and baby-sitting for my brother Bill, who lives 32
in Boston. He is my favorite brother and there is a strong bond
between us. Understanding my feelings of shame and ugliness he
and his wife take me to a local hospital, where the "glob" is
removed by a doctor named O. Henry. There is still a small bluish
crater where the scar tissue was, but the ugly white stuff is gone.
Almost immediately I become a different person from the girl who
does not raise her head. Or so I think. Now that I've raised my
head I win the boyfriend of my dreams. Now that I've raised my
head I have plenty of friends. Now that I've raised my head class-
work comes from my lips as faultlessly as Easter speeches did,
and I leave high school as valedictorian, most popular student,
and *queen,* hardly believing my luck. Ironically, the girl who was
voted most beautiful in our class (and was) was later shot twice
through the chest by a male companion, using a "real" gun, while
she was pregnant. But that's another story in itself. Or is it?

"You did not change," they say. 33

It is now thirty years since the "accident." A beautiful journal- 34
ist comes to visit and to interview me. She is going to write a cover
story for her magazine that focuses on my latest book. "Decide how
you want to look on the cover," she says. "Glamorous, or whatever."

Never mind "glamorous," it is the "whatever" that I hear. 35
Suddenly all I can think of is whether I will get enough sleep the
night before the photography session: If I don't, my eye will be
tired and wander, as blind eyes will.

At night in bed with my lover I think up reasons why I should 36
not appear on the cover of a magazine. "My meanest critics will
say I've sold out," I say. "My family will now realize I write scan-
dalous books."

"But what's the real reason you don't want to do this?" he asks. 37

"Because in all probability," I say in a rush, "my eye won't be 38
straight."

"It will be straight enough," he says. Then, "Besides, I thought 39
you'd made your peace with that."

And I suddenly remember that I have. 40

I remember: 41

I am talking to my brother Jimmy, asking if he remembers 42
anything unusual about the day I was shot. He does not know I

consider that day the last time my father, with his sweet home remedy of cool lily leaves, chose me, and that I suffered and raged inside because of this. "Well," he says, "all I remember is standing by the side of the highway with Daddy, trying to flag down a car. A white man stopped, but when Daddy said he needed somebody to take his little girl to the doctor, he drove off."

43   *I remember:*

44   I am in the desert for the first time. I fall totally in love with it. I am so overwhelmed by its beauty, I confront for the first time, consciously, the meaning of the doctor's words years ago: "Eyes are sympathetic. If one is blind, the other will likely become blind too." I realize I have dashed about the world madly, looking at this, looking at that, storing up images against the fading of the light. *But I might have missed seeing the desert!* The shock of that possibility—and gratitude for over twenty-five years of sight—sends me literally to my knees. Poem after poem comes— which is perhaps how poets pray.

45   *On Sight*

I am so thankful I have seen
The Desert
And the creatures in the desert
And the desert Itself.

The desert has its own moon
Which I have seen
With my own eye.
There is no flag on it.

Trees of the desert have arms
All of which are always up
That is because the moon is up
The sun is up
Also the sky
The Stars
Clouds
None with flags.

If there were flags, I doubt
the trees would point.
Would you?

But mostly, I remember this: 46

I am twenty-seven, and my baby daughter is almost three. 47
Since her birth I have worried about her discovery that her
mother's eyes are different from other people's. Will she be embarrassed? I think. What will she say? Every day she watches a television program called *Big Blue Marble*. It begins with a picture
of the earth as it appears from the moon. It is bluish, a little
battered-looking, but full of light, with whitish clouds swirling
around it. Every time I see it I weep with love, as if it is a picture
of Grandma's house. One day when I am putting Rebecca down
for her nap, she suddenly focuses on my eye. Something inside
me cringes, gets ready to try to protect myself. All children are
cruel about physical differences, I know from experience, and that
they don't always mean to be is another matter. I assume Rebecca
will be the same.

But no-o-o-o. She studies my face intently as we stand, her 48
inside and me outside her crib. She even holds my face mater-
nally between her dimpled little hands. Then, looking every bit as
serious and lawyerlike as her father, she says, as if it may just possibly have slipped my attention: "Mommy, there's a *world* in your
eye." (As in, "Don't be alarmed, or do anything crazy.") And then,
gently, but with great interest: "Mommy, where did you *get* that
world in your eye?"

For the most part, the pain left then. (So what, if my broth- 49
ers grew up to buy even more powerful pellet guns for their sons
and to carry real guns themselves. So what, if a young
"Morehouse man" once nearly fell off the steps of Trevor Arnett
Library because he thought my eyes were blue.) Crying and
laughing I ran to the bathroom, while Rebecca mumbled and
sang herself to sleep. Yes indeed, I realized, looking into the mirror. There *was* a world in my eye. And I saw that it was possible to love it: that in fact, for all it had taught me of shame and
anger and inner vision, I *did* love it. Even to see it drifting out
of orbit in boredom, or rolling up out of fatigue, not to mention
floating back at attention in excitement (bearing witness, a friend
has called it), deeply suitable to my personality, and even characteristic of me.

That night I dream I am dancing to Stevie Wonder's song 50
"Always" (the name of the song is really "As," but I hear it as
"Always"). As I dance, whirling and joyous, happier than I've

ever been in my life, another bright-faced dancer joins me. We dance and kiss each other and hold each other through the night. The other dancer has obviously come through all right, as I have done. She is beautiful, whole, and free. And she is also me.

1983

The Female Body

Margaret Atwood

1

1   I agree, it's a hot topic. But only one? Look around, there's a wide range. Take my own, for instance.

2   I get up in the morning. My topic feels like hell. I sprinkle it with water, brush parts of it, rub it with towels, powder it, add lubricant. I dump in the fuel and away goes my topic, my topical topic, my controversial topic, my capacious topic, my limping topic, my nearsighted topic, my topic with back problems, my badly behaved topic, my vulgar topic, my outrageous topic, my aging topic, my topic that is out of the question and anyway still can't spell, in its oversized coat and worn winter boots, scuttling along the sidewalk as if it were flesh and blood, hunting for what's out there, an avocado, an alderman, an adjective, hungry as ever.

2

3   The basic Female Body comes with the following accessories: garter belt, panti-girdle, crinoline, camisole, bustle, brassiere, stomacher, chemise, virgin zone, spike heels, nose ring, veil, kid gloves, fishnet stockings, fichu, bandeau, Merry Widow, weepers, chokers, barrettes, bangles, beads, lorgnette, feather boa, basic black, compact, Lycra stretch one-piece with modesty panel, designer peignoir, flannel nightie, lace teddy, bed, head.

3

The Female Body is made of transparent plastic and lights up 4
when you plug it in. You press a button to illuminate the different systems. The circulatory system is red, for the heart and
arteries, purple for the veins; the respiratory system is blue; the
lymphatic system is yellow; the digestive system is green, with
liver and kidneys in aqua. The nerves are done in orange and the
brain is pink. The skeleton, as you might expect, is white.

The reproductive system is optional, and can be removed. It 5
comes with or without a miniature embryo. Parental judgment
can thereby be exercised. We do not wish to frighten or offend.

4

He said, I won't have one of those things in the house. It gives a 6
young girl a false notion of beauty, not to mention anatomy. If a
real woman was built like that she'd fall on her face.

She said, If we don't let her have one like all the other girls she'll 7
feel singled out. It'll become an issue. She'll long for one and she'll
long to turn into one. Repression breeds sublimation. You know that.

He said, It's not just the pointy plastic tits, it's the wardrobes. 8
The wardrobes and that stupid male doll, what's his name, the
one with the underwear glued on.

She said, Better to get it over with when she's young. He said, 9
All right, but don't let me see it.

She came whizzing down the stairs, thrown like a dart. She 10
was stark naked. Her hair had been chopped off, her head was
turned back to front, she was missing some toes and she'd been
tattooed all over her body with purple ink in a scrollwork design.
She hit the potted azalea, trembled there for a moment like a
botched angel, and fell.

He said, I guess we're safe.   11

5

The Female Body has many uses. It's been used as a door knocker, 12
a bottle opener, as a clock with a ticking belly, as something to
hold up lampshades, as a nutcracker, just squeeze the brass legs

together and out comes your nut. It bears torches, lifts victorious wreaths, grows copper wings and raises aloft a ring of neon stars; whole buildings rest on its marble heads.

13 It sells cars, beer, shaving lotion, cigarettes, hard liquor; it sells diet plans and diamonds, and desire in tiny crystal bottles. Is this the face that launched a thousand products? You bet it is, but don't get any funny big ideas, honey, that smile is a dime a dozen.

14 It does not merely sell, it is sold. Money flows into this country or that country, flies in, practically crawls in, suitful after suitful, lured by all those hairless pre-teen legs. Listen, you want to reduce the national debt, don't you? Aren't you patriotic? That's the spirit. That's my girl.

15 She's a natural resource, a renewable one luckily, because those things wear out so quickly. They don't make 'em like they used to. Shoddy goods.

6

16 One and one equals another one. Pleasure in the female is not a requirement. Pair-bonding is stronger in geese. We're not talking about love, we're talking about biology. That's how we all got here, daughter.

17 Snails do it differently. They're hermaphrodites, and work in threes.

7

18 Each Female Body contains a female brain. Handy. Makes things work. Stick pins in it and you get amazing results. Old popular songs. Short circuits. Bad dreams.

19 Anyway: each of these brains has two halves. They're joined together by a thick cord; neural pathways flow from one to the other, sparkles of electric information washing to and fro. Like light on waves. Like a conversation. How does a woman know? She listens. She listens in.

20 The male brain, now, that's a different matter. Only a thin connection. Space over here, time over there, music and arithmetic in their own sealed compartments. The right brain doesn't know

what the left brain is doing. Good for aiming through, for hitting the target when you pull the trigger. What's the target? Who's the target? Who cares? What matters is hitting it. That's the male brain for you. Objective.

This is why men are so sad, why they feel so cut off, why they think of themselves as orphans cast adrift, footloose and stringless in the deep void. What void? she asks. What are you talking about? The void of the universe, he says, and she says Oh and looks out the window and tries to get a handle on it, but it's no use, there's too much going on, too many rustlings in the leaves, too many voices, so she says, Would you like a cheese sandwich, a piece of cake, a cup of tea? And he grinds his teeth because she doesn't understand, and wanders off, not just alone but Alone, lost in the dark, lost in the skull, searching for the other half, the twin who could complete him. 21

Then it comes to him: he's lost the Female Body! Look, it shines in the gloom, far ahead, a vision of wholeness, ripeness, like a giant melon, like an apple, like a metaphor for "breast" in a bad sex novel; it shines like a balloon, like a foggy noon, a watery moon, shimmering in its egg of light. 22

Catch it. Put it in a pumpkin, in a high tower, in a compound, in a chamber, in a house, in a room. Quick, stick a leash on it, a lock, a chain, some pain, settle it down, so it can never get away from you again. 23

1994

The Men We Carry in Our Minds

Scott Russell Sanders

The first men, besides my father, I remember seeing were black convicts and white guards, in the cottonfield across the road from our farm on the outskirts of Memphis. I must have been three or four. The prisoners wore dingy gray-and-black zebra suits, heavy as canvas, sodden with sweat. Hatless, stooped, they chopped weeds in the fierce heat, row after row, breathing the acrid dust 1 of boll-weevil poison. The overseers wore dazzling white shirts and broad shadowy hats. The oiled barrels of their shotguns flashed in the sunlight. Their faces in memory are utterly blank. Of course those men, white and black, have become for me an emblem of racial hatred. But they have also come to stand for the twin poles of my early vision of manhood—the brute toiling animal and the boss.

2   When I was a boy, the men I knew labored with their bodies. They were marginal farmers, just scraping by, or welders, steel workers, carpenters; they swept floors, dug ditches, mined coal, or drove trucks, their forearms ropy with muscle; they trained horses, stoked furnaces, built tires, stood on assembly lines wrestling parts onto cars and refrigerators. They got up before light, worked all day long whatever the weather, and when they came home at night they looked as though somebody had been whipping them. In the evenings and on weekends they worked on their own places, tilling gardens that were lumpy with clay, fixing broken-down cars, hammering on houses that were always too drafty, too leaky, too small.

3   The bodies of the men I knew were twisted and maimed in ways visible and invisible. The nails of their hands were black and split, the hands tattooed with scars. Some had lost fingers. Heavy lifting had given many of them finicky backs and guts weak from hernias. Racing against conveyor belts had given them ulcers. Their ankles and knees ached from years of standing on concrete. Anyone who had worked for long around machines was hard of hearing. They squinted, and the skin of their faces was creased like the leather of old work gloves. There were times, studying them, when I dreaded growing up. Most of them coughed, from dust or cigarettes, and most of them drank cheap wine or whiskey, so their eyes looked bloodshot and bruised. The fathers of my friends always seemed older than the mothers. Men wore out sooner. Only women lived into old age.

4   As a boy I also knew another sort of men, who did not sweat and break down like mules. They were soldiers, and so far as I could tell they scarcely worked at all. During my early school years we lived on a military base, an arsenal in Ohio, and every day I saw GIs in the guardshacks, on the stoops of barracks, at the wheels of olive drab Chevrolets. The chief fact of their lives

was boredom. Long after I left the Arsenal I came to recognize the sour smell the soldiers gave off as that of souls in limbo. They were all waiting—for wars, for transfers, for leaves, for promotions, for the end of their hitch—like so many braves waiting for the hunt to begin. Unlike the warriors of older tribes, however, they would have no say about when the battle would start or how it would be waged. Their waiting was broken only when they practiced for war. They fired guns at targets, drove tanks across the churned-up fields of the military reservation, set off bombs in the wrecks of old fighter planes. I knew this was all play. But I also felt certain that when the hour for killing arrived, they would kill. When the real shooting started, many of them would die. This was what soldiers were *for,* just as a hammer was for driving nails.

Warriors and toilers: those seemed, in my boyhood vision, to be   5 the chief destinies for men. They weren't the only destinies, as I learned from having a few male teachers, from reading books, and from watching television. But the men on television—the politicians, the astronauts, the generals, the savvy lawyers, the philosophical doctors, the bosses who gave orders to both soldiers and laborers— seemed as remote and unreal to me as the figures in tapestries. I could no more imagine growing up to become one of these cool, potent creatures than I could imagine becoming a prince.

A nearer and more hopeful example was that of my father,   6 who had escaped from a red-dirt farm to a tire factory, and from the assembly line to the front office. Eventually he dressed in a white shirt and tie. He carried himself as if he had been born to work with his mind. But his body, remembering the earlier years of slogging work, began to give out on him in his fifties, and it quit on him entirely before he turned sixty-five. Even such partial escape from man's fate as he had accomplished did not seem possible for most of the boys I knew. They joined the Army, stood in line for jobs in the smoky plants, helped build highways. They were bound to work as their fathers had worked, killing themselves or preparing to kill others.

A scholarship enabled me not only to attend college, a rare   7 enough feat in my circle, but even to study in a university meant for the children of the rich. Here I met for the first time young men who had assumed from birth that they would lead lives of comfort and power. And for the first time I met women who told me that men were guilty of having kept all the joys and privileges of the earth for themselves. I was baffled. What privileges? What joys? I thought about the maimed, dismal lives of most of the men back home. What had they stolen from their wives and daughters? The right to go five days a week, twelve months a year, for thirty or forty years to a steel mill or a coal mine? The right to drop bombs and die in war? The right to feel every leak in the roof, every gap in the fence, every cough in the engine, as a wound they must mend? The right to feel, when the layoff comes or the plant shuts down, not only afraid but ashamed?

8   I was slow to understand the deep grievances of women. This was because, as a boy, I had envied them. Before college, the only people I had ever known who were interested in art or music or literature, the only ones who read books, the only ones who ever seemed to enjoy a sense of ease and grace were the mothers and daughters. Like the menfolk, they fretted about money, they scrimped and made-do. But, when the pay stopped coming in, they were not the ones who had failed. Nor did they have to go to war, and that seemed to me a blessed fact. By comparison with the narrow, ironclad days of fathers, there was an expansiveness, I thought, in the days of mothers. They went to see neighbors, to shop in town, to run errands at school, at the library, at church. No doubt, had I looked harder at their lives, I would have envied them less. It was not my fate to become a woman, so it was easier for me to see the graces. Few of them held jobs outside the home, and those who did filled thankless roles as clerks and waitresses. I didn't see, then, what a prison a house could be, since houses seemed to me brighter, handsomer places than any factory. I did not realize—because such things were never spoken of—how often women suffered from men's bullying. I did learn about the wretchedness of abandoned wives, single mothers, widows; but I also learned about the wretchedness of lone men. Even then I could see how exhausting it was for a mother to cater all day to the needs of young children. But if I had been asked, as a boy, to choose between tending a baby and tending a machine, I think I would have chosen the baby. (Having now tended both, I know I would choose the baby.)

9   So I was baffled when the women at college accused me and my sex of having cornered the world's pleasures. I think something like my bafflement has been felt by other boys (and by girls as

well) who grew up in dirt-poor farm country, in mining country, in black ghettos, in Hispanic barrios, in the shadows of factories, in Third World nations—any place where the fate of men is as grim and bleak as the fate of women. Toilers and warriors. I realize now how ancient these identities are, how deep the tug they exert on men, the undertow of a thousand generations. The miseries I saw, as a boy, in the lives of nearly all men I continue to see in the lives of many—the body-breaking toil, the tedium, the call to be tough, the humiliating powerlessness, the battle for a living and for territory.

When the women I met at college thought about the joys and 10 privileges of men, they did not carry in their minds the sort of men I had known in my childhood. They thought of their fathers, who were bankers, physicians, architects, stockbrokers, the big wheels of the big cities. These fathers rode the train to work or drove cars that cost more than any of my childhood houses. They were attended from morning to night by female helpers, wives and nurses and secretaries. They were never laid off, never short of cash at month's end, never lined up for welfare. These fathers made decisions that mattered. They ran the world.

The daughters of such men wanted to share in this power, this 11 glory. So did I. They yearned for a say over their future, for jobs worthy of their abilities, for the right to live at peace, unmolested, whole. Yes, I thought, yes yes. The difference between me and these daughters was that they saw me, because of my sex, as destined from birth to become like their fathers, and therefore as an enemy to their desires. But I knew better. I wasn't an enemy, in fact or in feeling. I was an ally. If I had known, then, how to tell them so, would they have believed me? Would they now?

1984

9

Marriage and Family

The Making of a Divorce Culture

Barbara Dafoe Whitehead

1   Divorce is now part of everyday American life. It is embedded in our laws and institutions, our manners and mores, our movies and television shows, our novels and children's storybooks, and our closest and most important relationships. Indeed, divorce has become so pervasive that many people naturally assume it has seeped into the social and cultural mainstream over a long period of time. Yet this is not the case. Divorce has become an American way of life only as the result of recent and revolutionary change.

2   The entire history of American divorce can be divided into two periods, one evolutionary and the other revolutionary. For most of the nation's history, divorce was a rare occurrence and an insignificant feature of family and social relationships. In the first sixty years of the twentieth century, divorce became more common, but it was hardly commonplace. In 1960, the divorce rate stood at a still relatively modest level of nine per one thousand married couples. After 1960, however, the rate accelerated at a dazzling pace. It doubled in roughly a decade and continued its upward climb until the early 1980s, when it stabilized at the highest level among advanced Western societies. As a consequence of this sharp and sustained rise, divorce moved from the margins to the mainstream of American life in the space of three decades.

3   Ideas are important in revolutions, yet surprisingly little attention has been devoted to the ideas that gave impetus to the divorce revolution. Of the scores of books on divorce published in recent decades, most focus on its legal, demographic, economic, or (especially) psychological dimensions. Few, if any, deal fully

296

with its intellectual origins. Yet trying to comprehend the divorce revolution and its consequences without some sense of its ideological origins, is like trying to understand the American Revolution without taking into account the thinking of John Locke, Thomas Jefferson, or Thomas Paine. This more recent revolution, like the revolution of our nation's founding, has its roots in a distinctive set of ideas and claims.

This book is about the ideas behind the divorce revolution 4 and how these ideas have shaped a culture of divorce. The making of a divorce culture has involved three overlapping changes: first, the emergence and widespread diffusion of a historically new and distinctive set of ideas about divorce in the last third of the twentieth century; second, the migration of divorce from a minor place within a system governed by marriage to a freestanding place as a major institution governing family relationships; and third, a widespread shift in thinking about the obligations of marriage and parenthood.

Beginning in the late 1950s, Americans began to change their 5 ideas about the individual's obligations to family and society. Broadly described, this change was away from an ethic of obligation to others and toward an obligation to self. I do not mean that people suddenly abandoned all responsibilities to others, but rather that they became more acutely conscious of their responsibility to attend to their own individual needs and interests. At least as important as the moral obligation to look after others, the new thinking suggested, was the moral obligation to look after oneself.

This ethical shift had a profound impact on ideas about the 6 nature and purpose of the family. In the American tradition, the marketplace and the public square have represented the realms of life devoted to the pursuit of individual interest, choice, and freedom, while the family has been the realm defined by voluntary commitment, duty, and self-sacrifice. With the greater emphasis on individual satisfaction in family relationships, however, family well-being became subject to a new metric. More than in the past, satisfaction in this sphere came to be based on subjective judgments about the content and quality of individual happiness rather than on such objective measures as level of income, material nurture and support, or boosting children onto a higher rung on the socioeconomic ladder. People began to judge the strength and "health" of family bonds according to their capacity to promote individual fulfillment and personal growth. As a result, the conception of the family's role and place in the society began to change. The family began to lose its separate place and distinctive identity as the realm of duty, service, and sacrifice. Once the domain of the obligated self, the family was increasingly viewed as yet another domain for the expression of the unfettered self.

7   These broad changes figured centrally in creating a new conception of divorce which gained influential adherents and spread broadly and swiftly throughout the society—a conception that represented a radical departure from earlier notions. Once regarded mainly as a social, legal, and family event in which there were other stakeholders, divorce now became an event closely linked to the pursuit of individual satisfactions, opportunities, and growth.

8   The new conception of divorce drew upon some of the oldest, and most resonant, themes in the American political tradition. The nation, after all, was founded as the result of a political divorce, and revolutionary thinkers explicitly adduced a parallel between the dissolution of marital bonds and the dissolution of political bonds. In political as well as marital relationships, they argued, bonds of obligation were established voluntarily on the basis of mutual affection and regard. Once such bonds turned cold and oppressive, peoples, like individuals, had the right to dissolve them and to form more perfect unions.

9   In the new conception of divorce, this strain of eighteenth-century political thought mingled with a strain of twentieth-century psychotherapeutic thought. Divorce was not only an individual right but also a psychological resource. The dissolution of marriage offered the chance to make oneself over from the inside out, to refurbish and express the inner self, and to acquire certain valuable psychological assets and competencies, such as initiative, assertiveness, and a stronger and better self-image.

10   The conception of divorce as both an individual right and an inner experience merged with and reinforced the new ethic of obligation to the self. In family relationships, one had an obligation to be attentive to one's own feelings and to work toward improving the quality of one's inner life. This ethical imperative completed the rationale for a sense of individual entitlement to divorce.

Increasingly, mainstream America saw the legal dissolution of marriage as a matter of individual choice, in which there were no other stakeholders or larger social interests. This conception of divorce strongly argued for removing the social, legal, and moral impediments to the free exercise of the individual right to divorce.

Traditionally, one major impediment to divorce was the presence of children in the family. According to well-established popular belief, dependent children had a stake in their parents' marriage and suffered hardship as a result of the dissolution of the marriage. Because children were vulnerable and dependent, parents had a moral obligation to place their children's interests in the marital partnership above their own individual satisfactions. This notion was swiftly abandoned after the 1960s. Influential voices in the society, including child-welfare professionals, claimed that the happiness of individual parents, rather than an intact marriage, was the key determinant of children's family well-being. If divorce could make one or both parents happier, then it was likely to improve the well-being of children as well.

In the following decades, the new conception of divorce spread through the law, therapy, etiquette, the social sciences, popular advice literature, and religion. Concerns that had dominated earlier thinking on divorce were now dismissed as old-fashioned and excessively moralistic. Divorce would not harm children but would lead to greater happiness for children and their single parents. It would not damage the institution of marriage but would make possible better marriages and happier individuals. Divorce would not damage the social fabric by diminishing children's life chances but would strengthen the social fabric by improving the quality of affective bonds between parents and children, whatever form the structural arrangements of their families might happen to take.

As the sense of divorce as an individual freedom and entitlement grew, the sense of concern about divorce as a social problem diminished. Earlier in the century, each time the divorce rate increased sharply, it had inspired widespread public concern and debate about the harmful impact of divorce on families and the society. But in the last third of the century, as the divorce rate rose to once unthinkable levels, public anxiety about it all but vanished. At the very moment when divorce had its most profound impact on the society, weakening the institution of marriage, revolutionizing the structure of families and reorganizing parent-child relationships, it ceased to be a source of concern or debate.

14   The lack of attention to divorce became particularly striking after the 1980s, as a politically polarized debate over the state of the American family took shape. On one side, conservatives pointed to abortion, illegitimacy, and homosexuality as forces destroying the family. On the other, liberals cited domestic violence, economic insecurity, and inadequate public supports as the key problems afflicting the family. But politicians on both sides had almost nothing to say about divorce. Republicans did not want to alienate their upscale constituents or their libertarian wing, both of whom tended to favor easy divorce, nor did they want to call attention to the divorces among their own leadership. Democrats did not want to anger their large constituency among women who saw easy divorce as a hard-won freedom and prerogative, nor did they wish to seem unsympathetic to single mothers. Thus, except for bipartisan calls to get tougher with deadbeat dads, both Republicans and Democrats avoided the issue of divorce and its consequences as far too politically risky.

15   But the failure to address divorce carried a price. It allowed the middle class to view family breakdown as a "them" problem rather than an "us" problem. Divorce was not like illegitimacy or welfare dependency, many claimed. It was a matter of individual choice, imposing few, if any, costs or consequences on others. Thus, mainstream America could cling to the comfortable illusion that the nation's family problems had to do with the behavior of unwed teenage mothers or poor women on welfare rather than with the instability of marriage and family life within its own ranks.

16   Nonetheless, after thirty years of persistently high levels of divorce, this illusion, though still politically attractive, is increasingly difficult to sustain in the face of a growing body of experience and evidence. To begin with, divorce has indeed hurt children. It has created economic insecurity and disadvantage for many children who would not otherwise be economically vulnerable. It has led to more fragile and unstable family households. It has caused a mass exodus of fathers from children's households and, all too often, from their lives. It has reduced the levels of parental time and money invested in children. In sum, it has changed the

very nature of American childhood. Just as no patient would have designed today's system of health care, so no child would have chosen today's culture of divorce.

Divorce figures prominently in the altered economic fortunes [17] of middle-class families. Although the economic crisis of the middle class is usually described as a problem caused by global economic changes, changing patterns in education and earnings, and ruthless corporate downsizing, it owes more to divorce than is commonly acknowledged. Indeed, recent data suggest that marriage may be a more important economic resource than a college degree. According to an analysis of 1994 income patterns, the median income of married-parent households whose heads have only a high school diploma is ten percent higher than the median income of college-educated single-parent households.[1] Parents who are college graduates *and* married form the new economic elite among families with children. Consequently, those who are concerned about what the downsizing of corporations is doing to workers should also be concerned about what the downsizing of families through divorce is doing to parents and children.

Widespread divorce depletes social capital as well. Scholars [18] tell us that strong and durable family and social bonds generate certain "goods" and services, including money, mutual assistance, information, caregiving, protection, and sponsorship. Because such bonds endure over time, they accumulate and form a pool of social capital which can be drawn down upon, when needed, over the entire course of a life. An elderly couple, married for fifty years, is likely to enjoy a substantial body of social and emotional

---

[1]An analysis of income data provided by The Northeastern University Center for Labor Market Studies shows the following distribution by education and marital status:

MEDIAN INCOMES FOR U.S. FAMILIES WITH CHILDREN, 1994

Education of household head	Married Couple Families	Single Parent Families
College Graduate	$71,263	$36,006
High School Graduate	$40,098	$14,698

Based on 1994 Current Population Statistics. Families with one or more children under 18. Age of household head: 22–62.

capital, generated through their long-lasting marriage, which they can draw upon in caring for each other and for themselves as they age. Similarly, children who grow up in stable, two-parent married households are the beneficiaries of the social and emotional capital accumulated over time as a result of an enduring marriage bond. As many parents know, children continue to depend on these resources well into young adulthood. But as family bonds become increasingly fragile and vulnerable to disruption, they become less permanent and thus less capable of generating such forms of help, financial resources, and mutual support. In short, divorce consumes social capital and weakens the social fabric. At the very time that sweeping socioeconomic changes are mandating greater investment of social capital in children, widespread divorce is reducing the pool of social capital. As the new economic and social conditions raise the hurdles of child-rearing higher, divorce digs potholes in the tracks.

19   It should be stressed that this book is not intended as a brief against divorce as such. We must assume that divorce is necessary as a remedy for irretrievably broken marriages, especially those that are marred by severe abuse such as chronic infidelity, drug addiction, or physical violence. Nor is its argument directed against those who are divorced. It assumes that divorce is difficult, painful, and often unwanted by at least one spouse, and that divorcing couples require compassion and support from family, friends, and their religious communities. Nor should this book be taken as an appeal for a return to an earlier era of American family life. The media routinely portray the debate over the family as one between nostalgists and realists, between those who want to turn back the clock to the fifties and those who want to march bravely and resolutely forward into the new century. But this is a lazy and misguided approach, driven more by the easy availability of archival photos and footage from 1950s television sitcoms than by careful consideration of the substance of competing arguments.

20   More fundamentally, this approach overlooks the key issue. And that issue is not how today's families might stack up against those of an earlier era; indeed, no reliable empirical data for such a comparison exist. In an age of diverse family structures, the heart of the matter is what kinds of contemporary family arrangements have the greatest capacity to promote children's well-being,

and how we can ensure that more children have the advantages of growing up in such families.

In the past year or so, there has been growing recognition of 21 the personal and social costs of three decades of widespread divorce. A public debate has finally emerged. Within this debate, there are two separate and overlapping discussions.

The first centers on a set of specific proposals that are 22 intended to lessen the harmful impact of divorce on children: a federal system of child-support collection, tougher child-support enforcement, mandatory counseling for divorcing parents, and reform of no-fault divorce laws in the states. What is striking about this discussion is its narrow focus on public policy, particularly on changes in the system of no-fault divorce. In this, as in so many other crucial discussions involving social and moral questions, the most vocal and visible participants come from the world of government policy, electoral politics, and issue advocacy. The media, which are tongue-tied unless they can speak in the language of left-right politics, reinforce this situation. And the public is offered needlessly polarized arguments that hang on a flat yes-or-no response to this or that individual policy measure. All too often, this discussion of divorce poses what *Washington Post* columnist E. J. Dionne aptly describes as false choices.

Notably missing is a serious consideration of the broader 23 moral assumptions and empirical claims that define our divorce culture. Divorce touches on classic questions in American public philosophy—on the nature of our most important human and social bonds, the duties and obligations imposed by bonds we voluntarily elect, the "just causes" for the dissolution of those bonds, and the differences between obligations volunteered and those that must be coerced. Without consideration of such questions, the effort to change behavior by changing a few public policies is likely to founder.

The second and complementary discussion does try to place 24 divorce within a larger philosophical framework. Its proponents have looked at the decline in the well-being of the nation's children as the occasion to call for a collective sense of commitment by all Americans to all of America's children. They pose the challenging question: "What are Americans willing to do 'for the sake of *all* children'?" But while this is surely an important question, it addresses only half of the problem of declining commitment. The other half has to do with how we answer the question: "What are individual parents obliged to do 'for the sake of their own children'?"

25   Renewing a *social* ethic of commitment to children is an urgent goal, but it cannot be detached from the goal of strengthening the *individual* ethic of commitment to children. The state of one affects the standing of the other. A society that protects the rights of parents to easy, unilateral divorce, and flatly rejects the idea that parents should strive to preserve a marriage "for the sake of the children," faces a problem when it comes to the question of public sacrifice "for the sake of the children." To put it plainly, many of the ideas we have come to believe and vigorously defend about adult prerogatives and freedoms in family life are undermining the foundations of altruism and support for children.

26   With each passing year, the culture of divorce becomes more deeply entrenched. American children are routinely schooled in divorce. Mr. Rogers teaches toddlers about divorce. An entire children's literature is devoted to divorce. Family movies and videos for children feature divorced families. *Mrs. Doubtfire,* originally a children's book about divorce and then a hit movie, is aggressively marketed as a holiday video for kids. Of course, these books and movies are designed to help children deal with the social reality and psychological trauma of divorce. But they also carry an unmistakable message about the impermanence and unreliability of family bonds. Like romantic love, the children's storybooks say, family love comes and goes. Daddies disappear. Mommies find new boyfriends. Mommies' boyfriends leave. Grandparents go away. Even pets must be left behind.

27   More significantly, in a society where nearly half of all children are likely to experience parental divorce, family breakup becomes a defining event of American childhood itself. Many children today know nothing but divorce in their family lives. And although children from divorced families often say they want to avoid divorce if they marry, young adults whose parents divorced are more likely to get divorced themselves and to bear children outside of marriage than young adults from stable married-parent families.

Precisely because the culture of divorce has generational 28
momentum, this book offers no easy optimism about the prospects
for change. But neither does it counsel passive resignation or
acceptance of the culture's relentless advance. What it does offer
is a critique of the ideas behind current divorce trends. Its argument is directed against the ideas about divorce that have gained
ascendancy, won our support, and lodged in our consciousness as
"proven" and incontrovertible. It challenges the popular idea of
divorce as an individual right and freedom to be exercised in the
pursuit of individual goods and satisfactions, without due regard
for other stakeholders in the marital partnership, especially children.
This may be a fragile and inadequate response to a profoundly
consequential set of changes, but it seeks the abandonment of ideas
that have misled us and failed our children.

In a larger sense, this book is both an appreciation and a criti- 29
cism of what is peculiarly American about divorce. Divorce has
spread throughout advanced Western societies at roughly the same
pace and over roughly the same period of time. Yet nowhere else
has divorce been so deeply imbued with the larger themes of a
nation's political traditions. Nowhere has divorce so fully reflected
the spirit and susceptibilities of a people who share an extravagant
faith in the power of the individual and in the power of positive
thinking. Divorce in America is not unique, but what we have made
of divorce is uniquely American. In exploring the cultural roots of
divorce, therefore, we look at ourselves, at what is best and worst
in our traditions, what is visionary and what is blind, and how the
two are sometimes tragically commingled and confused.

1997

Why I [Still] Want a Wife

Judy Brady

I belong to that classification of people known as wives. I am A 1
Wife. And, not altogether incidentally, I am a mother. Not too
long ago a male friend of mine appeared on the scene fresh from

a recent divorce. He had one child; who is, of course, with his ex-wife. He is obviously looking for another wife. As I thought about him while I was ironing one evening, it suddenly occurred to me that I, too, would like to have a wife. Why do I want a wife?

2   I would like to go back to school so that I can become economically independent, support myself, and, if need be, support those dependent upon me. I want a wife who will work and send me to school. And while I am going to school I want a wife to take care of my children. I want a wife to keep track of the children's doctor and dentist appointments. And to keep track of mine, too. I want a wife to make sure my children eat properly and are kept clean. I want a wife who will wash the children's clothes and keep them mended. I want a wife who is a good nurturant attendant to my children, who arranges for their schooling, makes sure that they have an adequate social life with their peers, takes them to the park, the zoo, etc. I want a wife who takes care of the children when they are sick, a wife who arranges to be around when the children need special care, because, of course, I cannot miss classes at school. My wife must arrange to lose time at work and not lose the job. It may mean a small cut in my wife's income from time to time, but I guess I can tolerate that. Needless to say, my wife will arrange and pay for the care of the children while my wife is working.

3   I want a wife who will take care of *my* physical needs. I want a wife who will keep my house clean. A wife who will pick up after me. I want a wife who will keep my clothes clean, ironed, mended, replaced when need be, and who will see to it that my personal things are kept in their proper place so that I can find what I need the minute I need it. I want a wife who cooks the meals, a wife who is a *good* cook. I want a wife who will plan the menus, do the necessary grocery shopping, prepare the meals, serve them pleasantly, and then do the cleaning up while I do my studying. I want a wife who will care for me when I am sick and sympathize with my pain and loss of time from school. I want a wife to go along when our family takes a vacation so that someone can continue to care for me and my children when I need a rest and change of scene.

I want a wife who will not bother me with rambling com- 4
plaints about a wife's duties. But I want a wife who will listen to
me when I feel the need to explain a rather difficult point I have
come across in my course of studies. And I want a wife who will
type my papers for me when I have written them.

I want a wife who will take care of the details of my social 5
life. When my wife and I are invited out by my friends, I want
a wife who will take care of the babysitting arrangements. When
I meet people at school that I like and want to entertain, I want
a wife who will have the house clean, will prepare a special
meal, serve it to me and my friends, and not interrupt when I
talk about the things that interest me and my friends. I want a
wife who will have arranged that the children are fed and ready
for bed before my guests arrive so that the children do not
bother us.

And I want a wife who knows that sometimes I need a night 6
out by myself.

I want a wife who is sensitive to my sexual needs, a wife who 7
makes love passionately and eagerly when I feel like it, a wife
who makes sure I am satisfied. And, of course, I want a wife who
will not demand sexual attention when I am not in the mood for
it. I want a wife who assumes the complete responsibility for birth
control, because I do not want more children. I want a wife who
will remain sexually faithful to me so that I do not have to clut-
ter up my intellectual life with jealousies. And I want a wife who
understands that *my* sexual needs may entail more than strict
adherence to monogamy. I must, after all, be able to relate to people as fully as possible.

If, by chance, I find another person more suitable as a wife 8
than the wife I already have, I want the liberty to replace my present wife with another one. Naturally, I will expect a fresh, new
life; my wife will take the children and be solely responsible for
them so that I am left free.

When I am through with school and have a job, I want my 9
wife to quit working and remain at home so that my wife can
more fully and completely take care of a wife's duties.

My God, who *wouldn't* want a wife?   10

1970/Revised 1991

On Black Fathering

Cornel West

1   One of the most difficult tasks to accomplish in American society is to be a solid, caring, and loving black father. To be a good black father, first you have to negotiate all of the absurd attacks and assaults on your humanity and on your capacity and status as a human being. Second, you have to provide materially and economically, as well as nurture psychologically, personally, and existentially. All of this requires a deep level of maturity. By maturity I mean a solid understanding of who one is as a person, and a sense of sacrifice and courage. For black men to reach that level of maturity and understanding is almost miraculous given the dehumanizing context for black men, and yet millions and millions have done it. It is a tribute to fulfill the highest standards of fatherhood. When I think of my own particular case, I think of my father, my grandfather, and his father, because what they were able to do was to sustain some sense of dignity and sacrifice even as they dealt with all the arrows that were coming at them on every level in American society.

2   Let's consider the economic level. In America, generally speaking, patriarchal definitions of men in relation to the economic front mean you have a job and provide for your family. Many black men did not (and do not) make enough money to provide for their families adequately because of their exclusion from jobs with a living wage. They then oftentimes tended, and tend, to accent certain patriarchal identities (e.g., predatory or abusive behavior) in lieu of the fact that they could not perform the traditional patriarchal roles in American society.

3   Then on the home front, where black men had and have, oftentimes, wives who were and are subject to such white supremacist abuse, either at the white home where these sisters work(ed) or as a service worker in other parts of white society, most black men had to deal with the kinds of scars and bruises that come from knowing that you were supposed to protect your woman, as it were, which is also part of the patriarchal identity in America—a man ought to be able to protect his woman but could not protect her from the vicious abuse. Many black men also

recognized that there was a relation between their not being able to get a job given the discrimination and segregation on the one hand and the tremendous power wielded by those white men who were often condoning the abuse of their own wives.

How children perceive their father is another interesting 4 component of the dynamic that black fathers have to negotiate. How are black fathers able to convey to their children some affirmative sense of self, some sense of reality—given what is happening to these men on the economic front, given what many of them know is happening to their wives outside of the house, and given the perception by their own children that they are unable to fulfill the expected patriarchal role? In the tradition of the black father, the best ones—I think my grandfather and dad are good examples—came up with ways of negotiating a balance so that they would recognize that exclusion from the economic sphere was real, and recognize that possible abuse of their wives was real, and also recognize that they had to sustain a connection with their kids in which their kids could see the best in them despite the limited and dehumanizing circumstances under which they functioned.

My mother happened to be a woman who was not abused 5 in the fashion described above. I remember one incident when a white policeman disrespected my mother. Dad went at him verbally and, in the eyes of the police, ended up violating the law. At that point he just drew a line in the sand that said, "You're going too far." I thank God that a number of incidents like that didn't happen, or he would have ended up in jail forever— like so many other brothers who just do not allow certain levels of disrespect of their mother, wife, sister, or daughter. As a man, what I was able to see in Dad was his ability to transform his own pain with a sense of laughter, and a sense of empathy, and a sense of compassion for others. This was a real act of moral genius Dad accomplished, and I think that it is part of the best of a tradition of moral genius. Unfortunately, large numbers of black men do not reach that level because the rage and the anger are just too deep; they just burn them out and consume their soul. Fortunately, on the other hand, you do have many black men that achieve this level and some that go beyond it.

6   In my own case as a father, I certainly tried to emulate and imitate Dad's very ingenious ways of negotiating the balances between what was happening on these different fronts, but because of the sacrifices he and Mom made, I had access to opportunities that he did not. When my son Cliff was born, I was convinced that I wanted to try to do for him what Dad had done for me. But it was not to be—there was no way that I could be the father to my son that my dad was to me. Part of it was that my circumstances were very different. Another part was simply that I was not the man that my father was. My brother is actually the shining example of building on the rich legacy of my dad as a father much more than I am, because he gives everything—right across the board. He is there—whatever the circumstance—has spent time with the kids; he is always there in the same way that Dad was there for us. I'll always try to be a rich footnote to my brother, yet as a father I have certainly not been the person that he was. The effort has been there, the endeavor too, but the circumstances (as well as my not being as deep a person as he or my father) have not enabled me to measure up. On the other hand, my son Cliff turned out to be a decent and fascinating person—and he is still in process, of course.

7   The bottom line for my dad was always love, and he was a deeply Christian man—his favorite song was "I Will Trust in the Lord." He had a profound trust. His trust was much more profound than mine in some ways, even though I work at it. He had a deep love, and that's the thing I've tried to build on with Cliff. My hope and my inclination are that Cliff feels this love, but certainly it takes more than love to nurture and father a son or a daughter.

8   The most important things for black fathers to try to do are to give of themselves, to try to exemplify in their own behavior what they want to see in their sons and daughters, and, most important, to spend time with and give attention to their children. This is a big challenge, yet it is critical as we move into the twenty-first century.

9   The most difficult task of my life was to give the eulogy for my father. Everything else pales in the face of this challenge. Hence what Dad means to me—like my family, Cliff and Elleni—constitutes who and what I am and will be.

EULOGY

Clifton Lincoln West, Jr. What a man. What an individual. What 10
a person. What a servant. We gather here this afternoon in this
sacred place and this consecrated space to say good-bye. To bid
farewell to a good man, a great Christian who lived a grand and
loving life. When I think of my father, I cannot but think of what
he said to that reporter from the *Sacramento Bee* when they asked
him, "What is it about you and what is it about your family—do
you have a secret?" Dad said, "No, we live by Grace—in addition
to that, me and his mother, we try to *be there*." I shall never forget that my father was not simply a man of quiet dignity, steadfast
integrity, and high intelligence, but fundamentally and quintes-
sentially he was a man of love, and love means being there for
others. That's why when I think of Dad I recall that precious
moment in the fifteenth chapter of John in the eleventh and
twelfth verse: "These things have I given unto you that my joy
might remain in you, and that your joy might be full. This is my
commandment that ye love one another as I have loved you."

In the midst of Dad's sophistication and refinement he was 11
always for real. He was someone who was down-to-earth because
he took this commandment seriously, and it meant he had to cut
against the grain in a world in which he was going to endure lovingly and with compassion. Isn't that what the very core of the
gospel is about? The thirteenth chapter of I Corinthians—that
great litany of love that Dr. King talked about—deals with it. Dad
used to read it all the time. I will never forget when he took me
to college in Cambridge, the first time I ever flew on an airplane
(it cost about ninety-five dollars then). Dad told me, "Corn, we're
praying for you, and always remember: 'Though I speak with the
tongues of men and of angels and have not love, I become as a
sounding brass or a tinkling cymbal. And though I have the gift
of prophecy, and understand all mysteries, and all knowledge;
and though I have all faith, so that I could remove mountains, and
have not love, I am nothing.'"

As we stand here on these stormy banks of Jordan and watch 12
Dad's ship go by, may I remind each and every one of you that
we come from a loving family, a courageous people of African
descent, and a rich Christian tradition. We have seen situations in

which history has pushed our backs against the wall, and life has knocked us to our knees. In the face of despair and degradation sometimes we know that all we can do is sing a song, or crack a smile, or say a prayer. Yet we refuse to allow grief and misery to have the last word.

13   Dad was a man of love, and if I was to adopt his perspective at this very moment, he would say, "Corn, don't push me in the limelight, keep your mother in mind, don't focus on me, keep the family in mind—I'm just a servant passing through." That's the kind of father I had.

14   But he didn't come to it by himself, you see. He was part of a family, he was part of a people, he was part of a tradition that went all the way back to gut-bucket Jim Crow Louisiana, September 7, 1928. He was not supposed to make it, you see. Nobody would have believed that Clifton Lincoln West, Jr., the third child of C. L. West and Lovey West, would have been able to aspire to the heights that he did. No one would have predicted or projected that he would make it through the first three months in Louisiana—Cliff was not supposed to make that trip, you know. He was born the year before the stock market crashed. His family stayed three months in Louisiana, and Grandfather and Grandmother, with three young children in a snowstorm, journeyed on a train to Tulsa, Oklahoma. You all know what Tulsa, Oklahoma, was like. It was seven years after the major riot in this country in which over three hundred folks—black folks—were killed and Greenwood, Archer and Pine—that GAP corner—the Wall Street of black America was all burned out. But Grandmama had something else in mind, and the Lord did too.

15   Dad went on to Paul Laurence Dunbar Elementary School—to give you an idea of what side of town they were living on—and George Washington Carver Junior High School, and Booker T. Washington High School. It was there that he got to choose the idea of pulling from the best of the world but remaining not of the world. I like that about Dad. He wasn't so excessively pious or so excessively rigid that he became naive and got caught up in narrow doctrines and creeds and thought he was better than anybody else. That's not the kind of man he was. No. His faith was grounded in a love because he knew that he had fallen short of the glory of God. He knew he had inadequacies and shortcomings,

but he was going to struggle anyhow; he was going to keep keeping on anyway.

After high school he went on to the military for three years. [16] He could have easily given his life for this country. When he returned to Tulsa, Oklahoma, he was refused admission at the University of Tulsa, and then went on to that grand institution, Fisk University, where he met that indescribably wonderful, beautiful, lovable honor student from Orange, Texas—Irene Bias. I'll never forget when we were at Fisk together, he described the place right outside Jubilee Hall where they met. I said, "Dad, that's a special place," and he said, "Yes, that meeting was the beginning of the peak of my life." As their love began to grow and multiply, the army grabbed him back again for eighteen months, but in the years to come they had young Clifton, my brother, to whom I'm just a footnote; myself, of course; and Cynthia and Cheryl. We moved from Oklahoma through Topeka, Kansas, on our way to 8008 48th Avenue, Glen Elder. Yes, how proud we were driving up in that bright orange Mercury. We were at the cutting edge of residential breakdown in Sacramento, but along the way, for almost a decade, Dad, and the men of Glen Elder—Mr. Peters, Mr. Pool, Mr. Powell, Mr. Reed—these were black men who cared and who worked together. These overworked yet noble men built the little league diamond by themselves, and then they organized the league into ten teams—minor and major leagues for the neighborhood. They provided a means by which character and integrity could be shaped among the young brothers. Then every Sunday, onto Shiloh—"can't wait for the next sermon of Reverend Willie P. Cooke, just hope that he didn't go too long"—but we knew that the Lord was working in him. Dad would always tell us, "You know how blessed I am, how blessed we are. Never think that we've come as far as we have on our own."

When we were in trouble, there was Mr. Fields, Mrs. Ray, and [17] Mrs. Harris—there were hundreds of folks who made a difference. You all remember when Dad went to the hospital when he was thirty-one years old and the doctors had given up on him. There was a great sadness on Forty-eighth Avenue because he had left Mom with four little children. Granddad—the Reverend C. L. West, left his church for months to come and be with Mom— Grandmom came as well—and Dad was in the hospital in Oakland.

They had given up on him; the medical profession had reached its conclusion and said they could do nothing. And we said, "We know the power. Let Him step in." We knew that Reverend Cook hadn't been preaching that "Jesus is a rock in a weary land, and water in dry places, and food when you are hungry, and a mind regulator and a heart fixer" for nothing. And we came to Calvary in prayer.

18   Can you imagine how different our lives would have been if we had lost Dad then, in 1961, rather than 1994? Even in the midst of our fear we rejoice. It would have been a different world for each and every one of us, especially the children. Dad kept going after his recovery. He worked at McClellan Air Force Base— steadily missed some of those promotions he should have got, but he stayed convinced that he was going to teach people right no matter what, even given his own situation.

19   That's another thing I loved about him. People always ask me, "West, why do you still talk about love? It's played out. Why when you talk about blackness is it always linked to white brothers and sisters and yellow brothers and sisters and red brothers and sisters and brown brothers and sisters?" And I tell them about John 15:11–12. I tell them that I dedicated my life a long time ago to the same Jesus that Dad dedicated his life to, to the same Jesus that Reverend C. L. West dedicated his life, to the same Jesus that my grandfather on my mother's side and my grandmother on my mother's side dedicated their lives to, but, more important, I saw in the concrete, with Dad and Mom, a love that transcends skin pigmentation. I saw it on the ground. Dad taught us that even as you keep track of the injustice, you don't lose track of the humanity. That's what love and being there are all about. Dad made it a priority and preference to be there for us. He made a choice. It meant that he would live a life of interruptions because those who are fundamentally committed to being there are going to be continually interrupted—your own agenda, your own project, are going to be interfered with. Dad was always open to that kind of interruption. He was able to translate a kind of unpredictable interruption into a supportive intervention in somebody else's life. More important, Dad realized that a being-there kind of love meant that you had to have follow up and follow through. One could not just show up—one has to follow up and follow through. This is

the most difficult aspect of it. Love is inseparable from pain and hurt and sadness and sorrow and disappointment, but Dad knew that you had to have follow up and follow through. He knew that you had to struggle in the midst of that pain and that hurt—you had to have just not simply the high moments of love, but the funk of love, the stink and the stench of love. In all of his relationships Dad embodied precisely that struggle with the high moments of love and the low moments of love. He knew that the cross was not just about smiles and that it was not just about celebration—it was about sadness, stench, and funk. That is what the blood was about, not Kool-aid but blood. That's how inseparable scars, bruises, and wounds are from joy, affirmation, and wholeness. If you were serious about love, if you were serious about being there for people you were going to be there in in the midst of any situation, any circumstances, any condition. Dad realized that God being there for us in any situation and circumstance meant that if he was going to be Godlike, he had to be there in any situation for us. I've been alive now for forty years, and on Thursday I'll be forty-one years old, and *not once has my mother or father disappointed me.* They have always been there. That is a blessing, and I do not deserve it. It's a blessing, and I am thankful for it.

So as we bid farewell to Dad, I want you all to know that I am looking forward to a family reunion. I am looking forward to union together on the other side of the Jordan. I am looking forward to seeing Dad in a place where the wicked will cease their troubling and the weary shall be at rest. I tell you when I get there, I'm going down Revelation Boulevard to the corner of John Street, right around the corner from Mark's place. But I want to go to Nahum's place. I don't want to be in Jeremiah's house, it would be too crowded. I don't even want to be down on Peter Street, too many people there—I want some quiet time. I want to sit down with C. L. West, I want to sit down with Nick Bias, and I want to sit down with Aunt Juanita, and I want to sit down with Aunt Tiny. And I want to sit down with Dad! I want to let them know that we did the best that we could to keep alive the best of the legacy of love that they left to us. And when we come together, we will come together in a way in which there will be no more tears, no more heartache, no more heartbreak, no more sadness and sorrow, no more agony and anguish. We shall sit at the feet of the Lord and be blessed, and our souls will look back and wonder how we got over, how we got over.

1988

Evan's Two Moms

Anna Quindlen

1   Evan has two moms. This is no big thing. Evan has always had two moms—in his school file, on his emergency forms, with his friends. "Ooooh, Evan, you're lucky," they sometimes say. "You have two moms." It sounds like a sitcom, but until last week it was emotional truth without legal bulwark. That was when a judge in New York approved the adoption of a six-year-old boy by his biological mother's lesbian partner. Evan. Evan's mom. Evan's other mom. A kid, a psychologist, a pediatrician. A family.

2   The matter of Evan's two moms is one in a series of events over the last year that lead to certain conclusions. A Minnesota appeals court granted guardianship of a woman left a quadriplegic in a car accident to her lesbian lover, the culmination of a seven-year battle in which the injured woman's parents did everything possible to negate the partnership between the two. A lawyer in Georgia had her job offer withdrawn after the state attorney general found out that she and her lesbian lover were planning a marriage ceremony; she's brought suit. The computer company Lotus announced that the gay partners of employees would be eligible for the same benefits as spouses.

3   Add to these public events the private struggles, the couples who go from lawyer to lawyer to approximate legal protections their straight counterparts take for granted, the AIDS survivors who find themselves shut out of their partners' dying days by biological family members and shut out of their apartments by leases with a single name on the dotted line, and one solution is obvious.

4   Gay marriage is a radical notion for straight people and a conservative notion for gay ones. After years of being sledgehammered

by society, some gay men and lesbian women are deeply suspicious of participating in an institution that seems to have "straight world" written all over it.

But the rads of twenty years ago, straight and gay alike, have 5 other things on their minds today. Family is one, and the linchpin of family has commonly been a loving commitment between two adults. When same-sex couples set out to make that commitment, they discover that they are at a disadvantage: No joint tax returns. No health insurance coverage for an uninsured partner. No survivor's benefits from Social Security. None of the automatic rights, privileges, and responsibilities society attaches to a marriage contract. In Madison, Wisconsin, a couple who applied at the Y with their kids for a family membership were turned down because both were women. It's one of those small things that can make you feel small.

Some took marriage statutes that refer to "two persons" at 6 their word and applied for a license. The results were court decisions that quoted the Bible and embraced circular argument: marriage is by definition the union of a man and a woman because that is how we've defined it.

No religion should be forced to marry anyone in violation of 7 its tenets, although ironically it is now only in religious ceremonies that gay people can marry, performed by clergy who find the blessing of two who love each other no sin. But there is no secular reason that we should take a patchwork approach of corporate, governmental, and legal steps to guarantee what can be done simply, economically, conclusively, and inclusively with the words "I do."

"Fran and I chose to get married for the same reasons that 8 any two people do," said the lawyer who was fired in Georgia. "We fell in love; we wanted to spend our lives together." Pretty simple.

Consider the case of *Loving* v. *Virginia,* aptly named. At the 9 time, sixteen states had laws that barred interracial marriage, relying on natural law, that amorphous grab bag for justifying prejudice. Sounding a little like God throwing Adam and Eve out of paradise, the trial judge suspended the one-year sentence of Richard Loving, who was white, and his wife, Mildred, who was black, provided they got out of the State of Virginia.

10   In 1967 the Supreme Court found such laws to be unconstitutional. Only twenty-five years ago and it was a crime for a black woman to marry a white man. Perhaps twenty-five years from now we will find it just as incredible that two people of the same sex were not entitled to legally commit themselves to each other. Love and commitment are rare enough; it seems absurd to thwart them in any guise.

1992

Cinderella: A Story of Sibling Rivalry and Oedipal Conflicts

Bruno Bettelheim

1 By all accounts, "Cinderella" is the best-known fairy tale, and probably also the best-liked. It is quite an old story; when first written down in China during the ninth century A.D., it already had a history. The unrivaled tiny foot size as a mark of extraordinary virtue, distinction, and beauty, and the slipper made of precious material are facets which point to an Eastern, if not necessarily Chinese, origin. The modern hearer does not connect sexual attractiveness and beauty in general with extreme smallness of the foot, as the ancient Chinese did, in accordance with their practice of binding women's feet.

2   "Cinderella," as we know it, is experienced as a story about the agonies and hopes which form the essential content of sibling rivalry; and about the degraded heroine winning out over her siblings who abused her. Long before Perrault gave "Cinderella" the form in which it is now widely known, "having to live among the ashes" was a symbol of being debased in comparison to one's siblings, irrespective of sex. In Germany, for example, there were stories in which such an ash-boy later becomes king, which parallels Cinderella's fate. "Aschenputtel" is the title of the Brothers Grimm's version of the tale. The term originally designated a lowly, dirty kitchenmaid who must tend to the fireplace ashes.

There are many examples in the German language of how 3 being forced to dwell among the ashes was a symbol not just of degradation, but also of sibling rivalry, and of the sibling who finally surpasses the brother or brothers who have debased him. Martin Luther in his *Table Talks* speaks about Cain as the God-forsaken evildoer who is powerful, while pious Abel is forced to be his ash-brother *(Aschebrüdel)*, a mere nothing, subject to Cain; in one of Luther's sermons he says that Esau was forced into the role of Jacob's ash-brother. Cain and Abel, Jacob and Esau are Biblical examples of one brother being suppressed or destroyed by the other.

The fairy tale replaces sibling relations with relations between 4 stepsiblings—perhaps a device to explain and make acceptable an animosity which one wishes would not exist among true siblings. Although sibling rivalry is universal and "natural" in the sense that it is the negative consequence of being a sibling, this same relation also generates equally as much positive feeling between siblings, highlighted in fairy tales such as "Brother and Sister."

No other fairy tale renders so well as the "Cinderella" stories 5 the inner experiences of the young child in the throes of sibling rivalry, when he feels hopelessly outclassed by his brothers and sisters. Cinderella is pushed down and degraded by her stepsisters; her interests are sacrificed to theirs by her (step)mother; she is expected to do the dirtiest work and although she performs it well, she receives no credit for it; only more is demanded of her. This is how the child feels when devastated by the miseries of sibling rivalry. Exaggerated though Cinderella's tribulations and degradations may seem to the adult, the child carried away by sibling rivalry feels, "That's me; that's how they mistreat me, or would want to; that's how little they think of me." And there are moments—often long time periods—when for inner reasons a child feels this way even when his position among his siblings may seem to give him no cause for it.

When a story corresponds to how the child feels deep down— 6 as no realistic narrative is likely to do—it attains an emotional quality of "truth" for the child. The events of "Cinderella" offer him vivid images that give body to his overwhelming but nevertheless often vague and nondescript emotions; so these episodes seem more convincing to him than his life experiences.

7   The term "sibling rivalry" refers to a most complex constellation of feelings and their causes. With extremely rare exceptions, the emotions aroused in the person subject to sibling rivalry are far out of proportion to what his real situation with his sisters and brothers would justify, seen objectively. While all children at times suffer greatly from sibling rivalry, parents seldom sacrifice one of their children to the others, nor do they condone the other children's persecuting one of them. Difficult as objective judgments are for the young child—nearly impossible when his emotions are aroused—even he in his more rational moments "knows" that he is not treated as badly as Cinderella. But the child often feels mistreated, despite all his "knowledge" to the contrary. That is why he believes in the inherent truth of "Cinderella," and then he also comes to believe in her eventual deliverance and victory. From her triumph he gains the exaggerated hopes for his future which he needs to counteract the extreme misery he experiences when ravaged by sibling rivalry.

8   Despite the name "sibling rivalry," this miserable passion has only incidentally to do with a child's actual brothers and sisters. The real source of it is the child's feelings about his parents. When a child's older brother or sister is more competent than he, this arouses only temporary feelings of jealousy. Another child being given special attention becomes an insult only if the child fears that, in contrast, he is thought little of by his parents, or feels rejected by them. It is because of such an anxiety that one or all of a child's sisters or brothers may become a thorn in his flesh. Fearing that in comparison to them he cannot win his parents' love and esteem is what inflames sibling rivalry. This is indicated in stories by the fact that it matters little whether the siblings actually possess greater competence. The Biblical story of Joseph tells that it is jealousy of parental affection lavished on him which accounts for the destructive behavior of his brothers. Unlike Cinderella's, Joseph's parent does not participate in degrading him, and, on the contrary, prefers him to his other children. But Joseph, like Cinderella, is turned into a slave, and, like her, he miraculously escapes and ends by surpassing his siblings.

9   Telling a child who is devastated by sibling rivalry that he will grow up to do as well as his brothers and sisters offers little relief from his present feelings of dejection. Much as he would like to

trust our assurances, most of the time he cannot. A child can see things only with subjective eyes, and comparing himself on this basis to his siblings, he has no confidence that he, on his own, will someday be able to fare as well as they. If he could believe more in himself, he would not feel destroyed by his siblings no matter what they might do to him, since then he could trust that time would bring about a desired reversal of fortune. But since the child cannot, on his own, look forward with confidence to some future day when things will turn out all right for him, he can gain relief only through fantasies of glory—a domination over his siblings—which he hopes will become reality through some fortunate event.

Whatever our position within the family, at certain times in our lives we are beset by sibling rivalry in some form or other. Even an only child feels that other children have some great advantages over him, and this makes him intensely jealous. Further, he may suffer from the anxious thought that if he did have a sibling, his parents would prefer this other child to him. "Cinderella" is a fairy tale which makes nearly as strong an appeal to boys as to girls, since children of both sexes suffer equally from sibling rivalry, and have the same desire to be rescued from their lowly position and surpass those who seem superior to them.   10

On the surface, "Cinderella" is as deceptively simple as the story of "Little Red Riding Hood," with which it shares greatest popularity. "Cinderella" tells about the agonies of sibling rivalry, of wishes coming true, of the humble being elevated, of true merit being recognized even when hidden under rags, of virtue rewarded and evil punished—a straightforward story. But under this overt content is concealed a welter of complex and largely unconscious material, which details of the story allude to just enough to set our unconscious associations going. This makes a contrast between surface simplicity and underlying complexity which arouses deep interest in the story and explains its appeal to the millions over centuries. To begin gaining an understanding of these hidden meanings, we have to penetrate behind the obvious sources of sibling rivalry discussed so far.   11

As mentioned before, if the child could only believe that it is the infirmities of his age which account for his lowly position, he would not have to suffer so wretchedly from sibling rivalry,   12 because he could trust the future to right matters. When he thinks that his degradation is deserved, he feels his plight is utterly hopeless. Djuna Barnes's perceptive statement about fairy tales—that the child knows something about them which he cannot tell (such as that he likes the idea of Little Red Riding Hood and the wolf being in bed together)—could be extended by dividing fairy tales into two groups: one group where the child responds only unconsciously to the inherent truth of the story and thus cannot tell about it; and another large number of tales where the child preconsciously or even consciously knows what the "truth" of the story consists of and thus could tell about it, but does not want to let on that he knows. Some aspects of "Cinderella" fall into the latter category. Many children believe that Cinderella probably deserves her fate at the beginning of the story, as they feel they would, too; but they don't want anyone to know it. Despite this, she is worthy at the end to be exalted, as the child hopes he will be too, irrespective of his earlier shortcomings.

13   Every child believes at some period of his life—and this is not only at rare moments—that because of his secret wishes, if not also his clandestine actions, he deserves to be degraded, banned from the presence of others, relegated to a netherworld of smut. He fears this may be so, irrespective of how fortunate his situation may be in reality. He hates and fears those others—such as his siblings—whom he believes to be entirely free of similar evilness, and he fears that they or his parents will discover what he is really like, and then demean him as Cinderella was by her family. Because he wants others—most of all, his parents—to believe in his innocence, he is delighted that "everybody" believes in Cinderella's. This is one of the great attractions of this fairy tale. Since people give credence to Cinderella's goodness, they will also believe in his, so the child hopes. And "Cinderella" nourishes this hope, which is one reason it is such a delightful story.

14   Another aspect which holds large appeal for the child is the vileness of the stepmother and stepsisters. Whatever the shortcomings of a child may be in his own eyes, these pale into insignificance when compared to the stepsisters' and stepmother's falsehood and nastiness. Further, what these stepsisters do to Cinderella justifies whatever nasty thoughts one may have about one's siblings: they are so vile that anything one may wish would happen to them

is more than justified. Compared to their behavior, Cinderella is indeed innocent. So the child, on hearing her story, feels he need not feel guilty about his angry thoughts.

On a very different level—and reality considerations coexist [15] easily with fantastic exaggerations in the child's mind—as badly as one's parents or siblings seem to treat one, and much as one thinks one suffers because of it, all this is nothing compared to Cinderella's fate. Her story reminds the child at the same time how lucky he is, and how much worse things could be. (Any anxiety about the latter possibility is relieved, as always in fairy tales, by the happy ending.)

The behavior of a five-and-a-half-year-old girl, as reported by [16] her father, may illustrate how easily a child may feel that she is a "Cinderella." This little girl had a younger sister of whom she was very jealous. The girl was very fond of "Cinderella," since the story offered her material with which to act out her feelings, and because without the story's imagery she would have been hard pressed to comprehend and express them. This little girl had used to dress very neatly and liked pretty clothes, but she became unkempt and dirty. One day when she was asked to fetch some salt, she said as she was doing so, "Why do you treat me like Cinderella?"

Almost speechless, her mother asked her, "Why do you think [17] I treat you like Cinderella?"

"Because you make me do all the hardest work in the house!" [18] was the little girl's answer. Having thus drawn her parents into her fantasies, she acted them out more openly, pretending to sweep up all the dirt, etc. She went even further, playing that she prepared her little sister for the ball. But she went the "Cinderella" story one better, based on her unconscious understanding of the contradictory emotions fused into the "Cinderella" role, because at another moment she told her mother and sister, "You shouldn't be jealous of me just because I am the most beautiful in the family."

This shows that behind the surface humility of Cinderella lies [19] the conviction of her superiority to mother and sisters, as if she would think: "You can make me do all the dirty work, and I pretend that I am dirty, but within me I know that you treat me this way because you are jealous of me because I am so much better than you." This conviction is supported by the story's ending, which assures every "Cinderella" that eventually she will be discovered by her prince.

20   Why does the child believe deep within himself that Cinderella deserves her dejected state? This question takes us back to the child's state of mind at the end of the oedipal period. Before he is caught in oedipal entanglements, the child is convinced that he is lovable, and loved, if all is well within his family relationships. Psychoanalysis describes this stage of complete satisfaction with oneself as "primary narcissism." During this period the child feels certain that he is the center of the universe, so there is no reason to be jealous of anybody.

21   The oedipal disappointments which come at the end of this developmental stage cast deep shadows of doubt on the child's sense of his worthiness. He feels that if he were really as deserving of love as he had thought, then his parents would never be critical of him or disappoint him. The only explanation for parental criticism the child can think of is that there must be some serious flaw in him which accounts for what he experiences as rejection. If his desires remain unsatisfied and his parents disappoint him, there must be something wrong with him or his desires, or both. He cannot yet accept that reasons other than those residing within him could have an impact on his fate. In his oedipal jealousy, wanting to get rid of the parent of the same sex had seemed the most natural thing in the world, but now the child realizes that he cannot have his own way, and that maybe this is so because the desire was wrong. He is no longer so sure that he is preferred to his siblings, and he begins to suspect that this may be due to the fact that *they* are free of any bad thoughts or wrongdoing such as his.

22   All this happens as the child is gradually subjected to ever more critical attitudes as he is being socialized. He is asked to behave in ways which run counter to his natural desires, and he resents this. Still he must obey, which makes him very angry. This anger is directed against those who make demands, most likely his parents; and this is another reason to wish to get rid of them, and still another reason to feel guilty about such wishes. This is why the child also feels that he deserves to be chastised for his feelings, a punishment he believes he can escape only if nobody learns what he is thinking when he is angry. The feeling of being

unworthy to be loved by his parents at a time when his desire for their love is very strong leads to the fear of rejection, even when in reality there is none. This rejection fear compounds the anxiety that others are preferred and also maybe preferable—the root of sibling rivalry.

Some of the child's pervasive feelings of worthlessness have 23 their origin in his experiences during and around toilet training and all other aspects of his education to become clean, neat, and orderly. Much has been said about how children are made to feel dirty and bad because they are not as clean as their parents want or require them to be. As clean as a child may learn to be, he knows that he would much prefer to give free rein to his tendency to be messy, disorderly, and dirty.

At the end of the oedipal period, guilt about desires to be 24 dirty and disorderly becomes compounded by oedipal guilt, because of the child's desire to replace the parent of the same sex in the love of the other parent. The wish to be the love, if not also the sexual partner, of the parent of the other sex, which at the beginning of the oedipal development seemed natural and "innocent," at the end of the period is repressed as bad. But while this wish as such is repressed, guilt about it and about sexual feelings in general is not, and this makes the child feel dirty and worthless.

Here again, lack of objective knowledge leads the child to 25 think that he is the only bad one in all these respects—the only child who has such desires. It makes every child identify with Cinderella, who is relegated to sit among the cinders. Since the child has such "dirty" wishes, that is where he also belongs, and where he would end up if his parents knew of his desires. This is why every child needs to believe that even if he were thus degraded, eventually he would be rescued from such degradation and experience the most wonderful exaltation—as Cinderella does.

For the child to deal with his feelings of dejection and worth- 26 lessness aroused during this time, he desperately needs to gain some grasp on what these feelings of guilt and anxiety are all about. Further, he needs assurance on a conscious and an uncon scious level that he will be able to extricate himself from these predicaments. One of the greatest merits of "Cinderella" is that, irrespective of the magic help Cinderella receives, the child understands that essentially it is through her own efforts, and because of the person she is, that Cinderella is able to transcend magnificently her degraded state, despite what appear as insurmountable obstacles. It gives the child confidence that the same will be true for him, because the story relates so well to what has caused both his conscious and his unconscious guilt.

27   Overtly "Cinderella" tells about sibling rivalry in its most extreme form: the jealousy and enmity of the stepsisters, and Cinderella's sufferings because of it. The many other psychological issues touched upon in the story are so covertly alluded to that the child does not become consciously aware of them. In his unconscious, however, the child responds to these significant details which refer to matters and experiences from which he consciously has separated himself, but which nevertheless continue to create vast problems for him.

1975

Chapter

10

Political Science

The Qualities of the Prince

Niccolò Machiavelli

ON THOSE THINGS FOR WHICH MEN, AND PARTICULARLY PRINCES, ARE PRAISED OR BLAMED

Now there remains to be examined what should be the methods 1
and procedures of a prince in dealing with his subjects and
friends. And because I know that many have written about this,
I am afraid that by writing about it again I shall be thought of
as presumptuous, since in discussing this material I depart rad-
ically from the procedures of others. But since my intention is to
write something useful for anyone who understands it, it
seemed more suitable to me to search after the effectual truth of
the matter rather than its imagined one. And many writers have
imagined for themselves republics and principalities that have
never been seen nor known to exist in reality; for there is such
a gap between how one lives and how one ought to live that
anyone who abandons what is done for what ought to be done
learns his ruin rather than his preservation: for a man who
wishes to make a vocation of being good at all times will come
to ruin among so many who are not good. Hence it is necessary
for a prince who wishes to maintain his position to learn how not
to be good, and to use this knowledge or not to use it according
to necessity.

Leaving aside, therefore, the imagined things concerning a 2
prince, and taking into account those that are true, I say that all
men, when they are spoken of, and particularly princes, since
they are placed on a higher level, are judged by some of these

qualities which bring them either blame or praise. And this is
why one is considered generous, another miserly (to use a Tuscan
word, since "avaricious" in our language is still used to mean
one who wishes to acquire by means of theft; we call "miserly"
one who excessively avoids using what he has); one is considered a giver, the other rapacious; one cruel, another merciful; one
treacherous, another faithful; one effeminate and cowardly,
another bold and courageous; one humane, another haughty;
one lascivious, another chaste; one trustworthy, another cunning;
one harsh, another lenient; one serious, another frivolous; one
religious, another unbelieving; and the like. And I know that
everyone will admit that it would be a very praiseworthy thing
to find in a prince, of the qualities mentioned above, those that
are held to be good, but since it is neither possible to have them
nor to observe them all completely, because human nature does
not permit it, a prince must be prudent enough to know how to
escape the bad reputation of those vices that would lose the state
for him, and must protect himself from those that will not lose
it for him, if this is possible; but if he cannot, he need not concern himself unduly if he ignores these less serious vices. And,
moreover, he need not worry about incurring the bad reputation
of those vices without which it would be difficult to hold his
state; since, carefully taking everything into account, one will
discover that something which appears to be a virtue, if pursued, will end in his destruction; while some other thing which
seems to be a vice, if pursued, will result in his safety and his
well-being.

ON GENEROSITY AND MISERLINESS

3 Beginning, therefore, with the first of the above-mentioned qualities,
I say that it would be good to be considered generous; nevertheless, generosity used in such a manner as to give you a reputation for it will harm you; because if it is employed virtuously and
as one should employ it, it will not be recognized and you will
not avoid the reproach of its opposite. And so, if a prince wants
to maintain his reputation for generosity among men, it is necessary for him not to neglect any possible means of lavish display;

in so doing such a prince will always use up all his resources and he will be obliged, eventually, if he wishes to maintain his reputation for generosity, to burden the people with excessive taxes and to do everything possible to raise funds. This will begin to make him hateful to his subjects, and, becoming impoverished, he will not be much esteemed by anyone; so that, as a consequence of his generosity, having offended many and rewarded few, he will feel the effects of any slight unrest and will be ruined at the first sign of danger; recognizing this and wishing to alter his policies, he immediately runs the risk of being reproached as a miser.

A prince, therefore, unable to use this virtue of generosity in   4 a manner which will not harm himself if he is known for it, should, if he is wise, not worry about being called a miser; for with time he will come to be considered more generous once it is evident that, as a result of his parsimony, his income is sufficient, he can defend himself from anyone who makes war against him, and he can undertake enterprises without overburdening his people, so that he comes to be generous with all those from whom he takes nothing, who are countless, and miserly with all those to whom he gives nothing, who are few. In our times we have not seen great deeds accomplished except by those who were considered miserly; all others were done away with. Pope Julius II, although he made use of his reputation for generosity in order to gain the papacy, then decided not to maintain it in order to be able to wage war; the present King of France has waged many wars without imposing extra taxes on his subjects, only because his habitual parsimony has provided for the additional expenditures; the present King of Spain, if he had been considered generous, would not have engaged in nor won so many campaigns.

Therefore, in order not to have to rob his subjects, to be able to   5 defend himself, not to become poor and contemptible, and not to be forced to become rapacious, a prince must consider it of little importance if he incurs the name of miser, for this is one of those vices that permits him to rule. And if someone were to say: Caesar with his generosity came to rule the empire, and many others, because they were generous and known to be so, achieved very high positions; I reply: you are either already a prince or you are on the way to becoming one; in the first instance such generosity is damaging; in the second it is very necessary to be thought generous. And Caesar was one of those who wanted to gain the principality of Rome; but if, after obtaining this, he had lived and had not moderated his expenditures, he would have destroyed that empire. And if someone were to reply: there have existed many princes who have accomplished great deeds with their armies who have been reputed to be generous; I answer you: a prince either spends his own money and that of his subjects or that of others; in the first case he must be economical; in the second he must not restrain any part of his generosity. And for that prince who goes out with his soldiers and lives by looting, sacking, and ransoms, who controls the property of others, such generosity is necessary; otherwise he would not be followed by his troops. And with what does not belong to you or to your subjects you can be a more liberal giver, as were Cyrus, Caesar, and Alexander; for spending the wealth of others does not lessen your reputation but adds to it; only the spending of your own is what harms you. And there is nothing that uses itself up faster than generosity, for as you employ it you lose the means of employing it, and you become either poor or despised or, in order to escape poverty, rapacious and hated. And above all other things a prince must guard himself against being despised and hated; and generosity leads you to both one and the other. So it is wiser to live with the reputation of a miser, which produces reproach without hatred, than to be forced to incur the reputation of rapacity, which produces reproach along with hatred, because you want to be considered as generous.

ON CRUELTY AND MERCY AND WHETHER IT IS BETTER TO BE LOVED THAN TO BE FEARED OR THE CONTRARY

6 Proceeding to the other qualities mentioned above, I say that every prince must desire to be considered merciful and not cruel; nevertheless, he must take care not to misuse this mercy. Cesare Borgia was considered cruel; nonetheless, his cruelty had brought order to Romagna, united it, restored it to peace and obedience. If we examine this carefully, we shall see that he was more merciful than the Florentine people, who, in order to avoid being considered cruel, allowed the destruction of Pistoia. Therefore, a prince

must not worry about the reproach of cruelty when it is a matter of keeping his subjects united and loyal; for with a very few examples of cruelty he will be more compassionate than those who, out of excessive mercy, permit disorders to continue, from which arise murders and plundering; for these usually harm the community at large, while the executions that come from the prince harm one individual in particular. And the new prince, above all other princes, cannot escape the reputation of being called cruel, since new states are full of dangers. And Virgil, through Dido, states: "My difficult condition and the newness of my rule make me act in such a manner, and to set guards over my land on all sides."

Nevertheless, a prince must be cautious in believing and in 7 acting, nor should he be afraid of his own shadow; and he should proceed in such a manner, tempered by prudence and humanity, so that too much trust may not render him imprudent nor too much distrust render him intolerable.

From this arises an argument: whether it is better to be loved 8 than to be feared, or the contrary. I reply that one should like to be both one and the other; but since it is difficult to join them together, it is much safer to be feared than to be loved when one of the two must be lacking. For one can generally say this about men: that they are ungrateful, fickle, simulators and deceivers, avoiders of danger, greedy for gain; and while you work for their good they are completely yours, offering you their blood, their property, their lives, and their sons, as I said earlier, when danger is far away; but when it comes nearer to you they turn away. And that prince who bases his power entirely on their words, finding himself stripped of other preparations, comes to ruin; for friendships that are acquired by a price and not by greatness and nobility of character are purchased but are not owned, and at the proper moment they cannot be spent. And men are less hesitant about harming someone who makes himself loved than one who makes himself feared because love is held together by a chain of obligation which, since men are a sorry lot, is broken on every occasion in which their own self-interest is concerned; but fear is held together by a dread of punishment which will never abandon you.

A prince must nevertheless make himself feared in such a 9 manner that he will avoid hatred, even if he does not acquire love;

since to be feared and not to be hated can very well be combined; and this will always be so when he keeps his hands off the property and the women of his citizens and his subjects. And if he must take someone's life, he should do so when there is proper justification and manifest cause; but, above all, he should avoid the property of others; for men forget more quickly the death of their father than the loss of their patrimony. Moreover, the reasons for seizing their property are never lacking; and he who begins to live by stealing always finds a reason for taking what belongs to others; on the contrary, reasons for taking a life are rarer and disappear sooner.

10   But when the prince is with his armies and has under his command a multitude of troops, then it is absolutely necessary that he not worry about being considered cruel; for without that reputation he will never keep an army united or prepared for any combat. Among the praiseworthy deeds of Hannibal is counted this: that, having a very large army, made up of all kinds of men, which he commanded in foreign lands, there never arose the slightest dissension, neither among themselves nor against their prince, both during his good and his bad fortune. This could not have arisen from anything other than his inhuman cruelty, which, along with his many other abilities, made him always respected and terrifying in the eyes of his soldiers; and without that, to attain the same effect, his other abilities would not have sufficed. And the writers of history, having considered this matter very little, on the one hand admire these deeds of his and on the other condemn the main cause of them.

11   And that it be true that his other abilities would not have been sufficient can be seen from the example of Scipio, a most extraordinary man not only in his time but in all recorded history, whose armies in Spain rebelled against him; this came about from nothing other than his excessive compassion, which gave to his soldiers more liberty than military discipline allowed. For this he was censured in the senate by Fabius Maximus, who called him the corruptor of the Roman militia. The Locrians, having been ruined by one of Scipio's officers, were not avenged by him, nor was the arrogance of that officer corrected, all because of his tolerant nature; so that someone in the senate who tried to apologize for him said that there were many men who knew how not

to err better than they knew how to correct errors. Such a nature would have, in time, damaged Scipio's fame and glory if he had maintained it during the empire; but, living under the control of the senate, this harmful characteristic of his not only concealed itself but brought him fame.

I conclude, therefore, returning to the problem of being feared 12 and loved, that since men love at their own pleasure and fear at the pleasure of the prince, a wise prince should build his foundation upon that which belongs to him, not upon that which belongs to others: he must strive only to avoid hatred, as has been said.

HOW A PRINCE SHOULD KEEP HIS WORD

How praiseworthy it is for a prince to keep his word and to live 13 by integrity and not by deceit everyone knows; nevertheless, one sees from the experience of our times that the princes who have accomplished great deeds are those who have cared little for keeping their promises and who have known how to manipulate the minds of men by shrewdness; and in the end they have surpassed those who laid their foundations upon honesty.

You must, therefore, know that there are two means of fight- 14 ing: one according to the laws, the other with force; the first way is proper to man, the second to beasts; but because the first, in many cases, is not sufficient, it becomes necessary to have recourse to the second. Therefore, a prince must know how to use wisely the natures of the beast and the man. This policy was taught to princes allegorically by the ancient writers, who described how Achilles and many other ancient princes were given to Chiron the Centaur to be raised and taught under his discipline. This can only mean that, having a half-beast and half-man as a teacher, a prince must know how to employ the nature of the one and the other; and the one without the other cannot endure.

Since, then, a prince must know how to make good use of the 15 nature of the beast, he should choose from among the beasts the fox and the lion; for the lion cannot defend itself from traps and the fox cannot protect itself from wolves. It is therefore necessary to be a fox in order to recognize the traps and a lion in order to frighten the wolves. Those who play only the part of the lion do not understand matters. A wise ruler, therefore, cannot and should not keep his word when such an observance of faith would be to his disadvantage and when the reasons which made him promise are removed. And if men were all good, this rule would not be good; but since men are a sorry lot and will not keep their promises to you, you likewise need not keep yours to them. A prince never lacks legitimate reasons to break his promises. Of this one could cite an endless number of modern examples to show how many pacts, how many promises have been made null and void because of the infidelity of princes; and he who has known best how to use the fox has come to a better end. But it is necessary to know how to disguise this nature well and to be a great hypocrite and a liar: and men are so simpleminded and so controlled by their present necessities that one who deceives will always find another who will allow himself to be deceived.

16   I do not wish to remain silent about one of these recent instances. Alexander VI did nothing else, he thought about nothing else, except to deceive men, and he always found the occasion to do this. And there never was a man who had more forcefulness in his oaths, who affirmed a thing with more promises, and who honored his word less; nevertheless, his tricks always succeeded perfectly since he was well acquainted with this aspect of the world.

17   Therefore, it is not necessary for a prince to have all of the above-mentioned qualities, but it is very necessary for him to appear to have them. Furthermore, I shall be so bold as to assert this: that having them and practicing them at all times is harmful; and appearing to have them is useful; for instance, to seem merciful, faithful, humane, forthright, religious, and to be so; but his mind should be disposed in such a way that should it become necessary not to be so, he will be able and know how to change to the contrary. And it is essential to understand this: that a prince, and especially a new prince, cannot observe all those things by which men are considered good, for in order to maintain the state he is often obliged to act against his promise, against charity, against humanity, and against religion. And therefore, it is necessary that he have a mind ready to turn itself according to the way the winds of Fortune and the changeability of affairs require him;

and, as I said above, as long as it is possible, he should not stray from the good, but he should know how to enter into evil when necessity commands.

A prince, therefore, must be very careful never to let anything slip from his lips which is not full of the five qualities mentioned above: he should appear, upon seeing and hearing him, to be all mercy, all faithfulness, all integrity, all kindness, all religion. And there is nothing more necessary than to seem to possess this last quality. And men in general judge more by their eyes than their hands; for everyone can see but few can feel. Everyone sees what you seem to be, few perceive what you are, and those few do not dare to contradict the opinion of the many who have the majesty of the state to defend them; and in the actions of all men, and especially of princes, where there is no impartial arbiter, one must consider the final result.[1] Let a prince therefore act to seize and to maintain the state; his methods will always be judged honorable and will be praised by all; for ordinary people are always deceived by appearances and by the outcome of a thing; and in the world there is nothing but ordinary people; and there is no room for the few, while the many have a place to lean on. A certain prince of the present day, whom I shall refrain from naming, preaches nothing but peace and faith, and to both one and the other he is entirely opposed; and both, if he had put them into practice, would have cost him many times over either his reputation or his state.

ON AVOIDING BEING DESPISED AND HATED

But since, concerning the qualities mentioned above, I have spoken about the most important, I should like to discuss the others briefly in this general manner: that the prince, as was noted above, should think about avoiding those things which make him hated and despised; and when he has avoided this, he will have carried out his duties and will find no danger whatsoever in other vices. As I have said, what makes him hated above all else is being rapacious

---

[1]The Italian original, *si guarda al fine*, has often been mistranslated as "the ends justify the means," something Machiavelli never wrote. [Translators' note]

and a usurper of the property and the women of his subjects; he must refrain from this; and in most cases, so long as you do not deprive them of either their property or their honor, the majority of men live happily; and you have only to deal with the ambition of a few, who can be restrained without difficulty and by many means. What makes him despised is being considered changeable, frivolous, effeminate, cowardly, irresolute; from these qualities a prince must guard himself as if from a reef, and he must strive to make everyone recognize in his actions greatness, spirit, dignity, and strength; and concerning the private affairs of his subjects, he must insist that his decision be irrevocable; and he should maintain himself in such a way that no man could imagine that he can deceive or cheat him.

20   That prince who projects such an opinion of himself is greatly esteemed; and it is difficult to conspire against a man with such a reputation and difficult to attack him, provided that he is understood to be of great merit and revered by his subjects. For a prince must have two fears: one, internal, concerning his subjects; the other, external, concerning foreign powers. From the latter he can defend himself by his good troops and friends; and he will always have good friends if he has good troops; and internal affairs will always be stable when external affairs are stable, provided that they are not already disturbed by a conspiracy; and even if external conditions change, if he is properly organized and lives as I have said and does not lose control of himself, he will always be able to withstand every attack, just as I said that Nabis the Spartan did. But concerning his subjects, when external affairs do not change, he has to fear that they may conspire secretly: the prince secures himself from this by avoiding being hated or despised and by keeping the people satisfied with him; this is a necessary matter, as was treated above at length. And one of the most powerful remedies a prince has against conspiracies is not to be hated by the masses; for a man who plans a conspiracy always believes that he will satisfy the people by killing the prince; but when he thinks he might anger them, he cannot work up the courage to undertake such a deed; for the problems on the side of the conspirators are countless. And experience demonstrates that conspiracies have been many but few have been concluded successfully; for anyone who conspires cannot be alone, nor can he find

companions except from amongst those whom he believes to be dissatisfied; and as soon as you have uncovered your intent to one dissatisfied man, you give him the means to make himself happy, since he can have everything he desires by uncovering the plot; so much is this so that, seeing a sure gain on the one hand and one doubtful and full of danger on the other, if he is to maintain faith with you he has to be either an unusually good friend or a completely determined enemy of the prince. And to treat the matter briefly, I say that on the part of the conspirator there is nothing but fear, jealousy, and the thought of punishment that terrifies him; but on the part of the prince there is the majesty of the principality, the laws, the defenses of friends and the state to protect him; so that, with the good will of the people added to all these things, it is impossible for anyone to be so rash as to plot against him. For, where usually a conspirator has to be afraid before he executes his evil deed, in this case he must be afraid, having the people as an enemy, even after the crime is performed, nor can he hope to find any refuge because of this.

One could cite countless examples on this subject; but I want 21 to satisfy myself with only one which occurred during the time of our fathers. Messer Annibale Bentivoglio, prince of Bologna and grandfather of the present Messer Annibale, was murdered by the Canneschi family, who conspired against him; he left behind no heir except Messer Giovanni, then only a baby. As soon as this murder occurred, the people rose up and killed all the Canneschi. This came about because of the good will that the house of the Bentivoglio enjoyed in those days; this good will was so great that with Annibale dead, and there being no one of that family left in the city who could rule Bologna, the Bolognese people, having heard that in Florence there was one of the Bentivoglio blood who was believed until that time to be the son of a blacksmith, went to Florence to find him, and they gave him the control of that city; it was ruled by him until Messer Giovanni became of age to rule.

I conclude, therefore, that a prince must be little concerned 22 with conspiracies when the people are well disposed toward him; but when the populace is hostile and regards him with hatred, he must fear everything and everyone. And well-organized states and wise princes have, with great diligence, taken care not to anger the nobles and to satisfy the common people and keep them contented; for this is one of the most important concerns that a prince has.

1513

The Declaration of Independence

Thomas Jefferson

In Congress, July 4, 1776
The unanimous Declaration of the thirteen United States of America

1   When in the Course of human events it becomes necessary for one people to dissolve the political bands which have connected them with another, and to assume among the powers of the earth, the separate and equal station to which the Laws of Nature and of Nature's God entitle them, a decent respect to the opinions of mankind requires that they should declare the causes which impel them to the separation.

2   We hold these truths to be self-evident, that all men are created equal, that they are endowed by their Creator with certain unalienable Rights, that among these are Life, Liberty and the pursuit of Happiness. That to secure these rights, Governments are instituted among Men, deriving their just powers from the consent of the governed. That whenever any Form of Government becomes destructive of these ends, it is the Right of the People to alter or to abolish it, and to institute new Government, laying its foundation on such principles and organizing its powers in such form, as to them shall seem most likely to affect their Safety and Happiness. Prudence, indeed, will dictate that Governments long established should not be changed for light and transient causes; and accordingly all experience hath shewn that mankind are more disposed to suffer, while evils are sufferable, than to right themselves by abolishing the forms to which they are accustomed. But when a long train of abuses and usurpations, pursuing invariably the same Object evinces a design to reduce them under absolute

Despotism, it is their right, it is their duty, to throw off such Government, and to provide new Guards for their future security. Such has been the patient sufferance of these Colonies; and such is now the necessity which constrains them to alter their former Systems of Government. The history of the present King of Great Britain is a history of repeated injuries and usurpations, all having in direct object the establishment of an absolute Tyranny over these States. To prove this, let Facts be submitted to a candid world.

He has refused his Assent to Laws, the most wholesome and 3 necessary for the public good.

He has forbidden his Governors to pass laws of immediate 4 and pressing importance, unless suspended in their operation till his Assent should be obtained; and when so suspended, he has utterly neglected to attend to them.

He has refused to pass other Laws for the accommodation of 5 large districts of people, unless those people would relinquish the right of Representation in the Legislature, a right inestimable to them and formidable to tyrants only.

He has called together legislative bodies at places unusual, 6 uncomfortable, and distant from the depository of their Public Records, for the sole purpose of fatiguing them into compliance with his measures.

He has dissolved Representative Houses repeatedly, for oppos- 7 ing with manly firmness his invasions on the rights of the people.

He has refused for a long time, after such dissolutions, to cause 8 others to be elected; whereby the Legislative Powers, incapable of Annihilation, have returned to the People at large for their exercise; the State remaining in the mean time exposed to all the dangers of invasion from without, and convulsions within.

He has endeavored to prevent the population of these States; for 9 that purpose obstructing the Laws for Naturalization of Foreigners; refusing to pass others to encourage their migration hither, and raising the conditions of new Appropriations of Lands.

He has obstructed the Administration of Justice, by refusing 10 his Assent to Laws for Establishing Judiciary Powers.

He has made judges dependent on his Will alone, for the 11 tenure of their offices, and the amount and payment of their salaries.

12   He has erected a multitude of New Offices, and sent hither swarms of Officers to harass our people, and eat out their substance.

13   He has kept among us, in times of peace, Standing Armies without the Consent of our legislatures.

14   He has affected to render the Military independent of and superior to the Civil Power.

15   He has combined with others to subject us to a jurisdiction foreign to our constitution, and unacknowledged by our laws; giving his Assent to the Acts of pretended Legislation: For quartering large bodies of armed troops among us: For protecting them, by a mock Trial, from punishment for any Murders which they should commit on the Inhabitants of these States: For cutting off our Trade with all parts of the world: For imposing Taxes on us without our Consent: For depriving us in many cases, of the benefits of Trial by Jury: For Transporting us beyond Seas to be tried for pretended offenses: For abolishing the free System of English Laws in a neighboring Province, establishing therein an Arbitrary government, and enlarging its Boundaries so as to render it at once an example and fit instrument for introducing the same absolute rule into these Colonies: For taking away our Charters, abolishing our most valuable Laws and altering fundamentally the Forms of our Governments: For suspending our own Legislatures, and declaring themselves invested with power to legislate for us in all cases whatsoever.

16   He has abdicated Government here, by declaring us out of his Protection and waging War against us.

17   He has plundered our seas, ravaged our Coasts, burnt our towns, and destroyed the lives of our people.

18   He is at this time transporting large Armies of foreign Mercenaries to complete the works of death, desolation and tyranny, already begun with circumstances of Cruelty & Perfidy scarcely paralleled in the most barbarous ages, and totally unworthy the Head of a civilized nation.

19   He has constrained our fellow Citizens taken Captive on the high Seas to bear Arms against their Country, to become the executioners of their friends and Brethren, or to fall themselves by their Hands.

He has excited domestic insurrections amongst us, and has 20 endeavored to bring on the inhabitants of our frontiers, the merciless Indian Savages, whose known rule of warfare is an undistinguished destruction of all ages, sexes, and conditions.

In every stage of these Oppressions We have Petitioned for 21 Redress in the most humble terms: Our repeated petitions have been answered only by repeated injury. A Prince, whose character is thus marked by every act which may define a Tyrant, is unfit to be the ruler of a free people.

Nor have we been wanting in attention to our British brethren. 22 We have warned them from time to time of attempts by their legislature to extend an unwarrantable jurisdiction over us. We have reminded them of the circumstances of our emigration and settlement here. We have appealed to their native justice and magnanimity, and we have conjured them by the ties of our common kindred to disavow these usurpations, which would inevitably interrupt our connections and correspondence. They too have been deaf to the voice of justice and of consanguinity. We must, therefore, acquiesce in the necessity, which denounces our Separation, and hold them, as we hold the rest of mankind, Enemies in War, in Peace Friends.

We, THEREFORE, the Representatives of the UNITED 23 STATES OF AMERICA, in General Congress, Assembled, appealing to the Supreme Judge of the world for the rectitude of our intentions, do, in the Name, and by Authority of the good People of these Colonies, solemnly publish and declare, That these United Colonies are, and of Right ought to be FREE AND INDEPENDENT STATES: that they are Absolved from all Allegiance to the British Crown, and that all political connection between them and the State of Great Britain, is and ought to be totally dissolved; and that as Free and Independent States; they have full Power to levy War, conclude Peace, contract Alliances, establish Commerce, and to do all the Acts and Things which Independent States may of right do. And for the support of this Declaration, with a firm reliance on the protection of Divine Providence, we mutually pledge to each other our Lives, our Fortunes, and our sacred Honor.

1776

Declaration of Sentiments

Elizabeth Cady Stanton

1 When, in the course of human events, it becomes necessary for one portion of the family of man to assume among the people of the earth a position different from that which they have hitherto occupied, but one to which the laws of nature and of nature's God entitle them, a decent respect to the opinions of mankind requires that they should declare the causes that impel them to such a course.

2   We hold these truths to be self-evident: that all men and women are created equal; that they are endowed by their Creator with certain inalienable rights; that among these are life, liberty, and the pursuit of happiness; that to secure these rights governments are instituted, deriving their just powers from the consent of the governed. Whenever any form of government becomes destructive of these ends, it is the right of those who suffer from it to refuse allegiance to it, and to insist upon the institution of a new government, laying its foundation on such principles, and organizing its powers in such form, as to them shall seem most likely to effect their safety and happiness. Prudence, indeed, will dictate that governments long established should not be changed for light and transient causes; and accordingly all experience hath shown that mankind are more disposed to suffer, while evils are sufferable, than to right themselves by abolishing the forms to which they were accustomed. But when a long train of abuses and usurpations, pursuing invariably the same object evinces a design to reduce them under absolute despotism, it is their duty to throw off such government, and to provide new guards for their future security. Such has been the patient sufferance of the women under this government, and such is now the necessity which constrains them to demand the equal station to which they are entitled.

3   The history of mankind is a history of repeated injuries and usurpations on the part of man toward woman, having in direct object the establishment of an absolute tyranny over her. To prove this, let facts be submitted to a candid world.

4   He has never permitted her to exercise her inalienable right to the elective franchise.

He has compelled her to submit to laws, in the formation of 5 which she had no voice.

He has withheld from her rights which are given to the most 6 ignorant and degraded men—both natives and foreigners.

Having deprived her of this first right of a citizen, the elec- 7 tive franchise, thereby leaving her without representation in the halls of legislation, he has oppressed her on all sides.

He has made her, if married, in the eye of the law, civilly dead. 8

He has taken from her all right in property, even to the wages 9 she earns.

He has made her, morally, an irresponsible being, as she can 10 commit many crimes with impunity, provided they be done in the presence of her husband. In the covenant of marriage, she is com- pelled to promise obedience to her husband, he becoming, to all intents and purposes, her master—the law giving him power to deprive her of her liberty, and to administer chastisement.

He has so framed the laws of divorce, as to what shall be the 11 proper causes, and in case of separation, to whom the guardian- ship of the children shall be given, as to be wholly regardless of the happiness of women—the law, in all cases, going upon a false supposition of the supremacy of man, and giving all power into his hands.

After depriving her of all rights as a married woman, if single, 12 and the owner of property, he has taxed her to support a govern- ment which recognizes her only when her property can be made profitable to it.

He has monopolized nearly all the profitable employments, 13 and from those she is permitted to follow, she receives but a scanty remuneration. He closes against her all the avenues to wealth and distinction which he considers most honorable to himself. As a teacher of theology, medicine, or law, she is not known.

He has denied her the facilities for obtaining a thorough edu- 14 cation, all colleges being closed against her.

He allows her in Church, as well as State, but a subordinate 15 position, claiming Apostolic authority for her exclusion from the ministry, and, with some exceptions, from any public participa- tion in the affairs of the Church.

He has created a false public sentiment by giving to the world 16 a different code of morals for men and women, by which moral delinquencies which exclude women from society, are not only tolerated, but deemed of little account in man.

17   He has usurped the prerogative of Jehovah himself, claiming it as his right to assign for her a sphere of action, when that belongs to her conscience and to her God.

18   He has endeavored, in every way that he could, to destroy her confidence in her own powers, to lessen her self-respect, and to make her willing to lead a dependent and abject life.

19   Now in view of this entire disfranchisement of one-half the people of this country, their social and religious degradation—in view of the unjust laws above mentioned, and because women do feel themselves aggrieved, oppressed, and fraudulently deprived of their most sacred rights, we insist that they have immediate admission to all the rights and privileges which belong to them as citizens of the United States.

20   In entering upon the great work before us, we anticipate no small amount of misconception, misrepresentation, and ridicule; but we shall use every instrumentality within our power to effect our object. We shall employ agents, circulate tracts, petition the State and National legislatures, and endeavor to enlist the pulpit and the press in our behalf. We hope this Convention will be followed by a series of Conventions embracing every part of the country.

1848

The Meaning of Democracy

E. B. White

1 We received a letter from the Writers' War Board the other day asking for a statement on "The Meaning of Democracy." It presumably is our duty to comply with such a request, and it is certainly our pleasure.

2   Surely the Board knows what democracy is. It is the line that forms on the right. It is the don't in Don't Shove. It is the hole in the stuffed shirt through which the sawdust slowly trickles; it is

the dent in the high hat. Democracy is the recurrent suspicion that more than half of the people are right more than half of the time. It is the feeling of privacy in the voting booths, the feeling of communion in the libraries, the feeling of vitality everywhere. Democracy is the score at the beginning of the ninth. It is an idea which hasn't been disproved yet, a song the words of which have not gone bad. It's the mustard on the hot dog and the cream in the rationed coffee. Democracy is a request from a War Board, in the middle of a morning in the middle of a war, wanting to know what democracy is.

1944

Civil Disobedience

Henry David Thoreau

I heartily accept the motto—"That government is best which gov- 1
erns least;" and I should like to see it acted up to more rapidly and systematically. Carried out, it finally amounts to this, which also I believe,—"That government is best which governs not at all;" and when men are prepared for it, that will be the kind of government which they will have. Government is at best but an expedient; but most governments are usually, and all governments are sometimes, inexpedient. The objections which have been brought against a standing army, and they are many and weighty, and deserve to prevail, may also at last be brought against a standing government. The standing army is only an arm of the standing government. The government itself, which is only the mode which the people have chosen to execute their will, is equally liable to be abused and perverted before the people can act through it. Witness the present Mexican war, the work of comparatively a few individuals using the standing government as their tool; for, in the outset, the people would not have consented to this measure.

This American government,—what is it but a tradition, 2
though a recent one, endeavoring to transmit itself unimpaired to

posterity, but each instant losing some of its integrity? It has not the vitality and force of a single living man; for a single man can bend it to his will. It is a sort of wooden gun to the people themselves; and, if ever they should use it in earnest as a real one against each other, it will surely split. But it is not the less necessary for this; for the people must have some complicated machinery or other, and hear its din, to satisfy that idea of government which they have. Governments show thus how successfully men can be imposed on, even impose on themselves, for their own advantage. It is excellent, we must all allow; yet this government never of itself furthered any enterprise, but by the alacrity with which it got out of its way. *It* does not keep the country free. *It* does not settle the West. *It* does not educate. The character inherent in the American people has done all that has been accomplished; and it would have done somewhat more, if the government had not sometimes got in its way. For government is an expedient by which men would fain succeed in letting one another alone; and, as has been said, when it is most expedient, the governed are most let alone by it. Trade and commerce, if they were not made of India rubber, would never manage to bounce over the obstacles which legislators are continually putting in their way; and, if one were to judge these men wholly by the effects of their actions, and not partly by their intentions, they would deserve to be classed and punished with those mischievous persons who put obstructions on the railroads.

3   But, to speak practically and as a citizen, unlike those who call themselves no-government men, I ask for, not at once no government, but *at once* a better government. Let every man make known what kind of government would command his respect, and that will be one step toward obtaining it.

4   After all, the practical reason why, when the power is once in the hands of the people, a majority are permitted, and for a long period continue, to rule, is not because they are most likely to be in the right, nor because this seems fairest to the minority, but because they are physically the strongest. But a government in which the majority rule in all cases cannot be based on justice, even as far as men understand it. Can there not be a government in which majorities do not virtually decide right and wrong, but conscience?—in which majorities decide only those questions to

which the rule of expediency is applicable? Must the citizen ever for a moment, or in the least degree, resign his conscience to the legislator? Why has every man a conscience, then? I think that we should be men first, and subjects afterward. It is not desirable to cultivate a respect for the law, so much as for the right. The only obligation which I have a right to assume, is to do at any time what I think right. It is truly enough said, that a corporation has no conscience; but a corporation of conscientious men is a corporation *with* a conscience. Law never made men a whit more just; and, by means of their respect for it, even the well-disposed are daily made the agents of injustice. A common and natural result of an undue respect for law is, that you may see a file of soldiers, colonel, captain, corporal, privates, powder-monkeys and all, marching in admirable order over hill and dale to the wars, against their wills, aye, against their common sense and consciences, which makes it very steep marching indeed, and produces a palpitation of the heart. They have no doubt that it is a damnable business in which they are concerned; they are all peaceably inclined. Now, what are they? Men at all? or small moveable forts and magazines, at the service of some unscrupulous man in power? Visit the Navy Yard, and behold a marine, such a man as an American government can make, or such as it can make a man with its black arts, a mere shadow and reminiscence of humanity, a man laid out alive and standing, and already, as one may say, buried under arms with funeral accompaniments, though it may be

> "Not a drum was heard, nor a funeral note,
> As his corse to the ramparts we hurried;
> Not a soldier discharged his farewell shot
> O'er the grave where our hero we buried."

The mass of men serve the State thus, not as men mainly, but 5 as machines, with their bodies. They are the standing army, and the militia, jailers, constables, *posse comitatus*, &c. In most cases there is no free exercise whatever of the judgment or of the moral sense; but they put themselves on a level with wood and earth and stones; and wooden men can perhaps be manufactured that will serve the purpose as well. Such command no more respect than men of straw, or a lump of dirt. They have the same sort of worth only as horses and dogs. Yet such as these even are commonly esteemed good citizens. Others, as most legislators, politicians, lawyers, ministers, and office-holders, serve the State chiefly with their heads; and, as they rarely make any moral distinctions, they are as likely to serve the devil, without intending it, as God. A very few, as heroes, patriots, martyrs, reformers in the great sense, and *men*, serve the State with their consciences also, and so necessarily resist it for the most part; and they are commonly treated by it as enemies. A wise man will only be useful as a man, and will not submit to be "clay," and "stop a hole to keep the wind away," but leave that office to his dust at least:—

> "I am too high-born to be propertied,
> To be a secondary at control,
> Or useful serving-man and instrument
> To any sovereign state throughout the world."

6   He who gives himself entirely to his fellow-men appears to them useless and selfish; but he who gives himself partially to them is pronounced a benefactor and philanthropist.

7   How does it become a man to behave toward this American government to-day? I answer that he cannot without disgrace be associated with it. I cannot for an instant recognize that political organization as *my* government which is the *slave's* government also.

8   All men recognize the right of revolution; that is, the right to refuse allegiance to and to resist the government, when its tyranny or its inefficiency are great and unendurable. But almost all say that such is not the case now. But such was the case, they think, in the Revolution of '75. If one were to tell me that this was a bad government because it taxed certain foreign commodities brought to its ports, it is most probable that I should not make an ado about it, for I can do without them: all machines have their friction; and possibly this does enough good to counterbalance the evil. At any rate, it is a great evil to make a stir about it. But when the friction comes to have its machine, and oppression and robbery are organized, I say, let us not have such a machine any longer. In other words, when a sixth of the population of a nation

which has undertaken to be the refuge of liberty are slaves, and a whole country is unjustly overrun and conquered by a foreign army, and subjected to military law, I think that it is not too soon for honest men to rebel and revolutionize. What makes this duty the more urgent is the fact, that the country so overrun is not our own, but ours is the invading army.

Paley, a common authority with many on moral questions, in ₉ his chapter on the "Duty of Submission to Civil Government," resolves all civil obligation into expediency; and he proceeds to say, "that so long as the interest of the whole society requires it, that is, so long as the established government cannot be resisted or changed without public inconveniency, it is the will of God that the established government be obeyed, and no longer."—"This principle being admitted, the justice of every particular case of resistance is reduced to a computation of the quantity of the danger and grievance on the one side, and of the probability and expense of redressing it on the other." Of this, he says, every man shall judge for himself. But Paley appears never to have contemplated those cases to which the rule of expediency does not apply, in which a people, as well as an individual, must do justice, cost what it may. If I have unjustly wrested a plank from a drowning man, I must restore it to him though I drown myself. This, according to Paley, would be inconvenient. But he that would save his life, in such a case, shall lose it. This people must cease to hold slaves, and to make war on Mexico, though it cost them their existence as a people.

In their practice, nations agree with Paley; but does any one ₁₀ think that Massachusetts does exactly what is right at the present crisis?

> "A drab of state, a cloth-o'-silver slut,
>   To have her train borne up, and her soul trail
>   in the dirt."

Practically speaking, the opponents to a reform in Massachusetts are not a hundred thousand politicians at the South, but a hundred thousand merchants and farmers here, who are more interested in commerce and agriculture than they are in humanity, and are not prepared to do justice to the slave and to Mexico, *cost what it may.* I quarrel not with far-off foes, but with those who, near at home, co-operate with, and do the bidding of those far away, and without whom the latter would be harmless. We are accustomed to say, that the mass of men are unprepared; but improvement is slow, because the few are not materially wiser or better than the many. It is not so important that many should be as good as you, as that there be some absolute goodness somewhere; for that will leaven the whole lump. There are thousands who are *in opinion* opposed to slavery and to the war, who yet in effect do nothing to put an end to them; who, esteeming themselves children of Washington and Franklin, sit down with their hands in their pockets, and say that they know not what to do, and do nothing; who even postpone the question of freedom to the question of free-trade, and quietly read the prices-current along with the latest advices from Mexico, after dinner, and, it may be, fall asleep over them both. What is the price-current of an honest man and patriot to-day? They hesitate, and they regret, and sometimes they petition; but they do nothing in earnest and with effect. They will wait, well disposed, for others to remedy the evil, that they may no longer have it to regret. At most, they give only a cheap vote, and a feeble countenance and God-speed, to the right, as it goes by them. There are nine hundred and ninety-nine patrons of virtue to one virtuous man; but it is easier to deal with the real possessor of a thing than with the temporary guardian of it.

11   All voting is a sort of gaming, like chequers or backgammon, with a slight moral tinge to it, a playing with right and wrong, with moral questions; and betting naturally accompanies it. The character of the voters is not staked. I cast my vote, perchance, as I think right; but I am not vitally concerned that that right should prevail. I am willing to leave it to the majority. Its obligation, therefore, never exceeds that of expediency. Even voting *for the right* is *doing* nothing for it. It is only expressing to men feebly your desire that it should prevail. A wise man will not leave the right to the mercy of chance, nor wish it to prevail through the power of the majority. There is but little virtue in the action of masses of men. When the majority shall at length vote for the abolition of slavery, it will be because they are indifferent to slavery, or because there is but little slavery left to be abolished by their vote. *They* will then be the only slaves. Only *his* vote can hasten the abolition of slavery who asserts his own freedom by his vote.

I hear of a convention to be held at Baltimore, or elsewhere, 12 for the selection of a candidate for the Presidency, made up chiefly of editors, and men who are politicians by profession; but I think, what is it to any independent, intelligent, and respectable man what decision they may come to, shall we not have the advantage of his wisdom and honesty, nevertheless? Can we not count upon some independent votes? Are there not many individuals in the country who do not attend conventions? But no: I find that the respectable man, so called, has immediately drifted from his position, and despairs of his country, when his country has more reason to despair of him. He forthwith adopts one of the candidates thus selected as the only *available* one, thus proving that he is himself *available* for any purposes of the demagogue. His vote is of no more worth than that of any unprincipled foreigner or hireling native, who may have been bought. Oh for a man who is a *man*, and, as my neighbor says, has a bone in his back which you cannot pass your hand through! Our statistics are at fault: the population has been returned too large. How many *men* are there to a square thousand miles in this country? Hardly one. Does not America offer any inducement for men to settle here? The American has dwindled into an Odd Fellow,—one who may be known by the development of his organ of gregariousness, and a manifest lack of intellect and cheerful self-reliance; whose first and chief concern, on coming into the world, is to see that the alms-houses are in good repair; and, before yet he has lawfully donned the virile garb, to collect a fund for the support of the widows and orphans that may be; who, in short, ventures to live only by the aid of the mutual insurance company, which has promised to bury him decently.

It is not a man's duty, as a matter of course, to devote him- 13 self to the eradication of any, even the most enormous wrong; he may still properly have other concerns to engage him; but it is his duty, at least, to wash his hands of it, and, if he gives it no thought longer, not to give it practically his support. If I devote myself to other pursuits and contemplations, I must first see, at least, that I do not pursue them sitting upon another man's shoulders. I must get off him first, that he may pursue his contemplations too. See what gross inconsistency is tolerated. I have heard some of my townsmen say, "I should like to have them order me out to help

put down an insurrection of the slaves, or to march to Mexico,—
see if I would go;" and yet these very men have each, directly by
their allegiance, and so indirectly, at least, by their money, furnished a substitute. The soldier is applauded who refuses to serve
in an unjust war by those who do not refuse to sustain the unjust
government which makes the war; is applauded by those whose
own act and authority he disregards and sets at nought; as if the
State were penitent to that degree that it hired one to scourge it
while it sinned, but not to that degree that it left off sinning for a
moment. Thus, under the name of order and civil government, we
are all made at last to pay homage to and support our own meanness. After the first blush of sin, comes its indifference; and from
immoral it becomes, as it were, *un*moral, and not quite unnecessary
to that life which we have made.

14   The broadest and most prevalent error requires the most dis-
interested virtue to sustain it. The slight reproach to which the
virtue of patriotism is commonly liable, the noble are most likely
to incur. Those who, while they disapprove of the character and
measures of a government, yield to it their allegiance and support,
are undoubtedly its most conscientious supporters, and so frequently the most serious obstacles to reform. Some are petitioning
the State to dissolve the Union, to disregard the requisitions of the
President. Why do they not dissolve it themselves—the union
between themselves and the State,—and refuse to pay their quota
into its treasury? Do not they stand in the same relation to the
State, that the State does to the Union? And have not the same
reasons prevented the State from resisting the Union, which have
prevented them from resisting the State?

15   How can a man be satisfied to entertain an opinion merely,
and enjoy *it?* Is there any enjoyment in it, if his opinion is that he
is aggrieved? If you are cheated out of a single dollar by your
neighbor, you do not rest satisfied with knowing that you are
cheated, or with saying that you are cheated, or even with petitioning him to pay you your due; but you take effectual steps at
once to obtain the full amount, and see that you are never cheated
again. Action from principle,—the perception and the performance of right,—changes things and relations; it is essentially revolutionary, and does not consist wholly with any thing which was.
It not only divides states and churches, it divides families; aye, it

divides the *individual,* separating the diabolical in him from the divine.

Unjust laws exist: shall we be content to obey them, or shall 16 we endeavor to amend them, and obey them until we have succeeded, or shall we transgress them at once? Men generally, under such a government as this, think that they ought to wait until they have persuaded the majority to alter them. They think that, if they should resist, the remedy would be worse than the evil. But it is the fault of the government itself that the remedy is worse than the evil. *It* makes it worse. Why is it not more apt to anticipate and provide for reform? Why does it not cherish its wise minority? Why does it cry and resist before it is hurt? Why does it not encourage its citizens to be on the alert to point out its faults, and *do* better than it would have them? Why does it always crucify Christ, and excommunicate Copernicus and Luther, and pronounce Washington and Franklin rebels?

One would think, that a deliberate and practical denial of its 17 authority was the only offence never contemplated by government; else, why has it not assigned its definite, its suitable and proportionate penalty? If a man who has no property refuses but once to earn nine shillings for the State, he is put in prison for a period unlimited by any law that I know, and determined only by the discretion of those who placed him there; but if he should steal ninety times nine shillings from the State, he is soon permitted to go at large again.

If the injustice is part of the necessary friction of the machine 18 of government, let it go, let it go: perchance it will wear smooth,— certainly the machine will wear out. If the injustice has a spring, or a pulley, or a rope, or a crank, exclusively for itself, then perhaps you may consider whether the remedy will not be worse than the evil; but if it is of such a nature that it requires you to be the agent of injustice to another, then, I say, break the law. Let your life be a counter friction to stop the machine. What I have to do is to see, at any rate, that I do not lend myself to the wrong which I condemn.

As for adopting the ways which the State has provided for 19 remedying the evil, I know not of such ways. They take too much time, and a man's life will be gone. I have other affairs to attend to. I came into this world, not chiefly to make this a good place to live in, but to live in it, be it good or bad. A man has not every thing to do, but something; and because he cannot do *every thing*, it is not necessary that he should do *something* wrong. It is not my business to be petitioning the governor or the legislature any more than it is theirs to petition me; and, if they should not hear my petition, what should I do then? But in this case the State has provided no way: its very Constitution is the evil. This may seem to be harsh and stubborn and unconciliatory; but it is to treat with the utmost kindness and consideration the only spirit that can appreciate or deserves it. So is all change for the better, like birth and death which convulse the body.

20   I do not hesitate to say, that those who call themselves abolitionists should at once effectually withdraw their support, both in person and property, from the government of Massachusetts, and not wait till they constitute a majority of one, before they suffer the right to prevail through them. I think that it is enough if they have God on their side, without waiting for that other one. Moreover, any man more right than his neighbors, constitutes a majority of one already.

21   I meet this American government, or its representative the State government, directly, and face to face, once a year, no more, in the person of its tax-gatherer; this is the only mode in which a man situated as I am necessarily meets it; and it then says distinctly, Recognize me; and the simplest, the most effectual, and, in the present posture of affairs, the indispensablest mode of treating with it on this head, of expressing your little satisfaction with and love for it, is to deny it then. My civil neighbor, the tax-gatherer, is the very man I have to deal with,—for it is, after all, with men and not with parchment that I quarrel,—and he has voluntarily chosen to be an agent of the government. How shall he ever know well what he is and does as an officer of the government, or as a man, until he is obliged to consider whether he shall treat me, his neighbor, for whom he has respect, as a neighbor and well-disposed man, or as a maniac and disturber of the peace, and see if he can get over this obstruction to his neighborliness without a ruder and more impetuous thought or speech corresponding with his action? I know this well, that if one thousand, if one hundred, if ten men whom I could name,—if ten *honest* men only,— aye, if *one* HONEST man, in this State of Massachusetts, *ceasing to*

hold slaves, were actually to withdraw from this copartnership, and be locked up in the county jail therefor, it would be the abolition of slavery in America. For it matters not how small the beginning may seem to be: what is once well done is done for ever. But we love better to talk about it: that we say is our mission. Reform keeps many scores of newspapers in its service, but not one man. If my esteemed neighbor, the State's ambassador, who will devote his days to the settlement of the question of human rights in the Council Chamber, instead of being threatened with the prisons of Carolina, were to sit down the prisoner of Massachusetts, that State which is so anxious to foist the sin of slavery upon her sister,—though at present she can discover only an act of inhospitality to be the ground of a quarrel with her,—the Legislature would not wholly waive the subject the following winter.

Under a government which imprisons any unjustly, the true place for a just man is also a prison. The proper place to-day, the only place which Massachusetts has provided for her freer and less desponding spirits, is in her prisons, to be put out and locked out of the State by her own act, as they have already put themselves out by their principles. It is there that the fugitive slave, and the Mexican prisoner on parole, and the Indian come to plead the wrongs of his race, should find them; on that separate, but more free and honorable ground, where the State places those who are not *with* her but *against* her,—the only house in a slave-state in which a free man can abide with honor. If any think that their influence would be lost there, and their voices no longer afflict the ear of the State, that they would not be as an enemy within its walls, they do not know by how much truth is stronger than error, nor how much more eloquently and effectively he can combat injustice who has experienced a little in his own person. Cast your whole vote, not a strip of paper merely, but your whole influence. A minority is powerless while it conforms to the majority; it is not even a minority then; but it is irresistible when it clogs by its whole weight. If the alternative is to keep all just men in prison, or give up war and slavery, the State will not hesitate which to choose. If a thousand men were not to pay their tax-bills this year, that would not be a violent and bloody measure, as it would be to pay them, and enable the State to commit violence and shed innocent blood. This is, in fact, the definition of a peaceable revolution, if any such is possible. If the tax-gatherer, or any other public officer, asks me, as one has done, "But what shall I do?" my answer is, "If you really wish to do any thing, resign your office." When the subject has refused allegiance, and the officer has resigned his office, then the revolution is accomplished. But even suppose blood should flow. Is there not a sort of blood shed when the conscience is wounded? Through this wound a man's real manhood and immortality flow out, and he bleeds to an everlasting death. I see this blood flowing now.

23   I have contemplated the imprisonment of the offender, rather than the seizure of his goods,—though both will serve the same purpose,—because they who assert the purest right, and consequently are most dangerous to a corrupt State, commonly have not spent much time in accumulating property. To such the State renders comparatively small service, and a slight tax is wont to appear exorbitant, particularly if they are obliged to earn it by special labor with their hands. If there were one who lived wholly without the use of money, the State itself would hesitate to demand it of him. But the rich man—not to make any invidious comparison—is always sold to the institution which makes him rich. Absolutely speaking, the more money, the less virtue; for money comes between a man and his objects, and obtains them for him; and it was certainly no great virtue to obtain it. It puts to rest many questions which he would otherwise be taxed to answer; while the only new question which it puts is the hard but superfluous one, how to spend it. Thus his moral ground is taken from under his feet. The opportunities of living are diminished in proportion as what are called the "means" are increased. The best thing a man can do for his culture when he is rich is to endeavour to carry out those schemes which he entertained when he was poor. Christ answered the Herodians according to their condition. "Show me the tribute-money," said he;—and one took a penny out of his pocket;—If you use money which has the image of Caesar on it, and which he has made current and valuable, that is, *if you are men of the State,* and gladly enjoy the advantages of Caesar's government, then pay him back some of his own when he demands it; "Render therefore to Caesar that which is Caesar's, and to God those things which are God's,"—leaving them no wiser than before as to which was which; for they did not wish to know.

When I converse with the freest of my neighbors, I perceive 24
that, whatever they may say about the magnitude and seriousness
of the question, and their regard for the public tranquility, the long
and the short of the matter is, that they cannot spare the protection of the existing government, and they dread the consequences
of disobedience to it to their property and families. For my own
part, I should not like to think that I ever rely on the protection
of the State. But, if I deny the authority of the State when it presents its tax-bill, it will soon take and waste all my property, and
so harass me and my children without end. This is hard. This
makes it impossible for a man to live honestly and at the same
time comfortably in outward respects. It will not be worth the
while to accumulate property; that would be sure to go again. You
must hire or squat somewhere, and raise but a small crop, and eat
that soon. You must live within yourself, and depend upon yourself, always tucked up and ready for a start, and not have many
affairs. A man may grow rich in Turkey even, if he will be in all
respects a good subject of the Turkish government. Confucius
said,—"If a State is governed by the principles of reason, poverty
and misery are subjects of shame; if a State is not governed by the
principles of reason, riches and honors are the subjects of shame."
No: until I want the protection of Massachusetts to be extended to
me in some distant southern port, where my liberty is endangered,
or until I am bent solely on building up an estate at home by peaceful enterprise, I can afford to refuse allegiance to Massachusetts,
and her right to my property and life. It costs me less in every
sense to incur the penalty of disobedience to the State, than it
would to obey. I should feel as if I were worth less in that case.

Some years ago, the State met me in behalf of the church, and 25
commanded me to pay a certain sum toward the support of a clergyman whose preaching my father attended, but never I myself.
"Pay it," it said, "or be locked up in the jail." I declined to pay.
But, unfortunately, another man saw fit to pay it. I did not see
why the schoolmaster should be taxed to support the priest, and
not the priest the schoolmaster; for I was not the State's schoolmaster, but I supported myself by voluntary subscription. I did
not see why the lyceum should not present its tax-bill, and have
the State to back its demand, as well as the church. However, at
the request of the selectmen, I condescended to make some such

statement as this in writing:—"Know all men by these presents, that I, Henry Thoreau, do not wish to be regarded as a member of any incorporated society which I have not joined." This I gave to the town-clerk; and he has it. The State, having thus learned that I did not wish to be regarded as a member of that church, has never made a like demand on me since; though it said that it must adhere to its original presumption that time. If I had known how to name them, I should then have signed off in detail from all the societies which I never signed on to; but I did not know where to find a complete list.

26   I have paid no poll-tax for six years. I was put into a jail once on this account, for one night; and, as I stood considering the walls of solid stone, two or three feet thick, the door of wood and iron, a foot thick, and the iron grating which strained the light, I could not help being struck with the foolishness of that institution which treated me as if I were mere flesh and blood and bones, to be locked up. I wondered that it should have concluded at length that this was the best use it could put me to, and had never thought to avail itself of my services in some way. I saw that, if there was a wall of stone between me and my towns-men, there was a still more difficult one to climb or break through, before they could get to be as free as I was. I did not for a moment feel confined, and the walls seemed a great waste of stone and mortar. I felt as if I alone of all my townsmen had paid my tax. They plainly did not know how to treat me, but behaved like persons who are underbred. In every threat and in every compliment there was a blunder; for they thought that my chief desire was to stand the other side of that stone wall. I could not but smile to see how industriously they locked the door on my meditations, which followed them out again without let or hinderance, and *they* were really all that was dangerous. As they could not reach me, they had resolved to punish my body; just as boys, if they cannot come at some person against whom they have a spite, will abuse his dog. I saw that the State was half-witted, that it was timid as a lone woman with her silver spoons, and that it did not know its friends from its foes, and I lost all my remaining respect for it, and pitied it.

27   Thus the State never intentionally confronts a man's sense, intellectual or moral, but only his body, his senses. It is not armed

with superior wit or honesty, but with superior physical strength. I was not born to be forced. I will breathe after my own fashion. Let us see who is the strongest. What force has a multitude? They only can force me who obey a higher law than I. They force me to become like themselves. I do not hear of *men* being *forced* to live this way or that by masses of men. What sort of life were that to live? When I meet a government which says to me, "Your money or your life," why should I be in haste to give it my money? It may be in a great strait, and not know what to do: I cannot help that. It must help itself; do as I do. It is not worth the while to snivel about it. I am not responsible for the successful working of the machinery of society. I am not the son of the engineer. I perceive that, when an acorn and a chestnut fall side by side, the one does not remain inert to make way for the other, but both obey their own laws, and spring and grow and flourish as best they can, till one, perchance, overshadows and destroys the other. If a plant cannot live according to its nature, it dies; and so a man.

The night in prison was novel and interesting enough. The pris- 28 oners in their shirtsleeves were enjoying a chat and the evening air in the door-way, when I entered. But the jailer said, "Come, boys, it is time to lock up;" and so they dispersed, and I heard the sound of their steps returning into the hollow apartments. My room-mate was introduced to me by the jailer, as "a first-rate fellow and a clever man." When the door was locked, he showed me where to hang my hat, and how he managed matters there. The rooms were white-washed once a month; and this one, at least, was the whitest, most simply furnished, and probably the neatest apartment in the town. He naturally wanted to know where I came from, and what brought me there; and, when I had told him, I asked him in my turn how he came there, presuming him to be an honest man, of course; and, as the world goes, I believe he was. "Why," said he, "they accuse me of burning a barn; but I never did it." As near as I could discover, he had probably gone to bed in a barn when drunk, and smoked his pipe there; and so a barn was burnt. He had the reputation of being a clever man, had been there some three months waiting for his trial to come on, and would have to wait as much longer; but he was quite domesticated and contented, since he got his board for nothing, and thought that he was well treated.

29   He occupied one window, and I the other; and I saw, that if one stayed there long, his principal business would be to look out the window. I had soon read all the tracts that were left there, and examined where former prisoners had broken out, and where a grate had been sawed off, and heard the history of the various occupants of that room; for I found that even here there was a history and a gossip which never circulated beyond the walls of the jail. Probably this is the only house in the town where verses are composed, which are afterward printed in a circular form, but not published. I was shown quite a long list of verses which were composed by some young men who had been detected in an attempt to escape, who avenged themselves by singing them.

30   I pumped my fellow-prisoner as dry as I could, for fear I should never see him again; but at length he showed me which was my bed, and left me to blow out the lamp.

31   It was like travelling into a far country, such as I had never expected to behold, to lie there for one night. It seemed to me that I never had heard the town-clock strike before, nor the evening sounds of the village; for we slept with the windows open, which were inside the grating. It was to see my native village in the light of the middle ages, and our Concord was turned into a Rhine stream, and visions of knights and castles passed before me. They were the voices of old burghers that I heard in the streets. I was an involuntary spectator and auditor of whatever was done and said in the kitchen of the adjacent village-inn,—a wholly new and rare experience to me. It was a closer view of my native town. I was fairly inside of it. I never had seen its institutions before. This is one of its peculiar institutions; for it is a shire town. I began to comprehend what its inhabitants were about.

32   In the morning, our breakfasts were put through the hole in the door, in small oblong-square tin pans, made to fit, and holding a pint of chocolate, with brown bread, and an iron spoon. When they called for the vessels again, I was green enough to return what bread I had left; but my comrade seized it, and said that I should lay that up for lunch or dinner. Soon after, he was let out to work at haying in a neighboring field, whither he went every day, and would not be back till noon; so he bade me good-day, saying that he doubted if he should see me again.

When I came out of prison,—for some one interfered, and ₃₃ paid the tax,—I did not perceive that great changes had taken place on the common, such as he observed who went in a youth, and emerged a tottering and gray-headed man; and yet a change had to my eyes come over the scene,—the town, and State, and country,—greater than any that mere time could effect. I saw yet more distinctly the State in which I lived. I saw to what extent the people among whom I lived could be trusted as good neighbors and friends; that their friendship was for summer weather only; that they did not greatly purpose to do right; that they were a distinct race from me by their prejudices and superstitions, as the Chinamen and Malays are; that, in their sacrifices to humanity, they ran no risks, not even to their property; that, after all, they were not so noble but they treated the thief as he had treated them, and hoped, by a certain outward observance and a few prayers, and by walking in a particular straight though useless path from time to time, to save their souls. This may be to judge my neighbors harshly; for I believe that most of them are not aware that they have such an institution as the jail in their village.

It was formerly the custom in our village, when a poor debtor ₃₄ came out of jail, for his acquaintances to salute him, looking through their fingers, which were crossed to represent the grating of a jail window, "How do ye do?" My neighbors did not thus salute me, but first looked at me, and then at one another, as if I had returned from a long journey. I was put into jail as I was going to the shoemaker's to get a shoe which was mended. When I was let out the next morning, I proceeded to finish my errand, and, having put on my mended shoe, joined a huckleberry party, who were impatient to put themselves under my conduct; and in half an hour,—for the horse was soon tackled,—was in the midst of a huckleberry field, on one of our highest hills, two miles off; and then the State was nowhere to be seen.

This is the whole history of "My Prisons."   ₃₅

I have never declined paying the highway tax, because I am ₃₆ as desirous of being a good neighbor as I am of being a bad subject; and, as for supporting schools, I am doing my part to educate my fellow-countrymen now. It is for no particular item in the tax-bill that I refuse to pay it. I simply wish to refuse allegiance to the State, to withdraw and stand aloof from it effectually. I do not care to trace the course of my dollar, if I could, till it buys a man, or a musket to shoot one with,—the dollar is innocent,—but I am concerned to trace the effects of my allegiance. In fact, I quietly declare war with the State, after my fashion, though I will still make what use and get what advantage of her I can, as is usual in such cases.

37   If others pay the tax which is demanded of me, from a sympathy with the State, they do but what they have already done in their own case, or rather they abet injustice to a greater extent than the State requires. If they pay the tax from a mistaken interest in the individual taxed, to save his property or prevent his going to jail, it is because they have not considered wisely how far they let their private feelings interfere with the public good.

38   This, then, is my position at present. But one cannot be too much on his guard in such a case, lest his action be biassed by obstinacy, or an undue regard for the opinions of men. Let him see that he does only what belongs to himself and to the hour.

39   I think sometimes, Why, this people mean well; they are only ignorant; they would do better if they knew how: why give your neighbors this pain to treat you as they are not inclined to? But I think, again, this is no reason why I should do as they do, or permit others to suffer much greater pain of a different kind. Again, I sometimes say to myself, When many millions of men, without heat, without ill-will, without personal feeling of any kind, demand of you a few shillings only, without the possibility, such is their constitution, of retracting or altering their present demand, and without the possibility, on your side, of appeal to any other millions, why expose yourself to this overwhelming brute force? You do not resist cold and hunger, the winds and the waves, thus obstinately; you quietly submit to a thousand similar necessities. You do not put your head into the fire. But just in proportion as I regard this as not wholly a brute force, but partly a human force, and consider that I have relations to those millions as to so many millions of men, and not of mere brute or inanimate things, I see that appeal is possible, first and instantaneously, from them to the Maker of them, and, secondly, from them to themselves. But, if I put my head deliberately into the fire, there is no appeal to fire or to the Maker of fire, and I have only myself to blame. If I could

convince myself that I have any right to be satisfied with men as they are, and to treat them accordingly, and not according, in some respects, to my requisitions and expectations of what they and I ought to be, then, like a good Mussulman and fatalist, I should endeavor to be satisfied with things as they are, and say it is the will of God. And, above all, there is this difference between resisting this and a purely brute or natural force, that I can resist this with some effect; but I cannot expect, like Orpheus, to change the nature of the rocks and trees and beasts.

I do not wish to quarrel with any man or nation. I do not wish 40 to split hairs, to make fine distinctions, or set myself up as better than my neighbors. I seek rather, I may say, even an excuse for conforming to the laws of the land. I am but too ready to conform to them. Indeed I have reason to suspect myself on this head; and each year, as the tax-gatherer comes round, I find myself disposed to review the acts and position of the general and state governments, and the spirit of the people, to discover a pretext for conformity. I believe that the State will soon be able to take all my work of this sort out of my hands, and then I shall be no better a patriot than my fellow-countrymen. Seen from a lower point of view, the Constitution, with all its faults, is very good; the law and the courts are very respectable; even this State and this American government are, in many respects, very admirable and rare things, to be thankful for, such as a great many have described them; but seen from a point of view a little higher, they are what I have described them; seen from a higher still, and the highest, who shall say what they are, or that they are worth looking at or thinking of at all?

However, the government does not concern me much, and I 41 shall bestow the fewest possible thoughts on it. It is not many moments that I live under a government, even in this world. If a man is thought-free, fancy-free, imagination-free, that which is *not* never for a long time appearing *to be* to him, unwise rulers or reformers cannot fatally interrupt him.

I know that most men think differently from myself; but those 42 whose lives are by profession devoted to the study of these or kindred subjects, content me as little as any. Statesmen and legislators, standing so completely within the institution, never distinctly and nakedly behold it. They speak of moving society, but have no resting-place without it. They may be men of a certain experience and discrimination, and have no doubt invented ingenious and even useful systems, for which we sincerely thank them; but all their wit and usefulness lie within certain not very wide limits. They are wont to forget that the world is not governed by policy and expediency. Webster never goes behind government, and so cannot speak with authority about it. His words are wisdom to those legislators who contemplate no essential reform in the existing government; but for thinkers, and those who legislate for all time, he never once glances at the subject. I know of those whose serene and wise speculations on this theme would soon reveal the limits of his mind's range and hospitality. Yet, compared with the cheap professions of most reformers, and the still cheaper wisdom and eloquence of politicians in general, his are almost the only sensible and valuable words, and we thank Heaven for him. Comparatively, he is always strong, original, and, above all, practical. Still his quality is not wisdom, but prudence. The lawyer's truth is not Truth, but consistency, or a consistent expediency. Truth is always in harmony with herself, and is not concerned chiefly to reveal the justice that may consist with wrong-doing. He well deserves to be called, as he has been called, the Defender of the Constitution. There are really no blows to be given by him but defensive ones. He is not a leader, but a follower. His leaders are the men of '87. "I have never made an effort," he says, "and never propose to make an effort; I have never countenanced an effort, and never mean to countenance an effort, to disturb the arrangement as originally made, by which the various States came into the Union." Still thinking of the sanction which the Constitution gives to slavery, he says, "Because it was a part of the original compact,—let it stand." Notwithstanding his special acuteness and ability, he is unable to take a fact out of its merely political relations, and behold it as it lies absolutely to be disposed of by the intellect,—what, for instance, it behoves a man to do here in America to-day with regard to slavery, but ventures, or is driven, to make some such desperate answer as the following, while professing to speak absolutely, and as a private man,—from which what new and singular code of social duties might be inferred?— "The manner," says he, "in which the government of those States where slavery exists are to regulate it, is for their own consideration, under their responsibility to their constituents, to the general laws of propriety, humanity, and justice, and to God. Associations formed elsewhere, springing from a feeling of humanity, or any other cause, have nothing whatever to do with it. They have never received any encouragement from me, and they never will."

They who know of no purer sources of truth, who have traced 43 up its stream no higher, stand, and wisely stand, by the Bible and the Constitution, and drink at it there with reverence and humility; but they who behold where it comes trickling into this lake or that pool, gird up their loins once more, and continue their pilgrimage toward its fountain-head.

No man with a genius for legislation has appeared in America. 44 They are rare in the history of the world. There are orators, politicians, and eloquent men, by the thousand; but the speaker has not yet opened his mouth to speak, who is capable of settling the much-vexed questions of the day. We love eloquence for its own sake, and not for any truth which it may utter, or any heroism it may inspire. Our legislators have not yet learned the comparative value of free-trade and of freedom, of union, and of rectitude, to a nation. They have no genius or talent for comparatively humble questions of taxation and finance, commerce and manufactures and agriculture. If we were left solely to the wordy wit of legislators in Congress for our guidance, uncorrected by the seasonable experience and the effectual complaints of the people, America would not long retain her rank among the nations. For eighteen hundred years, though perchance I have no right to say it, the New Testament, has been written; yet where is the legislator who has wisdom and practical talent enough to avail himself of the light which it sheds on the science of legislation?

The authority of government, even such as I am willing to 45 submit to,—for I will cheerfully obey those who know and can do better than I, and in many things even those who neither know nor can do so well,—is still an impure one: to be strictly just, it must have the sanction and consent of the governed. It can have no pure right over my person and property but what I concede to it. The progress from an absolute to a limited monarchy, from a limited monarchy to a democracy, is a progress toward a true respect for the individual. Is a democracy, such as we know it, the last improvement possible in government? Is it not possible to take a step further towards recognizing and organizing the rights of man? There will never be a really free and enlightened State, until the State comes to recognize the individual as a higher and independent power, from which all its own power and authority are derived, and treats him accordingly. I please myself with imagining a State at last which can afford to be just to all men, and to treat the individual with respect as a neighbor; which even would not think it inconsistent with its own repose, if a few were to live aloof from it, not meddling with it, nor embraced by it, who fulfilled all the duties of neighbors and fellow-men. A State which bore this kind of fruit, and suffered it to drop off as fast as it ripened, would prepare the way for a still more perfect and glorious State, which also I have imagined, but not yet anywhere seen.

1848

Letter from Birmingham City Jail

Martin Luther King, Jr.

1 My dear Fellow Clergymen,
While confined here in the Birmingham city jail, I came across your recent statement calling our present activities "unwise and untimely." Seldom, if ever, do I pause to answer criticism of my work and ideas. If I sought to answer all of the criticisms that cross my desk, my secretaries would be engaged in little else in the course of the day, and I would have no time for constructive work. But since I feel that you are men of genuine good will and your criticisms are sincerely set forth, I would like to answer your statement in what I hope will be patient and reasonable terms.

2   I think I should give the reason for my being in Birmingham, since you have been influenced by the argument of "outsiders coming in." I have the honor of serving as president of the Southern Christian Leadership Conference, an organization operating in every southern state, with headquarters in Atlanta, Georgia. We have some eighty-five affiliate organizations all across the South—one being

the Alabama Christian Movement for Human Rights. Whenever necessary and possible we share staff, educational and financial resources with our affiliates. Several months ago our local affiliate here in Birmingham invited us to be on call to engage in a nonviolent direct-action program if such were deemed necessary. We readily consented and when the hour came we lived up to our promises. So I am here, along with several members of my staff, because we were invited here. I am here because I have basic organizational ties here.

Beyond this, I am in Birmingham because injustice is here. Just 3 as the eighth century prophets left their little villages and carried their "thus saith the Lord" far beyond the boundaries of their hometowns; and just as the Apostle Paul left his little village of Tarsus and carried the gospel of Jesus Christ to practically every hamlet and city of the Graeco-Roman world, I too am compelled to carry the gospel of freedom beyond my particular hometown. Like Paul, I must constantly respond to the Macedonian call for aid.

Moreover, I am cognizant of the interrelatedness of all com- 4 munities and states. I cannot sit idly by in Atlanta and not be concerned about what happens in Birmingham. Injustice anywhere is a threat to justice everywhere. We are caught in an inescapable network of mutuality, tied in a single garment of destiny. Whatever affects one directly affects all indirectly. Never again can we afford to live with the narrow, provincial "outside agitator" idea. Anyone who lives in the United States can never be considered an outsider anywhere in this country.

You deplore the demonstrations that are presently taking 5 place in Birmingham. But I am sorry that your statement did not express a similar concern for the conditions that brought the demonstrations into being. I am sure that each of you would want to go beyond the superficial social analyst who looks merely at effects, and does not grapple with underlying causes. I would not hesitate to say that it is unfortunate that so-called demonstrations are taking place in Birmingham at this time, but I would say in more emphatic terms that it is even more unfortunate that the white power structure of this city left the Negro community with no other alternative.

In any nonviolent campaign there are four basic steps: (1) col- 6 lection of the facts to determine whether injustices are alive,

(2) negotiation, (3) self-purification, and (4) direct action. We have gone through all of these steps in Birmingham. There can be no gainsaying of the fact that racial injustice engulfs this community.

7   Birmingham is probably the most thoroughly segregated city in the United States. Its ugly record of police brutality is known in every section of this country. Its unjust treatment of Negroes in the courts is a notorious reality. There have been more unsolved bombings of Negro homes and churches in Birmingham than any city in this nation. These are the hard, brutal and unbelievable facts. On the basis of these conditions Negro leaders sought to negotiate with the city fathers. But the political leaders consistently refused to engage in good faith negotiation.

8   Then came the opportunity last September to talk with some of the leaders of the economic community. In these negotiating sessions certain promises were made by the merchants—such as the promise to remove the humiliating racial signs from the stores. On the basis of these promises Rev. Shuttlesworth and the leaders of the Alabama Christian Movement for Human Rights agreed to call a moratorium on any type of demonstrations. As the weeks and months unfolded we realized that we were the victims of a broken promise. The signs remained. Like so many experiences of the past we were confronted with blasted hopes, and the dark shadow of a deep disappointment settled upon us. So we had no alternative except that of preparing for direct action, whereby we would present our very bodies as a means of laying our case before the conscience of the local and national community. We were not unmindful of the difficulties involved. So we decided to go through a process of self-purification. We started having workshops on nonviolence and repeatedly asked ourselves the questions, "Are you able to accept blows without retaliating?" "Are you able to endure the ordeals of jail?" We decided to set our direct-action program around the Easter season, realizing that with the exception of Christmas, this was the largest shopping period of the year. Knowing that a strong economic withdrawal program would be the by-product of direct action, we felt that this was the best time to bring pressure on the merchants for the needed changes. Then it occurred to us that the March election was ahead and so we speedily decided to postpone action until after election day. When we discovered that

Mr. Connor was in the run-off, we decided again to postpone action so that the demonstrations could not be used to cloud the issues. At this time we agreed to begin our nonviolent witness the day after the run-off.

This reveals that we did not move irresponsibly into direct 9 action. We too wanted to see Mr. Connor defeated; so we went through postponement after postponement to aid in this community need. After this we felt that direct action could be delayed no longer.

You may well ask, "Why direct action? Why sit-ins, marches, 10 etc.? Isn't negotiation a better path?" You are exactly right in your call for negotiation. Indeed, this is the purpose of direct action. Nonviolent direct action seeks to create such a crisis and establish such creative tension that a community that has constantly refused to negotiate is forced to confront the issue. It seeks so to dramatize the issue that it can no longer be ignored. I just referred to the creation of tension as a part of the work of the nonviolent resister. This may sound rather shocking. But I must confess that I am not afraid of the word tension. I have earnestly worked and preached against violent tension, but there is a type of constructive nonviolent tension that is necessary for growth. Just as Socrates felt that it was necessary to create a tension in the mind so that individuals could rise from the bondage of myths and half-truths to the unfettered realm of creative analysis and objective appraisal, we must see the need of having nonviolent gadflies to create the kind of tension in society that will help men to rise from the dark depths of prejudice and racism to the majestic heights of understanding and brotherhood. So the purpose of the direct action is to create a situation so crisis-packed that it will inevitably open the door to negotiation. We, therefore, concur with you in your call for negotiation. Too long has our beloved Southland been bogged down in the tragic attempt to live in monologue rather than dialogue.

One of the basic points in your statement is that our acts are 11 untimely. Some have asked, "Why didn't you give the new administration time to act?" The only answer that I can give to this inquiry is that the new administration must be prodded about as much as the outgoing one before it acts. We will be sadly mistaken if we feel that the election of Mr. Boutwell will bring the millennium to Birmingham. While Mr. Boutwell is much more articulate and gentle than Mr. Connor, they are both segregationists, dedicated to the task of maintaining the status quo. The hope I see in Mr. Boutwell is that he will be reasonable enough to see the futility of massive resistance to desegregation. But he will not see this without pressure from the devotees of civil rights. My friends, I must say to you that we have not made a single gain in civil rights without determined legal and nonviolent pressure. History is the long and tragic story of the fact that privileged groups seldom give up their privileges voluntarily. Individuals may see the moral light and voluntarily give up their unjust posture; but as Reinhold Niebuhr has reminded us, groups are more immoral than individuals.

12   We know through painful experience that freedom is never voluntarily given by the oppressor; it must be demanded by the oppressed. Frankly, I have never yet engaged in a direct action movement that was "well-timed," according to the timetable of those who have not suffered unduly from the disease of segregation. For years now I have heard the words "Wait!" It rings in the ear of every Negro with a piercing familiarity. This "Wait" has almost always meant "Never." It has been a tranquilizing thalidomide, relieving the emotional stress for a moment, only to give birth to an ill-formed infant of frustration. We must come to see with the distinguished jurist of yesterday that "justice too long delayed is justice denied." We have waited for more than 340 years for our constitutional and God-given rights. The nations of Asia and Africa are moving with jetlike speed toward the goal of political independence, and we still creep at horse and buggy pace toward the gaining of a cup of coffee at a lunch counter. I guess it is easy for those who have never felt the stinging darts of segregation to say, "Wait." But when you have seen vicious mobs lynch your mothers and fathers at will and drown your sisters and brothers at whim; when you have seen hate-filled policemen curse, kick, brutalize and even kill your black brothers and sisters with impunity; when you see the vast majority of your twenty million Negro brothers smothering in an airtight cage of poverty in the midst of an affluent society; when you suddenly find your tongue twisted and your speech stammering as you seek to explain to your six-year-old daughter why she can't go to the

public amusement park that has just been advertised on television, and see tears welling up in her little eyes when she is told that Funtown is closed to colored children, and see the depressing clouds of inferiority begin to form in her little mental sky, and see her begin to distort her little personality by unconsciously developing a bitterness toward white people; when you have to concoct an answer for a five-year-old son asking in agonizing pathos: "Daddy, why do white people treat colored people so mean?"; when you take a cross-country drive and find it necessary to sleep night after night in the uncomfortable corners of your automobile because no motel will accept you; when you are humiliated day in and day out by nagging signs reading "white" and "colored"; when your first name becomes "nigger" and your middle name becomes "boy" (however old you are) and your last name becomes "John," and when your wife and mother are never given the respected title "Mrs."; when you are harried by day and haunted by night by the fact that you are a Negro, living constantly at tiptoe stance never quite knowing what to expect next, and plagued with inner fears and outer resentments; when you are forever fighting a degenerating sense of "nobodiness"; then you will understand why we find it difficult to wait. There comes a time when the cup of endurance runs over, and men are no longer willing to be plunged into an abyss of injustice where they experience the blackness of corroding despair. I hope, sirs, you can understand our legitimate and unavoidable impatience.

You express a great deal of anxiety over our willingness to 13 break laws. This is certainly a legitimate concern. Since we so diligently urge people to obey the Supreme Court's decision of 1954 outlawing segregation in the public schools, it is rather strange and paradoxical to find us consciously breaking laws. One may well ask, "How can you advocate breaking some laws and obeying others?" The answer is found in the fact that there are two types of laws: there are *just* and there are *unjust* laws. I would agree with Saint Augustine that "An unjust law is no law at all."

Now what is the difference between the two? How does one 14 determine when a law is just or unjust? A just law is a man-made code that squares with the moral law or the law of God. An unjust law is a code that is out of harmony with the moral law. To put it in the terms of Saint Thomas Aquinas, an unjust law is a human law that is not rooted in eternal and natural law. Any law that uplifts human personality is just. Any law that degrades human personality is unjust. All segregation statutes are unjust because segregation distorts the soul and damages the personality. It gives the segregator a false sense of superiority, and the segregated a false sense of inferiority. To use the words of Martin Buber, the great Jewish philosopher, segregation substitutes an "I–it" relationship for the "I–thou" relationship, and ends up relegating persons to the status of things. So segregation is not only politically, economically and sociologically unsound, but it is morally wrong and sinful. Paul Tillich has said that sin is separation. Isn't segregation an existential expression of man's tragic separation, an expression of his awful estrangement, his terrible sinfulness? So I can urge men to disobey segregation ordinances because they are morally wrong.

15   Let us turn to a more concrete example of just and unjust laws. An unjust law is a code that a majority inflicts on a minority that is not binding on itself. This is difference made legal. On the other hand a just law is a code that a majority compels a minority to follow that it is willing to follow itself. This is sameness made legal.

16   Let me give another explanation. An unjust law is a code inflicted upon a minority which that minority had no part in enacting or creating because they did not have the unhampered right to vote. Who can say that the legislature of Alabama which set up the segregation laws was democratically elected? Throughout the state of Alabama all types of conniving methods are used to prevent Negroes from becoming registered voters and there are some counties without a single Negro registered to vote despite the fact that the Negro constitutes a majority of the population. Can any law set up in such a state be considered democratically structured?

17   These are just a few examples of unjust and just laws. There are some instances when a law is just on its face and unjust in its application. For instance, I was arrested Friday on a charge of parading without a permit. Now there is nothing wrong with an ordinance which requires a permit for a parade, but when the ordinance is used to preserve segregation and to deny citizens the First Amendment privilege of peaceful assembly and peaceful protest, then it becomes unjust.

I hope you can see the distinction I am trying to point out. In 18
no sense do I advocate evading or defying the law as the rabid
segregationist would do. This would lead to anarchy. One who
breaks an unjust law must do it *openly, lovingly* (not hatefully as
the white mothers did in New Orleans when they were seen on
television screaming, "nigger, nigger, nigger"), and with a willingness to accept the penalty. I submit that an individual who
breaks a law that conscience tells him is unjust, and willingly
accepts the penalty by staying in jail to arouse the conscience of
the community over its injustice, is in reality expressing the very
highest respect for law.

Of course, there is nothing new about this kind of civil dis- 19
obedience. It was seen sublimely in the refusal of Shadrach,
Meshach and Abednego to obey the laws of Nebuchadnezzar
because a higher moral law was involved. It was practiced
superbly by the early Christians who were willing to face hungry
lions and the excruciating pain of chopping blocks, before submitting to certain unjust laws of the Roman Empire. To a degree
academic freedom is a reality today because Socrates practiced
civil disobedience.

We can never forget that everything Hitler did in Germany 20
was "legal" and everything the Hungarian freedom fighters did
in Hungary was "illegal." It was "illegal" to aid and comfort a
Jew in Hitler's Germany. But I am sure that if I had lived in
Germany during that time I would have aided and comforted my
Jewish brothers even though it was illegal. If I lived in a Communist country today where certain principles dear to the Christian
faith are suppressed, I believe I would openly advocate disobey-
ing these anti-religious laws. I must make two honest confessions
to you, my Christian and Jewish brothers. First, I must confess
that over the last few years I have been gravely disappointed with
the white moderate. I have almost reached the regrettable conclusion that the Negro's great stumbling block in the stride
toward freedom is not the White Citizen's Counciler or the Ku
Klux Klanner, but the white moderate who is more devoted to
"order" than to justice; who prefers a negative peace which is the
absence of tension to a positive peace which is the presence of
justice; who constantly says, "I agree with you in the goal you
seek, but I can't agree with your methods of direct action"; who

paternalistically feels that he can set the timetable for another man's freedom; who lives by the myth of time and who constantly advised the Negro to wait until a "more convenient season." Shallow understanding from people of good will is more frustrating than absolute misunderstanding from people of ill will. Lukewarm acceptance is much more bewildering than outright rejection.

21   I had hoped that the white moderate would understand that law and order exist for the purpose of establishing justice, and that when they fail to do this they become dangerously structured dams that block the flow of social progress. I had hoped that the white moderate would understand that the present tension of the South is merely a necessary phase of the transition from an obnoxious negative peace, where the Negro passively accepted his unjust plight, to a substance-filled positive peace, where all men will respect the dignity and worth of human personality. Actually, we who engage in nonviolent direct action are not the creators of tension. We merely bring to the surface the hidden tension that is already alive. We bring it out in the open where it can be seen and dealt with. Like a boil that can never be cured as long as it is covered up but must be opened with all its pus-flowing ugliness to the natural medicines of air and light, injustice must likewise be exposed, with all of the tension its exposing creates, to the light of human conscience and the air of national opinion before it can be cured.

22   In your statement you asserted that our actions, even though peaceful, must be condemned because they precipitate violence. But can this assertion be logically made? Isn't this like condemning the robbed man because his possession of money precipitated the evil act of robbery? Isn't this like condemning Socrates because his unswerving commitment to truth and his philosophical delvings precipitated the misguided popular mind to make him drink the hemlock? Isn't this like condemning Jesus because His unique God-consciousness and never-ceasing devotion to His will precipitated the evil act of crucifixion? We must come to see, as federal courts have consistently affirmed, that it is immoral to urge an individual to withdraw his efforts to gain his basic constitutional rights because the quest precipitates violence. Society must protect the robbed and punish the robber.

I had also hoped that the white moderate would reject the 23
myth of time. I received a letter this morning from a white brother
in Texas which said: "All Christians know that the colored people will receive equal rights eventually, but it is possible that you
are in too great of a religious hurry. It has taken Christianity
almost two thousand years to accomplish what it has. The teachings of Christ take time to come to earth." All that is said here
grows out of a tragic misconception of time. It is the strangely
irrational notion that there is something in the very flow of time
that will inevitably cure all ills. Actually time is neutral. It can be
used either destructively or constructively. I am coming to feel
that the people of ill will have used time much more effectively
than the people of good will. We will have to repent in this generation not merely for the vitriolic words and actions of the bad
people, but for the appalling silence of the good people. We must
come to see that human progress never rolls in on wheels of
inevitability. It comes through the tireless efforts and persistent
work of men willing to be co-workers with God, and without this
hard work time itself becomes an ally of the forces of social stag-
nation. We must use time creatively, and forever realize that the
time is always ripe to do right. Now is the time to make real the
promise of democracy, and transform our pending national elegy
into a creative psalm of brotherhood. Now is the time to lift our
national policy from the quicksand of racial injustice to the solid
rock of human dignity.

You spoke of our activity in Birmingham as extreme. At first 24
I was rather disappointed that fellow clergymen would see my
nonviolent efforts as those of the extremist. I started thinking
about the fact that I stand in the middle of two opposing forces
in the Negro community. One is a force of complacency made up
of Negroes who, as a result of long years of oppression, have been
so completely drained of self-respect and a sense of "somebodi-
ness" that they have adjusted to segregation, and, of a few
Negroes in the middle class who, because of a degree of academic
and economic security, and because at points they profit by segregation, have unconsciously become insensitive to the problems
of the masses. The other force is one of bitterness and hatred, and
comes perilously close to advocating violence. It is expressed in
the various black nationalist groups that are springing up over the

nation, the largest and best known being Elijah Muhammad's Muslim movement. This movement is nourished by the contemporary frustration over the continued existence of racial discrimination. It is made up of people who have lost faith in America, who have absolutely repudiated Christianity, and who have concluded that the white man is an incurable "devil." I have tried to stand between these two forces, saying that we need not follow the "do-nothingism" of the complacent or the hatred and despair of the black nationalist. There is the more excellent way of love and nonviolent protest. I'm grateful to God that, through the Negro church, the dimension of nonviolence entered our struggle. If this philosophy had not emerged, I am convinced that by now many streets of the South would be flowing with floods of blood. And I am further convinced that if our white brothers dismiss us as "rabble-rousers" and "outside agitators" those of us who are working through the channels of nonviolent direct action and refuse to support our nonviolent efforts, millions of Negroes, out of frustration and despair, will seek solace and security in black nationalist ideologies, a development that will lead inevitably to a frightening racial nightmare.

25   Oppressed people cannot remain oppressed forever. The urge for freedom will eventually come. This is what happened to the American Negro. Something within has reminded him of his birthright of freedom; something without has reminded him that he can gain it. Consciously and unconsciously, he has been swept in by what the Germans call the *Zeitgeist,* and with his black brothers of Africa, and his brown and yellow brothers of Asia, South America and the Caribbean, he is moving with a sense of cosmic urgency toward the promised land of racial justice. Recognizing this vital urge that has engulfed the Negro community, one should readily understand public demonstrations. The Negro has many pent-up resentments and latent frustrations. He has to get them out. So let him march sometime; let him have his prayer pilgrimages to the city hall; understand why he must have sit-ins and freedom rides. If his repressed emotions do not come out in these nonviolent ways, they will come out in ominous expressions of violence. This is not a threat; it is a fact of history. So I have not said to my people "get rid of your discontent." But I have tried to say that this normal and healthy discontent can be

channelized through the creative outlet of nonviolent direct action. Now this approach is being dismissed as extremist. I must admit that I was initially disappointed in being so categorized.

But as I continued to think about the matter I gradually 26 gained a bit of satisfaction from being considered an extremist. Was not Jesus an extremist in love—"Love your enemies, bless them that curse you, pray for them that despitefully use you." Was not Amos an extremist for justice—"Let justice roll down like waters and righteousness like a mighty stream." Was not Paul an extremist for the gospel of Jesus Christ—"I bear in my body the marks of the Lord Jesus." Was not Martin Luther an extremist— "Here I stand; I can do none other so help me God." Was not John Bunyan an extremist—"I will stay in jail to the end of my days before I make a butchery of my conscience." Was not Abraham Lincoln an extremist—"This nation cannot survive half slave and half free." Was not Thomas Jefferson an extremist—"We hold these truths to be self-evident, that all men are created equal." So the question is not whether we will be extremist but what kind of extremist will we be. Will we be extremists for hate or will we be extremists for love? Will we be extremists for the preservation of injustice—or will we be extremists for the cause of justice? In that dramatic scene on Calvary's hill, three men were crucified. We must not forget that all three were crucified for the same crime— the crime of extremism. Two were extremists for immorality, and thusly fell below their environment. The other, Jesus Christ, was an extremist for love, truth and goodness, and thereby rose above his environment. So, after all, maybe the South, the nation and the world are in dire need of creative extremists.

I had hoped that the white moderate would see this. Maybe 27 I was too optimistic. Maybe I expected too much. I guess I should have realized that few members of a race that has oppressed another race can understand or appreciate the deep groans and passionate yearnings of those that have been oppressed and still fewer have the vision to see that injustice must be rooted out by strong, persistent and determined action. I am thankful, however, that some of our white brothers have grasped the meaning of this social revolution and committed themselves to it. They are still all too small in quantity, but they are big in quality. Some like Ralph McGill, Lillian Smith, Harry Golden and James Dabbs have written about our struggle in eloquent, prophetic and understanding terms. Others have marched with us down nameless streets of the South. They have languished in filthy roach-infested jails, suffering the abuse and brutality of angry policemen who see them as "dirty nigger-lovers." They, unlike so many of their moderate brothers and sisters, have recognized the urgency of the moment and sensed the need for powerful "action" antidotes to combat the disease of segregation.

28   Let me rush on to mention my other disappointment. I have been so greatly disappointed with the white church and its leadership. Of course, there are some notable exceptions. I am not unmindful of the fact that each of you has taken some significant stands on this issue. I commend you, Rev. Stallings, for your Christian stance on this past Sunday, in welcoming Negroes to your worship service on a non-segregated basis. I commend the Catholic leaders of this state for integrating Springhill College several years ago.

29   But despite these notable exceptions I must honestly reiterate that I have been disappointed with the church. I do not say that as one of the negative critics who can always find something wrong with the church. I say it as a minister of the gospel, who loves the church; who was nurtured in its bosom; who has been sustained by its spiritual blessings and who will remain true to it as long as the cord of life shall lengthen.

30   I had the strange feeling when I was suddenly catapulted into the leadership of the bus protest in Montgomery several years ago that we would have the support of the white church. I felt that the white ministers, priests and rabbis of the South would be some of our strongest allies. Instead, some have been outright opponents, refusing to understand the freedom movement and misrepresenting its leaders; all too many others have been more cautious than courageous and have remained silent behind the anesthetizing security of the stained-glass windows.

31   In spite of my shattered dreams of the past, I came to Birmingham with the hope that the white religious leadership of this community would see the justice of our cause, and with, deep moral concern, serve as the channel through which our just grievances would get to the power structure. I had hoped that each of you would understand. But again I have been disappointed. I have

heard numerous religious leaders of the South call upon their worshippers to comply with a desegregation decision because it is the *law*, but I have longed to hear white ministers say, "Follow this decree because integration is morally *right* and the Negro is your brother." In the midst of blatant injustices inflicted upon the Negro, I have watched white churches stand on the sideline and merely mouth pious irrelevancies and sanctimonious trivialities. In the midst of a mighty struggle to rid our nation of racial and economic injustice, I have heard so many ministers say, "Those are social issues with which the gospel has no real concern," and I have watched so many churches commit themselves to a completely otherworldly religion which made a strange distinction between body and soul, the sacred and the secular.

So here we are moving toward the exit of the twentieth cen- 32 tury with a religious community largely adjusted to the status quo, standing as a taillight behind other community agencies rather than a headlight leading men to higher levels of justice.

I have traveled the length and breadth of Alabama, Missis- 33 sippi and all the other southern states. On sweltering summer days and crisp autumn mornings I have looked at her beautiful churches with their lofty spires pointing heavenward. I have beheld the impressive outlay of her massive religious education buildings. Over and over again I have found myself asking: "What kind of people worship here? Who is their God? Where were their voices when the lips of Governor Barnett dripped with words of interposition and nullification? Where were they when Governor Wallace gave the clarion call for defiance and hatred? Where were their voices of support when tired, bruised and weary Negro men and women decided to rise from the dark dungeons of complacency to the bright hills of creative protest?"

Yes, these questions are still in my mind. In deep disappoint- 34 ment, I have wept over the laxity of the church. But be assured that my tears have been tears of love. There can be no deep disappointment where there is not deep love. Yes, I love the church; I love her sacred walls. How could I do otherwise? I am in the rather unique position of being the son, the grandson and the great-grandson of preachers. Yes, I see the church as the body of Christ. But, oh! How we have blemished and scarred that body through social neglect and fear of being nonconformists.

35   There was a time when the church was very powerful. It was
during that period when the early Christians rejoiced when they
were deemed worthy to suffer for what they believed. In those
days the church was not merely a thermometer that recorded the
ideas and principles of popular opinion; it was a thermostat that
transformed the mores of society. Wherever the early Christians
entered a town the power structure got disturbed and immediately sought to convict them for being "disturbers of the peace"
and "outside agitators." But they went on with the conviction that
they were "a colony of heaven," and had to obey God rather than
man. They were small in number but big in commitment. They
were too God-intoxicated to be "astronomically intimidated."
They brought an end to such ancient evils as infanticide and glad-
iatorial contest.

36   Things are different now. The contemporary church is often a
weak, ineffectual voice with an uncertain sound. It is so often the
arch-supporter of the status quo. Far from being disturbed by the
presence of the church, the power structure of the average community is consoled by the church's silent and often vocal sanction
of things as they are.

37   But the judgment of God is upon the church as never before.
If the church of today does not recapture the sacrificial spirit of
the early church, it will lose its authentic ring, forfeit the loyalty
of millions, and be dismissed as an irrelevant social club with no
meaning for the twentieth century. I am meeting young people
every day whose disappointment with the church has risen to
outright disgust.

38   Maybe again, I have been too optimistic. Is organized religion
too inextricably bound to the status quo to save our nation and
the world? Maybe I must turn my faith to the inner spiritual
church, the church within the church, as the true *ecclesia* and the
hope of the world. But again I am thankful to God that some
noble souls from the ranks of organized religion have broken
loose from the paralyzing chains of conformity and joined us as
active partners in the struggle for freedom. They have left their
secure congregations and walked the streets of Albany, Georgia,
with us. They have gone through the highways of the South on
tortuous rides for freedom. Yes, they have gone to jail with us.
Some have been kicked out of their churches, and lost support of

their bishops and fellow ministers. But they have gone with the faith that right defeated is stronger than evil triumphant. These men have been the leaven in the lump of the race. Their witness has been the spiritual salt that has preserved the true meaning of the gospel in these troubled times. They have carved a tunnel of hope through the dark mountain of disappointment.

I hope the church as a whole will meet the challenge of this 39 decisive hour. But even if the church does not come to the aid of justice, I have no despair about the future. I have no fear about the outcome of our struggle in Birmingham, even if our motives are presently misunderstood. We will reach the goal of freedom in Birmingham and all over the nation, because the goal of America is freedom. Abused and scorned though we may be, our destiny is tied up with the destiny of America. Before the Pilgrims landed at Plymouth we were here. Before the pen of Jefferson etched across the pages of history the majestic words of the Declaration of Independence, we were here. For more than two centuries our fore-parents labored in this country without wages; they made cotton king; and they built the homes of their masters in the midst of brutal injustice and shameful humiliation—and yet out of a bottomless vitality they continued to thrive and develop. If the inexpressible cruelties of slavery could not stop us, the opposition we now face will surely fail. We will win our freedom because the sacred heritage of our nation and the eternal will of God are embodied in our echoing demands.

I must close now. But before closing I am impelled to mention 40 one other point in your statement that troubled me profoundly. You warmly commended the Birmingham police force for keeping "order" and "preventing violence." I don't believe you would have so warmly commended the police force if you had seen its angry violent dogs literally biting six unarmed, nonviolent Negroes. I don't believe you would so quickly commend the policemen if you would observe their ugly and inhuman treatment of Negroes here in the city jail; if you would watch them push and curse old Negro women and young Negro girls; if you would see them slap and kick old Negro men and young boys; if you will observe them, as they did on two occasions, refuse to give us food because we wanted to sing our grace together. I'm sorry that I can't join you in your praise for the police department.

41   It is true that they have been rather disciplined in their public handling of the demonstrators. In this sense they have been rather publicly "nonviolent." But for what purpose? To preserve the evil system of segregation. Over the last few years I have consistently preached that nonviolence demands that the means we use must be as pure as the ends we seek. So I have tried to make it clear that it is wrong to use immoral means to attain moral ends. But now I must affirm that it is just as wrong, or even more so, to use moral means to preserve immoral ends. Maybe Mr. Connor and his policemen have been rather publicly nonviolent, as Chief Pritchett was in Albany, Georgia, but they have used the moral means of nonviolence to maintain the immoral end of flagrant racial injustice. T. S. Eliot has said that there is no greater treason than to do the right deed for the wrong reason.

42   I wish you had commended the Negro sit-inners and demonstrators of Birmingham for their sublime courage, their willingness to suffer and their amazing discipline in the midst of the most inhuman provocation. One day the South will recognize its real heroes. They will be the James Merediths, courageously and with a majestic sense of purpose facing jeering and hostile mobs and the agonizing loneliness that characterizes the life of the pioneer. They will be old, oppressed, battered Negro women, symbolized in a seventy-two-year-old woman of Montgomery, Alabama, who rose up with a sense of dignity and with her people decided not to ride the segregated buses, and responded to one who inquired about her tiredness with ungrammatical profundity: "My feet is tired, but my soul is rested." They will be the young high school and college students, young ministers of the gospel and a host of their elders courageously and nonviolently sitting-in at lunch counters and willingly going to jail for conscience's sake. One day the South will know that when these disinherited children of God sat down at lunch counters they were in reality standing up for the best in the American dream and the most sacred values in our Judeo-Christian heritage, and thusly, carrying our whole nation back to those great wells of democracy which were dug deep by the Founding Fathers in the formulation of the Constitution and the Declaration of Independence.

43   Never before have I written a letter this long (or should I say a book?). I'm afraid that it is much too long to take your precious

time. I can assure you that it would have been much shorter if I had been writing from a comfortable desk, but what else is there to do when you are alone for days in the dull monotony of a narrow jail cell other than write long letters, think strange thoughts, and pray long prayers?

If I have said anything in this letter that is an overstatement 44 of the truth and is indicative of an unreasonable impatience, I beg you to forgive me. If I have said anything in this letter that is an understatement of the truth and is indicative of my having a patience that makes me patient with anything less than brotherhood, I beg God to forgive me.

I hope this letter finds you strong in the faith. I also hope that 45 circumstances will soon make it possible for me to meet each of you, not as an integrationist or a civil rights leader, but as a fellow clergyman and a Christian brother. Let us all hope that the dark clouds of racial prejudice will soon pass away and the deep fog of misunderstanding will be lifted from our fear-drenched communities and in some not too distant tomorrow the radiant stars of love and brotherhood will shine over our great nation with all of their scintillating beauty.

Yours for the cause of Peace and Brotherhood,

Martin Luther King, Jr.

1963

Economics

A Modest Proposal

Jonathan Swift

1 It is a melancholy object to those who walk through this great town[1] or travel in the country, when they see the streets, the roads, and cabin doors, crowded with beggars of the female sex, followed by three, four, or six children, all in rags and importuning every passenger for an alms. These mothers, instead of being able to work for their honest livelihood, are forced to employ all their time in strolling to beg sustenance for their helpless infants, who, as they grow up, either turn thieves for want of work, or leave their dear native country to fight for the Pretender in Spain,[2] or sell themselves to the Barbadoes.

2   I think it is agreed by all parties that this prodigious number of children in the arms, or on the backs, or at the heels of their mothers, and frequently of their fathers, is in the present deplorable state of the kingdom a very great additional grievance; and therefore whoever could find out a fair, cheap, and easy method of making these children sound, useful members of the commonwealth would deserve so well of the public as to have his statue set up for a preserver of the nation.

3   But my intention is very far from being confined to provide only for the children of professed beggars; it is of a much greater extent, and shall take in the whole number of infants at a certain age who are born of parents in effect as little able to support them as those who demand our charity in the streets.

[1]Dublin, Ireland.
[2]The son James II, whose Catholic sympathies cost him the English throne.

As to my own part, having turned my thoughts for many years 4 upon this important subject, and maturely weighed the several schemes of other projectors, I have always found them grossly mistaken in their computation. It is true, a child just dropped from its dam may be supported by her milk for a solar year, with little other nourishment; at most not above the value of two shillings, which the mother may certainly get, or the value in scraps, by her lawful occupation of begging; and it is exactly at one year old that I propose to provide for them in such a manner as instead of being a charge upon their parents or the parish, or wanting food and raiment for the rest of their lives, they shall on the contrary contribute to the feeding, and partly to the clothing, of many thousands.

There is likewise another great advantage in my scheme, that 5 it will prevent those involuntary abortions, and that horrid practice of women murdering their bastard children, alas, too frequent among us, sacrificing the poor innocent babes, I doubt, more to avoid the expense than the shame, which would move tears and pity in the most savage and inhuman breast.

The number of souls in this kingdom being usually reckoned 6 one million and a half, of these I calculate there may be about two hundred thousand couples whose wives are breeders, from which number I subtract thirty thousand couples who are able to maintain their own children, although I apprehend there cannot be so many under the present distress of the kingdom; but this being granted, there will remain an hundred and seventy thousand breeders. I again subtract fifty thousand for those women who miscarry, or whose children die by accident or disease within the year. There only remain an hundred and twenty thousand children of poor parents annually born. The question therefore is, how this number shall be reared and provided for, which, as I have already said, under the present situation of affairs, is utterly impossible by all the methods hitherto proposed. For we can neither employ them in handicraft nor agriculture; we neither build houses (I mean in the country) nor cultivate land. They can very seldom pick up livelihood by stealing till they arrive at six years old, except where they are of towardly parts;[3] although I confess

---

[3]Mature for their age.

they learn the rudiments much earlier, during which time they can however be looked upon only as probationers, as I have been informed by a principal gentleman in the county of Cavan, who protested to me that he never knew above one or two instances under the age of six, even in a part of the kingdom so renowned for the quickest proficiency in that art.

7   I am assured by our merchants that a boy or a girl before twelve years old is no salable commodity; and even when they come to this age, they will not yield above three pounds, or three pounds and half a crown at most on the Exchange; which cannot turn to account either to the parents or the kingdom, the charge of nutriment and rags having been at least four times that value.

8   I shall now therefore humbly propose my own thoughts, which I hope will not be liable to the least objection.

9   I have been assured by a very knowing American of my acquaintance in London, that a young healthy child well nursed is at a year old a most delicious, nourishing, and wholesome food, whether stewed, roasted, baked, or boiled; and I make no doubt that it will equally serve in fricasee or a ragout.

10   I do therefore humbly offer it to public consideration that of the hundred and twenty thousand children, already computed, twenty thousand may be reserved for breed, whereof only one fourth part to be males, which is more than we allow to sheep, black cattle, or swine; and my reason is that these children are seldom the fruits of marriage, a circumstance not much regarded by our savages, therefore one male will be sufficient to serve four females. That the remaining hundred thousand may at a year old be offered in sale to the persons of quality and fortune through the kingdom, always advising the mother to let them suck plentifully in the last month, so as to render them plump and fat for a good table. A child will make two dishes at an entertainment for friends; and when the family dines alone, the fore or hind quarter will make a reasonable dish, and seasoned with a little pepper or salt will be very good boiled on the fourth day, especially in winter.

11   I have reckoned upon a medium that a child just born will weigh twelve pounds, and in a solar year if tolerably nursed increaseth to twenty-eight pounds.

I grant this food will be somewhat dear, and therefore very 12 proper for landlords, who, as they have already devoured most of the parents, seem to have the best title to the children.

Infant's flesh will be in season throughout the year, but more 13 plentiful in March, and a little before and after. For we are told by a grave author, an eminent French physician,[4] that fish being a prolific diet, there are more children born in Roman Catholic countries about nine months after Lent, than at any other season; therefore, reckoning a year after Lent, the markets will be more glutted than usual, because the number of popish infants is at least three to one in this kingdom; and therefore it will have one other collateral advantage, by lessening the number of Papists among us.

I have already computed the charge of nursing a beggar's 14 child (in which list I reckon all cottagers, laborers, and four fifths of the farmers) to be about two shillings per annum, rags included; and I believe no gentleman would repine to give ten shillings for the carcass of a good fat child, which, as I have said, will make four dishes of excellent nutritive meat, when he hath only some particular friend or his own family to dine with him. Thus the squire will learn to be a good landlord, and grow popular among the tenants; the mother will have eight shillings net profit, and be fit for work till she produces another child.

Those who are more thrifty (as I must confess the times require) 15 may flay the carcass; the skin of which artificially[5] dressed will make admirable gloves for ladies, and summer boots for fine gentlemen.

As to our city of Dublin, shambles[6] may be appointed for this 16 purpose in the most convenient parts of it, and butchers we may be assured will not be wanting; although I rather recommend buying the children alive, and dressing them hot from the knife as we do roasting pigs.

A very worthy person, a true lover of his country, and whose 17 virtues I highly esteem, was lately pleased in discoursing on this matter to offer a refinement upon my scheme. He said that many

[4]François Rabelais, doctor, monk, and scholar, who was also one of the greatest comic writers of the sixteenth century.
[5]Expertly.
[6]Places where animals are butchered.

gentlemen of his kingdom, having of late destroyed their deer, he conceived that the want of venison might be well supplied by the bodies of young lads and maidens, not exceeding fourteen years of age nor under twelve, so great a number of both sexes in every county being now ready to starve for want of work and service; and these to be disposed of by their parents, if alive, or otherwise by their nearest relations. But with due deference to so excellent a friend and so deserving a patriot, I cannot be altogether in his sentiments; for as to the males, my American acquaintance assured me from frequent experience that their flesh was generally tough and lean, like that of our schoolboys, by continual exercise, and their taste disagreeable; and to fatten them would not answer the charge. Then as to the females, it would, I think with humble submission, be a loss to the public, because they soon would become breeders themselves; and besides, it is not improbable that some scrupulous people might be apt to censure such a practice (although indeed very unjustly) as a little bordering upon cruelty; which, I confess, hath always been with me the strongest objection against any project, how well soever intended.

18   But in order to justify my friend, he confessed that this expedient was put into his head by the famous Psalmanazar,[7] a native of the island Formosa, who came from thence to London above twenty years ago, and in conversation told my friend that in his country when any young person happened to be put to death, the executioner sold the carcass to the persons of quality as a prime dainty; and that in his time the body of a plump girl of fifteen, who was crucified for an attempt to poison the emperor, was sold to his Imperial Majesty's prime minister of state, and other great mandarins of the court, in joints from the gibbet, at four hundred crowns. Neither indeed can I deny that if the same use were made of several plump young girls in this town, who without one single groat to their fortunes cannot stir abroad without a chair,[8] and appear at the playhouse and assemblies in foreign fineries which they never will pay for, the kingdom would not be the worse.

---

[7]A charlatan who fraudulently claimed to have come from Formosa.
[8]A conveyance carried by servants.

Some persons of a desponding spirit are in great concern 19
about that vast number of poor people who are aged, diseased,
or maimed, and I have been desired to employ my thoughts
what course may be taken to ease the nation of so grievous an
encumbrance. But I am not in the least pain upon that matter,
because it is very well known that they are every day dying
and rotting by cold and famine, and filth and vermin, as fast
as can be reasonably expected. And as to the younger laborers,
they are now in almost as hopeful a condition. They cannot get
work, and consequently pine away for want of nourishment to
a degree that if any time they are accidentally hired to common
labor, they have not strength to perform it; and thus the country and themselves are happily delivered from the evils to
come.

I have too long digressed, and therefore shall return to my 20
subject. I think the advantages by the proposal which I have made
are obvious and many, as well as of the highest importance.

For first, as I have already observed, it would greatly lessen 21
the number of Papists, with whom we are yearly overrun, being
the principal breeders of the nation as well as our most dangerous enemies; and who stay at home on purpose to deliver the
kingdom to the Pretender, hoping to take their advantage by the
absence of so many good Protestants, who have chosen rather to
leave their country than to stay at home and pay tithes against
their conscience to an Episcopal curate.

Secondly, the poorer tenants will have something valuable of 22
their own, which by law may be made liable to distress,[9] and help
to pay their landlord's rent, their corn and cattle being already
seized and money a thing unknown.

Thirdly, whereas the maintenance of an hundred thousand 23
children, from two years old and upwards, cannot be computed
at less than ten shillings a piece per annum, the nation's stock will
be thereby increased fifty thousand pounds per annum, besides
the profit of a new dish introduced to the tables of all gentlemen
of fortune in the kingdom who have any refinement in taste. And

---

[9]Confiscated as payment for debt.

the money will circulate among ourselves, the goods being entirely of our own growth and manufacture.

24   Fourthly, the constant breeders, besides the gain of eight shillings sterling per annum by the sale of their children, will be rid of the charge for maintaining them after the first year.

25   Fifthly, this food would likewise bring great custom to taverns, where the vintners will certainly be so prudent as to procure the best receipts for dressing it to perfection, and consequently have their houses frequented by all the fine gentlemen, who justly value themselves upon their knowledge in good eating; and a skillful cook, who understands how to oblige his guests, will contrive to make it as expensive as they please.

26   Sixthly, this would be a great inducement to marriage, which all wise nations have either encouraged by rewards or enforced by laws and penalties. It would increase the care and tenderness of mothers toward their children, when they were sure of a settlement for life to the poor babes, provided in some sort by the public, to their annual profit instead of expense. We should see an honest emulation among the married women, which of them could bring the fattest child to the market. Men would become as fond of their wives during the time of pregnancy as they are now of their mares in foal, their cows in calf, or sows when they are ready to farrow; nor offer to beat or kick them (as is too frequent a practice) for fear of a miscarriage.

27   Many other advantages might be enumerated. For instance, the addition of some thousand carcasses in our exportation of barreled beef, the propagation of swine's flesh, and improvements in the art of making good bacon, so much wanted among us by the great destruction of pigs, too frequent at our tables, which are no way comparable in taste or magnificence to a well-grown, fat, yearling child, which roasted whole will make a considerable figure at a lord mayor's feast or any other public entertainment. But this and many others I omit, being studious of brevity.

28   Supposing that one thousand families in this city would be constant customers for infants' flesh, besides others who might have it at merry meetings, particularly weddings and christenings, I compute that Dublin would take off annually about twenty thousand carcasses, and the rest of the kingdom (where

probably they will be sold somewhat cheaper) the remaining eighty thousand.

I can think of no one objection that will possibly be raised 29 against this proposal, unless it should be urged that the number of people will be thereby much lessened in the kingdom. This I freely own, and it was indeed one principal design in offering it to the world. I desire the reader will observe; that I calculate my remedy for this one individual kingdom of Ireland and for no other that ever was, is, or I think ever can be upon earth. Therefore, let no man talk to me of other expedients: of taxing our absentees at five shillings a pound: of using neither clothes nor household furniture except what is of our own growth and manufacture: of utterly rejecting the materials and instruments that promote foreign luxury: of curing the expensiveness of pride, vanity, idleness, and gaming in our women: of introducing a vein of parsimony, prudence, and temperance: of learning to love our country, in the want of which we differ even from Lowlanders and the inhabitants of Topinamboo:[10] of quitting our animosities and factions, nor acting any longer like the Jews,[11] who were murdering one another at the very moment their city was taken: of being a little cautious not to sell our country and conscience for nothing: of teaching landlords to have at least one degree of mercy toward their tenants: lastly, of putting a spirit of honesty, industry, and skill into our shopkeepers; who, if a resolution could now be taken to buy only our native goods, would immediately unite to cheat and exact upon us in the price, the measure, and the goodness, nor could ever yet be brought to make one fair proposal of just dealing, though often and earnestly invited to it.

Therefore, I repeat, let no man talk to me of these and the 30 like expedients, till he hath at least some glimpse of hope that there will ever be some hearty and sincere attempt to put them in practice.

But as to myself, having been wearied out for many years 31 with offering vain, idle, visionary thoughts, and at length utterly

---

[10]In Brazil.
[11]Rome conquered Jerusalem in 70 A.D. during civil war.

despairing of success, I fortunately fell upon this proposal, which, as it is wholly new, so it hath something solid and real, of no expense and little trouble, full in our own power, and whereby we can incur no danger in disobliging England. For this kind of commodity will not bear exportation, the flesh being of too tender a consistence to admit a long continuance in salt, although perhaps I could name a country which would be glad to eat up our whole nation without it.

32   After all, I am not so violently bent upon my own opinion as to reject any offer proposed by wise men, which shall be found equally innocent, cheap, easy, and effectual. But before something of that kind shall be advanced in contradiction to my scheme, and offering a better, I desire the author or authors will be pleased maturely to consider two points. First, as things now stand, how they will be able to find food and raiment for an hundred thousand useless mouths and backs. And secondly, there being a round million of creatures in human figure throughout this kingdom, whose sole subsistence put into a common stock would leave them in debt two millions of pounds sterling, adding those who are beggars by profession to the bulk of farmers, cottagers, and laborers, with their wives and children who are beggars in effect; I desire those politicians who dislike my overture, and may perhaps be so bold to attempt an answer, that they will first ask the parents of these mortals whether they would not at this day think it a great happiness to have been sold for food at a year old in this manner I prescribe, and thereby have avoided such a perpetual scene of misfortunes as they have since gone through by the oppression of landlords, the impossibility of paying rent without money or trade, the want of common sustenance, with neither house nor clothes to cover them from the inclemencies of the weather, and the most inevitable prospect of entailing the like or greater miseries upon their breed forever.

33   I profess, in the sincerity of my heart, that I have not the least personal interest in endeavoring to promote this necessary work, having no other motive than the public good of my country, by advancing our trade, providing for infants, relieving the poor, and giving some pleasure to the rich. I have no children by which I

can propose to get a single penny; the youngest being nine years old, and my wife past childbearing.

1729

Who Makes the Clothes We Wear?

Jesse Jackson

Would you spend $20 for a stylish Gap T-shirt if you knew it was 1 made by teen-age girls in El Salvador forced to work 18 hours a day in a sweatshop for about 16 cents a shirt?

Would you pay top dollar for designer fashions at Neiman 2 Marcus that were made by immigrant Thai women imprisoned behind barbed wire in forced-labor conditions?

Would you give Nike $80 for a pair of athletic shoes if you 3 knew they were made by teen-age girls in Indonesia working 60-hour weeks for less than Indonesia's miserable minimum wage? Would you buy them if you knew that one young woman who organized a strike to demand that Nike pay the statutory minimum wage in Indonesia was abducted, raped and murdered?

Across the world—including in the United States, the sweat- 4 shop is back in the press. High-profit, high-profile, high-priced retailers have grown callous and uncaring about the inhuman working conditions of the desperate—here and abroad—who make their products. Private companies turn their backs as their subcontractors routinely trample the basic rights of their workers—speech, association, the right to organize, the right to a living wage, the right to a bathroom break, to healthy and safe work conditions, to overtime, the prohibition of child and slave labor. Desperate workers have been too weak to resist.

Look, for instance, at the conditions in El Monte, Calif. On 5 Aug. 2, government officials raided a sweatshop filled with immigrant Thai women laboring for as little as 59 cents per hour for 16 to 22 hours a day. Discipline was enforced by threats of rape and beatings. The women were locked up day and night as they produced garments for Neiman Marcus, J.C. Penney and other U.S. retailers and manufacturers.

6   As these outrages have gained public attention, manufacturers and retailers are getting nervous. The $200 million or so that Nike spends each year to paste its symbol on everything from Pete Sampras at the U.S. Open to the Dallas Cowboy uniforms can be wasted by one powerful scandal that ignites consumers' moral sensibilities. "Just do it" is Nike's multimillion-dollar slogan. But many Americans, if informed of these sweatshop realities, just might not do it; and that has major clothing and shoe manufacturers terrified. A consumer time bomb has begun to tick.

7   Republicans are out of step with this growing popular concern. They are busy gutting what few government protections exist for working people. The budget to enforce U.S. labor laws and workplace health and safety is being slashed. Republicans are blocking efforts to codify minimal labor and environmental standards in global trade treaties and develop international investigation and reporting.

8   Their opposition isn't just about trimming "big government." They also oppose legislation that would empower workers to elect their own representatives to monitor workplace safety. Even House Speaker Newt Gingrich—self-styled Third Wave revolutionary—has had little to say about the growing consumer reaction.

9   Unions, consumer groups, and human-rights organizations are expanding their monitoring of labor conditions here and abroad. Many citizens would happily join a groundswell to hold one of these global corporate behemoths accountable for how they treat the least of their workers. If consumers spurn just one popular brand name, the other companies will rush to clean up their act.

10   Then the companies will push for government regulation and policing as insulation against independent consumer movements. Gingrich will scurry to get in front of the parade. Conservatives will shelve opposition to big government and line up to pass the laws and codes of conduct that businesses want.

Practices like those in El Monte aren't about reasonable profit; 11
they are about greed. These companies have grown arrogant in
their global reach. Like true cynics, they know the price of everything and the value of nothing. In 1993, the labor cost to Nike for
a pair of $80 sneakers was 12 cents; in 1994, the company had
more than $4.3 billion in sales. Nike paid more to give shoes away
in promotions than to pay 12,000 women in Indonesia who make
them. Organizers estimate that 1% of the Nike advertising budget
could double the wages paid to the women and lift them above
the poverty line.

Nike can afford minimal rights for their workers. Now 12
informed consumers may begin to make the trampling of basic
decency a whole lot more expensive than the cost of respecting it.

1995

Nickel-and-Dimed: On (Not) Getting By in America

Barbara Ehrenreich

At the beginning of June 1998 I leave behind everything that nor- 1
mally soothes the ego and sustains the body—home, career, companion, reputation, ATM card—for a plunge into the low-wage
workforce. There, I become another, occupationally much diminished "Barbara Ehrenreich"—depicted on job-application forms as
a divorced homemaker whose sole work experience consists of
housekeeping in a few private homes. I am terrified, at the beginning, of being unmasked for what I am: a middle-class journalist
setting out to explore the world that welfare mothers are entering,
at the rate of approximately 50,000 a month, as welfare reform kicks
in. Happily, though, my fears turn out to be entirely unwarranted:
during a month of poverty and toil, my name goes unnoticed and
for the most part unuttered. In this parallel universe where my
father never got out of the mines and I never got through college,
I am "baby," "honey," "blondie," and, most commonly, "girl."

2   My first task is to find a place to live. I figure that if I can earn $7 an hour—which, from the want ads, seems doable—I can afford to spend $500 on rent, or maybe, with severe economies, $600. In the Key West area, where I live, this pretty much confines me to flophouses and trailer homes—like the one, a pleasing fifteen-minute drive from town, that has no air-conditioning, no screens, no fans, no television, and, by way of diversion, only the challenge of evading the landlord's Doberman pinscher. The big problem with this place, though, is the rent, which at $675 a month is well beyond my reach. All right, Key West is expensive. But so is New York City, or the Bay Area, or Jackson Hole, or Telluride, or Boston, or any other place where tourists and the wealthy compete for living space with the people who clean their toilets and fry their hash browns.[1] Still, it is a shock to realize that "trailer trash" has become, for me, a demographic category to aspire to.

3   So I decide to make the common trade-off between affordability and convenience, and go for a $500-a-month efficiency thirty miles up a two-lane highway from the employment opportunities of Key West, meaning forty-five minutes if there's no road construction and I don't get caught behind some sundazed Canadian tourists. I hate the drive, along a roadside studded with white crosses commemorating the more effective head-on collisions, but it's a sweet little place—a cabin, more or less, set in the swampy back yard of the converted mobile home where my landlord, an affable TV repairman, lives with his bartender girlfriend. Anthropologically speaking, a bustling trailer park would be preferable, but here I have a gleaming white floor and a firm mattress, and the few resident bugs are easily vanquished.

4   Besides, I am not doing this for the anthropology. My aim is nothing so mistily subjective as to "experience poverty" or find

---

[1] According to the Department of Housing and Urban Development, the "fair-market rent" for an efficiency is $551 here in Monroe County, Florida. A comparable rent in the five boroughs of New York City is $704; in San Francisco, $713; and in the heart of Silicon Valley, $808. The fair-market rent for an area is defined as the amount that would be needed to pay rent plus utilities for "privately owned, decent, safe, and sanitary rental housing of a modest (non-luxury) nature with suitable amenities."

out how it "really feels" to be a long-term low-wage worker. I've had enough unchosen encounters with poverty and the world of low-wage work to know it's not a place you want to visit for touristic purposes; it just smells too much like fear. And with all my real-life assets—bank account, IRA, health insurance, multi-room home—waiting indulgently in the background, I am, of course, thoroughly insulated from the terrors that afflict the genuinely poor.

No, this is a purely objective, scientific sort of mission. The 5 humanitarian rationale for welfare reform—as opposed to the more punitive and stingy impulses that may actually have motivated it—is that work will lift poor women out of poverty while simultaneously inflating their self-esteem and hence their future value in the labor market. Thus, whatever the hassles involved in finding child care, transportation, etc., the transition from welfare to work will end happily, in greater prosperity for all. Now there are many problems with this comforting prediction, such as the fact that the economy will inevitably undergo a downturn, eliminating many jobs. Even without a downturn, the influx of a million former welfare recipients into the low-wage labor market could depress wages by as much as 11.9 percent, according to the Economic Policy Institute (EPI) in Washington, D.C.

But is it really possible to make a living on the kinds of jobs 6 currently available to unskilled people? Mathematically, the answer is no, as can be shown by taking $6 to $7 an hour, perhaps subtracting a dollar or two an hour for child care, multiplying by 160 hours a month, and comparing the result to the prevailing rents. According to the National Coalition for the Homeless, for example, in 1998 it took, on average nationwide, an hourly wage of $8.89 to afford a one-bedroom apartment, and the Preamble Center for Public Policy estimates that the odds against a typical welfare recipient's landing a job at such a "living wage" are about 97 to 1. If these numbers are right, low-wage work is not a solution to poverty and possibly not even to homelessness.

It may seem excessive to put this proposition to an experi- 7 mental test. As certain family members keep unhelpfully reminding me, the viability of low-wage work could be tested, after a fashion, without ever leaving my study. I could just pay myself $7 an hour for eight hours a clay, charge myself for room and board, and total up the numbers after a month. Why leave the people and work that I love? But I am an experimental scientist by training. In that business, you don't just sit at a desk and theorize; you plunge into the everyday chaos of nature, where surprises lurk in the most mundane measurements. Maybe, when I got into it, I would discover some hidden economies in the world of the low-wage worker. After all, if 30 percent of the workforce toils for less than $8 an hour, according to the EPI, they may have found some tricks as yet unknown to me. Maybe—who knows?— I would even be able to detect in myself the bracing psychological effects of getting out of the house, as promised by the welfare wonks at places like the Heritage Foundation. Or, on the other hand, maybe there would be unexpected costs—physical, mental, or financial—to throw off all my calculations. Ideally, I should do this with two small children in tow, that being the welfare average, but mine are grown and no one is willing to lend me theirs for a month-long vacation in penury. So this is not the perfect experiment, just a test of the best possible case: an unencumbered woman, smart and even strong, attempting to live more or less off the land.

8   On the morning of my first full day of job searching, I take a red pen to the want ads, which are auspiciously numerous. Everyone in Key West's booming "hospitality industry" seems to be looking for someone like me—trainable, flexible, and with suitably humble expectations as to pay. I know I possess certain traits that might be advantageous—I'm white and, I like to think, well-spoken and poised—but I decide on two rules: One, I cannot use any skills derived from my education or usual work—not that there are a lot of want ads for satirical essayists anyway. Two, I have to take the best-paid job that is offered me and of course do my best to hold it; no Marxist rants or sneaking off to read novels in the ladies' room. In addition, I rule out various occupations for one reason or another: Hotel front-desk clerk, for example, which to my surprise is regarded as unskilled and pays around $7 an hour, gets eliminated because it involves standing in one spot for eight hours a day.

Waitressing is similarly something I'd like to avoid, because I remember it leaving me bone tired when I was eighteen, and I'm decades of varicosities and back pain beyond that now. Telemarketing, one of the first refuges of the suddenly indigent, can be dismissed on grounds of personality. This leaves certain supermarket jobs, such as deli clerk, or housekeeping in Key West's thousands of hotel and guest rooms. Housekeeping is especially appealing, for reasons both atavistic and practical: it's what my mother did before I came along, and it can't be too different from what I've been doing part-time, in my own home, all my life.

So I put on what I take to be a respectful-looking outfit of 9 ironed Bermuda shorts and scooped-neck T-shirt and set out for a tour of the local hotels and supermarkets. Best Western, Econo Lodge, and HoJo's all let me fill out application forms, and these are, to my relief, interested in little more than whether I am a legal resident of the United States and have committed any felonies. My next stop is Winn-Dixie, the supermarket, which turns out to have a particularly onerous application process, featuring a fifteen-minute "interview" by computer since, apparently, no human on the premises is deemed capable of representing the corporate point of view. I am conducted to a large room decorated with posters illustrating how to look "professional" (it helps to be white and, if female, permed) and warning of the slick promises that union organizers might try to tempt me with. The interview is multiple choice: Do I have anything, such as child-care problems, that might make it hard for me to get to work on time? Do I think safety on the job is the responsibility of management? Then, popping up cunningly out of the blue: How many dollars' worth of stolen goods have I purchased in the last year? Would I turn in a fellow employee if I caught him stealing? Finally, "Are you an honest person?"

Apparently, I ace the interview, because I am told that all I 10 have to do is show up in some doctor's office tomorrow for a urine test. This seems to be a fairly general rule: if you want to stack Cheerio boxes or vacuum hotel rooms in chemically fascist America, you have to be willing to squat down and pee in front of some health worker (who has no doubt had to do the same thing herself). The wages Winn-Dixie is offering—$6 and a couple of dimes to start with—are not enough, I decide, to compensate for this indignity.[2]

11   I lunch at Wendy's, where $4.99 gets you unlimited refills at the Mexican part of the Superbar, a comforting surfeit of refried beans and "cheese sauce." A teenage employee, seeing me studying the want ads, kindly offers me an application form, which I fill out, though here, too, the pay is just $6 and change an hour. Then it's off for a round of the locally owned inns and guesthouses. At "The Palms," let's call it, a bouncy manager actually takes me around to see the rooms and meet the existing housekeepers, who, I note with satisfaction, look pretty much like me— faded ex-hippie types in shorts with long hair pulled back in braids. Mostly, though, no one speaks to one or even looks at me except to proffer an application form. At my last stop, a palatial B&B, I wait twenty minutes to meet "Max," only to be told that there are no jobs now but there should be one soon, since "nobody lasts more than a couple weeks." (Because none of the people I talked to knew I was a reporter, I have changed their names to protect their privacy and, in some cases perhaps, their jobs.)

12   Three days go by like this, and, to my chagrin, no one out of the approximately twenty places I've applied calls me for an interview. I had been vain enough to worry about coming across as too educated for the jobs I sought, but no one even seems interested in finding out how overqualified I am. Only later will I realize that the want ads are not a reliable measure of the actual jobs available at any particular time. They are, as I should have guessed from Max's comment, the employers' insurance policy against the relentless turnover of the low-wage workforce. Most of the big hotels run ads almost continually, just to build a supply of applicants to replace the current workers as they drift away or are fired, so

---

[2]According to the *Monthly Labor Review* (November 1996), 28 percent of work sites surveyed in the service industry conduct drug tests (corporate workplaces have much higher rates), and the incidence of testing has risen markedly since the Eighties. The rate of testing is highest in the South (56 percent of work sites polled), with the Midwest in second place (50 percent). The drug most likely to be detected—marijuana, which can be detected in urine for weeks—is also the most innocuous, while heroin and cocaine are generally undetectable three days after use. Prospective employees sometimes try to cheat the tests by consuming excessive amounts of liquids and taking diuretics and even masking substances available through the Internet.

finding a job is just a matter of being at the right place at the right time and flexible enough to take whatever is being offered that day. This finally happens to me at one of the big discount hotel chains, where I go, as usual, for housekeeping and am sent, instead, to try out as a waitress at the attached "family restaurant," a dismal spot with a counter and about thirty tables that looks out on a parking garage and features such tempting fare as "Pollish [sic] sausage and BBQ sauce" on 95-degree days. Phillip, the dapper young West Indian who introduces himself as the manager, interviews me with about as much enthusiasm as if he were a clerk processing me for Medicare, the principal questions being what shifts can I work and when can I start. I mutter something about being woefully out of practice as a waitress, but he's already on to the uniform: I'm to show up tomorrow wearing black slacks and black shoes; he'll provide the rust-colored polo shirt with HEARTHSIDE embroidered on it, though I might want to wear my own shirt to get to work, ha ha. At the word "tomorrow," something between fear and indignation rises in my chest. I want to say, "Thank you for your time, sir, but this is just an experiment, you know, not my actual life."

So begins my career at the Hearthside, I shall call it, one small profit center within a global discount hotel chain, where for two weeks I work from 2:00 till 10:00 P.M. for $2.43 an hour plus tips.[3] In some futile bid for gentility, the management has barred employees from using the front door, so my first day I enter through the kitchen, where a red-faced man with shoulder-length blond hair is throwing frozen steaks against the wall and yelling, "Fuck this shit!" "That's just Jack," explains Gail, the wiry middle-aged waitress who is assigned to train me. "He's on the rag again"—a condition occasioned, in this instance, by the fact that the cook on the morning shift had forgotten to thaw out the steaks. For the next eight hours, I run after the agile Gail, absorbing bits

[3]According to the Fair Labor Standards Act, employers are not required to pay "tipped employees," such as restaurant servers, more than $2.13 an hour in direct wages. However, if the sum of tips plus $2.13 an hour falls below the minimum wage, or $5.15 an hour, the employer is required to make up the difference. This fact was not mentioned by managers or otherwise publicized at either of the restaurants where I worked.

of instruction along with fragments of personal tragedy. All food must be trayed, and the reason she's so tired today is that she woke up in a cold sweat thinking of her boyfriend, who killed himself recently in an upstate prison. No refills on lemonade. And the reason he was in prison is that a few DUIs caught up with him, that's all, could have happened to anyone. Carry the creamers to the table in a monkey bowl, never in your hand. And after he was gone she spent several months living in her truck, peeing in a plastic pee bottle and reading by candlelight at night, but you can't live in a truck in the summer, since you need to have the windows down, which means anything can get in, from mosquitoes on up.

14　　At least Gail puts to rest any fears I had of appearing overqualified. From the first day on, I find that of all the things I have left behind, such as home and identity, what I miss the most is competence. Not that I have ever felt utterly competent in the writing business, in which one day's success augurs nothing at all for the next. But in my writing life, I at least have some notion of procedure: do the research, make the outline, rough out a draft, etc. As a server, though, I am beset by requests like bees: more iced tea here, ketchup over there, a to-go box for table fourteen, and where are the high chairs, anyway? Of the twenty-seven tables, up to six are usually mine at any time, though on slow afternoons or if Gail is off, I sometimes have the whole place to myself. There is the touch-screen computer-ordering system to master, which is, I suppose, meant to minimize server–cook contact, but in practice requires constant verbal fine-tuning: "That's gravy on the mashed, okay? None on the meatloaf," and so forth—while the cook scowls as if I were inventing these refinements just to torment him. Plus, something I had forgotten in the years since I was eighteen: about a third of a server's job is "side work" that's invisible to customers—sweeping, scrubbing, slicing, refilling, and restocking. If it isn't all done, every little bit of it, you're going to face the 6:00 P.M. dinner rush defenseless and probably go down in flames. I screw up dozens of times at the beginning, sustained in my shame entirely by Gail's support—"It's okay, baby, everyone does that sometime"—because, to my total surprise and despite the scientific detachment I am doing my best to maintain, I care.

15　　The whole thing would be a lot easier if I could just skate through it as Lily Tomlin in one of her waitress skits, but I was raised by the absurd Booker T. Washingtonian precept that says: If you're going to do something, do it well. In fact, "well" isn't good enough by half. Do it better than anyone has ever done it before. Or so said my father, who must have known what he was talking about because he managed to pull himself, and us with him, up from the mile-deep copper mines of Butte to the leafy suburbs of the Northeast, ascending from boilermakers to martinis before booze beat out ambition. As in most endeavors I have encountered in my life, doing it "better than anyone" is not a reasonable goal. Still, when I wake up at 4:00 A.M. in my own cold sweat, I am not thinking about the writing deadlines I'm neglecting; I'm thinking about the table whose order I screwed up so that one of the boys didn't get his kiddie meal until the rest of the family had moved on to their Key Lime pies. That's the other powerful motivation I hadn't expected—the customers, or "patients," as I can't help thinking of them on account of the mysterious vulnerability that seems to have left them temporarily unable to feed themselves. After a few days at the Hearthside, I feel the service ethic kick in like a shot of oxytocin, the nurturance hormone. The plurality of my customers are hard-working locals—truck drivers, construction workers, even housekeepers from the attached hotel—and I want them to have the closest to a "fine dining" experience that the grubby circumstances will allow. No "you guys" for me; everyone over twelve is "sir" or "ma'am." I ply them with iced tea and coffee refills; I return, mid-meal, to inquire how everything is; I doll up their salads with chopped raw mushrooms, summer squash slices, or whatever bits of produce I can find that have survived their sojourn in the cold-storage room mold-free.

There is Benny, for example, a short, tight-muscled sewer [16] repairman, who cannot even think of eating until he has absorbed a half hour of air-conditioning and ice water. We chat about hyperthermia and electrolytes until he is ready to order some finicky combination like soup of the day, garden salad, and a side of grits. There are the German tourists who are so touched by my pidgin "Willkommen" and "Ist alles gut?" that they actually tip. (Europeans, spoiled by their trade-union-ridden, high-wage welfare states, generally do not know that they are supposed to tip. Some restaurants, the Hearthside included, allow servers to "grat" their foreign customers, or add a tip to the bill. Since this amount is added before the customers have a chance to tip or not tip, the practice amounts to an automatic penalty for imperfect English.) There are the two dirt-smudged lesbians, just off their construction shift, who are impressed enough by my suave handling of the fly in the pina colada that they take the time to praise me to Stu, the assistant manager. There's Sam, the kindly retired cop, who has to plug up his tracheotomy hole with one finger in order to force the cigarette smoke into his lungs.

17   Sometimes I play with the fantasy that I am a princess who, in penance for some tiny transgression, has undertaken to feed each of her subjects by hand. But the non-princesses working with me are just as indulgent, even when this means flouting management rules—concerning, for example, the number of croutons that can go on a salad (six). "Put on all you want," Gail whispers, "as long as Stu isn't looking." She dips into her own tip money to buy biscuits and gravy for an out-of-work mechanic who's used up all his money on dental surgery, inspiring me to pick up the tab for his milk and pie. Maybe the same high levels of agape can be found throughout the "hospitality industry." I remember the poster decorating one of the apartments I looked at, which said "If you seek happiness for yourself you will never find it. Only when you seek happiness for others will it come to you," or words to that effect—an odd sentiment, it seemed to me at the time, to find in the dank one-room basement apartment of a bellhop at the Best Western. At the Hearthside, we utilize whatever bits of autonomy we have to ply our customers with the illicit calories that signal our love. It is our job as servers to assemble the salads and desserts, pouring the dressings and squirting the whipped cream. We also control the number of butter patties our customers get and the amount of sour cream on their baked potatoes. So if you wonder why Americans are so obese, consider the fact that waitresses both express their humanity and earn their tips through the covert distribution of fats.

18   Ten days into it, this is beginning to look like a livable lifestyle. I like Gail, who is "looking at fifty" but moves so fast she can alight in one place and then another without apparently being anywhere between them. I clown around with Lionel, the teenage Haitian busboy, and catch a few fragments of conversation with Joan, the svelte fortyish hostess and militant feminist who is the only one

of us who dares to tell Jack to shut the fuck up. I even warm up to Jack when, on a slow night and to make up for a particularly unwarranted attack on my abilities, or so I imagine, he tells me about his glory days as a young man at "coronary school"—or do you say "culinary"?—in Brooklyn, where he dated a knock-out Puerto Rican chick and learned everything there is to know about food. I finish up at 10:00 or 10:30, depending on how much side work I've been able to get done during the shift, and cruise home to the tapes I snatched up at random when I left my real home— Marianne Faithfull, Tracy Chapman, Enigma, King Sunny Ade, the Violent Femmes—just drained enough for the music to set my cranium resonating but hardly dead. Midnight snack is Wheat Thins and Monterey Jack, accompanied by cheap white wine on ice and whatever AMC has to offer. To bed by 1:30 or 2:00, up at 9:00 or 10:00, read for an hour while my uniform whirls around in the landlord's washing machine, and then it's another eight hours spent following Mao's central instruction, as laid out in the Little Red Book, which was: Serve the people.

I could drift along like this, in some dreamy proletarian idyll, except for two things. One is management. If I have kept this subject on the margins thus far it is because I still flinch to think that I spent all those weeks under the surveillance of men (and later women) whose job it was to monitor my behavior for signs of sloth, theft, drug abuse, or worse. Not that managers and especially "assistant managers" in low-wage settings like this are exactly the class enemy. In the restaurant business, they are mostly former cooks or servers, still capable of pinch-hitting in the kitchen or on the floor, just as in hotels they are likely to be former clerks, and paid a salary of only about $400 a week. But everyone knows they have crossed over to the other side, which is, crudely put, corporate as opposed to human. Cooks want to prepare tasty meals; servers want to serve them graciously; but managers are there for only one reason—to make sure that money is made for some theoretical entity that exists far away in Chicago or New York, if a corporation can be said to have a physical existence at all. Reflecting on her career, Gail tells me ruefully that she had sworn, years ago, never to work for a corporation again. "They don't cut you no slack. You give and you give, and they take."

20   Managers can sit—for hours at a time if they want—but it's their job to see that no one else ever does, even when there's nothing to do, and this is why, for servers, slow times can be as exhausting as rushes. You start dragging out each little chore, because if the manager on duty catches you in an idle moment, he will give you something far nastier to do. So I wipe, I clean, I consolidate ketchup bottles and recheck the cheesecake supply, even tour the tables to make sure the customer evaluation forms are all standing perkily in their places—wondering all the time how many calories I burn in these strictly theatrical exercises. When, on a particularly dead afternoon, Stu finds me glancing at a *USA Today* a customer has left behind, he assigns me to vacuum the entire floor with the broken vacuum cleaner that has a handle only two feet long, and the only way to do that without incurring orthopedic damage is to proceed from spot to spot on your knees.

21   On my first Friday at the Hearthside there is a "mandatory meeting for all restaurant employees," which I attend, eager for insight into our overall marketing strategy and the niche (your basic Ohio cuisine with a tropical twist?) we aim to inhabit. But there is no "we" at this meeting. Phillip, our top manager except for an occasional "consultant" sent out by corporate headquarters, opens it with a sneer: "The break room—it's disgusting. Butts in the ashtrays, newspapers lying around, crumbs." This windowless little room, which also houses the time clock for the entire hotel, is where we stash our bags and civilian clothes and take our half-hour meal breaks. But a break room is not a right, he tells us. It can be taken away. We should also know that the lockers in the break room and whatever is in them can be searched at any time. Then comes gossip; there has been gossip; gossip (which seems to mean employees talking among themselves) must stop. Off-duty employees are henceforth barred from eating at the restaurant, because "other servers gather around them and gossip." When Phillip has exhausted his agenda of rebukes, Joan complains about the condition of the ladies' room and I throw in my two bits about the vacuum cleaner. But I don't see any backup coming from my fellow servers, each of whom has subsided into her own personal funk; Gail, my role model, stares sorrowfully at a point six inches from her nose. The meeting ends when Andy, one of the cooks, gets up, muttering about breaking up his day off for this almighty bullshit.

Just four days later we are suddenly summoned into the 22 kitchen at 3:30 P.M., even though there are live tables on the floor. We all—about ten of us—stand around Phillip, who announces grimly that there has been a report of some "drug activity" on the night shift and that, as a result, we are now to be a "drug-free" workplace, meaning that all new hires will be tested, as will possibly current employees on a random basis. I am glad that this part of the kitchen is so dark, because I find myself blushing as hard as if I had been caught toking up in the ladies' room myself: I haven't been treated this way—lined up in the corridor, threatened with locker searches, peppered with carelessly aimed accusations—since junior high school. Back on the floor, Joan cracks, "Next they'll be telling us we can't have sex on the job." When I ask Stu what happened to inspire the crackdown, he just mutters about "management decisions" and takes the opportunity to upbraid Gail and me for being too generous with the rolls. From now on there's to be only one per customer, and it goes out with the dinner, not with the salad. He's also been riding the cooks, prompting Andy to come out of the kitchen and observe—with the serenity of a man whose customary implement is a butcher knife—that "Stu has a death wish today."

Later in the evening, the gossip crystallizes around the the- 23 ory that Stu is himself the drug culprit, that he uses the restaurant phone to order up marijuana and sends one of the late servers out to fetch it for him. The server was caught, and she may have ratted Stu out or at least said enough to cast some suspicion on him, thus accounting for his pissy behavior. Who knows? Lionel, the busboy, entertains us for the rest of the shift by standing just behind Stu's back and sucking deliriously on an imaginary joint.

The other problem, in addition to the less-than-nurturing 24 management style, is that this job shows no sign of being financially viable. You might imagine, from a comfortable distance, that people who live, year in and year out, on $6 to $10 an hour have discovered some survival stratagems unknown to the middle class. But no. It's not hard to get my co-workers to talk about their living situations, because housing, in almost every case, is the principal source of disruption in their lives, the first thing they fill you in on when they arrive for their shifts. After a week, I have compiled the following survey:

25 • Gail is sharing a room in a well-known downtown flophouse for which she and a roommate pay about $250 a week. Her roommate, a male friend, has begun hitting on her, driving her nuts, but the rent would be impossible alone.

26 • Claude, the Haitian cook, is desperate to get out of the two-room apartment he shares with his girlfriend and two other, unrelated, people. As far as I can determine, the other Haitian men (most of whom only speak Creole) live in similarly crowded situations.

27 • Annette, a twenty-year-old server who is six months pregnant and has been abandoned by her boyfriend, lives with her mother, a postal clerk.

28 • Marianne and her boyfriend are paying $170 a week for a one-person trailer.

29 • Jack, who is, at $10 an hour, the wealthiest of us, lives in the trailer he owns, paying only the $400-a-month lot fee.

30 • The other white cook, Andy, lives on his dry-docked boat, which, as far as I can tell from his loving descriptions, can't be more than twenty feet long. He offers to take me out on it, once it's repaired, but the offer comes with inquiries as to my marital status, so I do not follow up on it.

31 • Tina and her husband are paying $60 a night for a double room in a Days Inn. This is because they have no car and the Days Inn is within walking distance of the Hearthside. When Marianne, one of the breakfast servers, is tossed out of her trailer for subletting (which is against the trailer-park rules), she leaves her boyfriend and moves in with Tina and her husband.

32 • Joan, who had fooled me with her numerous and tasteful outfits (hostesses wear their own clothes), lives in a van she parks behind a shopping center at night and showers in Tina's motel room. The clothes are from thrift shops.[4]

---

[4]I could find no statistics on the number of employed people living in cars or vans, but according to the National Coalition for the Homeless's 1997 report "Myths and Facts About Homelessness," nearly one in five homeless people (in twenty-nine cities across the nation) is employed in a full- or part-time job.

It strikes me, in my middle-class solipsism, that there is gross 33 improvidence in some of these arrangements. When Gail and I are wrapping silverware in napkins—the only task for which we are permitted to sit—she tells me she is thinking of escaping from her roommate by moving into the Days Inn herself. I am astounded: How can she even think of paying between $40 and $60 a day? But if I was afraid of sounding like a social worker, I come out just sounding like a fool. She squints at me in disbelief, "And where am I supposed to get a month's rent and a month's deposit for an apartment?" I'd been feeling pretty smug about my $500 efficiency, but of course it was made possible only by the $1,300 I had allotted myself for start-up costs when I began my low-wage life: $1,000 for the first month's rent and deposit, $100 for initial groceries and cash in my pocket, $200 stuffed away for emergencies. In poverty, as in certain propositions in physics, starting conditions are everything.

There are no secret economies that nourish the poor; on the 34 contrary, there are a host of special costs. If you can't put up the two months' rent you need to secure an apartment, you end up paying through the nose for a room by the week. If you have only a room, with a hot plate at best, you can't save by cooking up huge lentil stews that can be frozen for the week ahead. You eat fast food, or the hot dogs and styrofoam cups of soup that can be microwaved in a convenience store. If you have no money for health insurance—and the Hearthside's niggardly plan kicks in only after three months—you go without routine care or prescription drugs and end up paying the price. Gail, for example, was fine until she ran out of money for estrogen pills. She is supposed to be on the company plan by now, but they claim to have lost her application form and need to begin the paperwork all over again. So she spends $9 per migraine pill to control the headaches she wouldn't have, she insists, if her estrogen supplements were covered. Similarly, Marianne's boyfriend lost his job as a roofer because he missed so much time after getting a cut on his foot for which he couldn't afford the prescribed antibiotic.

My own situation, when I sit down to assess it after two weeks 35 of work, would not be much better if this were my actual life. The seductive thing about waitressing is that you don't have to wait for payday to feel a few bills in your pocket, and my tips usually cover meals and gas, plus something left over to stuff into the kitchen drawer I use as a bank. But as the tourist business slows in the summer heat, I sometimes leave work with only $20 in tips (the gross is higher, but servers share about 15 percent of their tips with the busboys and bartenders). With wages included, this amounts to about the minimum wage of $5.15 an hour. Although the sum in the drawer is piling up, at the present rate of accumulation it will be more than a hundred dollars short of my rent when the end of the month comes around. Nor can I see any expenses to cut. True, I haven't gone the lentil-stew route yet, but that's because I don't have a large cooking pot, pot holders, or a ladle to stir with (which cost about $30 at Kmart, less at thrift stores), not to mention onions, carrots, and the indispensable bay leaf. I do make my lunch almost every day—usually some slow-burning, high-protein combo like frozen chicken patties with melted cheese on top and canned pinto beans on the side. Dinner is at the Hearthside, which offers its employees a choice of BLT, fish sandwich, or hamburger for only $2. The burger lasts longest, especially if it's heaped with gut-puckering jalapeños, but by midnight my stomach is growling again.

36   So unless I want to start using my car as a residence, I have to find a second, or alternative, job. I call all the hotels where I filled out housekeeping applications weeks ago—the Hyatt, Holiday Inn, Econo Lodge, HoJo's, Best Western, plus a half dozen or so locally run guesthouses. Nothing. Then I start making the rounds again, wasting whole mornings waiting for some assistant manager to show up, even dipping into places so creepy that the front-desk clerk greets you from behind bulletproof glass and sells pints of liquor over the counter. But either someone has exposed my real-life housekeeping habits—which are, shall we say, mellow— or I am at the wrong end of some infallible ethnic equation: most, but by no means all, of the working housekeepers I see on my job searches are African Americans, Spanish-speaking, or immigrants from the Central European post-Communist world, whereas servers are almost invariably white and monolingually English-speaking. When I finally get a positive response, I have been identified once again as server material. Jerry's, which is part of a well-known national family restaurant chain and physically attached here to another budget hotel chain, is ready to use me at once. The prospect is both exciting and terrifying, because, with about the same number of tables and counter seats, Jerry's attracts

three or four times the volume of customers as the gloomy old Hearthside.

Picture a fat person's hell, and I don't mean a place with no 37 food. Instead there is everything you might eat if eating had no bodily consequences—cheese fries, chicken-fried steaks, fudge-laden desserts—only here every bite must be paid for, one way or another, in human discomfort. The kitchen is a cavern, a stomach leading to the lower intestine that is the garbage and dishwashing area, from which issue bizarre smells combining the edible and the offal: creamy carrion, pizza barf, and that unique and enigmatic Jerry's scent—citrus fart. The floor is slick with spills, forcing us to walk through the kitchen with tiny steps, like Susan McDougal in leg irons. Sinks everywhere are clogged with scraps of lettuce, decomposing lemon wedges, waterlogged toast crusts. Put your hand down on any counter and you risk being stuck to it by the film of ancient syrup spills, and this is unfortunate, because hands are utensils here, used for scooping up lettuce onto salad plates, lifting out pie slices, and even moving hash browns from one plate to another. The regulation poster in the single unisex restroom admonishes us to wash our hands thoroughly and even offers instructions for doing so, but there is always some vital substance missing—soap, paper towels, toilet paper—and I never find all three at once. You learn to stuff your pockets with napkins before going in there, and too bad about the customers, who must eat, though they don't realize this, almost literally out of our hands.

The break room typifies the whole situation: there is none, 38 because there are no breaks at Jerry's. For six to eight hours in a row, you never sit except to pee. Actually, there are three folding chairs at a table immediately adjacent to the bathroom, but hardly anyone ever sits here, in the very rectum of the gastro-architectural system. Rather, the function of the peritoilet area is to house the ashtrays in which servers and dishwashers leave their cigarettes burning at all times, like votive candles, so that they don't have to waste time lighting up again when they dash back for a puff. Almost everyone smokes as if his or her pulmonary well-being depended on it—the multinational mélange of cooks, the Czech dishwashers, the servers, who are all American natives—creating an atmosphere in which oxygen is only an occasional pollutant. My first morning at Jerry's, when the hypoglycemic shakes set in, I complain to one of my fellow servers that I don't understand how she can go so long without food. "Well, I don't understand how you can go so long without a cigarette," she responds in a tone of reproach—because work is what you do for others; smoking is what you do for yourself. I don't know why the antismoking crusaders have never grasped the element of defiant self-nurturance that makes the habit so endearing to its victims—as if, in the American workplace, the only thing people have to call their own is the tumors they are nourishing and the spare moments they devote to feeding them.

39   Now, the Industrial Revolution is not an easy transition, especially when you have to zip through it in just a couple of days. I have gone from craft work straight into the factory, from the air-conditioned morgue of the Hearthside directly into the flames. Customers arrive in human waves, sometimes disgorged fifty at a time from their tour buses, peckish and whiny. Instead of two "girls" on the floor at once, there can be as many as six of us running around in our brilliant pink-and-orange Hawaiian shirts. Conversations, either with customers or fellow employees, seldom last more than twenty seconds at a time. On my first day, in fact, I am hurt by my sister servers' coldness. My mentor for the day is an emotionally uninflected twenty-three-year-old, and the others, who gossip a little among themselves about the real reason someone is out sick today and the size of the bail bond someone else has had to pay, ignore me completely. On my second day, I find out why. "Well, it's good to see you again," one of them says in greeting. "Hardly anyone comes back after the first day." I feel powerfully vindicated— a survivor—but it would take a long time, probably months, before I could hope to be accepted into this sorority.

40   I start out with the beautiful, heroic idea of handling the two jobs at once, and for two days I almost do it: the breakfast/lunch shift at Jerry's, which goes till 2:00, arriving at the Hearthside at 2:10, and attempting to hold out until 10:00. In the ten minutes between jobs, I pick up a spicy chicken sandwich at the Wendy's drive-through window, gobble it down in the car, and change from khaki slacks to black, from Hawaiian to rust polo. There is a problem, though. When during the 3:00 to 4:00 P.M. dead time I finally sit down to wrap silver, my flesh seems to bond to the seat. I try to refuel with a purloined cup of soup, as I've seen Gail and Joan do dozens of times, but a manager catches me and hisses

"No eating!" though there's not a customer around to be offended by the sight of food making contact with a server's lips. So I tell Gail I'm going to quit, and she hugs me and says she might just follow me to Jerry's herself.

But the chances of this are minuscule. She has left the flop- 41 house and her annoying roommate and is back to living in her beat-up old truck. But guess what? She reports to me excitedly later that evening: Phillip has given her permission to park overnight in the hotel parking lot, as long as she keeps out of sight, and the parking lot should be totally safe, since it's patrolled by a hotel security guard! With the Hearthside offering benefits like that, how could anyone think of leaving?

Gail would have triumphed at Jerry's, I'm sure, but for me it's 42 a crash course in exhaustion management. Years ago, the kindly fry cook who trained me to waitress at a Los Angeles truck stop used to say: Never make an unnecessary trip; if you don't have to walk fast, walk slow; if you don't have to walk, stand. But at Jerry's the effort of distinguishing necessary from unnecessary and urgent from whenever would itself be too much of an energy drain. The only thing to do is to treat each shift as a one-time-only emergency: you've got fifty starving people out there, lying scattered on the battlefield, so get out there and feed them! Forget that you will have to do this again tomorrow, forget that you will have to be alert enough to dodge the drunks on the drive home tonight—just burn, burn, burn! Ideally, at some point you enter what servers call "a rhythm" and psychologists term a "flow state," in which signals pass from the sense organs directly to the muscles, bypassing the cerebral cortex, and a Zen-like emptiness sets in. A male server from the Hearthside's morning shift tells me about the time he "pulled a triple"—three shifts in a row, all the way around the clock—and then got off and had a drink and met this girl, and maybe he shouldn't tell me this, but they had sex right then and there, and it was like, beautiful.

But there's another capacity of the neuromuscular system, 43 which is pain. I start tossing back drugstore-brand ibuprofen pills as if they were vitamin C, four before each shift, because an old mouse-related repetitive-stress injury in my upper back has come back to full-spasm strength, thanks to the tray carrying. In my ordinary life, this level of disability might justify a day of ice packs and stretching. Here I comfort myself with the Aleve commercial in which the cute blue-collar guy asks: If you quit after working four hours, what would your boss say? And the not-so-cute blue-collar guy, who's lugging a metal beam on his back, answers: He'd fire me, that's what. But fortunately, the commercial tells us, we workers can exert the same kind of authority over our painkillers that our bosses exert over us. If Tylenol doesn't want to work for more than four hours, you just fire its ass and switch to Aleve.

44 True, I take occasional breaks from this life, going home now and then to catch up on e-mail and for conjugal visits (though I am careful to "pay" for anything I eat there), seeing *The Truman Show* with friends and letting them buy my ticket. And I still have those what-am-I-doing-here moments at work, when I get so homesick for the printed word that I obsessively reread the six-page menu. But as the days go by, my old life is beginning to look exceedingly strange. The e-mails and phone messages addressed to my former self come from a distant race of people with exotic concerns and far too much time on their hands. The neighborly market I used to cruise for produce now looks forbiddingly like a Manhattan yuppie emporium. And when I sit down one morning in my real home to pay bills from my past life, I am dazzled at the two- and three-figure sums owed to outfits like Club BodyTech and Amazon.com.

45 Management at Jerry's is generally calmer and more "professional" than at the Hearthside, with two exceptions. One is Joy, a plump, blowsy woman in her early thirties, who once kindly devoted several minutes to instructing me in the correct one-handed method of carrying trays but whose moods change disconcertingly from shift to shift and even within one. Then there's B. J., a.k.a. B. J.-the-bitch, whose contribution is to stand by the kitchen counter and yell, "Nita, your order's up, move it!" or, "Barbara, didn't you see you've got another table out there? Come on, girl!" Among other things, she is hated for having replaced the whipped-cream squirt cans with big plastic whipped-cream-filled baggies that have to be squeezed with both hands—because, reportedly, she saw or thought she saw employees trying to inhale the propellant gas from the squirt cans, in the hope that it might be nitrous oxide. On my third night, she pulls me aside abruptly

and brings her face so close that it looks as if she's planning to butt me with her forehead. But instead of saying, "You're fired," she says, "You're doing fine." The only trouble is I'm spending time chatting with customers: "That's how they're getting you." Furthermore I am letting them "run me," which means harassment by sequential demands: you bring the ketchup and they decide they want extra Thousand Island; you bring that and they announce they now need a side of fries; and so on into distraction. Finally she tells me not to take her wrong. She tries to say things in a nice way, but you get into a mode, you know, because everything has to move so fast.[5]

I mumble thanks for the advice, feeling like I've just been 46 stripped naked by the crazed enforcer of some ancient sumptuary law: No chatting for you, girl. No fancy service ethic allowed for the serfs. Chatting with customers is for the beautiful young college-educated servers in the downtown carpaccio joints, the kids who can make $70 to $100 a night. What had I been thinking? My job is to move orders from tables to kitchen and then trays from kitchen to tables. Customers are, in fact, the major obstacle to the smooth transformation of information into food and food into money—they are, in short, the enemy. And the painful thing is that I'm beginning to see it this way myself. There are the traditional asshole types—frat boys who down multiple Buds and then make a fuss because the steaks are so emaciated and the fries so sparse—as well as the variously impaired—due to age, diabetes, or literacy issues—who require patient nutritional counseling. The worst, for some reason, are the Visible Christians—like the ten-person table, all jolly and sanctified after Sunday-night service, who run me mercilessly and then leave me $1 on a $92 bill. Or the guy with the crucifixion T-shirt (SOMEONE TO LOOK UP TO) who complains that his baked potato is too hard and his iced tea too icy (I cheerfully fix both) and leaves no

---

[5]In *Workers in a Lean World: Unions in the International Economy* (Verso, 1997), Kim Moody cites studies finding an increase in stress-related workplace injuries and illness between the mid-1980s and the early 1990s. He argues that rising stress levels reflect a new system of "management by stress," in which workers in a variety of industries are being squeezed to extract maximum productivity, to the detriment of their health.

tip. As a general rule, people wearing crosses or WWJD? (What Would Jesus Do?) buttons look at us disapprovingly no matter what we do, as if they were confusing waitressing with Mary Magdalene's original profession.

47   I make friends, over time, with the other "girls" who work my shift: Nita, the tattooed twenty-something who taunts us by going around saying brightly, "Have we started making money yet?" Ellen, whose teenage son cooks on the graveyard shift and who once managed a restaurant in Massachusetts but won't try out for management here because she prefers being a "common worker" and not "ordering people around." Easy-going fiftyish Lucy, with the raucous laugh, who limps toward the end of the shift because of something that has gone wrong with her leg, the exact nature of which cannot be determined without health insurance. We talk about the usual girl things—men, children, and the sinister allure of Jerry's chocolate peanut-butter cream pie— though no one, I notice, ever brings up anything potentially expensive, like shopping or movies. As at the Hearthside, the only recreation ever referred to is partying, which requires little more than some beer, a joint, and a few close friends. Still, no one here is homeless, or cops to it anyway, thanks usually to a working husband or boyfriend. All in all, we form a reliable mutual-support group: If one of us is feeling sick or overwhelmed, another one will "bev" a table or even carry trays for her. If one of us is off sneaking a cigarette or a pee,[6] the others will do their best to conceal her absence from the enforcers of corporate rationality.

[6]Until April 1998, there was no federally mandated right to bathroom breaks. According to Marc Linder and Ingrid Nygaard, authors of *Void Where Prohibited: Rest Breaks and the Right to Urinate on Company Time* (Cornell University Press, 1997), "The right to rest and void at work is not high on the list of social or political causes supported by professional or executive employees, who enjoy personal workplace liberties that millions of factory workers can only daydream about. . . . While we were dismayed to discover that workers lacked an acknowledged legal right to void at work, [the workers] were amazed by outsiders' naive belief that their employers would permit them to perform this basic bodily function when necessary. . . . A factory worker, not allowed a break for six-hour stretches, voided into pads worn inside her uniform; and a kindergarten teacher in a school without aides had to take all twenty children with her to the bathroom and line them up outside the stall door when she voided."

But my saving human connection—my oxytocin receptor, as 48 it were—is George, the nineteen-year-old, fresh-off-the-boat Czech dishwasher. We get to talking when he asks me, tortuously, how much cigarettes cost at Jerry's. I do my best to explain that they cost over a dollar more here than at a regular store and suggest that he just take one from the half-filled packs that are always lying around on the break table. But that would be unthinkable. Except for the one tiny earring signaling his allegiance to some vaguely alternative point of view, George is a perfect straight arrow—crew-cut, hardworking, and hungry for eye contact. "Czech Republic," I ask, "or Slovakia?" and he seems delighted that I know the difference. "Václav Havel," I try. "Velvet Revolution, Frank Zappa?" "Yes, yes, 1989," he says, and I realize we are talking about history.

My project is to teach George English. "How are you today, 49 George?" I say at the start of each shift. "I am good, and how are you today, Barbara?" I learn that he is not paid by Jerry's but by the "agent" who shipped him over—$5 an hour, with the agent getting the dollar or so difference between that and what Jerry's pays dishwashers. I learn also that he shares an apartment with a crowd of other Czech "dishers," as he calls them, and that he cannot sleep until one of them goes off for his shift, leaving a vacant bed. We are having one of our ESL sessions late one afternoon when B.J. catches us at it and orders "Joseph" to take up the rubber mats on the floor near the dishwashing sinks and mop underneath. "I thought your name was George," I say loud enough for B.J. to hear as she strides off back to the counter. Is she embarrassed? Maybe a little, because she greets me back at the counter with "George, Joseph—there are so many of them!" I say nothing, neither nodding nor smiling, and for this I am punished later when I think I am ready to go and she announces that I need to roll fifty more sets of silverware and isn't it time I mixed up a fresh four-gallon batch of blue-cheese dressing? May you grow old in this place, B.J., is the curse I beam out at her when I am finally permitted to leave. May the syrup spills glue your feet to the floor.

I make the decision to move closer to Key West. First, because 50 of the drive. Second and third, also because of the drive: gas is eating up $4 to $5 a day, and although Jerry's is as high-volume as you can get, the tips average only 10 percent, and not just for a newbie like me. Between the base pay of $2.15 an hour and the obligation to share tips with the busboys and dishwashers, we're averaging only about $7.50 an hour. Then there is the $30 I had to spend on the regulation tan slacks worn by Jerry's servers—a setback it could take weeks to absorb. (I had combed the town's two downscale department stores hoping for something cheaper but decided in the end that these marked-down Dockers, originally $49, were more likely to survive a daily washing.) Of my fellow servers, everyone who lacks a working husband or boyfriend seems to have a second job: Nita does something at a computer eight hours a day; another welds. Without the forty-five-minute commute, I can picture myself working two jobs and having the time to shower between them.

51   So I take the $500 deposit I have coming from my landlord, the $400 I have earned toward the next month's rent, plus the $200 reserved for emergencies, and use the $1,100 to pay the rent and deposit on trailer number 46 in the Overseas Trailer Park, a mile from the cluster of budget hotels that constitute Key West's version of an industrial park. Number 46 is about eight feet in width and shaped like a barbell inside, with a narrow region—because of the sink and the stove—separating the bedroom from what might optimistically be called the "living" area, with its two-person table and half-sized couch. The bathroom is so small my knees rub against the shower stall when I sit on the toilet, and you can't just leap out of the bed, you have to climb down to the foot of it in order to find a patch of floor space to stand on. Outside, I am within a few yards of a liquor store, a bar that advertises "free beer tomorrow," a convenience store, and a Burger King—but no supermarket or, alas, laundromat. By reputation, the Overseas park is a nest of crime and crack, and I am hoping at least for some vibrant, multicultural street life. But desolation rules night and day, except for a thin stream of pedestrian traffic heading for their jobs at the Sheraton or 7-Eleven. There are not exactly people here but what amounts to canned labor, being preserved from the heat between shifts.

52   In line with my reduced living conditions, a new form of ugliness arises at Jerry's. First we are confronted—via an announcement

on the computers through which we input orders—with the new rule that the hotel bar is henceforth off-limits to restaurant employees. The culprit, I learn through the grapevine, is the ultra-efficient gal who trained me—another trailer-home dweller and a mother of three. Something had set her off one morning, so she slipped out for a nip and returned to the floor impaired. This mostly hurts Ellen, whose habit it is to free her hair from its rubber band and drop by the bar for a couple of Zins before heading home at the end of the shift, but all of us feel the chill. Then the next day, when I go for straws, for the first time I find the dry-storage room locked. Ted, the portly assistant manager who opens it for me, explains that he caught one of the dishwashers attempting to steal something, and, unfortunately, the miscreant will be with us until a replacement can be found—hence the locked door. I neglect to ask what he had been trying to steal, but Ted tells me who he is—the kid with the buzz cut and the earring. You know, he's back there right now.

I wish I could say I rushed back and confronted George to get   53 his side of the story. I wish I could say I stood up to Ted and insisted that George be given a translator and allowed to defend himself, or announced that I'd find a lawyer who'd handle the case pro bono. The mystery to me is that there's not much worth stealing in the dry-storage room, at least not in any fenceable quantity: "Is Gyorgi here, and am having 200—maybe 250— ketchup packets. What do you say?" My guess is that he had taken—if he had taken anything at all—some Saltines or a can of cherry-pie mix, and that the motive for taking it was hunger.

So why didn't I intervene? Certainly not because I was held   54 back by the kind of moral paralysis that can pass as journalistic objectivity. On the contrary, something new—something loathsome and servile—had infected me, along with the kitchen odors that I could still sniff on my bra when I finally undressed at night. In real life I am moderately brave, but plenty of brave people shed their courage in concentration camps, and maybe something similar goes on in the infinitely more congenial milieu of the low-wage American workplace. Maybe, in a month or two more at Jerry's, I might have regained my crusading spirit. Then again, in a month or two I might have turned into a different person altogether—say, the kind of person who would have turned George in.

55   But this is not something I am slated to find out. When my month-long plunge into poverty is almost over, I finally land my dream job—housekeeping. I do this by walking into the personnel office of the only place I figure I might have some credibility, the hotel attached to Jerry's, and confiding urgently that I have to have a second job if I am to pay my rent and, no, it couldn't be front-desk clerk. "All right," the personnel lady fairly spits, "So it's housekeeping," and she marches me back to meet Maria, the house-keeping manager, a tiny, frenetic Hispanic woman who greets me as "babe" and hands me a pamphlet emphasizing the need for a positive attitude. The hours are nine in the morning till whenever, the pay is $6.10 an hour, and there's one week of vacation a year. I don't have to ask about health insurance once I meet Carlotta; the middle-aged African-American woman who will be training me. Carla, as she tells me to call her, is missing all of her top front teeth.

56   On that first day of housekeeping and last day of my entire project—although I don't yet know it's the last—Carla is in a foul mood. We have been given nineteen rooms to clean, most of them "checkouts," as opposed to "stay-overs," that require the whole enchilada of bed-stripping, vacuuming, and bathroom-scrubbing. When one of the rooms that had been listed as a stay-over turns out to be a checkout, Carla calls Maria to complain, but of course to no avail. "So make up the motherfucker," Carla orders me, and I do the beds while she sloshes around the bathroom. For four hours without a break I strip and remake beds, taking about four and a half minutes per queen-sized bed, which I could get down to three if there were any reason to. We try to avoid vacuuming by picking up the larger specks by hand, but often there is noth-ing to do but drag the monstrous vacuum cleaner—it weighs about thirty pounds—off our cart and try to wrestle it around the floor. Sometimes Carla hands me the squirt bottle of "BAM" (an acronym for something that begins, ominously, with "butyric"; the rest has been worn off the label) and lets me do the bathrooms. No service ethic challenges me here to new heights of performance. I just concentrate on removing the pubic hairs from the bathtubs, or at least the dark ones that I can see.

57   I had looked forward to the breaking-and-entering aspect of cleaning the stay-overs, the chance to examine the secret, physical

existence of strangers. But the contents of the rooms are always banal and suprisingly neat—zipped-up shaving kits, shoes lined up against the wall (there are no closets), flyers for snorkeling trips, maybe an empty wine bottle or two. It is the TV that keeps us going, from *Jerry* to *Sally* to *Hawaii Five-O* and then on to the soaps. If there's something especially arresting, like "Won't Take No for an Answer" on *Jerry*, we sit down on the edge of a bed and giggle for a moment as if this were a pajama party instead of a terminally dead-end job. The soaps are the best, and Carla turns the volume up full blast so that she won't miss anything from the bathroom or while the vacuum is on. In room 503, Marcia confronts Jeff about Lauren. In 505, Lauren taunts poor cuckolded Marcia. In 511, Helen offers Amanda $10,000 to stop seeing Eric, prompting Carla to emerge from the bathroom to study Amanda's troubled face. "You take it, girl," she advises. "I would for sure."

The tourists' rooms that we clean and, beyond them, the far 58 more expensively appointed interiors in the soaps, begin after a while to merge. We have entered a better world—a world of comfort where every day is a day off, waiting to be filled up with sexual intrigue. We, however, are only gatecrashers in this fantasy, forced to pay for our presence with backaches and perpetual thirst. The mirrors, and there are far too many of them in hotel rooms, contain the kind of person you would normally find pushing a shopping cart down a city street—bedraggled, dressed in a damp hotel polo shirt two sizes too large, and with sweat dribbling down her chin like drool. I am enormously relieved when Carla announces a half-hour meal break, but my appetite fades when I see that the bag of hot-dog rolls she has been carrying around on our cart is not trash salvaged from a checkout but what she has brought for her lunch.

When I request permission to leave at about 3:30, another 59 housekeeper warns me that no one has so far succeeded in combining housekeeping at the hotel with serving at Jerry's: "Some kid did it once for five days, and you're no kid." With that helpful information in mind, I rush back to number 46, down four Advils (the name brand this time), shower, stooping to fit into the stall, and attempt to compose myself for the oncoming shift. So much for what Marx termed the "reproduction of labor power," meaning the things a worker has to do just so she'll be ready to work again.

The only unforeseen obstacle to the smooth transition from job to job is that my tan Jerry's slacks, which had looked reasonably clean by 40-watt bulb last night when I handwashed my Hawaiian shirt, prove by daylight to be mottled with ketchup and ranch-dressing stains. I spend most of my hour-long break between jobs attempting to remove the edible portions with a sponge and then drying the slacks over the hood of my car in the sun.

60   I can do this two-job thing, is my theory, if I can drink enough caffeine and avoid getting distracted by George's ever more obvious suffering.[7] The first few days after being caught he seemed not to understand the trouble he was in, and our chirpy little conversations had continued. But the last couple of shifts he's been listless and unshaven, and tonight he looks like the ghost we all know him to be, with dark half-moons hanging from his eyes. At one point, when I am briefly immobilized by the task of filling little paper cups with sour cream for baked potatoes, he comes over and looks as if he'd like to explore the limits of our shared vocabulary, but I am called to the floor for a table. I resolve to give him all my tips that night and to hell with the experiment in low-wage money management. At eight, Ellen and I grab a snack together standing at the mephitic end of the kitchen counter, but I can only manage two or three mozzarella sticks and lunch had been a mere handful of McNuggets. I am not tired at all, I assure myself, though it may be that there is simply no more "I" left to do the tiredness monitoring. What I would see, if I were more alert to the situation, is that the forces of destruction are already massing against me. There is only one cook on duty, a young man named Jesus ("Hay-Sue," that is) and he is new to the job. And there is Joy, who shows up to take over in the middle of the shift, wearing high heels and a long, clingy white dress and fuming as if she'd just been stood up in some cocktail bar.

---

[7]In 1996, the number of persons holding two or more jobs averaged 7.8 million, or 6.2 percent of the workforce. It was about the same rate for men and for women (6.1 versus 6.2), though the kinds of jobs differ by gender. About two thirds of multiple jobholders work one job full-time and the other part-time. Only a heroic minority—4 percent of men and 2 percent of women—work two full-time jobs simultaneously. (From John F. Stinson Jr., "New Data on Multiple Jobholding Available from the CPS," in the *Monthly Labor Review*, March 1997.)

Then it comes, the perfect storm. Four of my tables fill up at 61 once. Four tables is nothing for me now, but only so long as they are obligingly staggered. As I bev table 27, tables 25, 28, and 24 are watching enviously. As I bev 25, 24 glowers because their bevs haven't even been ordered. Twenty-eight is four yuppyish types, meaning everything on the side and agonizing instructions as to the chicken Caesars. Twenty-five is a middle-aged black couple, who complain, with some justice, that the iced tea isn't fresh and the tabletop is sticky. But table 24 is the meteorological event of the century: ten British tourists who seem to have made the decision to absorb the American experience entirely by mouth. Here everyone has at least two drinks—iced tea and milk shake, Michelob and water (with lemon slice, please)—and a huge promiscuous orgy of breakfast specials, mozz sticks, chicken strips, quesadillas, burgers with cheese and without, sides of hash browns with cheddar, with onions, with gravy, seasoned fries, plain fries, banana splits. Poor Jesus! Poor me! Because when I arrive with their first tray of food—after three prior trips just to refill bevs—Princess Di refuses to eat her chicken strips with her pancake-and-sausage special, since, as she now reveals, the strips were meant to be an appetizer. Maybe the others would have accepted their meals, but Di, who is deep into her third Michelob, insists that everything else go back while they work on their "starters." Meanwhile, the yuppies are waving me down for more decaf and the black couple looks ready to summon the NAACP.

Much of what happened next is lost in the fog of war. Jesus 62 starts going under. The little printer on the counter in front of him is spewing out orders faster than he can rip them off, much less produce the meals. Even the invincible Ellen is ashen from stress. I bring table 24 their reheated main courses, which they immediately reject as either too cold or fossilized by the microwave. When I return to the kitchen with their trays (three trays in three trips), Joy confronts me with arms akimbo: "What is this?" She means the food—the plates of rejected pancakes, hash browns in assorted flavors, toasts, burgers, sausages, eggs. "Uh, scrambled with cheddar," I try, "and that's . . ." "NO," she screams in my face. "Is it a traditional, a super-scramble, an eye-opener?" I pretend to study my check for a clue, but entropy has been up to its tricks, not only on the plates but in my head, and I have to admit that the original order is beyond reconstruction. "You don't know an eye-opener from a traditional?" she demands in outrage. All I know, in fact, is that my legs have lost interest in the current venture and have announced their intention to fold. I am saved by a yuppie (mercifully not one of mine) who chooses this moment to charge into the kitchen to bellow that his food is twenty-five minutes late. Joy screams at him to get the hell out of her kitchen, please, and then turns on Jesus in a fury, hurling an empty tray across the room for emphasis.

63   I leave. I don't walk out, I just leave. I don't finish my side work or pick up my credit-card tips, if any, at the cash register or, of course, ask Joy's permission to go. And the surprising thing is that you *can* walk out without permission, that the door opens, that the thick tropical night air parts to let me pass, that my car is still parked where I left it. There is no vindication in this exit, no fuck-you surge of relief, just an overwhelming, dank sense of failure pressing down on me and the entire parking lot. I had gone into this venture in the spirit of science, to test a mathematical proposition, but somewhere along the line, in the tunnel vision imposed by long shifts and relentless concentration, it became a test of myself, and clearly I have failed. Not only had I flamed out as a housekeeper/server, I had even forgotten to give George my tips, and, for reasons perhaps best known to hardworking, generous people like Gail and Ellen, this hurts. I don't cry, but I am in a position to realize, for the first time in many years, that the tear ducts are still there, and still capable of doing their job.

64   When I moved out of the trailer park, I gave the key to number 46 to Gail and arranged for my deposit to be transferred to her. She told me that Joan is still living in her van and that Stu had been fired from the Hearthside. I never found out what happened to George.

65   In one month, I had earned approximately $1,040 and spent $517 on food, gas, toiletries, laundry, phone, and utilities. If I had remained in my $500 efficiency, I would have been able to pay the rent and have $22 left over (which is $78 less than the cash I had in my pocket at the start of the month). During this time I bought no clothing except for the required slacks and no prescription drugs or medical care (I did finally buy some vitamin B to

compensate for the lack of vegetables in my diet). Perhaps I could have saved a little on food if I had gotten to a supermarket more often, instead of convenience stores, but it should be noted that I lost almost four pounds in four weeks, on a diet weighted heavily toward burgers and fries.

How former welfare recipients and single mothers will (and 66 do) survive in the low-wage workforce, I cannot imagine. Maybe they will figure out how to condense their lives—including child-raising, laundry, romance, and meals—into the couple of hours between fulltime jobs. Maybe they will take up residence in their vehicles, if they have one. All I know is that I couldn't hold two jobs and I couldn't make enough money to live on with one. And I had advantages unthinkable to many of the long-term poor—health, stamina, a working car, and no children to care for and support. Certainly nothing in my experience contradicts the conclusion of Kathryn Edin and Laura Lein, in their recent book *Making Ends Meet: How Single Mothers Survive Welfare and Low-Wage Work*, that low-wage work actually involves more hardship and deprivation than life at the mercy of the welfare state. In the coming months and years, economic conditions for the working poor are bound to worsen, even without the almost inevitable recession. As mentioned earlier, the influx of former welfare recipients into the low-skilled workforce will have a depressing effect on both wages and the number of jobs available. A general economic downturn will only enhance these effects, and the working poor will of course be facing it without the slight, but nonetheless often saving, protection of welfare as a backup.

The thinking behind welfare reform was that even the hum- 67 blest jobs are morally uplifting and psychologically buoying. In reality they are likely to be fraught with insult and stress. But I did discover one redeeming feature of the most abject low-wage work—the camaraderie of people who are, in almost all cases, far too smart and funny and caring for the work they do and the wages they're paid. The hope, of course, is that someday these people will come to know what they're worth, and take appropriate action.

1999

What Is Poverty?

Jo Goodwin Parker

1   You ask me what is poverty? Listen to me. Here I am, dirty, smelly, and with no "proper" underwear on and with the stench of my rotting teeth near you. I will tell you. Listen to me. Listen without pity. I cannot use your pity. Listen with understanding. Put yourself in my dirty, worn out, ill-fitting shoes, and hear me.

2   Poverty is getting up every morning from a dirt- and illness-stained mattress. The sheets have long since been used for diapers. Poverty is living in a smell that never leaves. This is a smell of urine, sour milk, and spoiling food sometimes joined with the strong smell of long-cooked onions. Onions are cheap. If you have smelled this smell, you did not know how it came. It is the smell of the outdoor privy. It is the smell of young children who cannot walk the long dark way in the night. It is the smell of the mattresses where years of "accidents" have happened. It is the smell of the milk which has gone sour because the refrigerator long has not worked, and it costs money to get it fixed. It is the smell of rotting garbage. I could bury it, but where is the shovel? Shovels cost money.

3   Poverty is being tired. I have always been tired. They told me at the hospital when the last baby came that I had chronic anemia caused from poor diet, a bad case of worms, and that I needed a corrective operation. I listened politely—the poor are always polite. The poor always listen. They don't say that there is no money for iron pills, or better food, or worm medicine. The idea of an operation is frightening and costs so much that, if I had dared, I would have laughed. Who takes care of my children? Recovery from an operation takes a long time. I have three children. When I left them with "Granny" the last time I had a job, I came home to find the baby covered with fly specks, and a diaper that had not been changed since I left. When the dried diaper came off, bits of my baby's flesh came with it. My other child was playing with a sharp bit of broken glass, and my oldest was playing alone at the edge of a lake. I made twenty-two dollars a week, and a good nursery school costs twenty dollars a week for three children. I quit my job.

Poverty is dirt. You can say in your clean clothes coming from 4
your clean house, "Anybody can be clean." Let me explain about
housekeeping with no money. For breakfast I give my children
grits with no oleo or cornbread without eggs and oleo. This does
not use up many dishes. What dishes there are, I wash in cold
water and with no soap. Even the cheapest soap has to be saved
for the baby's diapers. Look at my hands, so cracked and red.
Once I saved for two months to buy a jar of Vaseline for my hands
and the baby's diaper rash. When I had saved enough, I went to
buy it and the price had gone up two cents. The baby and I suffered on. I have to decide every day if I can bear to put my
cracked sore hands into the cold water and strong soap. But you
ask, why not hot water? Fuel costs money. If you have a wood
fire it costs money. If you burn electricity, it costs money. Hot
water is a luxury. I do not have luxuries. I know you will be surprised when I tell you how young I am. I look so much older. My
back has been bent over the wash tubs every day for so long. I
cannot remember when I ever did anything else. Every night I
wash every stitch my school age child has on and just hope her
clothes will be dry by morning.

Poverty is staying up all night on cold nights to watch the fire 5
knowing one spark on the newspaper covering the walls means
your sleeping child dies in flames. In summer, poverty is watching gnats and flies devour your baby's tears when he cries. The
screens are torn and you pay so little rent you know they will
never be fixed. Poverty means insects in your food, in your nose,
in your eyes, and crawling over you when you sleep. Poverty is
hoping it never rains because diapers won't dry when it rains and
soon you are using newspapers. Poverty is seeing your children
forever with runny noses. Paper handkerchiefs cost money and all
your rags you need for other things. Even more costly are anti-
histamines. Poverty is cooking without food and cleaning without
soap.

Poverty is asking for help. Have you ever had to ask for help, 6
knowing your children will suffer unless you get it? Think about
asking for a loan from a relative, if this is the only way you can
imagine asking for help. I will tell you how it feels. You find out
where the office is that you are supposed to visit. You circle that
block four or five times. Thinking of your children, you go in.

Everyone is very busy. Finally, someone comes out and you tell her that you need help. That never is the person you need to see. You go see another person, and after spilling the whole shame of your poverty all over the desk between you, you find that this isn't the right office after all—you must repeat the whole process, and it never is any easier at the next place.

7   You have asked for help, and after all it has a cost. You are again told to wait. You are told why, but you don't really hear because of the red cloud of shame and the rising cloud of despair.

8   Poverty is remembering. It is remembering quitting school in junior high because "nice" children had been so cruel about my clothes and my smell. The attendance officer came. My mother told him I was pregnant. I wasn't, but she thought that I could get a job and help out. I had jobs off and on, but never long enough to learn anything. Mostly I remember being married. I was so young then. I am still young. For a time, we had all the things you have. There was a little house in another town, with hot water and every thing. Then my husband lost his job. There was unemployment insurance for a while and what few jobs I could get. Soon, all our nice things were repossessed and we moved back here. I was pregnant then. This house didn't look so bad when we first moved in. Every week it gets worse. Nothing is ever fixed. We now had no money. There were a few odd jobs for my husband, but everything went for food then, as it does now. I don't know how we lived through three years and three babies, but we did. I'll tell you something, after the last baby I destroyed my marriage. It had been a good one, but could you keep on bringing children in this dirt? Did you ever think how much it costs for any kind of birth control? I knew my husband was leaving the day he left, but there were no goodbys between us. I hope he has been able to climb out of this mess somewhere. He never could hope with us to drag him down.

9   That's when I asked for help. When I got it, you know how much it was? It was, and is, seventy-eight dollars a month for the four of us; that is all I ever can get. Now you know why there is no soap, no needles and thread, no hot water, no aspirin, no worm medicine, no hand cream, no shampoo. None of these things for-ever and ever and ever. So that you can see clearly, I pay twenty dollars a month rent, and most of the rest goes for food. For grits

and cornmeal, and rice and milk and beans. I try my best to use only the minimum electricity. If I use more, there is that much less for food.

Poverty is looking into a black future. Your children won't 10 play with my boys. They will turn to other boys who steal to get what they want. I can already see them behind the bars of their prison instead of behind the bars of my poverty. Or they will turn to the freedom of alcohol or drugs, and find themselves enslaved. And my daughter? At best, there is for her a life like mine.

But you say to me, there are schools. Yes, there are schools. 11 My children have no extra books, no magazines, no extra pencils, or crayons, or paper and most important of all, they do not have health. They have worms, they have infections, they have pink-eye all summer. They do not sleep well on the floor, or with me in my one bed. They do not suffer from hunger, my seventy-eight dollars keeps us alive, but they do suffer from malnutrition. Oh yes, I do remember what I was taught about health in school. It doesn't do much good. In some places there is a surplus com-modities program. Not here. The county said it cost too much. There is a school lunch program. But I have two children who will already be damaged by the time they get to school.

But, you say to me, there are health clinics. Yes, there are 12 health clinics and they are in the towns. I live out here eight miles from town. I can walk that far (even if it is sixteen miles both ways), but can my little children? My neighbor will take me when he goes; but he expects to get paid, *one way or another*. I bet you know my neighbor. He is that large man who spends his time at the gas station, the barbershop, and the corner store complaining about the government spending money on the immoral mothers of illegitimate children.

Poverty is an acid that drips on pride until all pride is worn 13 away. Poverty is a chisel that chips on honor until honor is worn away. Some of you say that you would do *something* in my situ-ation, and maybe you would, for the first week or the first month, but for year after year after year?

Even the poor can dream. A dream of a time when there is 14 money. Money for the right kinds of food, for worm medicine, for iron pills, for toothbrushes, for hand cream, for a hammer and nails and a bit of screening, for a shovel, for a bit of paint, for some sheeting, for needles and thread. Money to pay *in money* for a trip to town. And, oh, money for hot water and money for soap. A dream of when asking for help does not eat away the last bit of pride. When the office you visit is as nice as the offices of other governmental agencies, when there are enough workers to help you quickly, when workers do not quit in defeat and despair. When you have to tell your story to only one person, and that person can send you for other help and you don't have to prove your poverty over and over and over again.

15   I have come out of my despair to tell you this. Remember I did not come from another place or another time. Others like me are all around you. Look at us with an angry heart, anger that will help you help me. Anger that will let you tell of me. The poor are always silent. Can you be silent too?

1971

Gilded Lilies and Liberal Guilt

Patricia J. Williams

1 The original vehicle for my interest in the intersection of commerce and the Constitution was my family history. A few years ago, I came into the possession of what may have been the contract of sale for my great-great-grandmother. It is a very simple but lawyerly document, describing her as "one female" and revealing her age as eleven; no price is specified, merely "value exchanged." My sister also found a county census record taken two years later; on a list of one Austin Miller's personal assets she appears again, as "slave, female"—thirteen years old now with an eight-month infant.

2   Since then I have tried to piece together what it must have been like to be my great-great-grandmother. She was purchased, according to matrilineal recounting, by a man who was extremely temperamental and quite wealthy. I try to imagine what it would have been like to have a discontented white man buy me, after a

fight with his mother about prolonged bachelorhood. I wonder what it would have been like to have a thirty-five-year-old man own the secrets of my puberty, which he bought to prove himself sexually as well as to increase his livestock of slaves. I imagine trying to please, with the yearning of adolescence, a man who truly did not know I was human, whose entire belief system resolutely defined me as animal, chattel, talking cow. I wonder what it would have been like to have his child, pale-faced but also animal, before I turned thirteen. I try to envision being casually threatened with sale from time to time, teeth and buttocks bared to interested visitors.

Family legend has it that my great-great-grandmother was 3 very lazy, that she sat on the bank of the river all day and fished. According to the census, she was at least two decades younger than any other slave on the estate; family legend says that no one liked her. What could it have been like for my stunned, raped great-great-grandmother—an unwed teenage mother in today's parlance—so disliked and isolated from even her own children that the stones they purveyed were of her laziness? Her children were the exclusive property of their father (though that's not what they called him). They grew up in his house, taken from her as she had been taken from her mother. They became haughty, favored, frightened house servants who were raised playing with, caring for, and envying this now-married man's legitimate children, their half brothers and sister. Her children grew up reverent of and obedient to this white man—my great-great-grandfather—and his other children, to whom they were taught they owed the debt of their survival. It was a mistake from which the Emancipation Proclamation never fully freed any of them.

Her children must have been something of an ultimate 4 betrayal; it could not have been easy to see in them the hope of her own survival. Freed from slavery by the Civil War, they went on to establish respected black Episcopal churches and to learn to play the piano. They grew up clever and well-bred. They grew up to marry other frightened, refined, master-blooded animals; they grew up good people, but alien.

Austin Miller, one of Tennessee's finest lawyers according to 5 other records, went on to become a judge; and the sons by his wife went on to become lawyers as well. There is no surviving record of what happened to my great-great-grandmother, no account of how or when she died.

6   This story is what inspired my interest in the interplay of notions of public and private, of family and market; of male and female, of molestation and the law. I track meticulously the dimension of meaning in my great-great-grandmother as chattel: the meaning of money; the power of consumerist world view, the deaths of those we label the unassertive and the inefficient. I try to imagine where and who she would be today. I am engaged in a long-term project of tracking his words—through his letters and opinions—and those of his sons who were also lawyers and judges, of finding the shape described by her absence in all this.

7   I see her shape and his hand in the vast networking of our society, and in the evils and oversights that plague our lives and laws. The control he had over her body. The force he was in her life, in the shape of my life today. The power he exercised in the choice to breed her or not. The choice to breed slaves in his image, to choose her mate and be that mate. In his attempt to own what no man can own, the habit of his power and the absence of her choice.

8   I look for her shape and his hand.

1991

Work in Corporate America

Russell Baker

1 It is not surprising that modern children tend to look blank and dispirited when informed that they will someday have to "go to work and make a living." The problem is that they cannot visualize what work is in corporate America.

2   Not so long ago, when a parent said he was off to work, the child knew very well what was about to happen. His parent was going to make something or fix something. The parent could take his offspring to his place of business and let him watch while he repaired a buggy or built a table.

When a child asked, "What kind of work do you do, Daddy?" 3
his father could answer in terms that a child could come to grips
with. "I fix steam engines." "I make horse collars."

Well, a few fathers still fix steam engines and build tables, but 4
most do not. Nowadays, most fathers sit in glass buildings doing
things that are absolutely incomprehensible to children. The
answers they give when asked, "What kind of work do you do,
Daddy?" are likely to be utterly mystifying to a child.

"I sell space." "I do market research." "I am a data proces- 5
sor." "I am in public relations." "I am a systems analyst." Such
explanations must seem nonsense to a child. How can he possibly envision anyone analyzing a system or researching a market?

Even grown men who do market research have trouble visu- 6
alizing what a public relations man does with his day, and it is a
safe bet that the average systems analyst is as baffled about what
a space salesman does at the shop as the average space salesman
is about the tools needed to analyze a system.

In the common everyday job, nothing is made any more. 7
Things are now made by machines. Very little is repaired. The
machines that make things make them in such a fashion that they
will quickly fall apart in such a way that repairs will be prohibitively expensive. Thus the buyer is encouraged to throw the thing
away and buy a new one. In effect, the machines are making
junk.

The handful of people remotely associated with these machines 8
can, of course, tell their inquisitive children "Daddy makes junk."
Most of the work force, however, is too remote from junk production to sense any contribution to the industry. What do these
people do?

Consider the typical twelve-story glass building in the typical 9
American city. Nothing is being made in this building and nothing is being repaired, including the building itself. Constructed as
a piece of junk, the building will be discarded when it wears out,
and another piece of junk will be set in its place.

Still, the building is filled with people who think of them- 10
selves as working. At any given moment during the day perhaps
one-third of them will be talking into telephones. Most of these
conversations will be about paper, for paper is what occupies
nearly everyone in this building.

11 Some jobs in the building require men to fill paper with words. There are persons who type neatly on paper and persons who read paper and jot notes in the margins. Some persons make copies of paper and other persons deliver paper. There are persons who file paper and persons who unfile paper.

12 Some persons mail paper. Some persons telephone other persons and ask that paper be sent to them. Others telephone to ascertain the whereabouts of paper. Some persons confer about paper. In the grandest offices, men approve of some paper and disapprove of other paper.

13 The elevators are filled throughout the day with young men carrying paper from floor to floor and with vital men carrying paper to be discussed with other vital men.

14 What is a child to make of all this? His father may be so eminent that he lunches with other men about paper. Suppose he brings his son to work to give the boy some idea of what work is all about. What does the boy see happening?

15 His father calls for paper. He reads paper. Perhaps he scowls at paper. Perhaps he makes an angry red mark on paper. He telephones another man and says they had better lunch over paper.

16 At lunch they talk about paper. Back at the office, the father orders the paper retyped and reproduced in quintuplicate, and then sent to another man for comparison with paper that was reproduced in triplicate last year.

17 Imagine his poor son afterwards mulling over the mysteries of work with a friend, who asks him, "What's your father do?" What can the boy reply? "It beats me," perhaps, if he is not very observant. Or if he is, "Something that has to do with making junk, I think. Same as everybody else."

1971

PART 3

Sciences

12

Brave New World

Virtual Students, Digital Classroom

Neil Postman

1   If one has a trusting relationship with one's students (let us say, graduate students), it is not altogether gauche to ask them if they believe in God (with a capital G). I have done this three or four times and most students say they do. Their answer is preliminary to the next question: If someone you love were desperately ill, and you had to choose between praying to God for his or her recovery or administering an antibiotic (as prescribed by a competent physician), which would you choose?

2   Most say the question is silly since the alternatives are not mutually exclusive. Of course. But suppose they were—which would you choose? God helps those who help themselves, some say in choosing the antibiotic, therefore getting the best of two possible belief systems. But if pushed to the wall (e.g., God does not always help those who help themselves; God helps those who pray and who believe), most choose the antibiotic, after noting that the question is asinine and proves nothing. Of course, the question was not asked, in the first place, to prove anything but to begin a discussion of the nature of belief. And I do not fail to inform the students, by the way, that there has recently emerged evidence of a "scientific" nature that when sick people are prayed for they do better than those who aren't.

3   As the discussion proceeds, important distinctions are made among the different meanings of "belief," but at some point it becomes far from asinine to speak of the god of Technology—in the sense that people believe technology works, that they rely on it, that it makes promises, that they are bereft when denied access

436

to it, that they are delighted when they are in its presence, that for most people it works in mysterious ways, that they condemn people who speak against it, that they stand in awe of it and that, in the "born again" mode, they will alter their life-styles, their schedules, their habits, and their relationships to accommodate it. If this be not a form of religious belief, what is?

In all strands of American cultural life, you can find so many 4 examples of technological adoration that it is possible to write a book about it. And I would if it had not already been done so well. But nowhere do you find more enthusiasm for the god of Technology than among educators. In fact, there are those, like Lewis Perelman, who argue (for example, in his book, *School's Out*) that modern information technologies have rendered schools entirely irrelevant since there is now much more information available outside the classroom than inside it. This is by no means considered an outlandish idea. Dr. Diane Ravitch, former Assistant Secretary of Education, envisions, with considerable relish, the challenge that technology presents to the tradition that "children (and adults) should be educated in a specific place, for a certain number of hours, and a certain number of days during the week and year." In other words, that children should be educated in school. Imagining the possibilities of an information superhighway offering perhaps a thousand channels, Dr. Ravitch assures us that:

> In this new world of pedagogical plenty, children and adults will be able to dial up a program on their home television to learn whatever they want to know, at their own convenience. If Little Eva cannot sleep, she can learn algebra instead. At her home-learning station, she will tune in to a series of interesting problems that are presented in an interactive medium, much like video games. . . .
>
> Young John may decide that he wants to learn the history of modern Japan, which he can do by dialing up the greatest authorities and teachers on the subject, who will not only use dazzling graphs and illustrations, but will narrate a historical video that excites his curiosity and imagination.

In this vision there is, it seems to me, a confident and typical 5 sense of unreality. Little Eva can't sleep, so she decides to learn a little algebra? Where does Little Eva come from? Mars? If not, it is more likely she will tune in to a good movie. Young John decides that he wants to learn the history of modern Japan? How did young John come to this point? How is it that he never visited a library up to now? Or is that he, too, couldn't sleep and decided that a little modern Japanese history was just what he needed?

6 What Ravitch is talking about here is not a new technology but a new species of child, one who, in any case, no one has seen up to now. Of course, new technologies do make new kinds of people, which leads to a second objection to Ravitch's conception of the future. There is a kind of forthright determinism about the imagined world described in it. The technology is here or will be; we must use it because it is there; we will become the kind of people the technology requires us to be, and whether we like it or not, we will remake our institutions to accommodate technology. All of this must happen because it is good for us, but in any case, we have no choice. This point of view is present in very nearly every statement about the future relationship of learning to technology. And, as in Ravitch's scenario, there is always a cheery, gee-whiz tone to the prophecies. Here is one produced by the National Academy of Sciences, written by Hugh McIntosh.

> School for children of the Information Age will be vastly different than it was for Mom and Dad.
>
> Interested in biology? Design your own life forms with computer simulation.
>
> Having trouble with a science project? Teleconference about it with a research scientist.
>
> Bored with the real world? Go into a virtual physics lab and rewrite the laws of gravity.
>
> These are the kinds of hands-on learning experiences schools could be providing right now. The technologies that make them possible are already here, and today's youngsters, regardless of economic status, know how to use them. They spend hours with them every week—not in the classroom, but in their own homes and in video game centers at every shopping mall.

7 It is always interesting to attend to the examples of learning, and the motivations that ignite them, in the songs of love that technophiles perform for us. It is, for example, not easy to imagine

research scientists all over the world teleconferencing with thousands of students who are having difficulty with their science projects. I can't help thinking that most research scientists would put a stop to this rather quickly. But I find it especially revealing that in the scenario above we have an example of a technological solution to a psychological problem that would seem to be exceedingly serious. We are presented with a student who is "bored with the real world." What does it mean to say someone is bored with the real world, especially one so young? Can a journey into virtual reality cure such a problem? And if it can, will our troubled youngster want to return to the real world? Confronted with a student who is bored with the real world, I don't think we can solve the problem so easily by making available a virtual reality physics lab.

The role that new technology should play in schools or any- 8 where else is something that needs to be discussed without the hyperactive fantasies of cheerleaders. In particular, the computer and its associated technologies are awesome additions to a culture, and are quite capable of altering the psychic, not to mention the sleeping, habits of our young. But like all important technologies of the past, they are Faustian bargains,[1] giving and taking away, sometimes in equal measure, sometimes more in one way than the other. It is strange—indeed, shocking—that with the twenty-first century so close, we can still talk of new technologies as if they were unmixed blessings—gifts, as it were, from the gods. Don't we all know what the combustion engine has done for us and against us? What television is doing for us and against us? At the very least, what we need to discuss about Little Eva, Young John, and McIntosh's trio is what they will lose, and what we will lose, if they enter a world in which computer technology is their chief source of motivation, authority, and, apparently, psychological sustenance. Will they become, as Joseph Weizenbaum warns,[2] more impressed by calculation than human judgment? Will speed of response become, more than ever, a defining quality of intelligence? If, indeed, the idea of a school will be dramatically altered,

---

[1]The legendary Doctor Faustus exchanged his soul for infinite knowledge in a pact with the Devil.

[2]Weizenbaum's 1976 book, *Computer Power and Human Reason: From Judgment to Calculation*, raises these questions.

what kinds of learning will be neglected, perhaps made impossible? Is virtual reality a new form of therapy? If it is, what are its dangers?

9   These are serious matters, and they need to be discussed by those who know something about children from the planet Earth, and whose vision of children's needs, and the needs of society, go beyond thinking of school mainly as a place for the convenient distribution of information. Schools are not now and have never been largely about getting information to children. That has been on the schools' agenda, of course, but has always been way down on the list. For technological utopians, the computer vaults information access to the top. This reshuffling of priorities comes at a most inopportune time. The goal of giving people greater access to more information faster, more conveniently, and in more diverse forms was the main technological thrust of the nineteenth century. Some folks haven't noticed it but that problem was largely solved, so that for almost a hundred years there has been more information available to the young outside the school than inside. That fact did not make the schools obsolete, nor does it now make them obsolete. Yes, it is true that Little Eva, the insomniac from Mars, could turn on an algebra lesson, thanks to the computer, in the wee hours of the morning. She could also, if she wished, read a book or magazine, watch television, turn on the radio or listen to music. All of this she could have done before the computer. The computer does not solve any problem she has but does exacerbate one. For Little Eva's problem is not how to get access to a well-structured algebra lesson but what to do with all the information available to her during the day, as well as during sleepless nights. Perhaps this is why she couldn't sleep in the first place. Little Eva, like the rest of us, is overwhelmed by information. She lives in a culture that has 260,000 billboards, 17,000 newspapers, 12,000 periodicals, 27,000 video outlets for renting tapes, 400 million television sets, and well over 500 million radios, not including those in automobiles. There are 40,000 new book titles published every year, and each day 41 million photographs are taken. And thanks to the computer, more than 60 billion pieces of advertising junk come into our mailboxes every year. Everything from telegraphy and photography in the nineteenth century

to the silicon chip in the twentieth has amplified the din of information intruding on Little Eva's consciousness. From millions of sources all over the globe, through every possible channel and medium—light waves, air waves, ticker tape, computer banks, telephone wires, television cables, satellites, and printing presses—information pours in. Behind it in every imaginable form of storage—on paper, on video, on audiotape, on disks, film, and silicon chips—is an even greater volume of information waiting to be retrieved. In the face of this we might ask: What can schools do for Little Eva besides making still more information available? If there is nothing, then new technologies will indeed make schools obsolete. But in fact, there is plenty.

One thing that comes to mind is that schools can provide her 10 with a serious form of technology education. Something quite different from instruction in using computers to process information, which, it strikes me, is a trivial thing to do, for two reasons. In the first place, approximately 35 million people have already learned how to use computers without the benefit of school instruction. If the schools do nothing, most of the population will know how to use computers in the next ten years, just as most of the population learns how to drive a car without school instruction. In the second place, what we needed to know about cars—as we need to know about computers, television, and other important technologies—is not how to use them but how they use *us*. In the case of cars, what we needed to think about in the early twentieth century was not how to drive them but what they would do to our air, our landscape, our social relations, our family life, and our cities. Suppose in 1946 we had started to address similar questions about television: What will be its effects on our political institutions, our psychic habits, our children, our religious conceptions, our economy? Would we be better positioned today to control TV's massive assault on American culture? I am talking here about making technology itself an object of inquiry so that Little Eva and Young John are more interested in asking questions about the computer than getting answers from it.

I am not arguing against using computers in school. I am 11 arguing against our sleepwalking attitudes toward it, against allowing it to distract us from important things, against making a god of it. This is what Theodore Roszak warned against in *The*

Cult of Information: "Like all cults," he wrote, "this one also has the intention of enlisting mindless allegiance and acquiescence. People who have no clear idea of what they mean by information or why they should want so much of it are nonetheless prepared to believe that we live in an Information Age, which makes every computer around us what the relics of the True Cross were in the Age of Faith: emblems of salvation." To this, I would add the sage observation of Alan Kay of Apple Computer. Kay is widely associated with the invention of the personal computer, and certainly has an interest in schools using them. Nonetheless, he has repeatedly said that any problems the schools cannot solve without computers, they cannot solve with them. What are some of those problems? There is, for example, the traditional task of teaching children how to behave in groups. One might even say that schools have never been essentially about individualized learning. It is true, of course, that groups do not learn, individuals do. But the idea of a school is that individuals must learn in a setting in which individual needs are subordinated to group interests. Unlike other media of mass communication, which celebrate individual response and are experienced in private, the classroom is intended to tame the ego, to connect the individual with others, to demonstrate the value and necessity of group cohesion. At present, most scenarios describing the uses of computers have children solving problems alone; Little Eva, Young John, and the others are doing just that. The presence of other children may, indeed, be an annoyance.

12   Like the printing press before it, the computer has a powerful bias toward amplifying personal autonomy and individual problem-solving. That is why educators must guard against computer technology's undermining some of the important reasons for having the young assemble (to quote Ravitch) "in a specific place, for a certain number of hours, and a certain number of days during the week and year."

13   Although Ravitch is not exactly against what she calls "state schools," she imagines them as something of a relic of a pretechnological age. She believes that the new technologies will offer all children equal access to information. Conjuring up a hypothetical Little Mary who is presumably from a poorer home than

Little Eva, Ravitch imagines that Mary will have the same opportunities as Eva "to learn any subject, and to learn it from the same master teachers as children in the richest neighborhood." For all of its liberalizing spirit, this scenario makes some important omissions. One is that though new technologies may be a solution to the learning of "subjects," they work against the learning of what are called "social values," including an understanding of democratic processes. If one reads the first chapter of Robert Fulghum's *All I Really Need to Know I Learned in Kindergarten,* one will find an elegant summary of a few things Ravitch's scenario has left out. They include learning the following lessons: Share everything, play fair, don't hit people, put things back where you found them, clean up your own mess, wash your hands before you eat, and, of course, flush. The only thing wrong with Fulghum's book is that no one has learned all these things at kindergarten's end. We have ample evidence that it takes many years of teaching these values in school before they have been accepted and internalized. That is why it won't do for children to learn in "settings of their own choosing." That is also why schools require children to be in a certain place at a certain time and to follow certain rules, like raising their hands when they wish to speak, not talking when others are talking, not chewing gum, not leaving until the bell rings, exhibiting patience toward slower learners, etc. This process is called making civilized people. The god of Technology does not appear interested in this function of schools. At least, it does not come up much when technology's virtues are enumerated.

The god of Technology may also have a trick or two up its 14 sleeve about something else. It is often asserted that new technologies will equalize learning opportunities for the rich and poor. It is devoutly to be wished for, but I doubt it will happen. In the first place, it is generally understood by those who have studied the history of technology that technological change always produces winners and losers. There are many reasons for this, among them economic differences. Even in the case of the automobile, which is a commodity most people can buy (although not all), there are wide differences between the rich and poor in the quality of what is available to them. It would be quite astonishing if computer technology equalized all learning opportunities, irrespective of economic differences. One may be delighted that Little Eva's parents could afford the technology and software to make it possible for her to learn algebra at midnight. But Little Mary's parents may not be able to, may not even know such things are available. And if we say that the school could make the technology available to Little Mary (at least during the day), there may [be] something else Little Mary is lacking.

15   It turns out, for example, that Little Mary may be having sleepless nights as frequently as Little Eva but not because she wants to get a leg up on her algebra. Maybe because she doesn't know who her father is, or, if she does, where he is. Maybe we can understand why McIntosh's kid is bored with the real world. Or is the child confused about it? Or terrified? Are there educators who seriously believe that these problems can be addressed by new technologies?

16   I do not say, of course, that schools can solve the problems of poverty, alienation, and family disintegration, but schools can *respond* to them. And they can do this because there are people in them, because these people are concerned with more than algebra lessons or modern Japanese history, and because these people can identify not only one's level of competence in math but one's level of rage and confusion and depression. I am talking here about children as they really come to us, not children who are invented to show us how computers may enrich their lives. Of course, I suppose it is possible that there are children who, waking at night, want to study algebra or who are so interested in their world that they yearn to know about Japan. If there be such children, and one hopes there are, they do not require expensive computers to satisfy their hunger for learning. They are on their way, with or without computers. Unless, of course, they do not care about others or have no friends, or little respect for democracy or are filled with suspicion about those who are not like them. When we have machines that know how to do something about these problems, that is the time to rid ourselves of the expensive burden of schools or to reduce the function of teachers to "coaches" in the uses of machines (as Ravitch envisions). Until then, we must be more modest about this god of Technology and certainly not pin our hopes on it.

17   We must also, I suppose, be empathetic toward those who search with good intentions for technological panaceas. I am a

teacher myself and know how hard it is to contribute to the making of a civilized person. Can we blame those who want to find an easy way, through the agency of technology? Perhaps not. After all, it is an old quest. As early as 1918, H. L. Mencken[3] (although completely devoid of empathy) wrote, "There is no sure-cure so idiotic that some superintendent of schools will not swallow it. The aim seems to be reduce the whole teaching process to a sort of automatic reaction, to discover some master formula that will not only take the place of competence and resourcefulness in the teacher but that will also create an artificial receptivity in the child."

Mencken was not necessarily speaking of technological 18 panaceas but he may well have been. In the early 1920s a teacher wrote the following poem:

> Mr. Edison says
> That the radio will supplant the teacher.
> Already one may learn languages by means of
> Victrola records.
> The moving picture will visualize
> What the radio fails to get across.
> Teachers will be relegated to the backwoods,
> With fire-horses,
> And long-haired women;
> Or, perhaps shown in museums.
> Education will become a matter
> Of pressing the button.
> Perhaps I can get a position at the switchboard.

I do not go as far back as the radio and Victrola, but I am old 19 enough to remember when 16-millimeter film was to be the sure-cure. Then closed-circuit television. Then 8-millimeter film. Then teacher-proof textbooks. Now computers.

I know a false god when I see one. 20

1995

[3]American journalist (1880–1956).

The Virtual Community

Howard Rheingold

1 In the summer of 1986, my then-two-year-old daughter picked up a tick. There was this blood-bloated *thing* sucking on our baby's scalp, and we weren't quite sure how to go about getting it off. My wife, Judy, called the pediatrician. It was eleven o'clock in the evening. I logged onto the WELL. I got my answer online within minutes from a fellow with the improbable but genuine name of Flash Gordon, M.D. I had removed the tick by the time Judy got the callback from the pediatrician's office.

2 What amazed me wasn't just the speed with which we obtained precisely the information we needed to know, right when we needed to know it. It was also the immense inner sense of security that comes with discovering that real people—most of them parents, some of them nurses, doctors, and midwives—are available, around the clock, if you need them. There is a magic protective circle around the atmosphere of this particular conference. We're talking about our sons and daughters in this forum, not about our computers or our opinions about philosophy, and many of us feel that this tacit understanding sanctifies the virtual space.

3 The atmosphere of the Parenting conference—the attitudes people exhibit to each other in the tone of what they say in public— is part of what continues to attract me. People who never have much to contribute in political debate, technical argument, or intellectual gamesmanship turn out to have a lot to say about raising children. People you knew as fierce, even nasty, intellectual opponents in other contexts give you emotional support on a deeper level, parent to parent, within the boundaries of Parenting, a small but warmly human corner of cyberspace.

4 Here is a short list of examples from the hundreds of separate topics available for discussion in the Parenting conference. Each of these entries is the name of a conversation that includes scores or hundreds of individual contributions spread over a period of days or years, like a long, topical cocktail party you can rewind back to the beginning to find out who said what before you got there.

Great Expectations: You're Pregnant: Now What? Part III
What's Bad About Children's TV?
Movies: The Good, the Bad, and the Ugly
Initiations and Rites of Passage
Brand New Well Baby!!
How Does Being a Parent Change Your Life?
Tall Teenage Tales (cont.)
Guilt
MOTHERS
Vasectomy—Did It Hurt?
Introductions! Who Are We?
Fathers (Continued)
Books for Kids, Section Two
Gay and Lesbian Teenagers
Children and Spirituality
Great Parks for Kids
Quality Toys
Parenting in an Often-Violent World
Children's Radio Programming
New WELL Baby
Home Schooling
Newly Separated/Divorced Fathers
Another Well Baby—Carson Arrives in Seattle!
Single Parenting
Uncle Philcat's Back Fence: Gossip Here!
Embarrassing Moments
Kids and Death
All the Poop on Diapers
Pediatric Problems—Little Sicknesses and Sick Little Ones
Talking with Kids About the Prospect of War
Dealing with Incest and Abuse

*Other People's Children
When They're Crying
Pets for Kids*

5   People who talk about a shared interest, albeit a deep one such as being a parent, don't often disclose enough about themselves as whole individuals online to inspire real trust in others. In the case of the subcommunity of the Parenting conference, a few dozen of us, scattered across the country, few of whom rarely if ever saw the others face-to-face, had a few years of minor crises to knit us together and prepare us for serious business when it came our way. Another several dozen read the conference regularly but contribute only when they have something important to add. Hundreds more every week read the conference without comment, except when something extraordinary happens. . . .

6   Many people are alarmed by the very idea of a virtual community, fearing that is another step in the wrong direction, substituting more technological ersatz for yet another natural resource or human freedom. These critics often voice their sadness at what people have been reduced to doing in a civilization that worships technology, decrying the circumstances that lead some people into such pathetically disconnected lives that they prefer to find their companions on the other side of a computer screen. There is a seed of truth in this fear, for virtual communities require more than words on a screen at some point if they intend to be other than ersatz.

7   Some people—many people—don't do well in spontaneous spoken interaction, but turn out to have valuable contributions to make in a conversation in which they have time to think about what to say. These people, who might constitute a significant proportion of the population, can find written communication more authentic than the face-to-face kind. Who is to say that this preference for one mode of communication—informal written text— is somehow less authentically human than audible speech? Those who critique CMC because some people use it obsessively hit an important target, but miss a great deal more when they don't take into consideration people who use the medium for genuine human interaction. Those who find virtual communities cold places point at the limits of the technology, its most dangerous

pitfalls, and we need to pay attention to those boundaries. But these critiques don't tell us how Philcat and Lhary and the Allisons and my own family could have found the community of support and information we found in the WELL when we needed it. And those of us who do find communion in cyberspace might do well to pay attention to the way the medium we love can be abused. . . .

Because we cannot see one another in cyberspace, gender, age, 8 national origin, and physical appearance are not apparent unless a person wants to make such characteristics public. People whose physical handicaps make it difficult to form new friendships find that virtual communities treat them as they always wanted to be treated—as thinkers and transmitters of ideas and feeling beings, not carnal vessels with a certain appearance and way of walking and talking (or not walking and not talking).

One of the few things that enthusiastic members of virtual 9 communities in Japan, England, France, and the United States all agree on is that expanding their circle of friends is one of the most important advantages of computer conferencing. CMC is a way to *meet* people, whether or not you feel the need to affiliate with them on a community level. It's a way of both making contact with and maintaining a distance from others. The way you meet people in cyberspace puts a different spin on affiliation: in traditional kinds of communities, we are accustomed to meeting people, then getting to know them; in virtual communities, you can get to know people and then choose to meet them. Affiliation also can be far more ephemeral in cyberspace because you can get to know people you might never meet on the physical plane.

How does anybody find friends? In the traditional commu- 10 nity, we search through our pool of neighbors and professional colleagues, of acquaintances and acquaintances of acquaintances, in order to find people who share our values and interests. We then exchange information about one another, disclose and discuss our mutual interests, and sometimes we become friends. In a virtual community we can go directly to the place where our favorite subjects are being discussed, then get acquainted with people who share our passions or who use words in a way we find attractive. In this sense, the topic is the address: you can't simply pick up a phone and ask to be connected with someone who wants to talk about Islamic art or California wine, or someone with a three-year-old daughter or a forty-year-old Hudson; you can, however, join a computer conference on any of those topics, then open a public or private correspondence with the previously unknown people you find there. Your chances of making friends are magnified by orders of magnitude over the old methods of finding a peer group.

11   You can be fooled about people in cyberspace, behind the cloak of words. But that can be said about telephones or face-to-face communication as well; computer-mediated communications provide new ways to fool people, and the most obvious identity swindles will die out only when enough people learn to use the medium critically. In some ways, the medium will, by its nature, be forever biased toward certain kinds of obfuscation. It will also be a place that people often end up revealing themselves far more intimately than they would be inclined to do without the intermediation of screens and pseudonyms. . . .

12   Three different kinds of social criticisms of technology are relevant to claims of CMC as a means of enhancing democracy. One school of criticism emerges from the longer-term history of communications media, and focuses on the way electronic communications media already have preempted public discussions by turning more and more of the content of the media into advertisements for various commodities—a process these critics call commodification. Even the political process, according to this school of critics, has been turned into a commodity. The formal name for this criticism is "the commodification of the public sphere." The public sphere is what these social critics claim we used to have as citizens of a democracy, but have lost to the tide of commodization. The public sphere is also the focus of the hopes of online activists, who see CMC as a way of revitalizing the open and widespread discussions among citizens that feed the roots of democratic societies.

13   The second school of criticism focuses on the fact that high-bandwidth interactive networks could be used in conjunction with other technologies as a means of surveillance, control, and disinformation as well as a conduit for useful information. This direct assault on personal liberty is compounded by a more diffuse erosion of old social values due to the capabilities of new

technologies; the most problematic example is the way traditional notions of privacy are challenged on several fronts by the ease of collecting and disseminating detailed information about individuals via cyberspace technologies. When people use the convenience of electronic communication or transaction, we leave invisible digital trails; now that technologies for tracking those trails are maturing, there is cause to worry. The spreading use of computer matching to piece together the digital trails we all leave in cyberspace is one indication of privacy problems to come.

Along with all the person-to-person communications exchanged 14 on the world's telecommunications networks are vast flows of other kinds of personal information—credit information, transaction processing, health information. Most people take it for granted that no one can search through all the electronic transactions that move through the world's networks in order to pin down an individual for marketing—or political—motives. Remember the "knowbots" that would act as personal servants, swimming in the info-tides, fishing for information to suit your interests? What if people could turn loose knowbots to collect all the information digitally linked to *you?* What if the Net and cheap, powerful computers give that power not only to governments and large corporations but to everyone?

Every time we travel or shop or communicate, citizens of the 15 credit-card society contribute to streams of information that travel between point of purchase, remote credit bureaus, municipal and federal information systems, crime information databases, central transaction databases. And all these other forms of cyberspace interaction take place via the same packet-switched, high-bandwidth network technology—those packets can contain transactions as well as video clips and text files. When these streams of information begin to connect together, the unscrupulous or would-be tyrants can use the Net to catch citizens in a more ominous kind of net.

The same channels of communication that enable citizens 16 around the world to communicate with one another also allow government and private interests to gather information about them. This school of criticism is known as Panoptic in reference to the perfect prison proposed in the eighteenth century by Jeremy Bentham—a theoretical model that happens to fit the real capabilities of today's technologies.

17   Another category of critical claim deserves mention, despite the rather bizarre and incredible imagery used by its most well known spokesmen—the hyper-realist school. These critics believe that information technologies have already changed what used to pass for reality into a slicked-up electronic simulation. Twenty years before the United States elected a Hollywood actor as president, the first hyper-realists pointed out how politics had become a movie, a spectacle that raised the old Roman tactic of bread and circuses to the level of mass hypnotism. We live in a hyper-reality that was carefully constructed to mimic the real world and extract money from the pockets of consumers: the forests around the Matterhorn might be dying, but the Disneyland version continues to rake in the dollars. The television programs, movie stars, and theme parks work together to create global industry devoted to maintaining a web of illusion that grows more lifelike as more people buy into it and as technologies grow more powerful.

18   Many other social scientists have intellectual suspicions of the hyper-realist critiques, because so many are abstract and theoretical, based on little or no direct knowledge of technology itself. Nevertheless, this perspective does capture something about the way the effects of communications technologies have changed our modes of thought. One good reason for paying attention to the claims of the hyper-realists is that the society they predicted decades ago bears a disturbingly closer resemblance to real life than do the forecasts of the rosier-visioned technological utopians. While McLuhan's image of the global village has taken on a certain irony in light of what has happened since his predictions of the 1960s, "the society of the spectacle"—another prediction from the 1960s, based on the advent of electronic media—offered a far less rosy and, as events have proved, more realistic portrayal of the way information technologies have changed social customs. . . .

19   What should those of us who believe in the democratizing potential of virtual communities do about the technological critics? I believe we should invite them to the table and help them see the flaws in our dreams, the bugs in our designs. I believe we should study what the historians and social scientists have to say about the illusions and power shifts that accompanied the diffusion of previous technologies. CMC and technology in general have real limits; it's best to continue to listen to those who understand the

limits, even as we continue to explore the technologies' positive capabilities. Failing to fall under the spell of the "rhetoric of the technological sublime," actively questioning and examining social assumptions about the effects of new technologies, reminding ourselves that electronic communication has powerful illusory capabilities, are all good steps to take to prevent disasters.

If electronic democracy is to succeed, however, in the face of all the obstacles, activists must do more than avoid mistakes. Those who would use computer networks as political tools must go forward and actively apply their theories to more and different kinds of communities. If there is a last good hope, a bulwark against the hyper-reality of Baudrillard or Forster, it will come from a new way of looking at technology. Instead of falling under the spell of a sales pitch, or rejecting new technologies as instruments of illusion, we need to look closely at new technologies and ask how they can help build stronger, more humane communities—and ask how they might be obstacles to that goal. The late 1990s may eventually be seen in retrospect as a narrow window of historical opportunity, when people either acted or failed to act effectively to regain control over communications technologies. Armed with knowledge, guided by a clear, human-centered vision, governed by a commitment to civil discourse, we the citizens hold the key levers at a pivotal time. What happens next is largely up to us.

1993

Cyberspace and Identity

Sherry Turkle

We come to see ourselves differently as we catch sight of our images in the mirror of the machine. Over a decade ago, when I first called the computer a "second self" (1984), these identity-transforming relationships were most usually one-on-one, a person alone with a machine. This is no longer the case. A rapidly expanding system of networks, collectively known as the Internet, links millions of people together in new spaces that are changing the way we think, the nature of our sexuality, the form of our communities, our very identities. In cyberspace, we are learning to live in virtual worlds. We may find ourselves alone as we navigate virtual oceans, unravel virtual mysteries, and engineer virtual skyscrapers. But increasingly, when we step through the looking glass, other people are there as well.

2   Over the past decade, I have been engaged in the ethnographic and clinical study of how people negotiate the virtual and the "real" as they represent themselves on computer screens linked through the Internet. For many people, such experiences challenge what they have traditionally called "identity," which they are moved to recast in terms of multiple windows and parallel lives. Online life is not the only factor that is pushing them in this direction; there is no simple sense in which computers are causing a shift in notions of identity. It is, rather, that today's life on the screen dramatizes and concretizes a range of cultural trends that encourage us to think of identity in terms of multiplicity and flexibility.

VIRTUAL PERSONAE

3 In this essay, I focus on one key element of online life and its impact on identity: the creation and projection of constructed personae into virtual space. In cyberspace, it is well known, one's body can be represented by one's own textual description: The obese can be slender, the beautiful plain. The fact that self-presentation is written in text means that there is time to reflect upon and edit one's "composition," which makes it easier for the shy to be outgoing, the "nerdy" sophisticated. The relative anonymity of life on the screen—one has the choice of being known only by one's chosen "handle" or online name—gives people the chance to express often unexplored aspects of the self. Additionally, multiple aspects of self can be explored in parallel. Online services offer their users the opportunity to be known by several different names. For example, it is not unusual for someone to be BroncoBill in one online community, ArmaniBoy in another, and MrSensitive in a third.

The online exercise of playing with identity and trying out 4 new identities is perhaps most explicit in "role playing" virtual communities (such as Multi-User Domains, or MUDs) where participation literally begins with the creation of a persona (or several); but it is by no means confined to these somewhat exotic locations. In bulletin boards, newsgroups, and chat rooms, the creation of personae may be less explicit than on MUDs, but it is no less psychologically real. One IRC (Internet Relay Chat) participant describes her experience of online talk: "I go from channel to channel depending on my mood. . . . actually feel a part of several of the channels, several conversations . . . I'm different in the different chats. They bring out different things in me." Identity play can happen by changing names and by changing places.

For many people, joining online communities means crossing 5 a boundary into highly charged territory. Some feel an uncomfortable sense of fragmentation, some a sense of relief. Some sense the possibilities for self-discovery. A 26-year-old graduate student in history says, "When I log on to a new community and I create a character and know I have to start typing my description, I always feel a sense of panic. Like I could find out something I don't want to know." A woman in her late thirties who just got an account with America Online used the fact that she could create five "names" for herself on her account as a chance to "lay out all the moods I'm in—all the ways I want to be in different places on the system."

The creation of site-specific online personae depends not only 6 on adopting a new name. Shifting of personae happens with a change of virtual place. Cycling through virtual environments is made possible by the existence of what have come to be called "windows" in modern computing environments. Windows are a way to work with a computer that makes it possible for the machine to place you in several contexts at the same time. As a user, you are attentive to just one of [the] windows on your screen at any given moment, but in a certain sense, you are a presence in all of them at all times. You might be writing a paper in bacteriology and using your computer in several ways to help you: You are "present" to a word processing program on which you are taking notes and collecting thoughts, you are "present" to communications software that is in touch with a distant computer for collecting reference materials, you are "present" to a simulation program that is charting the growth of bacterial colonies when a new organism enters their ecology, and you are "present" to an online chat session where participants are discussing recent research in the field. Each of these activities takes place in a "window," and your identity on the computer is the sum of your distributed presence.

7   The development of the windows metaphor for computer interfaces was a technical innovation motivated by the desire to get people working more efficiently by "cycling through" different applications, much as time-sharing computers cycle through the computing needs of different people. But in practice, windows have become a potent metaphor for thinking about the self as a multiple, distributed, "time-sharing" system.

8   The self no longer simply plays different roles in different settings—something that people experience when, for example, one wakes up as a lover; makes breakfast as a mother; and drives to work as a lawyer. The windows metaphor suggests a distributed self that exists in many worlds and plays many roles at the same time. The "windows" enabled by a computer operating system support the metaphor, and cyberspace raises the experience to a higher power by translating the metaphor into a life experience of "cycling through."

IDENTITY, MORATORIA, AND PLAY

9 Cyberspace, like all complex phenomena, has a range of psychological effects. For some people, it is a place to "act out" unresolved conflicts, to play and replay characterological difficulties on a new and exotic stage. For others, it provides an opportunity to "work through" significant personal issues, to use the new materials of cybersociality to reach for new resolutions. These more positive identity effects follow from the fact that for some, cyberspace provides what Erik Erikson ([1950] 1963) would have called a "psychosocial moratorium," a central element in how he thought about identity development in adolescence. Although the term moratorium implies a "time out," what Erikson had in mind was not withdrawal. On the contrary, the adolescent moratorium is a time of intense interaction with people and ideas. It is a time of passionate friendships and experimentation. The adolescent

falls in and out of love with people and ideas. Erikson's notion of the moratorium was not a "hold" on significant experiences but on their consequences. It is a time during which one's actions are, in a certain sense, not counted as they will be later in life. They are not given as much weight, not given the force of full judgment. In this context, experimentation can become the norm rather than a brave departure. Relatively consequence-free experimentation facilitates the development of a "core self," a personal sense of what gives life meaning that Erikson called "identity."

Erikson developed these ideas about the importance of a 10 moratorium during the late 1950s and early 1960s. At that time, the notion corresponded to a common understanding of what "the college years" were about. Today, 30 years later, the idea of the college years as a consequence-free "time out" seems of another era. College is pre-professional, and AIDS has made consequence-free sexual experimentation an impossibility. The years associated with adolescence no longer seem a "time out." But if our culture no longer offers an adolescent moratorium, virtual communities often do. It is part of what makes them seem so attractive.

Erikson's ideas about stages did not suggest rigid sequences. 11 His stages describe what people need to achieve before they can move ahead easily to another developmental task. For example, Erikson pointed out that successful intimacy in young adulthood is difficult if one does not come to it with a sense of who one is, the challenge of adolescent identity building. In real life, however, people frequently move on with serious deficits. With incompletely resolved "stages," they simply do the best they can. They use whatever materials they have at hand to get as much as they can of what they have missed. Now virtual social life can play a role in these dramas of self-reparation. Time in cyberspace reworks the notion of the moratorium because it may now exist on an always-available "window."

EXPANDING ONE'S RANGE IN THE REAL

Case, a 34-year-old industrial designer happily married to a 12 female co-worker, describes his real-life (RL) persona as a "nice guy," a "Jimmy Stewart type like my father." He describes his outgoing, assertive mother as a "Katharine Hepburn type." For Case, who views assertiveness through the prism of this Jimmy Stewart/Katharine Hepburn dichotomy, an assertive man is quickly perceived as "being a bastard." An assertive woman, in contrast, is perceived as being "modern and together." Case says that although he is comfortable with his temperament and loves and respects his father, he feels he pays a high price for his own low-key ways. In particular, he feels at a loss when it comes to confrontation, both at home and at work. Online, in a wide range of virtual communities, Case presents himself as females whom he calls his "Katharine Hepburn types." These are strong, dynamic, "out there" women who remind Case of his mother, who "says exactly what's on her mind." He tells me that presenting himself as a woman online has brought him to a point where he is more comfortable with confrontation in his RL as a man.

13   Case describes his Katharine Hepburn personae as "externalizations of a part of myself." In one interview with him, I used the expression "aspects of the self," and he picked it up eagerly, for his online life reminds him of how Hindu gods could have different aspects or subpersonalities, all the while being a whole self. In response to my question "Do you feel that you call upon your personae in real life?" Case responded:

> Yes, an aspect sort of clears its throat and says, "I can do this. You are being so amazingly conflicted over this and I know exactly what to do. Why don't you just let me do it?" . . . In real life, I tend to be extremely diplomatic, non-confrontational. I don't like to ram my ideas down anyone's throat. [Online] I can be, "Take it or leave it." All of my Hepburn characters are that way. That's probably why I play them. Because they are smartmouthed, they will not sugarcoat their words.

In some ways, Case's description of his inner world of actors who address him and are able to take over negotiations is reminiscent of the language of people with multiple-personality disorder. But the contrast is significant: Case's inner actors are not split off from each other or from his sense of "himself." He experiences himself very much as a collective self, not feeling that he must goad or repress this or that aspect of himself into conformity. He is at ease, cycling through from Katharine Hepburn to Jimmy Stewart. To use analyst Philip Bromberg's language (1994), online life has helped Case learn how to "stand in the spaces between selves and still feel one, to see the multiplicity and still feel a unity." To use computer scientist Marvin Minsky's (1987) phrase, Case feels at ease cycling through his "society of mind," a notion of identity as distributed and heterogeneous. Identity, from the Latin *idem*, has been used habitually to refer to the sameness between two qualities. On the Internet, however, one can be many, and one usually is.

AN OBJECT TO THINK WITH FOR THINKING ABOUT IDENTITY

In the late 1960s and early 1970s, I was first exposed to notions of 14 identity and multiplicity. These ideas—most notably that there is no such thing as "the ego," that each of us is a multiplicity of parts, fragments, and desiring connections—surfaced in the intellectual hothouse of Paris; they presented the world according to such authors as Jacques Lacan, Gilles Deleuze, and Felix Guattari. But despite such ideal conditions for absorbing theory, my "French lessons" remained abstract exercises. These theorists of poststructuralism spoke words that addressed the relationship between mind and body, but from my point of view had little to do with my own.

In my lack of personal connection with these ideas, I was not 15 alone. To take one example, for many people it is hard to accept any challenge to the idea of an autonomous ego. While in recent years, many psychologists, social theorists, psychoanalysts, and philosophers have argued that the self should be thought of as essentially decentered, the normal requirements of everyday life exert strong pressure on people to take responsibility for their actions and to see themselves as unitary actors. This disjuncture between theory (the unitary self is an illusion) and lived experience (the unitary self is the most basic reality) is one of the main reasons why multiple and decentered theories have been slow to catch on—or when they do, why we tend to settle back quickly into older, centralized ways of looking at things.

When, 20 years later, I used my personal computer and modem 16 to join online communities, I had an experience of this theoretical perspective which brought it shockingly down to earth. I used language to create several characters. My textual actions are my actions—my words make things happen. I created selves that were made and transformed by language. And different personae were exploring different aspects of the self. The notion of a decentered identity was concretized by experiences on a computer screen. In this way, cyberspace becomes an object to think with for thinking about identity—an element of cultural bricolage.

17   Appropriable theories—ideas that capture the imagination of the culture at large—tend to be those with which people can become actively involved. They tend to be theories that can be "played" with. So one way to think about the social appropriability of a given theory is to ask whether it is accompanied by its own objects-to-think-with that can help it move out beyond intellectual circles.

18   For example, the popular appropriation of Freudian ideas had little to do with scientific demonstrations of their validity. Freudian ideas passed into the popular culture because they offered robust and down-to-earth objects to think with. The objects were not physical but almost-tangible ideas, such as dreams and slips of the tongue. People were able to play with such Freudian "objects." They became used to looking for them and manipulating them, both seriously and not so seriously. And as they did so, the idea that slips and dreams betray an unconscious began to feel natural.

19   In Freud's work, dreams and slips of the tongue carried the theory. Today, life on the computer screen carries theory. People decide that they want to interact with others on a computer network. They get an account on a commercial service. They think that this will provide them with new access to people and information, and of course it does. But it does more. When they log on, they may find themselves playing multiple roles; they may find themselves playing characters of the opposite sex. In this way, they are swept up by experiences that enable them to explore previously unexamined aspects of their sexuality or that challenge their ideas about a unitary self. The instrumental computer, the computer that does things for us, has revealed another side: a subjective computer that does things *to* us as people, to our view of ourselves and our relationships, to our ways of looking at our minds. In simulation, identity can be fluid and multiple, a signifier no longer clearly points to a thing that is signified, and

understanding is less likely to proceed through analysis than by navigation through virtual space.

Within the psychoanalytic tradition, many "schools" have 20 departed from a unitary view of identity, among these the Jungian, object-relations; and Lacanian. In different ways, each of these groups of analysts was banished from the ranks of orthodox Freudians for such suggestions, or somehow relegated to the margins. As the United States became the center of psychoanalytic politics in the mid-twentieth century, ideas about a robust executive ego began to constitute the psychoanalytic mainstream.

But today, the pendulum has swung away from that compla- 21 cent view of a unitary self. Through the fragmented selves presented by patients and through theories that stress the decentered subject, contemporary social and psychological thinkers are confronting what has been left out of theories of the unitary self. It is asking such questions as, What is the self when it functions as a society? What is the self when it divides its labors among its constituent "alters"? Those burdened by posttraumatic dissociative disorders suffer these questions; I am suggesting that inhabitants of virtual communities play with them. In our lives on the screen, people are developing ideas about identity as multiplicity through new social *practices* of identity as multiplicity.

With these remarks, I am not implying that chat rooms or MUDs 22 or the option to declare multiple user names on America Online are causally implicated in the dramatic increase of people who exhibit symptoms of multiple-personality disorder (MPD), or that people on MUDs have MPD, or that MUDding (or online chatting) is like having MPD. I am saying that the many manifestations of multiplicity in our culture, including the adoption of online personae, are contributing to a general reconsideration of traditional, unitary notions of identity. Online experiences with "parallel lives" are part of the significant cultural context that supports new theorizing about nonpathological, indeed healthy, multiple selves.

In thinking about the self, *multiplicity* is a term that carries 23 with it several centuries of negative associations, but such authors as Kenneth Gergen (1991), Emily Martin (1994), and Robert Jay Lifton (1993) speak in positive terms of an adaptive, "flexible" self. The flexible self is not unitary, nor are its parts stable entities. A person cycles through its aspects, and these are themselves ever-changing and in constant communication with each other. Daniel Dennett (1991) speaks of the flexible self by using the metaphor of consciousness as multiple drafts, analogous to the experience of several versions of a document open on a computer screen, where the user is able to move between them at will. For Dennett, knowledge of these drafts encourages a respect for the many different versions, while it imposes a certain distance from them. Donna Haraway (1991), picking up on this theme of how a distance between self states may be salutory, equates a "split and contradictory self" with a "knowing self." She is optimistic about its possibilities: "The knowing self is partial in all its guises, never finished, whole, simply there and original; it is always constricted and stitched together imperfectly; and therefore able to join with another, to see together without claiming to be another." What most characterizes Haraway's and Dennett's models of a knowing self is that the lines of communication between its various aspects are open. The open communication encourages an attitude of respect for the many within us and the many within others.

24   Increasingly, social theorists and philosophers are being joined by psychoanalytic theorists in efforts to think about healthy selves whose resilience and capacity for joy comes from having access to their many aspects. For example, Philip Bromberg (1994) insists that our ways of describing "good parenting" must now shift away from an emphasis on confirming a child in a "core self" and onto helping a child develop the capacity to negotiate fluid transitions between self states. The healthy individual knows how to be many but to smooth out the moments of transition between states of self. Bromberg says: "Health is when you are multiple but feel a unity. Health is when different aspects of self can get to know each other and reflect upon each other." Here, within the psychoanalytic tradition, is a model of multiplicity as a state of easy traffic across selves, a conscious, highly articulated "cycling through."

FROM A PSYCHOANALYTIC TO A COMPUTER CULTURE?

25 Having literally written our online personae into existence, they can be a kind of Rorschach test. We can use them to become more aware of what we project into everyday life. We can use the

virtual to reflect constructively on the real. Cyberspace opens the possibility for identity play, but it is very serious play. People who cultivate an awareness of what stands behind their screen personae are the ones most likely to succeed in using virtual experience for personal and social transformation. And the people who make the most of their lives on the screen are those who are able to approach it in a spirit of self-reflection. What does my behavior in cyberspace tell me about what I want, who I am, what I may not be getting in the rest of my life?

As a culture, we are at the end of the Freudian century. Freud, 26 after all, was a child of the nineteenth century; of course, he was carrying the baggage of a very different scientific sensibility than our own. But faced with the challenges of cyberspace, our need for a practical philosophy of self-knowledge, one that does not shy away from issues of multiplicity, complexity, and ambivalence, that does not shy away from the power of symbolism, from the power of the word, from the power of identity play, has never been greater as we struggle to make meaning from our lives on the screen. It is fashionable to think that we have passed from a psychoanalytic culture to a computer culture—that we no longer need to think in terms of Freudian slips but rather of information processing errors. But the reality is more complex. It is time to rethink our relationship to the computer culture and psychoanalytic culture as proudly held joint citizenship.

1999

REFERENCES

Bromberg, Philip. 1994. "Speak that I May See You: Some Reflections on Dissociation, Reality, and Psychoanalytic Listening." *Psychoanalytic Dialogues* 4 (4): 517–47.
Dennett, Daniel. 1991. *Consciousness Explained.* Boston: Little, Brown.
Erikson, Erik. [1950] 1963. *Childhood and Society,* 2nd Ed. New York: Norton.
Haraway, Donna. 1991. "The Actors are Cyborg, Nature is Coyote, and the Geography is Elsewhere: Postscript to 'Cyborgs at Large.'" In *Technoculture,* edited by Constance Penley and Andrew Ross. Minneapolis: University of Minnesota Press.

Gergen, Kenneth. 1991. *The Saturated Self-Dilemmas of Identity in Contemporary Life*. New York: Basic Books.

Lifton, Robert Jay. 1993. *The Protean Self: Human Resilience in an Age of Fragmentation*. New York: Basic Books.

Martin, Emily. 1994. *Flexible Bodies: Tracking Immunity in American Culture from the Days of Polio to the Days of AIDS*. Boston: Beacon Press.

Minsky, Martin. 1987. *The Society of Mind*. New York: Simon & Schuster.

Turkle, Sherry. [1978] 1990. *Psychoanalytic Politics: Jacques Lacan and Freud's French Revolution*. 2nd Ed. New York: Guilford Press.

—1984. *The Second Self: Computers and the Human Spirit*. New York: Simon & Schuster.

—1995. *Life on the Screen: Identity in the Age of the Internet*. New York: Simon & Schuster.

The Intimacy of Blogs

Michael Snider

1 When Plain Layne suddenly pulled her site down in early June, a little corner of the blogosphere went nuts. Instead of the 26-year-old Minnesotan's poignant daily entries on her Weblog, an on-line journal, a blunt one-line message greeted visitors: "Take very good care of you." No more honestly introspective narratives of her life. No more unbridled entries detailing the search for her birth parents, sessions with her therapist or her disappointing love affair with Violet, the stubby-tongued Dragon Lady. Comments flooded cyberspace. "Her surprising, unannounced departure is sending me and my overactive imagination into a frenzy of worry," wrote Gudy Two Shoes on his own Weblog. "If she's gone then I wish her well," posted Intellectual Poison. "She got me started with this whole blogging thing, something that I am truly grateful for." And Daintily Dirty asked, "Are the relationships we create by our blogging of any value?"

2   That's a good question. It turned out that Plaine Layne, aka Layne Johnson, wasn't gone for good. She'd just had a week during which she moved into a new house and witnessed the birth of her surrogate little sister's baby before getting her site back up (*http://plainlayne.dreamhost.com*). But the reaction from her readers

was genuine. One of the prime reasons people blog is to make connections with others, and when Plain Layne went missing, it was like a neighbour had just up and moved in the middle of the night, with no forwarding address.

Weblogs are independent Web sites usually operated by a sin- 3 gle person or by a small group of people. They serve as frequently updated forums to discuss whatever the blogger wants to discuss. Unmonitored, each blogger is author, editor and publisher, beholden solely to his or her own whims and desires. There are political blogs, media blogs, gay blogs, sports blogs, war blogs, antiwar blogs, tech blogs, photo blogs—hundreds of thousands of blogs, actually (estimates are as high as two million). "Blogging is not people wasting other people's time talking about the minutiae of their lives," says Joe Clark, 38, a Toronto author who operates several blogs. "The thing that's attractive about reading Weblogs is that you know there is one human being or a group of human beings behind them."

Free and easy-to-use publishing programs with names like 4 Blogger, Movable Type and Live Journal spurred the phenomenon. Now, anyone with a computer and an Internet connection can set up their own blog with relative ease. Paul Martin blogs, journalists blog, pundits, critics and social misfits blog. And what can you find there? Well, imagine standing in front of a library of gargantuan magazine racks loaded with glossy covers with everything from newsweeklies to girlie mags.

Blogs break down into two very general groups: linking blogs 5 and personal online journals. Political blogs like Glenn Reynolds' *Instapundit.com,* media blogs like Jim Romenesko's Poynter Online (*www.poynter.org/medianews*), or tech blogs like *slashdot.com* are of the former kind. They're link-driven sites that connect readers to theme-related news stories and sometimes add a little commentary along with it. A personal blog is more like a diary entry or column in a daily newspaper, *a la* Rebecca Eckler of the *National Post* or Leah McLaren of the *Globe and Mail*—all about "me and what I think." Writers recount events in their lives—sometimes very private ones—and air their thoughts to a public audience.

Reasons vary. Sometimes, the practice is therapeutic. For some, 6 like Ryan Rhodes, who runs Rambling Rhodes (*http://ramblingrhodes. blogspot.com*), blogging has some functional purposes. Rhodes, from Rochester, Minn., is news editor for an IBM publication called *eServer Magazine* but also writes humour columns for some local newspapers. He figured blogging would be a good writing exercise that might offer him instant feedback from readers. "I like knowing the stuff I write is being read," says Rhodes, "and I like it when it hits someone in a positive way and they tell me, so I can use it later for my column."

7   Personal blogs are famous for breaking usual standards of disclosure, revealing details considered by some to be very private. Dan Gudy, a 29-year-old Berliner, kept a diary when he was a teenager but gave it up, unhappy with the results. "My first experience was a total failure," says Gudy. "It was only myself talking about myself and I do that enough." But last year, when he created his site, Gudy Two Shoes (*http://gudy.blogspot.com*), the self-described introvert discovered that blogging opened a release valve. "I had to deal with some problems at the time and somehow needed to let it out. Part of me asked, why not use a blog for that?" Now, Gudy blogs about the books he reads and bike-riding through the German countryside. He also blogs about his sex life with his wife. "People can talk about what a nice bike ride they had or what a nice meal they had, but why can't they talk about what a nice f—they had last night?

8   For many, that very willingness to discuss intimate details is one of the most alluring facets of blogging. "Your Weblog becomes an exterior part of you," says Clark, "so you can have some distance from your feelings, even though you're putting them out for everyone to read. But then all your readers are right up close and they know you because you're writing directly to them." In turn, readers can offer their own feedback: personal blogs frequently allow them to comment after each post, with something as easy as clicking a link that opens a pop-up box where they can add their own two cents' worth. "When I first started blogging," writes Daintily Dirty (*http://www.blogdreams.blogspot.com*), an anonymous 32-year-old blogger who chatted with *Macleans* via instant messenger, "I had no idea what I was getting into with the personal nature of the interactions. But the connections you find are what keep you coming back."

9   Layne Johnson's readers can attest to that. An excellent narrative writer who opens her soul to her readers, Plain Layne's daily entries regularly receive dozens of comments. "I hopped

from one blog to the next and somewhere found Plain Layne," says Gudy. "What made me stay was her brutal honesty and intimacy of sharing, her very beautiful way of writing." Rhodes echoes the sentiment. "Layne is digital crack," he says. "Hands down, as far as I've read, she's got the best personal blog. I have to read her every day."

Johnson politely turned down a request for an interview, 10 explaining her bloging is a personal exercise that's meant to be cathartic. And somehow, that's the way it should be. Plain Layne does her talking, or typing, on her blog. "I think the hardest thing about sharing your life on-line is that at some point you discover people know you," Johnson wrote in a June post. "They know you from the inside out, the way your mind works, what makes you laugh or cry, your hopes and fears." It's clear to see she uses her blog as an outlet, a place to dump her anxiety and frustration in a search for identity and understanding. It's also a place of amusement and mirth, with stories of stupefying office meetings and uproarious golf outings, all told with a flair and talent that would make some "me" columnists envious.

Blogs might seem too revealing for people who prefer their 11 diaries to remain private. But more and more strangers are inviting millions of other strangers into their lives, with a willingness to share just about anything, finding their own shelf space on the world's most accessible magazine rack, open to anyone who cares to pick up a copy. Welcome to the blogosphere.

2003

Cyberspace: If You Don't Love It, Leave It

Esther Dyson

Something in the American psyche loves new frontiers. We hanker 1 after wide-open spaces; we like to explore; we like to make rules instead of follow them. But in this age of political correctness and other intrusions on our national cult of independence, it's hard to find a place where you can go and be yourself without worrying about the neighbors.

2   There is such a place: cyberspace. Lost in the furor over porn on the Net is the exhilarating sense of freedom that this new frontier once promised—and still does in some quarters. Formerly a playground for computer nerds and techies, cyberspace now embraces every conceivable constituency: schoolchildren, flirtatious singles, Hungarian-Americans, accountants—along with pederasts and porn fans. Can they all get along? Or will our fear of kids surfing for cyberporn behind their bedroom doors provoke a crackdown?

3   The first order of business is to grasp what cyberspace *is*. It might help to leave behind metaphors of highways and frontiers and to think instead of real estate. Real estate, remember, is an intellectual, legal, artificial environment constructed *on top of* land. Real estate recognizes the difference between parkland and shopping mall, between red-light zone and school district, between church, state and drugstore.

4   In the same way, you could think of cyberspace as a giant and unbounded world of virtual real estate. Some property is privately owned and rented out; other property is common land; some places are suitable for children, and others are best avoided by all but the kinkiest citizens. Unfortunately, it's those places that are now capturing the popular imagination: places that offer bomb-making instructions, pornography, advice on how to procure stolen credit cards. They make cyberspace sound like a nasty place. Good citizens jump to a conclusion: Better regulate it.

5   The most recent manifestation of this impulse is the Exon-Coats Amendment, a well-meaning but misguided bill drafted by Senators Jim Exon, Democrat of Nebraska, and Daniel R. Coats, Republican of Indiana, to make cyberspace "safer" for children. Part of the telecommunications reform bill passed by the Senate and awaiting consideration by the House, the amendment would outlaw making "indecent communication" available to anyone under 18.[1]

---

[1]The Communications Decency Act (CDA) was passed by Congress, but the Supreme Court ruled that it was unconstitutional in 1996. [This note is the author's.]

Then there's the Amateur Action bulletin board case, in which the owners of a porn service in Milpitas, Calif., were convicted in a Tennessee court of violating "community standards" after a local postal inspector requested that the material be transmitted to him.

Regardless of how many laws or lawsuits are launched, 6 regulation won't work.

Aside from being unconstitutional, using censorship to counter 7 indecency and other troubling "speech" fundamentally misinterprets the nature of cyberspace. Cyberspace isn't a frontier where wicked people can grab unsuspecting children, nor is it a giant television system that can beam offensive messages at unwilling viewers. In this kind of real estate, users have to *choose* where they visit, what they see, what they do. It's optional, and it's much easier to bypass a place on the Net than it is to avoid walking past an unsavory block of stores on the way to your local 7-Eleven.

Put plainly, cyberspace is a voluntary destination—in reality, 8 many destinations. You don't just get "onto the net"; you have to go someplace in particular. That means that people can choose where to go and what to see. Yes, community standards should be enforced, but those standards should be set by cyberspace communities themselves, not by the courts or by politicians in Washington. What we need isn't Government control over all these electronic communities: We need self-rule.

What makes cyberspace so alluring is precisely the way in which 9 it's *different* from shopping malls, television, highways and other terrestrial jurisdictions. But let's define the territory:

First, there are private e-mail conversations, akin to the con- 10 versations you have over the telephone or voice mail. These are private and consensual and require no regulation at all.

Second, there are information and entertainment services, where 11 people can download anything from legal texts and lists of "great new restaurants" to game software or dirty pictures. These places are like bookstores, malls and movie houses—places where you go to buy something. The customer needs to request an item or sign up for a subscription; stuff (especially pornography) is not sent out to people who don't ask for it. Some of these services are free or included as part of a broader service like Compuserve or America Online; others charge and may bill their customers directly.

12   Third, there are "real" communities—groups of people who communicate among themselves. In real-estate terms, they're like bars or restaurants or bathhouses. Each active participant contributes to a general conversation, generally through posted messages. Other participants may simply listen or watch. Some are supervised by a moderator; others are more like bulletin boards—anyone is free to post anything. Many of these services started out unmoderated but are now imposing rules to keep out unwanted advertising, extraneous discussions or increasingly rude participants. Without a moderator, the decibel level often gets too high.

13   Ultimately, it's the rules that determine the success of such places. Some of the rules are determined by the supplier of content; some of the rules concern prices and membership fees. The rules may be simple: "Only high-quality content about oil-industry liability and pollution legislation: $120 an hour." Or: "This forum is unmoderated, and restricted to information about copyright issues. People who insist on posting advertising or unrelated material will be asked to desist (and may eventually be barred)." Or: "Only children 8 to 12, on school-related topics and only clean words. The moderator will decide what's acceptable."

14   Cyberspace communities evolve just the way terrestrial communities do: people with like-minded interests band together. Every cyberspace community has its own character. Overall, the communities on Compuserve tend to be more techy or professional; those on America Online, affluent young singles; Prodigy, family oriented. Then there are independents like Echo, a hip, downtown New York service, or Women's Wire, targeted to women who want to avoid the male culture prevalent elsewhere on the Net. There's SurfWatch, a new program allowing access only to locations deemed suitable for children. On the Internet itself, there are lots of passionate noncommercial discussion groups on topics ranging from Hungarian politics (Hungary-Online) to copyright law.

15   And yes, there are also porn-oriented services, where people share dirty pictures and communicate with one another about all kinds of practices, often anonymously. Whether these services encourage the fantasies they depict is subject to debate—the same debate that has raged about pornography in other media. But the point is that no one is forcing this stuff on anybody.

What's unique about cyberspace is that it liberates us from the   16
tyranny of government, where everyone lives by the rule of the
majority. In a democracy, minority groups and minority prefer-
ences tend to get squeezed out, whether they are minorities of
race and culture or minorities of individual taste. Cyberspace
allows communities of any size and kind to flourish; in cyberspace, communities are chosen by the users, not forced on them
by accidents of geography. This freedom gives the rules that pre-
side in cyberspace a moral authority that rules in terrestrial environments don't have. Most people are stuck in the country of their
birth, but if you don't like the rules of a cyberspace community,
you can just sign off. Love it or leave it. Likewise, if parents don't
like the rules of a given cyberspace community, they can restrict
their children's access to it.

What's likely to happen in cyberspace is the formation of new   17
communities, free of the constraints that cause conflict on earth.
Instead of a global village, which is a nice dream but impossible
to manage, we'll have invented another world of self-contained
communities that cater to their own members' inclinations without interfering with anyone else's. The possibility of a real market-
style evolution of governance is at hand. In cyberspace, we'll
be able to test and evolve rules governing what needs to be
governed—intellectual property, content and access control, rules
about privacy and free speech. Some communities will allow anyone in; others will restrict access to members who qualify on one
basis or another. Those communities that prove self-sustaining
will prosper (and perhaps grow and split into subsets with ever-
more-particular interests and identities). Those that can't survive—
either because people lose interest or get scared off—will simply
wither away.

In the near future, explorers in cyberspace will need to get   18
better at defining and identifying their communities. They will
need to put in place—and accept—their own local governments,
just as the owners of expensive real estate often prefer to have
their own security guards rather than call in the police. But they
will rarely need help from any terrestrial government.

Of course, terrestrial governments may not agree. What to do,   19
for instance, about pornography? The answer is labeling—not
banning—questionable material. In order to avoid censorship and

lower the political temperature, it makes sense for cyberspace participants themselves to agree on a scheme for questionable items, so that people or automatic filters can avoid them. In other words, posting pornography in "alt.sex.bestiality" would be OK; it's easy enough for software manufacturers to build an automatic filter that would prevent you—or your child—from ever seeing that item on a menu. (It's as if all the items were wrapped with labels on the wrapper.) Someone who posted the same material under the title "Kid-Fun" could be sued for mislabeling.

20   Without a lot of fanfare, private enterprises and local groups are already producing a variety of labeling and ranking services, along with kid-oriented sites like Kidlink, EdWeb and Kids' Space. People differ in their tastes and values and can find services or reviewers on the Net that suit them in the same way they select books and magazines. Or they can wander freely if they prefer, making up their own itinerary.

21   In the end, our society needs to grow up. Growing up means understanding that there are no perfect answers, no all-purpose solutions, no government-sanctioned safe havens. We haven't created a perfect society on earth and we won't have one in cyberspace either. But at least we can have individual choice—and individual responsibility.

1995

13

Environment

Can We Know the Universe?
Reflections on a Grain of Salt

Carl Sagan

*Nothing is rich but the inexhaustible wealth of
nature. She shows us only surfaces, but she is a
million fathoms deep.*

—*Ralph Waldo Emerson*

Science is a way of thinking much more than it is a body of know- 1
ledge. Its goal is to find out how the world works, to seek what
regularities there may be, to penetrate to the connections of
things—from subnuclear particles, which may be the constituents
of all matter, to living organisms, the human social community,
and thence to the cosmos as a whole. Our intuition is by no means
an infallible guide. Our perceptions may be distorted by training
and prejudice or merely because of the limitations of our sense
organs, which, of course, perceive directly but a small fraction of
the phenomena of the world. Even so straightforward a question
as whether in the absence of friction a pound of lead falls faster
than a gram of fluff was answered incorrectly by Aristotle and
almost everyone else before the time of Galileo. Science is based
on experiment, on a willingness to challenge old dogma, on an
openness to see the universe as it really is. Accordingly, science
sometimes requires courage—at the very least the courage to
question the conventional wisdom.

Beyond this the main trick of science is to *really* think of some- 2
thing: the shape of clouds and their occasional sharp bottom edges
at the same altitude everywhere in the sky; the formation of a

473

dewdrop on a leaf; the origin of a name or a word—Shakespeare, say, or "philanthropic"; the reason for human social customs—the incest taboo, for example; how it is that a lens in sunlight can make paper burn; how a "walking stick" got to look so much like a twig; why the Moon seems to follow us as we walk; what prevents us from digging a hole down to the center of the Earth; what the definition is of "down" on a spherical Earth; how it is possible for the body to convert yesterday's lunch into today's muscle and sinew; or how far is up—does the universe go on forever, or if it does not, is there any meaning to the question of what lies on the other side? Some of these questions are pretty easy. Others, especially the last, are mysteries to which no one even today knows the answer. They are natural questions to ask. Every culture has posed such questions in one way or another. Almost always the proposed answers are in the nature of "Just So Stories," attempted explanations divorced from experiment, or even from careful comparative observations.

3   But the scientific cast of mind examines the world critically as if many alternative worlds might exist, as if other things might be here which are not. Then we are forced to ask why what we see is present and not something else. Why are the Sun and the Moon and the planets spheres? Why not pyramids, or cubes, or dodecahedra? Why not irregular, jumbly shapes? Why so symmetrical, worlds? If you spend any time spinning hypotheses, checking to see whether they make sense, whether they conform to what else we know, thinking of tests you can pose to substantiate or deflate your hypotheses, you will find yourself doing science. And as you come to practice this habit of thought more and more you will get better and better at it. To penetrate into the heart of the thing— even a little thing, a blade of grass, as Walt Whitman said—is to experience a kind of exhilaration that, it may be, only human beings of all the beings on this planet can feel. We are an intelligent species and the use of our intelligence quite properly gives us pleasure. In this respect the brain is like a muscle. When we think well, we feel good. Understanding is a kind of ecstasy.

4   But to what extent can we *really* know the universe around us? Sometimes this question is posed by people who hope the answer will be in the negative, who are fearful of a universe in which everything might one day be known. And sometimes we

hear pronouncements from scientists who confidently state that everything worth knowing will soon be known—or even is already known—and who paint pictures of a Dionysian or Polynesian age in which the zest for intellectual discovery has withered, to be replaced by a kind of subdued languor, the lotus eaters drinking fermented coconut milk or some other mild hallucinogen. In addition to maligning both the Polynesians, who were intrepid explorers (and whose brief respite in paradise is now sadly ending), as well as the inducements to intellectual discovery provided by some hallucinogens, this contention turns out to be trivially mistaken.

Let us approach a much more modest question: not whether 5 we can know the universe or the Milky Way Galaxy or a star or a world. Can we know, ultimately and in detail, a grain of salt? Consider one microgram of table salt, a speck just barely large enough for someone with keen eyesight to make out without a microscope. In that grain of salt there are about 10^{16} sodium and chlorine atoms. This is a 1 followed by 16 zeros, 10 million billion atoms. If we wish to know a grain of salt, we must know at least the three-dimensional positions of each of these atoms. (In fact, there is much more to be known—for example, the nature of the forces between the atoms—but we are making only a modest calculation.) Now, is this number more or less than the number of things which the brain can know?

How much *can* the brain know? There are perhaps 10^{11} neu- 6 rons in the brain, the circuit elements and switches that are responsible in their electrical and chemical activity for the functioning of our minds. A typical brain neuron has perhaps a thousand little wires, called dendrites, which connect it with its fellows. If, as seems likely, every bit of information in the brain corresponds to one of these connections, the total number of things knowable by the brain is no more than 10^{14}, one hundred trillion. But this number is only one percent of the number of atoms in our speck of salt.

So in this sense the universe is intractable, astonishingly 7 immune to any human attempt at full knowledge. We cannot on this level understand a grain of salt, much less the universe.

But let us look a little more deeply at our microgram of salt. 8 Salt happens to be a crystal in which, except for defects in the structure of the crystal lattice, the position of every sodium and chlorine atom is predetermined. If we could shrink ourselves into this crystalline world, we would see rank upon rank of atoms in an ordered array, a regularly alternating structure—sodium, chlorine, sodium, chlorine, specifying the sheet of atoms we are standing on and all the sheets above us and below us. An absolutely pure crystal of salt could have the position of every atom specified by something like 10 bits of information.[1] This would not strain the information-carrying capacity of the brain.

9   If the universe had natural laws that governed its behavior to the same degree of regularity that determines a crystal of salt, then, of course, the universe would be knowable. Even if there were many such laws, each of considerable complexity, human beings might have the capability to understand them all. Even if such knowledge exceeded the information-carrying capacity of the brain, we might store the additional information outside our bodies—in books, for example, or in computer memories—and still, in some sense, know the universe.

10   Human beings are, understandably, highly motivated to find regularities, natural laws. The search for rules, the only possible way to understand such a vast and complex universe, is called science. The universe forces those who live in it to understand it. Those creatures who find everyday experience a muddled jumble of events with no predictability, no regularity, are in grave peril. The universe belongs to those who, at least to some degree, have figured it out.

11   It is an astonishing fact that there *are* laws of nature, rules that summarize conveniently—not just qualitatively but quantitatively— how the world works. We might imagine a universe in which there are no such laws, in which the 10^{80} elementary particles that make up a universe like our own behave with utter and uncompromising abandon. To understand such a universe we would need a brain at least as massive as the universe. It seems unlikely

---

[1]Chlorine is a deadly poison gas employed on European battlefields in World War I. Sodium is a corrosive metal which upon contact with water. Together they make a placid and unpoisonous material, table salt. Why each of these substances has the properties it does is a subject called chemistry, which requires more than 10 bits of information to understand. [This note is the author's.]

that such a universe could have life and intelligence, because beings and brains require some degree of internal stability and order. But even if in a much more random universe there were such beings with an intelligence much greater than our own, there could not be much knowledge, passion or joy.

Fortunately for us, we live in a universe that has at least 12 important parts that are knowable. Our common-sense experience and our evolutionary history have prepared us to understand something of the workaday world. When we go into other realms, however, common sense and ordinary intuition turn out to be highly unreliable guides. It is stunning that as we go close to the speed of light our mass increases indefinitely, we shrink toward zero thickness in the direction of motion, and time for us comes as near to stopping as we would like. Many people think that this is silly, and every week or two I get a letter from someone who complains to me about it. But it is a virtually certain consequence not just of experiment but also of Albert Einstein's brilliant analysis of space and time called the Special Theory of Relativity. It does not matter that these effects seem unreasonable to us. We are not in the habit of traveling close to the speed of light. The testimony of our common sense is suspect at high velocities.

Or consider an isolated molecule composed of two atoms 13 shaped something like a dumbbell—a molecule of salt, it might be. Such a molecule rotates about an axis through the line connecting the two atoms. But in the world of quantum mechanics, the realm of the very small, not all orientations of our dumbbell molecule are possible. It might be that the molecule could be oriented in a horizontal position, say, or in a vertical position, but not at many angles in between. Some rotational positions are forbidden. Forbidden by what? By the laws of nature. The universe is built in such a way as to limit, or quantize, rotation. We do not experience this directly in everyday life; we would find it startling as well as awkward in sitting-up exercises, to find arms outstretched from the sides or pointed up to the skies permitted but many intermediate positions forbidden. We do not live in the world of the small, on the scale of 10^{-13} centimeters, in the realm where there are twelve zeros between the decimal place and the one. Our common-sense intuitions do not count. What does count is experiment—in this case observations from the far infrared spectra of molecules. They show molecular rotation to be quantized.

14   The idea that the world places restrictions on what humans might do is frustrating. Why *shouldn't* we be able to have intermediate rotational positions? Why *can't* we travel faster than the speed of light? But so far as we can tell, this is the way the universe is constructed. Such prohibitions not only press us toward a little humility; they also make the world more knowable. Every restriction corresponds to a law of nature, a regularization of the universe. The more restrictions there are on what matter and energy can do, the more knowledge human beings can attain. Whether in some sense the universe is ultimately knowable depends not only on how many natural laws there are that encompass widely divergent phenomena, but also on whether we have the openness and the intellectual capacity to understand such laws. Our formulations of the regularities of nature are surely dependent on how the brain is built, but also, and to a significant degree, on how the universe is built.

15   For myself, I like a universe that includes much that is unknown and, at the same time, much that is knowable. A universe in which everything is known would be static and dull, as boring as the heaven of some weak-minded theologians. A universe that is unknowable is no fit place for a thinking being. The ideal universe for us is one very much like the universe we inhabit. And I would guess that this is not really much of a coincidence.

1979

The Obligation to Endure
Rachel Carson

1 The history of life on earth has been a history of interaction between living things and their surroundings. To a large extent, the physical form and the habits of the earth's vegetation and its animal life have been molded by the environment. Considering

the whole span of earthly time, the opposite effect, in which life actually modifies its surroundings, has been relatively slight. Only within the moment of time represented by the present century has one species—man—acquired significant power to alter the nature of his world.

During the past quarter century this power has not only 2 increased to one of disturbing magnitude but it has changed in character. The most alarming of all man's assaults upon the environment is the contamination of air, earth, rivers, and sea with dangerous and even lethal materials. This pollution is for the most part irrecoverable; the chain of evil it initiates not only in the world that must support life but in living tissues is for the most part irreversible. In this now universal contamination of the environment, chemicals are the sinister and little-recognized partners of radiation in changing the very nature of the world—the very nature of its life. Strontium 90, released through nuclear explosions into the air, comes to earth in rain or drifts down as fallout, lodges in soil, enters into the grass or corn or wheat grown there, and in time takes up its abode in the bones of a human being, there to remain until his death. Similarly, chemicals sprayed on croplands or forests or gardens lie long in soil, entering into living organisms, passing from one to another in a chain of poisoning and death. Or they pass mysteriously by underground streams until they emerge and, through the alchemy of air and sunlight, combine into new forms that kill vegetation, sicken cattle, and work unknown harm on those who drink from once pure wells. As Albert Schweitzer has said, "Man can hardly even recognize the devils of his own creation."

It took hundreds of millions of years to produce the life that 3 now inhabits the earth—eons of time in which that developing and evolving and diversifying life reached a state of adjustment and balance with its surroundings. The environment, rigorously shaping and directing the life it supported, contained elements that were hostile as well as supporting. Certain rocks gave out dangerous radiation; even within the light of the sun, from which all life draws its energy, there were shortwave radiations with power to injure. Given time—time not in years but in millennia— life adjusts, and a balance has been reached. For time is the essential ingredient; but in the modern world there is no time.

4   The rapidity of change and the speed with which new situations are created follow the impetuous and heedless pace of man rather than the deliberate pace of nature. Radiation is no longer merely the background radiation of rocks, the bombardment of cosmic rays, the ultraviolet of the sun that have existed before there was any life on earth; radiation is now the unnatural creation of man's tampering with the atom. The chemicals to which life is asked to make its adjustment are no longer merely the calcium and silica and copper and all the rest of the minerals washed out of the rocks and carried in rivers to the sea; they are the synthetic creations of man's inventive mind, brewed in his laboratories, and having no counterparts in nature.

5   To adjust to these chemicals would require time on the scale that is nature's; it would require not merely the years of a man's life but the life of generations. And even this, were it by some miracle possible, would be futile, for the new chemicals come from our laboratories in an endless stream; almost five hundred annually find their way into actual use in the United States alone. The figure is staggering and its implications are not easily grasped— 500 new chemicals to which the bodies of men and animals are required somehow to adapt each year, chemicals totally outside the limits of biologic experience.

6   Among them are many that are used in man's war against nature. Since the mid-1940s over 200 basic chemicals have been created for use in killing insects, weeds, rodents, and other organisms described in the modern vernacular as "pests"; and they are sold under several thousand different brand names.

7   These sprays, dusts, and aerosols are now applied almost universally to farms, gardens, forests, and homes—nonselective chemicals that have the power to kill every insect, the "good" and the "bad," to still the song of birds and the leaping of fish in the streams, to coat the leaves with a deadly film, and to linger on in soil—all this though the intended target may be only a few weeds or insects. Can anyone believe it is possible to lay down such a barrage of poisons on the surface of the earth without making it unfit for all life? They should not be called "insecticides," but "biocides."

8   The whole process of spraying seems caught up in an endless spiral. Since DDT was released for civilian use, a process of

escalation has been going on in which ever more toxic materials must be found. This has happened because insects, in a triumphant vindication of Darwin's principle of the survival of the fittest, have evolved super races immune to the particular insecticide used, hence a deadlier one has always to be developed—and then a deadlier one than that. It has happened also because, for reasons to be described later, destructive insects often undergo a "flareback," or resurgence, after spraying in numbers greater than before. Thus the chemical war is never won, and all life is caught in its violent crossfire.

Along with the possibility of the extinction of mankind by 9 nuclear war, the central problem of our age has therefore become the contamination of man's total environment with such substances of incredible potential for harm—substances that accumulate in the tissues of plants and animals and even penetrate the germ cells to shatter or alter the very material of heredity upon which the shape of the future depends.

Some would-be architects of our future look toward a time 10 when it will be possible to alter the human germ plasm by design. But we may easily be doing so now by inadvertence, for many chemicals, like radiation, bring about gene mutations. It is ironic to think that man might determine his own future by something so seemingly trivial as the choice of an insect spray.

All this has been risked—for what? Future historians may 11 well be amazed by our distorted sense of proportion. How could intelligent beings seek to control a few unwanted species by a method that contaminated the entire environment and brought the threat of disease and death even to their own kind? Yet this is precisely what we have done. We have done it, moreover, for reasons that collapse the moment we examine them. We are told that the enormous and expanding use of pesticides is necessary to maintain farm production. Yet is our real problem not one of *overproduction?* Our farms, despite measures to remove acreages from production and to pay farmers *not* to produce, have yielded such a staggering excess of crops that the American taxpayer in 1962 is paying out more than one billion dollars a year as the total carrying cost of the surplus-food storage program. And is the situation helped when one branch of the Agriculture Department tries to reduce production while another states, as it did in 1958,

"It is believed generally that reduction of crop acreages under provisions of the Soil Bank will stimulate interest in use of chemicals to obtain maximum production on the land retained in crops."

12   All this is not to say there is no insect problem and no need of control. I am saying, rather, that control must be geared to realities, not to mythical situations, and that the methods employed must be such that they do not destroy us along with the insects.

13   The problem whose attempted solution has brought such a train of disaster in its wake is an accompaniment of our modern way of life. Long before the age of man, insects inhabited the earth— a group of extraordinarily varied and adaptable beings. Over the course of time since man's advent, a small percentage of the more than half a million species of insects have come into conflict with human welfare in two principal ways: as competitors for the food supply and as carriers of human disease.

14   Disease-carrying insects become important where human beings are crowded together, especially under conditions where sanitation is poor, as in times of natural disaster or war or in situations of extreme poverty and deprivation. Then control of some sort becomes necessary. It is a sobering fact, however, as we shall presently see, that the method of massive chemical control has had only limited success, and also threatens to worsen the very conditions it is intended to curb.

15   Under primitive agricultural conditions the farmer had few insect problems. These arose with the intensification of agriculture— the devotion of immense acreages to a single crop. Such a system set the stage for explosive increases in specific insect populations. Single-crop farming does not take advantage of the principles by which nature works; it is agriculture as an engineer might conceive it to be. Nature has introduced great variety into the landscape, but man has displayed a passion for simplifying it. Thus he undoes the built-in checks and balances by which nature holds the species within bounds. One important natural check is a limit on the amount of suitable habitat for each species. Obviously then, an insect that lives on wheat can build up its population to much higher levels on a farm devoted to wheat than on one in which wheat is intermingled with other crops to which the insect is not adapted.

The same thing happens in other situations. A generation or 16
more ago, the towns of large areas of the United States lined their
streets with the noble elm tree. Now the beauty they hopefully
created is threatened with complete destruction as disease sweeps
through the elms, carried by a beetle that would have only limited chance to build up large populations and to spread from tree
to tree if the elms were only occasional trees in a richly diversified planting.

Another factor in the modern insect problem is one that must 17
be viewed against a background of geologic and human history:
the spreading of thousands of different kinds of organisms from
their native homes to invade new territories. This worldwide
migration has been studied and graphically described by the
British ecologist Charles Elton in his recent book *The Ecology of
Invasions*. During the Cretaceous Period, some hundred million
years ago, flooding seas cut many land bridges between conti-
nents and living things found themselves confined in what Elton
calls "colossal separate nature reserves." There, isolated from others of their kind, they developed many new species. When some
of the land masses were joined again, about 15 million years ago,
these species began to move out into new territories—a movement
that is not only still in progress but is now receiving considerable
assistance from man.

The importation of plants is the primary agent in the modern 18
spread of species, for animals have almost invariably gone along
with the plants, quarantine being a comparatively recent and not
completely effective innovation. The United States Office of Plant
Introduction alone has introduced almost 200,000 species and
varieties of plants from all over the world. Nearly half of the 180
or so major insect enemies of plants in the United States are accidental imports from abroad, and most of them have come as
hitchhikers on plants.

In new territory, out of reach of the restraining hand of the 19
natural enemies that kept down its numbers in its native land, an
invading plant or animal is able to become enormously abundant.
Thus it is no accident that our most troublesome insects are
introduced species.

These invasions, both the naturally occurring and those 20
dependent on human assistance, are likely to continue indefinitely.

Quarantine and massive chemical campaigns are only extremely expensive ways of buying time. We are faced, according to Dr. Elton, "with a life-and-death need not just to find new technological means of suppressing this plant or that animal"; instead we need the basic knowledge of animal populations and their relations to their surroundings that will "promote an even balance and damp down the explosive power of outbreaks and new invasions."

21   Much of the necessary knowledge is now available but we do not use it. We train ecologists in our universities and even employ them in our governmental agencies but we seldom take their advice. We allow the chemical death rain to fall as though there were no alternative, whereas in fact there are many, and our ingenuity could soon discover many more if given opportunity.

22   Have we fallen into a mesmerized state that makes us accept as inevitable that which is inferior or detrimental, as though having lost the will or the vision to demand that which is good? Such thinking, in the words of the ecologist Paul Shepard, "idealizes life with only its head out of water, inches above the limits of toleration of the corruption of its own environment. . . . Why should we tolerate a diet of weak poisons, a home in insipid surroundings, a circle of acquaintances who are not quite our enemies, the noise of motors with just enough relief to prevent insanity? Who would want to live in a world which is just not quite fatal?"

23   Yet such a world is pressed upon us. The crusade to create a chemically sterile, insect-free world seems to have engendered a fanatic zeal on the part of many specialists and most of the so-called control agencies. On every hand there is evidence that those engaged in spraying operations exercise a ruthless power. "The regulatory entomologists . . . function as prosecutor, judge and jury, tax assessor and collector and sheriff to enforce their own orders," said Connecticut entomologist Neely Turner. The most flagrant abuses go unchecked in both state and federal agencies.

24   It is not my contention that chemical insecticides must never be used. I do contend that we have put poisonous and biologically potent chemicals indiscriminately into the hands of persons largely or wholly ignorant of their potentials for harm. We have subjected enormous numbers of people to contact with these poisons, without their consent and often without their knowledge. If the Bill of Rights contains no guarantee that a citizen shall be secure against

lethal poisons distributed either by private individuals or by public officials, it is surely only because our forefathers, despite their considerable wisdom and foresight, could conceive of no such problem.

I contend, furthermore, that we have allowed these chemicals 25 to be used with little or no advance investigation of their effect on soil, water, wildlife, and man himself. Future generations are unlikely to condone our lack of prudent concern for the integrity of the natural world that supports all life.

There is still very limited awareness of the nature of the threat. 26 This is an era of specialists, each of whom sees his own problem and is unaware of or intolerant of the larger frame into which it fits. It is also an era dominated by industry, in which the right to make a dollar at whatever cost is seldom challenged. When the public protests, confronted with some obvious evidence of damaging results of pesticide applications, it is fed little tranquilizing pills of half truth. We urgently need an end to these false assurances, to the sugar coating of unpalatable facts. It is the public that is being asked to assume the risks that the insect controllers calculate. The public must decide whether it wishes to continue on the present road, and it can do so only when in full possession of the facts. In the words of Jean Rostand, "The obligation to endure gives us the right to know."

1962

Saving Nature, But Only for Man

Charles Krauthammer

Environmental sensitivity is now as required an attitude in polite 1 society as is, say, belief in democracy or aversion to polyester. But now that everyone from Ted Turner to George Bush, Dow to Exxon has professed love for Mother Earth, how are we to choose among the dozens of conflicting proposals, restrictions, projects, regulations and laws advanced in the name of the environment? Clearly not everything with an environmental claim is worth doing. How to choose?

2   There is a simple way. First, distinguish between environmental luxuries and environmental necessities. Luxuries are those things it would be nice to have if costless. Necessities are those things we must have regardless. Then apply a rule. Call it the fundamental axiom of sane environmentalism: Combatting ecological change that directly threatens the health and safety of people is an environmental necessity. All else is luxury.

3   For example: preserving the atmosphere—stopping ozone depletion and the greenhouse effect—is an environmental necessity. In April scientists reported that ozone damage is far worse than previously thought. Ozone depletion not only causes skin cancer and eye cataracts, it also destroys plankton, the beginning of the food chain atop which we humans sit.

4   The reality of the greenhouse effect is more speculative, though its possible consequences are far deadlier: melting ice caps, flooded coastlines, disrupted climate, parched plains and, ultimately, empty breadbaskets. The American Midwest feeds the world. Are we prepared to see Iowa acquire New Mexico's desert climate? And Siberia acquire Iowa's?

5   Ozone depletion and the greenhouse effect are human disasters. They happen to occur in the environment. But they are urgent because they directly threaten man. A sane environmentalism, the only kind of environmentalism that will win universal public support, begins by unashamedly declaring that nature is here to serve man. A sane environmentalism is entirely anthropocentric: it enjoins man to preserve nature, but on the grounds of self-preservation.

6   A sane environmentalism does not sentimentalize the earth. It does not ask people to sacrifice in the name of other creatures. After all, it is hard enough to ask people to sacrifice in the name of other humans. (Think of the chronic public resistance to foreign aid and welfare.) Ask hardworking voters to sacrifice in the name of the snail darter, and, if they are feeling polite, they will give you a shrug.

7   Of course, this anthropocentrism runs against the grain of a contemporary environmentalism that indulges in earth worship to the point of idolatry. One scientific theory—Gaia theory—actually claims that Earth is a living organism. This kind of environmentalism likes to consider itself spiritual. It is nothing more than

sentimental. It takes, for example, a highly selective view of the benignity of nature. My nature worship stops with the April twister that came through Kansas or the May cyclone that killed more than 125,000 Bengalis and left 10 million (!) homeless.

A nonsentimental environmentalism is one founded on Protagoras' maxim that "Man is the measure of all things." Such a principle helps us through the thicket of environmental argument. Take the current debate raging over oil drilling in a corner of the Alaska National Wildlife Refuge. Environmentalists, mobilizing against a bill working its way through the U.S. Congress to permit such exploration, argue that Americans should be conserving energy instead of drilling for it. This is a false either/or proposition. The U.S. does need a sizable energy tax to reduce consumption. But it needs more production too. Government estimates indicate a nearly fifty-fifty chance that under the ANWR lies one of the five largest oil fields ever discovered in America. 8

The U.S. has just come through a war fought in part over oil. Energy dependence costs Americans not just dollars but lives. It is a bizarre sentimentalism that would deny oil that is peacefully attainable because it risks disrupting the calving grounds of Arctic caribou. 9

I like the caribou as much as the next man. And I would be rather sorry if their mating patterns are disturbed. But you can't have everything. And if the choice is between the welfare of caribou and reducing an oil dependency that gets people killed in wars, I choose man over caribou every time. 10

Similarly the spotted owl in Oregon. I am no enemy of the owl. If it could be preserved at no or little cost, I would agree: the variety of nature is a good, a high aesthetic good. But it is no more than that. And sometimes aesthetic goods have to be sacrificed to the more fundamental ones. If the cost of preserving the spotted owl is the loss of livelihood for 30,000 logging families, I choose family over owl. 11

The important distinction is between those environmental goods that are fundamental and those that are merely aesthetic. Nature is our ward. It is not our master. It is to be respected and even cultivated. But it is man's world. And when man has to choose between his well-being and that of nature, nature will have to accommodate. 12

13   Man should accommodate only when his fate and that of nature are inextricably bound up. The most urgent accommodation must be made when the very integrity of man's habitat—e.g., atmospheric ozone—is threatened. When the threat to man is of a lesser order (say, the pollutants from coal- and oil-fired generators that cause death from disease but not fatal damage to the ecosystem), a more modulated accommodation that balances economic against health concerns is in order. But in either case the principle is the same: protect the environment—because it is man's environment.

14   The sentimental environmentalists will call this saving nature with a totally wrong frame of mind. Exactly. A sane—a humanistic—environmentalism does it not for nature's sake but for our own.

1991

The Clan of the One-Breasted Women

Terry Tempest Williams

EPILOGUE

1   I belong to a Clan of One-Breasted Women. My mother, my grandmothers, and six aunts have all had mastectomies. Seven are dead. The two who survive have just completed rounds of chemotherapy and radiation.

2   I've had my own problems: two biopsies for breast cancer and a small tumor between my ribs diagnosed as a "borderline malignancy."

3   This is my family history.

4   Most statistics tell us breast cancer is genetic, hereditary, with rising percentages attached to fatty diets, childlessness, or becoming pregnant after thirty. What they don't say is living in Utah may be the greatest hazard of all.

We are a Mormon family with roots in Utah since 1847. The 5 "word of wisdom" in my family aligned us with good foods—no coffee, no tea, tobacco, or alcohol. For the most part, our women were finished having their babies by the time they were thirty. And only one faced breast cancer prior to 1960. Traditionally, as a group of people, Mormons have a low rate of cancer.

Is our family a cultural anomaly? The truth is, we didn't think 6 about it. Those who did, usually the men, simply said, "bad genes." The women's attitude was stoic. Cancer was part of life. On February 16, 1971, the eve of my mother's surgery, I accidentally picked up the telephone and overheard her ask my grandmother what she could expect.

"Diane, it is one of the most spiritual experiences you will 7 ever encounter."

I quietly put down the receiver. 8

Two days later, my father took my brothers and me to the hos- 9 pital to visit her. She met us in the lobby in a wheelchair. No bandages were visible. I'll never forget her radiance, the way she held herself in a purple velvet robe, and how she gathered us around her.

"Children, I am fine. I want you to know I felt the arms of 10 God around me."

We believed her. My father cried. Our mother, his wife, was 11 thirty-eight years old.

A little over a year after Mother's death, Dad and I were hav- 12 ing dinner together. He had just returned from St. George, where the Tempest Company was completing the gas lines that would service southern Utah. He spoke of his love for the country, the sandstoned landscape, bare-boned and beautiful. He had just finished hiking the Kolob trail in Zion National Park. We got caught up in reminiscing, recalling with fondness our walk up Angel's Landing on his fiftieth birthday and the years our family had vacationed there.

Over dessert, I shared a recurring dream of mine. I told my 13 father that for years, as long as I could remember, I saw this flash of light in the night in the desert—that this image had so permeated my being that I could not venture south without seeing it again, on the horizon, illuminating buttes and mesas.

"You did see it," he said. 14

"Saw what?" 15

16 "The bomb. The cloud. We were driving home from Riverside, California. You were sitting on Diane's lap. She was pregnant. In fact, I remember the day, September 7, 1957. We had just gotten out of the Service. We were driving north, past Las Vegas. It was an hour or so before dawn, when this explosion went off. We not only heard it, but felt it. I thought the oil tanker in front of us had blown up. We pulled over and suddenly, rising from the desert floor, we saw it, clearly, this golden-stemmed cloud, the mushroom. The sky seemed to vibrate with an eerie pink glow. Within a few minutes, a light ash was raining on the car."

17 I stared at my father.

18 "I thought you knew that," he said. "It was a common occurrence in the fifties."

19 It was at this moment that I realized the deceit I had been living under. Children growing up in the American Southwest, drinking contaminated milk from contaminated cows, even from the contaminated breasts of their mothers, my mother—members, years later, of the Clan of One-Breasted Women.

20 It is a well-known story in the Desert West, "The Day We Bombed Utah," or more accurately, the years we bombed Utah: above ground atomic testing in Nevada took place from January 27, 1951, through July 11, 1962. Not only were the winds blowing north covering "low-use segments of the population" with fallout and leaving sheep dead in their tracks, but the climate was right. The United States of the 1950s was red, white, and blue. The Korean War was raging. McCarthyism was rampant. Ike was it, and the cold war was hot. If you were against nuclear testing, you were for a communist regime.

21 Much has been written about this "American nuclear tragedy." Public health was secondary to national security. The Atomic Energy Commissioner, Thomas Murray, said, "Gentlemen, we must not let anything interfere with this series of tests, nothing."

22 Again and again, the American public was told by its government, in spite of burns, blisters, and nausea, "It has been found that the tests may be conducted with adequate assurance of safety under conditions prevailing at the bombing reservations." Assuaging public fears was simply a matter of public relations. "Your best action," an Atomic Energy Commission booklet read, "is not to be

worried about fallout." A news release typical of the times stated, "We find no basis for concluding that harm to any individual has resulted from radioactive fallout."

On August 30, 1979, during Jimmy Carter's presidency, a suit 23 was filed, *Irene Allen v. The United States of America*. Mrs. Allen's case was the first on an alphabetical list of twenty-four test cases, representative of nearly twelve hundred plaintiffs seeking compensation from the United States government for cancers caused by nuclear testing in Nevada.

Irene Allen lived in Hurricane, Utah. She was the mother of 24 five children and had been widowed twice. Her first husband, with their two oldest boys, had watched the tests from the roof of the local high school. He died of leukemia in 1956. Her second husband dies of pancreatic cancer in 1978.

In a town meeting conducted by Utah Senator Orrin Hatch, 25 shortly before the suit was filed, Mrs. Allen said, "I am not blaming the government, I want you to know that, Senator Hatch. But I thought if my testimony could help in any way so this wouldn't happen again to any of the generations coming up after us . . . I am happy to be here this day to bear testimony of this."

God-fearing people. This is just one story in an anthology of 26 thousands.

On May 10, 1984, Judge Bruce S. Jenkins handed down his 27 opinion. Ten of the plaintiffs were awarded damages. It was the first time a federal court had determined that nuclear tests had been the cause of cancers. For the remaining fourteen test cases, the proof of causation was not sufficient. In spite of the split decision, it was considered a landmark ruling. It was not to remain so for long.

In April 1987, the Tenth Circuit Court of Appeals over- 28 turned Judge Jenkins's ruling on the ground that the United States was protected from suit by the legal doctrine of sovereign immunity, a centuries-old idea from England in the days of absolute monarchs.

In January 1988, the Supreme Court refused to review the 29 Appeals Court decision. To our court system it does not matter whether the United States government was irresponsible, whether it lied to its citizens, or even that citizens died from the fallout of nuclear testing. What matters is that our government is immune: "The King can do no wrong."

30   In Mormon culture, authority is respected, obedience is revered, and independent thinking is not. I was taught as a young girl not to "make waves" or "rock the boat."

31   "Just let it go," Mother would say. "You know how you feel, that's what counts."

32   For many years, I have done just that—listened, observed, and quietly formed my own opinions, in a culture that rarely asks questions because it has all the answers. But one by one, I have watched the women in my family die common, heroic deaths. We sat in waiting rooms hoping for good news, but always receiving the bad. I cared for them, bathed their scarred bodies, and kept their secrets. I watched beautiful women become bald as Cytoxan, cisplatin, and Adriamycin were injected into their veins. I held their foreheads as they vomited green-black bile, and I shot them with morphine when the pain became inhuman. In the end, I witnessed their last peaceful breaths, becoming a midwife to the rebirth of their souls.

33   The price of obedience has become too high.

34   The fear and inability to question authority that ultimately killed rural communities in Utah during atmospheric testing of atomic weapons is the same fear I saw in my mother's body. Sheep. Dead sheep. The evidence is buried.

35   I cannot prove that my mother, Diane Dixon Tempest, or my grandmothers, Lettie Romney Dixon and Kathryn Blackett Tempest, along with my aunts developed cancer from nuclear fallout in Utah. But I can't prove they didn't.

36   My father's memory was correct. The September blast we drove through in 1957 was part of Operation Plumbbob, one of the most intensive series of bomb tests to be initiated. The flash of light in the night in the desert, which I had always thought was a dream, developed into a family nightmare. It took fourteen years, from 1957 to 1971, for cancer to manifest in my mother—the same time, Howard L. Andrews, an authority in radioactive fallout at the National Institutes of Health, says radiation cancer requires to become evident. The more I learn about what it means to be a "downwinder," the more questions I drown in.

What I do know, however, is that as a Mormon woman of the 37 fifth generation of Latter-day Saints, I must question everything, even if it means losing my faith, even it if means becoming a member of a border tribe among my own people. Tolerating blind obedience in the name of patriotism or religion ultimately takes our lives.

When the Atomic Energy Commission described the country 38 north of the Nevada Test Site as "virtually uninhabited desert terrain," my family and the birds at Great Salt Lake were some of the "virtual uninhabitants."

One night, I dreamed women from all over the world circled 39 a blazing fire in the desert. They spoke of change, how they hold the moon in their bellies and wax and wane with its phases. They mocked the presumption of even-tempered beings and made promises that they would never fear the witch inside themselves. The women danced wildly as sparks broke away from the flames and entered the night sky as stars.

And they sang a song given to them by Shoshone grandmothers: 40

Ah ne nah, nah	Consider the rabbits
nin nah nah—	How gently they walk on the earth—
ah ne nah, nah	Consider the rabbits
nin nah nah—	How gently they walk on the earth—
Nyaga mutzi	We remember them
oh ne nay—	We can walk gently also—
Nyaga mutzi	We remember them
oh ne nay—	We can walk gently also—

The women danced and drummed and sang for weeks, preparing themselves for what was to come. They would reclaim the desert for the sake of their children, for the sake of the land.

A few miles downwind from the fire circle, bombs were being 41 tested. Rabbits felt the tremors. Their soft leather pads on paws and feet recognized the shaking sands, while the roots of mesquite and sage were smoldering. Rocks were hot from the inside out and dust devils hummed unnaturally. And each time there was another nuclear test, ravens watched the desert heave. Stretch marks appeared. The land was losing its muscle.

42   The women couldn't bear it any longer. They were mothers. They had suffered labor pains but always under the promise of birth. The red hot pains beneath the desert promised death only, as each bomb became a stillborn. A contract had been made and broken between human beings and the land. A new contract was being drawn by the women, who understood the fate of the earth as their own.

43   Under the cover of darkness, ten women slipped under a barbed-wire fence and entered the contaminated country. They were trespassing. They walked toward the town of Mercury, in moonlight, taking their cues from coyote, kit fox, antelope squirrel, and quail. They moved quietly and deliberately through the maze of Joshua trees. When a hint of daylight appeared they rested, drinking tea and sharing their rations of food. The women closed their eyes. The time had come to protest with the heart, that to deny one's genealogy with the earth was to commit treason against one's soul.

44   At dawn, the women draped themselves in mylar, wrapping long streamers of silver plastic around their arms to blow in the breeze. They wore clear masks, that became the faces of humanity. And when they arrived at the edge of Mercury, they carried all the butterflies of a summer day in their wombs. They paused to allow their courage to settle.

45   The town that forbids pregnant women and children to enter because of radiation risks was asleep. The women moved through the streets as winged messengers, twirling around each other in slow motion, peeking inside homes and watching the easy sleep of men and women. They were astonished by such stillness and periodically would utter a shrill note or low cry just to verify life.

46   The residents finally awoke to these strange apparitions. Some simply stared. Others called authorities, and in time, the women were apprehended by wary soldiers dressed in desert fatigues. They were taken to a white, square building on the other edge of Mercury. When asked who they were and why they were there,

the women replied, "We are mothers and we have come to reclaim the desert for our children."

The soldiers arrested them. As the ten women were blindfolded 47 and handcuffed, they began singing.

> *You can't forbid us everything*
> *You can't forbid us to think—*
> *You can't forbid our tears to flow*
> *And you can't stop the songs that we sing.*

The women continued to sing louder and louder, until they heard the voices of their sisters moving across the mesa:

> *Ah ne nah, nah*
> *nin nah nah—*
> *Ah ne nah, nah*
> *nin nah nah—*
> *Nyaga mutzi*
> *oh ne nay—*
> *Nyaga mutzi*
> *oh ne nay—*

"Call for reinforcements," one soldier said.

"We have," interrupted one woman, "we have—and you have 48 no idea of our numbers."

I crossed the line at the Nevada Test Site and was arrested 49 with nine other Utahns for trespassing on military lands. They are still conducting nuclear tests in the desert. Ours was an act of civil disobedience. But as I walked toward the town of Mercury, it was more than a gesture of peace. It was a gesture on behalf of the Clan of One-Breasted Women.

As one officer cinched the handcuffs around my wrists, 50 another frisked my body. She found a pen and a pad of paper tucked inside my left boot.

"And these?" she asked sternly.   51

"Weapons," I replied.   52

Our eyes met. I smiled. She pulled the leg of my trousers back 53 over my boot.

54   "Step forward, please," she said as she took my arm.

55   We were booked under an afternoon sun and bused to Tonopah, Nevada. It was a two-hour ride. This was familiar country. The Joshua trees standing their ground had been named by my ancestors, who believed they looked like prophets pointing west to the Promised Land. These were the same trees that bloomed each spring, flowers appearing like white flames in the Mojave. And I recalled a full moon in May, when Mother and I had walked among them, flushing out mourning doves and owls.

56   The bus stopped short of town. We were released.

57   The officials thought it was a cruel joke to leave us stranded in the desert with no way to get home. What they didn't realize was that we were home, soul-centered and strong, women who recognized the sweet smell of sage as fuel for our spirits.

1991

The Stone Horse

Barry Lopez

I

1 The deserts of southern California, the high, relatively cooler and wetter Mojave and the hotter, dryer Sonoran to the south of it, carry the signatures of many cultures. Prehistoric rock drawings in the Mojave's Coso Range, probably the greatest concentration of petroglyphs in North America, are at least three thousand years old. Big-game-hunting cultures that flourished six or seven thousand years before that are known from broken spear tips, choppers, and burins left scattered along the shores of great Pleistocene lakes, long since evaporated. Weapons and tools discovered at China Lake may be thirty thousand years old; and worked stone from a quarry in the Calico Mountains is, some

argue, evidence that human beings were here more than 200,000 years ago.

Because of the long-term stability of such arid environments, ₂ much of this prehistoric stone evidence still lies exposed on the ground, accessible to anyone who passes by—the studious, the acquisitive, the indifferent, the merely curious. Archaeologists do not agree on the sequence of cultural history beyond about twelve thousand years ago, but it is clear that these broken bits of chalcedony, chert, and obsidian, like the animal drawings and geometric designs etched on walls of basalt throughout the desert, anchor the earliest threads of human history, the first record of human endeavor here.

Western man did not enter the California desert until the end ₃ of the eighteenth century, 250 years after Coronado brought his soldiers into the Zuni pueblos in a bewildered search for the cities of Cibola. The earliest appraisals of the land were cursory, hurried. People traveled *through* it, en route to Santa Fe or the California coastal settlements. Only miners tarried. In 1823 what had been Spain's became Mexico's, and in 1848 what had been Mexico's became America's; but the bare, jagged mountains and dry lake beds, the vast and uniform plains of creosote bush and yucca plants, remained as obscure as the northern Sudan until the end of the nineteenth century.

Before 1940 the tangible evidence of twentieth-century man's ₄ passage here consisted of very little—the hard tracery of travel corridors; the widely scattered, relatively insignificant evidence of mining operations; and the fair expanse of irrigated fields at the desert's periphery. In the space of a hundred years or so the wagon roads were paved, railroads were laid down, and canals and high-tension lines were built to bring water and electricity across the desert to Los Angeles from the Colorado River. The dark mouths of gold, talc, and tin mines yawned from the bony flanks of desert ranges. Dust-encrusted chemical plants stood at work on the lonely edges of dry lake beds. And crops of grapes, lettuce, dates, alfalfa, and cotton covered the Coachella and Imperial valleys, north and south of the Salton Sea, and the Palo Verde Valley along the Colorado.

These developments proceeded with little or no awareness ₅ of earlier human occupations by cultures that preceded those of the historic Indians—the Mohave, the Chemehuevi, the Quechan. (Extensive irrigation began actually to change the climate of the Sonoran Desert, and human settlements, the railroads, and farming introduced many new, successful plants into the region.)

6   During World War II, the American military moved into the desert in great force, to train troops and to test equipment. They found the clear weather conducive to year-round flying, the dry air and isolation very attractive. After the war, a complex of training grounds, storage facilities, and gunnery and test ranges was permanently settled on more than three million acres of military reservations. Few perceived the extent or significance of the destruction of the aboriginal sites that took place during tank maneuvers and bombing runs or in the laying out of highways, railroads, mining districts, and irrigated fields. The few who intuited that something like an American Dordogne Valley lay exposed here were (only) amateur archaeologists; even they reasoned that the desert was too vast for any of this to matter.

7   After World War II, people began moving out of the crowded Los Angeles basin into homes in Lucerne, Apple, and Antelope valleys in the western Mojave. They emigrated as well to a stretch of resort land at the foot of the San Jacinto Mountains that included Palm Springs, and farther out to old railroad and military towns like Twenty-nine Palms and Barstow. People also began exploring the desert, at first in military-surplus jeeps and then with a variety of all-terrain and off-road vehicles that became available in the 1960s. By the mid-1970s, the number of people using such vehicles for desert recreation had increased exponentially. Most came and went in innocent curiosity; the few who didn't wreaked a havoc all out of proportion to their numbers. The disturbance of previously isolated archaeological sites increased by an order of magnitude. Many sites were vandalized before archaeologists, themselves late to the desert, had any firm grasp of the bounds of human history in the desert. It was as though in the same moment an Aztec library had been discovered intact various lacunae had begun to appear.

8   The vandalism was of three sorts: the general disturbance usually caused by souvenir hunters and by the curious and the oblivious; the wholesale stripping of a place by professional

thieves for black-market sale and trade; and outright destruction, in which vehicles were actually used to ram and trench an area. By 1980, the Bureau of Land Management estimated that probably 35 percent of the archaeological sites in the desert had been vandalized. The destruction at some places by rifles and shotguns, or by power winches mounted on vehicles, was, if one cared for history, demoralizing to behold.

In spite of public education, land closures, and stricter law enforcement in recent years, the BLM estimates that, annually, about 1 percent of the archaeological record in the desert continues to be destroyed or stolen. 9

II

A BLM archaeologist told me, with understandable reluctance, where to find the intaglio. I spread my Automobile Club of Southern California map of Imperial County out on his desk, and he traced the route with a pink felt-tip pen. The line crossed Interstate 8 and then turned west along the Mexican border. 10

"You can't drive any farther than about here," he said, marking a small X. "There's boulders in the wash. You walk up past them." 11

On a separate piece of paper he drew a route in a smaller scale that would take me up the arroyo to a certain point where I was to cross back east, to another arroyo. At its head, on higher ground just to the north, I would find the horse. 12

"It's tough to spot unless you know it's there. Once you pick it up . . ." He shook his head slowly, in a gesture of wonder at its existence. 13

I waited until I held his eye. I assured him I would not tell anyone else how to get there. He looked at me with stoical despair, like a man who had been robbed twice, whose belief in human beings was offered without conviction. 14

I did not go until the following day because I wanted to see it at dawn. I ate breakfast at four A.M. in El Centro and then drove south. The route was easy to follow, though the last section of road proved difficult, broken and drifted over with sand in some spots. I came to the barricade of boulders and parked. It was light enough by then to find my way over the ground with little trouble. The 15 contours of the landscape were stark, without any masking vegetation. I worried only about rattlesnakes.

16   I traversed the stone plain as directed, but, in spite of the frankness of the land, I came on the horse unawares. In the first moment of recognition I was without feeling. I recalled later being startled, and that I held my breath. It was laid out on the ground with its head to the east, three times life size. As I took in its outline I felt a growing concentration of all my senses, as though my attentiveness to the pale rose color of the morning sky and other peripheral images had now ceased to be important. I was aware that I was straining for sound in the windless air, and I felt the uneven pressure of the earth hard against my feet. The horse, outlined in a standing profile on the dark ground, was as vivid before me as a bed of tulips.

17   I've come upon animals suddenly before, and felt a similar tension, a precipitate heightening of the senses. And I have felt the inexplicable but sharply boosted intensity of a wild moment in the bush, where it is not until some minutes later that you discover the source of electricity—the warm remains of a grizzly bear kill, or the still moist tracks of a wolverine.

18   But this was slightly different. I felt I had stepped into an unoccupied corridor. I had no familiar sense of history, the temporal structure in which to think: This horse was made by Quechan people three hundred years ago. I felt instead a headlong rush of images: people hunting wild horses with spears on the Pleistocene veld of southern California; Cortés riding across the causeway into Montezuma's Tenochtitlán; a short-legged Comanche, astride his horse like some sort of ferret, slashing through cavalry lines of young men who rode like farmers; a hood exploding past my face one morning in a corral in Wyoming. These images had the weight and silence of stone.

19   When I released my breath, the images softened. My initial feeling, of facing a wild animal in a remote region, was replaced with a calm sense of antiquity. It was then that I became conscious, like an ordinary tourist, of what was before me, and thought: this horse was probably laid out by Quechan people. But when? I wondered. The first horses they saw, I knew, might have been those that came north from Mexico in 1692 with Father Eusebio Kino. But Cocopa people, I recalled, also came this far north on

occasion, to fight with their neighbors, the Quechan. And *they* could have seen horses with Melchior Diaz, at the mouth of the Colorado River in the fall of 1540. So, it could be four hundred years old. (No one in fact knows.)

I still had not moved. I took my eyes off the horse for a 20 moment to look south over the desert plain into Mexico, to look east past its head at the brightening sunrise, to situate myself. Then, finally, I brought my trailing foot slowly forward and stood erect. Sunlight was running like a thin sheet of water over the stony ground and it threw the horse into relief. It looked as though no hand had ever disturbed the stones that gave it its form.

The horse had been brought to life on ground called desert 21 pavement, a tight, flat matrix of small cobbles blasted smooth by sand-laden winds. The uniform, monochromatic blackness of the stones, a patina of iron and magnesium oxides called desert varnish, is caused by long-term exposure to the sun. To make this type of low-relief ground glyph, or intaglio, the artist either selectively turns individual stones over to their lighter side or removes areas of stone to expose the lighter soil underneath, creating a negative image. This horse, about eighteen feet from brow to rump and eight feet from withers to hoof, had been made in the latter way, and its outline was bermed at certain points with low ridges of stone a few inches high to enhance its three-dimensional qualities. (The left side of the horse was in full profile; each leg was extended at 90 degrees to the body and fully visible, as though seen in three-quarter profile.)

I was not eager to move. The moment I did I would be back 22 in the flow of time, the horse no longer quivering in the same way before me. I did not want to feel again the sequence of quotidian events—to be drawn off into deliberation and analysis. A human being, a four-footed animal, the open land. That was all that was present—and a "thoughtless" understanding of the very old desires bearing on this particular animal: to hunt it, to render it, to fathom it, to subjugate it, to honor it, to take it as a companion.

What finally made me move was the light. The sun now filled 23 the shallow basin of the horse's body. The weighted line of the stone berm created the illusion of a mane and the distinctive roundness of an equine belly. The change in definition impelled me. I moved to the left, circling past its rump, to see how the light might flesh the horse out from various points of view. I circled it completely before squatting on my haunches. Ten or fifteen minutes later I chose another view. The third time I moved, to a point near the rear hooves, I spotted a stone tool at my feet. I stared at it a long while, more in awe than disbelief, before reaching out to pick it up. I turned it over in my left palm and took it between my fingers to feel its cutting edge. It is always difficult, especially with something so portable, to rechannel the desire to steal.

24   I spent several hours with the horse. As I changed positions and as the angle of the light continued to change I noticed a number of things. The angle at which the pastern carried the hoof away from the ankle was perfect. Also, stones had been placed within the image to suggest at precisely the right spot the left shoulder above the foreleg. The line that joined thigh and hock was similarly accurate. The muzzle alone seemed distorted—but perhaps these stones had been moved by a later hand. It was an admirably accurate representation, but not what a breeder would call perfect conformation. There was the suggestion of a bowed neck and an undershot jaw, and the tail, as full as a winter coyote's, did not appear to be precisely to scale.

25   The more I thought about it, the more I felt I was looking at an individual horse, a unique combination of generic and specific detail. It was easy to imagine one of Kino's horses as a model, or a horse that ran off from one of Coronado's columns. What kind of horses would these have been? I wondered. In the sixteenth century the most sought-after horses in Europe were Spanish, the offspring of Arabian stock and Barbary horses that the Moors brought to Iberia and bred to the older, eastern European strains brought in by the Romans. The model for this horse, I speculated, could easily have been a palomino, or a descendant of horses trained for lion hunting in North Africa.

26   A few generations ago, cowboys, cavalry quartermasters, and draymen would have taken this horse before me under consideration and not let up their scrutiny until they had its heritage fixed to their satisfaction. Today, the distinction between draft and harness horses is arcane knowledge, and no image may come to mind for a blue roan or a claybank horse. The loss of such refinement in everyday conversation leaves me unsettled. People praise the Eskimo's ability to distinguish among forty types of snow but

forget the skill of others who routinely differentiate between overo and tobiano pintos. Such distinctions are made for the same reason. You have to do it to be able to talk clearly about the world.

For parts of two years I worked as a horse wrangler and 27 packer in Wyoming. It is dim knowledge now; I would have to think to remember if a buckskin was a kind of dun horse. And I couldn't throw a double-diamond hitch over a set of panniers—the packer's basic tie-down—without guidance. As I squatted there in the desert, however, these more personal memories seemed tenuous in comparison with the sweep of this animal in human time. My memories had no depth. I thought of the Hittite cavalry riding against the Syrians 3,500 years ago. And the first of the Chinese emperors, Ch'in Shih Huang, buried in Shensi Province in 210 B.C. with thousands of life-size horses and soldiers, a terra-cotta guardian army. What could I know of what was in the mind of whoever made this horse? Was there some racial memory of it as an animal that had once fed the artist's ancestors and then disappeared from North America? And then returned in this strange alliance with another race of men?

Certainly, whoever it was, the artist had observed the animal 28 very closely. Certainly the animal's speed had impressed him. Among the first things the Quechan would have learned from an encounter with Kino's horses was that their own long-distance runners—men who could run down mule deer—were no match for this animal.

From where I squatted I could look far out over the Mexican 29 plain. Juan Bautista de Anza passed this way in 1774, extending El Camino Real into Alta California from Sinaloa. He was followed by others, all of them astride the magical horse; *gente de razón*, the people of reason, coming into the country of *los primitivos*. The horse, like the stone animals of Egypt, urged these memories upon me. And as I drew them up from some forgotten corner of my mind—huge horses carved in the white chalk downs of southern England by an Iron Age people; Spanish horses rearing and wheeling in fear before alligators in Florida—the images seemed tethered before me. With this sense of proportion, a memory of my own— the morning I almost lost my face to a horse's hoof—now had somewhere to fit.

30   I rose up and began to walk slowly around the horse again. I had taken the first long measure of it and was now looking for a way to depart, a new angle of light, a fading of the image itself before the rising sun, that would break its hold on me. As I circled, feeling both heady and serene at the encounter, I realized again how strangely vivid it was. It had been created on a barren bajada between two arroyos, as nondescript a place as one could imagine. The only plant life here was a few wands of ocotillo cactus. The ground beneath my shoes was so hard it wouldn't take the print of a heavy animal even after a rain. The only sounds I heard here were the voices of quail.

31   The archaeologist had been correct. For all its forcefulness, the horse is inconspicuous. If you don't care to see it you can walk right past it. That pleases him, I think. Unmarked on the bleak shoulder of the plain, the site signals to no one; so he wants no protective fences here, no informative plaque, to act as beacons. He would rather take a chance that no motorcyclist, no aimless wanderer with a flair for violence and a depth of ignorance, will ever find his way here.

32   The archaeologist had given me something before I left his office that now seemed peculiar—an aerial photograph of the horse. It is widely believed that an aerial view of an intaglio provides a fair and accurate depiction. It does not. In the photograph the horse looks somewhat crudely constructed; from the ground it appears far more deftly rendered. The photograph is of a single moment, and in that split second the horse seems vaguely impotent. I watched light pool in the intaglio at dawn; I imagine you could watch it withdraw at dusk and sense the same animation I did. In those prolonged moments its shape and so, too, its general character change—noticeably. The living quality of the image, its immediacy to the eye, was brought out by the light-in-time, not, at least here, in the camera's frozen instant.

33   Intaglios, I thought, were never meant to be seen by gods in the sky above. They were meant to be seen by people on the ground, over a long period of shifting light. This could even be true of the huge figures on the Plain of Nazca in Peru, where people could walk for the length of a day beside them. It is our own impatience that leads us to think otherwise.

This process of abstraction, almost unintentional, drew me 34
gradually away from the horse. I came to a position of attention
at the edge of the sphere of its influence. With a slight bow I paid
my respects to the horse, its maker, and the history of us all,
and departed.

III

A short distance away I stopped the car in the middle of the road 35
to make a few notes. I could not write down what I was thinking
when I was with the horse. It would have seemed disrespectful,
and it would have required another kind of attention. So now I
patiently drained my memory of the details it had fastened itself
upon. The road I'd stopped on was adjacent to the All American
Canal, the major source of water for the Imperial and Coachella
valleys. The water flowed west placidly. A disjointed flock of
coots, small, dark birds with white bills, was paddling against the
current, foraging in the rushes.

I was peripherally aware of the birds as I wrote, the only 36
movement in the desert, and of a series of sounds from a village
a half-mile away. The first sounds from this collection of ramshackle houses in a grove of cottonwoods were the distracted
dawn voices of dogs. I heard them intermingled with the cries of
a rooster. Later, the high-pitched voices of children calling out to
each other came disembodied through the dry desert air. Now, a
little after seven, I could hear someone practicing on the trumpet,
the same rough phrases played over and over. I suddenly remembered how as children we had tried to get the rhythm of a gal-
loping horse with hands against our thighs, or by fluttering our
tongues against the roofs of our mouths.

After the trumpet, the impatient calls of adults summoning 37
children. Sunday morning. Wood smoke hung like a lens in the
trees. The first car starts—a cold eight-cylinder engine, of Chrysler
extraction perhaps, goosed to life, then throttled back to murmur
through dual mufflers, the obbligato music of a shade-tree
mechanic. The rote bark of mongrel dogs at dawn, the jagged out-
cries of men and women, an engine coming to life. Like a thousand
villages from West Virginia to Guadalajara.

38   I finished my notes—where was I going to find a description of
the horses that came north with the conquistadors? Did their manes
come forward prominently over the brow, like this one's, like the
forelocks of Blackfeet and Assiniboin men in nineteenth-century
paintings? I set the notes on the seat beside me.

39   The road followed the canal for a while and then arced north,
toward Interstate 8. It was slow driving and I fell to thinking how
the desert had changed since Anza had come through. New plants
and animals—the MacDougall cottonwood, the English house
sparrow, the chukar from India—have about them now the air of
the native born. Of the native species, some—no one knows how
many—are extinct. The populations of many others, especially the
animals, have been sharply reduced. The idea of a desert impoverished by agricultural poisons and varmint hunters, by off-road
vehicles and military operations, did not seem as disturbing to
me, however, as this other horror, now that I had been those hours
with the horse. The vandals, the few who crowbar rock art off the
desert's walls, who dig up graves, who punish the ground that
holds intaglios, are people who devour history. Their self-centered
scorn, their disrespect for ideas and images beyond their ken, create the awful atmosphere of loose ends in which totalitarianism
thrives, in which the past is merely curious or wrong.

40   I thought about the horse sitting out there on the unprotected
plain. I enumerated its qualities in my mind until a sense of its
vulnerability receded and it became an anchor for something else.
I remembered that history, a history like this one, which ran deeper
than Mexico, deeper than the Spanish, was a kind of medicine. It
permitted the great breadth of human expression to reverberate,
and it did not urge you to locate its apotheosis in the present.

41   Each of us, individuals and civilizations, has been held upside
down like Achilles in the River Styx. The artist mixing his colors
in the dim light of Altamira; an Egyptian ruler lying still now,
wrapped in his byssus, stored against time in a pyramid; the faded
Dorset culture of the Arctic; the Hmong and Samburu and Walbiri
of historic time; the modern nations. This great, imperfect stretch
of human expression is the clarification and encouragement, the
urging and the reminder, we call history. And it is inscribed
everywhere in the face of the land, from the mountain passes of
the Himalayas to a nameless bajada in the California desert.

Small birds rose up in the road ahead, startled, and flew off. 42
I prayed no infidel would ever find that horse.

1988

The Greenest Campuses:
An Idiosyncratic Guide

Noel Perrin

About 1,100 American colleges and universities run at least a 1
token environmental-studies program, and many hundreds of
those programs offer well-designed and useful courses. But only
a drastically smaller number practice even a portion of what they
teach. The one exception is recycling. Nearly every institution that
has so much as one lonely environmental-studies course also does
a little halfhearted recycling. Paper and glass, usually.

There are some glorious exceptions to those rather churlish 2
observations, I'm glad to say. How many? Nobody knows. No one
has yet done the necessary research (though the National Wildlife
Federation's Campus Ecology program is planning a survey).

Certainly *U.S. News & World Report* hasn't. Look at the rank- 3
ings in their annual college issue. The magazine uses a complex
formula something like this: Institution's reputation, 25 percent;
student-retention rate, 20 percent; faculty resources, 20 percent;
and so on, down to alumni giving, 5 percent. The lead criterion
may help explain why Harvard, Yale, and Princeton Universities
so frequently do a little dance at the top of the list.

But *U.S. News* has nothing at all to say about the degree to 4
which a college or university attempts to behave sustainably—
that is, to manage its campus and activities in ways that promote
the long-term health of the planet. The magazine is equally mum
about which of the institutions it is ranking can serve as models
to society in a threatened world.

And, of course, the world is threatened. When the Royal 5
Society in London and the National Academy of Sciences in

Washington issued their first-ever joint statement, it ended like this: "The future of our planet is in the balance. Sustainable development can be achieved, but only if irreversible degradation of the environment can be halted in time. The next 30 years may be crucial." They said that in 1992. If all those top scientists are right, we have a little more than 20 years left in which to make major changes in how we live.

6   All this affects colleges. I have one environmentalist friend who loves to point out to the deans and trustees she meets that if we don't make such changes, and if the irreversible degradation of earth does occur, Harvard's huge endowment and Yale's lofty reputation will count for nothing.

7   But though *U.S. News* has nothing to say, fortunately there is a fairly good grapevine in the green world. I have spent considerable time in the past two years using it like an organic cell phone. By that means I have come up with a short, idiosyncratic list of green colleges, consisting of six that are a healthy green, two that are greener still, and three that I believe are the greenest in the United States.

8   Which approved surveying techniques have I used? None at all. Some of my evidence is anecdotal, and some of my conclusions are affected by my personal beliefs, such as that electric and hybrid cars are not just a good idea, but instruments of salvation.

9   Obviously I did not examine, even casually, all 1,100 institutions. I'm sure I have missed some outstanding performers. I hope I have missed a great many.

10   Now, here are the 11, starting with **Brown University.**

11   It is generally harder for a large urban university to move toward sustainable behavior than it is for a small-town college with maybe a thousand students. But it's not impossible. Both Brown, in the heart of Providence, R.I., and Yale University (by no means an environmental leader in other respects), in the heart of New Haven, Conn., have found a country way of dealing with food waste. Pigs. Both rely on pigs.

12   For the past 10 years, Brown has been shipping nearly all of its food waste to a Rhode Island piggery. Actually, not shipping it—just leaving it out at dawn each morning. The farmer comes to the campus and gets it. Not since Ralph Waldo Emerson took

food scraps out to the family pig have these creatures enjoyed such a high intellectual connection.

But there is a big difference in scale. Where Emerson might 13 have one pail of slops now and then, Brown generates 700 tons of edible garbage each year. Haulage fee: $0. Tipping fee: $0. (That's the cost of dumping the garbage into huge cookers, where it is heated for the pigs.) Annual savings to Brown: about $50,000. Addition to the American food supply: many tons of ham and bacon each year.

Of course, Brown does far more than feed a balanced diet to 14 a lot of pigs. That's just the most exotic (for an urban institution) of its green actions "Brown is Green" became the official motto of the university in August 1990. It was accurate then, and it remains accurate now.

Yale is the only other urban institution I'm aware of that sup- 15 ports a pig population. Much of the credit goes to Cyril May, the university's environmental coordinator, just as much of the credit at Brown goes to its environmental coordinator, Kurt Teichert.

May has managed to locate two Connecticut piggeries. The 16 one to which he sends garbage presents problems. The farmer has demanded—and received—a collection fee. And he has developed an antagonistic relationship with some of Yale's food-service people. (There are a lot of them: The campus has 16 dining facilities.) May is working on an arrangement with the second piggery. But if it falls through, he says, "I may go back on semibended knee to the other."

Yale does not make the list as a green college, for reasons you 17 will learn later in this essay. But it might in a few more years

Carleton College is an interesting example of an institution 18 turning green almost overnight. No pig slops here; the dining halls are catered by Marriott. But change is coming fast.

In the summer of 1999, Carleton appointed its first-ever 19 environmental coordinator, a brand-new graduate named Rachel Smit. The one-year appointment was an experiment, with a cobbled-together salary and the humble title of "fifth-year intern." The experiment worked beyond anyone's expectation.

Smit began publishing an environmental newsletter called *The* 20 *Green Bean* and organized a small committee of undergraduates to explore the feasibility of composting the college's food waste, an effort that will soon begin. A surprised Marriott has already found itself serving organic dinners on Earth Day.

21   Better yet, the college set up an environmental-advisory committee of three administrators, three faculty members, and three students to review all campus projects from a green perspective. Naturally, many of those projects will be buildings, and to evaluate them, Carleton is using the Minnesota Sustainable Design Guide, itself cowritten by Richard Strong, director of facilities.

22   The position of fifth-year intern is now a permanent one-year position, and its salary is a regular part of the budget.

23   What's next? If Carleton gets a grant it has applied for, there will be a massive increase in environmental-studies courses and faculty seminars and, says the dean of budgets, "a whole range of green campus projects under the rubric of 'participatory learning.'"

24   And if Carleton doesn't get the grant? Same plans, slower pace.

25   Twenty years ago, **Dartmouth College** would have been a contender for the title of greenest college in America, had such a title existed. It's still fairly green. It has a large and distinguished group of faculty members who teach environmental studies, good recycling, an organic farm that was used last summer in six courses, years of experience with solar panels, and a fair number of midlevel administrators (including three in the purchasing office) who are ardent believers in sustainability.

26   But the college has lost ground. Most troubling is its new $50-million library, which has an actual anti-environmental twist: A portion of the roof requires steam from the power plant to melt snow off of it. The architect, Robert Venturi, may be famous, but he's no environmentalist.

27   Dartmouth is a striking example of what I shall modestly call Perrin's Law: No college or university can move far toward sustainability without the active support of at least two senior administrators. Dartmouth has no such committed senior administrators at all. It used to. James Hornig, a former dean of sciences, and Frank Smallwood, a former provost, were instrumental in creating the environmental-studies program, back in 1970. They are now emeriti. The current senior administrators are not in the least hostile to sustainability; they just give a very low priority to the college's practicing what it preaches.

Emory University is probably further into the use of nonpol- 28
luting and low-polluting motor vehicles than any other college in
the country. According to Eric Gaither, senior associate vice president for business affairs, 60 percent of Emory's fleet is powered by
alternative fuels. The facilities-management office has 40 electric
carts, which maintenance workers use for getting around campus.
The community-service office (security and parking) has its own
electric carts and an electric patrol vehicle. There are five electric
shuttle buses and 14 compressed–natural-gas buses on order, plus
one natural-gas bus in service.

Bill Chace, Emory's president, has a battery-charging station 29
for electric cars in his garage, and until recently an electric car to
charge. Georgia Power, which lent the car, has recalled it, but
Chace hopes to get it back. Meanwhile, he rides his bike to work
most of the time.

How has Emory made such giant strides? "It's easy to do," 30
says Gaither, "when your president wants you to."

If Carleton is a model of how a small college turns green, the 31
University of Michigan at Ann Arbor is a model of how a big
university does. Carleton is changing pretty much as an entity,
while Michigan is more like the Electoral College—50 separate
entities. The School of Natural Resources casts its six votes for sustainability, the English department casts its 12 for humanistic
studies, the recycling coordinator casts her 1, the electric-vehicle
program casts its 2, and so on. An institution of Michigan's size
changes in bits and pieces.

Some of the bits show true leadership. For example, the 32
university is within weeks of buying a modest amount of green
power. It makes about half of its own electricity (at its heating
plant) and buys the other half. Five percent of that other half soon
will come from renewable sources: hydro (water power) and bio-
mass (so-called fuel crops, which are grown specifically to be
burned for power).

The supporters of sustainability at Michigan would like to see 33
the university adopt a version of what is known as the Kyoto Protocol. The agreement, which the United States so far has refused
to sign, requires that by 2012 each nation reduce its emission of
greenhouse gases to 7 percent below its 1990 figure. Michigan's
version of the protocol, at present a pipe dream, would require

the university to do what the government won't—accept that reduction as a goal.

34   The immediate goal of "sustainabilists" at Ann Arbor is the creation of a universitywide environmental coordinator, who would work either in the president's or the provost's office.

35   Giants are slow, but they are also strong.

36   **Tulane University** has the usual programs, among green institutions, in recycling, composting, and energy efficiency. But what sets it apart is the Tulane Environmental Law Clinic, which is staffed by third-year law students. The director is a faculty member, and there are three law "fellows," all lawyers, who work with the students. The clinic does legal work for environmental organizations across Louisiana and "most likely has had a greater environmental impact than all our other efforts combined," says Elizabeth Davey, Tulane's first-ever environmental coordinator.

37 At least two campuses of the **University of California** (Berkeley is not among them) have taken a first and even a second step toward sustainable behavior. First step: symbolic action, like installing a few solar panels, to produce clean energy and to help educate students. With luck, one of those little solar arrays might produce as much as a 20th of a percent of the electricity the university uses. It's a start.

38   The two campuses are Davis and Santa Cruz, and I think Davis nudges ahead of Santa Cruz. That is primarily because Davis the city and Davis the university have done something almost miraculous. They have brought car culture at least partially under control, greatly reducing air pollution as a result.

39   The city has a population of about 58,000, which includes 24,000 students. According to reliable estimates, there are something over 50,000 bikes in town or on the campus, all but a few hundred owned by their riders. Most of the bikes are used regularly on the city's 45 miles of bike paths (closed to cars) and the 47 miles of bike lanes (cars permitted in the other lanes). The university maintains an additional 14 miles of bike paths on its large campus

40   What happens on rainy days? "A surprising number continue to bike," says David Takemoto-Weerts, coordinator of Davis's bicycle program.

If every American college in a suitable climate were to behave 41 like Davis, we could close a medium-sized oil refinery. Maybe we could even get rid of one coal-fired power plant, and thus seriously improve air quality.

The **University of New Hampshire** is trying to jump straight 42 from symbolic gestures, like installing a handful of solar panels, to the hardest task of all for an institution trying to become green— establishing a completely new mind-set among students, administrators, and faculty and staff members. It may well succeed.

Campuses that have managed to change attitudes are rare. 43 Prescott College, in Prescott, Ariz., and Sterling College, in Craftsbury Common, Vt., are rumored to have done so, and there may be two or three others. They're not on my list—because they're so small, because their students tend to be bright green even before they arrive, and because I have limited space.

New Hampshire has several token green projects, including a 44 tiny solar array, able to produce one kilowatt at noon on a good day. And last April it inaugurated the Yellow Bike Cooperative. It is much smaller than anything that happens at Davis, where a bike rack might be a hundred yards long. But it's also more original and more communitarian. Anyone in Durham—student, burger flipper, associate dean—can join the Yellow Bike program by paying a $5 fee.

What you get right away is a key that unlocks all 50 bikes 45 owned by the cooperative. (They are repaired and painted by student volunteers.) Want to cross campus? Just go to the nearest bike rack, unlock a Yellow, and pedal off. The goal, says Julie Newman, of the Office of Sustainability Programs, is "to greatly decrease one-person car trips on campus."

But the main thrust at New Hampshire is consciousness-raising. 46 When the subject of composting food waste came up, the university held a seminar for its food workers.

New Hampshire's striking vigor is partly the result of a special 47 endowment—about $12.8-million—exclusively for the sustainability office. Tom Kelly, the director, refuses to equate sustainability with greenness. Being green, in the sense of avoiding pollution and promoting reuse, is just one aspect of living sustainably, which involves "the balancing of economic viability with ecological health and human well-being," he says.

48   **Oberlin College** is an exception to Perrin's Law. The college has gotten deeply into environmental behavior without the active support of two or, indeed, any senior administrators. As at Dartmouth, the top people are not hostile; they just have other priorities.

49   Apparently, until this year, Oberlin's environmental-studies program was housed in a dreary cellar. Now it's in the $8.2-million Adam Joseph Lewis Environmental Studies Center, which is one of the most environmentally benign college buildings in the world. The money for it was raised as a result of a deal that the department chairman, David Orr, made with the administration: He could raise money for his own program, provided that he approached only people and foundations that had never shown the faintest interest in Oberlin.

50   It's too soon for a full report on the building. It is loaded with solar panels—690 of them, covering the roof (for a diagram of the building, see www.oberlin.edu/newserv/esc/escabout.html). In about a year, data will be available on how much energy the panels have saved and whether, as Orr hopes, the center will not only make all its own power, but even export some.

51   **Northland College,** in Wisconsin, also goes way beyond tokenism. Its McLean Environmental Living and Learning Center, a two-year-old residence hall for 114 students, is topped by a 120-foot wind tower that, with a good breeze coming off Lake Superior, can generate 20 kilowatts of electricity. The building also includes three arrays of solar panels. They are only token-size, generating a total of 3.2 kilowatts at most. But one array does heat most of the water for one wing of McLean, while the other three form a test project.

52   One test array is fixed in place—it can't be aimed. Another is like that sunflower in Blake's poem—it countest the steps of the sun. Put more prosaically, it tracks the sun across the sky each day. The third array does that and can also be tilted to get the best angle for each season of the year.

53   Inside the dorm is a pair of composting toilets—an experiment, to see if students will use them. Because no one is forced to try the new ones if they don't want to—plenty of conventional toilets are close by—it means something when James Miller, vice president and dean of student development and

enrollment, reports, "Students almost always choose the composting bathrooms."

From the start, the college's goal has been to have McLean oper- 54 ate so efficiently that it consumes 40 percent less outside energy than would a conventional dormitory of the same dimensions. The building didn't reach that goal in its first year; energy use dropped only 34.2 percent. But anyone dealing with a new system knows to expect bugs at the beginning. There were some at Northland, including the wind generator's being down for three months. (As I write, it's turning busily.) Dean Miller is confident that the building will meet or exceed the college's energy-efficiency goal.

There is no room here to talk about the octagonal classroom 55 structure made of bales of straw, built largely by students. Or about the fact that Northland's grounds are pesticide- and herbicide-free.

If Oberlin is a flagrant exception to Perrin's Law, **Middlebury** 56 **College** is a strong confirmation. Middlebury is unique, as far as I know, in having not only senior administrators who strongly back environmentalism, but one senior administrator right inside the program. What Michigan wants, Middlebury has.

Nan Jenks-Jay, director of environmental affairs, reports 57 directly to the provost. She is responsible for both the teaching side and the living-sustainably side of environmentalism. Under her are an environmental coordinator, Amy Self, and an academic-program coordinator, Janet Wiseman.

The program has powerful backers, including the president, 58 John M. McCardell Jr.; the provost and executive vice president, Ronald D. Liebowitz; and the executive vice president for facilities planning, David W. Ginevan. But everyone I talked with at Middlebury, except for the occasional student who didn't want to trouble his mind with things like returnable bottles—to say nothing of acid rain—seemed at least somewhat committed to sustainable living.

Middlebury has what I think is the oldest environmental- 59 studies program in the country; it began back in 1965. It has the best composting program I've ever seen. And, like Northland, it is pesticide- and herbicide-free.

Let me end as I began, with Harvard, Yale, and Princeton. And with 60 *U.S. News*'s consistently ranking them in the top five, accompanied from time to time by the California Institute of Technology, Stanford University, and the Massachusetts Institute of Technology

61   What if *U.S. News* did a green ranking? What if it based the listings on one of the few bits of hard data that can be widely compared: the percentage of waste that a college recycles?

62   Harvard would come out okay, though hardly at the top. The university recycled 24 percent of its waste last year, thanks in considerable part to the presence of Rob Gogan, the waste manager. He hopes to achieve 28 percent this year. That's feeble compared with Brown's 35 percent, and downright puny against Middlebury's 64 percent.

63   But compared with Yale and Princeton, it's magnificent. Most of the information I could get from Princeton is sadly dated. It comes from the 1995 report of the Princeton Environmental Reform Committee, whose primary recommendation was that the university hire a full-time waste manager. The university has not yet done so. And if any administrators on the campus know the current recycling percentage, they're not telling.

64   And Yale—poor Yale! It does have a figure. Among the performances of the 20 or so other colleges and universities whose percentages I'm aware of, only Carnegie Mellon's is worse. Yale: 19 percent. Carnegie Mellon: 11 percent.

65   What should universities—and society—be shooting for? How can you ask? One-hundred-percent retrieval of everything retrievable, of course.

2001

Chapter 14

Medicine

The Terrifying Normalcy of AIDS
Stephen Jay Gould

Disney's Epcot Center in Orlando, Fla., is a technological tour de 1
force and a conceptual desert. In this permanent World's Fair,
American industrial giants have built their versions of an unblem-
ished future. These masterful entertainments convey but one message, brilliantly packaged and relentlessly expressed: progress
through technology is the solution to all human problems. G.E. proclaims from Horizons: "If we can dream it, we can do it." A.T.&T.
speaks from on high within its giant golf ball: We are now
"unbounded by space and time." United Technologies bubbles
from the depths of Living Seas: "With the help of modern technology, we feel there's really no limit to what can be accomplished."

Yet several of these exhibits at the Experimental Prototype 2
Community of Tomorrow, all predating last year's space disaster,
belie their stated message from within by using the launch of the
shuttle as a visual metaphor for technological triumph. The Chal-
lenger disaster may represent a general malaise, but it remains an
incident. The AIDS pandemic, an issue that may rank with nuclear
weaponry as the greatest danger of our era, provides a more striking proof that mind and technology are not omnipotent and that
we have not canceled our bond to nature.

In 1984, John Platt, a biophysicist who taught at the Univer- 3
sity of Chicago for many years, wrote a short paper for private
circulation. At a time when most of us were either ignoring AIDS,
or viewing it as a contained and peculiar affliction of homosexual
men, Platt recognized that the limited data on the origin of AIDS

517

and its spread in America suggested a more frightening prospect: we are all susceptible to AIDS, and the disease has been spreading in a simple exponential manner.

4   Exponential growth is a geometric increase. Remember the old kiddy problem: if you place a penny on square one of a checkerboard and double the number of coins on each subsequent square—2, 4, 8, 16, 32 . . .—how big is the stack by the sixty-fourth square? The answer: about as high as the universe is wide. Nothing in the external environment inhibits this increase, thus giving to exponential processes their relentless character. In the real, noninfinite world, of course, some limit will eventually arise, and the process slows down, reaches a steady state, or destroys the entire system: the stack of pennies falls over, the bacterial cells exhaust their supply of nutrients.

5   Platt noticed that data for the initial spread of AIDS fell right on an exponential curve. He then followed the simplest possible procedure of extrapolating the curve unabated into the 1990's. Most of us were incredulous, accusing Platt of the mathematical gamesmanship that scientists call "curve fitting." After all, aren't exponential models unrealistic? Surely we are not all susceptible to AIDS. Is it not spread only by odd practices to odd people? Will it not, therefore, quickly run its short course within a confined group?

6 Well, hello 1987—worldwide data still match Platt's extrapolated curve. This will not, of course, go on forever. AIDS has probably already saturated the African areas where it probably originated, and where the sex ratio of afflicted people is 1-to-1, male-female. But AIDS still has far to spread, and may be moving exponentially, through the rest of the world. We have learned enough about the cause of AIDS to slow its spread, if we can make rapid and fundamental changes in our handling of that most powerful part of human biology—our own sexuality. But medicine, as yet, has nothing to offer as a cure and precious little even for palliation.

7   This exponential spread of AIDS not only illuminates its, and our, biology, but also underscores the tragedy of our moralistic misperception. Exponential processes have a definite time and place of origin, an initial point of "inoculation"—in this case, Africa. We didn't notice the spread at first. In a population of billions, we pay little attention when one increases to two, or eight

to sixteen, but when one million becomes two million, we panic, even though the *rate* of doubling has not increased.

The infection has to start somewhere, and its initial locus may 8 be little more than an accident of circumstance. For a while, it remains confined to those in close contact with the primary source, but only by accident of proximity, not by intrinsic susceptibility. Eventually, given the power and lability of human sexuality, it spreads outside the initial group and into the general population. And now AIDS has begun its march through our own heterosexual community.

What a tragedy that our moral stupidity caused us to lose pre- 9 cious time, the greatest enemy in fighting an exponential spread, by down-playing the danger because we thought that AIDS was a disease of three irregular groups of minorities: minorities of life style (needle users), of sexual preference (homosexuals) and of color (Haitians). If AIDS had first been imported from Africa into a Park Avenue apartment, we would not have dithered as the exponential march began.

The message of Orlando—the inevitability of technological 10 solutions—is wrong, and we need to understand why.

Our species has not won its independence from nature, and 11 we cannot do all that we can dream. Or at least we cannot do it at the rate required to avoid tragedy, for we are not unbounded from time. Viral diseases are preventable in principle, and I suspect that an AIDS vaccine will one day be produced. But how will this discovery avail us if it takes until the millennium, and by then AIDS has fully run its exponential course and saturated our population, killing a substantial percentage of the human race? A fight against an exponential enemy is primarily a race against time.

We must also grasp the perspective of ecology and evolu- 12 tionary biology and recognize, once we reinsert ourselves properly into nature, that AIDS represents the ordinary workings of biology, not an irrational or diabolical plague with a moral meaning. Disease, including epidemic spread, is a natural phenomenon, part of human history from the beginning. An entire subdiscipline of my profession, paleopathology, studies the evidence of ancient diseases preserved in the fossil remains of organisms. Human history has been marked by episodic plagues. More native peoples died of imported disease than ever fell before the gun during the era of colonial expansion. Our memories are short, and we have had a respite, really, only since the influenza pandemic at the end of World War I, but AIDS must be viewed as a virulent expression of an ordinary natural phenomenon.

13   I do not say this to foster either comfort or complacency. The evolutionary perspective is correct, but utterly inappropriate for our human scale. Yes, AIDS is a natural phenomenon, one of a recurring class of pandemic diseases. Yes, AIDS may run through the entire population, and may carry off a quarter or more of us. Yes, it may make no *biological* difference to Homo sapiens in the long run: there will still be plenty of us left and we can start again. Evolution cares as little for its agents—organisms struggling for reproductive success—as physics cares for individual atoms of hydrogen in the sun. But we care. These atoms are our neighbors, our lovers, our children and ourselves. AIDS is both a natural phenomenon and, potentially, the greatest natural tragedy in human history.

14   The cardboard message of Epcot fosters the wrong attitudes: we must both reinsert ourselves into nature and view AIDS as a natural phenomenon in order to fight properly. If we stand above nature and if technology is all-powerful, then AIDS is a horrifying anomaly that must be trying to tell us something. If so, we can adopt one of two attitudes, each potentially fatal. We can either become complacent, because we believe the message of Epcot and assume that medicine will soon generate a cure, or we can panic in confusion and seek a scapegoat for something so irregular that it must have been visited upon us to teach us a moral lesson.

15   But AIDS is not irregular. It is part of nature. So are we. This should galvanize us and give us hope, not prompt the worst of all responses: a kind of "new-age" negativism that equates natural with what we must accept and cannot, or even should not, change. When we view AIDS as natural, and when we recognize both the exponential property of its spread and the accidental character of its point of entry into America, we can break through our destructive tendencies to blame others and to free ourselves of concern.

16   If AIDS is natural, then there is no message in its spread. But by all that science has learned and all that rationality proclaims,

AIDS works by a *mechanism*—and we can discover it. Victory is not ordained by any principle of progress, or any slogan of technology, so we shall have to fight like hell, and be watchful. There is no message, but there is a mechanism.

1987

Active and Passive Euthanasia

James Rachels

The distinction between active and passive euthanasia is thought 1 to be crucial for medical ethics. The idea is that it is permissible, at least in some cases, to withhold treatment and allow a patient to die, but it is never permissible to take any direct action designed to kill the patient. This doctrine seems to be accepted by most doctors, and it is endorsed in a statement adopted by the House of Delegates of the American Medical Association on December 4, 1973:

> The intentional termination of the life of one human being by another—mercy killing—is contrary to that for which the medical profession stands and is contrary to the policy of the American Medical Association. The cessation of the employment of extraordinary means to prolong the life of the body when there is irrefutable evidence that biological death is imminent is the decision of the patient and/or his immediate family. The advice and judgment of the physician should be freely available to the patient and/or his immediate family.

However, a strong case can be made against this doctrine. In what follows I will set out some of the relevant arguments, and urge doctors to reconsider their views on this matter.

To begin with a familiar type of situation, a patient who is 2 dying of incurable cancer of the throat is in terrible pain, which can no longer be satisfactorily alleviated. He is certain to die within a few days, even if present treatment is continued, but he does not want to go on living for those days since the pain is unbearable. So he asks the doctor for an end to it, and his family joins in the request.

3   Suppose the doctor agrees to withhold treatment, as the conventional doctrine says he may. The justification for his doing so is that the patient is in terrible agony, and since he is going to die anyway, it would be wrong to prolong his suffering needlessly. But now notice this. If one simply withholds treatment, it may take the patient longer to die, and so he may suffer more than he would if more direct action were taken and a lethal injection given. This fact provides strong reason for thinking that, once the initial decision not to prolong his agony has been made, active euthanasia is actually preferable to passive euthanasia, rather than the reverse. To say otherwise is to endorse the option that leads to more suffering rather than less, and is contrary to the humanitarian impulse that prompts the decision not to prolong his life in the first place.

4   Part of my point is that the process of being "allowed to die" can be relatively slow and painful, whereas being given a lethal injection is relatively quick and painless. Let me give a different sort of example. In the United States about one in six hundred babies is born with Down's syndrome. Most of these babies are otherwise healthy—that is, with only the usual pediatric care, they will proceed to an otherwise normal infancy. Some, however, are born with congenital defects such as intestinal obstructions that require operations if they are to live. Sometimes, the parents and the doctor will decide not to operate, and let the infant die. Anthony Shaw describes what happens then:

> When surgery is denied [the doctor] must try to keep the infant from suffering while natural forces sap the baby's life away. As a surgeon whose natural inclination is to use the scalpel to fight off death, standing by and watching a salvageable baby die is the most emotionally exhausting experience I know. It is easy at a conference, in a theoretical discussion to decide that such infants should be allowed to die. It is altogether different to stand by in the nursery and watch as dehydration and infection wither a tiny being over hours and days. This is a terrible ordeal for me and the hospital staff—much more so than for the parents who never set foot in the nursery.[1]

[1]Anthony Shaw, "Doctor Do We Have a Choice?" *New York Times Magazine,* January 30, 1972, p. 54.

I can understand why some people are opposed to all euthanasia, and insist that such infants must be allowed to live. I think I can also understand why other people favor destroying these babies quickly and painlessly. But why should anyone favor letting "dehydration and infection wither a tiny being over hours and days"? The doctrine that says that a baby may be allowed to dehydrate and wither, but may not be given an injection that would end its life without suffering, seems so patently cruel as to require no further refutation. The strong language is not intended to offend, but only to put the point in the clearest possible way.

My second argument is that the conventional doctrine leads to 5 decisions concerning life and death made on irrelevant grounds.

Consider again the case of the infants with Down's syndrome 6 who need operations for congenital defects unrelated to the syndrome to live. Sometimes, there is no operation, and the baby dies, but when there is no such defect, the baby lives on. Now, an operation such as that to remove an intestinal obstruction is not prohibitively difficult. The reason why such operations are not performed in these cases is, clearly, that the child has Down's syndrome and the parents and the doctor judge that because of that fact it is better for the child to die.

But notice that this situation is absurd, no matter what view 7 one takes of the lives and potentials of such babies. If the life of such an infant is worth preserving, what does it matter if it needs a simple operation? Or, if one thinks it better that such a baby should not live on, what difference does it make that it happens to have an unobstructed intestinal tract? In either case, the matter of life and death is being decided on irrelevant grounds. It is the Down's syndrome, and not the intestines, that is the issue. The matter should be decided, if at all, on that basis, and not be allowed to depend on the essentially irrelevant question of whether the intestinal tract is blocked.

What makes this situation possible, of course, is the idea that 8 when there is an intestinal blockage, one can "let the baby die," but when there is no such defect there is nothing that can be done, for one must not "kill" it. The fact that this idea leads to such results as deciding life or death on irrelevant grounds is another good reason why the doctrine would be rejected.

9   One reason why so many people think that there is an important moral difference between active and passive euthanasia is that they think killing someone is morally worse than letting someone die. But is it? Is killing, in itself, worse than letting die? To investigate this issue, two cases may be considered that are exactly alike except that one involves killing whereas the other involves letting someone die. Then, it can be asked whether this difference makes any difference to the moral assessments. It is important that the cases be exactly alike, except for this one difference, since otherwise one cannot be confident that it is this difference and not some other that accounts for any variation in the assessments of the two cases. So, let us consider this pair of cases:

10   In the first, Smith stands to gain a large inheritance if anything should happen to his six-year-old cousin. One evening while the child is taking his bath, Smith sneaks into the bathroom and drowns the child, and then arranges things so that it will look like an accident.

11   In the second, Jones also stands to gain if anything should happen to his six-year-old cousin. Like Smith, Jones sneaks in planning to drown the child in his bath. However, just as he enters the bathroom Jones sees the child slip and hit his head, and fall face down in the water. Jones is delighted; he stands by, ready to push the child's head back under if it is necessary, but it is not necessary. With only a little thrashing about, the child drowns all by himself, "accidentally," as Jones watches and does nothing.

12   Now Smith killed the child, whereas Jones "merely" let the child die. That is the only difference between them. Did either man behave better, from a moral point of view? If the difference between killing and letting die were in itself a morally important matter, one should say that Jones's behavior was less reprehensible than Smith's. But does one really want to say that? I think not. In the first place, both men acted from the same motive, personal gain, and both had exactly the same end in view when they acted. It may be inferred from Smith's conduct that he is a bad man, although the judgment may be withdrawn or modified if certain further facts are learned about him—for example, that he is mentally deranged. But would not the very same thing be inferred about Jones from his conduct? And would not the same further considerations also be relevant to any modification of this

judgment? Moreover, suppose Jones pleaded, in his own defense, "After all, I didn't do anything except just stand there and watch the child drown. I didn't kill him; I only let him die." Again, if letting die were in itself less bad than killing, this defense should have at least some weight. But it does not. Such a "defense" can only be regarded as a grotesque perversion of moral reasoning. Morally speaking, it is no defense at all.

Now, it may be pointed out, quite properly, that the cases of 13 euthanasia with which doctors are concerned are not like this at all. They do not involve personal gain or the destruction of normal healthy children. Doctors are concerned only with cases in which the patient's life is of no further use to him, or in which the patient's life has become or will soon become a terrible burden. However, the point is the same in these cases: The bare difference between killing and letting die does not, in itself, make a moral difference. If a doctor lets a patient die, for humane reasons, he is in the same moral position as if he had given the patient a lethal injection for humane reasons. If his decision was wrong—if, for example, the patient's illness was in fact curable—the decision would be equally regrettable no matter which method was used to carry it out. And if the doctor's decision was the right one, the method used is not in itself important.

The AMA policy statement isolates the crucial issue very well; 14 the crucial issue is "the intentional termination of the life of one human being by another." But after identifying this issue, and forbidding "mercy killing," the statement goes on to deny that the cessation of treatment is the intentional termination of life. This is where the mistake comes in, for what is the cessation of treatment, in these circumstances, if it is not "the intentional termination of life of one human being by another"? Of course it is exactly that, and if it were not, there would be no point to it.

Many people will find this judgment hard to accept. One rea- 15 son, I think, is that it is very easy to conflate the question of whether killing is, in itself, worse than letting die, with the very different question of whether most actual cases of killing are more reprehensible than most actual cases of letting die. Most actual cases of killing are clearly terrible (think, for example, of all the murders reported in the newspapers), and one hears of such cases every day. On the other hand, one hardly ever hears of a case of letting die, except for the actions of doctors who are motivated by humanitarian reasons. So one learns to think of killing in a much worse light than of letting die. But this does not mean that there is something about killing that makes it in itself worse than letting die, for it is not the bare difference between killing and letting die that makes the difference in these cases. Rather, the other factors— the murderer's motive of personal gain, for example, contrasted with the doctor's humanitarian motivation—account for different reactions to the different cases.

16   I have argued that killing is not in itself any worse than let-ting die; if my contention is right, it follows that active euthana-sia is not any worse than passive euthanasia. What arguments can be given on the other side? The most common, I believe, is the following:

> The important difference between active and passive euthanasia is that, in passive euthanasia, the doctor does not do anything to bring about the patient's death. The doctor does nothing, and the patient dies of whatever ills already afflict him. In active euthanasia, however, the doctor does something to bring about the patient's death: He kills him. The doctor who gives the patient with cancer a lethal injection has himself caused his patient's death; whereas if he merely ceases treatment, the can-cer is the cause of the death.

A number of points need to be made here. This first is that it is not exactly correct to say that in passive euthanasia the doctor does nothing, for he does do one thing that is very important: He lets the patient die. "Letting someone die" is certainly different, in some respects, from other types of action—mainly in that it is a kind of action that one may perform by way of not performing certain other actions. For example, one may let a patient die by way of not giving medication, just as one may insult someone by way of not shaking his hand. But for any purpose of moral assess-ment, it is a type of action nonetheless. The decision to let a patient die is subject to moral appraisal in the same way that a decision to kill him would be subject to moral appraisal: It may be assessed as wise or unwise, compassionate or sadistic, right or wrong. If a doctor deliberately let a patient die who was suffer-ing from a routinely curable illness, the doctor would certainly be to blame for what he had done, just as he would be to blame if he had needlessly killed the patient. Charges against him would then be appropriate. If so, it would be no defense at all for him to insist that he didn't "do anything." He would have done something very serious indeed, for he let his patient die.

Fixing the cause of death may be very important from a legal [17] point of view, for it may determine whether criminal charges are brought against the doctor. But I do not think that this notion can be used to show a moral difference between active and passive euthanasia. The reason why it is considered bad to be the cause of someone's death is that death is regarded as a great evil—and so it is. However, if it has been decided that euthanasia—even passive euthanasia—is desirable in a given case, it has also been decided that in this instance death is not greater an evil than the patient's continued existence. And if this is true, the usual reason for not wanting to be the cause of someone's death simply does not apply.

Finally, doctors may think that all of this is only of academic [18] interest—the sort of thing that philosophers may worry about but that has no practical bearing on their own work. After all, doctors must be concerned about the legal consequences of what they do, and active euthanasia is clearly forbidden by the law. But even so, doctors should also be concerned with the fact that the law is forcing upon them a moral doctrine that may be indefensible, and has a considerable effect on their practices. Of course, most doctors are not now in the position of being coerced in this matter, for they do not regard themselves as merely going along with what the law requires. Rather, in statements such as the AMA policy statement that I have quoted, they are endorsing this doctrine as a central point of medical ethics. In that statement, active euthanasia is condemned not merely as illegal but as "contrary to that for which the medical profession stands," whereas passive euthanasia is approved. However, the preceding considerations suggest that there is really no moral difference between the two, considered in themselves (there may be important moral differences in some cases in their *consequences*, but, as I pointed out, these differences may make active euthanasia, and not passive euthanasia, the morally preferable option). So, whereas doctors may have to discriminate between active and passive euthanasia to satisfy the law, they should not do any more than that. In particular, they should not give the distinction any added authority and weight by writing it into official statements of medical ethics.

1975

We Do Abortions Here

Sallie Tisdale

1   We do abortions here; that is all we do. There are weary, grim moments when I think I cannot bear another basin of bloody remains, utter another kind phrase of reassurance. So I leave the procedure room in the back and reach for a new chart. Soon I am talking to an eighteen-year-old woman pregnant for the fourth time. I push up her sleeve to check her blood pressure and find row upon row of needle marks, neat and parallel and discolored. She has been so hungry for her drug for so long that she has taken to using the loose skin of her upper arms; her elbows are already a permanent ruin of bruises. She is surprised to find herself nearly four months pregnant. I suspect she is often surprised, in a mild way, by the blows she is dealt. I prepare myself for another basin, another brief and chafing loss.

2   "How can you stand it?" Even the clients ask. They see the machine, the strange instruments, the blood, the final stroke that wipes away the promise of pregnancy. Sometimes I see that too: I watch a woman's swollen abdomen sink to softness in a few stuttering moments and my own belly flip-flops with sorrow. But all it takes for me to catch my breath is another interview, one more story that sounds so much like the last one. There is a numbing sameness lurking in this job: the same questions, the same answers, even the same trembling tone in the voices. The worst is the sameness of human failure, of inadequacy in the face of each day's dull demands.

3   In describing this work, I find it difficult to explain how much I enjoy it most of the time. We laugh a lot here, as friends and as professional peers. It's nice to be with women all day. I like the

sudden, transient bonds I forge with some clients: moments when I am in my strength, remembering weakness, and a woman in weakness reaches out for my strength. What I offer is not power, but solidness, offered almost eagerly. Certain clients waken in me every tender urge I have—others make me wince and bite my tongue. Both challenge me to find a balance. It is a sweet brutality we practice here, a stark and loving dispassion.

I look at abortion as if I am standing on a cliff with a tele- 4 scope, gazing at some great vista. I can sweep the horizon with both eyes, survey the scene in all its distance and size. Or I can put my eye to the lens and focus on the small details, suddenly so close. In abortion the absolute must always be tempered by the contextual, because both are real, both valid, both hard. How can we do this? How can we refuse? Each abortion is a measure of our failure to protect, to nourish our own. Each basin I empty is a promise—but a promise broken a long time ago.

I grew up on the great promise of birth control. Like many 5 women my age, I took the pill as soon as I was sexually active. To risk pregnancy when it was so easy to avoid seemed stupid, and my contraceptive success, as it were, was part of the promise of social enlightenment. But birth control fails, far more frequently than laboratory trials predict. Many of our clients take the pill; its failure to protect them is a shocking realization. We have clients who have been sterilized, whose husbands have had vasectomies; each one is a statistical misfit, fine print come to life. The anger and shame of these women I hold in one hand, and the basin in the other. The distance between the two, the length I pace and try to measure, is the size of an abortion.

The procedure is disarmingly simple. Women are surprised, 6 as though the mystery of conception, a dark and hidden genesis, requires an elaborate finale. In the first trimester of pregnancy, it's a mere few minutes of vacuuming, a neat tidying up. I give a woman a small yellow Valium, and when it has begun to relax her, I lead her into the back, into bareness, the stirrups. The doctor reaches in her, opening the narrow tunnel to the uterus with a succession of slim, smooth bars of steel. He inserts a plastic tube and hooks it to a hose on the machine. The woman is framed against white paper that crackles as she moves, the light bright in her eyes. Then the machine rumbles low and loud in the small windowless room; the doctor moves the tube back and forth with an efficient rhythm, and the long tail of it fills with blood that spurts and stumbles along into a jar. He is usually finished in a few minutes. They are long minutes for the woman; her uterus frequently reacts to its abrupt emptying with a powerful, unceasing cramp, which cuts off the blood vessels and enfolds the irritated, bleeding tissue.

7   I am learning to recognize the shadows that cross the faces of the women I hold. While the doctor works between her spread legs, the paper drape hiding his intent expression, I stand beside the table. I hold the woman's hands in mine, resting them just below her ribs. I watch her eyes, finger her necklace, stroke her hair. I ask about her job, her family; in a haze she answers me; we chatter, faces close, eyes meeting and sliding apart.

8   I watch the shadows that creep up unnoticed and suddenly darken her face as she screws up her features and pushes a tear out each side to slide down her cheeks. I have learned to anticipate the quiver of chin, the rapid intake of breath and the surprising sobs that rise soon after the machine starts to drum. I know this is when the cramp deepens, and the tears are partly the tears that follow pain—the sharp, childish crying when one bumps one's head on a cabinet door. But a well of woe seems to open beneath many women when they hear that thumping sound. The anticipation of the moment has finally come to fruit; the moment has arrived when the loss is no longer an imagined one. It has come true.

9   I am struck by the sameness and I am struck every day by the variety here—how this commonplace dilemma can so display the differences of women. A twenty-one-year-old woman, unemployed, uneducated, without family, in the fifth month of her fifth pregnancy. A forty-two-year-old mother of teenagers, shocked by her condition, refusing to tell her husband. A twenty-three-year-old mother of two having her seventh abortion, and many women in their thirties having their first. Some are stoic, some hysterical, a few giggle uncontrollably, many cry.

10   I talk to a sixteen-year-old uneducated girl who was raped. She has gonorrhea. She describes blinding headaches, attacks of breathlessness, nausea. "Sometimes I feel like two different people," she tells me with a calm smile, "and I talk to myself."

I pull out my plastic models. She listens patiently for a time, 11
and then holds her hands wide in front of her stomach.

"When's the baby going to go up into my stomach?" she asks. 12
I blink. "What do you mean?" 13

"Well," she says, still smiling, "when women get so big, isn't 14
the baby in your stomach? Doesn't it hatch out of an egg there?"

My first question in an interview is always the same. As I 15
walk down the hall with the woman, as we get settled in chairs
and I glance through her files, I am trying to gauge her, to get a
sense of the words, and the tone, I should use. With some I joke,
with others I chat, sometimes I fall into a brisk, business-like patter. But I ask every woman, "Are you sure you want to have an
abortion?" Most nod with grim knowing smiles. "Oh yes," they
sigh. Some seek forgiveness, offer excuses. Occasionally a woman
will flinch and say, "Please don't use that word."

Later I describe the procedure to come, using care with my 16
language. I don't say "pain" any more than I would say "baby."
So many are afraid to ask how much it will hurt. "My sister told
me—" I hear. "A friend of mine said—" and the dire expectations
unravel. I prick the index finger of a woman for a drop of blood to
test, and as the tiny lancet approaches the skin she averts her eyes,
holding her trembling hand out to me and jumping at my touch.

It is when I am holding a plastic uterus in one hand, a suc- 17
tion tube in the other, moving them together in imitation of the
scrubbing to come, that women ask the most secret question. I am
speaking in a matter-of-fact voice about "the tissue" and "the contents" when the woman suddenly catches my eye and asks, "How
big is the baby now?" These words suggest a quiet need for a definition of the boundaries being drawn. It isn't so odd, after all,
that she feels relief when I describe the growing bud's bulbous
shape, its miniature nature. Again I gauge, and sometimes lie a
little, weaseling around its infantile features until its clinging
power slackens.

But when I look in the basin, among the curdlike blood clots, 18
I see an elfin thorax, attenuated, its pencilline ribs all in parallel
rows with tiny knobs of spine rounding upwards. A translucent
arm and hand swim beside.

A sleepy-eyed girl, just fourteen, watched me with a slight 19
and goofy smile all through her abortion. "Does it have little feet

and little fingers and all?" she'd asked earlier. When the suction was over she sat up woozily at the end of the table and murmured, "Can I see it?" I shook my head firmly.

20 "It's not allowed," I told her sternly, because I knew she didn't really want to see what was left. She accepted this statement of authority, and a shadow of confused relief crossed her plain, pale face.

21 Privately, even grudgingly, my colleagues might admit the power of abortion to provoke emotion. But they seem to prefer the broad view and disdain the telescope. Abortion is a matter of choice, privacy, control. Its uncertainty lies in specific cases: retarded women and girls too young to give consent for surgery, women who are ill or hostile or psychotic. Such common dilemmas are met with both compassion and impatience: they slow things down. We are too busy to chew over ethics. One person might discuss certain concerns, behind closed doors, or describe a particularly disturbing dream. But generally there is to be no ambivalence.

22 Every day I take calls from women who are annoyed that we cannot see them, cannot do their abortion today, this morning, now. They argue the price, demand that we stay after hours to accommodate their job or class schedule. Abortion is so routine that one expects it to be like a manicure: quick, cheap, and painless.

23 Still, I've cultivated a certain disregard. It isn't negligence, but I don't always pay attention. I couldn't be here if I tried to judge each case on its merits; after all, we do over a hundred abortions a week. At some point each individual in this line of work draws a boundary and adheres to it. For one physician the boundary is a particular week of gestation; for another, it is a certain number of repeated abortions. But these boundaries can be fluid too: one physician overruled his own limit to abort a mature but severely malformed fetus. For me, the limit is allowing my clients to carry their own burden, shoulder the responsibility themselves. I shoulder the burden of trying not to judge them.

24 This city has several "crisis pregnancy centers" advertised in the Yellow Pages. They are small offices staffed by volunteers, and they offer free pregnancy testing, glossy photos of dead fetuses, and movies. I had a client recently whose mother is active in the

anti-abortion movement. The young woman went to the local crisis center and was told that the doctor would make her touch her dismembered baby, that the pain would be the most horrible she could imagine, and that she might, after an abortion, never be able to have children. All lies. They called her at home and at work, over and over and over, but she had been wise enough to give a false name. She came to us a fugitive. We who do abortions are marked, by some, as impure. It's dirty work.

When a deliveryman comes to the sliding glass window by 25 the reception desk and tilts a box toward me, I hesitate. I read the packing slip, assess the shape and weight of the box in light of its supposed contents. We request familiar faces. The doors are carefully locked; I have learned to half glance around at bags and boxes, looking for a telltale sign. I register with security when I arrive, and I am careful not to bang a door. We are all a little on edge here.

Concern about size and shape seems to be natural, and so is 26 the relief that follows. We make the powerful assumption that the fetus is different from us, and even when we admit the similarities, it is too simplistic to be seduced by form alone. But the form is enormously potent—humanoid, powerless, palm-sized, and pure, it evokes an almost fierce tenderness when viewed simply as what it appears to be. But appearance, and even potential, aren't enough. The fetus, in becoming itself, can ruin others; its utter dependence has a sinister side. When I am struck in the moment by the contents in the basin, I am careful to remember the context, to note the tearful teenager and the woman sighing with something more than relief. One kind of question, though, I find considerably trickier.

"Can you tell what it is?" I am asked, and this means gender. 27 This question is asked by couples, not women alone. Always couples would abort a girl and keep a boy. I have been asked about twins, and even if I could tell what race the father was.

An eighteen-year-old woman with three daughters brought 28 her husband to the interview. He glared first at me, then at his wife, as he sank lower and lower in the chair, picking his teeth with a toothpick. He interrupted a conversation with his wife to ask if I could tell whether the baby would be a boy or a girl. I told him I could not.

29   "Good," he replied in a slow and strangely malevolent voice, "'cause if it was a boy I'd wring her neck."

30   In a literal sense, abortion exists because we are able to ask such questions, able to assign a value to the fetus which can shift with changing circumstances. If the human bond to a child were as primitive and unflinchingly narrow as that of other animals, there would be no abortion. There would be no abortion because there would be nothing more important than caring for the young and perpetuating the species, no reason for sex but to make babies. I sense this sometimes, this wordless organic duty, when I do ultrasounds.

31   We do ultrasound, a sound-wave test that paints a faint, gray picture of the fetus, whenever we're uncertain of gestation. Age is measured by the width of the skull and confirmed by the length of the femur or thighbone; we speak of a pregnancy as being a certain "femur length" in weeks. The usual concern is whether a pregnancy is within the legal limit for an abortion. Women this far along have bellies which swell out round and tight like trim muscles. When they lie flat, the mound rises softly above the hips, pressing the umbilicus upward.

32   It takes practice to read an ultrasound picture, which is grainy and etched as though in strokes of charcoal. But suddenly a rapid rhythmic motion appears—the beating heart. Nearby is a soft oval, scratched with lines—the skull. The leg is harder to find, and then suddenly the fetus moves, bobbing in the surf. The skull turns away, an arm slides across the screen, the torso rolls. I know the weight of a baby's head on my shoulder, the whisper of lips on ears, the delicate curve of a fragile spine in my hand. I know how heavy and correct a newborn cradled feels. The creature I watch in secret requires nothing from me but to be left alone, and that is precisely what won't be done.

33   These inadvertently made beings are caught in a twisting web of motive and desire. They are at least inconvenient, sometimes quite literally dangerous in the womb, but most often they fall somewhere in between—consequences never quite believed in come to roost. Their virtue rises and falls outside their own nature: they become only what we make them. A fetus created by accident is the most absolute kind of surprise. Whether the blame lies in a failed IUD, a slipped condom, or a false impression of

safety, that fetus is a thing whose creation has been actively worked against. Its existence is an error. I think this is why so few women, even late in a pregnancy, will consider giving a baby up for adoption. To do so means making the fetus real—imagining it as something whole and outside oneself. The decision to terminate a pregnancy is sometimes so difficult and confounding that it creates an enormous demand for immediate action. The decision is a rejection; the pregnancy has become something to be rid of, a condition to be ended. It is a burden, a weight, a thing separate.

Women have abortions because they are too old, and too 34 young, too poor, and too rich, too stupid, and too smart. I see women who berate themselves with violent emotions for their first and only abortion, and others who return three times, five times, hauling two or three children, who cannot remember to take a pill or where they put the diaphragm. We talk glibly about choice. But the choice for what? I see all the broken promises in lives lived like a series of impromptu obstacles. There are the sweet, light promises of love and intimacy, the glittering promise of education and progress, the warm promise of safe families, long years of innocence and community. And there is the promise of freedom: freedom from failure, from faithlessness. Freedom from biology. The early feminist defense of abortion asked many questions, but the one I remember is this: Is biology destiny? And the answer is yes, sometimes it is. Women who have the fewest choices of all exercise their right to abortion the most.

Oh, the ignorance. I take a woman to the back room and ask 35 her to undress; a few minutes later I return and find her positioned discreetly behind a drape, still wearing underpants. "Do I have to take these off too?" she asks, a little shocked. Some swear they have not had sex, many do not know what a uterus is, how sperm and egg meet, how sex makes babies. Some late seekers do not believe themselves pregnant; they believe themselves *impregnable.* I was chastised when I began this job for referring to some clients as girls: it is a feminist heresy. They come so young, snapping gum, sockless and sneakered, and their shakily applied eyeliner smears when they cry. I call them girls with maternal benignity. I cannot imagine them as mothers.

The doctor seats himself between the woman's thighs and 36 reaches into the dilated opening of a five-month pregnant uterus.

Quickly he grabs and crushes the fetus in several places, and the room is filled with a low clatter and snap of forceps, the click of the tanaculum, and a pulling, sucking sound. The paper crinkles as the drugged and sleepy woman shifts, the nurse's low, honey-brown voice explains each step in delicate words.

37   I have fetus dreams, we all do here: dreams of abortions one after the other; of buckets of blood splashed on the walls; trees full of crawling fetuses. I dreamed that two men grabbed me and began to drag me away. "Let's do an abortion," they said with a sickening leer, and I began to scream, plunged into a vision of sucking, scraping pain, of being spread and torn by impartial instruments that do only what they are bidden. I woke from this dream barely able to breathe and thought of kitchen tables and coat hangers, knitting needles striped with blood, and women all alone clutching a pillow in their teeth to keep the screams from piercing the apartment-house walls. Abortion is the narrowest edge between kindness and cruelty. Done as well as it can be, it is still violence—merciful violence, like putting a suffering animal to death.

38   Maggie, one of the nurses, received a call at midnight not long ago. It was a woman in her twentieth week of pregnancy; the necessarily gradual process of cervical dilation begun the day before had stimulated labor, as it sometimes does. Maggie and one of the doctors met the woman at the office in the night. Maggie helped her onto the table, and as she lay down the fetus was delivered into Maggie's hands. When Maggie told me about it the next day, she cupped her hands into a small bowl—"It was just like a little kitten," she said softly, wonderingly. "Everything was still attached."

39   At the end of the day I clean out the suction jars, pouring blood into the sink, splashing the sides with flecks of tissue. From the sink rises a rich and humid smell, hot, earthy, and moldering; it is the smell of something recently alive beginning to decay. I take care of the plastic tub on the floor, filled with pieces too big to be trusted to the trash. The law defines the contents of the bucket I hold protectively against my chest as "tissue." Some would say my complicity in filling that bucket gives me no right to call it anything else. I slip the tissue gently into a bag and place it in the freezer, to be burned at another time. Abortion requires of me an entirely new set of assumptions. It requires a willingness

to live with conflict, fearlessness, and grief. As I close the freezer door, I imagine a world where this won't be necessary, and then return to the world where it is.

1990

The Technology of Medicine
Lewis Thomas

Technology assessment has become a routine exercise for the sci- 1
entific enterprises on which the country is obliged to spend vast sums for its needs. Brainy committees are continually evaluating the effectiveness and cost of doing various things in space, defense, energy, transportation, and the like, to give advice about prudent investments for the future.

Somehow medicine, for all the $80-odd billion that it is said 2
to cost the nation, has not yet come in for much of this analytical treatment. It seems taken for granted that the technology of medicine simply exists, take it or leave it, and the only major technologic problem which policy-makers are interested in is how to deliver today's kind of health care, with equity, to all the people.

When, as is bound to happen sooner or later, the analysts get 3
around to the technology of medicine itself, they will have to face the problem of measuring the relative cost and effectiveness of all the things that are done in the management of disease. They make their living at this kind of thing, and I wish them well, but I imagine they will have a bewildering time. For one thing, our methods of managing disease are constantly changing—partly under the influence of new bits of information brought in from all corners of biologic science. At the same time, a great many things are done that are not so closely related to science, some not related at all.

In fact, there are three quite different levels of technology in 4
medicine, so unlike each other as to seem altogether different undertakings. Practitioners of medicine and the analysts will be in trouble if they are not kept separate.

5 1. First of all, there is a large body of what might be termed "nontechnology," impossible to measure in terms of its capacity to alter either the natural course of disease or its eventual outcome. A great deal of money is spent on this. It is valued highly by the professionals as well as the patients. It consists of what is sometimes called "supportive therapy." It tides patients over through diseases that are not, by and large, understood. It is what is meant by the phrases "caring for" and "standing by." It is indispensable. It is not, however, a technology in any real sense, since it does not involve measures directed at the underlying mechanism of disease.

6 It includes the large part of any good doctor's time that is taken up with simply providing reassurance, explaining to patients who fear that they have contracted one or another lethal disease that they are, in fact, quite healthy.

7 It is what physicians used to be engaged in at the bedside of patients with diphtheria, meningitis, poliomyelitis, lobar pneumonia, and all the rest of the infectious diseases that have since come under control.

8 It is what physicians must now do for patients with intractable cancer, severe rheumatoid arthritis, multiple sclerosis, stroke, and advanced cirrhosis. One can think of at least twenty major diseases that require this kind of supportive medical care because of the absence of an effective technology. I would include a large amount of what is called mental disease, and most varieties of cancer, in this category.

9 The cost of this nontechnology is very high, and getting higher all the time. It requires not only a great deal of time but also very hard effort and skill on the part of physicians; only the very best of doctors are good at coping with this kind of defeat. It also involves long periods of hospitalization, lots of nursing, lots of involvement of nonmedical professionals in and out of the hospital. It represents, in short, a substantial segment of today's expenditures for health.

10 2. At the next level up is a kind of technology best termed "halfway technology." This represents the kinds of things that must be done after the fact, in efforts to compensate for the incapacitating effects of certain diseases whose course one is unable to do very much about. It is a technology designed to make up for disease, or to postpone death.

The outstanding examples in recent years are the transplan- 11
tations of hearts, kidneys, livers, and other organs, and the equally
spectacular inventions of artificial organs. In the public mind, this
kind of technology has come to seem like the equivalent of the
high technologies of the physical sciences. The media tend to present each new procedure as though it represented a breakthrough
and therapeutic triumph, instead of the makeshift that it really is.

In fact, this level of technology is, by its nature, at the same 12
time highly sophisticated and profoundly primitive. It is the kind
of thing that one must continue to do until there is a genuine
understanding of the mechanisms involved in disease. In chronic
glomerulonephritis, for example, a much clearer insight will be
needed into the events leading to the destruction of glomeruh by
the immunologic reactants that now appear to govern this disease,
before one will know how to intervene intelligently to prevent the
process, or turn it around. But when this level of understanding
has been reached, the technology of kidney replacement will not
be much needed and should no longer pose the huge problem of
logistics, cost, and ethics that it poses today.

An extremely complex and costly technology for the man- 13
agement of coronary heart disease has evolved—involving specialized ambulances and hospital units, all kinds of electronic
gadgetry, and whole platoons of new professional personnel—to
deal with the end results of coronary thrombosis. Almost everything offered today for the treatment of heart disease is at this
level of technology, with the transplanted and artificial hearts as
ultimate examples. When enough has been learned to know what
really goes wrong in heart disease, one ought to be in a position
to figure out ways to prevent or reverse the process, and when
this happens the current elaborate technology will probably be set
to one side.

Much of what is done in the treatment of cancer, by surgery, 14
irradiation, and chemotherapy, represents halfway technology, in
the sense that these measures are directed at the existence of
already established cancer cells, but not at the mechanisms by
which cells become neoplastic.

It is a characteristic of this kind of technology that it costs an 15
enormous amount of money and requires a continuing expansion
of hospital facilities. There is no end to the need for new, highly

trained people to run the enterprise. And there is really no way out of this, at the present state of knowledge. If the installation of specialized coronary-care units can result in the extension of life for only a few patients with coronary disease (and there is no question that this technology is effective in a few cases), it seems to me an inevitable fact of life that as many of these as can be will be put together, and as much money as can be found will be spent. I do not see that anyone has much choice in this. The only thing that can move medicine away from this level of technology is new information, and the only imaginable source of this information is research.

16   3. The third type of technology is the kind that is so effective that it seems to attract the least public notice; it has come to be taken for granted. This is the genuinely decisive technology of modern medicine, exemplified best by modern methods for immunization against diphtheria, pertussis, and the childhood virus diseases, and the contemporary use of antibiotics and chemotherapy for bacterial infections. The capacity to deal effectively with syphilis and tuberculosis represents a milestone in human endeavor, even though full use of this potential has not yet been made. And there are, of course, other examples: the treatment of endocrinologic disorders with appropriate hormones, the prevention of hemolytic disease of the newborn, the treatment and prevention of various nutritional disorders, and perhaps just around the corner the management of Parkinsonism and sickle-cell anemia. There are other examples, and everyone will have his favorite candidates for the list, but the truth is that there are nothing like as many as the public has been led to believe.

17   The point to be made about this kind of technology—the real high technology of medicine—is that it comes as the result of a genuine understanding of disease mechanisms, and when it becomes available, it is relatively inexpensive, and relatively easy to deliver.

18   Offhand, I cannot think of any important human disease for which medicine possesses the outright capacity to prevent or cure where the cost of the technology is itself a major problem. The price is never as high as the cost of managing the same diseases during the earlier stages of no-technology or halfway technology. If a case of typhoid fever had to be managed today by the best

methods of 1935, it would run to a staggering expense. At, say, around fifty days of hospitalization, requiring the most demanding kind of nursing care, with the obsessive concern for details of diet that characterized the therapy of that time, with daily laboratory monitoring, and, on occasion, surgical intervention for abdominal catastrophe, I should think $10,000 would be a conservative estimate for the illness, as contrasted with today's cost of a bottle of chloramphenicol and a day or two of fever. The halfway technology that was evolving for poliomyelitis in the early 1950s, just before the emergence of the basic research that made the vaccine possible, provides another illustration of the point. Do you remember Sister Kenny, and the cost of those institutes for rehabilitation, with all those ceremonially applied hot fomentations, and the debates about whether the affected limbs should be totally immobilized or kept in passive motion as frequently as possible, and the masses of statistically tormented data mobilized to support one view or the other? It is the cost of that kind of technology, and its relative effectiveness, that must be compared with the cost and effectiveness of the vaccine.

Pulmonary tuberculosis had similar episodes in its history. 19 There was a sudden enthusiasm for the surgical removal of infected lung tissue in the early 1950s, and elaborate plans were being made for new and expensive installations for major pulmonary surgery in tuberculosis hospitals, and then INH and streptomycin came along and the hospitals themselves were closed up.

It is when physicians are bogged down by their incomplete 20 technologies, by the innumerable things they are obliged to do in medicine when they lack a clear understanding of disease mechanisms, that the deficiencies of the healthcare system are most conspicuous. If I were a policy-maker, interested in saving money for health care over the long haul, I would regard it as an act of high prudence to give high priority to a lot more basic research in biologic science. This is the only way to get the full mileage that biology owes to the science of medicine, even though it seems, as used to be said in the days when the phrase still had some meaning, like asking for the moon.

1974

Remarks by the President on Stem Cell Research

George W. Bush

1 Good evening. I appreciate you giving me a few minutes of your time tonight so I can discuss with you a complex and difficult issue, an issue that is one of the most profound of our time.

2   The issue of research involving stem cells derived from human embryos is increasingly the subject of a national debate and dinner table discussions. The issue is confronted every day in laboratories as scientists ponder the ethical ramifications of their work. It is agonized over by parents and many couples as they try to have children, or to save children already born.

3   The issue is debated within the church, with people of different faiths, even many of the same faith coming to different conclusions. Many people are finding that the more they know about stem cell research, the less certain they are about the right ethical and moral conclusions.

4   My administration must decide whether to allow federal funds, your tax dollars, to be used for scientific research on stem cells derived from human embryos. A large number of these embryos already exist. They are the product of a process called in vitro fertilization, which helps so many couples conceive children. When doctors match sperm and egg to create life outside the womb, they usually produce more embryos than are planted in the mother. Once a couple successfully has children, or if they are unsuccessful, the additional embryos remain frozen in laboratories.

5   Some will not survive during long storage; others are destroyed. A number have been donated to science and used to create privately funded stem cell lines. And a few have been implanted in an adoptive mother and born, and are today healthy children.

6   Based on preliminary work that has been privately funded, scientists believe further research using stem cells offers great promise that could help improve the lives of those who suffer from many terrible diseases—from juvenile diabetes to Alzheimer's, from Parkinson's to spinal cord injuries. And while scientists admit

they are not yet certain, they believe stem cells derived from embryos have unique potential.

You should also know that stem cells can be derived from 7 sources other than embryos—from adult cells, from umbilical cords that are discarded after babies are born, from human placenta. And many scientists feel research on these type of stem cells is also promising. Many patients suffering from a range of diseases are already being helped with treatments developed from adult stem cells.

However, most scientists, at least today, believe that research 8 on embryonic stem cells offer the most promise because these cells have the potential to develop in all of the tissues in the body.

Scientists further believe that rapid progress in this research 9 will come only with federal funds. Federal dollars help attract the best and brightest scientists. They ensure new discoveries are widely shared at the largest number of research facilities and that the research is directed toward the greatest public good.

The United States has a long and proud record of leading the 10 world toward advances in science and medicine that improve human life. And the United States has a long and proud record of upholding the highest standards of ethics as we expand the limits of science and knowledge. Research on embryonic stem cells raises profound ethical questions, because extracting the stem cell destroys the embryo, and thus destroys its potential for life. Like a snowflake, each of these embryos is unique, with the unique genetic potential of an individual human being.

As I thought through this issue, I kept returning to two fun- 11 damental questions: First, are these frozen embryos human life, and therefore, something precious to be protected? And second, if they're going to be destroyed anyway, shouldn't they be used for a greater good, for research that has the potential to save and improve other lives?

I've asked those questions and others of scientists, scholars, 12 bioethicists, religious leaders, doctors, researchers, members of Congress, my Cabinet, and my friends. I have read heartfelt letters from many Americans. I have given this issue a great deal of thought, prayer and considerable reflection. And I have found widespread disagreement.

13   On the first issue, are these embryos human life—well, one researcher told me he believes this five-day-old cluster of cells is not an embryo, not yet an individual, but a pre-embryo. He argued that it has the potential for life, but it is not a life because it cannot develop on its own.

14   An ethicist dismissed that as a callous attempt at rationalization. Make no mistake, he told me, that cluster of cells is the same way you and I, and all the rest of us, started our lives. One goes with a heavy heart if we use these, he said, because we are dealing with the seeds of the next generation.

15   And to the other crucial question, if these are going to be destroyed anyway, why not use them for good purpose—I also found different answers. Many argue these embryos are byproducts of a process that helps create life, and we should allow couples to donate them to science so they can be used for good purpose instead of wasting their potential. Others will argue there's no such thing as excess life, and the fact that a living being is going to die does not justify experimenting on it or exploiting it as a natural resource.

16   At its core, this issue forces us to confront fundamental questions about the beginnings of life and the ends of science. It lies at a difficult moral intersection, juxtaposing the need to protect life in all its phases with the prospect of saving and improving life in all its stages.

17   As the discoveries of modern science create tremendous hope, they also lay vast ethical mine fields. As the genius of science extends the horizons of what we can do, we increasingly confront complex questions about what we should do. We have arrived at that brave new world that seemed so distant in 1932, when Aldous Huxley wrote about human beings created in test tubes in what he called a "hatchery."

18   In recent weeks, we learned that scientists have created human embryos in test tubes solely to experiment on them. This is deeply troubling, and a warning sign that should prompt all of us to think through these issues very carefully.

19   Embryonic stem cell research is at the leading edge of a series of moral hazards. The initial stem cell researcher was at first reluctant to begin his research, fearing it might be used for human cloning. Scientists have already cloned a sheep. Researchers are telling us the next step could be to clone human beings to create

individual designer stem cells, essentially to grow another you, to be available in case you need another heart or lung or liver.

I strongly oppose human cloning, as do most Americans. We 20 recoil at the idea of growing human beings for spare body parts, or creating life for our convenience. And while we must devote enormous energy to conquering disease, it is equally important that we pay attention to the moral concerns raised by the new frontier of human embryo stem cell research. Even the most noble ends do not justify any means.

My position on these issues is shaped by deeply held beliefs. 21 I'm a strong supporter of science and technology, and believe they have the potential for incredible good—to improve lives, to save life, to conquer disease. Research offers hope that millions of our loved ones may be cured of a disease and rid of their suffering. I have friends whose children suffer from juvenile diabetes. Nancy Reagan has written me about President Reagan's struggle with Alzheimer's. My own family has confronted the tragedy of child-hood leukemia. And, like all Americans, I have great hope for cures.

I also believe human life is a sacred gift from our Creator. 22 I worry about a culture that devalues life, and believe as your President I have an important obligation to foster and encourage respect for life in America and throughout the world. And while we're all hopeful about the potential of this research, no one can be certain that the science will live up to the hope it has generated.

Eight years ago, scientists believed fetal tissue research 23 offered great hope for cures and treatments—yet, the progress to date has not lived up to its initial expectations. Embryonic stem cell research offers both great promise and great peril. So I have decided we must proceed with great care.

As a result of private research, more than 60 genetically 24 diverse stem cell lines already exist. They were created from embryos that have already been destroyed, and they have the ability to regenerate themselves indefinitely, creating ongoing opportunities for research. I have concluded that we should allow federal funds to be used for research on these existing stem cell lines, where the life and death decision has already been made.

Leading scientists tell me research on these 60 lines has great 25 promise that could lead to breakthrough therapies and cures. This allows us to explore the promise and potential of stem cell research without crossing a fundamental moral line, by providing taxpayer funding that would sanction or encourage further destruction of human embryos that have at least the potential for life.

26   I also believe that great scientific progress can be made through aggressive federal funding of research on umbilical cord placenta, adult and animal stem cells which do not involve the same moral dilemma. This year, your government will spend $250 million on this important research.

27   I will also name a President's council to monitor stem cell research, to recommend appropriate guidelines and regulations, and to consider all of the medical and ethical ramifications of biomedical innovation. This council will consist of leading scientists, doctors, ethicists, lawyers, theologians and others, and will be chaired by Dr. Leon Kass, a leading biomedical ethicist from the University of Chicago.

28   This council will keep us apprised of new developments and give our nation a forum to continue to discuss and evaluate these important issues. As we go forward, I hope we will always be guided by both intellect and heart, by both our capabilities and our conscience.

29   I have made this decision with great care, and I pray it is the right one.

30   Thank you for listening. Good night, and God bless America.

Acknowledgments

"Language and Literature from a Pueblo Indian Perspective" reprinted with the permission of Simon & Schuster Adult Publishing Group from *Yellow Woman and a Beauty of the Spirit* by Leslie Marmon Silko. Copyright © 1996 by Leslie Marmon Silko.

Angelou, Maya. "Graduation", copyright © 1969 and renewed 1997 by Maya Angelou, from *I Know Why the Caged Bird Sings* by Maya Angelou. Used by permission of Random House, Inc.

Anzaldua, Gloria. "How to Tame a Wild Tongue" from *Borderlands/ LA Frontera: The New Mestiza*. Copyright © 1987, 1999 by Gloria Anzaldua. Reprinted by permission of Aunt Lute Books.

Atwood, Margaret. "The Female Body" from *Good Bones and Simple Murders* by Margaret Atwood, copyright © 1983, 1992, 1994, by O.W. Toad Ltd. A Nan A. Talese Book. Used by permission of Doubleday, a division of Random House, Inc. and McClelland & Stewart Ltd.

Baker, Russell. "Observer: The Paper Workinstiff" by Russell Baker from *The New York Times*, October 15, 1969. Copyright © 1969 The New York Times Co. Reprinted by permission.

Baldwin, James. From *Notes of a Native Son* by James Baldwin. Copyright © 1955, renewed 1983, by James Baldwin. Reprinted by permission of Beacon Press, Boston.

Barry, Dave. "Red, White and Beer" from *Dave Barry's Greatest Hits* by Dave Barry, copyright © 1988 by Dave Barry. Used by permission of Crown Publishers, a division of Random House, Inc.

bell hooks. "keeping close to home: class and education" by bell hooks from *Talking Back: Thinking Feminist*. Reprinted by permission of South End Press and Between the Lines Publishers.

Bennett, William J. "What Really Ails America" by William J. Bennett as appeared in *Reader's Digest*. Reprinted by permission of William J. Bennett.

Bettleheim, Bruno. Credit to come.

Goodman, Ellen. "A Reasonable Woman Standard" by Ellen Goodman. Copyright © 1991, The Washington Post Writers Group. Reprinted with permission.

Gould, Stephen Jay. "Darwin's Middle Road". Copyright © 1979 by Stephen Jay Gould, from *The Panda's Thumb: More Reflections in Natural History* by Stephen Jay Gould. Used by permission of W. W. Norton & Company, Inc.

Gould, Stephen Jay. "The Terrifying Normalcy of AIDS" by Stephen Jay Gould. Reprinted by permission.

Heaton and Wilson. Credit to come.

Highet, Gilbert. "The Mystery of Zen" from *Talent and Geniuses* by Gilbert Highet. Copyright © 1957 by Gilbert Highet. Reprinted by permission of Curtis Brown, Ltd.

Hong, Maxine. From *The Woman Warrior* by Maxine Hong Kingston, copyright © 1975, 1976 by Maxine Hong Kingston. Used by permission of Alfred A. Knopf, a division of Random House, Inc.

Hughes, Langston. "Salvation" from *The Big Sea* by Langston Hughes. Copyright 1940 by Langston Hughes. Copyright renewed 1968 by Arna Bontemps and George Houston Bass. Reprinted by permission of Hill and Want, a division of Farrar, Straus and Giroux, LLC.

Hurston, Zora Neale. "How It Feels to Be Colored Me" by Zora Neale Hurston. Used with the permission of the Estate of Zora Neale Hurston.

Ignatiev, Noel. "How the Irish Became White" from *How the Irish Became White* by Noel Ignatiev. Reprinted by permission of Routledge/ Taylor & Francis Group, LLC.

Jackson, Jesse. "Who Makes the Clothes We Wear?" by Jesse Jackson, September 17, 1995. Reprinted by permission of TMSReprints.

Jowett, Benjamin. "Allegory of the Cave" by Plato from *Dialogues of Plato*, 4th Edition translated by Benjamin Jowett. Copyright 1953. Reprinted by permission of Oxford University Press.

Kincaid, Jamaica. Credit to come.

King, Martin Luther, Jr. "Letter from Birmingham Jail" and "I have a Dream." Reprinted by arrangement with the Estate of Martin Luther King Jr., c/o Writers House as agent for the proprietor, New York NY. Copyright 1963 Martin Luther King Jr., copyright renewed 1991 Coretta Scott King.

King, Stephen. Credit to come.

Koch, Edward I. "Death and Justice" by Edward I. Koch from *The New Republic*, April 15, 1985. Reprinted by permission of The New Republic, © 1985, The New Repubic, LLC.

Perrin, Noel. "The Greenest Campuses" by Noel Perrin. Reprinted by permission of Elizabeth Perrin.

Postman, Neil. From *The End of Education* by Neil Postman, copyright © 1995 by Neil Postman. Used by permission of Alfred A. Knopf, a division of Random House, Inc.

Quindlen, Anna. From *Thinking Out Loud* by Anna Quindlen, copyright © 1993 by Anna Quindlen. Used by permission of Random House, Inc.

Rachels, James. "Active and Passive Euthanasia" by James Rachels. Copyright © 1975. Reprinted by permission of Massachusetts Medical Society.

Rheingold, Howard. "The Virtual Community" by Howard Rheingold from *The Virtual Community.* Reprinted by permission of The MIT Press.

Rich, Adrienne. "Claiming an Education" from *On Lies, Secrets, and Silence: Selected Prose 1966–1978* by Adrienne Rich. Copyright © 1979 by W. W. Norton & Company, Inc. Used by permission of W. W. Norton & Company, Inc.

Rodriguez, Richard. "Aria" from *Hunger of Memory* by Richard Rodriguez. Copyright © 1981 by Richard Rodriguez (Boston: David Godine, 1981). Reprinted by permission of Georges Borchardt, Inc., on behalf of the author.

Rose, Mike. Chapter 2, "I Just Wanna Be Average", pp. 11–37 reprinted with the permission of The Free Press, a Division of Simon & Schuster Adult Publishing Group, from *Lives on the Boundary:* The Struggles and Achievements of America's Underprepared by Mike Rose. Copyright © 1989 by Mike Rose. All rights reserved.

Russell, Bertrand. From *The Problems of Philosophy* by Bertrand Russell. Oxford University Press.

Sagan, Carl. Credit to come.

Sanders, Scott Russell. "The Men We Carry in Our Minds" by Scott Russell Sanders. Copyright © 1984 by Scott Russell Sanders. First appeared in Milkweed Chronicle, from *The Paradise of Bombs.* Reprinted by permission of the author and the author's agents, the Virginia Kidd Agency.

Snider, Michael. "The Intimacy of Blogs" by Michael Snider from *Maclean's,* 15 September 2003. Reprinted by permission of Maclean's.

Staples, Brent. Credit to come.

Steele, Shelby. From *The Content of Our Character* by Shelby Steele. Copyright © 1990 by the author and reprinted by permission of St. Martin's Press, LLC.

Steinem, Gloria. "Sex, Lies and Advertising" by Gloria Steinem from MS Magazine, July/August 1990. Reprinted by permission of the author.

Takaki, Ronald. "The Harmful Myth of Asian Superiority" by Ronald Takaki from *The New York Times*, June 16, 1990. Copyright © 1990 The New York Times Co. Reprinted by permission.

Tannen, Deborah. Excerpt from *You Just Don't Understand* by Deborah Tannen. Copyright © 1990 by Deborah Tannen. Reprinted by permission of HarperCollins Publishers.

Tempest, Terry. "The Clan of One-Breasted Women" from *Refuge: An Unnatural History of Family and Place* by Terry Tempest Williams, copyright © 1991 by Terry Tempest Williams. Used by permission of Pantheon Books, a division of Random House, Inc.

Terkel, Studs. "Who Built the Pyramids: Mike Lefevre" by Studs Terkel from WORKING. Copyright © 1972 Studs Terkel. Reprinted by permission of Donadio & Olson, Inc.

Thomas, Lewis. "The Lives of a Cell", copyright © 1971 by The Massachusetts Medical Society, from *The Lives of a Cell* by Lewis Thomas. Used by permission of Viking Penguin, a division of Penguin Group (USA) Inc.

Tisdale, Sallie. "We Do Abortions Here" by Sallie Tisdale as appeared in HARPER'S, October 1990. Reprinted by permission of the author.

Turkle, Sherry. "Cyberspace and Identity" reprinted with the permission of Simon & Schuster Adult Publishing Group from *Life on the Screen: Identity in the Age of the Internet* by Sherry Turkle. Copyright © 1995 by Sherry Turkle.

Twitchell, James B. "But First, a Word from Our Sponsor" by James B. Twitchell. Reprinted by permission of the author.

Walker, Alice. "Beauty: When the Other Dancer is the Self" from *In Search of Our Mothers' Gardens: Womanist Prose*, copyright © 1983 by Alice Walker, reprinted by permission of Harcourt, Inc.

West, Cornel. "On Black Fathering" by Cornel West, copyright © 1996 by Cornel West, from *Faith of Our Fathers*, edited by Andre C. Willis. Used by permission of Dutton, a division of Penguin Group (USA) Inc.

White, E.B. "The Meaning of Democracy" by E. B. White. Reprinted by permission of The Estate of E. B. White.

Williams, Patricia. Reprinted by permission of the publisher form *The Alchemy of Race and Rights: Diary of A Law Professor* by Patricia J. Williams, pp. 17–19, Cambridge, Mass.: Harvard University Press, Copyright © 1991 by the President and Fellows of Harvard College.

Wilson, James Q. "Cars and Their Enemies" by James Q. Wilson reprinted from *Commentary*, July 1997, by permission; all rights reserved.

Woolf, Virginia. "The Death of the Moth" from *The Death of the Moth and Other Essays* by Virgina Woolf, copyright 1942 by Harcourt, Inc. and renewed 1970 by Marjorie T. Parsons, Executrix, reprinted by permission of the publisher

X, Malcom. "Coming to an Awareness of Language" from *The Autobiography of Malcolm X* by Malcolm X and Alex Haley, copyright © 1964 by Alex Haley and Malcolm X. Copyright © 1965 by Alex Haley and Betty Shabazz. Used by permission of Random House, Inc.

Index